Managing (e)Business Transformation

A global perspective

Ali Farhoomand

First published 2005 by
PALGRAVE MACMILLAN
Houndmills, Basingstoke, Hampshire RG21 6XS and
175 Fifth Avenue, New York, N. Y. 10010
Companies and representatives throughout the world

PALGRAVE MACMILLAN is the global academic imprint of the Palgrave
Macmillan division of St. Martin's Press, LLC and of Palgrave Macmillan Ltd.
Macmillan® is a registered trademark in the United States, United Kingdom
and other countries. Palgrave is a registered trademark in the European
Union and other countries.

ISBN 1–4039–4437–7 hardback
ISBN 1–4039–3604–8 paperback

This book is printed on paper suitable for recycling and
made from fully managed and sustained forest sources.

A catalogue record for this book is available from the British Library.

Library of Congress Cataloging-in-Publication Data
Farhoomand, Ali F.
    Managing (e)business transformation : a global perspective / Ali Farhoomand.
        p. cm.
        Includes bibliogaphical references and index.
        ISBN 1–4039–4437–7 (cloth) — ISBN 1–439–3604–8 (paper)
    1. Electronic commerce—Management. 2. Industrial management.
    3. Electronic commerce—Management—Case studies. 4. Industrial
    management—Case studies. I. Title: Managing e-business
    transformation. II. Title.
HF5548.32.F37 2004
658'.5—dc22   2004044792

10   9   8   7   6   5   4   3   2   1
14   13   12   11   10   09   08   07   06   05
Printed and bound in China

Contents

List of figures

List of tables

Preface

Almost every company today is trying to find out how best to deploy the Internet throughout its value chain to improve operational efficiency, entrench strategic position, and ultimately create economic value. In their e-business transformational initiatives, companies must grapple with a whole host of strategic, organisational, technical and increasingly global issues.

This book explains what is involved in e-business transformation: from tightly aligning e-business strategy with business strategy, to setting up the necessary infrastructure, to streamlining and integrating front-end and back-end business processes, to considering implementation and emerging global issues. More specifically, *Managing (e)Business Transformation: A Global Perspective* provides a roadmap for companies planning to transform into an e-business where proprietary and shared infrastructures are used to link customers, suppliers, partners and employees to create superior economic value. This book is written based on the premise that integrating Internet technologies throughout the value chain is crucial in building and managing business relationships. It also underscores the importance of basic business and economic principles within the context of a networked environment.

This book takes a strong managerial perspective and argues that the Internet is just an enabling, albeit principal, technology that allows firms to build the infrastructure needed to operate in an evolving business order. It builds on established business and economic theories, concepts and fundamentals to show that e-business has fast become synonymous with business. The book is distinctively written to provide a systematic, empirically based and theoretically grounded guide on "how to manage e-business transformation."

The book is unique in several ways. First, we have stayed away from hype emanating from public media and trade publications by relying on basic business and economic concepts. We have deliberately enclosed in brackets the "e" in the title to signify our philosophy and conviction that businesses are still guided by basic economic principles and that e-business transformation is indeed business transformation. Second, the material in the book is an outgrowth of our empirical, longitudinal field studies of dozens of companies over the last couple of years. These studies are presented in the form of full-fledged case studies written by a team of professional case-writers. Third, we have based the material presented in the book on a conceptual structure called the **Dynamic**

Organisational Tension Framework to guide the reader through the phases of the transformation process.

The structure of the book is as follows. We start with an introductory chapter about change and transformation to gain an appreciation of why transformational efforts are so difficult to pull off. **Chapter 1 Change and transformation in business** explores past attempts at organisational transformation and considers why many of these efforts have been unsuccessful. Particular attention is given to the hope placed in the Total Quality Management (TQM) and Business Process Reengineering (BPR) movements as an elixir for organisational problems. We then introduce the concepts of chaos and complexity as effective ways to study organisations in terms of relationships, rather than the mere sum of their tangible parts. We argue that the impact of information technology must be viewed within the context of its interaction with the other four major organisational components: strategy, processes, structure, and people. In order to develop a holistic view of e-business transformation, we use the DOT framework to organise and tie together the material in the book through the following four parts:

Part 1: e-Business strategy and valuation provides a review of key issues related to e-business strategy and valuation. We discuss how the Internet can be used to improve operational effectiveness, how companies can align their e-business strategy with business strategy, and how they must go about making sound investment decisions when valuating e-business initiatives.

● **Chapter 2 e-Business strategy** is designed to introduce the reader to basic strategy concepts that are shaped by market and technological factors. It shows how customers and partners are aligned along business processes to create sustainable competitive advantage. It explains how companies can leverage e-business to achieve superior operational efficiency and enhanced economic value. We take the view that e-business strategy should address the fundamental question of *where* a company wants to go, and *how* it intends to get there. The chapter also presents the concept of business architecture and how it can be used to draft an e-business strategy.

● **Chapter 3 Valuing e-business investments and managing performance** is designed to develop an understanding of e-business-related investments, costs, and profitability. With the recent failure of dot-coms, an increased focus is emerging on how to think about measurable value in e-business and how to devise methods for determining the financial valuation of e-business investments. Various valuation methodologies discussed.

Part 2: e-Business infrastructure development provides an analysis of what it takes to develop and manage the technical infrastructure necessary for integrating internal and external business processes.

● **Chapter 4 e-Business infrastructure: the building blocks** highlights the rising stature of the IT function in modern organisations and emphasises the strategic significance of the role that senior management should play in e-business infrastructure decisions. We briefly examine the evolution of organisational computing from the early mainframe era through to present-day e-business transformation. We then turn our attention to the key e-business applications as they relate to the essential organisational processes and relationships between a company and three major stakeholder groups: customers, suppliers, and employees. We also discuss how emerging wireless technologies add yet another dimension to the potential of e-business, particularly with respect to enhancing enterprise productivity.

● **Chapter 5 e-Business infrastructure: integration, standards and security** shows how successful e-business implementation involves weaving together various information technologies to ensure that the solution in place is functional, secure, and scalable. It explains how companies competing in the e-business landscape need to consider the key issues of infrastructure implementation in integrating various parts of e-business mosaic, setting up appropriate standards, and putting in place security measures. We delve into the promise of the XML messaging standard and the potential of XML-based frameworks to succeed electronic data interchange as the means to exchange business data between businesses and their partners.

Part 3: e-Business process management presents a review of the three major areas involved in process management: enterprise management (through ERP systems), customer relationship management, and supply chain management. We explain what it takes to integrate the selling chain and supply chain with enterprise-level processes. We argue that to achieve sustainable strategic advantage, firms need to configure their value chain distinctively such that it would be difficult for competitors to imitate.

● **Chapter 6 Enterprise resource planning systems** examines ERP's role as the backbone of a firm's e-business capability. We examine how ERP systems are evolving and consider potential costs and benefits of maintaining an ERP implementation. A case is made for a strong back-office as the launching pad for an organisation's e-business aspirations.

● **Chapter 7 e-CRM: evolution from traditional relationships** explores how a relationship strategy is driven by business focus, organisational structure, and customer orientation. The major emphasis is on existing customer relationships. We show how structured, embedded CRM processes enable firms to build long-term sustainable business advantage not only through improved operational effectiveness but more importantly through unique strategic positioning.

● **Chapter 8 Supply chain management** shows how businesses can improve the bottom line by creating tighter relationships with vendors, suppliers, and customers. We highlight the importance of streamlining logistics processes in enhancing coordination among various players in the supply chain. The evolution of traditional SCM, integrated SCM, and collaborative SCM is discussed in detail; the importance of establishing metrics in measuring SCM performance is highlighted.

Part 4: e-Business implementation and globalisation examines e-business implementation strategies, the requisite structural changes, and legal aspects of doing e-business globally.

● **Chapter 9 e-Business change management: effective implementation of e-business strategies** provides a conceptualisation of e-business change management in terms of the DOT framework. A number of change management scenarios are presented to highlight situations in which people typically resist e-business initiatives. We argue that the success of e-business transformation entails rethinking the roles and responsibilities of managers and employees in terms of information processes. We explain that change management involves an ongoing series of tradeoffs between the design and implementation of e-business initiatives; we also pay attention to the cultural aspects of transformation.

● **Chapter 10 Legal considerations of global e-business** demonstrates why companies need to think about idiosyncratic legal frameworks across markets. The discussion also focuses on the regulatory environment and business variables which need to be understood when undertaking a global business perspective. Also, we discuss the critical issues of privacy and intellectual property rights.

Each chapter starts with a short synopsis to help the reader approach the material in systematic fashion. This is followed by specific topical learning objectives of the chapter. Throughout each chapter we use, as much as possible, well-known academic theories and concepts to provide the reader with a conceptual underpinning of the topics under study. We also provide a rich collection of examples and vignettes to expose the reader to interesting real-world issues through highlighting a particular problem, example, or method.

We finish each chapter with one or two real-life case studies, most of which are written by expert case-writers at the University of Hong Kong's Centre for Asian Business Cases (CABC). All the case study are anchored in solid teaching and learning objectives, and revolve around particular e-business concepts and theories; they are:

● decision and action-oriented, forcing the reader to assume an accountable decision-making role;

● analytical, encouraging readers to apply analytical techniques for choice-making and problem resolution; and

● global, covering real-life e-business operations of companies doing business across the world.

In compiling the case studies in the book we have tried to ensure diversity and richness by choosing 14 companies representing different industries and operating in different geographies. Such eclectic set of American, European, and Pan-Pacific cases should help the reader gain a better appreciation of the complexities involved in undertaking e-business transformation initiatives in today's inter-dependent global business environment. Two of the case studies specifically relate to the issues faced by small and medium sized enterprises.

Like any major writing effort, the successful fruition of this book would not have been possible without significant contributions by many people. First, my deepest thanks go to Amir Hoosain who oversaw the overall progress of the project. This book has benefited from his intellectual prowess, keen insights, and unbending dedication; he was indeed a delight to work with. Next, I am indebted to my three co-authors: Guy Gable, Shamza Khan, and Lynne Markus, who worked hard to ensure that their contributed chapters fit tightly with the DOT framework that holds the book together. I would also like to acknowledge the support of our capable team of professional case-writers at the CABC: Mary Ho, Phoebe Ho, Andrew Lee, Marissa McCauley, Vincent Mak, and Pauline Ng, as well as Greg Timbrell. Finally, the contributions of John Mooney, Fiacre Hensey, and Scott L. Schneberger, for providing the *Green Pastures Agribusiness* and *STATER NV* case studies, Guy Gable for supervising the *Return of the Jebi* case study, Lynne Markus for co-supervising the *Electronic Tendering System* case study, Julie Yu for co-supervising the *Citibank* and *Grey Worldwide* case studies, and Ben Yen for co-supervising the *Eastman Chemical* case study are duly recognised.

I should point out that in order to test the real-life viability of the concepts and theories used in this book we spent a significant amount of time with executives from the many organisations that participated in our case studies. We have materially benefited from the insight provided by these managers, and as such, acknowledge their contributions.

ALI F. FARHOOMAND
2004

Change and transformation in business

To explore the concept of success and how it can be assessed ❏

To recognize why transformation efforts often fail ❏

To learn about the concepts of complexity and chaos ❏

To find out how companies can manage increased complexity ❏
and chaos

To learn about organizational transformation processes ❏

To study the framework of Dynamic Organizational Tension ❏

To learn how this framework can be used as a springboard to study ❏
various issues associated with e-business transformation

> When change within a business is slower than that without, you're in real trouble. You can't predict the future but we can learn to react a lot faster than our adversaries.
>
> – Jack Welch, former General Electric CEO[1]

---

1. Pascale et al. (2000, p. 28).

We have all heard that contemporary businesses are facing an increasingly *complex* and *chaotic* world characterized by uncertainty, randomness, interdependence, and constant change. We have also heard that in order to survive in this complex and chaotic world, companies need to reinvent themselves, change from within, and transform.[2] But:

- What exactly do we mean by complexity and chaos?

- How do *complex adaptive systems*, such as organizations, change?

- Can companies deal with increased complexity through organizational transformation?

- Are there any patterns of order in today's seemingly chaotic business environment that can help companies in their transformational initiatives?

- How can companies manage complexity by building organizational structures that are fluid and adaptive?

- What role does technology play in structural transformations?

- How can companies leverage complexity and chaos to build and sustain competitive advantage?

In this chapter we address these issues by examining how companies can make order out of disorder through the effective management of their complex environment. In the process, we introduce a conceptual framework to show the intricate dynamic interplay among the major organizational dimensions: strategy, structure, processes, people, and technology.

We start the chapter by probing the question of what actually constitutes success in an e-business effort. We then proceed with a discussion of why so many organization transformation initiatives fall short of achieving success. Specifically we discuss the reason behind the failure of two very popular transformation efforts – total quality management (TQM) and business process reengineering (BPR). Because of the ambiguities ingrained in today's business lexicon, we then provide a brief introduction to the concepts of chaos, complexity, and complex adaptive systems with a view to highlighting their implications for e-business transformation. Next we discuss the steps involved in organizational transformation. This is followed by an introduction of the Dynamic Organizational Tension (DOT) framework. We use this framework to show how companies walk "at the edge of chaos" by maintaining dynamic tension among major forces within and outside their organizational bounds. We show that in order to manage e-business transformation successfully, companies need to strike a balance between their desire for stability,

---

2. *American Heritage Dictionary* defines the term *change* as "[t] the act, process, or result of altering or modifying", and the term *transformation* as "[a] marked change, as in appearance or character, usually for the better".

on the one hand, and the destabilizing forces in the market, on the other. Understanding the tradeoffs involved in this as well as other paradoxes is of paramount importance in transformational initiatives.

Success: a moving yardstick

Success: The accomplishment of what was aimed at.

– Oxford English Dictionary

Success: The favourable or prosperous termination of attempts and endeavours.

– Random House Dictionary

e-Business initiatives are increasingly vital to many organizations and typically involve a range of stakeholders – people with vested interests in what the technology promises to deliver. Different stakeholder groups have different needs and distinctive viewpoints on what type of outcome will constitute success. From a solution provider's point of view, a successful initiative is likely one that delivers the functional requirements and is completed within budgetary and time constraints. For senior executives, the expected benefit may involve improving visibility throughout the value chain and better managing the organization's resources; to the everyday user, a successful system may be one that enhances efficiency and job satisfaction. Perceptions of success in e-business are subject to multiple perspectives – thus the decision-makers behind an initiative must delve into the question of what criteria lead to success and, more importantly, how to balance the needs of different stakeholders and gauge how an initiative is progressing.

As a prelude to our exploration of the organizational transformation process, we begin by taking a critical look at the concept of business success. The two definitions given above serve as a basic illustration of the most common notions of what constitutes a successful endeavour. The first of the definitions hinges on attaining a pre-established goal: so long as this goal is accomplished, the endeavour may be considered a success. The second definition focuses instead on a favourable termination of the endeavour, irrespective of previous expectations. Since the effects of business transformation efforts are felt by many people, it can only be expected that both the original justification and the ongoing progress of transformation efforts will be subjected to close scrutiny. How then can a top decision-maker strike a balance between the goals established at the onset of an initiative and the evolving needs and expectations of different stakeholders?

The development of any business system is rooted in an organization's history. As such in order to assess the success of a system, we should first understand the pertinent context within which the system is developed before we can judge whether or not it has achieved its basic goals. The goals can be based on single- or multi-component criteria. Let us look to sports and other competitive activities as examples.[3]

---

3. Farhoomand (1992).

Some sports such as running, skiing, car racing, and swimming are judged according to one evaluative component: the time that it takes the participant(s) to finish a race. Similarly, the victor in sports such as hockey, football, and basketball is determined by only one evaluative component: the number of points (or goals) obtained within a fixed amount of time. Yet another set of sports such as volleyball, tennis, and golf depends on the attainment of pre-determined points, irrespective of time. All of these sports are easy to administer, provided that the players adhere to the rules. Apart from incidents that may lead to disagreement over the course of a game, by and large the role of an expert's judgement (i.e. a referee) in these games is kept to a minimum. The factor discriminating between winners and losers is the single evaluative component (e.g. time or score) on which the game is being assessed.

On the other hand, there are sports such as skating, gymnastics, and diving that are judged by a multi-criteria process. Several judges evaluate the performance of competitors based on their collective experiences and a set of pre-established criteria. For this category of sports, the subjective evaluation of the judges often plays a relatively large role in determining outcomes. Athletes act in concert with their environments by dynamically changing their behaviours and perceived goals in relation to changes in their surroundings (e.g. the behaviour of teammates and competitors or the goal itself).

The two types of evaluation functions we have outlined in the realm of competitive sports point to the potential for performance measures based on single, multiple, and composite criteria. As we shall see in our discussion of performance management (see Chapter 3), in business as in sports, well-chosen gauges of performance – whether based on single, multiple, or composite measures (so-called "portfolio" measurement techniques such as the balanced scorecard) – are critical for effective performance management.

Because it is usually difficult to assess a business decision based on a single evaluation criterion, organizations often seek to develop a number of criteria in order to focus attention on various aspects of the decision. In modern business, intense competition is the norm and managers face an immense set of ever-changing factors – the effects of innovation and competition lead to a moving-yardstick effect. As a result, perceptions of success may change from moment to moment as new developments occur. The use of a single determining criterion may fail to reflect important constraints that arise over the course of an initiative. The use of composite measurements of performance in determining success often serves as a more realistic barometer, but requires careful determination and weightings of the criteria, which are prone to changing priorities and a dynamic environment.

Measuring performance requires a clear understanding of the criteria used in the process of assessing success and may be developed through a four-step procedure.[4]

---

4. Nagle (1953).

1 *Defining the problem*: In what activities are we trying to determine success?

2 *Analyzing activities*: What are the goals of the activity? What performance standards are required? What is the relative importance of various related behaviours?

3 *Defining success*: What elements of the activity differentiate a successful system from an unsuccessful one? What are the weightings of these elements?

4 *Development of sub-criteria to measure the elements of success*: Are there any sub-criteria measures?

The crux of this approach is that one should first specify the goals or objectives before asking why some initiatives are successful while others are not. In other words, the approach leads to a focus on the "why" and "how" aspects of success.

Returning to our sports metaphor, we observe that competitors within almost all sports are ultimately assessed on a relative basis against some pre-defined benchmark. Drivers in the qualifying rounds of major car races enter the finals only if they beat a certain pre-specified time limit. So do athletes participating in swimming, running, and skiing. It should be noted that even though the winners of these sports may be selected based on their performance relative to the competition, their performance is also routinely judged against pre-established touchstones in the form of records. Obviously, records are not permanent and are improved over time. Here too we find a corollary in the business practice of continual improvement – the recurring activity aimed at increasing the organization's ability to fulfil customer requirements and exceed expectations.

A framework for e-business success

To understand the concept of e-business success, there is a need for a framework that highlights the basic properties of a successful system. To this end, we can extrapolate the premises underlying the general concepts of success – that is, goal-driven orientation, observers' attitudes, and time dependency – to further our understanding. We present a framework that reflects an e-business initiative as a system with *existing and attainable goals*. Furthermore, as we will explain in our discussion of e-business infrastructure in Chapters 4 and 5, the technical specifics of an initiative are also critical to a manager's stewardship in leading the organization to success.

As shown in the conceptual framework of e-business success (Figure 1.1), user and customer requirements dictate management's goals and business objectives, which in turn determine the choices made in terms of strategy, infrastructure, expenditures and implementation of the initiative. In addition, the perceived *quality* of the e-business initiative as well as the organizational *outcomes* resulting from it will also influence management's view of the system's success. In effect e-business success is a multi-faceted and complex concept, and its measurement entails the differing viewpoints of different stakeholders. Taken together we define

Figure 1.1 A conceptual framework of e-business success

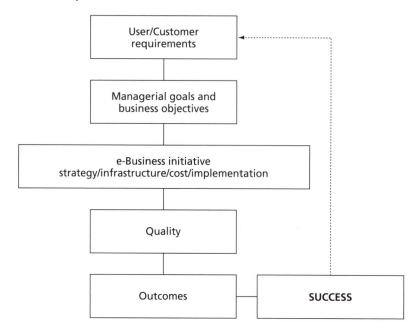

e-business success as the "correspondence between the stated goals (transactional, informational strategic) and the system's outcomes, taking into account the initiative's characteristics and perceived quality."

During the 1980s and 1990s researchers spent a great deal of effort trying to find ways to measure information systems' success. A majority of this work concentrated on user satisfaction as a proxy for system success. It was argued that if the end users of a system are satisfied, the system is successful. With the proliferation of the Internet, however, companies have increasingly come to the realization that e-business success hinges upon both internal and external factors.

Because e-business initiatives usually have multiple objectives, we should first understand why companies invest in information technology (IT). Lederer and associates (2001) divide the management objectives for IT investments into three groups: transactional benefits, informational benefits, and strategic benefits:[5]

1 Companies make *transactional IT* investment with the objective of automating their financial events such as payroll. The focus is on reducing costs and labour, and improving organizational efficiency and communications, in terms of both speed and quality of the information produced.

2 *Informational IT* investments are undertaken to improve management and operational control of the firm. The focus is on improving information quality, access, and flexibility.

---

5. Lederer et al. (2001).

3 Companies also make *strategic IT* investments with a view to gaining competitive advantage. Investments in this type of systems are made with the objective of attaining certain strategic goals such as enhancing competitiveness, responding to environmental changes or improving customer relations. We will further elaborate on these strategic objectives in the next chapter.

What causes transformation initiatives to fail?

Complexities involved in satisfying multiple goals and potential conflicts among various stakeholders with regard to these goals make it difficult for firms to successfully undertake transformational initiatives. But organizations' very existence depends on their ability to change and self-renew in order to deal with constant changes in their ecosystem. They need to transform continuously in order to grow, develop competitive advantage, or merely survive.

Transformation initiatives have gone under different names: downsizing, right sizing, de-layering, cultural change, restructuring, turnaround, TQM, BPR and so on. Even while these change efforts may have different focuses or take different approaches, they are all undertaken in response to changes in environmental conditions and with a view to sustaining strategic advantage. Given the prevalence and importance of change, then, why is it that findings show as much as 70 per cent of organizational change initiatives are unsuccessful?[6]

In the following section we examine TQM and BPR – the most widely applied transformation approaches of the last two decades – to explore why change efforts often do not succeed.

Total quality management

The concept of TQM swept corporate America in the early 1980s before spreading to the rest of the world. While some firms launching TQM initiatives saw modest improvements in key performance indicators, it has been estimated that as much as 80 per cent have been disappointed with their results. Below is a list of the major reasons why TQM did not work:[7]

- *Top management's failure to change*: The success of TQM depends on a paradigm shift in management thinking; TQM works only if senior management develops a deep and comprehensive understanding of the initiative.

- *Rigid corporate culture*: For TQM to work, it requires a participatory management style. However, many companies are bound by hierarchical, command-and-control structures and are unable to empower employees. This in turn hampers the free flow of information between management and employees.

---

6. Beer and Nohria (2001).
7. Gunneson (1997).

- *Fear and distrust*: In the absence of clear communication, employees often grow suspicious of change initiatives. They grow concerned about the impact of the change on their jobs, develop anxiety over job security and thus exhibit resistance to change.

- *Limited focus*: Many TQM initiatives have focused on certain processes without studying the holistic impact of changes brought about to the entire organization.

- *Credibility of implementation*: Because of an incomplete focus, employees may not understand the rationale behind the transformation process, how it works, how they can participate, and what is in it for them.

- *Lack of strategic fit*: Many TQM initiatives did not succeed because they were not integrally linked to the organization's basic strategic processes, particularly the key customer processes.

- *Inadequate management process*: Management processes are required to measure the progress of the transformation initiative. Beginning with top management, each executive should be accountable for monitoring the progress of change.

Business process reengineering

In the early 1990s, BPR emerged as the latest elixir to invigorate an underperforming business.[8] The basic idea was to link IT with processes that cut across functional boundaries. Michael Hammer and John Champy defined the term as "... the fundamental rethinking and radical redesign of business processes to achieve dramatic results improvements in contemporary measures of performance, such as cost, quality, service and speed."[9] The concept came with much appeal as it promised business transformation from the ground level and in a short timeframe – something that other change efforts such as TQM failed to deliver.

By the mid-1990s, over 70 per cent North American and European companies were engaged in some form of reengineering, creating a $51 billion business.[10] By the late 1990s, however, with inconclusive evidence about the effectiveness of BPR, its allure started to fade. Even its primary champions conceded that 70 per cent of all reengineering projects failed.[11] BPR had become associated with downsizing, leading to employees' demoralization and other dysfunctional behaviour. Indeed, a late 1990s survey of companies found that efforts to reengineer solely on cost-cutting grounds severely undercut morale without any compensating benefit in the long term.[12]

---

8. For a good discussion of the status of BPR, consult Sarker and Lee (2002).
9. Hammer and Champy (1993).
10. CSC Index (1994).
11. Davenport (1995).
12. Balachandran and Thiagarajan (1999).

Why did such a promising transformation approach lead to such lacklustre results? Major reasons include:

- *Cost-driven*: During the economic recession of the 1980s, firms were keen to find ways to restructure their businesses. With the emergence of BPR, corporate executives seized the opportunity to deal with redundancy problems. Cost-cutting and lay-offs were packaged under the lofty banner of reengineering; instead of the overhaul of basic processes, immediate and tangible cost reduction became the goal. These short-term measures in turn led not only to the rapid loss of human capital and employee loyalty, but also to organizational "memory". Companies were unable to replace the knowledge, know-how, skills, and experiences that had resided in the laid-off individuals.

- *Myth of the clean slate*: To senior management who had become frustrated with incremental improvements, the notion of a "clean-slate" approach to reengineering had particular appeal. Under this approach, design teams attempted to build best practices into all processes, without regard to constraints of existing information systems or other organizational factors. This clean-slate approach is rarely found in practice, however, because few firms can afford to "obliterate" their existing business environments and start from scratch,[13] something espoused by the original iteration of the BPR doctrine.

- *Insufficient breadth*: In contrast to the clean-slate myth, many reengineering projects did not succeed because of insufficient process breadth. Corporate issues are often defined in very narrow functional terms such as sales problem or human resources conflict. This type of functional view prevents companies from fully understanding the cross-functional, inter-organizational nature of processes. Discarding, or paying lip service to intrinsic interdependence, resulted in incremental, patched solutions. Successful process requires that all dimensions of the solution space have been properly aligned to deliver some strategic value.

- *Unclear or non-existent performance measures*: Based on a McKinsey Consulting study of BPR projects, most companies did not achieve measurable performance impacts.[14] Paradoxically, many managers involved in these change projects never learnt that their reengineering efforts did not have measurable impacts. They analyzed improvements relative to the process being redesigned, rather than the organization as a whole.

- *Technology as the solution*: IT-driven transformation, when viewed as the solution to fix an organizational problem, can ultimately lead to disappointing results. Process designers, usually led by IT specialists, identify new technologies and, based on their understanding of the properties and

---

13. Stoddard and Jarvenpaa (1995).
14. Hall et al. (1994).

capabilities of the new technologies, formulate solutions and designed improvements to existing business problems. This type of "engineering" view of the firm can be restrictive because it focuses on problem-solving as an end in itself. In Chapter 2 we show that for transformations to be successful, companies need to take an "architectural" view of business by focusing on relationships within and between processes and other organizational dimensions.

IT specialists often steer BPR change projects into proofs-of-concept for leading-edge technologies, assuming that the effective design and creation of enabling technology is a sufficient condition for successful implementation of the business redesign. These IT-driven reengineering efforts usually tend to focus on incremental improvement in automating existing processes, undermining the "obliteration" concept behind the original BPR idea. Another drawback of this approach is the pre-conceived fixation on a technology-based solution. This occurs when management pre-selects a technology solution based on the successful implementation of that technology by a major competitor or a recommendation from a long-standing technology partner, without a methodological study of the involved business processes.[15]

- *Lack of senior management support*: As in any major change effort, objections and disagreements that can only be solved through senior management intervention arise in reengineering projects. In addition, unless senior executives are personally involved in the design of new processes, they may be unwilling to authorize major expenditures to implement those designs. It is estimated that 30–50 per cent of a very senior executive's time is necessary to achieve major change across broad, cross-functional processes.[16]

- *Lack of empowerment*: While senior management support is crucial, project success will ultimately depend on how quickly and effectively employees themselves embrace change. Half of the companies undertaking BPR efforts report that the most difficult aspect is dealing with fear and anxiety in their organizations.[17] Transformations yield anticipated results only if employees are empowered to thoroughly understand the rationale behind the change, are part of the change, and have a sense of ownership of the transformation effort. It is only then that companies can keep employees accountable for results.

- *Excessive reliance on consultants*: Given the scale and complexity of reengineering projects, it is rare that companies can carry out the implementation internally. Most reengineering projects involve outside consultants who act as knowledge experts in the definition and execution of the BPR project. The value of the consultants lies in their capability to introduce best practices from other projects, and to influence the strategic thinking of the

---

15. Orr and Crowfoot (1992).
16. Hall et al. (1994).
17. Davenport (1995).

organization. Being brought in from the outside, however, consultants cannot be expected to have in-depth understanding of the structural and human capitals that are embedded in the organization. Because non-codified organizational knowledge is not amenable to direct management consultant influence, it tends to be neglected in the analysis and implementation processes.

In sum, successful organizational transformation requires a holistic approach that focuses on the dynamic interplay between the actors, the context, and the technology.[18] The following is an abbreviated list of the major pitfalls in transformation efforts:

- studying processes in isolation

- treating technology as a panacea

- insufficient management involvement throughout the change effort

- neglecting the organization's cultural legacy

- inappropriate or unclear performance measures

- lack of integration with the organization's basic strategic processes.

The proliferation of advanced information and communication technologies, the accelerated rate of globalization in business, and the increased interdependence among organizations present both challenges and opportunities to businesses. In response, companies are keenly aware that they should *change* in order to survive, but recognize that it is not easy to bring transformation efforts to fruition. The statistics reflecting the huge failure of change efforts inform us that something is amiss: that we need more effective change strategies in order to achieve the desired outcomes from transformation initiatives; and that we need to gain a better understanding of the complexities embedded in today's rugged business landscape.

Things appear complex because we do not *understand* them. When we understand something, it no longer appears complex. An understanding of chaos and complexity theories will help us in our journey to understand the chaotic and complex environment that we live in.

Chaos, complexity and complex adaptive systems

She who wants to have right without wrong, order without disorder,
Does not understand the principles of heaven and earth.
She does not know how things hang together.
            – Chuang Tzu, third century BC philosopher

---

18. Markus and Robey (1988).

DID YOU KNOW

- We tend to regard things we cannot control as chaotic. However the precise definition of *chaos* is ". . . that unlikely occurrence in which we cannot find patterns or understand interrelationships. It is the state within which things appear to proceed according to chance but in fact their behavior is determined by precise laws" (Pascale, 2000, p. 6). For example, even though a swarm of ants in a colony may seem chaotic at first glance, they are actually part of a complex adaptive system. In other words, "order and chaos are mirror images, two states that contain the other . . . A system can descend into chaos and unpredictability, yet within that state of chaos the system is held within boundaries that are well ordered and predictable. Without partnering of these two great forces, no change or progress is possible. Chaos is necessary to new creative ordering" (Wheatley, p. 13).

- *Complexity* ". . . occurs when systems are beyond linear understanding, beyond simple cause/effect, and beyond particular analysis, but have not yet 'spilled over' into the area of chaos" (McMaster, 1996, p. 13). It is the state of being "at the edge of chaos," a desired place between rigidity and chaos. We can understand systems by looking for patterns within their complexity, patterns that describe potential evolutions of the system. Companies can use complexity to transform the chaotic and complicated into something simple, to bring order out of disorder.

- Through *self-organization*, members of a company keep their individual identities while, at the same time, function in a web of relationships. In the face of threat or a compelling opportunity, self-organization takes place only at the edge of chaos. Self-organization refers to the important principle of self-renewal, the ability to adapt and reorganize as needed. The viability and resiliency of self-organizing systems come from their capacity to adapt rapidly and to create flexible transitory structures that allow them to reorganize into different forms in order to maintain their identity. In other word, self-organized systems are fluid; they adopt structures that suit the present situation.

In order to study e-business transformation, we first need to gain a good understanding of complex adaptive systems. In the process, we must also get insights into the concepts of chaos and complexity.

Let us start our discussion with a routine example: the weather. One time or another we have all experienced inaccuracies in weather forecasting. Why are meteorologists unable to predict weather with perfect accuracy in spite of the sophisticated arsenal of technologies they have at their disposal: satellites, complex and elaborate simulation models, and some of the world's most powerful computers?

The short answer is, "the butterfly effect," a term attributed to the meteorologist Martin Lorenz. "Does the flap of a butterfly's wings in Brazil set off a tornado in Texas?" he pondered.[19] While Lorenz declined answering the question directly, he noted that, ". . . if a single flap could lead to a tornado that would not otherwise have formed, it could equally well prevent a tornado that would otherwise have formed." In other words, Lorenz relied on chaos theory to observe that in complex systems a very small event may have unpredictable yet consequential effects on the whole system. The **butterfly effect** is at the heart of chaos theory; it illustrates that most things in life are non-linear, and that in order to understand the cause and effect of a phenomenon we need to go beyond obvious linear relationships.

Chaos theory takes a holistic view of the world within which **relationship** is the key. Nothing exists except in relation to everything else. In the chaotic world, order emerges through a web of relationships that constitute the whole. That is why in studying organizations we must focus on relationships, rather than analyzing merely the tangible parts. This focus is of fundamental significance in any initiative relating to organizational transformation; no single process is meaningful unless it is studied within the realm of relationships with other parts of the system.

We can observe the importance of relationship in all aspects of life, including the arts and sciences: "I don't paint things, I paint only relationships between things," said Henry Matisse, the famed impressionist. In the same vein, organizational designers, those responsible for devising the business architecture,[20] should not treat individual processes as "things" that can be studied in isolation. Rather, the roles and impacts of individual processes should be examined in the realm of their dynamic fit in the whole system. As we just discussed, one of the main reasons TQM and BPR projects have not succeeded is because of a focus on individual processes rather than on the whole organization.

Chaos theory embodies many paradoxes observed in our daily lives. It allows us to better understand the disorder that underlies apparent order. It is about keeping individual identities within a web of relationships. As with all living organisms we try, on the one hand, to maintain a clear sense of individual identity within a larger network of relationships that help shape our identity. On the other hand, our individual survival depends on how we learn to participate in a web of relationships. At the same time we produce ourselves, we change in order to preserve, we self-organize.[21]

Complex adaptive systems

Organizations are open, non-linear systems that use feedback systems to co-evolve and survive. Like other complex adaptive systems, organizations share the following common characteristics:[22]

---

19. The paper was presented at a conference in Washington in 1972, but was never published in any journal. It is reproduced in Lorenz, M. *The Essence of Chaos*, UCL Press, 1993, London.
20. For details of business architecture see the next chapter.
21. Wheatley (1999).
22. For detailed discussion of complexity, see Kelly and Allison (1999) and Wheatley (1999).

- They are **open systems** that interact with their environment through the exchange of energy, material, and feedback (in the form of information).

- Each organization forms a part of the environment for other organizations. This **co-evolution** is particularly true in today's networked business environment where the action of a given company triggers action and reaction in other companies.

- Contrary to popular belief, equilibrium is a precursor to organizational decline because organizations are less likely to respond to change when in a state of equilibrium.[23] Companies need to have **disequilibrium**-generating devices to deter complacency. The case study following this chapter, *Global Recycle Ltd: An e-Business Strategy*, deals with a young Scottish entrepreneur's efforts to develop an online exchange and take the age-old business of scrap dealing to a new dimension by changing established modes of business practice. Later on we see how companies can use diversity and variety as a means of reinvigorating their systems. We also discuss how inertia, the subtle yet lingering drive for persevering equilibrium, can lead to the erosion of strategic advantage.

- Organizations are **non-linear**. Simple cause-and-effect fails to explain organizational complexity. Chaos theory tells us a small change in a system's initial condition can have a vast effect on the final outcome of the system. As such, a small misstep in the beginning of a business project or initiative may have a substantive impact on the final outcome of the project. For example, we have seen how a small misunderstanding in analyzing users' requirements in a proposed system could drastically affect the usefulness of that system; an innocuous rumour can blow up into uncontrollable self-feeding frenzy; or an action by a small group could put the whole organization in jeopardy, as was in the Enron case.

- Organizations use information as a **feedback** mechanism to see how well they are doing compared with their stated objectives. Sales reports of a newly launched product, for example, tell a company how well they are doing against their sales target. Feedback loops can be either *balancing* (negative) or *amplifying* (positive). Balancing feedback loops use information to prevent a system deviating from desired goals. The objective is to achieve stability by regulating and controlling various operations. For example, the information related to a project's cost overrun is fed back into the system, prompting management to curtail costs. Like thermostats, managers use negative loops to evaluate performance against standards.

---

23. Pascale et al. (2000).

In contrast, amplifying feedback loops use information to see if there is something new and amplify it to signal a need to change. In amplifying loops, information increases and disturbances grow, prompting change to avoid system deterioration. In effect, disequilibrium is used to the system's advantage, it is used as a vehicle for growth. By employing an amplifying feedback loop, for example, companies can reward individual creativity, thus fostering organizational innovations.

The implications of a feedback loop for e-business transformation should be obvious. They can be used for better organizational control and, at the same time, for faster market responsiveness.

● GE's senior executives routinely go through **workouts** – meetings during which employees rebuke top executives over unwanted bureaucracy and redundant work practices.[24] This workout programme not only improves communication up and down the organizational echelons, but more importantly, it rids the company of outmoded and counter-productive habits.

● Organizations have *fractal* structures, forms in which nested parts are shaped into the same pattern as the whole (self-similarity). In essence, **self-similarity** happens when the functional relationships among a system's subsystems are similar to the relationships between the elements in each subsystem. Fractals show the partnering of chaos and order; they are the emergent patterns underlying the order in disorder. Try to get hold of a fern and examine it very closely. You would be amazed to find out that the whole structure of the leaf is based on repetition of a *simple* shape comprising only four straight lines. This pattern is repeated over and over, free to change in size but not shape, to create fern trees and forests.[25]

● Companies can increase organizational flexibility and agility by building self-similarity in their structures. Faced with a sudden threat or opportunity, companies with self-similar structures can change direction quickly because of their ability to assemble effective teams.[26] Companies can achieve self-similarity usually by building culture, values, and processes that are self-similar. *Emerson Electric* embedded self-similar processes throughout its organization by successfully drilling the essential elements of management processes into every manager at the company.

24. Tichy and Charan (1989).
25. Like any other self-organizing system ferns reproduce themselves by small spores, which are single-celled reproductive bodies capable of growing into a new organism. See Wheatley (1999) for detailed discussion of *fractals*.
26. Kelly and Allison (1999).

EMERSON ELECTRIC

When I meet with people outside Emerson, I'm often asked: What makes Emerson tick? That question typically reflects an interest in the company's consistent financial performance over the past three-and-a-half decades – but my answer deals with issues that go far beyond financial statements.

Simply put, what makes us "tick" at Emerson is an effective management process. We believe that we can shape our future through careful planning and strong follow-up. Our managers plan for improved results and execute to get them. Driving this process is a set of shared values, including involvement, intensity, discipline, and persistence. We adhere to few policies or techniques that could be called unique or even unusual. But we do act on our policies, and that may indeed make us unusual.

It is crucial to "keep it simple." A corporation has to have a simple plan, simple communications, simple programs, and simple organizations. It takes real discipline to keep things simple.

The first pieces of our management process were put in place during the 1950s, when (we) established two fundamental principles –

continuous cost-reduction and open communication – as central to everyday management. The first of the two has correctly been described as a "religion" and "a way of life" at Emerson. Every year for the past three-and-half decades (in good times and bad), the company has set cost-reduction goals at every level and required plant personnel to identify the specific measures necessary to achieve those objectives. The second principle – open communication – is also fundamental to the management process. For decades, Emerson division presidents and plant managers have met regularly with all employees to discuss the specifics of our business and our competition. We continue this practice today because we believe people are more likely to be receptive to change if they know why, when, and how it's coming; they need to be involved in the process.

Organizational transformation

Organizational change is commonly divided into incremental and radical (evolutionary and revolutionary). Incremental change relates to a series of continuous progressions that affect only part of the organization, while radical change entails a frame-breaking burst that blows out the established organizational equilibrium.[27]

Transformation is more closely related to radical change because it usually affects the entire organization. However, transformation is not an on–off event because it does not necessarily happen through sudden bursts. Rather, transformation is usually accompanied by a series of continuous progressions that involve putting in place fundamental technologies, creating new structures and processes, developing new products/services, or creating new markets. As discussed above, transformation projects are bound to fail if they do not account for the dynamic tension between various organizational components, including employees affected by such organizational change. The case study following this

---

27. Daft (1998).

chapter, *Green Pastures Agribusiness*, illustrates how a business competing in the long-established fertilizer industry grappled with differing objectives and perceptions among its business units during its efforts to embark on major sourcing and procurement initiatives.

Organizational transformation entails dissecting the familiar relics of the past with a view to moving the company towards the edge of chaos, thus allowing a higher level of organizational mutation and experimentation. Typified by marked changes in form and character, transformation is about becoming something that has a new form, but at the same time it is identifiable as a realization of the original. Transformation implies a major change, but at the same it entails continuation. In transformation process, the history of self-organizing systems matters a great deal because new events are influenced by all past decisions and events.

Many management gurus have craftily discussed the importance of history in organizational learning – the ability to build good theories based on past experiences to explain organizational behaviour. "History is a process of transformation through conservation . . . Keeping a few essential parts as a base and allowing change to occur," Peter Drucker commends.[28] Henry Mintzberg also highlighted the importance of history:[29]

> The French term for medical operation is 'intervention'. Intervening is what all surgeons and too many managers do. Managers keep operating on their systems, radically altering them in the hope of fixing them, usually by cutting things out. Then they leave the consequences of their messy business to the nurses of the corporate world . . .

So companies should initiate transformation projects not only for diagnostic reasons, trying to "fix" emerging dysfunctional processes, but more importantly as a means for self-renewal, growth, and development. The success of such initiatives depends on the dynamic synchronization of the key organizational dimensions with the environment.

Transformation process phases

The transformation process can be divided into six broad phases:[30]

1 *Initiation*: The organizational transformation process is initiated by the realization that something is needed, wanted and is possible beyond the ordinary. The "antennas" of self-organizing companies are instinctively up because continuous transformation is essential to the evolutionary process of self-renewal. They constantly scan their environment, examine market

---

28. For an interesting coverage watch the video, "Leading in a time of change: a conversation with Peter F. Drucker & Peter M. Senge," the Drucker Foundation, San Francisco, CA: Jossey-Bass, 2001.
29. Mintzberg (1996, p. 10).
30. Kotter (1995) and McMaster (1996) provide excellent coverage of this topic.

forces, and identify potential threats and opportunities. The crucial thing at this stage is establishing a sense of urgency. John Kotter, a Harvard professor, found that over 50 per cent of transformation projects falter at this stage because of senior management's impatience or inability to create a sense of urgency.[31] It is not usually easy to bring people out of their comfort zones and drum up support for a potentially destabilizing initiative.

2   *Coalition*: The next step relates to assembling a powerful coalition. In the absence of an initial critical mass of people with commitment, transformation projects fail even before they start. Initially, the size of coalition should be around three to five people based on the size of the company. However for large companies, the size of coalition needs to be expanded to the 20–50 range in order for the project to grow.

     In recent years because transformation efforts usually extend the organizational boundaries, coalitions have come to involve external parties. In Chapter 2 we will discuss the role of partnerships in e-business strategic formulation.

3   *Formulation of a vision*: The new ideas must be communicated and promoted widely and iteratively in order to heighten the organization's awareness and understanding. Using the right "language" is very important in this phase. Many transformational initiatives get stuck here because of the inability of the initiators to articulate and share their ideas with the rest of the organization. Formulation of a vision can be possible only if the language used to describe the new phenomenon is integrated with the existing language and practice. It is the job of the guiding coalition to communicate the new vision by "walking the talk," becoming an embodiment, a symbol of the transformation vision and culture. In the *Green Pastures* case, we will see that when senior managers fail to manage the interplay between employees and technology, the prospects of transformation efforts can become seriously jeopardized. Let us not forget that in the final analysis there would be no transformation unless hundreds or thousands of people who are being affected by the change are going to buy into the transformation initiative. Many obstacles, including inflexibility in structures or systems, and stonewalling by employees who are threatened by the transformation, should first be removed before the organization can proceed to the next step.

4   *Experimentation*: When an idea is attractive enough to require action, it enters this phase. Through experimentation, companies can test the viability of new ideas and theories. Innovativeness requires a culture that is amenable to continuous experimentation; companies that do not encourage experimentation are not usually innovative. But since excess experimentation may lead to the disruption of the core business, a viable strategy is to

---

31. Kotter (1995).

cultivate fringes around the company. The success of this type of strategy, however, depends on a company's ability to promote the new ideas internally.

Consider the case of the Xerox research and development lab, Palo Alto Research Centre (PARC), which invented many familiar technologies including the first personal computer (Alto), the mouse, Ethernet, laser printer, flat screen and so on. Xerox failed to reap the economic benefits of these innovations because of its inability to integrate the new inventions into its mainstream business.[32] A company that may have been a technology powerhouse is now relegated to the bottom of product food chain, manufacturing commoditized products such as generic copiers. The company's market valuation reflects this sorry state of affairs.[33]

5 *Integration and implementation*: During this phase, new ideas are implemented and integrated into the mainstream organization. Successful integration, however, is possible only if the new way of doing things is anchored in and, at the same time, subsumes the old system. In this process, the daunting challenge is the deep understanding of the business architecture, mapping form to function by focusing on holistic relationships between processes rather than on individual processes.

6 *Institutionalization*: Transformation is a continuous process that requires constant fine-tuning and improvement; it is a never-ending process because self-renewal is an intrinsic attribute of complex systems such as organizations. After successful integration and implementation, companies need to imprint what they have learned in the transformation process into their "DNA" so that the new processes can begin to reinvent themselves.

Paradoxes surrounding organizational transformation

A **paradox** is a seemingly contradictory statement that may nonetheless be true. By posing a tension between two apparently contradictory statements, we induce creative thinking about how such contradictions can exist in reality.[34]

As complex systems, organizations need to grapple with numerous paradoxes that entail tradeoffs. Understanding and reconciling these paradoxes is a difficult but necessary part of organizational transformation.

Diversity vs uniformity

Companies need to strike a balance between uniformity and diversity. Whereas uniformity perpetuates a winning formula, diversity weakens that formula.

32. Pascale et al. (2000).
33. In the last 25 years, shares of Xerox have significantly under performed those of Hewlett Packard, Compaq, and IBM.
34. Robey (1997).

In the next chapter we show that one of the sources of erosion of competitive advantage is sub-optimization, a term used to describe people's resistance to change in the face of their previous successes. "If it ain't broke, why fix it?" is the mantra encouraging and advancing sub-optimization in organizations.

But, paradoxically, diversity is indispensable to the firm's survival. In Cybernetics, the Law of Requisite Variety states that the long-term survival of an open system depends on variety and diversity within the system. Similarly, in the world of the new science, it is widely accepted that the evolution of complex systems is accelerated in the presence of parasites. As parasites attack their host, the host will evolve to protect itself, but the parasites will in turn find a new line of attack for which the host will find a new way of defending itself. In this type of "evolutionary arms race," the ability to change faster than the rivals, then, becomes a source of sustainable advantage.

Jack Welch, the former CEO of General Electric and one of the most influential and celebrated executives of the past century, used "genetic diversity" as a disequilibrium-generating device to increase GE's immune system.[35] When he took over as GE's CEO in 1980, Welch recognized that even while its major divisions were profitable, most did not have any competitive advantage, mainly because they were too comfortable in their oligopolistic markets. In response to this complacency, Welch set a new agenda: Every division had to become number one or two in its respective market. Similarly, just before retiring, in 1999 he challenged each GE business head to "(1) hire 30 to 60 people with e-commerce or other non-traditional backgrounds, (2) protect them from the organization's immune defence response, and (3) come up with viable 'Destroy-Your-Business.com' options within six to nine months."[36] By doing so, Welch unleashed "parasites" into the GE's ecosystem in order to increase its resiliency so that it could turn potential threats into opportunities.

Today, GE is one of the most "e-business ready" companies in the world. A large proportion of traditional companies, however, reacted to the proliferation of the Internet too slowly; some even ignored it altogether. In the absence of champions (internal parasites), these companies succumbed to competitors and new entrants (external parasites) who seized the opportunity brought about by the Internet to cannibalize incumbents' existing businesses.

Simplicity vs complexity

> Business isn't complicated. The complications arise when people are cut off from information they need ... Ironically, it's hard to keep things simple ... Simple doesn't mean easy.
>
> – Jack Welch[37]

---

35. Trisoglio (1995, p. 24).
36. Pascale et al. (2000, p. 30).
37. Tichy and Charan (1989).

Art students soon learn that one of the most fundamental principles of composition and design is simplicity. Less is more. To understand this concept, take a look at a painting you are fond of. One that exudes dynamic tension through a vibrant interplay of colours, hues, light, shapes, lines, contrasts, movement, and pattern: a painting that whets your visual appetite. Now "study" the picture by squinting your eyes slightly so that you are not distracted by its details. Let your eyes wander around the canvas by following the "rhythm" underlying the painting. Ask yourself, "What makes the painting appealing?"

You will perhaps come up with many reasons. Invariably, though, you will find the answer in *simplicity*. Of course, many design principles influence the quality of an artwork, but simplicity usually stands out as a guiding light in art. In a way, art is about making simplicity out of complex things: to use a few decisive and bold brush strokes to capture the complexity of a forest, intricacies of a crowded market, dynamism of a facial expression and so on. That is not to say that art is easy. In contrast, mastering any art is an arduous task, requiring years of studying and practice. Indeed, it is rather difficult but necessary to derive simplicity out of complexity. Creating dynamic tension in art requires the ability to see the deep structure between various parts; not to see things but the relationships between them (see *All that Jazz*).

The same is true in organizational design: complexity and simplicity mirror one another; one contains the other. In our discussion of approaches to strategy presented in the next chapter, we discuss how companies can treat strategy as simple rules when dealing with today's complex business world.

ALL THAT JAZZ

Like wine, it takes time and a little curiosity to develop an effective "palate" for listening to Jazz, the truly great 20th century contribution to the world of music. At first listening we are overwhelmed by complexity and often a seemingly chaotic cacophony. Jazz sounds complex because so much of the art form relies on recognition of elements of the music which often do not reveal themselves to the undiscriminating listener. Like most art forms, the true inspiration of the music to those that create, perform and listen to it is the delightful simplicity that emerges from these seemingly complex and chaotic underlying elements in combination.

Good jazz, like all good music, is indeed much more than the sum of its elements. It conveys the real intent of the composition, its emotion: be it drama, fun, longing, exuberance, melancholy, joy, loneliness; the fusion of sound and spirit. Jazz appreciation grows from

identifying the relationships between the three principal building blocks of composition: conception, integration and execution. Conception is the emotion or message that the composer intends to convey, the emergent whole. Integration is the design of the various elements together to create the mood. Execution is the expression of the composer's intent within the technical limits of the instruments and the musicians' skills, but also crucially, the way the musicians become immersed in the whole. Because none of these three elements have much meaning on their own, the listener has to explore how these elements combine in complex ways to create emergent yet simple themes.

Jazz becomes less of a mystery when we can identify and appreciate its underlying elements. We have to develop the right "palate" by training our ears to discern simplicity out of complexity. To appreciate the whole, the composition, we must first learn to deconstruct the music by recognizing and identifying the various audible elements emanating from combinations of instruments. We can form the foundations by identifying the underlying rhythmic structures from base and percussion. At the same time, we should watch for the introduction of counterpoints to rhythmic structures by leading instruments – piano, saxophone, trumpet, voice, the full onslaught of brass. The growing complexity generated by the confluence of the rhythmic structure and the leading instruments would eventually lead to the emergence of a dominant theme. With the theme, simplicity typically emerges as individual elements disappear and the whole comes out. It is only then that we start hearing the essence of the whole – the purpose of the composition.

Jazz is simple, yet complex; complex, yet simple: a paradox.

Source: Fredrik Pretorius, The University of Hong Kong.

Organizational legacy vs need for change

On one hand, organizations need to change in order to grow. On the other hand, they are shackled by inflexibilities embedded in their legacy – the existing systems, processes, structures, and culture. Without the stewardship of a flexible and far-sighted management team, companies in traditionally low-tech industries (as in our *Green Pastures Agribusiness case study*) are often too content with simple proven technologies that have served them well to date. While all businesses are deeply reliant on their organizational legacy, this complacency retards the pace of change and adaptation, and can eventually lead to the firm's demise. In the face of a rapidly changing environment, many companies stick to the winning formulas of the past, rather than changing their legacy systems. This strategy usually fails because it assumes stable market conditions; it ignores the fact that at turbulent times the rules of the game may drastically change, rendering their legacy systems obsolete.

Not long ago, many companies grappled with the paradox surrounding the so-called *channel conflict*, wondering how to deal with the thorny issue of cannibalization in their existing channels of distribution. This paradox was – and still is – based on the tenuous assumption that multiple channels cannot co-exist. In hindsight, though, we know that this assumption was an outgrowth of entrenched organizational legacy, preventing companies from breaking free from inflexibilities built into their traditional distribution channels.

In the late 1990s, Wall Street shunned Merrill Lynch because analysts thought Merrill was losing ground to discount brokerage Charles Schwab. e-Commerce gurus attributed Merrill's dilemma to its inability to resolve the channel conflict triggered by online trading. What they did not realize was that Merrill had undertaken a massive transformation initiative, which included the distribution channel problem. It first acquired D.E. Shaw, an innovative investment company with a highly regarded discount broker. More impressively, it then quietly set in motion an e-business transformation program to integrate and synchronize various types of information used by its army of traders, financial and research analysts, as well as its customers.[38] Even though the transformation initiative was a daunting and massive task, it was strategically necessary. All in all, the Internet provided an opportunity for Merrill to bring order and speed where there had been chaos. Today, Merrill is vindicated and cited as a case study on successful e-business transformation. In contrast, many firms lacked the vision or missed an opportunity to use the Internet to set free from the shackles of legacy.

A framework of DOT

Equilibrium: A condition in which all acting influences are canceled by others, resulting in a stable, balanced, or unchanging system.[39]

Not long ago, organization scientists and business executives alike agreed – and some still do – that equilibrium and stability serve as prerequisites for effective organizational design and development. It was argued – incorrectly – that equilibrium is a necessary precursor for good organizational design; that a change in environment or any internal dimensions has to be counterbalanced (cancelled) by corresponding changes in other organizational dimensions. The proponents of this view argued that the desired state is a stable, balanced, and unchanging system; equilibrium is the end state for which organizations strived.

This tenuous view, however, is grounded in a "mechanical" view of the world. According to the second law of thermodynamics, equilibrium is the final stage in the evolution of *closed* systems, a point when the system has done all its work and can produce nothing more. At equilibrium, a closed system has dissipated all its energy, thus exhausting its capacity to change.[40]

More recently the debilitating shortcoming of equilibrium for open systems has become clear. Unlike deterministic systems like machines that thrive only under stable conditions, equilibrium is neither the goal nor the fate of organizations. In contrast, because companies constantly interact with their environment, they actually seek disequilibrium as a necessary condition for growth and development. Change is regarded as an adaptive response to some tension within the business ecosystem. When some part of the system changes, a tension between this and other parts of the system is created, which will be resolved by the adaptive change of the other parts. Put differently, organizations continuously keep themselves off balance so that they can change in order to grow. At the same time they organize themselves so that they are ready for unexpected environmental changes.

---

38. *The Economist* (2001, pp. 85–86).
39. American Heritage Dictionary.
40. Wheatley (1999).

STRUCTURAL ENGINEERS DESIGN WELD-FREE STEEL FRAME

Researchers at the University of California, San Diego have applied post-tensioning, a technique commonly used in the construction of concrete buildings and bridges, to create a new class of weld-free steel-framed structures. The initial test indicated that the post-tensioned steel frames could absorb strong earthquake motions with little or no damage.

By adding tremendous tension to rods that run horizontally through the beams and columns, squeezing them together like an elastic band, a steel frame can be constructed without welded joints. Strong post-tensioned rods clamp the beams to the columns, holding them together. These high-strength rods provide the spring force, which allows the system to return to its initial position after it is deformed during an earthquake. Another unique feature is that the behaviors of the structure can be modified as its function changes over time – something that cannot be done with welded joints.

Source: http://www.soe.ucsd.edu/news_events/news_2002/20020402.html, 2 April 2002

In the remainder of this chapter we introduce the framework of DOT as a springboard to discuss how this book is organized. The framework (shown in Figure 1.2) is based on the premise that for companies to grow, they need to keep dynamic tension among the five major organization dimensions (strategy, structure, people, technology, processes) and five major external forces (customers, suppliers, partners, competitors, regulators). Because a change in any internal dimension or external force results in tension between that factor and

Figure 1.2 Framework of DOT

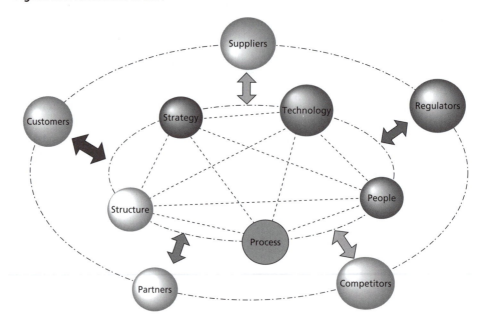

all other factors, organizations need to put in place fluid, flexible, and agile networked organizational forms so that they can respond to market changes faster than rivals in order to gain a business advantage. Using this reconfigurable structure, companies can quickly combine skills and resources across the firm to respond to changes in the external environment.

Whereas firms could previously try to avoid complexity, today they have to learn to embrace and manage complexity. Traditional top-down structures are simply incapable of accounting for interdependence among organizations because they slow down the flow of information between and within organizations. On a similar note, strategies ingrained in protected or stable markets are no longer adequate in today's ever-changing global markets; companies need to adopt innovative approaches in their strategy. Whereas in times of relative stability, companies can reinforce their existing dominant organizational form by *exploiting* the existing markets and relationships, during periods of relative disorder and turbulence, firms need to develop new and enhanced capabilities for dealing with higher levels of complexity and disorder. Such *exploration* strategies include merger and acquisitions, increasing alliances, and increasing rate of research and development.[41]

Organization of this book

Before going further, let us first examine what exactly we mean by the term "e-business." In this book we use the term to refer to the organization and management of major business processes around the Internet. It was originally coined by IBM in 1997 as part of a very successful advertising campaign. Subsequently, "e-business" achieved immense popularity as a buzzword du jour and this has led to frequent confusion with the term "e-commerce" – which refers exclusively to buying and selling products and services online. e-Commerce may be considered the selling component of e-business. In contrast, e-business encompasses all the major functions of a business, including human resources, customer service, and supply chain management. Virtually any type of business process that involves interaction with customers, suppliers, employees, and other companies falls within the realm of e-business. The term is especially important because it applies Web-based technology to the entire value chain, extending even beyond corporate boundaries.

The process of e-business transformation is concerned with much more than just investing in the necessary technology. An enterprise operating as an e-business must anticipate its customers' demands and use the appropriate technologies to enhance its business performance. e-Business requires the integration of Internet-based technologies with business processes and managerial practices. Managers involved in an e-business transformation effort must think first about their core business processes and then look at the available technology; business should not be driven by technology, instead it should leverage technology to address its needs.

---

41. See Lewin et al. (1999) and Galbraith et al. (2002).

By its nature, "e-business" entails doing things differently and investing in new systems to web-enable core processes. As we shall see in Chapter 5, e-business relies on open, public communications infrastructure that allows a company to connect and exchange information without the need for establishing and maintaining costly proprietary networks.

This book contains four parts.

Part 1: e-Business strategy and valuation relates to *structure* and *strategy* in the DOT framework. It consists of two chapters. In Chapter 2, "e-Business strategy," we outline the forces transforming strategy, discuss how companies achieve sustainable competitive advantage, explain what forces erode competitive advantage, and outline the steps involved in e-business strategy. We argue that successful e-business transformation requires a holistic approach to help companies put together various components of e-business into a coherent system. More specifically, we discuss how strategy acts as the guiding principle in setting in motion a firm's journey in transforming its business processes around the Internet. Not only do we discuss the issues related to the external forces, we also examine the dynamic relationships between strategy and the other four internal dimensions in the DOT framework. In Chapter 3, "Valuing e-business investments and managing performance," we show that while limitations exist, e-business implementations must be subjected to close scrutiny and accountability in terms of both their tangible and intangible benefits, and introduce various valuation methodologies and approaches for appraising e-business initiatives.

Part 2: e-Business infrastructure development relates to *technology* issues in the DOT framework. The purpose of this part is to introduce the subject of infrastructure and integration to a non-technical audience. We aim to cover the crucial trends and technologies that must be grasped by managers facing the question of e-business transformation. It consists of two chapters. Chapter 4, "e-Business infrastructure: the building blocks," establishes the case for greater senior-management involvement in charting the course for enterprise infrastructure. A brief overview of technological progress in organizational computing is presented, leading to the present e-business era. We then focus on the core building blocks of e-business infrastructure as represented in an e-business components pyramid and introduce the key e-business applications and technologies relating to the essential relationships of the enterprise. Chapter 5, "e-Business infrastructure: integration, standards and security" establishes the importance of integration for achieving a successful e-business implementation. The facilitating role of open XML-based standards is discussed, particularly with respect to the potential for such standards to supersede traditional Electronic Data Interchange (EDI) for Business-to-Business (B2B) transactions. An overview of security considerations and solutions is presented, and the issue of payment is examined. Finally, the trend towards wireless e-business is discussed.

Part 3: e-Business process management focuses on *processes* in the DOT framework. It is comprised of three chapters. In this part we highlight the interdependence of internal and external processes and the challenges related to integration within and across the enterprise. In Chapter 6, "Enterprise resource planning systems," we discuss the primary corporate-wide application and the architectural framework into which most other applications plug. Chapter 7, "e-CRM: evolution from traditional relationships," discusses the ever-important topic of consumer relationship management (CRM). Specifically we identify CRM as a *process*, explain how businesses can benefit from CRM processes, and discuss how CRM can affect a company's competitive position. Chapter 8, "Supply Chain Management," examines supply chain management (SCM), its components, planning and execution issues, and integration challenges.

Part 4: e-Business implementation and globalisation relates not only to the *people* dimension in the DOT framework, but more importantly centres on the change management and cross-border regulatory issues brought about by e-business transformation. In this part we try to put all the pieces together. In Chapter 9, "e-Business change management: effective implementation of e-business strategies," we establish the importance of e-business change management, conceptualize e-business change management as the joint optimization of technology, processes, and people, and outline common e-business change strategies. Chapter 10, "Legal Considerations of Global e-Business," relates to e-business regulatory environment. It examines the multi-jurisdictional issues surrounding global, cross-border transactions, such as taxation, intellectual property rights, and privacy.

Summary

Every time we hear that a proposal will destroy society, as we know it, we should have the courage to say: "Thank God; at last"

Stafford Beer, Systems thinker and philosopher[42]

In this chapter we set the stage to argue that e-business transformation is a dynamic and holistic process. Faced with threats or galvanized by opportunities, companies can no longer afford the luxury of equilibrium and stability. Today, changes are sweeping every corner of the corporate world. No industry is protected; no business process is sheltered. Change is indeed integral to doing business. In response to customers' never-quenching predilection for speed and agility and faced with an ever-increasing flow of information within and without their bounds, today's organizations have no choice but to embrace change: changes brought about by technology, changes in demography, changes in consumer preferences, changes in strategic landscape. Change is the order of the day.

In this fast-moving environment, the traditional view of organizations as deterministic systems that strive for stability and equilibrium is no longer valid. Nor are the concepts underlying such organizations: vertical hierarchies, rigid structures, inflexible divisions of labour, precise task descriptions and operating

---

42. Beer (1975).

procedures. By bringing down the artificial boundaries between companies, the Internet has further rendered these concepts invalid. Today, every company is part of a business web within which increasing complexity can only be managed by embracing change. Indeed, change has become the lever that turns the growth engine.

e-Business transformation is yet another form of organizational change, albeit an important one. In this chapter we briefly discussed that the successful e-business transformation depends, among other things, on a company's ability to:

- continuously scan the environment to identify potential threats as well as emerging opportunities;

- drum up wide organizational support by creating a critical mass of people committed to the transformation initiative;

- set up the necessary infrastructure;

- revamp the existing business processes;

- manage the implementation process; and

- provide valuation rationale for the initiative.

We conclude this chapter by examining how courier giant Federal Express Corporation (FedEx) successfully transformed into an e-business. Two cases follow this introductory chapter and both involve e-business-driven change within age-old industries. *Green Pastures Agribusiness* examines a company in the fertilizer industry that underwent its transformation effort while beleaguered by an outmoded closed-door management style. By contrast, in *Global Recycle: An e-Business Strategy for the Recycling Industry*, an innovative young entrepreneur develops an online trading platform that becomes an essential facilitator in deal-making for the recycling industry and eliminates the need for costly intermediaries.

Building an e-business at FedEx[43]

> The information about a package is just as important as the delivery of the package itself. That's why FedEx is dedicated to integrated transportation and information services so we can deliver meaningful solutions for customers in today's complex business environment . . . FedEx has built superior physical, virtual and people networks not just to prepare for change, but to shape change on a global scale . . .[44]

Federal Express Corporation was founded in 1973. It has often been credited as the inventor of the express transportation industry and customer logistics

---

43. Adapted from Conley et al. (2000).
44. FedEx *Annual Report*.

management. In over 29 years of operation, FedEx has earned a myriad of accolades and won over 194 awards for operational excellence. In 1983, FedEx became the first American company to achieve the US$1 billion revenues mark within a single decade, without corporate acquisitions and mergers. Today, with annual revenues of $20 billion, FedEx is the premier global provider of transportation, e-commerce and supply chain management services, holding about 30 per cent of the market share.

FedEx has transformed itself from an express delivery company to a global logistics and supply chain management company. The transformation was triggered by a growing awareness that competition in the transportation/express delivery industry was intensifying, and by reports that FedEx's transportation volume growth would slow, even with the surge in traffic that e-tailing and e-commerce was expected to generate. Action had to be taken if FedEx was to stay ahead of the competition.

The visionary behind the business

> If we're all operating in a day-to-day environment, we're thinking one to two years out. Fred's thinking five, ten, fifteen years out.
>
> – William Conley, VP, FedEx Logistics, Managing Director, Europe

Fundamental to the success of the FedEx business has been the visionary leadership of its founder. Fred Smith, Chairman, President and CEO of FedEx, anticipated the changing demands of the business environment over the years. He identified three main trends that were pushing the industry to change in the 1980s and 1990s: the globalization of businesses, advances in IT and the application of new technology to generate process efficiencies, and the changing market demand for more value-added services. As businesses expanded beyond national boundaries and extended their global reach to take advantage of new markets and cheaper resources, the movement of goods created new demands for the transportation and logistics industry. With this, the competitiveness of transportation companies depended upon a global network of distribution centres, and the ability of those companies to deliver to wherever their customers conducted business. Speed became crucial to achieving competitiveness, not only for transportation companies but also for their customers. The ability to deliver goods quickly shortened the order-to-payment cycle, improved cash flow, and created customer satisfaction.

By capitalizing on the fact that businesses needed speedy and reliable deliveries, FedEx shortened lead times for companies. Its next-day delivery service revolutionized the industry. The success of FedEx's distribution business in those early days rested on Smith's belief that the opportunities were excellent for a company that could provide reliable overnight delivery of time-sensitive documents and packages. To compete on a global basis, the key components of the physical infrastructure of his express delivery business had to be in place. The underlying philosophy was that wherever business was conducted, the movement of physical goods would follow.

Under Smith's leadership, the Company has transformed itself from a conventional business to an e-business. By continually applying new technologies to the business, FedEx has leapfrogged the rest of the industry over and over again. The ability to share information was a major breakthrough for the express transportation industry. FedEx's response was to place emphasis not only on the physical transportation, but also on the co-ordination and control of the storage and movement of parts and finished goods. Logistics came to include value-added activities such as order processing, distribution-centre operations, inventory control, purchasing, production, and customer and sales services. Interconnectivity through the Internet and intranets and the integration of systems enabled businesses to redefine themselves and re-engineer their selling and supply chains. Information came to replace inventory.

Smith has been a visionary, forcing his Company and other companies to think outside the proverbial box. The core of FedEx's corporate strategy has been to use IT to help customers take advantage of international markets.

The information infrastructure

FedEx has strategically positioned itself to provide physical transportation, coupled with information intelligence, from anywhere to anywhere, around the globe. It has established a sound information infrastructure that handles more than 100 million transactions per day. This scalable e-business infrastructure supports FedEx's core business by (a) addressing the need to improve internal operations and (b) foreseeing its customers' needs for integrated supply chain services.

The linking of back- and front-end processes has been made possible through a three-tier IT architecture, as shown in Figure 1.3. The database tier is located in Memphis, Tennessee. Various databases reside in a mainframe, and a data warehouse program made up of various systems applications, such as billing, customer records, and package-tracking, enables any department within the company to access and compile data and reports that are needed to run its operations.

The applications tier consists of distributed application servers that make up wide area networks. The application servers, which perform functions such as transportation and warehouse management based on customer requests, either retrieve data from or write to the data repositories that reside in the mainframe. The total available capacity across its wide area networks is 16 billion bits per second. These application servers are distributed among countries within a region to serve regional business operations such as Europe and Asia-Pacific. They are physically located at different hubs and accessed through inter-country connections via international leased lines.

The access tier encompasses the media via which customers and remote FedEx employees can access the FedEx infrastructure to use the applications on the servers and retrieve real-time information from various databases. Access is made possible through four access media: Web-based, non-Web-based, dumb, and radio data terminals.

Figure 1.3 FedEX's three-tier architecture

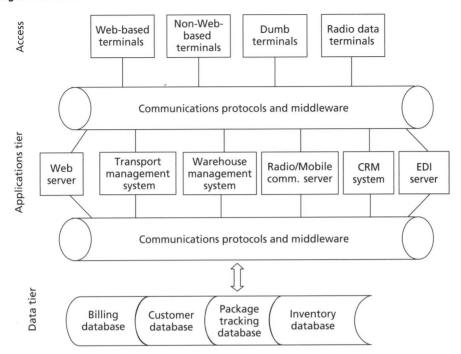

The communications protocols between each layer allow for the exchange of messages between systems. The Microsoft Message Queuing Services, for example, enable applications running at different times to communicate across heterogeneous networks and systems and allow for many ways of sending and receiving messages. The overall architecture also relies on a set of middleware that glues together various inter-enterprise applications.

Integrating business processes

FedEx's information infrastructure has enabled it to redesign its own business processes and those of its customers. It has permitted FedEx to look beyond the sequential and linear mode of operation to discover innovative business relationships and processes that create competitive advantages for FedEx and its customers. However, fundamental to establishing such relationships has been the need for integration.

FedEx's information infrastructure has allowed it to extend its services beyond pure transportation to address other supply chain service needs of its customers. From managing internal efficiencies, FedEx has seen the value of applying its systems and knowledge to its customers' businesses. The proliferation of the Internet has meant that FedEx has been able to build one-to-one relationships with its customers. Over the years, FedEx has established a corporate culture based on delivering quality customer service. This attitude of "doing whatever it takes to serve customers" has filtered down from the top. The Internet, therefore, has been crucial in helping FedEx take its service levels to new heights. It has allowed FedEx not only to let its customers pull real-time information and data into their internal systems, but also to become more involved in the internal processes of its customers.

Through its sophisticated information infrastructure, FedEx has been able to pull in its customers, and in many cases lock them in, with an unprecedented level of technological integration. By tracking back along the supply chain to the point of raw materials to identify the points where it can provide management services, FedEx has built on its expertise in applying technology to shorten the order-to-delivery cycle. Often, these services include transportation, order processing and related distribution centre operations, fulfilment, inventory control, purchasing, production, and customer and sales services. The ability to interconnect and distribute information to all the players in a supply chain has become the focus of FedEx's strategy. Through its information infrastructure, FedEx has been able to add value to other companies by providing better logistics management services. Thanks to FedEx's efforts to improve, tighten, and synchronize the various processes in the supply chain, customers have seen the benefits of reducing time and inventory. By integrating its services within the selling and supply chains of its customers, thus generating increases in customer loyalty and in customers' switching costs, FedEx has managed to effectively raise the entry barriers for competitors. No longer is it viewed simply as a transportation business; it is now recognized as a channel logistics business. FedEx's information infrastructure has underpinned this transformation.

Aligning organizational structure with systems and processes

In early 2000, FedEx announced a new branding strategy that involved changing the Company's name and extending the "FedEx" brand to three additional operating subsidiary companies. The intention was to take advantage of one of its greatest assets, the FedEx brand name; the name that customers count on for "absolutely, positively" reliable service and cutting-edge innovation. The renaming of the company as FedEx Corporation and the extension of the brand to its subsidiaries was in line with its intention to provide customers with an integrated set of business solutions. Customers would want to deal with one company to meet their transportation and logistics needs.

Apart from branding, there were also major reorganizations that resulted in a single point of access to sales, customer services, billing, and automation systems. Previously, these services were performed separately by the five subsidiary companies. With these consolidations, the company announced the formation of another subsidiary, called FedEx Corporate Services. Knowledge generation and use is at the heart of this new subsidiary, which pools together the marketing, sales, customer services, IT, and e-commerce resources of the Group.

Each operating subsidiary continues to operate independently, but collectively, to provide a wide range of business solutions. Independently, the subsidiaries can retain focus on meeting customers' specific logistics needs. But it is this collective synergy of solutions, built on an integrated knowledge base that gives FedEx its distinct competitive advantage. The new organization aims to use its rich knowledge base as the major pillar of its brand equity to help businesses of all sizes to achieve their shipping, logistics, supply chain, and e-business objectives. This is made possible through its integrated information infrastructure.

The reorganization served to align the organizational structure with the information infrastructure and integrated inter-organizational processes that FedEx has established. In so doing, FedEx aimed to leverage its cross-company customer knowledge base and its IT infrastructure to create better e-business solutions for its customers. This has opened up the opportunity for knowledge integration between business units within the Group, and has allowed FedEx to exploit its brand equity as well as its customer equity. The bundling strategy has made FedEx more convenient and accessible to customers, such that regardless of the choice of FedEx services, customers benefit from an integrated information platform. Whether customers contact FedEx in person, by phone or over the Internet, they are routed to one "touch point" for all services. Front-line staff has access to all previous records about every customer, kept in the Company's central databases. By gaining access to such information, staff is able to customize their service to each customer. They can also suggest integrated solutions for complete supply chain and e-commerce needs, and can cross-sell services and choreograph customer solutions. Customers can access up-to-the-minute information on package/consignment delivery status regardless of the mode of transportation, the type of service chosen, or the geographical location.

By bringing its organizational structure into line with its information infrastructure, FedEx is realizing the power of its brand equity. FedEx's integrated knowledge base is also helping other businesses to bridge the physical world and the virtual world, thus improving their operational efficiency and potentially enhancing their strategic position.

Questions for discussion

1   Why is organizational transformation so difficult?

2   How can complexity and chaos theories help companies in their e-business transformation efforts?

3   What are the characteristics of complex adaptive systems?

4   What are the major steps in transformation process?

5   What are some of the major paradoxes facing today's businesses?

6   What are the five organization dimensions? What are the five major external forces? How do these relate to one another?

7   Do you think e-business transformation is yet another management fad?

References

Balachandran, B.V. and Thiagarajan, S.M. (1999) *Reengineering Revisited*, Financial Executive Research Foundation.

Beer, S. (1975) *Platform of Change*, New York: John Wiley.

Beer, M. and Nohria, N. (2001) "Cracking the code of change", *Harvard Business Review*, May–June.

Conley, W.L., Farhoomand, A.F. and Ng, P. (2000) "Building an e-business at FedEx Corporation", 2nd place winner of the 2000 Paper Award Competition, *Society for Information Management*. Also in *Communication of the ACM*, March 2003.

CSC Index (1994) "State of reengineering report executive summary", Cambridge, MA.

Daft, R. (1998) *Organization Theory and Design*, 6th edn, Cincinnati, OH: South-Western College Publishing.

Davenport, T.H. (1995) "The fad that forgot people", *Fast Company Issue*, No. 1, November.

Drucker Foundation (2001) "Leading in a time of change: a conversation with Peter F. Drucker & Peter M. Senge", San Francisco, CA: Jossey-Bass.

Farhoomand, A.F. (1992) "A dynamic hierarchical structural model of information systems success: the case of electronic data interchange", Unpublished doctoral dissertation, McGill University, Montreal, Canada.

Galbraith, J., Downey, D. and Kates, A. (2002) *Designing Dynamic Organizations*, New York: AMACOM.

Gunneson, A.O. (1997) *Transitioning to Agility*, New York: Addison-Wesley Publishing.

Hall, E.A., Rosenthal, J. and Wade, J. (1994) "How to make reengineering really work", *The McKinsey Quarterly*, vol. 2.

Hammer, M. and Champy, J. (1993) *Reengineering the Corporation: A Manifesto for Business Revolution*, New York: HarperCollins.

Kelly, S. and Allison, M.A. (1999) *The Complexity Advantage*, New York: McGraw Hill.

Kotter, J. (1995), "Leading change: why transformation efforts fail", *HBR*, March–April.

Lederer, A.L., Mirchandani, D.A. and Sims, K. (2001) "The search for strategic advantage from the World Wide Web", *International Journal of Electronic Commerce*, vol. 5, no. 4, Summer.

Lewin, Arie Y., Long, Chris P. and Carroll, Timothy N. (1999) "The coevolution of the new organizational forms", *Organization Science*, vol. 10, no. 5, September–October.

Markus, M.L. and Robey, D. (1988) "Information technology and organizational change: causal structure in theory and research", *Management Science*, vol. 34.

McMaster, M.D. (1996) *The Intelligence Advantage: Organizing for Complexity*, Boston, MA: Butterworth-Heinemann.

Mintzberg, H. (1996) "Musings on management", *HBR*, July–August, p. 10.

Nagle, B.F. (1953) "Criterion development", *Personnel Psychology*, vol. 6.

Orr, J. and Crowfoot, N. (1992) *Design by Anecdote: The Use of Ethnography to Guide the Application of Technology to Practice*, Palo Alto Research Corporation.

Pascale, R.T., Millemann, M. and Gioja, L. (2000) *Surfing the Edge of Chaos: The Laws of Nature and the New Laws of Business*, New York: Crown Business, p. 28.

Robey, D. (1997) "The paradox of transformation: using contradictory logic to manage the organizational consequences of information technology", in *Steps to Future: Fresh Thinking on the Dynamics of Organizational Transformation*, C. Sauer and P. Yetton (eds), San Francisco: Jossey-Bass.

Sarker, S. and Lee, A.S. (2002) "Using a positivist case research methodology to test three competing theories-in-use of business process redesign", *Journal of the Association for Information Systems*, vol. 2, no. 7, January.

Stoddard, D.B. and Jarvenpaa, S.L. (1995) "Business process redesign: tactics for managing radical change", *Journal of Management Information Systems*, vol. 12, no. 1, 1995, pp. 223–50.

The Economist (2001) "A reluctant success", 9 June, pp. 85–86.

The Economist (2002) "A survey of the real-time economy", 2 February, pp. 3–5.

Tichy, N. and Charan, R. (1989) "Speed, simplicity, self-confidence: an interview with Jack Welch", *HBR*, September–October.

Trisoglio, A. (1995) "The strategy and complexity seminar", unpublished, London School of Economics, p. 24.

Wheatley, M. (1999) *Leadership and the New Science: Discovering Order in a Chaotic World*, 2nd edn, San Francisco: Barrett-Koehler Publishers.

Case study 1   Green pastures agribusiness

By 2003, Green Pastures Agribusiness (GPA) had evolved into a global leader in the mature fertilizer industry. The organization was a large, asset-intensive corporation whose success depended on complex networking relationships. Now top management at GPA faced the challenge to recognize successful e-business strategies and transform its traditional business model by successfully integrating internet-based technologies and institutionalizing new work processes. However, in the post-dot.com era, they wondered if any commercial competitive advantage could be derived in a low-tech industry or if e-business initiatives could reinforce its global leadership position.

Top management decided to hire consultants to advise them on main issues to rise at its AGM in two months helping them decide whether any future e-business strategy would be outlined. Also, they wanted to decide if e-business could be further integrated into its business model; the consultant team would help decide which implementation strategies would be optimal, how to implement them, and strategies to overcome organizational resistances they were facing from business unit managers.

Company

In 1989, GPA established its corporate headquarters in France, providing fertilizer raw materials. Through several acquisitions over the past fourteen years, the organization evolved into a vertically integrated global fertilizer company and as a result, inherited all challenges of a "multi-cultured" organization, where internal politics could affect the ultimate success or failure of any (e-business) initiative.

Green pastures agribusiness's six business units included: Business Development, Strategy, Purchasing, Logistics, Sales and Marketing, and Support Services (see Exhibit 1). The e-commerce department was a new addition to Support Services, which along with Purchasing, Logistics, Strategy, and Business Development were organizationally and physically separated from commercial activities (Sales and Marketing). Support service offices were located in Northern

Exhibit 1 Green pastures' organisation chart

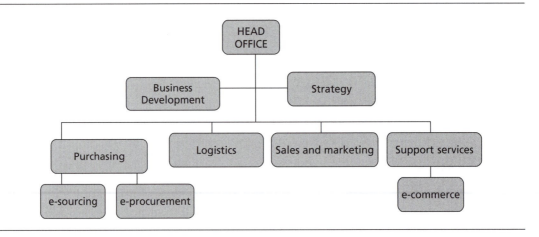

Europe, well distanced both physically and culturally from commercial headquarters in Western Europe.

Green pastures agribusiness's main activities included the sourcing, production, storage, transportation, and marketing of fertilizers to its end user – the farmers. Its traditional business model involved using raw materials, labour, and capital to produce a range of fertilizers. GPA had established its market presence and strength largely from economies of scales of manufacturing plants and its logistical capabilities. The main business activities were divided into four business processes: raw material sourcing and procurement, fertilizer production, fertilizer storage and transportation, and fertilizer marketing as shown in Figure 1.

The business processes mainly involved raw material sourcing and procurement of natural resources, including nitrogen and ammonium to manufacture fertilizers, therefore the value chain was simple: fertilizers were produced and delivered to the farmer. Gas and electricity were GPA's largest inputs Figure 2; these were used to run plants and manufacture chemicals and fertilizers. As a result, the company faced significant exposure to fluctuating gas and electricity prices. The risk was intensified, given industry margins were razor thin and any cost increases significantly impacted on operating margins.

The value chain was based on complex logistics; since logistics-related costs represented over 20 per cent of GPA's delivered product, by reducing these costs

Figure 1 Green pastures business processes

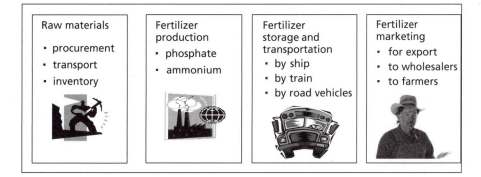

Figure 2 Fertilizer market business drivers

Business drivers	Which affects:
Gas price	Ammonia price
Ammonium price	Urea price
Grain prices	Urea price
European market segmentation	Value-added margins
Oil prices	European gas costs

Source: Adapted from 'Kemira GrowHow' presentation 2003, http://streaming2.visualsystems.com/rmcc/kcmd/slides/CMD2003Sirvio.pdf.

existed an opportunity to obtain a competitive advantage.

Changing face of the fertilizer industry

Fertilizers improved crop and pasture productivity; this in turn helped sustain agricultural production. A few major international players and myriads of smaller more localized activities typified the sector.

The fertilizer industry was a major consumer of natural gas, sulfuric acid, ammonium sulfate, and phosphate rock. Therefore, local minerals extraction and processing industries and chemical industries were important suppliers for fertilizer manufacturing. For any business to run smoothly, a number of peripheral parties were involved including transporters, bag producers, technology licensors and fabricators, insurers, financiers, and so on. Investment in exploitation or production was generally capital-intensive and while state participation had been a common practice, there was a growing trend towards privatization.

The fertilizer sector's asset-intensive nature resulted in relatively low involvement in IT in general and Internet-based technologies specifically. Typically, smaller market players relied on traditional technologies such as telephone and fax, which were believed by many to adequately address business needs.

However, larger players were quick to adopt cutting-edge technology; for example, American farmers used GPS systems long before urban America caught onto it. Other trends in the agricultural sector included "Precision Agriculture" or "Site-Specific Application" mainly applied by Europeans; both techniques deployed soil analysis and yielded data with computer-aided blending as the machines, guided by GPS, applied the fertilizers.

Some firms even used the Internet to track weather and together market information, while other fertilizer businesses were managing

their exposure to lending and exchange rate fluctuations (due to the capital intensity) through online financial tools. The extremely challenging business climate of farming – which was seasonal, highly fragmented, and operating on very low margins – seemed ideal to some industry analysts for the sector's adoption of online businesses.

Goldman Sachs argued that B2B e-commerce potential was greater in industries with the following characteristics:[1]

- a highly diffused supply chain; pressure to control costs;
- complex product specifications;
- processes accounting for at least 20 per cent of total costs; and
- technological innovation as part of the industry's culture.

The most compelling aspect was potential savings gained from implementing technology. An Aberdeen Group study found e-procurement could reduce purchasing costs and time by more than 70 per cent or almost $2 million per year, for a midsize company. In 2001, IDC reported that by implementing e-procurement initiatives, procurement departments saved five to seven per cent of their total budget. Forrester Research survey found that corporate buyers expected to save eight per cent by buying via b-to-b e-marketplaces in 2001.[2] David Watt, an economist, highlighted his opinion on the e-business issue:

> Farming is not just about planting and reaping crops, just as the information revolution driven by the New Economy is not just about taking traditional pursuits such as watching

---

1. Thompson, S.J., Hayenga, M., Hayes, D., 'E-AGRIBUSINESS', *International Food and Agribusiness Management Association, 2000 Agribusiness Forum Papers*, July 4, 2000. http://agecon.tamu.edu/iama/2000Congress/Forum%20-%20Final%20PAPERS/Area%20III/Thompson_Shelly2.PDF.
2. "B-to-B-ing Optimistic", *Industry Standard's Metric Report*, April 17, 2001.

commodity markets and giving them a new 24/7 twist with the Internet and instant messaging on cellphones and Palm Pilots. There are deeper issues at play. Corporations are now using sophisticated "management software" that will have implications for how the entire economy works, including agriculture. This management software will not only look at demand in the past, but also predict how it might go in the future. So if you're looking at how you might modify your products in the future, you've got a very strong idea of where your customer base is, how it's changed over time, and where it may go in the future.[3]

In the past, for example, most agri-businesses interested in distant or larger markets required intermediary services such as wholesalers, distributors, or brokers. With e-commerce, an agri-business could link directly to global customers through its website. However, major industry players were focusing primarily on e-Procurement, and some had developed EDI-type arrangements with their dealer networks, in an endeavour to exploit efficiencies and reduce transaction costs.

The industry focus was to use technology to transform business areas where transaction costs could be reduced within existing systems, and not develop new business models as such. Few companies had embarked on structural transformations because many new business models had failed (e.g. failure of auction portal XSAG.com). Insiders blamed it on the fertilizer industry's uniqueness where producers "collaborated." By not delivering products to these auctions, firms avoided head-on price competition, acted to maintain prices at levels that returned reasonable margins and avoided the risk of channel conflicts. Although various industry players had participated in such auctions, it was mostly to occasionally "offload" any surplus products.

Another reason for business transformation failures within the industry was attributed to senior management's lack of support for new business processes and unwillingness and inability to deal with organizational change. Prior to the new economy, fertilizer companies never faced change-management challenges since firms conducted businesses traditionally and were not faced with dynamic industry.

However, business transformation was becoming necessary and there was a need to identify new business models due to intense pressure on margins. Technology was driving new initiatives in the agri-business sector and advanced logistics methodologies were becoming popular, such as "Just-in-Time," "Vendor-Managed Inventory," and "Collaborative Planning Forecasting and Replenishment." From an implementation point of view, these solutions required an open environment to support information exchanges and transactions between clients and suppliers, something that was contrary to how business was traditionally done.

In addition, the digital economy was pressuring the agribusiness sector to extend its enterprise and exchange information automatically with trading partners and suppliers, to integrate their systems and applications. Since, in the fertilizer business, the entire supply chain revolved around manufacturing, effective integration meant plant systems must be integrated with the company. This full spectrum of business processes could be managed by ERP systems to drive the enterprise.

Pressure to enhance supply management also created the ASP model in which firms participate in emerging supply-chain networks in order to energize their core competencies and enable e-partnerships of the supply chain to function in the agribusiness sector. The provider would engage in typical activities of procurement, order fulfilment, product design and development, distribution, and delivery. Technology adoption became even more compelling considering over 80 per cent of logistics processes, although firms in the sector were

3. "Turning information into profit: a new vision for farming", *Canadian Farm Manager*, December-January 2002/2003.

similar and there was proof that e-business initiatives, for example e-procurement, reduced acquisition and transaction costs, it could also raise the whole industry's efficiency status quo. On the other hand, the industry's solidarity could ensure that no one player would gain true competitive advantage over others through utilization of new technologies.

GPA's e-business initiatives

The business-change process was initiated because GPA needed to reinforce its global position; its incremental change strategy entailed embarking on two major e-business initiatives: e-sourcing and e-procurement (the e-Commerce department was entirely new). The IT investments were strategic and transactional in nature; while the e-sourcing group focused on lowering costs through better-structured online sourcing arrangements, the e-commerce team saw its potential contributions in terms of downstream activities, supporting links between the company and customer with a view to gaining competitive advantage.

Top management debated how it could successfully implement and integrate e-business initiatives into its current business model. Although operating in a low-tech industry, they felt that to retain and enhance its global leadership position, it would need to implement technologies to gain competitive advantage. These ideas were initiated during the dot.com hype and since then, management implemented two major business transformation initiatives undertaken by the purchasing department: e-sourcing and e-procurement.

e-Sourcing

In 2000, the Agri-Purchasing Department established a contract with "Freemarkets," a business to business (B2B) portal and auction company. A reverse auction could be defined as "a supply-aggregating event that lowers the price of goods for a buyer." Reverse auctioning could also be considered as a negotiation tool or alternate pricing mechanism.[4] Up to late 2001, GPA had run eight reverse auctions, it acted like a consultant in structuring auction tenders and also hosted the auctions. GPA used the auction platform to significantly drive down contract costs. Results so far indicated that the purchasing processes became more efficient and effective, resulting in reduced costs (by pooling volume), fewer transaction errors, larger contracts negotiation, supplier reduction and "adding value" by reducing GPA's invoices and designing clever ways of buying. A manager at the purchasing department commented:

> The e-Sourcing tool takes us through the process of collecting data on whatever we want to buy, finding suppliers and pre-qualifying them; structuring data and our line-items in packages to attract the most competition (lotting), and devising a contract strategy.

So far, the e-sourcing tool was only used to buy "indirect" materials, such as electricity, but the aim was to integrate e-sourcing into GPA's entire business processes. The purchasing department's goal was to establish an optimal supplier and contract portfolio online for the whole division, and manage purchases on contract with suppliers using tools such as e-sourcing and e-procurement.

e-Procurement

This was a corporate-level project (i.e. the umbrella organization over the various divisions); distinct from e-sourcing's divisional initiative. Its overall goal was essentially to *e-Enable* the transaction side, or the order-to-payment cycle: sending orders and receiving goods, getting invoices, communicating with suppliers, and digitizing this information into

---

4. Wyld, D.C., 'How can reverse auctions affect the supply chain', *Supply Chain Planet*, http://www.supplychainplanet.com/e_article000179744.cfm.

the company's Enterprise Resource Planning (ERP).[5] Suppliers were large and chosen on the basis of their being technically able to link up with the company, not unlike a more traditional EDI system. As a result, the suppliers were integrated into the SAP/ERP system.

The e-Commerce Department

The purchasing department was considering what role the e-commerce department could play, whether they could work together and how its activities might be incorporated if full-spectrum e-business transformation was implemented. The e-commerce department, created in 2000 amid the "e-Business hype", was part of a comprehensive overall organizational restructuring process. So far, it had created two major information products: TopCrops and Agri Information Market (AIM). The TopCrops product aimed to provide agricultural information online, in addition to providing farmers and professionals' advice on machinery, seeds, crop protection, and fertilizers. Previously, this advice was available in pamphlets and brochures, or as tacit knowledge in the heads of a select band of roving agronomists. However, with the exception of a few markets, this information facility was not yet integrated into the firm's commercial activities. Meanwhile AIM was a dedicated information portal, which networked all the division's support and production facilities with business units; this product was accessible by all employees and some select partners. While response to the product was positive, management felt better implementation was critical before information was available organization-wide and the change was institutionalized.

Another objective for the e-commerce department was to *e-Enable* all commercial activities along the company's value chain

with the aim to develop cost-effective electronic channels, as replacements for the more traditional marketing systems. However, focus on the e-commerce initiative changed dramatically over the past twelve months, as the realization that what was being proposed was perceived (by the markets) as threatening to existing systems, and would be strongly opposed.

In addition, differences of opinion existed between business units about success of the two e-business initiatives already undertaken; the purchasing team believed simpler solutions were just as efficient, even though suppliers had limited access to the company's ERP-selected pages, where purchase orders were made. GPA implemented B2B software, which enabled purchasers to buy its fertilizers off catalogues (although it was expensive to link a few suppliers who were technically apt). On the other hand, the corporate e-sourcing initiative was more complex and aimed to integrate all activities across divisions and with external parties; it was seen as a broad-spectrum initiative encompassing all sourcing activities within GPA.

However, Business Unit managers showed little enthusiasm for any further e-business implementation; they were pessimistic about results of existing e-business implementation and doubted successful integration on any new work processes. It had been a year since GPA embarked on its e-procurement initiative, and the pilot phase was over and top management agreed to continue the initiative but had not decided whether to implement a more tightly aligned e-business system.

The lack of enthusiasm was attributed to two major reasons: management's inability to take a holistic approach towards its business transformation process and also their inability to manage the interplay between employees and technology. Top management's primary focus centred on its European activities and a return to profitability for those Business Units; this meant an emergent strategy was evident but did not accommodate any specific e-business strategy.

---

5. ERP systems are the mission-critical backbone through which most, if not all business transactions flow. Besides providing the core transaction processing that large, complex enterprises require, ERP systems are often the launchpad for strategic initiatives, such as e-business and B2B commerce.

Management began realizing that organizational resistances were driven by fear of change, loss of autonomy at the department and individual level or fear of "big brother" taking over (i.e. here the e-commerce department or the Corporate establishing direct access to the customers of the Business Units). In addition, the e-commerce department's position had become precarious since the Head of e-commerce department no longer participated in the top management's monthly meetings under the new organisational structure; the department became further removed from an inner-circle of decision-makers and with this management change, e-business's status dropped significantly.

A major issue involved employees; redundancies were something alien to the company. Historically, people joined the company for life and there was little staff turnover; implementing an e-business system would eradicate operational positions, as Internet-based technologies replaced repetitive activities. One manager said, "Anything that disturbs the status quo would likely be met with some degree of resistance. That's just human nature. People are not interested in increased efficiencies and streamlining through e-business or anything else, if it causes them or their friends to lose their jobs!" But, the Business Units' resistance to the e-commerce department's earlier efforts could also be attributed to its initial threatening approach because certain individuals had strongly believed that successful e-enablment meant abandonment of the traditional model and the sales and marketing team still felt that the e-commerce department held this view.

Marketing team's resistance to change

Most Business Unit managers were unclear on the e-business initiative's objectives. On the other hand, employees were neither involved nor consulted on any technology implementations, hence they did not understand the rationale behind the transformation process.

A major issue with the e-commerce department was its location; being in Northern Europe, it felt isolated and believed that it militated against effective liaison with Business Units abroad, whom they saw as their primary client. Also, being positioned under the "administrative corporate umbrella", as opposed to being integrated with commercial headquarters was viewed as a barrier to effective relations with Business Units. The finance and marketing departments simply viewed it as another support function based at corporate headquarters and essentially a provider of some online agro-technical advice on fertilizer products and crops. Therefore, for a majority of GPA's Business Unit managers, e-commerce's role was largely seen as an extra-organizational activity; a "link" between the company and the outside world of suppliers and customers.

Within the e-commerce division though, there was controversy on how e-business might enhance the traditional business model. Apart from those in both the purchasing and e-commerce departments, few managers voiced an appreciation for e-business or Internet-based technologies potential contributions to intra-organizational activities.

The e-commerce department suggested that a primary role for them was information digitalization, essentially providing agronomic advice and support online to business units and their selected clients' front offices. Although possibilities for online sales were mentioned, they faced strong market resistance arising from channel conflict fears with the well-established dealer/distributor networks. The sales and marketing department felt different from other departments; it was particularly resistant to implementing any change. This group was responsible for all marketing operations including, sales, farm advisory services (helping farmers achieve their crop objectives with optimized fertilizer use) and typically, its success depended on intermediaries, channel management, and building strong networking relationships. As a result, its teams felt technology could not replace relationships humans established and no part of the sales process should be automated.

The Sales and Marketing department had been identified by the e-commerce department as their primary client, but it claimed it had not availed support services offered. Reasons given for this "lack of active cooperation" by Business Units in general also pinpointed to four major issues:

1 Fear of upsetting existing, established networks and channels, given Sales and Marketing's reliance on dealers.

2 Teams unwilling to invest time in an unproven system; given performance-based rewards, the sales and marketing team were unwilling to experiment with untested business models.

3 Focus on the bottom line in Europe, particularly on a return to profitability in the short-term. e-Business was perceived as a more long-term agenda.

4 Top management's failure to communicate and integrate its vision into the organization's working culture.

An influx of Internet-based technologies threatened to revolutionize Sales and Marketing, and many employed in these functions felt vulnerable. This inevitable breach of their "comfort zone" by new e-business channels resulted in stiff resistance towards these initiatives and they admitted it was a natural "knee-jerk" reaction to resist when one's security is threatened. As Business Unit heads were highly accountable for the bottom line, and given the fact that margins were tight, embarking on entirely new and unproven e-business endeavours was viewed as high-risk.

Organizational resistance to technological change

While management felt the two e-business initiatives implemented in the past few years were generally successful, they failed to assemble a workforce coalition to support the initiatives. For example, in 2001, management simply introduced the e-business concept (during the company's restructuring), by depicting the e-commerce department in a "new" corporate organizational chart. No explanation was given on the division's role within the organization, its objectives, or any implementation plan. Although subsequently, the e-commerce department, as a team, embarked on a profiling and publicity exercise via a dedicated website and through presentations at management forums and Business Units meetings, new practices were not fully institutionalized and Business Unit managers took advantage of Top Management's lack of communication to resist any business process transformations.

Therefore, top management's inability to communicate its vision cost GPA internal support and resistance to any further transformation initiatives. The e-procurement and e-sourcing experiments had generated many ideas, but Business Unit managers worried that weak implementation of new business processes would create chaos since the workforce would not support new techniques enough to subsume the old business system.

Conclusion

Analyzing these issues, the consultants decided to bring attention of key issues to Top Management: first, they wanted to point at their failure to communicate its vision and successfully integrate new business processes. Secondly failure to obtain buy-in and ongoing support of Business Unit managers but also involved underestimating the enormity of e-business implementation and not openly informing ground level workforces. The consultants felt this closed-door management style threatened even existing traditional, but successful techniques. Finally, the consultants repeatedly identified the top management as the primary causal agent for failure of institutionalizing existing e-business initiatives' or gathering support for any further e-business initiatives.

Case study 2   Global Recycle Ltd.: an e-business strategy for the recycling industry

I'm confident that we've touched upon a global opportunity, but we haven't lost sight of the fact that we're a small developing business and are focusing primarily on building a self-sustaining business model.
– Warren MacLeod, Managing Director, Global Recycle[1]

When Pat Daly formed Eurecycle.com in 2000 at the tender age of 21, he had no idea that within a year it would become the largest online trading exchange for the recycling industry in Europe. The success of the business attracted a team of investors, directors and staff, and Global Recycle Ltd. was formed in 2001. Conducting its business through globalrecycle.com, the Company's business grew rapidly to become the largest online trading exchange for the recycling industry in the world. Membership increased to over 900 companies, including several multinationals, based in over 81 countries.

Primarily, the online trading platform provided three areas of service: (i) a place for members to post buy-and-sell requests; (ii) matching buyers and sellers, and starting negotiations between them; and (iii) offering instant online introductions between members. By initially charging a one per cent transaction fee on all introductions that resulted in a deal, the Company's revenue stream showed healthy growth. In 2002, its achievements were recognized with a number of national and international awards.

Building on this success, the board of directors was due to meet in early 2003 at the Company's offices in Glasgow to map out plans for building a more sophisticated system that would provide its members with a platform for the entire transaction process,

from introductions through to the delivery of materials to buyers. They were wondering what additional services globalrecycle.net could provide. Could there be opportunities for collaboration with other players in the industry? However, in considering these possibilities, Global Recycle was well aware that the US$400 billion industry was not ready to do everything online just yet, and that the pace of change and direction of growth would have to be dictated by its members. With this in mind, the directors debated the need to fine-tune the business model, build member confidence and ensure a position of market dominance.

Industry background

Recycling was not new. The practice was as old as humanity, and could be dated back to the Stone Age, when fragments splinted from flint axes were used to make arrowheads. Since then, an industry had formed and flourished on the principle that scrap, a by-product primarily brought on by the Industrial Revolution, could be of economic value as a secondary raw material. Recycling was therefore known as the process of transforming old or new scrap into new secondary raw materials that could be fed back into the manufacturing process.[2] In more recent decades, the world had become more aware of the need for conservation. Thus the demand for recyclable raw material grew considerably. The industry had also become fully international. Since secondary materials were not available uniformly around the world, it had to be transported from one area of abundance to

1. "2002 Overall National Winner", E-Commerce Awards, URL: http://ecommerce-awards.co.uk/ past_winners/ 2002/globalrecycle.html, accessed 18 September 2003.

2. "About Recycling", *Bureau of International Recycling*, URL: http://www.bir.org/aboutrecycling/index.asp, accessed on 29 September 2003.

another area of demand. The industry was responsible for collecting, sorting, processing, and marketing a vast range of materials. Secondary materials were produced to critical specifications and marketed to industries around the world.

The process of collecting, sorting, processing, and marketing secondary raw materials was complex and involved many parties and considerable negotiation. The lines of communication were long, and control rested with those who had the appropriate contacts. This created many inefficiencies in matching supply with demand; getting the best price on a purchase, and gaining knowledge of who the market players were and what the market conditions were that could affect a trade decision.

By 2003, the recycling industry employed 1.5 million people across more than 50 countries. Over 600 million tonnes of commodities were processed annually by the industry.[3] However, of that, only one-third was traded internationally.

Company background

> Our goal is to become the daily procurement and marketing tool for our members to build their international business networks. This is a goal we feel we are well on the way to achieving as evidenced by our unsurpassed member loyalty and their repeated daily use of the Trading Exchange.[4]

Pat Daly was a third-generation scrap dealer. Learning the trade from his father and grandfather at a young age, he took the business of scrap trading into a whole new dimension. For starters, Daly recognized the inefficiencies inherent in the industry. His idea was to provide one central meeting place that would allow transparency, so people could be confident of finding what they wanted, and of negotiating a fair price. Short of having to physically transport the scrap, he envisioned the process of shifting it around the world on the Web by introducing buyers to sellers. He would take a commission for facilitating the connection. Simple! Hence, in January 2000, Eurecycle.com was formed. The low start-up costs and the philosophy of low operating costs ensured the development of the exchange in incremental stages. However, the business grew rapidly to become the largest online exchange for the industry in Europe. Since the trade was global in nature, and since Daly recognized the need to tap into the wider market with better software and more business experience, in February 2001 he teamed up with Warren MacLeod, a senior mining executive from Canada with a formal education in e-business.

International mining financier Dennis MacLeod (father) and Warren MacLeod (son) contributed to the first round of financing for Daly's business. With this, Global Recycle Ltd. was formed in July 2002. Warren MacLeod (hereafter referred to as "MacLeod") gained control of the Company and became managing director. MacLeod was able to provide the business expertise, financing and e-business know-how to take Daly's ideas to the global stage. In addition to Daly and MacLeod, other members of the board of directors included Jim Mathers (Chairman) and Alasdair Paton.

globalrecycle.net

> As a scrap dealer, I have always relied on my phone and fax, but in a global industry that never sleeps, they had their limitations.
>   – Pat Daly, Director[5]

Launched on 1 May 2001, www.globalrecycle.net provided a meeting place for recycling companies to post

3. "About Recycling", *Bureau of International Recycling*, URL: http://www.bir.org/aboutrecycling/ index.asp, accessed on 29 September 2003.
4. "About Global Recycle", Global Recycle, URL: http://www.globalrecycle.net/about.asp?contentid=18, accessed on 18 September 2003.
5. "Website full of waste is a winner", Recycling Product News, URL://www.baumpub.com/publications/rpn/Features/RPNOctF5.htm, accessed on 26 September 2003.

information about material they wanted to buy or sell, engage in negotiations with other members and be introduced to other members (see Exhibit 1). After just a couple of weeks, the first online transaction, worth over US$35,000, was completed between a medium-sized non-ferrous metal processor and one of the world's major aluminium consumers. Daly's reaction: "We are particularly pleased to see completed transactions involving high-profile companies at such an early stage."[6]

The name of the game was simplicity, thus appealing to a wide range of clients, from small three-man shows to huge multinational corporations. The online exchange connected the traders, the foundries, and the processors. In doing so, the customer connected directly

to end users "without touching the four or five guys in between," said Daly.[7] Registered membership had the greatest representation from the US, the UK, India, China, the Netherlands, Canada, Germany, Hong Kong, and Pakistan. Product categories traded on the exchange are listed in Exhibit 2.

The speed and access of the Internet combined with traditional knowledge of the industry and constant customer support were factors that commentators claimed had led to business success. The Company outperformed its expectations in four areas: (i) membership registrations; (ii) the number of buy-and-sell requests posted on the site; (iii) the number of negotiations between members; and (iv) the number of introductions between members.

Exhibit 1 Global Recycle's homepage

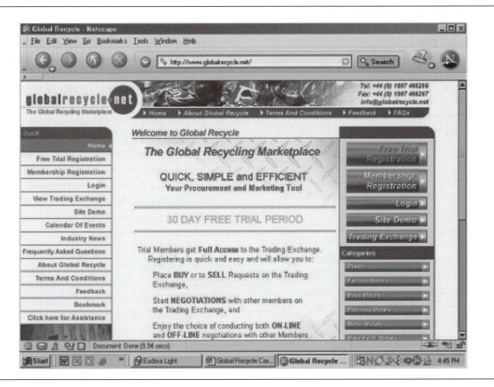

6. "Global completes first online transaction", Global Recycle Ltd., 22 May 2001 URL: http://www.globalrecycle.net/press.asp?ID=2&Type=R&contentid=21, accessed on 18 September 2003.

7. Clark, R., "All the World's a Deal", Global Recycle Ltd., 13 May 2002 URL: http://www.globalrecycle.net/press.asp?ID=14&Type=A&contentid=22, accessed on 18 September 2003.

Exhibit 2 Product categories traded through globalrecycle.net

1 Plastic
2 Ferrous metals
3 Basic metals
4 Precious metals
5 Minor metals
6 Rare earth metals
7 Minerals
8 Automotive
9 Batteries
10 Electronics
11 Tyres and rubber
12 Waste paper
13 Wood
14 Textiles and leather
15 Glass and fibreglass
16 Liquids, oils and chemicals
17 Used building materials
18 Used equipment.

Services offered

The Company offered a 30-day free trial membership period, aimed at encouraging long-term customers. Interested companies would simply register online, which took only a minute or two. Within 24 hours the company would receive a user ID and password confirming registration as a trial member. Trial members were offered full membership privileges and unlimited access to the trading exchange. This meant they could gain access to the trading exchange, post as many Requests for Quotes (RFQs) as they liked and engage in as many negotiations with members as they wished. On the last three days of the trial period, the trial member would receive daily notifications that the trial period would soon expire. A link would also be provided to allow them to upgrade to full membership status. The transition between trial and full membership status was smooth and no RFQs posted or negotiations initiated were lost or deactivated. However, if the trial member decided not to upgrade, all RFQs and negotiations were deactivated. Nevertheless, the trial member would still be able to continue negotiations outside the exchange with Global Recycle members.

Members could post buy-or-sell requests on the trading exchange. They could browse through to look for RFQs posted and start negotiations. The exchange sought to match the interests of buyers and sellers. Once two members opened a negotiation, contact details of the other party were provided by Global Recycle to the two companies concerned. Thus the negotiating parties had the opportunity and flexibility to decide how and when they wanted to negotiate with each other. Global Recycle did not concern itself with the negotiations or any agreed transactions between the parties.

The website also included a calendar of events around the world that might be of interest to members. A list of members and their area of specialization was also available.

A user-friendly system

The simple theories of business have been overlooked by 70% of B2B exchanges and that is why none of these can boast of having

completed even one transaction despite throwing millions down the drain. . . . While others are happy to put their efforts solely into technology, we focus on customer care and making sure our members get the best deal they can. Of course the technology is important but if the customer is fearful of it then no amount of money will change that.
– Pat Daly, Director[8]

Once a member logged into the exchange using his/her user ID and password, a personalised "My Global Recycle" page would open. From this page, members could manage their buy/sell RFQs (to post, edit or delete them), review negotiations, post responses to negotiations or abort them. Full contact details of all members with whom the user had entered into negotiation with were also accessible through this page. Members could choose to negotiate through the exchange, directly via e-mail or by telephone. Negotiating through the exchange, the "My Global Recycle" page was connected to an e-mail system whereby each time a member posted a response in a negotiation, an e-mail notification would go to the other member and provide a link back to the negotiation. This line of communication could continue indefinitely. Members were not charged any transaction fees on agreed deals between members. All members were responsible for their own negotiations, agreed transactions and any relationships they developed with other members. Members were free to cancel their membership at any time.

Since there were 18 product categories to choose from, sellers could post RFQs on the pages of a number of categories and sub-categories. Up to six product photographs could be uploaded for every RFQ posted. New RFQs posted on the exchange would be notified through live e-mail to members who had specified their product categories of interest. In addition, members could choose to receive a daily summary e-mail.

Real value to members

Global Recycle saw that its competitive advantage lay in being able to connect buyers and sellers in a timely manner, providing full contact details to the negotiating parties, and providing an active forum for large national and multinational companies around the world. At any time while members were navigating through its website, they could click on an Assistance Button to post any queries to the Company. The Company promised a response within 24 hours.

Apart from time savings, members realised increased competitiveness, lower transaction costs and major reductions in telephone and fax charges. The *My Global Recycle* page also helped them to manage their negotiations and orders. There were new opportunities for its members to do business.

Costs to Members

Prior to November 2002, the Company charged a one per cent transaction fee on each completed deal. This was an honour-based system that relied on members contacting Global Recycle when a transaction was completed. The Company would contact sellers after introductions were made to confirm whether transactions had been agreed or completed. Buyers found to have breached trust were asked to leave the exchange.

With effect from November 2002, Global Recycle started a new charging system. Each new member was charged a monthly membership fee of US$29.99, automatically debited from the member's credit card. Members requesting introductions to buyers/sellers were charged US$9.99 per introduction. Monthly account statements were available to members. For existing members, a fee of US$20 per introduction was charged. They were not required to pay a monthly registration fee until 12 months later.

8. "Global completes first online transaction", Global Recycle Ltd., 22 May 2001, URL: http://www.globalrecycle.net/press.asp?ID=2&Type=R&contentid=21, accessed on 18 September 2003.

However, the transaction fee of one per cent remained effective for buyers.

Achievements

> We're just a few guys in an office in Glasgow, but the CIO award put us up there in the company of Cisco, Ernst & Young, and JP Morgan. That provides us with many hours of laughter.
> – Pat Daly, Director[9]

In November 2001, Global Recycle became the only non-American-based winner of the prestigious CIO Web Business 50 Award, run by IDG's *CIO* magazine. Fifty outstanding websites across businesses, government and non-profit platforms won awards. Editor in chief of the magazine, Abbie Lundberg, said, "Winning sites have combined excellence in design and functionality to create a top notch experience for the consumers, business partners and other users."[10]

Then, in June 2002, the Company walked away with two of the nine awards presented at the 2002 Winners of the Web ("Wow") Awards organised by Scottish Enterprise. The award recognised and rewarded the most impressive and creative businesses, companies and organisations that demonstrated real business success through the imaginative use of Internet technologies.

On a daily basis, Global Recycle traded between 5000 and 20,000 tonnes of goods between companies. Yet the company remained lean, with a team of fewer than 10 staff. The Company took pride in being a Scottish company with traditional Scottish values of hard work, honesty, fairness, frugality and sound business practices as

guiding principles for doing business. The directors firmly believed that these values were the underlying reasons for the success of the Company.

A Roadmap for the Future: Goals and Hurdles

As the directors met to discuss the strategic plan for the future growth and development of the business, a number of areas of concern came to mind. The Company had undoubtedly seized an opportunity in an industry previously dominated by traditional relationships. As the industry was beginning to realise the benefits of technology, Global Recycle had to find ways to stay ahead of the competition, particularly as other Internet trading sites were rapidly emerging.[11] One consideration would be to build a more sophisticated system that would provide a platform for the entire transaction process from introductions through to the delivery of materials to buyers. What other services could globalrecycle.net offer? What kind of partnerships might be helpful to deliver the required services? How could these new services be introduced to members in a way that would not create complexity, or that would not jeopardise the user-friendly attributes of the exchange?

Global Exchange was also interested in tapping into more lucrative and emerging markets such as China and Russia. Increasingly, traders tended to send scrap to such countries, where environmental and labour laws were relaxed, and where the recycling process could be done by cheap labour. The move from West to East aroused Global Recycle's interest in

9. Clark, R., "All the World's a Deal", Global Recycle Ltd., 13 May 2002 URL: http://www.globalrecycle.net/ press.asp?ID=14&Type=A&contentid=22, accessed on 18 September 2003.
10. "Global receives CIO Magazine Top 50 Award", Global Recycle Ltd., 30 November 2001 URL: http://www.globalrecycle.net/press.asp?ID=3& Type=R&contentid=21, accessed on 18 September 2003.

11. "E-scrap becomes a reality", *Purchasing Magazine Online*, 5 October 2000 URL: http://www.manufacturing.net/ pur/index.asp? layout=articlePrint&art, accessed on 30 September 2003.

establishing some collaborative links with international traders. What were the options?

Pauline Ng prepared this case under the supervision of Ali Farhoomand for class discussion. This case is not intended to show effective or ineffective handling of decision or business processes.

e-Business strategy and valuation

e-Business strategy

Objectives

- ❏ To learn what strategy is
- ❏ To recognize forces transforming strategy
- ❏ To understand how companies achieve sustainable competitive advantage
- ❏ To recognize the major factors influencing strategic IT investment decisions
- ❏ To learn about forces that erode competitive advantage
- ❏ To find out what is involved in e-business strategy

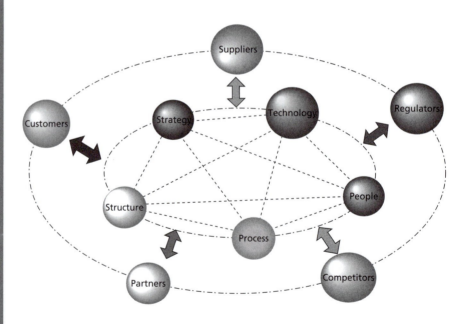

In Chapter 1, we established that e-business transformation is a dynamic process that should be understood by senior managers doing business amid sweeping changes in the corporate world. Management's ability to embrace rather than avoid chaos and complexity was viewed as a foundation and precursor for devising strategies conducive to competition in ever-changing global markets.

In this chapter, we proceed with an examination of e-business strategy as the first and foremost component of the DOT framework. Strategy comprises management's elaborate and systematic plan of action that takes into account *where* a company should be headed and *how* it intends to get there. In order to stay one step ahead of the competition, management can view the Internet as the backbone that can assist it in coordinating the activities along its value chain. With a sound and reasoned strategy in place, managers are better positioned to make intelligent choices about how they can configure organizational dimensions (*technology*, *people*, *processes*, and *structure*) to sustain competitive advantage.

Thus, strategy serves as the key determinant of success – today's manager must understand the forces that threaten to erode competitive advantage, and outline the steps necessary to counter this danger. Given the speed by which markets are moving and changing today, firms are under pressure to adopt strategies that allow them to seize fleeting opportunities. Broadly speaking, there are three major forces that have important strategic implications for companies. In this chapter, we will delve into an examination of these forces and also explore the concept of sustainable advantage and various issues associated with e-business strategy.

What is strategy, anyway? And why should it matter?

Strategy is about *tradeoffs*: tradeoffs a company makes in deciding *where* it wants to go, and tradeoffs it makes in determining *how* to get there. These tradeoffs are influenced by basic competitive forces as well as the market dynamics within which a firm operates.[1]

Not only does strategy help determine the destination (where) one is trying to reach, it also provides a roadmap (how) to guide the traveller in his/her journey. In other words, strategy allows a firm to distinguish itself, to be *different* from competitors with a view to achieving a competitive advantage.

In the late 1990s many traditional companies adopted misguided strategies in crafting their online presence. It was not that they did not know where they wanted to go; rather their actions stemmed from a misunderstanding of the role that technology plays in the strategic process. Most dotcoms and many traditional firms failed to see the Internet as merely an *enabling technology* that could help their overall business strategy. These companies crafted their online strategy in a vacuum, detached from their corporate strategy. The implicit and flawed assumption was that most online ventures would eventually yield sustainable competitive advantage. As we know in hindsight, this did not materialize. Why?

Consider the traditional newspaper industry. Not long ago, almost every major newspaper in the country was struggling to come up with a new "business model" for its online initiative. It was argued that the Internet had changed

---

1. Porter (1996).

the rules of the game inexorably in the way newspapers created content, produced, distributed and marketed its products and services, and generated profits. The idea was that a *new* business order had been born, that a new mindset was needed to explore emerging opportunities. After all, the Internet had transformed businesses inside out by:

- Introducing non-traditional *revenue streams* such as online advertising

- Extending *reach* beyond local markets

- Improving *operational effectiveness* through shortening the production and marketing cycles and reducing transaction costs.

Some newspapers did not embark on online initiatives, fearing possible cannibalization of their existing products and services. Many created an online presence, but considered it separate from their mainstream business. Some even considered spinning off their online ventures, heralding the arrival of a new market. In retrospect, these newspapers and many other businesses in other industries were on target as to *where* they wanted to take their businesses; they all wanted to have an online presence. However, flawed assumptions about market dynamics fogged the vision of many companies as to *how* to execute their online strategy. One such assumption related to the "network effect," a term attributed to Ethernet inventor and cyberspace visionary Bob Metcalfe who observed that the value of a network is proportional to the square of the number of people using it. However, this is true only if there is no cost associated with attracting new members to the network. So the common strategy of trying to gain market share at any cost proved unsuccessful as it ignored, among other things, the simple arithmetic that in the long run, profits generated by a customer should be more than the cost of acquiring that customer!

In this chapter we focus on the first organizational dimension of the DOT framework: strategy. We continue the chapter by providing an overview of three different approaches to strategy before discussing the major factors transforming strategy. We then explain what leads to sustainable competitive advantage, what factors affect strategic IT investment decisions, and what factors erode competitive advantage. Finally, we introduce the concept of business architecture with an eye to explaining what it takes to formulate and execute a sound e-business strategy.

Approaches to strategy

In general, companies follow one of the three approaches to strategy shown in Table 2.1. More precisely, companies can compete by:

- Building a fortress and defending it

- Nurturing and leveraging resources

- Flexibly pursuing fleeting opportunities within simple rules.

Table 2.1 Three approaches to strategy

	Position	Resources	Simple rules
Strategic logic	Establish position	Leverage resources	Pursue opportunities
Strategic steps	● Identify an attractive market ● Locate a defensible position ● Fortify and defend	● Establish a vision ● Build resources ● Leverage across markets	● Jump into the confusion ● Keep moving ● Seize opportunities ● Finish strong
Strategic question	Where should we be?	What should we be?	How should we proceed?
Source of advantage	Unique, valuable position with tightly integrated activity system	Unique, valuable, inimitable resources	Key processes and unique simple rules
Works best in	Slowly changing, well-structured markets	Moderately changing, well-structured markets	Rapidly changing, ambiguous markets
Duration of advantage	Sustained	sustained	Unpredictable
Risk	It will be too difficult to alter position as conditions change	Company will be too slow to build new resources as conditions change Long-term dominance	Managers will be too tentative in executing on promising opportunities
Performance goal	Profitability	Long-term dominance	Growth

Each of these approaches requires a different skill set and works best under different circumstances.

By treating strategy as *simple rules*, companies can first define and zero in on their unique *strategic processes*, and then guide those processes through a handful of *simple rules*.[2] The main strategic logic behind simple rules is to seize fleeting opportunities successfully, as opposed to leveraging resources or establishing a stable market position.

As we discussed in Chapter 1, leading companies have long appreciated the usefulness of simplicity. For example, in mid-1980s Jack Welch asked GE's 14 business leaders to each prepare one-page answers to the following five questions. Through these five questions Welch was able to communicate GE's strategy to the rank and file of his $50 billion company in a swift manner:[3]

---

2. Eisenhardt and Sull (2001).
3. Tichy and Charan (1989).

"Strategy answers two questions," says Kathleen Eisenhardt, professor of strategy and organization at Stanford University: "*Where do you want to go*? and *how do you want to get there*?" In static markets, the emphasis is on the *where*, but in high-velocity markets, the *how* becomes vital. In fact, to succeed in complex markets, the counterintuitive insight is to keep strategy simple – centered on a few strategic processes and a couple of simple rules. It also means paying close attention to timing and rhythm – your own, your customers', and your competitors'. It is this simplicity and focus that allow managers to capture the opportunities that create unexpected and valuable advantage.

1   What are your market dynamics globally today, and where are they going to be over the next several years?

2   What actions have your competitors taken in the last three years to upset those global dynamics?

3   What have you done in the last three years to affect those dynamics?

4   What are the most dangerous things your competitor could do in the next three years to upset those dynamics?

5   What are the most effective things you could do to bring your desired impact on those dynamics?

In addition to simplicity, speed of execution is also taking center stage in the strategy-making process. Increasingly, companies are influenced by a business environment where speed is God and time the devil! But in order to react to fleeting opportunities, companies first need to identify and define their key strategic processes.

Factors transforming strategy

The Internet is an infrastructural backbone that can help companies coordinate various activities within and outside their bounds. Figure 2.1 shows how the Internet influences industry structure through five forces of competition. There are several aspects of the new business order that have important implications for the strategy-making process.

Transaction costs

Over six decades ago Nobel laureate Ronald Coase observed that businesses face a wide variety of costs associated with the preparation and monitoring of various agreements with their suppliers, employees, and customers.[4] He argued that firms *exist* because of their ability to reduce such transaction costs. The true

---

4. Coase (1937).

Figure 2.1 How the Internet influences industry structure

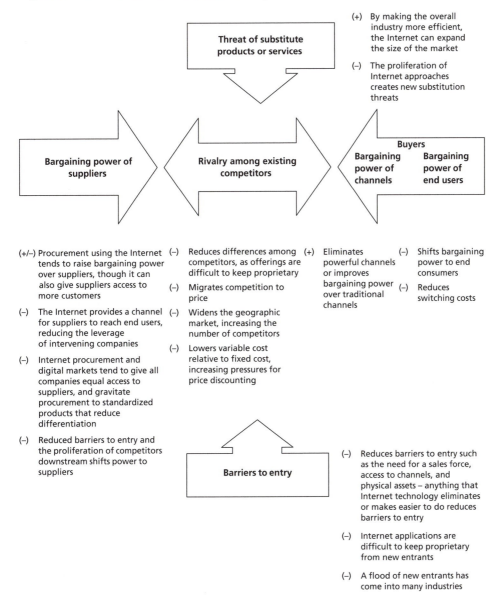

elegance of Coase's thesis can be felt today when we account for the new challenges brought about by the dramatic decline in transaction costs:

● *Searching for buyers and sellers*: The Internet generally reduces search costs. Using search engines and e-markets, it is now less costly than before to find the right buyer or seller.

- *Coordinating various transactional activities*: The Internet allows for more efficient coordination of geographically dispersed resources and processes.

- *Negotiating and carrying out contractual aspects of transactions*: The Internet may eventually help reduce the contractual costs of transactions using intelligent agents and bots.

Because the Internet is based on open standards, the adoption of a cost-reducing Internet-based technology by a market participant is likely followed by widespread adoption of that technology. This would in time lead to a downward shift of transaction costs for the industry as a whole because extensive diffusion of the technology would lead to more efficient production for the entire industry. Efficient firms are able to pass along to their customers the resulting cost savings, as Dell and Wal-Mart have been doing for a long time. Inefficient firms, on the other hand, could see their profit margins and market shares squeezed. In extreme cases where incumbents are not quick to catch up, they could eventually be driven out of the market altogether, as was the case for companies such as Compaq and K-Mart.

In tandem with the downward trend of transaction costs, the Internet removes the traditional advantages of scale enjoyed by large players. In the level-playing field, small businesses can compete with large firms more effectively.

Deconstruction of business structure

The value chain is the set of activities through which a product or service is created and delivered to customers. In general, companies can extract competitive advantage by the way they perform a number of discrete but interconnected value-adding activities. The Internet has powerful impacts not only on individual activities (Figure 2.2) but also on the way the whole chain is configured and its various parts are integrated.

Information is the glue that holds the value chain together, and the Internet is a powerful tool that allows for disaggregation and reaggregation of the value chain. Increasingly, the way companies configure and manage their value chains becomes a source of competitive advantage.

Unbundling and reconfiguring the value chain, however, presents interesting challenges and opportunities. On one hand, firms can use the Internet to create sustainable advantage through cross-activity integration. But to do so companies need to use the Internet to integrate different activities and to configure their value chain with a view to making imitation by competitors difficult. As we will discuss later in the chapter, sustainability of any advantage resulting from an innovation is almost always directly proportional to the length of time it takes rivals to copy that innovation.[5] Since copying a process innovation is

---

5. Occasionally firms use patents to protect their competitive advantage.

Figure 2.2 Applications of the Internet in the value chain

Firm infrastructure

- Web-based, distributed financial and ERP systems
- On-line investor relations (e.g. information dissemination, broadcast conference calls)

Human resources management

- Self-service personnel and benefits administration
- Web-based training
- Internet-based sharing and dissemination of company information
- Electronic time and expense reporting

Technology development

- Collaborative product design across locations and among multiple value-system participants
- Knowledge directories accessible from all parts of the organization
- Real-time access by R&D to on-line sales and service information

Procurement

- Internet-enabled demand planning; real-time available-to-promise/capable-to-promise and fulfillment
- Other linkage of purchase, inventory, and forecasting systems with suppliers
- Automated "requisition to pay"
- Direct and indirect procurement via marketplaces, exchanges, auctions, and buyer-seller matching

Inbound logistics	Operations	Outbound logistics	Marketing and sales	After-sales service
• Real-time integrated scheduling, shipping, warehouse management, demand management and planning, and advanced planning and scheduling across the company and its suppliers • Dissemination throughout the company of real-time inbound and in-progress inventory data	• Integrated information exchange, scheduling, and decision making in in-house plants, contract assemblers, and components suppliers • Real-time available-to-promise and capable-to-promise information available to the sales force and channels	• Real-time transaction of orders whether initiated by an end consumer, a sales person, or a channel partner • Automated customer-specific agreements and contract terms • Customer and channel access to product development and delivery status • Collaborative integration with customer forecasting system • Integrated channel management including information exchange, warranty claims, and contract management (versioning, process control)	• On-line sales channels including Web sites and marketplaces • Real-time inside and outside access to customer information, product catalogs, dynamic pricing, inventory availability, on-line submission of quotes, and order entry • On-line product configurators • Customer-tailored marketing via customer profiling • Push advertising • Tailored on-line access • Real-time customer feed-back through Web surveys, opt-in/opt-out marketing, and promotion response tracking	• On-line support of customer service representatives through e-mail response management, billing integration, co-browse, chat, "call me now," voice-over-IP, and other uses of video streaming • Customer self-service via Web sites and intelligent service request processing including updates to billing and shipping profiles • Real-time field service access to customer account review, schematic review, parts availability and ordering, work-order update, and service parts management

Web-distributed supply chain management

Reprinted by permission of *Harvard Business Review,* from "Strategy and the Internet" by Michael E. Porter, March 2001.© 2001 by the Harvard Business School Publishing Corporation, all rights reserved.

generally more difficult than imitating technological innovations, companies must strive to integrate the Internet into the entire value chain rather than applying it only to individual activities. On the other hand, unbundling the value chain could paradoxically lead to the loss of any existing advantage because of the risk of de-averaging this advantage.

De-averaging competitive advantage

Evans and Wurster present a compelling idea in regard to competitive advantage and the Internet.[6] They observe that since firms perform some activities well and some not so well, advantages in some activities are offset by disadvantages in others. As long as a firm has competitive advantage over the *entire* value chain, it is advantaged. It does not matter where the advantage specifically comes from. In a way, firms "subsidize" poor performance in one activity by combining it with advantaged activities.

But as we just showed, the Internet deconstructs the value chain by allowing firms to unbundle various activities involved in sourcing, production, and marketing. This type of deconstruction in turn leads to the exposure of all activities – both disadvantaged and advantaged. Since the activities in the value chain are open to rivals and new entrants, competition intensifies. Competitive advantage over the entire chain no longer matters as new competitors focus on maximizing performance in specific activities.

Consider traditional car dealerships. In addition to selling cars, dealers usually provide other services like financing. A dealer's competitive advantage comes from the *sum* of advantages resulting from all the activities pertaining to sourcing, selling, servicing, and financing. Now consider the deconstruction of the dealers' value chain. As new entrants (e.g. online car dealerships) see the inefficiencies in the existing value chain, they reconfigure the value chain so that performance in *each* activity is maximized. This can be done, for example, through outsourcing of different activities to parties most advantaged in those areas. Incumbents could in turn lose the most advantageous parts of their business to new competitors, left behind with those parts of the value chain that are least value adding.

In the absence of a proactive strategic response by incumbents, what would happen to the less attractive activities performed by them? What would be the ultimate result of such deconstruction?

In situations where market incumbents are not in tune with market forces, they lose the most advantageous parts of the value chain to competitors. This would initially lead to a decline in incumbents' profit margins because the most advantageous company in each activity would take up the most profitable parts of the chain. A prolonged inertia by incumbents would put a further squeeze on profit margins and would eventually lead to market consolidation (think of automobile industry).

In contrast, proactive incumbents respond by deconstructing the value chain themselves. Weak points in the chain are identified, appropriate alliances are formed to remove existing inefficiencies, and a new, integrated configuration is created. e-Business integration usually involves other market participants – customers, suppliers, partners, and even competitors. Each participant in the new value chain would try to maximize performance in one or more activities. This

---

6. Evans and Wurster (2000).

pre-emptive strike would consequently make it difficult for new entrants to deconstruct the chain to extract value from individual activities, or to copy it altogether.

As a direct consequence of the above three factors – reduced transaction costs, unbundled value chain, and de-averaged competitive advantage – competition intensifies. These forces influence the e-business strategy-making process in two important ways. First, since operational advantages resulting from the adoption of Internet-based technologies and applications are not usually long lasting, firms need to pay more attention to their strategic positioning as a source of sustainable competition.[7] Second, in the light of a deconstructed value chain, incumbents need to find innovative ways to use the Internet to configure their value chain so that various internal and external activities can be integrated dynamically. It is more difficult to copy integrated business processes than single processes.

Sustainable competitive advantage

According to Michael Porter competitive advantage would be enduring only if a firm can do:[8]

- things its competitors do, but better (operational effectiveness); or

- things differently than its competitors (strategic positioning).

Advantages in business, however, are almost always temporary. Advanced technologies can provide new opportunities for firms to experiment with new ways of doing their business or doing new businesses. In this role, technology is a pre-emptive strategic lever, enabling companies to achieve their strategic objectives. At the same time, it is increasingly easy to use advanced technologies to reverse engineer or simply copy new innovations. Globalization and the adoption of open standards such as HTML and XML have further facilitated copying. In this role, technology is a defensive weapon usually used to "catch up" with innovating market leaders.

This schizophrenic nature of technology places innovative companies in a quandary. On one hand, they recognize the enabling role of technology in achieving strategic objectives. They know they must innovate in order to survive. On the other hand, they are painfully aware of the perils of spending large sums of money on an innovation just to realize that the competition can readily copy what they have done.[9] The tradeoffs are somewhat thorny. Businesses are

---

7. For more information on strategic positioning, consult Porter (1996).
8. Porter (2001).
9. One way to protect innovations is to patent them. However, as an increasing number of innovations are based on "soft" processes involving know-how and intellectual property, it is not always feasible to use the patent laws to prevent competitors from replicating new innovations.

damned if they do not innovate, because distinctions brought about by innovations are usually good sources of competitive advantage. Yet they are also damned, albeit less severely, if they do innovate because it is likely that someone else would replicate the innovation. The choice should be clear, however.

In realizing lasting competitive advantage, the trick lies in (a) rapid and continuous innovation and (b) dynamic coupling of processes so that they cannot be duplicated easily. In effect, in order to be ahead of the pack, a firm increasingly needs to leverage new technologies, in rapid and continuous cycles, to do *different things*. Time has indeed become a strategic imperative permeating the sourcing, production, and marketing cycles. And competing on time and innovation has become the cornerstone of successful business strategies. Such was the case with *Stater NV* (see accompanying case study), the Dutch mortgage business which was the first in the European market to have created an electronic infrastructure for the mortgage process. This first-mover advantage gave Stater the market power to impose standards on the nascent market – yet it was under continued pressure to innovate as the "service-grid" of mortgage players grew.

Consider Intel. At any given point in time 100 per cent of Intel's revenues are generated from products introduced in the previous three years. Similarly, 30 per cent of revenues at 3M come from new products every year.[10] Time has brought a new sense of urgency to business: faster research and development, faster production, faster distribution, and faster marketing. This is as true in high-tech industries (Intel) as in traditional manufacturing and chemical industries (3M).

In addition to continuous innovation, companies can also ward off competition by making it difficult for their innovations to be replicated. This can best be achieved by integrating various processes involved in an innovation. As mentioned before, replication of an integrated system is usually far more difficult than copying single processes. Many people are in awe to see how Dell has consistently been able to year after year trump the competition using its seemingly straightforward "direct model." Ask customers what they want, produce the product, then sell it directly at the lowest price possible. One would expect to see widespread duplication of such a seemingly "simple" model by all the powerhouses competing in the PC space. But this has not happened. Indeed in 2001 Dell became the world's largest PC manufacturer, at the expense of all the other top-sellers (Compaq, HP, IBM, and NEC).[11] Why have not other vendors not been able to replicate Dell's model? Is this because the competition lacks a sense of direction? Or is it because they know what needs to be done but are simply unable to execute it properly?

The ability to execute a strategy in a timely fashion is perhaps as important as deciding on the direction a firm takes. As business environments become increasingly complex and unpredictable, and as certain technologies affect the

---

10. Eisenhardt and Brown (1998).
11. According to IDC, in the third quarter of 2003 Dell captured a 17.4 per cent market share in worldwide PC shipments, slightly higher than HP's 17.1 per cent. IBM, Fujitsu, and Toshiba, the other top three vendors, each had single-digit market shares.

way businesses operate more pervasively than before, companies are forced to manage their strategic process dynamically. Dynamic strategic process entails an undivided focus, rapid response to market forces, and a penchant for pursuing sustainable advantage. Long-lasting distinction is generated through a competitive cost structure capable of providing superior *customer value*. This can be achieved by delivering greater value to customers or comparable value at lower cost, or both.[12] Notice how craftily Dell has been able to successfully do both simultaneously!

Using technology to achieve operational excellence is usually easier than using it to establish new positions that attract new customers or steal customers away from incumbents. Rivals – at least the competitive ones – can usually emulate superior operational performance by copying the underlying technology. As a growing number of players adopt the new technology, the effects of these innovations gradually diminish. This dynamic equilibrium first leads to dilution and then to elimination of any initial advantage the innovating firm may have been able to reap from that technology. At this stage, the new technology becomes an essential part of doing business; it becomes a *strategic necessity*, changing the cost structure of the whole industry, and raising the bar for everyone.

Consider the introduction of automatic teller machines (ATM) in the 1970s. Citibank was able to reap the "first-mover" benefits for some time. The innovation was so revolutionary that not only did it result in improved operational effectiveness, but it also allowed Citibank to reposition its retail operations. Improved operational performance manifested itself in terms of convenience, access, speed, and cost. Customers could access their accounts faster and at any time through conveniently located machines. At the same time, Citibank successfully entrenched its strategic position by wooing established customers from other banks and simultaneously creating new demand for 24-hour banking services. Moreover, the introduction of ATMs reduced the cost of a typical transaction by almost 75 per cent (from slightly over $1.00 per branch transaction to about $0.27 for an ATM transaction). Eventually all competing banks invested billions of dollars in their ATM infrastructure. This in turn led to structural changes in the entire retail banking industry.

Competitive advantage and strategic investment decisions

An important question senior management has to deal with relates to cost justification and valuation of new technologies, a topic we will discuss in the following chapter. Suffice it to say that IT expenditure now comprises more than 50 per cent of new capital investment made by many companies.[13] At the same time most companies are frustrated by the elusive payoffs of IT because, as we saw in the case of ATMs, new applications of the emerging technologies can usually be copied easily. In these dynamic environments, the valuation of technology is not an easy task.

---

12. Porter (1996).
13. Westland (2002).

In order to facilitate more effective decision-making, it is imperative that managers have the skills to quantify and understand the impact of the risks, uncertainties, and options associated with their e-business initiatives. A poor decision relating to e-business investment may have disastrous effects on costs, productivity, and the customer service capabilities of the enterprise. In extreme cases it may have irreparable impacts. Similarly, the decision not to go with a particular e-business initiative may have profound negative repercussions. The need for a valuation and measurement programme has increased dramatically as management is facing the challenge of balancing projects against limited resources while at the same time recognizing the strategic importance of e-business.

The measurement of any given e-business implementation depends on numerous factors that, taken together, result in a complex environment. However, we can use a greatly simplified formula to put in perspective the IT-investment decision process. Broadly speaking, we can divide IT investments (see Chapter 1) into non-strategic and strategic decisions. The majority of IT investments are not strategic in that they do not give the adopting firm any competitive advantage. These investments are triggered either by technology push or by the demand to improve various operations in terms of speed, cost, and quality.

In contrast, strategic IT investments should bring advantage to the adopting firm – at least for some time. Since the payoffs for these investments are not usually quantifiable, firms need to find general yardsticks to measure the efficacy of their investments. Such a measure can be obtained by looking at the ratio of the amount of investment to the time it takes rivals to copy that technology. A high ratio signifies a poorly justified investment because it implies that a company has invested large sums in a technology just to find out that its competitors can copy it relatively easily. A low ratio, on the other hand, indicates a good investment because it gives the pioneer a relatively longer time to enjoy competitive advantages ensuing from the new technology. In sum, we should take note that it is increasingly difficult to enjoy "first mover" advantages in a sustainable manner because new technologies can be copied readily.

Erosion of competitive advantage

Gharajedaghi identifies five factors that erode competitive advantage:[14]

1 Imitation

2 Inertia

3 Suboptimization

4 Change of the game

5 Shift of paradigm.

---

14. Gharajedaghi (1999).

So far we have focused our discussion on the potential for imitation to erode competitive advantage; in the remainder of this section we cover the remaining four forces.

Inertia

A delay in reacting to technological innovation is the second cause of erosion of competitive advantage. Sometimes a firm's structural and bureaucratic rigidity delays reaction to new innovations. More often, though, firms fail to respond to a critical technology because, paradoxically, they are unable to break away from a previously dominant and successful technology. The more success a company has with a given technology, the more unlikely it is to adopt a new technology! It is often difficult for companies to see that success at times can be the impetus for future failure.

Inertia usually manifests itself first in terms of denial followed by incremental patching. Consider the case of Xerox, patent-holder of the photocopier until 1974. As the world's market leader, Xerox saw its market share drop from 49 to 22 per cent during the early 1980s when Japanese companies produced copiers that were sold at a price that would cost Xerox to produce! What was Xerox' reaction to this? Denial: "It is impossible. They must be dumping their products . . ." But initial denial was soon followed by the realization that the source of the problem was internal and not outside the firm. Subsequently, the path the company undertook was one of patching things up through incremental change. This type of incrementalism, however, invariably compromised the output quality. It also wasted time by giving rivals a window of opportunity to further solidify their market position.[15]

Suboptimization

Suboptimization refers to the fallacy that if X is good, more X is even better. It constitutes the tendencies and behaviours that destroy a proven advantage. Drawing from the Icarus mythology,[16] Miller shows how companies could fall into the trap of overestimating their strengths.[17] He calls the phenomenon a *paradox* because Icarus's greatest asset (his wings) finally led to his demise.

Digital Equipment Corporation (DEC) serves as a telling story of a company that so engrossed itself in minute technical tinkering that it lost sight of

---

15. According to IDC, Xerox copier market share in the US in 2002 had shrunk to 14 per cent compared to 30 per cent for Canon, the market leader. The stock price of Xerox in 2003 was floating around $10, almost what it was in the late 1970s. The Dow Jones Index had increased by about 1000 per cent during the same period.
16. In Greek mythology, *Icarus* and his father decide to escape prison using wax and feathers to built wings so that they can fly over the prison's walls. The father, being wise and experienced, flied over the wall and landed safely outside. *Icarus*, however, become emboldened to fly higher and higher and eventually got so close to the sun that his artificial wings melted and he plunged to his death.
17. Miller (1990).

its consumer. DEC invented minicomputers, a cheaper and more flexible alternative to mainframes, to become the world's second largest computer vendor in the 1980s. DEC was known for producing the most reliable and highest quality computers in the world, but gradually turned into an engineering monoculture. At the height of its success, DEC became so obsessed with technical fine-tuning of its products that it ignored consumers' needs for more economical and user-friendly systems. DEC slowly waned until Compaq eventually acquired it in 1998, to become then the world's largest PC maker. Interestingly, in the light of this acquisition and other debacles Compaq also saw its fortunes dwindle. HP acquired Compaq in 2002.

Change of the game

> Without changing our pattern of thought, we will not be able to solve the problems we have created with our current pattern of thought.

So brilliantly said Albert Einstein to articulate a persistent dilemma facing human beings: that playing a game successfully could invariably change the game itself. In assessing competitive advantage, this force is the most difficult to manage and predict because of our propensity to solve problems based on our current assumptions and worldview.

Henry Ford created mass production machines to build economical cars. This innovation successfully solved the production problem and resulted in an initial competitive advantage for Ford. However, Ford did not foresee that by solving the production problem, the nature of the game would change – in this case to one of marketing. As competitors widely imitated mass production, concern for markets replaced concern for production. Alfred Sloan of GM detected this shift and introduced the concept of a product-based divisional structure as an organizational design tool to manage growth and market diversity.[18]

Shift of paradigm

The highest-level tendencies and behaviours that destroy a proven advantage result in a shift of paradigm. The cumulative effects of imitation, inertia, sub-optimization, and change of the game display themselves in the form of a paradigm shift: the highest-level processes that diminish an existing advantage. During a paradigmatic shift, companies learn that the existing assumptions and mental models no longer provide adequate and convincing explanations. They start questioning the conventional wisdom and re-evaluate the emerging opportunities and threats. Usually the older an organization, the more difficult it is to break away from the rigid assumptions underlying legacy. As we saw in Chapter 1, in the face of radical technologies such as the Internet, most companies are ill equipped to make the necessary transformational changes largely as a result of

---

18. Gharajedaghi (1999).

rigidity inherent in their existing business architectures. This inflexibility in turn prevents incumbents from deconstructing and reconfiguring their value chain, opening the door for competitors to extract advantage from individual activities.

In summary, companies should identify the above hierarchy of forces to combat the erosion of their competitive position. We have discussed amply the risks and dangers of imitation. Companies should also be aware of the threats of inertia and suboptimization to avert complacency and exaggeration of previous successes. Businesses should also have their antennas up to scan their environment to see if the solution to an outstanding problem would indeed lead to a change in the nature of the problem itself. In such situations companies need to re-evaluate the efficacy of the current assumptions in solving the emerging problems.

e-Business strategy

What strategies should companies adopt in their e-business initiatives? In answering this question, let us first take stock of what we have covered so far. We discussed that strategy is creating fit among a company's activities. We also observed that the success of a strategy depends on doing many things well and integrating them. Because how a company creates fit among its activities influences its distinctive strategy and sustainability, the degree to which various activities in the value chain are integrated becomes a source of competitive advantage.

In formulating an e-business strategy, then, it is critical to think in terms of the *business architecture*, a concept that refers to how a company puts together various components into a coherent system. Similar to design of buildings, the principal role of architecture is to map form to function. As shown in Figure 2.3, the business architecture also maps form to function by providing a roadmap to link a firm's value proposition (function) to its offerings, processes, capabilities, and relationships (form). By examining various components of the business architecture we can see how tightly e-business strategy is linked to business strategy.

In the remaining parts of this section we will describe the dimensions of the business architecture along with the application of these concepts to electronic banking.

The value proposition

e-Business strategy starts with a firm's articulation of its value proposition. Over the course of identifying unmet and underserved needs, the value proposition helps a company to answer the following questions:

● Who are our customers that will be affected by the e-business initiative?

● What are their needs?

Figure 2.3 Dimensions of the business architecture

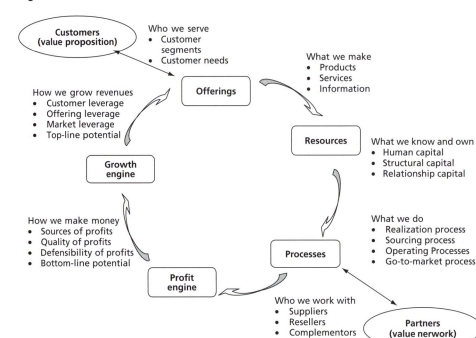

Source: Sawhney and Zabin, The Seven Steps to Nirvana: Strategic insights into e-Business Transformation, 2001, McGraw Hill, New York. Reprinted with permission.

● Why are the existing alternatives inadequate in satisfying these needs?

● What distinctive value can the e-business initiative create for customers?

As you may have noticed, all these questions relate to *customers*. The value proposition is driven by customers' needs and should be conceived based on customers' processes, not the company's processes. In essence, the value proposition should be designed so that it allows customers to conduct business their way, not the company's way.[19] By coupling its value chain dynamically to those of individual customers, not only can a company woo customers from rivals, it can also increase its customer retention rate. Attracting new customers and retaining existing customers can both be sources of sustainable advantage.

One of the case studies following this chapter details Citibank's efforts to transform its traditional money management function into a single Web-based platform for the corporate market. Citibank was facing a new breed of

---

19. Tapscott et al. (2000).

aggressive competitors with B2B e-payment offerings. Citibank's strategic response involved a careful consideration of the Internet's impact on its industry structure and how a newly devised e-business strategy could fit into the company's overall strategy. Crafting an online strategy for Citibank's position began with articulating its value proposition, and focusing on fundamental questions such as the following:

- What segments of the market will be affected by e-banking?

- What are the customers' online needs (e.g. 7×24, 365 days, location-free access)?

- How can traditional assets be used in conjunction with the Internet to create a strategic position in the industry?

- Why are the traditional offline alternatives inadequate in satisfying these needs (e.g. limited access)?

- What distinctive value would an e-business offering create for customers (e.g. convenience, extended reach)?

The offerings

The offerings of a company relate to the benefits that a company creates for its customer, and is defined as "seamless bundles of products, services, and information that a firm creates along its trading partners to solve a customer problem, and to create an end-to-end customer experience."[20]

An offering is not a product or a service but bundles of products and services that involve various partners. Recall that companies try to sustain their competitive advantage by making it difficult for rivals to copy their products and services. Having differentiated offerings that involve multi-parties, then, enhances a firm's strategic positioning.

The resources

Resources are all the capabilities, skills, people, and assets that a company uses to create economic value. We can divide resources into three broad groups: (1) structural capital; (2) human capital; and (3) relationship capital.[21]

Structural capital concerns explicit knowledge of the organization. It consists of codified knowledge and includes systems, processes, technologies, and any other physical asset. Increasingly structural capital is tied up in the networked knowledge, processes, and tools.

---

20. Sawhney and Zabin (2001, p. 91).
21. Stewart (1998).

Human capital relates to tacit knowledge in the organization. It consists of all the knowledge, know-how, skills, and experiences that reside in individuals. Because human capital is not embedded in organizational processes – it resides in people's brains – it is lost when people leave a company. Nonetheless, because the Internet has created an environment within which human capital is increasingly extending to people across companies, in formulating e-business strategy companies need to find ways to leverage knowledge shared by participants across enterprises.

Relationship capital relates to relationships and knowledge of customers, suppliers, distributors, partners, and competitors; it includes, among other things, brand equity and trust.

Companies use their resources as a platform to launch their strategic initiatives both in terms of growth and reinvention. In effect resources are tools used in configuring an organization's activities with a view to creating and leveraging competitive advantage. It is important to note that a firm's capital is increasingly tied up in its non-physical capital. Figure 2.4 shows how a company's resources are decapitalized and recapitalized in the networked economy. As companies become more customer-centric, brand equity becomes central to their profitability and growth, thus leading to a continuing flight of tangible assets to intangibles. In fact, recent research shows that more than 78 per cent of the S&P500's market value now flows from intangible capitals.[22]

Can you categorize all the resources involved in an e-banking initiative in terms of structural, human, and relationship capital? Which of these capabilities and assets are likely to be decapitalized and recapitalized? Which ones enhance the bank's competitive advantage?

Figure 2.4 Decapitalization/Recapitalization of the firm

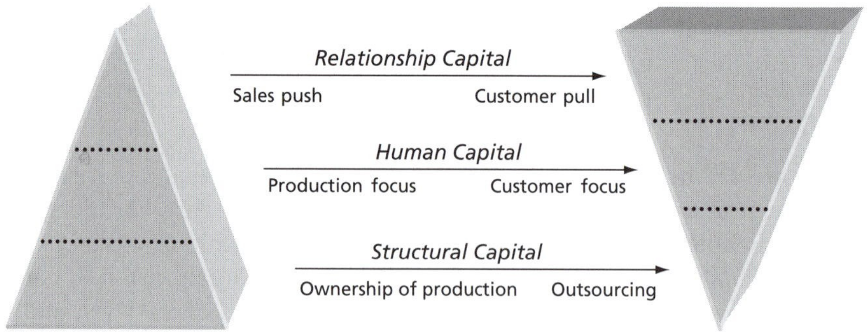

Source: Adapted from Read et al. (2001).

22. Read, C. et al. (2001).

The processes

Processes are the activities that a firm performs with its resources to produce a set of outcomes. Sawhney and Zabin identify nine categories of core processes:[23]

1 *New offering realization processes*: how a firm defines, designs, and markets new offerings.

2 *Customer relationship management process*: how a company builds and maintains relationship with its customers.

3 *Fulfillment of management process*: how a company sources its inputs and markets its products and services.

4 *Market sensing process*: how a firm collects market information and disseminates such information internally.

5 *Operations management process*: how a company transforms inputs to outputs.

6 *Business development process*: how a firm finds ways to grow.

7 *Strategy development process*: how a company defines its goals and the means to achieve those goals.

8 *Partner management process*: how a firm selects, manages, and maintains relationship with external partners.

9 *Financial management process*: how a company deploys its financial resources and allocates capital within the firm.

Whereas optimizing individual processes is usually easy, joint design and optimization of processes is indeed challenging. As we discussed previously, the way a firm configures and integrates processes involved in a transaction could be a source of sustainable advantage. Such was the case with *STATER NV* in its goal of becoming a hub for all stakeholders in the mortgage value chain – going so far as to grant external parties control over their parts of the process. Such process synchronization though is difficult because it has to take place at the system level, and it involves tight coordination among operation processes, logistics management processes, and marketing processes.

Can you take an inventory of all the processes that are involved in Citibank's e-banking initiative? Because these processes are interdependent on one another, how can the bank ensure that they are interfaced optimally?

The partners

According to Coase's thesis, a firm expands as long as the cost of organizing an extra transaction within the firm is less than the cost of carrying out the same

---

23. Sawhney and Zabin (2001).

transaction by means of an exchange on the open market. In the face of falling transaction costs, though, it is increasingly cheaper to outsource parts of business than to perform those activities inside the firm. In crafting the business architecture, then, firms need to decide which processes and activities should be kept inside the company, which ones outside.

It is helpful to examine partnerships within the realm of a *business web*[24] to describe how internetworked partnerships are formed to create value for their customers. Such partnerships can be vertical or horizontal. *Vertical partnerships* are formed along supply and demand chains and relate to the sourcing and fulfillment network that a firm creates. In contrast, *horizontal partnerships* do not involve direct inputs and outputs of the firm; rather, they complement the firm's offerings. Whereas vertical partnerships can improve operational effectiveness in terms of sourcing inputs and delivering outputs, horizontal partnerships may play a more important role in terms of strategic positioning by augmenting a firm's offerings or improving customer relationships. In deciding the breadth and depth of partnerships, firms must pay particular attention to the link between the business web they try to create and their value proposition. A different value proposition entails a different business architecture, which in turn requires different partners.

Some Internet strategists believe that a specific configuration of partnerships could itself be a source of competitive advantage. Consider the well-known story of how the PC industry was born. Traditional strategists argue that because IBM "gave away" various parts of its PC, including the operating system, to other companies to design, it helped to commoditize its PCs, thus leading to lower profitability not only for IBM but also for the PC industry as a whole. This view is in contrast to those of some Internet gurus who see partnering as an indispensable part of economic growth. IBM's partnering strategy in the 1980s, they argue, indeed expedited the diffusion of PCs, leading to the widespread use of information technology and networking, helping IBM to increase overall revenues. Partnering allowed IBM to leverage its business network to significantly boost sales, particularly in software and services areas. Compare that with Apple's vertically integrated strategy of designing and manufacturing most of the components of its computers, leading to a significant loss of Apple's market share.

An important partnering consideration relates to the outsourcing of IT application development and services. A recent survey of CIO's showed that about 80 per cent of companies outsource their application development and IT services, citing a lack of internal staff, lack of internal expertise, and the need for speed as the three main reasons. To gain better insights into outsourcing issues, you can refer to Appendix.

Can you identify the business web of the Citibank's e-banking initiative? How do you ensure that there is a cumulative logic in such partnerships in terms of sourcing, delivering, and augmentation of the e-banking offerings? Which partners would help to improve the bank's operational effectiveness?

---

24. Tapscott et al. (2000).

Which ones would help it to entrench its strategic position? To answer these questions you need to go back and re-examine the value proposition of the e-banking initiative.

The engines

Sawhney and Zabin's final dimensions of the business architecture – profit and growth engines – relate to evaluation and measurement. In formulating e-business strategy these engines are used to assess the efficacy of the whole business architecture in terms of profit and growth sustainability. Sustainable profits can be derived from ownership of proprietary structural capital, from relationships with customers, suppliers and partners, and from increasing returns to scale, as is the case for most software houses.[25] Profit engines tend to wind down over time. Therefore companies should try to have multiple profit engines in order to defend themselves in a sustainable manner against the erosion of a specific profit stream.

Sustainable growth can be derived along the offerings the firm creates (what), along the markets in which it participates (where), or along the customer base it serves (who). Growth along the offerings has traditionally been the most common form of growth engine. The Internet allows companies to collaborate with their partners to leverage their business architecture to introduce new products and services that create value for their customers.

Another time-tested growth engine is geographical expansion. Growing along markets, however, used to require vast investments, something available only to large players. The Internet has facilitated geographical expansion regardless of a company's size. Now smaller companies can use the shared infrastructure made possible by the Internet to also expand into global markets.

Finally, expanding along the customer base has taken center stage in the battle for growth. We will discuss in Chapter 5 (e-CRM) how companies can leverage Web-based technologies to finely segment their customer base, understand their needs, and evaluate the lifetime value of the customer with a view to growing along the segments that have most promising economic potentials in the long run.

Can you outline the profit and growth engines of Citibank's e-banking initiative?

Summary

In this chapter we discussed various issues surrounding strategy – the first organization dimension in the DOT framework – and how they relate to e-business transformation initiatives. We explained that strategy answers two fundamental

---

25. Companies whose main business relates to handing, producing, and marketing of information have usually high cost of production, but low cost of reproduction. Scaling then has a profound effect on profitability of such companies. It is not uncommon to see gross profit margins of 80–90 per cent among large software companies such as Microsoft and Adobe.

questions as to *where* a company wants to go and *how* it intends to get there. We then presented three approaches to strategy, each with a different strategic logic: establishing position, leveraging resources, and pursuing opportunities. Given the speed by which the markets are moving and changing today, we argued that firms may find it easier to respond to market forces by adopting a strategy that allows them to seize fleeting opportunities. We also maintained that even though the fundamentals of business are still the same, there are at least three major forces that have important strategic implications for companies: lower transaction costs made possible by the Internet, unbundling and reconfiguration of the value chain – or more appropriately value web, and de-averaging of competitive advantage. We also examined sources of sustainable advantage, as well as sources that erode such advantage: imitation, inertia, sub-optimization, change of the game, and shift of paradigm. Finally, we examined the concept of business architecture as a springboard to discuss various issues associated with e-business strategy.

Questions for discussion

???

1   What is strategy?

2   Compare and contrast the three approaches to strategy.

3   Why has the Internet allowed companies to reduce their transaction costs?

4   What are the implications of unbundling and reconfiguration of the value chain?

5   Under what circumstances does de-averaging of competitive advantage occur?

6   Under what conditions can firms sustain their competitive advantage?

7   What are the sources of erosion of sustainable advantage? Which ones are most difficult to predict and manage?

8   What issues should companies take into consideration when deciding on strategic IT investments?

9   What is business architecture? Why is it important? How can it help companies in their e-business strategy?

10   What issues do companies need to consider when entering outsourcing agreements?

Appendix: Information technology outsourcing

Outsourcing is not a new concept. In one form or another, it has existed for decades as a management tool. The economic recession of the 1980s brought forth a renewed attention towards outsourcing, particularly in the area of IT outsourcing. Internally, firms were in dire need to cut cost, downsize, and focus on their core businesses. The slowing of the economy prompted an increased interest to work with outside partners to increase efficiency and reduce in-house capital spending. Externally, the IT environment was undergoing revolutionary growth from the stand-alone mainframe environment to the inter-networked user-centric workstations. Firms found themselves having to network and integrate both internal and external computer systems to adapt to the new form of competition in the global marketplace. This integration had placed extraordinary pressures on firms having to run existing businesses and develop new capabilities simultaneously. It was under this economic landscape that outsourcing rose to the surface as a viable alternative.

In 1989, Kodak's $250 million outsourcing contract with IBM Corp., Digital Equipment Corp., and Businessland Inc. represented the landmark event where IT outsourcing was employed in a strategic sense. Instead of pure cost-cutting, outsourcing was used for strategic alliances with state-of-the-art IT service providers. Since then, the outsourcing industry has been growing at a staggering rate of 20 per cent a year.[26]

Simply stated, outsourcing is the purchase of a good or service that was previously provided internally. IT outsourcing is therefore the carrying-out of IT functions and activities by third parties. Over the years, IT outsourcing has evolved from a facility management model to the farming out of tasks, services, or functions to third-party vendors. Facility management refers to a company paying for another company to operate its computer centre. With the dawn of data processing, outsourcing practices have included such diverse functions as system programming, application development, system and application maintenance, network management, and end-user computer support and services.

Current state

In the last few years, the realities of outsourcing have changed rapidly. The plummeting cost of communications, the widespread use of standardized interfaces such as Internet browsers, and the quickening pace at which companies are automating data have cut interaction costs sharply. The workplace's dependence on information has also increased the use of outsourcing tremendously. Outsourcing is no longer limited to large and established corporations. Small to medium enterprises are making use of outsourcing to leverage the skills and expertise of outside vendors that they could not have developed on their own.

In an increasing number of cases, companies are opting to form partnerships with their service providers. The Kodak–IBM deal changed the common perception of IT outsourcing from an "arm's length" transaction to one of strategic partnership. Strategic partnerships are typically long-term commitments allowing the firms to share risks and rewards and to better manage complex interrelationships. The objective is to align the interests of both buyers and suppliers that the contract provisions fail to address. EDS, a leading IT-services provider, paid $250 million in 1990 for a 50 per cent stake in Texas Air Corp.'s System One before signing the $4 billion outsourcing contract with the company. However, much skepticism has been found in practice regarding the effectiveness

---

26. Caldwell and McGee (1997).

of this approach. It is believed that outsourcing suppliers cannot be strategic partners because they do not share the same profit motives, and that the outsourcing vendor's profits are inevitably maximized at the customer's expense. Partnership is a concept used to stress vendors' cooperative attitude, flexibility and willingness not to be constrained by precise contractual provision. In practice, only a small portion of organizations regard their outsourcing arrangements as partnerships, while all are aware of the primacy of the contract.[27]

Today outsourcing is expanding beyond pure IT services into business process outsourcing (BPO). Under such arrangement, instead of a single operation, a third-party provider is responsible for performing an entire business function for the client organization. Common examples are human resource management and payroll processing. IDC claims that BPO currently represents 60 per cent of all outsourcing spending worldwide.

In recent years companies have engaged in new Internet-based outsourcing services, such as Web hosting, Internet Service Providers (ISP), Web services, and Application Service Providers (ASP). For example, companies can use the Internet to access applications and related services provided by third parties. Sometimes referred to as "apps-on-tap," ASP services are hailed to become an important alternative, especially for smaller companies with low IT budgets and expertise.

Despite the popularity of outsourcing in the last decade, the results have been mixed. In a recent survey, one-fifth of the executives involved in some sort of outsourcing indicated that they were dissatisfied with the results of their outsourcing arrangements, while another fifth of the respondents were neither satisfied nor dissatisfied, implying that they were not seeing clear benefits.[28] Dun & Bradstreet reported that 20–25 per cent of all outsourcing relationships failed within two years and that 50 per cent failed within five. Nearly 70 per cent of the companies responding to the Dun & Bradstreet survey asserted that suppliers did not understand what they were supposed to do and that the cost of outsourcing was too high and the service provided was of poor quality.[29] In such cases, it has often been forgotten that outsourcing is not an end in itself, but rather a strategic tool for enhancing overall performance.

Why outsourcing?

It is argued that a company's overarching objective should be to maximize flexibility and control so that it can pursue different options as circumstances change. Competitiveness comes from the ability to manage change. Instead of making a one-time decision whether to outsource or not, companies should create an environment that will best accommodate the changes resulting from the outsourcing decision. One way to maximize both flexibility and control is to

---

27. Hancox and Hackney (1999).
28. Corbett and Associates (1999).
29. Ozanne (2000).

maximize competition, which in this case refers to the competition between potential external suppliers and internal IT departments battling to provide IT services.

Companies outsource parts of their operations for many different reasons. A survey by the Outsourcing Institute identifies the following top reasons.[30]

1   Reduce and control operating costs

2   Improve company focus

3   Gain access to world-class capabilities

4   Free internal resources for other purposes

5   Accelerate re-engineering benefits

6   Share risks

7   Make capital funds available

8   Get help to manage out-of-control functions

9   Get cash infusion

10   Get access to resources not available internally.

An important consideration in an outsourcing strategy is cost reduction. Companies hope to reduce their operating costs through outsourcing. However, there are substantial hidden costs that can easily escape management attention: costs associated with managing the relationship, monitoring the delivery of services, and coordinating the exchange of information between the buyer and supplier. A recent study of outsourcing contracts cited hidden costs as the biggest outsourcing problem.[31]

The conventional wisdom is that companies should focus on their set of "core competencies" and outsource other non-core activities. Core competencies define the company's unique competitive advantage in the marketplace. Instead of focusing on products and functions, core competencies should be viewed in terms of specific skills, knowledge sets, and management systems that actually create a sustainable competitive edge. Product and service offerings can be easily duplicated, back-engineered, or replaced by substitutes. Competencies, on the other hand, are set of strategies, skills, and infrastructure that cut across traditional functions.

Nike Inc., recognizing branding as its core competency, outsources 100 per cent of its shoe production, and manufactures only key technical components of its Nike Air system. Nike creates maximum value by concentrating on pre-production (research and development) and post-production (marketing,

---

30. The Outsourcing Institute (1998).
31. Willcocks and Fitzgerald (1994).

distribution, and sales), linked together by a central marketing information system. It even outsources the advertising component of its marketing program to Wieden & Kennedy, whose creative efforts have driven Nike to the top of the product recognition scale.[32]

By focusing on core competencies and shedding other non-core activities to qualified suppliers, a company can leverage its resources in four ways:

1   maximizing returns on internal resources by focusing on what the company does best;

2   creating barriers against competitors encroaching into the company's strategic stronghold;

3   fully utilizing external suppliers' investments, innovations, and specialized capabilities; and

4   reducing risk, shortening cycle times including time to market.

Knowledge transfer

Companies need to build management capabilities in monitoring and evaluating the outsourced products and services. Management needs a solid understanding of the objectives of the outsourcing arrangement before defining appropriate matrices in measuring the results on a regular basis.

An important issue is to put an appropriate knowledge transfer mechanism in place. Knowledge transfer, on a strategic level, will prevent management from over-reliance on a particular supplier, thus losing its bargaining power in future arrangements. After outsourcing, companies may find themselves having lost the very skills and processes that have distinguished them in the marketplace. In the 1980s, many US companies outsourced manufacture of what at the time seemed to be only minor components, such as semiconductor chips or bicycle frames. Later, the suppliers took ownership of the manufacture knowledge and skills, and refused to supply the components as individual parts. The companies lost the skills to manufacture the parts themselves and could not prevent their suppliers from either assisting competitors or entering the downstream market on their own.

At an operational level, knowledge transfer will ensure a smooth transition from the outsourced team to the internal team. Mechanisms such as job shadowing, documentation, and knowledge capture systems have been used to this effect. In addition, informal knowledge transfer, through the daily interactions of both employee groups, should not be overlooked. The interaction between skilled people in different functional groups often leads to unexpected insights or solutions. To nurture the continued development of cross-functional skills, companies should consciously ensure that their remaining employees interact

---

32. Quinn and Hilmer (1994).

constantly and closely with the outsourced experts. Co-location of employee offices and employee secondments are used for such purposes.

Conflict management

Conflicts of interest surface when the buyer demands exclusive rights to the outsourced products or services, while the supplier desires the ability to repackage and resell its expertise to other potential buyers, some of them direct competitors of the original buyer. Serious difficulties arise when the buyer does not have sufficient market power relative to the supplier. In such scenario, the buyer may become hostage to the supplier which could gradually raise prices and reduce service. Companies who contract all their IT needs could also become vulnerable to escalating fees and inflexible services. Dividing the IT operations into discrete slices and outsourcing to different suppliers may seem to be an attractive option, but this strategy entails extensive resources required to manage the disparate contracts. Outsourcing companies often try to manage these conflicting interests by tight contract control, using such measurement tools as service level agreements, charge-backs, and non-performance specifications. Although contract control cannot promote a true congruence of interests between the parties, it is recognized as an effective mechanism to ensure outsourcing success. In unbalanced market situations, tight contracts are particularly crucial to limit the buyer's vulnerability to suppliers' opportunistic behaviours.[33]

Future trends

Although the traditional drivers of outsourcing (e.g. cost reduction, focus on core competencies, and increased efficiency) still stand, there is mounting evidence that companies have turned to outsourcing for more strategic reasons, including keeping up with cutting-edge technology, building partnerships, creating value for the organization and its customers, and broadening infrastructure and operations reach.[34] The growing interest in broader goals seems to suggest that companies continue to see IT as a critical resource, and as such view outsourcing as a way to meet both immediate cost-reduction needs and long-term strategic growth.

There is also an emerging shift to outsource intellectual-based service activities, such as research, product development, human relations, legal work, and marketing. As companies increasingly become aware of the strategic potential of specialized knowledge and business networks, new outsourcing suppliers are likely to be more knowledge-based and less asset-intensive than those that are already in operation. The management of outsourcing will see a shift to rely on relationship management, rather than contractual terms and punitive measures for non-delivery.

---

33. Saunders et al. (1997).
34. *IT Index*, The Outsourcing Institute (2001).

On another front, globalization is increasing the range of options available to outsourcing buyers. More and more companies in Europe and North America are looking across borders for suppliers. The supplier market in the developing economies is one of the fastest-growing areas in outsourcing. The trend began in India, and now suppliers can be found in countries ranging from Pakistan and Indonesia, to Ireland and some of the former Soviet republics.

References

Caldwell, B. and McGee, M.K. (1997) "Outsourcing backlash", *Information Week*, September.

Coase, R. (1937) "The nature of the firm", *Economica*.

Corbett, M.F. and Associates (1999) *The 1999 Outsourcing Trends Report*, New York: LaGrangeville, March.

Gharajedaghi, J. (1999) *Systems Thinking: Managing Chaos and Complexity*, Boston, MA: Butterworth-Heinemann.

Eisenhardt, K. and Brown, S. (1998) "Time pacing: competing in markets that won't stand still", *Harvard Business Review*, March–April.

Eisenhardt, K. and Sull, D. (2001) "Strategy as simple rules", *Harvard Business Review*, January.

Evans, P. and Wurster, T.S. (2000) *Blown to Bits*, Harvard Business School Press, Boston.

Hancox, M. and Hackney, R. (1999) "Information technology outsourcing: conceptualizing practice in the public and private sector", Proceedings of the 32nd Hawaii International Conference on Systems Sciences.

IT Index, The Outsourcing Institute (2001) "*It's no Longer about Saving Money*" (Online). The Fifth Annual Outsourcing Index. Available from http://www.outsourcinginstitute.com/oi_index/no_longer.html.2001.

Miller, D. (1990) *Icarus Paradox: How Exceptional Companies Bring about their Own Downfall*, New York: HarperBusiness.

The Outsourcing Institute Membership (1998) "*Survey of Current and Potential Outsourcing End-Users*".

Ozanne, M.R. (2000) *D&B Barometer of Global Outsourcing*, Short Hills, NJ: Dun & Bradstreet.

Porter, M.E. (1996) "What is strategy?" *Harvard Business Review*, November–December.

Porter, M.E. (2001) "Strategy and the Internet", *Harvard Business Review*, March.

Quinn, J.B. and Hilmer, F.G. (1994) "Strategic outsourcing", *Sloan Management Review*, vol. 35, no. 4, Summer.

Read, C., Ross, J., Dunleavy, J., Schulman, D. and Bramante, J. (2001) *eCFO*, Pricewaterhousecoopers, New York: John Wiley & Sons.

Saunders, C., Gebelt, M. and Hu, Q. (1997) "Achieving success in information systems outsourcing", *California Management Review*, Berkeley, Winter.

Sawhney, M. and Zabin, J. (2001) *The Seven Steps to Nirvana: Strategic insights into eBusiness Transformation*, New York: McGraw Hill.

Stewart, T. (1998) *Intellectual Capital: The New Wealth of Organizations*, New York: Bantam Books.

Tapscott, D. Ticoll, D. and Lowy, A. (2000) *Digital Capital: Harnessing the Power of Business Webs*, Boston, Mass.: Harvard Business School Press.

Tichy, N. and Charan, R. (1989) "Speed, simplicity, self-confidence: an interview with Jack Welsh", *Harvard Business Review*.

Westland, C. (2002) *Valuing Technology: The New Science of Wealth in the Knowledge Economy*, New York: John Wiley & Sons.

Willcocks, L. and Fitzgerald, G. (1994) *A Business Guide to IT Outsourcing*, Business Intelligence, London.

Case study 1   Citibank's e-business strategy for global corporate banking

Citibank's Global Cash and Trade division was in the business of managing the flow of money for its corporate customers. It provided the tools and channels for its customers to receive money efficiently and to make payment in a timely fashion. In 2000, intense competition and the dot-com boom put pressure on Citibank and its competitors to transform their business in the new economy. In response to these challenges, Citibank made a serious push to deliver integrated solutions that would enable its corporate customers to conduct transactions on-line. Citibank's e-business strategy – *Connect, Transform and Extend* – was to Web-enable its core services, develop integrated solutions, and reach new markets. The ultimate goal was to build a single Web-enabled platform for all customers with similar needs.

To transform its Global Cash and Trade Division into an e-business, Citibank faced challenges in serving its corporate customers who had discrepant needs. Sophisticated clients, such as multinational companies (MNCs), required custom-built host-to-host product interface. Other customers, such as the small-and-medium-sized enterprises (SMEs), were more conservative and were not ready for Web-based solutions. How could Citibank build a flexible and agile e-business product that could capture their total cash management and trade service needs? Given Citibank's enormous global reach, how could it integrate the Internet initiatives into its overall strategy and create sustainable competitive advantages?

Global corporate banking at Citibank[1]

Citibank was incorporated in 1812 under the name of City Bank of New York. The bank had experienced several mergers since inception. The name Citibank N.A. was adopted in 1976. Following the merger with Travellers Group in 1998, the holding company changed its name to Citigroup Inc. In 2001, the Group employed 2,68,000 staff across over 100 countries serving 192 million customers.

Since the 1990s, Citibank's corporate banking activities evolved from a highly decentralised set of operation to a more centralised one, with much attention focused on 1400 large global corporations and institutional investors. By 1997, Citibank was one of the most profitable banks in the US. Its profits in 1997 were US$3.59 billion, with global corporate banking accounting for US$2.56 billion. By most measures, Citibank was the most global US bank.

For corporate customers, Citibank traditionally provided a full range of financial services, except for investment banking services in the US. The core products were broadly grouped into three categories:

1 *Transaction services*: such as cash management, trade and custody services

2 *Corporate finance services*: such as working capital finance, trade finance and asset-based financing

3 *Treasury market services*: such as hedging and foreign exchange.

Citibank's cash management and trade services (2000)

Citibank had a defined strategy for its corporate banking operations. Its target corporate client base included multi-nationals, financial institutions, government sectors, local corporations and the SME businesses. Cash and Trade service was a core product offered to these clients. Citibank's Cash and Trade division cleared approximately US$1 trillion worth of financial transactions for customers and

1. Baron, D. and Besanko, D. (2001) "Strategy, organization and incentives: global corporate banking at Citibank", *Industrial and Corporate Change*, vol. 10, no. 1, pp. 12–14.

counterparts around the world daily. These included foreign exchange transactions, equities, deposits, settlement of a trade transaction or payment of insurance policies. Where there were transactions between buyers and sellers, Citibank always wanted to be in the middle acting as an intermediary.

Citibank understood that many banks had similar product offerings. It differentiated itself through customer service across the spectrum, by offering telephone hotlines, relationship managers who understood clients' needs, product consultants who provided service expertise, and most importantly, continuous investment in technology to support both the front-end and back-end electronic banking systems.

Cash and treasury management products

The main focus of cash management was to find ways to move money around in the most efficient manner possible in supporting customers' requirement. Two crucial aspects of a corporate treasurer's needs were accounts payable and accounts receivable. Citibank focused on developing solutions to address three process areas: (1) Accounts Receivable Process Management; (2) Accounts Payable Process Management; and (3) Liquidity Management (see Exhibit 1).

Trade products

Citibank offered Trade Finance, Trade Services and Trade Support Services. Product offering covered the banking service and financing needs of customers who had import and/or export trade transactions (see Exhibit 2).

Pricing and customer service

Citibank set a standard price for each service, but price discrimination was discretionary based on client volume and value. While some banks competed on price, Citibank preferred to emphasise its customer service – response time, technology and

support – which gave customers full confidence to use Citibank. Citibank had moved beyond traditional boundaries of banking service by taking over some of the back-office functions of its customers. Customers could move away from the paper-based, highly manual intensive payment and collection process, and focus resources on their core business of generating sales and revenue. The value to Citibank in offering outsourcing services was to lock in its corporate customers: when a customer outsourced all of its back-end processes, Citibank secured all the business from the customer and gained a total relationship with the customer. Also, managing the processes for a large number of customers provided Citibank with economies of scale.

> We have the economy of scale and it is viable for us to do all the back-end processes – because the more processes we do for more customers, the lower the unit cost. So our strategy is to get as many outsourcing customers as we can, and by providing the outsourcing, we get the total wallet of the client.
> – Caroline Wong, Head of e-Business Group (Cash and Trade), Citibank Hong Kong[2]

A changing global environment
Smarter and tougher customers

Citibank had developed expertise and had specific coverage models to serve different market segments. However, as more of Citibank's clients expanded their businesses globally and became e-enabled, it became necessary for Citibank to shift to e-space. In particular, corporations that historically dealt largely through wholesale channels found that the Internet allowed them to sell directly to customers. Sophisticated corporate customers began to look for an additional range of services. They wanted to collect

---

2. Interview with Citibank e-Business Group in Hong Kong in July 2001.

Exhibit 1 Citibank's treasury and cash management objectives

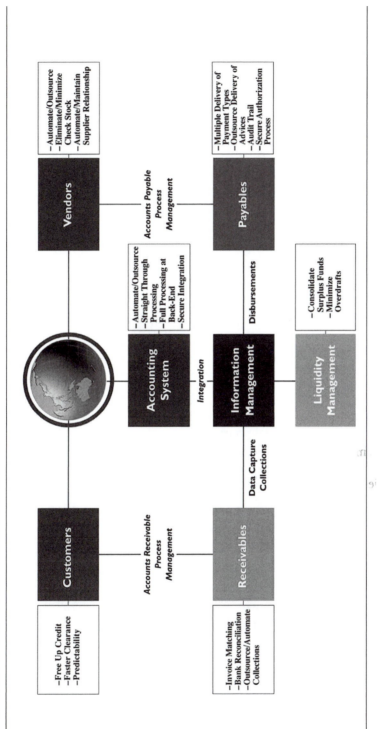

Exhibit 2 Citibank's trade service products

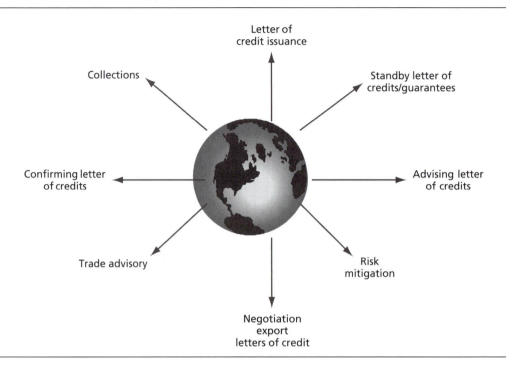

payment on-line and had access to more efficient Web-enabled financial processes.[3]

Middle markets were also driving the growing need for Internet banking capabilities. A study by Greenwich Associates in May–June 2001 showed that over half of the middle-market companies in the US and Canada were using their financial institutions' on-line banking facilities more often. Nearly 50 per cent of respondents said on-line offerings represented an important component of their banking relationships and cash management had the steepest gain in usage among mid-size companies.[4] Banks

were therefore pressured to identify what companies were looking for and to keep up with the customers with whom they were supposed to develop "consultative" relationships.

The B2B market in 2000

Sophisticated clients were looking for ways to streamline and improve their traditional payment processes. They demanded electronic invoicing, automatic application of payments to accounts receivable, on-line payment guarantees and non-repudiation of transactions that could be enabled by digital receipts stored in archives. On the payment side of the transaction, businesses required multi-currency payment management and payment aggregation by invoice and currency. Most companies were interested in technological solutions that allowed them to avoid paper disputes, which meant that the information flowing with a payment

3. Cockerill, C. (2001) "Cash management takes to the Internet", *Euromoney*, no. 381, London, January, p. 105.
4. Greenwich Associates is an international research and consulting firm specialising in financial services. Greenwich interviewed 500 corporate treasurers and other executives at middle-market companies in the US and Canada in May–June 2001. See also Rountree, D. (2001) "Importance of on-line banking", *Bank Technology News*, vol. 14, no. 11, New York, 2 November, p. 86.

was deemed to be as important as the payment.[5]

TowerGroup predicted that payment activities would migrate to the Internet and that there would be US$4 trillion in B2B e-payments activities by 2010. TowerGroup also reported that in 2000 more than 90 per cent of all B2B payments were made by cheque, with 7 per cent occurring over automated clearinghouse (ACH) network, a non-Internet system designed to handle large payments, and the rest using financial EDI services such as Fedwire.[6] The majority of small businesses used traditional payments such as cheques; large companies that used ACH did not have the complete data that surrounded a B2B payment. In addition to cheques, various payment methods were available, with clearance time varying according to the method:

- *Notes and coins*: Notes and coins paid into an account did not require clearing; it had no particular attraction to a bank, especially in large volumes, because they were a non-interest-bearing item
- *Banker's draft*: A cheque drawn on a bank. A payment by banker's draft was guaranteed.
- *Credit cards*: Made by voucher or electronically; voucher payments were processed in a similar way to cheques.
- *Special presentation of cheques*: Taken only in cases of extreme doubt about the customer; for example, the payee company could ask its bank to make a special presentation of the cheque by posting the cheque to the paying customer's bank.

- *Transfers*: Funds were transferred from one bank account to another on receipt of instructions (through telephone, subsequently confirmed by writing, on paper, sent by cable, telex or electronic processing centre) by the paying bank to make the payment.

Competition

Some multinational companies could not wait for banks to develop Web-enabled financial products so they started building their own systems and looking for ways to disintermediate banks. Other corporations approached the banks and signified their interest in participating in future developments. New technology, however, required major investments in people and technological services, a risk that some banks were not ready to take. The banking industry's trend towards consolidation meant that fewer banks were competing at the global transactions services marketplace. Deutsche Bank and Citibank were two leading banks that had invested hundreds of millions of dollars in the infrastructure required to move and monitor cash balances on-line. ABN AMRO was also making a serious push to develop its product range.

In early 2001, Deutsche Bank was seeking to outdo its competitors by building a global payment system capable of accommodating many currencies, languages and local business practices, a service called db-eBills. More large banks were seeking partnerships to provide a total, global business solution. In international cash management (ICM), companies either partnered with a lead bank that put together a solution for them, or dealt directly with local banks. The majority of companies used a lead bank to provide a solution in four ways: using correspondent banks, acting as an overlay bank, becoming a member of a banking club or bringing together a network of standardised service providers (refer to Exhibit 3 for trends in international cash management in 2000).

---

5. For example, if a company shipped a buyer 100 products at US$10 per piece, but five of the products were defective, the company might simply remit US$950 electronically without any information about the defective products. In such a case, there would be greater possibility of costly payment processes because of back and forth inquiries. The solution would be to send a paper explanation; however this could translate to additional billing inquiries and disputes.
6. To use the ACH network, a company is required to have US$10 million to US$50 million in annual revenues.

Exhibit 3 The main trends in international cash management (ICM) in 2000

- The centralisation of cash management and the introduction of shared service centres has continued in large companies and is spreading to medium-sized and small companies.
- A growing acceptance of the need to outsource ICM operations.
- Companies realising that the company–bank relationship is more important than whether or not a bank can offer Internet-based or e-commerce services.
- Companies increasingly wanting to understand and be comfortable with a bank's e-commerce strategy before they are prepared to award them business.
- The use of cross-border zero-balance accounts growing much faster than notional pooling, because many companies now have sophisticated in-house cash and treasury management systems to manage them.
- A growing realisation in some of the major banks that a network of standardised service provider banks is not always enough; it is also important to have a local branch or branches in countries around the world.
- Banks walking away from the ICM business when it has ceased to be profitable, producing a growing understanding and acceptance in large companies that banks need to make reasonable returns otherwise the standard and quality of services will inevitably suffer.
- As banks' ICM products and memberships of local clearings become similar, the key differentiator in the business will be delivery.

Source: Adapted from Large, J. (2001) "Moving into the business solution management area", *Corporate Finance*, London, September, pp. 4–14.

Most of the Fortune 500 companies preferred Citibank when making international e-payments.[7] Although Citibank established itself as a strong contender in the e-payment space, technology companies competed heavily by using their technological expertise and interests in providing new services.

Citibank e-business strategy

We are here to serve our clients: whatever our clients want us to do we'll do it for them. We're into e-business not because we're into the dotcom business; we're here because our clients want us to continue performing the basic banking functions for them on the web.

— Caroline Wong, Head of e-Business Group (Cash and Trade), Citibank Hong Kong[8]

Citibank's vision was to become the world's leading e-business enabler. It aimed to empower local, regional and global customers and the B2B2C marketplace and provide solutions to help them take advantage of the efficiencies and opportunities created by e-commerce. Citibank's e-business strategy to connect, transform and extend was a means to deliver on its vision (refer to Figures 1 and 2 for details of Citibank's e-business strategy).

Citibank e-business structure

In March 2000, Citigroup Chief Executive Officer Mr Sanford Weill announced the formation of the Internet Operation Group, a high-level committee charged with spreading responsibility for Internet activities more evenly between e-Citi, an incubator for Internet initiatives, and the bank's business units. In April 2000, the group announced the second phase of Citigroup's Internet activity – the creation of two units aimed at infusing the Internet into all consumer and corporate banking activities: e-Consumer and e-Business. Both units were intended to complement e-Citi.[9] In May 2000 two new

---

7. Clark, P. (2001), "No longer banking on exchanges", *B to B*, vol. 86, no. 13, 25 June, p. 13.
8. Interview with Citibank e-Business Group in Hong Kong in July 2001.

9. Mr Robert Willumstad was head of e-Consumer while Mr Edward Horowitz was head of e-Citi.

Figure 1 Citibank's e-business strategy

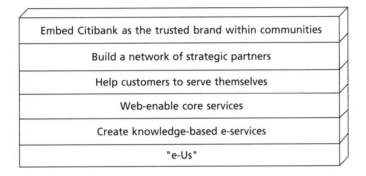

CONNECT	TRANSFORM	EXTEND
Web-enable its core services to connect with its customers	Draw the full range of Citibank's capabilities to deliver integrated solutions	Reach new markets, new customers and new products

Source: Asiamoney (2001) "CitiDirect online banking: a new era in business banking", *Asiamoney,* May, p. 84.

Figure 2 The six key elements of Citibank's e-business strategy

Embed Citibank as the trusted brand within communities

Build a network of strategic partners

Help customers to serve themselves

Web-enable core services

Create knowledge-based e-services

"e-Us"

business units, e-Capital Markets and e-Asset Management, were added.

Mr. Jorge Bermudez, Executive Vice President and Head of Global Cash Management and Trade Services, was appointed to lead the e-Business unit.[10] Mr. Bermudez's e-Business unit was responsible for developing Internet software for corporate clients setting up B2B electronic commerce exchanges.

The new business units brought people from the business lines together with people from the Internet side of operations, which combined resources and eliminated duplication and competition. The new strategy of forming high-level committees reversed the centralised approach that Citigroup had pursued under Mr. John Reed, the driving force behind the formation of e-Citi.[11] Citigroup's new structure involved traditional business units in formulating Internet strategies and forming committees to co-ordinate and synthesise, an approach that mirrored that of other banks[12]. In the early days of the Internet, banks erroneously managed e-business as a separate project.

Citibank's alliance strategy

Before 2000, Citibank had tried to excel at all facets of e-business – a strategy that failed. The Company invested millions of dollars and tried to specialise in each area such as software development, systems development and front-end services; however clients and software technology were constantly changing and Citibank was struggling to keep pace with client needs. By 2000, Citibank's strategy focused on alliances and the use of its partners' strengths. Specifically, Citibank partnered with companies that had

10. Mr Bermudez reported to Mr Victor Menezes, Chairman and Chief Executive of Citibank, and to the IOG.
11. Mr Reed resigned from his co-CEO post on 18 April 2000.

12. For example, Wells Fargo & Co. and Chase Manhattan Corp. integrated their Internet efforts more closely with their business units.

complementary technology or infrastructure or access to markets. Mr Tom Edgerton, Alliances Head for Citibank e-business, explained the need for forming alliances:

> In the future, it won't be what your company can do, but what the network of companies you work with can provide.[13]

Citibank's key technology players included Oracle, Commerce One Inc., SAP AG, Wisdom Technologies and Bolero.net. In August 2000, four companies teamed up with Citibank to form FinancialSettlementMatrix.com, a company that connected buyers and sellers in e-marketplaces with payment processing, credit and other services through multiple participating banks and financial service companies.[14] Citibank's challenge was how to manage the vendors and suppliers and ensure that they understand Citibank's strategy and would not exploit the Bank's strengths of the information base. Mr. Edgerton said of companies that had approached Citibank to partner them: "Citibank brings considerable value to potential alliance partners. They're interested in our brand, our financial services expertise, our global presence, our strong customer relationships and position as a trusted provider, as well as our knowledge of specific industries and international markets."

Connect

Customer convenience had been the thrust of Citibank's continuous evolution of its products and services. Key to this goal was providing clients with more channels to access Citibank, and the Internet provided Citibank the flexibility to meet this demand.

> A core part of our e-business strategy is Web-enabling our current services. With CitiDirect, we are building the infrastructure that will serve as the foundation for many of the value-added services we are developing on the Internet.
> – Jorge Bermudez, Citibank Executive Vice President and e-Business Head[15]

CitiDirect was designed for corporate customers to do full transactions on-line anywhere around the world.[16] It was a browser-based delivery channel designed to deliver on-line all of Citibank's cash management and trade products and services, enabling customers to make inquiries about their account balances, request statements, provide transaction initiation details and request statement transaction reports on-line and in real time. CitiDirect allowed customers to perform these functions at any location with internet access. This was particularly useful for global companies with operations spread out in many countries but wished to maintain control at regional or global treasury centres.

CitiDirect was piloted in October 2000. In Asia, it was piloted in Singapore, Hong Kong, Australia, Japan and Malaysia.[17] By December 2000, CitiDirect was already operating in 36 countries and four languages. In 2000, CitiDirect was available in five languages; it was expected to be operating in 80 countries and 20 languages – and doing a trillion dollars worth of business a day by 2002.[18] In May 2001, CitiDirect was already serving 1000 customers world-wide.

---

13. Citibank (2000) "Citi seeks alliances to accelerate into the e-space", *The Citibank Globe*, November–December, at URL: http://www.citibank.com/e-business/, 3 December.
14. Citibank partner companies were Enron Broadband Services (a delivery platform), i2 Technologies (an integrated open-architecture solution), S1 Corporation (Internet-based payment processing) and Wells Fargo & Company (provided complementary services to the entire e-business market).
15. Citibank (2000) "CitiDirect putting banking at customers' fingertips", *The Citibank Globe*, November–December, at URL: http://www.citibank.com/e-business/, 3 December.
16. Citibank asked its customers what they wanted from e-commerce and the Internet throughout the development of CitiDirect; customers put a premium on security, stability, speed, accuracy and user-friendliness. CitiDirect was designed with the customers' needs in mind.
17. Asiamoney (2001) "CitiDirect online banking: a new era in business banking", *Asiamoney*, May, p. 83.
18. Power, C. (2000) "Citi deploys its web troops into business lines", *American Banker*, 165(230), New York, 1 December, p. 1.

Transform

Transaction processing, such as cash management, trade finance and derivatives, were back-office activities that were not at the forefront of a customer's mind. Traditionally, transaction processing for a corporate customer, for example the transactional work involved in loan processing, was a function of the bank–customer relationship. Citibank's global presence translated to a huge transactional business and required supporting more than 200 data centres, which were doing basic, repeatable processes. In 1998, Citibank realised that, similar to any other factory product, this could be commoditised. Starting in 1998, Citibank began the transformation.

Regionalisation

The transformation process involved consolidating all the data centres within each country and moving them to Singapore. Data were centralised and systems were developed to manage the automatic processing of transactions. By May 1999, the data centres were rationalised to 60. On the operations side, Citibank began with the regionalisation of cash and trade, which afforded Citibank a complete focus on the process. Approaches that Citibank had taken in deciding the location for the regionalised centres were not mutually exclusive. It had considered the following in various combinations:

- take the biggest infrastructure already existing and build it up to replace all the smaller centres (e.g. Singapore);
- greenfield approach – ask where to get the best balance of all factors of production and start there from scratch (e.g. Penang);
- available people and skills (e.g. Sydney); and
- pure cost of labour; for lower-skilled areas such as voucher processing.

Singapore, which had back-office operations of several of the bank's business units, was the first processing centre that was regionalised; it was followed by Penang.[19] Next to be regionalised was Sydney's foreign exchange and derivatives centre. The centres used to be time-zone centric, such that decisions were based on the three continental time zones of Europe, Asia and the Americas. By 2001, the largest centres were in Penang, Malaysia; Singapore; Mumbai, India; Dublin in Europe; and Delaware and Buffalo in the US.

The regionalised and specialised processing centres provided Citibank scale and continual improvement opportunities. They reduced the cycle time for transactions, minimised error rates to near zero and yielded new efficiencies for Citibank and its customers.

> We're now able to fragment the process and focus on the little pieces that make the difference, this also means that there's a lot of exchange of information and standardisation of processes.
>
> – Venry Krishnakumar, Citibank Vice President and Regional Director, Operation and Technology (O&T) Asia Pacific & Japan[20]

Internalising the Web

Within Citibank, there was a programme to promote the e-workplace; the processing centres in particular had taken off with internalising the Web. The transformations in the processing cycle were taken further to focus on transforming workflow automation; employees had access to information without the need to make phone calls, check paper files or send faxes. By contrast, old-style processing centres required millions of cheques and huge reconcilement departments, which were paper-based and labour-intensive. The centralised and specialised location of processing made it

---

19. In Singapore, front-end securities processing was also regionalised; however, due to local settlement issues the back-end processing of securities transactions still needed to be done in individual countries.
20. Finance Asia (2001) "Processing comes to the fore", *Finance Asia*, May, p. 83.

easier for Citibank to secure databases into the processing of a transaction, for example, signature verification and digital imaging systems were linked into the funds-transfer system.[21]

Straight-through automation

Citibank was continuously pushing the limits of straight-through automation by constantly deploying various initiatives. For example, Citibank had conducted some artificial intelligence projects such as pre-populating forms with historical data, which dramatically reduced error rates. It could select rejected transactions and take a look at a customer's previous history with similar transactions and try to predict what the customer would try to do.[22] The effective implementation of such projects was attributable to the qualified and experienced staff at Citibank.

The benefits of efficiency and cost savings also trickled down to Citibank's customers. In traditional transactions customers deposit a cheque into an ATM or opened an LC by submitting all paperwork to a bank, but they did not know when the bank actually performed the task. With Citibank's straight-through processing, customers' expectations and need to know were matched because the processes were on-line and in real time.

Achievements

Proof that Citibank was at the top of the league was the awards it received (see Exhibit 4). Citibank was the first in the financial services industry to receive a quality award through its Singapore cash processing centre or regional cash process management unit (officially known as RCPMU).[23] Customers seemed to value Citibank's efforts; customer surveys showed that RCPMU was rated better than its competitors in the areas of accuracy, timeliness, accessibility and responsiveness, for several years in a row. Processing was fast becoming one of Citibank's unique selling propositions. Citibank's commitment to excellence in its processing business translated to greater transparency of the process for customers, allowing them full access to information about the status of their transaction.

Extend

CitiDirect's roll-out was evidence of Citibank's vision of delivering transaction services on-line anywhere in the world, any time. Building a new global infrastructure gave Citibank the opportunity to deliver e-products at scale more quickly and more efficiently to customers, and any capability improvements in one region would be seamlessly deployed world-wide. Citibank

---

Exhibit 4 Citibank awards in Asia – 2001

- Best Cash Management Bank, Best Foreign Exchange Bank, Best Project Finance House, Best Commercial Bank in Asia – *The Assets*, 2001.
- Best Bank in Asia – *Euromoney*, 2001.
- Best Cash Management Bank (1997–2001), Best Foreign Exchange Bank, Best Project Fiance House, Best Syndicated Loan House, Best Commercial Bank in Asia, Best Foreign Commercial Bank in Hong Kong (1997, 1999–2001) – *Finance Asia*, 2001.
- Best Bank of the Year (1998, 1999, 2001) – *IFR*, 2001.
- Best Cash Management Bank in Asia, Best Global Custodian in Asia Pacific – *Asiamoney*, 2001.

---

21. A system similar to SWIFT and forex systems.
22. Finance Asia (2001) "Processing comes to the fore", *Finance Asia*, May, p. 83.

23. The Centre processed up to US$20 billion worth of transactions daily.

expected CitiDirect to evolve constantly, which would give Citibank the flexibility to continuously enhance the system according to the changing needs of its customers. Other European banks focused mainly on providing pan-European solutions; fewer banks wanted to deliver global services.

Citibank's priority was to move all its corporate customers onto CitiDirect, because its main goal was to retire the legacy systems of the old-style electronic banking. Citibank had to contend, however, with difficulties in migrating certain customers from using traditional means to using the new products and services. Citibank's corporate clients included top-tier MNCs as well as SMEs. Previously, Citibank had not focused on SMEs; it was in 1997 that it started to consider the SME segment and introduced CitiBusiness.[24] While MNCs with an e-business focus knew what they wanted, SMEs that wanted an e-business presence were unsure how to move on. Some were not even e-enabled and were still tied up with the legacy systems of the 1970s, 1980s and 1990s. The greatest concern of most customers was security. Some resisted making the transformation because they were sceptical about security, and such old behaviour was entrenched. In part, these concerns about security hindered Citibank to roll out the Web-based applications despite Citibank's readiness. CitiDirect had already developed sophisticated security procedures using the latest encryption techniques. Its

multi-layered security architecture included public and private access keys, single-use passwords and multiple authorisation controls.

In 2001, Citibank was still providing services using legacy systems for conservative SME customers, while at the same time serving global customers such as MNCs that demanded to transact through the Internet. Citibank was aware that building customers' trust in the Web entailed a long education process. To encourage conservative customers to embrace CitiDirect, Citibank's plan was to build a strategy that included a pricing incentive scheme.

The Citibank advantage

Global reach

As part of a global financial institution that employed over 2,68,000 employees across 100 countries, Citibank was uniquely positioned to serve its customers' global needs. In the emerging markets where 86 per cent of the world's population lived, accounting for 43 per cent of the world's purchasing power, Citibank had implemented an Embedded Bank strategy. That was, a bank that had roots in the country as deep as any local indigenous bank, building a broad customer base, offering diverse products, actively participating in the community and recruiting staff and senior management from the local population. This local commitment and history together with the global reach and expertise was a powerful combination that set Citibank apart from its competitors. In 2002, Citibank celebrated its 100th year of operations in China, Hong Kong, India, Japan, the Philippines and Singapore.

Strong brand

Citibank had developed a strong brand recognition. Customers regarded Citibank as an innovative, global bank offering excellent customer service.

---

24. CitiBusiness was a one-stop financing solution offered to small- and medium-sized entrepreneurs. Products and services included CitiBusiness Direct (Internet banking); Cash Management; Trade Services and Trade Finance (trade products); CitiCorp Commercial Finance (asset-based finance); treasury products such as Spot and Forward Foreign Exchange, Interest Rate Hedging and Yield Enhancement Investment Products; and a Customer Centre. The Customer Centre provided CitiService (an integrated customer inquiry line for after-sales service), Document Collection (an express collection service), CitiFax (a convenient way to update account information) and CitiBusiness Direct (providing on-line access to account information and transaction initiation).

Continuous investment in technology

Citibank was committed to upholding its position as a premier supplier of cash management and transactional banking services and was investing heavily on technology to improve its services. The main goal was to provide corporate customers the most cost-effective, cutting-edge, reliable and secure solutions. A Citibank senior executive outlined one of the bank's competitive advantages:[25]

> We continuously invest in technology and it's one of our competitive advantages. We've been around a long time, we have been able to invest year after year and we have seen compounded value from that. A new entrant would have a difficult time investing all at once, but by spending money on infrastructure – not on salespeople or front ends – I think that's how you stay in the position we're in. If there's any trick at all that's it. I think this is an incredibly relevant issue for the Internet in general. It's not about building the new front end, although we're doing that too, it's about what you're doing to connect to it.

Conclusion

The Internet had touched so many areas in banking and changed how institutions make strategic decisions. At the same time, technology changed customers' expectations and needs. It was a challenge for Citibank to translate its traditional strengths to the Internet that would add value to its customers. Citibank was responding to this challenge by:

- Web-enabling access points to allow customers to connect seamlessly to Citibank;

- building a new global infrastructure to deliver products and services on-line; and

- integrating products in new ways.

In a business environment where change was inevitable, Citibank needed a distinctive strategic direction that would create competitive advantages that would not be easily replicated by its competitors. In addition, Citibank would need to make global transformation to deliver its e-business strategy and create a culture that would embrace the e-concept, a key element of a highly integrated e-business.

Marissa McCauley prepared this case in conjunction with Shamza Khan under the supervision of Prof. Julie H. Yu and Dr. Ali Farhoomand for class discussion. This case is not intended to show effective or ineffective handling of decision or business processes.

This case is part of a project funded by a teaching development grant from the University Grants Committee (UGC) of Hong Kong.

---

25. Finance Asia (2001), "Processing comes to the fore," *Finance Asia*, May, p. 83.

Case study 2   STATER NV: e-servicing strategies

After two years of online experiments, Tom van Vianen, CEO, felt certain it was time to fully implement STATER NV's new "e-servicing" concept with a cohesive strategy. Established in 1997 in the Netherlands and headquartered in Amersfoort, STATER had 27 business clients and serviced over 80 different mortgage portfolios of more than 450,000 mainly residential loans in the Netherlands, Belgium, and Germany. Their mortgage service operations and information systems were considered state-of-the-art in 2002, but they were moving business online while simultaneously increasing the types of services provided *and* expanding operations into Spain, France, and Italy – within the next five years. In a land known for taming the forces of the sea, Tom faced what seemed like a sea of "e-uncertainty." What exact roles should STATER play in an online loan market? How should they position themselves to lead in those roles? The E-Servicing Steering Committee looked to Tom to direct them, and he knew he needed a clear vision for the next steering committee meeting in two months, in May 2002.

eventually became the fifth largest lender in the Dutch market. In 1997, Bouwfonds launched an effort to "unbundle" the residential mortgage business by creating STATER NV. In 1999, STATER opened its first office abroad in Bonn, Germany – a country with a residential loan market five times the Dutch market. In 2001, ABN-AMRO (the eighth largest bank in Europe and the seventeenth in the world with over 3400 branches in more than 60 countries) became the majority share holder of STATER. STATER in turn acquired the back office of CBHK in Belgium, thereby establishing its second international office. In April 2001, US-based General Motors Acceptance Corporation (GMAC) began originating mortgages in the Netherlands through STATER NV. By the end of 2001, STATER had 435 employees, 27 business clients, serviced over 80 different mortgage portfolios with more than 450,000 loans, and gained revenue of more than US$49million ($55.4M Euros at January 1, 2002 exchange rates). The STATER corporate organization chart is shown in Appendix I. Significant financial data is presented in Appendix II.[1]

STATER NV

STATER NV was the leading provider of independent, third party residential mortgage servicing in continental Europe in 2001. It focused on managing all payment and ancillary back-office functions – streamlining the origination, servicing, and securitization of residential mortgage loans in a completely automated and paperless format.

STATER was established in 1997 as a spin-off of the mortgage business unit of Bouwfonds Nederlandse Gemeenten, one of the largest mortgage lenders in the Netherlands. Bouwfonds was established in 1946 by the Dutch municipalities to rebuild Holland after World War II by providing low-cost housing and financing. Bouwfonds' residential mortgage subsidiary, Bouwfonds Hypotheken,

STATER information system

The STATER mortgage information system (SHS, for Stater Hypotheek System) was the very heart of the business and was considered to be state-of-the-art in the mortgage servicing business. The SHS supported the complete mortgage process from loan origination to servicing (the primary market) to securitizing (a secondary market). While the mortgage system was developed during 1994–7 for Bouwfonds to support a single mortgage lender, it was subsequently adapted to service multiple lenders. In 1999, STATER developed a German version of the SHS for its German operations based on a copy of the Dutch system. Not only

---

1. From STATER NV Annual Report, 2001.

Appendix I STATER NV Organization

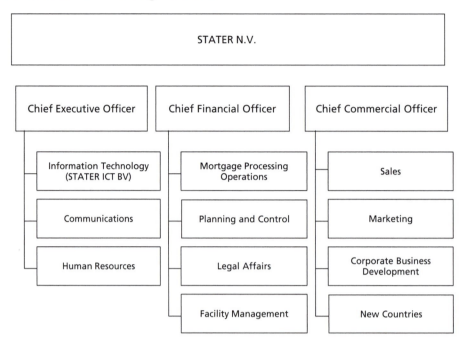

was system text translated into German, but system functions were also adapted to the requirements of the German mortgage market.

Appendix II Selected STATER NV financials for 2001(in euros times 1,000)

Revenue	10,573
Operating expenses	10,438
Profit participating interests after taxes	2,469
Net profit after taxes	2,757
STATER mortgage system	
Balance January 1	9,882
Investments	1,532
Shareholders' equity	16,759
Long-term liabilities	11,345
Tangible fixed assets	16,002
Number of loans in handling	451,278
Number of personnel (average)	394

SHS was developed for the traditional mortgage value chain (see Appendix III):

Process step	Involved parties
Marketing	Independent brokers, lenders, consumers
Origination, processing applications, generating offers, closing	Lenders, brokers, notaries, consumers
Servicing	Lenders, consumers
Funding, underwriting	Lenders, investors
Trading	Lenders, investors

This process flow was reflected in the original SHS functional structure:

Process	Functions
Origination	Application processing through closing
Servicing	Servicing until full redemption of a loan
Funding	Supporting lenders and investors

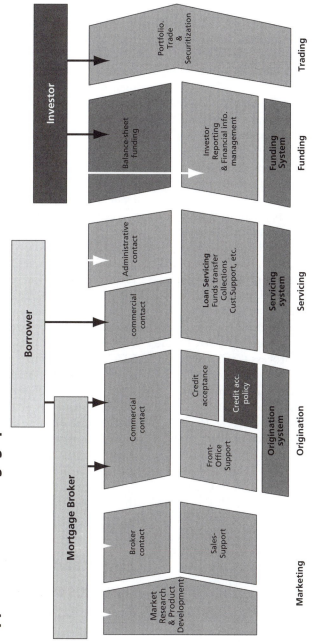

Appendix III The mortgage process

Mortgage Broker

Borrower

Investor

Market Research & Product Development

Broker contact

Commercial contact

Front-Office Support

Credit acceptance

Credit acc. policy

commercial contact

Administrative contact

Balance-sheet funding

Portfolio, Trade & Securitization

Sales-Support

Loan Servicing
Funds transfer
Collections
Cust.Support, etc.

Investor Reporting & Financial Info. management

Origination system

Servicing system

Funding System

Marketing

Origination

Servicing

Funding

Trading

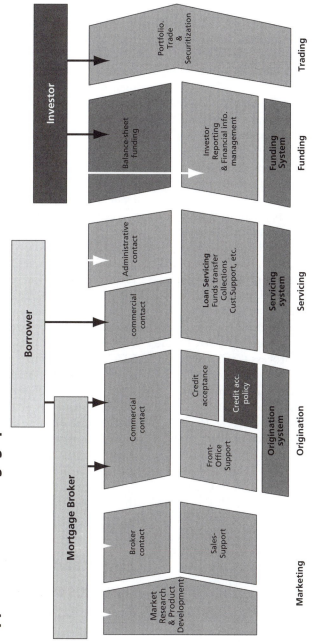

97

(Appendix IV gives an overview of the SHS application architecture and the main subsystems of the SHS in 2002.)

With small, competitive margins in the mortgage business, one of the most important SHS system design principles was to achieve cost efficiency in the mortgage process by taking the process flow as a starting point in the design and automating, where possible, all process steps. The workflow concept had a central role in the origination process that had a fixed sequence of steps; in the servicing module this workflow was embedded in events that triggered automated actions, both from the system and the user (based on tasks in a work list).

The most crucial subsystem of the SHS was the automated underwriting subsystem (called Capstone). This subsystem could make automated credit decisions based on rule-based and credit risk models developed using neural artificial intelligence and data mining technologies. Capstone contained the credit rules and risk models of each lender, making it possible to significantly streamline the loan origination process – tailored for each lender. When an application was entered into the system and an employee wanted to generate an offer, Capstone compared the application with the lender's credit rules as well as performed an automated check with a credit bureau. Lender employees could see the results of the credit check on a system monitor, but the built-in rules were determinant. If the system did not approve the loan, it was impossible to generate an offer without the approval of an authorized credit officer; if the system approved the loan, it automatically generated a conditional offer. During the fulfilment process, derived customer data were compared with the submitted customer documentation. If these data were consistent, the loan received final approval and was closed.

In practice, the system automatically generated over 90 per cent of STATER's loan offers; lender credit officers intervened with and analyzed only 10 per cent. This was tremendously efficient and made it possible to send an offer (or a rejection) to all consumers within 24 hours.

Most importantly, however, automated underwriting created opportunities to outsource part of the loan process to brokers because the system ensured compliance with their own credit rules. STATER could capitalize on its SHS investment by providing SHS processing to brokers, on behalf of its clients, as an outsourcer. Instead of just servicing existing loans, STATER could support the entire loan process as the information processing hub for brokers and lenders.

As a loan service hub, STATER could take the lead in other, wider initiatives. In the Netherlands, STATER led lenders and brokers to develop a standard Electronic Data Interchange (EDI) format for submitting electronic mortgage applications. Loan applications in EDI format were sent over a dedicated communications network to lenders and to STATER as the third party servicer. STATER developed a subsystem that validated EDI messages and then fed them automatically into Capstone for generating offers. The success rate of these EDI-formatted applications was initially very low – due to data inconsistencies and missing fields in the messages – but it showed it was possible to fully automate the process from application through generating an offer as a third party servicer.

STATER and the Internet

The EUBOS website[2]

STATER's initial leap into servicing the loan process through the Internet happened

---

2. The name was changed in 2002 for commercial reasons to www.bankofscotland.nl.

Appendix IV The SHS architecture

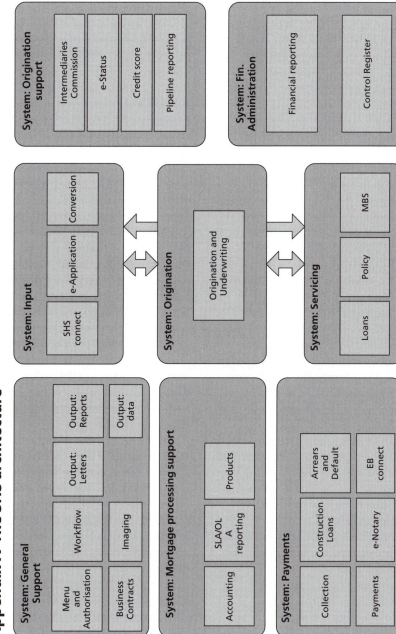

almost by accident. STATER did not have a clear Internet strategy in 1999 when the Bank of Scotland approached STATER with their intent to use STATER and the Internet as its main distribution channel in foreign markets. Aware of STATER's SHS and its potential benefits, the Bank of Scotland wanted to create a dedicated website with STATER in the Netherlands where consumers could get information on Bank of Scotland products, use calculators and other software to determine their mortgage options, and apply online for a mortgage. Ideally, consumers would then receive a return electronic offer by e-mail or through the website within a very short period. A call centre would be set up to answer customer questions or contact a customer in case of missing information or documents, or to offer personal advice.

By using STATER, the Bank of Scotland could quickly establish a lender presence – albeit virtual – in the Netherlands. By eliminating human brokers in the loan process value chain, the Bank of Scotland could also avoid paying loan commissions – and could thus reduce the loan rates charged to consumers. They hoped these reduced rates would provide them a competitive advantage over other Dutch lenders. It was clear to the Bank of Scotland that the capability of STATER's SHS to electronically process loan applications could be used with the concept of online Web-based mortgage applications to achieve business presence, reduce costs, and hopefully offer other business opportunities.

STATER and the Bank of Scotland formed a combined project team to implement the online capability. They agreed that the Bank of Scotland would be responsible for designing the website and the Web infrastructure, and that the STATER team

would be responsible for receiving and processing web-based applications through SHS-Connect.[3] To reduce SHS-Connect software changes, they also agreed early on that the format of the web-based application would comply with the existing EDI application format. Handling the applications that did not pass the formatting validation checks or the Capstone credit checks, however, would be very different. In the EUBOS Web-based model, there would be no broker involved to contact a consumer in the case of a rejected application. This would be, in essence, a direct business-to-customer (B2C) model – and such a model was totally new for STATER. Moreover, retaining potential customers was very important to the Bank of Scotland. So they decided to extend the SHS with a database of invalidly formatted and rejected applications that could then be accessed by call centre personnel. The customer fulfilment personnel could work on adding or correcting data fields by contacting customers and then re-submitting the application for validation and credit check. Throughout the process, consumers could track their application in a secure part of the EUBOS site. The SHS system would send electronic status messages and – if the application was approved – a mortgage offer.

The launch of the website at the end of 1999 attracted a lot of media attention – and shocked the incumbent banks because a foreign bank had succeeded in entering "their" market without having to set up a complete "on the ground" operation. The Internet, a call centre, and a third party servicer (STATER NV) were all the Bank of Scotland needed to enter the local residential loan market. The entry barrier to the Dutch mortgage market suddenly appeared to be disturbingly low. Willie Donald, Director of European Operations at Bank of Scotland commented:

EUBOS has proved very successful so far. The number of hits to the site has exceeded all

---

3. SHS-Connect was the subsystem that processed the electronic applications and performed validity checks. The credit check was performed in the next stage by Capstone.

expectations. The virtual age is truly upon us when a business can operate to such an extent, and profitably, with such a small core team of three people.[4]

Application service providers

Not only did STATER want to provide consumers with fast, effective loan servicing, STATER wanted to provide clients like the Bank of Scotland with business information. As STATER's business increased, so would the burden of implementing an increasing number of system connections with brokers, lenders, investor credit officers, and employees that worked from their homes. In the beginning, individual users had to dial in to connect, and multiple user environments used dedicated point-to-point connections. Both created an increasing burden on systems processing and information technology personnel – raising costs substantially. IT people had to install equipment and software, provide training, and in most cases give on-site technical support. Connecting through the Internet offered a much simpler and less costly communications alternative – and it allowed STATER to take advantage of application service providers.

Application service providers (or ASPs) were essentially outsourcers for information systems that ASP clients or client customers accessed through the Internet. ASP services ranged from complete system development, implementation, operation, and maintenance to simply hosting a website. While there were many potential benefits and risks in using ASPs, most of the benefits were tied to the benefits of the Internet as a communications channel and to ASP

economies of scale. STATER thought it could take advantage of both.

It seemed possible to have an ASP host the full SHS interface (the mortgage system and electronic loan files), making SHS available to a very wide range (and reach) of potential clients. As long as a client had an Internet connection, a computer with common Internet browser software, and authorized access, the client could access the SHS at anytime and from anywhere in the world. This could quickly create enormous business value for STATER's SHS and Capstone system – and for business clients who could use their existing Internet infrastructure to access and use STATER services. From STATER's perspective, the Bank of Scotland could be the beginning of a wide range of loan business relations with STATER's SHS at the core.

It was clear to Tom and STATER management that SHS and the Internet provided enormous business opportunities. STATER could be the hub of all the stakeholders in the mortgage value chain (Appendix III), and the Internet appeared to be the perfect way to connect STATER and the stakeholders – and give them data access to their part of the mortgage value chain. This vision became known as "e-servicing" and it was the umbrella for all STATER Internet-related projects.

e-Servicing

In 2000, STATER defined e-servicing this way:

> E-servicing is to give business relations and consumers access to data and functionalities of the SHS, anytime and anywhere, provided that they have the appropriate authorization. The use of Internet technology is essential for realizing the e-servicing concept.

An e-Servicing Steering Committee was formed to guide and monitor

---

4. Wednesday, 12 January 2000. Press release, Bank of Scotland. http://www.hbosplc.com/media/pressreleases/articles/bos/2000/eubos.doc.

STATER's move into online mortgage servicing:

Name	Corporate Position	Responsibilities
Tom van Vianen	CEO, STATER NV	Chair, corporate strategy
Richard Jansen	Senior VP, STATER Netherlands	Business clients
Harry Mulder	Senior VP, STATER Information Technology	IT strategy and implementation
Caroline Meyer	Director, Corporate Business Development	Corporate expansion strategies
Wilma Flohr	Director, Corporate Communications	Public relations
Johan Gessel	Program manager, e-Servicing	Project development and implementation

The committee met every two weeks. They decided they needed an integrated framework or e-strategy for the projects to guide project prioritization.

e-Servicing applications

It was apparent to Tom and the Steering Committee that business relations, or clients, could potentially use STATER's information systems in three basic ways:

Business function	Business relation
Information upload to SHS	STATER Brokers Lenders Front-office support Notaries Consumers
Information modification in SHS	STATER Brokers (applications, offers) Front-office support Notaries
Information retrieval from SHS	All business relations

The Committee then turned their attention to developing specific applications to perform e-servicing functions, initially focused on the home market (the Netherlands). These were, in chronological order:

- *e-Application*: A simple Web page where all the necessary data for a mortgage application could be entered and validated. It was to be used by brokers and lenders to quickly enter application data using an ordinary browser communicating with the SHS. e-Application data would be processed using the same technology infrastructure used by EUBOS.

- *e-Notary*: Notaries played a pivotal role in the loan process by closing the deal, and were hired by loan consumers. If the e-servicing hub could automate and improve the efficiency of the notary task, STATER could then more easily branch into the other loan process steps. The simply stated objective of this project was: "to optimize and speed up the information exchange between a notary and STATER using the Internet." Tom set out to build the capability for notaries to go to the STATER website using a browser and access a secure part of the site to see the status of all the loans the notary had been appointed to complete. When all requirements for closing were fulfilled, the notary would be able to request – online – release of funds for a closed mortgage. Before e-Notary, a notary had to send a fax to STATER to request disbursement; with e-Notary, a notary could directly control this part of the process. This was a benefit for the notary – more direct control over personal workloads – and for STATER in gaining a much more efficient process, speeding up loan closings, and reducing costs. STATER could also strengthen business associations with brokers, reducing broker relations with other loan servicers and thereby raising competitive barriers. After 12 months, over 50 per cent of the notary payments were handled through e-Notary.

And there was a secondary objective to this project. e-Notary was the first public, operational test of the new e-servicing applications and technical infrastructure. This not only made it a test case for the e-servicing program and the IT department, but it allowed the e-servicing team to gain experience and knowledge to apply to follow-on e-servicing projects.

From STATER's business side, however, it was a significant first step. For the first time, an external party in STATER's mortgage process would actively gain control over their own part of that process. This brought significant opportunities and risks. The opportunities included very favourable response by the notary community, including more notaries signing up for service with STATER. There was also the favourable public relations image of being "the first" with leading-edge technologies applied to the everyday loan business process. On the other hand, the risks of allowing external, non-STATER employees direct access to STATER databases filled with private financial data seemed dangerous – but essential to the entire concept of e-servicing. This project helped to "test the waters" of not only the technical infrastructure, but the entire virtual loan process – while limiting the scope of any damage before implementing more e-servicing projects.

- *e-Broker*: A loan or mortgage broker advised customers about loan options and costs, submitted loan applications, and tracked customer delivery of required documentation. To perform these tasks, a broker needed current information on the customer application status. Before e-Broker, STATER sent brokers a weekly status report on their applications. It was, of course, often out of date the moment it arrived. With e-Broker, this status report information was not only available in

detail on the STATER website from any Internet connection worldwide at any time, but was as instantaneously current as the information in STATER's databases.

Like e-Notary, e-Broker not only helped brokers conduct business more efficiently and possibly give them a competitive edge, but e-Broker made STATER's loan process more efficient and less costly by eliminating the reports and reducing the number of calls from brokers requesting or questioning information on a customer. And like e-Notary, it helped cement relationships with brokers; the more advantages it gave the brokers, the more dependent they became on e-Broker and STATER.

Possible applications

By March 2002, the e-Servicing Steering Committee was considering a number of other possible applications for the next e-servicing projects, including:

- *e-Capstone*: pre-qualifying loan applications online without requiring full processing in the SHS.
- *e-Consumer*: giving consumers direct access to their application data, loan data, and payment history – and perhaps calculate pre-payment penalties or provide other helpful functionality.
- *e-Advice*: integrating e-Application into e-Broker for a seamless process from customer advice through mortgage offer.

Strategic issues

The most important objective for STATER in 2002 was "growth in Europe" through 2005. The volume of outstanding mortgage loans in the European Union more than doubled in the previous ten years to over € 3.9 trillion in 2001 – more than 40 per cent of Europe's gross domestic product – and STATER wanted to be a major player. STATER intended to focus on countries with large, attractive residential loan markets – namely,

Spain, Italy, and France. Within the Netherlands and Belgium, STATER intended to concentrate on improving the efficiency of existing clients and aim for significant (20 per cent per year) growth in Germany. e-Servicing was the key part of its objectives; STATER aimed to furnish all mortgage stakeholders with the right information and services via the Internet.

But how? The profound "reach and range" of the Internet seemed to offer dozens of attractive, viable opportunities where there were few players. The STATER Steering Committee recognized that a complete e-servicing strategy was necessary to help them choose appropriate projects, coordinate organizational business units, guide them through the development process, and anticipate external events – like competitive reaction. The Steering Committee saw many issues, opportunities, and risks.

- **Market Position**. The Steering Committee felt that STATER could be positioned somewhere within three different models:

  1. *The "specialist originator"*:[5] STATER would standardize and automate the buyer decision-making process for complex and relatively expensive products, then send transactions to an exchange for execution.

  2. *A complete service provider*: STATER would facilitate an end-to-end mortgage process.

  3. *Business intelligence provider*: STATER had one of the most extensive mortgage databases in the Dutch mortgage industry; they could mine that data and sell market information – although, to date, STATER's business clients had not allowed STATER to use their data for these purposes.

STATER's competitive advantage had been based on its operational excellence, operating at a lower cost than the back-offices of lenders. e-Servicing could allow STATER to deliver new, premium services at even lower costs. Although brokers tended to be not willing to pay for services, the Steering Committee believed they would for effective, additional value provided.

Moreover, although the concept of "straight-through processing" with mortgages was first implemented by STATER, it was not invented by STATER – many service organizations and financial institutions were developing the concept with new technologies and Web-based architectures. Sustaining competitive market advantage would likely be a constant issue.

The Steering Committee had many questions. What were the potential advantages and risks of each model? Should STATER try to position itself in just one, a combination, or all three? If not all three, which one or ones? If more than one, what priority should STATER assign to them? Which should it try to tackle first – the easy one, the one with the quickest payoff, or the one with the biggest payoff? Which model was the competition most and least able to react to? Which was most likely to pay off in the short run; which in the long run? Which model was the one most likely to allow STATER to defend its present strengths? Which model was the one most likely to spawn new opportunities?

- **A portal for the mortgage industry.** e-Notary and e-Broker raised the issue of how to position these applications in the market. They were intended to deliver value-added services to the business relations with STATER's clients through the STATER website. One of the major discussions with their clients was whether or not a broker should be allowed to see

---

5. Described in Richard Wise and David Morrison, "Beyond the exchange: the future of B2B", *Harvard Business Review*, November–December 2000, pp. 86–96.

the status of all their offers or only the ones through a particular lender. Some lenders did not want brokers to have an overview that included lender competitors; they wanted brokers to access their information through the lender's website. Other lenders wanted to create the most efficient market and did not insist on access through lender websites.

STATER wanted to create its own mortgage portal; a one-entry point for all mortgage related services available to all mortgage participants. STATER would provide mortgage e-services on this site, but also links to other companies like auction sites. The Steering Committee wondered: would the market accept STATER as the central, driving force behind this concept? Or should STATER try to form alliances with different stakeholders to build the site – based on STATER applications?

- **Client obligations.** The existing e-servicing applications had created direct relationships with brokers and notaries who were participants in the process, but not employees or legal contractors with STATER. The scope of STATER's services had increased dramatically as had its responsibility to maintain and properly operate the e-infrastructure. But what rights did these third parties have? Could they launch claims or lawsuits against STATER in case of infrastructure failures or software errors? What if STATER was successfully hacked, causing the loss of confidential financial data – or worse – loan manipulation and fraud? If STATER launched the mortgage portal, to what extent would it be responsible for all the activity that occurred through its website? Could STATER control and manage what it had created?

- **Industry standard maker.** In the Dutch mortgage market, STATER was the front-runner and the first to have created an electronic infrastructure for the mortgage process. This appeared to give STATER the market power to impose their standards on this nascent market. But as the "service grid" of linked mortgage players grew – each with their own technology preferences and agendas – the industry would need a leader that had the influence and the capability to create and compel industry standards. Could STATER fulfil this ambitious role? Would STATER *want* to fulfil this role?

- **e-Business model.** For e-Application, STATER charged a fee for each application; for e-Broker, a fee per inquiry up to a certain limit per broker. The Committee wondered if STATER should charge an "admission" fee and a monthly fee for access to the service. Charging a broker was difficult (they were used to getting everything freely), but charging a notary was possible since STATER made notarys' work process more efficient and less costly.

The next steering committee meeting

Tom laid out the business strategy issues – as well as the technology issues – and attempted to first plot how he would identify STATER's alternatives and the criteria for his recommendations to the Steering Committee on an e-services strategy. He also wondered: Who should be involved in this process? Should they focus on a few areas, or attempt an overall, comprehensive strategy? How should the process occur?

As Tom looked out his office window pondering these questions, he could see fields of famous Dutch tulips beginning to bloom in swaths of primary colours. They bloom each year in spite of endangering seas and usually miserable winters, he thought, and yet they are beautiful. Perhaps they are a metaphor for the challenges, opportunities, and our own blooming in the European mortgage servicing market – starting with a good e-servicing business strategy.

Valuing e-business investments and managing performance

To demonstrate that while limitations exist, e-business implementations must be ❑ subjected to close scrutiny and accountability

To illustrate the significance of intangible benefits characteristic of an ❑ e-business investment

To introduce financial, hybrid, ratio, and portfolio valuation methodologies and ❑ approaches for appraising benefits ranging from quantifiable to intangible

To focus on performance measurement as a basis for comparing outcomes against ❑ initial performance targets

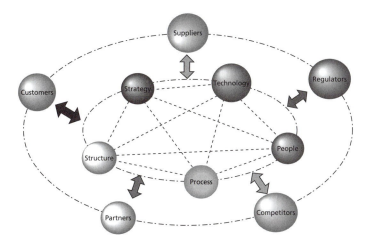

> The fact that the capital spending boom is still going strong indicates that businesses continue to find a wide array of potential high-rate-of-return, productivity-enhancing investments. And I see nothing to suggest that these opportunities will peter out anytime soon.
> – U.S. Federal Reserve Chairman Alan Greenspan in March 2000[1]

1. As quoted in CFO.com (2001), "ROI: Mad to Measure".

In Chapter 2, we touched upon the importance of cost justification of new technologies. Paradoxically, as IT is increasingly becoming essential for doing business, its benefits are becoming more intangible and thus difficult to measure. A manager charged with assessing the business value of a new technology will have to go through the process of assigning *measurable* values to a variety of benefits that are usually unquantifiable. Today's managers need to have the skills to quantify and recognise the impact of the risks, uncertainties and options associated with their company's e-business investments. To evaluate the overall efficacy of IT capital investments, managers need to adopt appropriate assessment methodologies to devise a selection of efficiency and effectiveness measures to compare outcomes against initial performance targets.

Within the framework of *Dynamic Organisation Tension* (DOT), pre-investment assessments of business value and subsequently, the ongoing measurement and management of performance constitute a vital feedback mechanism to regulate the dynamic bonds that exist among the five major organisational dimensions (strategy, structure, people, technology and processes). The importance of this two-fold process (consisting of valuation and performance management) has increased dramatically as managers face the challenge of pursuing strategic projects under budgetary limitations and a challenging economy.

In this chapter you will learn that accounting-based analytical tools that have been traditionally used to determine the payback period of investments do not adequately reflect the added uncertainty, extended timeframes and the importance of secondary benefits that are typical of most e-business investments. We will present a conceptual framework for performance management and highlight the principles and practices that are conducive to effective management of an e-business transformation effort. Most importantly, we will highlight the importance of linking valuation and measurement methodologies with the overall enterprise goals, and ensuring that the initiative is aligned with the organisation's e-business strategy.

Issues of technology spending and the need to track performance against expectations have always been the subject of some controversy. Organisational computing is now fifty years old and for most of this period, management's perception of the function has been essentially technical in nature. In the first two decades of corporate automation, simple analytical tools such as the "payback period" were widely used to determine the length of time it would take for the gains generated by an investment – that is, the cost-savings or extra revenue – to cover all initial costs.

With high inflation in the 1970s, distinctions between the present and future values of cash (i.e., time value of money) rose to the forefront of managerial consciousness.[2] As a result, investment analyses grew in sophistication and the straightforward payback period computation was improved upon by taking into account the cost of capital. From a financial standpoint, the future cash flows resulting from the IT investment were *discounted* to determine a net present

---

2. Norris et al. (2000).

value (NPV). Also of relevance was the *opportunity cost* of an investment – in essence, the return on the monetary investment that the company could earn through other means at a similar level of risk. If investment analysts were all-knowing, such calculations would be straightforward. In reality, however, numerous uncertainties exist and the usefulness of any analysis hinges on the accuracy of the underlying estimations.

Since the 1980s, the nature of IT implementations has shifted from merely automating information intensive tasks, to more far-reaching projects aimed at ultimately creating economic value. With the rise of e-business, technology spending has come to represent over half of new capital investments in US firms.[3] It is more imperative than ever for managers to have the skills to quantify and understand the impact of risks, uncertainties and options associated with their e-business initiatives. Simple measures based on cash flow do not reflect indirect benefits of new technology or added uncertainty.

This chapter highlights the core issues surrounding e-business evaluation by putting forth a conceptual framework for performance measurement. Our aim is to illustrate possible types of measures available to firms undergoing e-business transformation, not to prescribe a comprehensive measure or list of metrics that all organisations should be using. The appropriate measures for any given e-business implementation depend on many factors. Nevertheless, certain principles and best practices are always of paramount importance. The case study that follows this chapter, *e-Procurement at Cathay Pacific Airways: e-Business Valuation*, highlights some of these principles by illustrating how a leading international airline designed an evaluation methodology for a major e-procurement initiative.

Technology and the organisation

In the early days of organisational computing, the extent of technology valuation and performance measurement was often limited to payback period and internal technical measurements within the information systems function. As the use of technology became widespread, some observers began to point to an apparent *productivity paradox* in IT. It was argued that despite enormous advances in the underlying technology and a surge in technology spending, concrete benefits had not materialised in output statistics or measures of productivity.[4]

To counter these dire assessments, MIT Sloan professors Erik Brynjolfsson and Lorin Hitt affirmed the potential of IT for reducing costs and enhancing competitiveness. They contended that previous findings of a productivity paradox may have overlooked the time needed to realise the benefits of IT. Their estimates indicated that, "dollar for dollar, spending on computer capital created more value than spending on other types of capital."[5] In addition,

---

3. Westland (2002).
4. The idea was most prominently put forth by the economics Nobel laureate, Robert Solow, and information management expert, Paul Strassman.
5. Brynjolfsson and Hitt (1998).

the effects of IT are widely believed to result in further, less tangible benefits to the business at large. Among such benefits are improving management decision making, facilitating process management, enhancing group-work dynamics and so on. With an increased awareness of the complex role of technology in affecting firm operations and financial performance, new imperatives for capturing the true business value of technology and actively managing performance were born.

At the height of the dot-com boom, many IT executives once again questioned the need for determining the return on investment of e-business initiatives when the strategic importance of these projects seemed so self-evident! However, with the dot-com collapse, managers have been under pressure to develop frameworks to evaluate the success of their firm's e-business strategies. The push to establish such valuation and measurement programs has increased lately as managers face the challenge of balancing projects against limited resources. Today, in the light of the increasing importance of e-business technology for the realisation of enterprise strategy, the economic aspects of IT are receiving more attention than ever before.

As we argued in *Chapter 2* companies should undertake e-business transformation initiatives only as part of their overall properly aligned enterprise strategy. Before investment in any particular e-business project is approved, a satisfactory business case must articulate the requirements for derived value – both the quantifiable and unquantifiable benefits.

The expansion of IT infrastructure throughout organisational value chains has increased the impact of IT-spending on overall profitability. In addition, the need to reduce the time-to-market of technology implementations has also resulted in new requirements for reliable feedback mechanisms that can gauge the status of ongoing projects. Figure 3.1 depicts a simple framework of the sequence of expectations and actions that result in alignment between enterprise strategy and e-business implementation. Senior management's expectations of the value of an e-business investment are an outgrowth of the greater enterprise strategy and determine the level of funding allocated to the transformation effort. The project team must then establish performance targets and devise measurement techniques to assess progress on a continual basis.

Figure 3.1 An e-business value framework

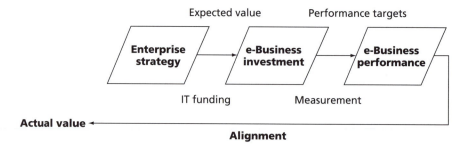

Source: Adapted from Howard Rubin Associates (1991).

The nature of e-business investments

Many organisations apply different standards for assessing IT investment decisions than for their other investment decisions. Decision-making authority is usually limited to IT staff, or to the heads of individual business units. Alternately, authority may rest with special groups, such as steering committees, responsible for approving all capital investment requests. In some companies, e-business initiatives may be subjected to stringent appraisal given the typically higher risk of technology investment. Other organisations may have established strategic imperatives to encourage the use of technology and thus reduce the required return criteria for e-business projects.

Over the course of corporate computerisation, technology investments have characteristically followed a sequential progression.[6] In the early days of computerisation, investments were made in technology that sought to automate basic processes. The benefits of these projects were relatively easy to quantify. For example, the responsibilities of a dozen high-salaried stockbrokers could be replaced by a shift to electronic brokering. Once a certain level of automation had been achieved, further investment allocations tended to focus on projects aimed at enhancing management information or supporting decision making. As the enterprise focus shifted into investments of an "informational" or "decisional" nature, the benefits sought from systems such as Management Information Systems (MIS) and Decision Support Systems (DSS) become less quantifiable. Today, as organisations increasingly use IT in their transformational initiatives, the methodology for quantifying benefits becomes even less clear. Projects are no longer driven by straightforward cost advantages, but instead by top management's overall vision for the enterprise (see Figure 3.2).

A poor decision relating to e-business infrastructure investment may have disastrous effects on costs, productivity and the customer service capabilities of the enterprise. A bad decision may destroy the business in more extreme cases. On a similar note, a decision not to go with a particular e-business initiative may also have very negative repercussions. In this sense, it can be said that the gravity of e-business investment decisions have similarities with other types of

Figure 3.2 Sequential phases of IT investment

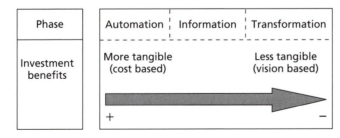

---

6. Remenyi et al. (2000).

"make or break" decisions taken by the firm, such as launching a new product. A variety of factors make the typical investment decision for e-business initiatives especially challenging:[7]

- spending on an e-business initiative will likely constitute a considerable proportion of an organisation's total capital expenditure;

- the e-business initiative comes with a hefty price tag and substantial risk, even so, potential benefits or environmental conditions are such that it must be given serious consideration;

- the technology under consideration is undergoing change in a rapid pace, and its intended use will involve several working departments; and

- in most instances, the business will have little experience in making reliable cost estimates, measuring performance or thoroughly analysing the costs and benefits of major technological initiatives.

On the enterprise scale, an IT investment can usually be classified by its scope and by underlying motivations. If an investment is a *strategic necessity* the organisation has no choice but to proceed and will generally decide on the option available at the lowest cost. Such investments would typically include IT initiatives necessary for compliance with legal and procedural requirements (e.g. electronic documentation), standardising interfaces with partners and suppliers (e.g. implementing partner interface processes through the RosettaNet standard) or in some instances catching up with market leaders (e.g. establishing automated teller machines).

Often the need for new capital investments would have come about as a result of earlier decisions regarding the direction of the business and as such, there are relatively few options available for consideration and the benefits from going ahead will be clearly apparent. Examples of such investments might include projects to update hardware, improve systems security or the development of systems to support a new product. The observable benefits from such projects typically include reduced costs of maintenance, protection of data from unauthorised access, improvements to cycle times in the delivery of products and services or lower reject ratios. Further, less tangible benefits may include improved worker morale from technological advancement or updated skills from new training associated with the project. With the organisation largely committed to an initiative, the option of maintaining status quo is often overlooked, but this too should be subjected to costing analysis, if merely for the sake of comparison.

IT managers are usually most knowledgeable about investments affecting the firm's core business. The benefits from such investments are usually quite evident and closely tied to the operational effectiveness of the business (see Chapter 2).

---

7. Ibid.

The decision to invest in undertaking e-business transformation may entail large investment and can be problematic owing to the difficulty of quantifying the investment returns. Many corporations enlist the expertise of external consultants who offer non-traditional (and often proprietary) strategic and financial tools for assessing both quantifiable and qualitative benefits of an e-business implementation.

The overall e-business vision is so closely tied to the very way an organisation engages its many stakeholders that it is not unusual for projects to show an initial negative NPV by conventional analysis. Owing to the many uncertainties involved and the intangible nature of most benefits, some may argue that determining e-business returns is a pointless exercise. But the effective management of any resource requires appropriate, albeit imperfect, measurement scales. A sensible way of approaching e-business implementations is to understand that there is no universal approach to valuation that can apply to every situation.

The following vignette illustrates the tailored approaches taken by various companies to assess the business value of their e-business ventures.

ROI IN PRACTICE

A few years ago, the traditional requirement to establish credible estimates of investment payback for an organisation's e-business ambitions was largely ignored. However, recent economic conditions have refocused attention on the need for more rigorous efforts to ensure the value delivered by major projects. The following are some ways in which companies competing in different arenas are meeting this challenge:

- Alaska Air Group Inc., the holding company for Alaska Airlines and Horizon Air Industries employs a straightforward ROI calculation in assessing its online presence. While many airlines look to the percentage of total revenue booked over the Internet as an indication of how many customers are opting to purchase online, Alaska Air computes the amount that selling tickets on the Web is saving in distribution costs, namely agency commissions and fees to reservation systems such as Sabre or Apollo. The cost of maintaining online sales capabilities are deducted from the amount

Alaska Air is saving on distribution costs. While this proves a handy and relatively trouble-free method, it does not account for secondary cost savings (e.g. savings in the cost of maintaining a toll-free line for bookings or itinerary information); nor does it reflect any incremental sales directly resulting from the Web.[8]

- Freight company, Yellow Corporation, applies a cost/benefit matrix to all IT projects, including MyYellow.com, a multifunctional portal the company developed to provide customers with a single point of access to satisfy needs ranging from calculating shipping rates to tracking the status of deliveries. The company began by studying sites operated by competitors such as Federal Express and UPS in order to understand what features would appeal most to customers and which would make the most sense to pursue. The company estimated that by using MyYellow.com it saved US$20 million in operational costs over traditional phone-based customer

---

8. Lewis (2000).

interaction. In addition to cost savings, the company saw an increase in customer retention rate (see Chapter 7). Customers conducting business through MyYellow.com were 23 per cent more likely to repeat business as compared with traditional customers.[9]

● Verizon Communications, the US$129 billion telecom giant applies two sets of criteria for assessing ROI.[10] Short- and medium-term e-business investments are measured by aggregating cost savings from conducting B2C and B2B business online, cost savings from paperless operations, increased revenue due to the technology-enabled capability of doing after-hours business, and a component of customer satisfaction measured through standard surveys. In addition, Verizon assesses "long-term equity" benefits from its online initiatives by counting the total number of transactions and volume of business conducted online, as well as the number of unique visitors to its website.

Valuation/Appraisal methodologies

Let us now turn our attention to some specific methodologies for evaluating the benefits derived from e-business investments. The crux of the problem faced by any manager in the position of assessing the business value of technology is that of assigning measurable values to a variety of benefits, which can range from easily quantifiable to distinctly intangible. We will use the term "value" as a reference to the utility or relative importance of any commodity associated with the implementation of technology. By extension, "business value" refers to the sum total of financial (quantifiable, tangible) and non-financial (qualitative, intangible) impacts. We explore the earning capability of an initiative from the perspective of a given organisation's objectives and requirements; similar businesses with equal resources may have very different views of the value of a particular initiative.

For any process of valuation to be of use, management must first come to a sense of what it considers good investment performance. This is usually a function of the industry in which the enterprise operates and the organisation's past investment performance. An ROI of 18 per cent might be outstanding for a corporation in a commodities-based industry, but decidedly mediocre for an organisation engaged in electronics distribution. A pragmatic approach is through reference to industry benchmarks or by adopting a longitudinal view whereby the trends in investment returns are examined over a fixed time period as a means of establishing expectations. Here, it is essential to take note of accounting issues that may have an impact on the calculation of ROI or other financial ratios. Periodic depreciation of technological assets may result in increasing ROI figures without an actual improvement in investment performance.

---

9. Banham and Rosenberg (2001).
10. As quoted in Lewis (2000).

Financial appraisal

Valuation methods are most commonly classified as being either of a *financial* or *non-financial* nature. Financial methods of appraisal are concerned with the monetary values that may be attributed to the impacts of an investment. We began this chapter by citing the *payback period* and *net present value* as measures that have long been applied in appraising potential investments. To elaborate:

- **Payback period** is the time between when an investment is funded and the time when the total cost of the investment is recovered through incoming cash flows (i.e. cash receipts: cost-savings or revenue generated, minus cash payments). Managers must determine the period in which their investment must be recovered – if this length of time falls within the calculated payback period, the investment is then justified by this criterion.

- **Net present value** is based on time value of money, and refers to an investment's future net cash flows, discounted at the cost of raising funds or at the opportunity cost of capital,[11] minus the initial investment. If positive, the investment is considered feasible. Generally speaking, the higher the NPV, the greater the preference given to the investment option.

In addition to the payback period and the NPV of an investment, other financial appraisals include the *average accounting rate of return* and the *internal rate of return*:

- An average rate of return is the rate that would make the present value of all financial returns from the investment (future cash flow) plus the final market value of an investment equal to its current market price. Financial estimates are made for each year and the sum is then divided by the anticipated lifetime of the investment. The result is then divided by the original investment cost to give an average rate of return. The average *accounting* rate of return requires that the average yearly depreciation be deducted from the average yearly net cash flow and divided by the average investment amount for the lifetime of the investment.

- The Internal Rate of Return (IRR) is defined as the discount rate which results in a net present value of zero:

$$\text{NPV} = CF_0 + \frac{CF_1}{\left(1 + \text{IRR}\right)^1} + \frac{CF_2}{\left(1 + \text{IRR}\right)^2} + \cdots + \frac{CF_n}{\left(1 + \text{IRR}\right)^n} = 0$$

If the IRR is found to exceed the cost of raising funds to finance the investment (or alternately, some measure of the opportunity cost of capital), it may be considered worthwhile to pursue the investment.

---

11. The formula for discounting cash flows is $CF_v = \Sigma\, CF_n/(1 + d)^n$; where CF_v = discounted cash flow, CF_n = cash flow in year n, d = discount rate and n = the specific year.

Because investments in e-business technology are characterised by a high degree of uncertainty, the effect of non-financial impacts must be given serious consideration when reviewing investment proposals. For a clearer picture of the strategic potentials of new technology investment, it is prudent to employ methods that do not assume a steady stream of cash flows, but expand upon purely financial appraisal to address risk and uncertainty. Examples of "expanded" financial approaches that are suited to e-business valuation include:

● **Sensitivity analysis** is an appraisal methodology that projects how investment performance can vary as changes occur in the underlying assumptions. The premise behind this approach lies in the fact that the variables affecting the cash flows generated by an investment (and thus, NPV) are not known to a certainty, but lie on a probability distribution. This form of analysis begins with a base scenario using the most likely values behind projected cash flow to determine a base NPV. Each variable is then adjusted by an amount to either side of the expected value, according to a series of alternative scenarios (e.g. "What if the cost of maintaining hardware is 10 per cent higher than expected?" "What if software license fees do not increase as anticipated?"). A set of calculations for NPV is made to reflect each revised-variable scenario and a set of NPV's may be plotted for graphical depiction (as in Figure 3.3). The gradient of the lines reflects how sensitive NPV is to variations in each factor – that is the higher the gradient (the steeper the slope), the greater the risk of deviation. With the assistance of spreadsheet models, multiple investment options can be compared using sensitivity analysis to gain insights into relative risk.

● **A decision tree** is a tool that allows for the analysis of investments as a series of sequential decisions. They aim to account for risks and uncertainties by addressing the changing conditions that occur over the lifetime of an

Figure 3.3 Sensitivity analysis: Graphical representation of sensitivity analysis for an e-learning system

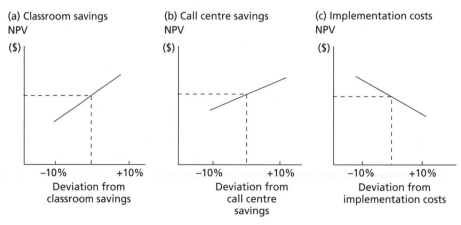

(a) Classroom savings
NPV
($)

−10%   +10%
Deviation from
classroom savings

(b) Call centre savings
NPV
($)

−10%   +10%
Deviation from
call centre
savings

(c) Implementation costs
NPV
($)

−10%   +10%
Deviation from
implementation costs

investment. Using this method, a listing of possible outcomes (NPV values with associated probabilities) can be projected when considering a proposal. Each node on a decision tree represents a point at which a decision must be made, while each diagonal "branch" bears an estimated probability.

● **Real options:** an option is an opportunity to respond to changing circumstances in an effort to influence investment performance. The valuation of options is a complicated subject that goes beyond the scope of this chapter.[12] Decision tree analysis is only a first step in assessing potential outcomes over the lifespan of an investment. Practitioners are increasingly employing options pricing models based upon economic modeling methods for valuing the price of financial market options. The *real options* approach is based on the view that any corporate real assets can be regarded in the same way as call options, thus addressing the effects of uncertainty over the duration of a project. Purely cash flow based calculations of NPV do not capture the economic worth of these options (which can be considerable when the underlying source of risk is high). Thus the true NPV of an investment can be equated with the sum of the NPV of real options and the purely cash flow based NPV figure.

Non-financial appraisal methods

Hybrid appraisals

A hybrid appraisal method aims to craft a single measure reflecting both financial and non-financial consequences of an investment based on quantitative and qualitative tools. Many variations of such methods exist and generally require a structure of thoughtfully selected decision criteria, which are then scored and assigned a relative weight. A widely used hybrid method is the "information economics" method.[13] The information economics methodology breaks the business down into *business* and *technology domains*. The technology domain offers IT opportunities to the business domain, while the business domain compensates the technology domain for the use of resources. Separate criteria are then applied to each domain (see Table 3.1).

Ratio-based methods of appraisal

Ratios are often used as a quantitative tool for the purposes of comparing organisational effectiveness. IT expenditures can be related to measures such as total number of employees, or to output measures involving products or services. A recent ratio-based measure that can offer qualitative insight, however, is the *Return on Management* (ROM) concept popularised by Paul Strassmann that has particular relevance to e-business scenarios.[14] ROM

---

12. For an overview on using real options to price strategic investments, consult Amram and Kulatilaka, "Real Options", Harvard Business School Publishing, 1999.
13. Parker et al. (1988).
14. Strassmann (1985; 1990).

Table 3.1 Business and technology domain criteria

Appraisal criteria	Meaning
Business domain	
Strategic match	The extent to which the investment matches the strategic business goals.
Competitive advantage	The extent to which the investment contributes to an improvement of positioning in the market (e.g. changes in industry structure, improvements of competitive positioning in the industry)
Management information	The extent to which the investment will inform management on core activities of the firm
Competitive response	The extent to which not investing implies a risk; a timely investment contributes to strategic advantage
Organisational risk	The extent to which new competencies are required
Technology domain	
Strategic information systems architecture	The extent to which the investment matches the IT plan and the required integration of IT applications
Definitional uncertainty	The extent to which user requirements can be clearly defined
Technical uncertainty	The extent to which new technical skills, hardware and software are required.
Infrastructure risk	The extent to which the investment requires additional infrastructure investments and the IT department is capable of supporting the proposed system.

Source: The Information Economics Method (Parker et al. 1988). Reprinted by permission of Pearson Education, Inc.

is built on the premise that in modern information economies, the time and effort of management can be considered a company's most important resources. It is sound management that determines what business value can be derived from an IT investment. As such, managers must think strategically about how best to focus their efforts. The ROM method can be expressed by the simple formula:

$$\text{ROM} = \frac{\text{Productive organizational energy released}}{\text{Management time and attention}}$$

Consideration of the ROM ratio is useful in helping managers understand if their efforts towards implementing the e-business strategy are leading to fruition. This approach is a departure from classical valuation, as it attributes value added to managerial factors rather than to capital.

Portfolio-based methods of assessment[15]

Portfolio-based methods are drawn from decision-making tools used in management consulting. They usually involve plotting the various investment alternatives against decision criteria. The method of *Investment Mapping* proposed by Glen Peters is a useful means of evaluating technology investments within the context of the overall corporate strategy.

A company's portfolio of e-business investments may be mapped on a matrix with two major dimensions, **benefits** and **investment orientation** constituting the two axes, as shown in Figure 3.4. A range of benefit and orientation values are approximated on a scale of values for existing and prospective investments and these are then plotted to represent the company's technology-investment strategy.

Figure 3.4 An investment map

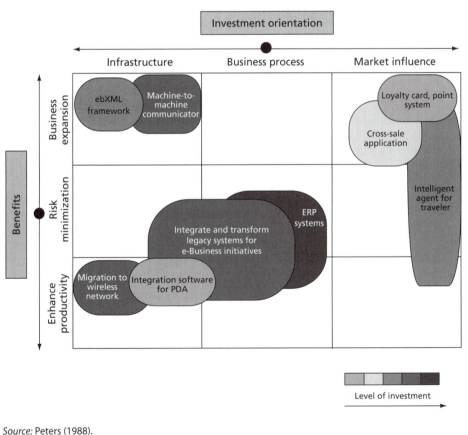

Source: Peters (1988).

15. The material in this section is adapted from Peters, G. (1988), Evaluating your computer investment strategy, *Journal of Information Technology*, vol. 3, pp. 178–88 (available online at http://www.tandf.co.uk/journals/routledge/02683962.html). Reproduced by permission of Taylor & Francis Ltd.

Connections may be found between investment maps and a company's e-business investment strategy. Companies with a preponderance of investments in the bottom left region of the matrix tend to be focused on cost reduction, often operating in volume/commodity-oriented markets where competition is predominantly price-driven. Those with investments erring towards the upper right tend to function in more specialised markets where value-added products and services are the cornerstone for a strategy of differentiation. Taking a longitudinal view, it can also be said that companies tend to progress diagonally "up the matrix" as use of IT grows more sophisticated and management begins adopting a vision of building upon traditional infrastructure components to align enterprise information systems with a value-chain orientation.

The benefits dimension

In a review of IT projects conducted in different industries, Peters identified three categories of benefits frequently sought by executives from their technology investments as shown in Figure 3.5.

Figure 3.5 Benefits of technology investments

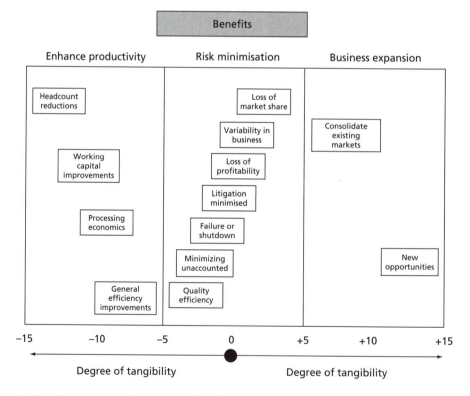

Position of investment attributes used to identify the range of anticipated benefits for an IT investment
(Please note (–) does not denote negative benefit)

Source: Peters (1988).

1 *Enhanced productivity*: Benefits that are targeted at improving the firm's operational efficiency, for example, systems integration projects that reduce the need for data entry, or logistics systems that reduce distribution costs. The benefits stemming from enhancing productivity can be subdivided into:

● *Headcount reduction*: productivity gains resulting from headcount reductions.

● *Working capital improvements*: productivity gains resulting from better inventory management (finished goods, work in progress, raw materials) and lower interest charges.

● *Processing economies*: productivity gains resulting from more efficient technology utilisation.

● *General efficiency improvements*: productivity gains through faster response to changes in supply and demand.

2 *Risk minimisation*: Benefits accrued through effective risk management. for example a statistical control system that gives early warning of potential failure in equipment performance. The categories of benefits contributing to risk minimisation are outlined in Table 3.2.

Table 3.2 Benefits contributing to risk minimisation

Benefit	Description/Examples
Minimising risk through improvements in quality	Investments in technology that result in a reduction in errors
Minimising unaccounted losses	Systems able to detect fraud or provide enhanced information on product movements
Reducing risks of failure or shutdown	Maintenance systems or reinforcements of systems against total or partial shutdown
Minimising risk of litigation	Implementing systems such as project control systems that reduce the risk of liquidated damages for failing to complete a project on time
Minimising loss of profitability	Information systems that provide management with performance reporting may minimise the risk of losing profitability
Minimising variability in the business profile	Automatic re-ordering systems on customer premises to minimise variability in market demand
Minimising risk of losing market share	Executive information systems that provide information on a company's performance compared with competitors; systems that add value to the company's products and services

3 *Business expansion*: Benefits resulting from IT initiatives that involve some form of innovation towards creating new products, providing new services or establishing new ways of doing business, for example offering insurance products through an auto-sales portal. Such benefits fall into two major areas:

   (a) *Consolidating existing markets* through systems that lead to better customer service or add value to existing products. For instance, a mobile service provider may offer customer feedback channels and value-added services through its online portal.

   (b) *Creating new opportunities* through systems that lead to new product innovation or access to new markets. For example, initiatives by financial institutions to create a single point of access for tracking and processing a range of personal finance and investment activities.

These benefits may be assigned values along a continuum according to a perceived degree of tangibility, for example ranging from -15 to $+15$. It is also important to note that a particular e-business investment may lead to more than one type of benefit for the company; this would be reflected by a range of values for the investment (e.g. ranging from 0 to $+10$ for an investment that brings benefits of risk minimisation and business expansion).

Investment orientation dimension

Peters calls the other major criterion for appraising the value of an IT project the *investment orientation* – the way in which a prospective investment corresponds with the objectives of the business. Companies operating in different industries are predisposed to pay greater attention to investments that correspond with the reality of their business. Investment orientation may be divided into three board categories:

1 *Infrastructure* refers to investments identified with the mainstay hardware, software, data, networks and human resources constituting the underlying foundation of an enterprise. For the purposes of investment analysis, prospective infrastructure investments tend to fall under the following three categories: telecommunications, software and hardware.

2 *Business processes* refer to investments associated with the firm's business processes, for example order processing, logistics systems, purchasing automation and so on. Table 3.3 shows the types of business process-related investments.

3 *Market-influencing* investments often receive the most attention from companies seeking to streamline their distribution channels and are oriented to:

   ● *improve distribution channels*, for example through e-commerce initiatives, electronic kiosks or smart card implementations.

Table 3.3 Business process investments

Investment	Description/Examples
Finance and accounts	Systems supporting reporting processes; systems providing information on budgets and sales targets
Corporate management	Systems developed to provide performance information
Processing orders	Systems supporting fundamental processes of the enterprise – e.g. customer enquiries
Production and distribution logistics	Systems geared towards automating distribution schedules
Processing goods/services	Systems necessary for processing goods or services – e.g. clearing systems in a bank
Purchasing/procurement	Systems that lend administrative support to the purchasing function, or which provide information to buyers
Office and administrative	Office & administrative support systems – e.g. payroll systems, email, HR management

Source: Peters (1988).

- *increase the percentage of repeat-sales* by building loyalty or providing value-added services. Investment in applications that manage customer service interactions such as website personalisation technology would also fall under this category.

- *change customer perceptions* by enhancing the image of a product, for example electronic ticketing technology for air travel, smart-card based identification and so on.

As with the benefits criterion, e-business investments may often span more than one category of orientation. Investment in smart card technology, for example, may require substantial capital expenditures for IT infrastructure, but also stand to alter customer perceptions of the underlying service and improve a company's distribution channels.

As shown in Figure 3.6 the investment orientation of various investment options may be assigned values along a continuum spanning from how closely the investment can be identified with basic infrastructure (*involvement with infrastructure*) at one extreme and at the other, how much the investment influences the market in which the company operates (*proximity to market*).

Through investment mapping, managers can compare prospective investments against one another and assess the orientation of their e-business and IT investment portfolios to the business value chain. The benefits and investment

Figure 3.6 Investment orientations

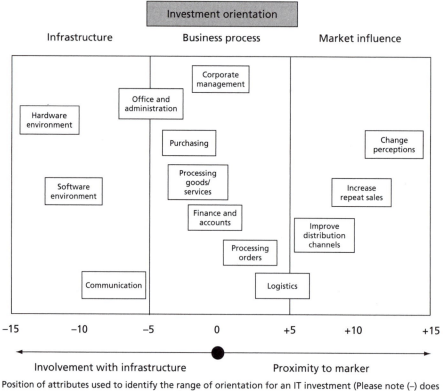

Position of attributes used to identify the range of orientation for an IT investment (Please note (–) does not denote negative benefit)

Source: Peters (1988).

orientation dimensions may be mapped against each other (as in Figure 3.4) to offer insight into how an e-business investment matches enterprise strategy. Investment mapping may also be used to gain an understanding of competitor strategies and investment allocation practices.

The methods of appraisal we have outlined are but a sampling of possible approaches using a variety of assessment criteria. Financial appraisal tools are well suited for assessing the monetary value of individual investment projects, while hybrid, ratio- and portfolio-based methods attempt to expand the breadth of purely financial tools by looking at the effect of investments on particular business processes or at the level of the entire firm.

In Chapter 1 we defined "success" as the accomplishment of what we aim at. In the remainder of this chapter, we will turn our attention to how management may track the progress of e-business initiatives for the purpose of comparing the actual value of investments against expected values and to assist in further decision-making.

Performance management

Successful companies have long employed appraisal methodologies to operationalise business objectives, determine the most advantageous allocation of resources and evaluate alternative courses of investment. In an e-business climate, the valuation process leading to a "green-light" for an investment initiative represents only the starting point of a cycle of assessment that must include the design of efficiency and effectiveness measures to form a basis for comparing outcomes against initial performance targets. A process of ongoing measurement also serves as a vehicle for providing early warnings of problems, valuable information towards further resource allocation and a channel for periodic feedback from stakeholder groups.

In the case study following this chapter, *e-Procurement at Cathay Pacific Airways: e-Business Valuation*, we see that a performance management regimen often also serves the political purpose of demonstrating that benefits have been realised from a major expenditure (and that further expenditures on related projects may be endorsed).

The requirement of tracking IT progress within the organisation has traditionally been a result of forces that include:[16]

- a need to justify substantial capital expenditure;

- internal or customer dissatisfaction traceable to the performance of IT functions;

- company-wide interest in meeting quality and performance standards (e.g. adherence to ISO certification);

- cost control initiatives driven internally by the finance or human resources departments;

- the need to address uncertainty and respond to concerns about the true business value of technology investments; IT investments may not be perceived as being linked to the profit-making aspects of the business; and

- a desire by the IT department itself to improve its service offerings or internal image

Ultimately, the process of measurement is undertaken to provide information for decision-making. There is no simple approach to measuring IT performance that can be effective for every e-business scenario. Traditional measures like network availability, lines of code and code re-usage provide only modest insight to upper management on the overall success of e-business investments. Further confusion arises with the addition of intangible factors, such as employee satisfaction, to the consideration of an initiative's success: Are more satisfied employees more

---

16. Compiled from Remenyi et al. (2000).

productive? Can monetary values be ascribed? When measurement encompasses employee use of technology, there is possibility of harmful consequences resulting from the very act of measurement. Such *measurement dysfunction* can be described as:

> The designers of a measurement system are usually powerless to guarantee information will be used in accord with their original intentions. People working on activities that are being measured understand that dictating the uses of measurement is difficult and will choose their behaviors accordingly. Claims that measurement will only be used in a particular way are not always credible. In preparing for motivational measurement, people being measured will glean information from the design of the measurement system.[17]

An effective measurement programme may itself constitute a noteworthy proportion of the IT budget. With this in mind, it is generally advisable to rely on a few well-chosen gauges of performance rather than to gather an overabundance of data that may be subject to misinterpretation or manipulation by employees concerned with assessment of personal merit or assignment of blame.

Developing a measurement framework

A crucial prerequisite for crafting an effective e-business measurement system lies in addressing a series of fundamental questions through close cooperation between senior management and the enterprise IT department or provider:

● What are the enterprise's major e-business performance expectations?

● Given these expectations, what are the key IT objectives and targets?

● What are the most appropriate measures for capturing these targets?

● What is the current baseline performance for these measures, what improvement is expected?

● How will the IT function collaborate with enterprise management and stakeholders to use these measures for enhancing performance?

By examining these crucial questions, three core facets of the measurement challenge may be discerned:

1 the **alignment** of IT objectives with the essential e-business mission of the enterprise;

2 the meticulous **construction** of measures to capture the performance of IT in serving the needs of the enterprise; and

---

17. Austin, Robert D. (1996).

3 The **implementation** of measurement systems at various levels of the
organisation.

To make possible these three aspects of performance measurement, the
organisation must also institute reliable data collection and analysis capabilities and affirm a commitment to continuous improvement in the delivery of
e-business solutions. Figure 3.7 shows a simple model illustrating this measurement framework. Using this model as a frame of reference, we now
review suitable practices for approaching the three facets of the measurement
challenge.

Aligning IT objectives with the e-business mission

The alignment of specific project goals with the enterprise-level e-business mission
requires close analysis of a chain of events leading from the mission statement
to the performance expectations for specific e-business initiatives. By charting a
systematic linkage of needs and responses (for the enterprise at large, and for
internal and external stakeholders), it becomes possible to identify the most essential goals relating to e-business transformation and subsequently, to determine the
most appropriate measures for evaluating performance. As such, it is crucial that
senior management begin with clear definitions of what the organisation intends

Figure 3.7 The e-business measurement challenge

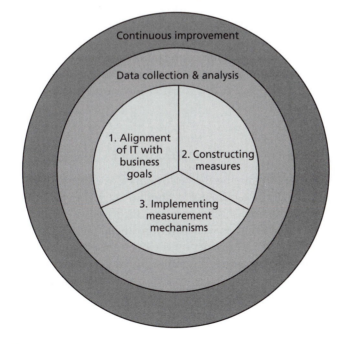

Source: Adapted from GAO Executive Guide (1998).

Figure 3.8 An e-business chain of alignment

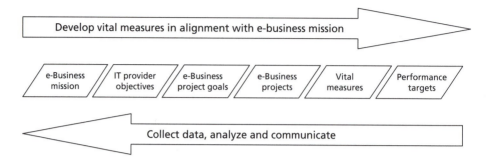

Source: Adapted from GAO Executive Guide (1998).

to accomplish, so that this may be rendered into a conceptualisation of how IT investments can lead to these goals. Throughout this process, senior management, IT managers and all other stakeholders must be in agreement over the e-business mission, resulting IT mission, project goals, chosen measures and expected targets. Figure 3.8 illustrates this sequence:

It is important that organisations attempt to isolate the vital measures for gauging the alignment of an e-business initiative, as an excessive number of measures increases expense, data collection complexity, confusion and the potential for dysfunction. The measures selected must in turn map back to the e-business project goals and enterprise mission. To further illustrate, Table 3.4 presents representative IT missions, project goals and possible measures for a hypothetical e-business scenario.

With careful consideration, performance measures can indicate how closely specific initiatives are aligned to the enterprise e-business mission. An effective performance measurement regimen should aim to capture indicators at the enterprise, project and process levels using both quantitative and qualitative measures.

Constructing measures to capture performance

An effective approach for gauging the performance of e-business investments must address the broad impact of e-business technology on all facets of the organisation. The system of measurement should strive to incorporate quantifiable measures suited to conventional analysis as well as non-financial factors that may be hard to quantify but have a significant impact on the outcomes of an e-business initiative. In strategic management literature, a popular framework for translating the enterprise mission into specific measurable objectives has been the Balanced Scorecard technique created by Robert Kaplan and David Norton.[18]

---

18. Kaplan and Norton (1992;1996).

Table 3.4 Representative mission, goals and measures

IT mission	Project goals	Possible measures
Reduce information spending	● Retire outdated infrastructure ● Increase allocation of IT spending to e-business infrastructure development	● IT spending as a percentage of revenues reduced ● Percentage reduction in costs of legacy systems ● Distributed computing cost per user ● Enterprise telecommunications costs per minute ● Cost per line of code developed
Improve IT infrastructure management	● Increase use of enterprise-wide solutions ● Increase interoperability	● Percentage new infra structure installed ● Percentage cost spent on maintenance versus percentage spent on new initiatives
Leverage enterprise-wide human capital, hardware and software resources	● Improved staff productivity ● Improved IT resource allocation	● Ratio productive : non-productive time ● Training costs per employee ● Percentage reduction in personnel impacted by e-business initiatives
Develop process-driven solutions	● Accelerated delivery of new solutions ● Focus IT resources on business process needs	● Compliance with industry standards ● Percentage reused code for in-house applications ● Customer survey ratings for development projects

The balanced scorecard method avoids placing too much emphasis on any single area of performance and targets measures at various levels of operation. Kaplan and Norton's scorecard tracks performance in four key areas as shown in Figure 3.9.

1 *Financial criteria* that determine the organisation's value to shareholders, for example revenue growth, cost reduction, asset utilisation and so on.

2 *Customer perspective* components such as customer satisfaction, retention, new customer acquisition and market share growth.

3 *Internal business processes* that enable the pursuit of organisational objectives.

4 *Learning and growth* – the infrastructure that must be in place so that the organisation can continue to improve and create value.

Figure 3.9 The balanced scorecard approach

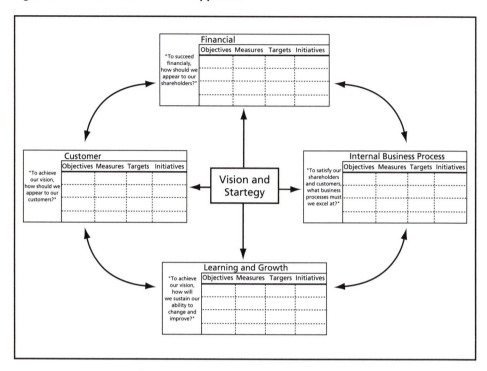

These four scorecard areas may be refined and adapted to better reflect an e-business transformation scenario:

1 accomplishing the e-business mission of the enterprise;

2 satisfying customers of e-business products and services;

3 internal IT processes necessary for e-business performance; and

4 ongoing learning and innovation.

As with the measurement framework for ensuring alignment of IT objectives, a set of customised objectives and vital measures must be devised for each scorecard area, striking a balance between shorter-term cost goals and non-financial variables. Under each area, measures are selected to capture performance at the enterprise, IT mission and e-business project levels. The measures used may be refined and replaced over time as management gains experience as to which are of greatest importance for decision-making.

Table 3.5 presents sample scorecard objectives and performance measures for the four scorecard areas we have outlined.

Table 3.5 Sample balanced scorecard objectives and measures

Objectives	Sample measures
Accomplishing the e-business mission of the enterprise	
Accomplishing e-business project goals	● Percentage of cost/time/quality improvements attributable to e-business solutions ● Percentage of performance targets met; percentage of benefits realised
e-Business technology portfolio management	● Percentage of old applications/legacy systems retired ● Percentage of reusable application parts ● New e-business investment as a percentage of total spending
Management of e-business costs and returns	● Cost (as a percentage) of in-house IT services vs industry benchmarks ● Financial indicators – for example NPV, IRR, return on net assets
Optimising e-business resource usage	● Percentage of Hardware/Software with interoperability capabilities ● Maintenance Hours vs industry standard
e-Business customer measures	
Cooperation between IT providers and customers	● Percentage of projects comprising integrated teams
Customer satisfaction	● Percentage of customers satisfied ● Percentage of services launched on time
e-Business technology support of business process improvements	● Percentage of new users proficient in use of e-business solutions ● Percentage of e-business solutions supporting process improvement projects
Internal IT processes in support of e-business	
Development and maintenance of e-business solutions	● Percentage of decrease in application failures ● Cycle time for development ● Mean time for resolving critical defects
Assuring project performance	● Percentage of projects meeting functionality requirements ● Percentage of projects completed on time/under budget
e-Business infrastructure availability	● Percentage of applications availability ● Percentage of network downtime
e-Business standards compliance	● Number of deviations from standards detected through reviews and audits ● Percentage of staff trained in standards ➤

Table 3.5 (cont'd)

Objectives	Sample measures
Ongoing Learning and Innovation	
Capable and competent work force	● Percentage of staff trained in use of e-business technology ● Percentage of budget reserved for training and development ● Percentage of staff professionally certified
Use of advanced technology	● Amount budgeted for advancing technological skills
Employee satisfaction and retention	● Percentage of employee turnover

Implementing performance measurement systems at multiple levels

Under the balanced scorecard method, measures were selected to capture performance at the enterprise, IT mission and e-business project levels as shown in Figure 3.10. This tiered approach allows for a better understanding of performance measurement throughout the organisation and close alignment with the enterprise e-business mission. Performance measurement at different levels of the organisation is undertaken for different purposes – an understanding of these purposes is essential in ensuring that appropriate metrics are selected for each decision-making level.

Most IT managers have the greatest experience in establishing measurement programmes at the project level where the focus of measurement is largely on technical outcomes. Key measures are designed for assessing systems and application

Figure 3.10 Summary of the graduating levels of performance measurement

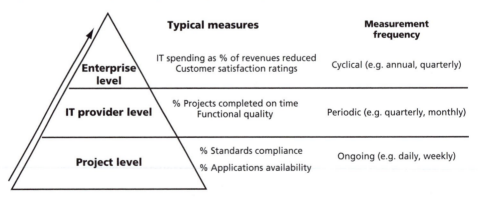

	Typical measures	**Measurement frequency**
Enterprise level	IT spending as % of revenues reduced Customer satisfaction ratings	Cyclical (e.g. annual, quarterly)
IT provider level	% Projects completed on time Functional quality	Periodic (e.g. quarterly, monthly)
Project level	% Standards compliance % Applications availability	Ongoing (e.g. daily, weekly)

processes in terms of quality, productivity and impacts on internal and external satisfaction. Typical measures at this level include productivity-oriented ratios, instances of defects or failure, and network availability. Technical metrics generally fall under the following categories:[19]

1 *Productivity metrics*: measures such as software delivery rates and the organisation's ability to support applications.

2 *Quality metrics*: measuring the technical quality of the organisation's e-business infrastructure.

3 *Delivery metrics*: measuring the ability to complete projects on schedule and within budget.

4 *Penetration metrics*: measuring the diffusion of technological solutions.

5 *Work profile metrics*: measuring the time it takes for IT efforts to advance through life-cycle stages.

6 *Demand metrics*: measuring request backlogs and the organisation's ability to service them.

7 *Technology assimilation metrics*: measuring the organisation's ability to identify and incorporate new technology.

8 *Work distribution metrics*: measuring the balance between development and maintenance.

9 *Capability metrics*: measuring the ability of the IT organisation to measure and improve itself.

At the IT provider level, the focus is on relating technical measures with e-business performance. Managers want to assess how particular e-business initiatives or processes are performing against expectations. The measures used are often drawn from technical metrics categories (especially quality and delivery metrics) and are used to improve operations within a line of business.

At the enterprise level, performance measures focus on e-business mission outcomes and how effectively the component initiatives are supporting enterprise-wide objectives. Information is reported to senior management, and in some instances, the company's shareholders or even the general public. The "yield" of technology investments to the business is the main issue under consideration, which is to say, the ratio of actual performance against expected value, weighted by customer satisfaction.[20]

---

19. Rubin (1991).
20. Ibid. – See Figure 1.

Targeted performance measures should be linked to the organisation's balanced scorecard, or other multivariable approach to ensure that an inclusive range of measures make up management's view of the organisation's progress towards e-business transformation. Although senior management and external stakeholders may never ask for performance indicators from the project levels, this data nevertheless provides crucial feedback on how well specific projects are supporting IT objectives and ultimately, desired outcomes such as customer satisfaction and shareholder value.

Summary

The magnitude and scope of e-business investment requires new perspectives on valuation. We have presented a variety of appraisal approaches drawn from traditional financial valuation techniques, which may be extended in an effort to account for investment alternatives and to capture the range of non-financial consequences that are highly pertinent to the success or failure of an e-business initiative. The justification of an investment option represents only a starting point that must be backed up by the design of a measurement program to demonstrate results and assist decision-making.

The measurement process is a value-adding part of the implementation process, which may itself require considerable expense, or constitute a significant administrative burden – as we see in the ensuing case study, *e-Procurement at Cathay Pacific Airways*. There is no "best" metric or approach to measurement appropriate to all business scenarios – the ultimate success of any measurement program lies in its alignment with project goals and the enterprise mission. The measures themselves may be used to establish a baseline for performance and should be revised, reconsidered or supplemented according to changing management requirements.

Questions for discussion

1 What is the "productivity paradox?"

2 Explain why the benefits of IT investments become more difficult to quantify as they become geared more towards e-business.

3 What are the shortcomings of traditional financial analysis techniques for evaluating e-business investments?

4 Why are real options relevant to the valuation of technology investments?

5 How can investments be evaluated within the context of overall corporate strategy?

6 What questions should be considered when crafting a performance measurement system?

7 How can a chain of alignment be used to derive performance measures from the e-business mission?

References

Amran, M. and Kulatilaka, N. (1999) "Real options", *Managing Strategic Investment in an Uncertain World*, Boston, MA: Harvard Business School Press.

Austin, R.D. (1996) *Measuring and managing performance in organisations*, New York: Dorset House Publishing.

Banham, R. and Rosenberg, H. (2001) "ROI mad to measure: calculating the return on e-business investments isn't easy, but that doesn't stop companies from trying", CFO.com, 15 September.

Brynjolfsson, E. and Hitt, L. (1998) "Beyond the productivity paradox: computers are the catalyst for bigger changes", *Communications of the ACM*, vol. 41, no. 8 (August), pp. 49–55.

GAO (1998) *Measuring Performance and Demonstrating Results of Information Technology Investments*, United States General Accounting Office Executive Guide.

Kaplan, Robert S. and Norton, David P. (1992) "The balanced scorecard: measures that drive performance", *Harvard Business Review*, vol. 70, no. 2 (January–February).

Kaplan, Robert S. and Norton, David P. (1996) "Using the balanced scorecard as a strategic management system", *Harvard Business Review*, vol. 74, no. 1 (January–February).

Lewis, D. (2000) "Pressure mounts to gauge e-Biz ROI", Internetweek online, Monday, 30 October, available from http://www.internetweek.com/transformation2000/issues/roi.htm [accessed 11 April 2002].

Norris, G., Hurley, J.R., Hartley, K.M., Dunleavy, J.R., Balls, J.D. and Dunleavy, J. (2000) *e-Business and ERP*, New York: John Wiley & Sons, Inc.

Parker, M.M., Benson, R.J. and Trainor, H.E. (1988) *Information Economics, Linking Business Performance to Information Technology*, Englewood Cliffs: Prentice-Hall.

Peters, G. (1988) "Evaluating your computer investment strategy", *Journal of Information Technology*, vol. 3, pp. 178–88.

Remenyi, D., Money, A., Sherwood-Smith, M. and Irani, Z. (2000) *The Effective Measurement and Management of IT Costs and Benefits*, Oxford: Butterworth-Heinemann.

Rubin, H. (1991) "Measure for measure", *Computerworld*, 15 April, Framingham, MA.

Strassmann, P.A. (1990) *The Business Value of Computers*, Information Economics Press.

Strassmann, P.A. (1985) *Information Payoff: The Transformation of Work in the Electronic Age*, Information Economics Press.

Westland, C. (2002) *Valuing Technology*, Singapore: John Wiley & Sons (Asia).

Further reading

Evans, C. (1981) *The Making of the Micro: A History of the Computer*, London: Victor Gollancz.

Renkema, T.J.W. (2000) *The IT Value Quest: How to Capture the Business Value of IT-Based Infrastructure*, Chichester: John Wiley & Sons.

Ridgway, V.F. (1956) "Dysfunctional consequences of performance measurements", *Administrative Science Quarterly* (September), pp. 240–7.

Case study   e-Procurement at Cathay Pacific Airways: e-business valuation

Experts should be aware that the technology they choose must be able to demonstrate its value to the institution and its shareholders.[1]

At the end of 2001, Cathay Pacific's CXeBuy electronic procurement system was fully operational for its headquarters in Hong Kong. The 14-month implementation project aimed at applying Internet-based technology to build the most efficient purchasing process and capability in the industry. The strategy was to Web-enable the procurement of goods and services for five of the airline spend categories, namely: in-flight service, cargo, information technology, marketing and office supplies. Users would access electronic catalogues hosted on either CXeBuy, electronic marketplaces or supplier Websites, using the Internet to transmit order information between Cathay and the 400-plus suppliers providing goods and services under the five spend categories.

While the project was far from complete, and as Cathay had just embarked on the next stage of rolling out CXeBuy to its outports, a member of the Project Steering Committee (PSC) raised a valuable but difficult question at that stage of system deployment. He queried the actual benefits realised so far as a result of e-procurement implementation. He wanted the project team to evaluate the cost savings and efficiency gains that were a direct consequence of implementing CXeBuy. He felt that it was important to gauge the results so far, so that department heads of each affected department could make appropriate decisions concerning the redeployment of staffing and resources, and therefore match the expected results stated

in the initial business case. At the same time, the PSC wanted assurances that the new e-procurement system lived up to expectations within the context of the initial project benefits estimates, and clearly supported the airline's corporate mission to be Asia's leading e-business airline. For Robert Lamoureux, manager in charge of the e-procurement initiative, the task of valuing and measuring the full benefits of CXeBuy throughout Cathay seemed premature at this deployment stage. Furthermore, with over 4000 spend items on the system and over 200 system users and approvers in its head office alone, the exercise could become a time-consuming and academic project in itself. As an alternative to conducting such an exercise, he proposed to the PSC to formulate a methodology that user departments could apply at will to assess the impact of CXeBuy on their operations. However, some members of the Committee raised concerns that such a voluntary approach would serve only a limited purpose, and would fall short of providing department heads with an overview of the impact of CXeBuy on the overall corporate mission. As these issues began to filtrate through the Airline, defensive arguments were raised by other PSC members, who were unsure of the need for such a valuation exercise at this early stage. They questioned the need to validate the benefits estimates and suggested that department heads would have difficulty and probably refuse to act on such theoretical results. Something had to be done to reinstate the need for accountability and support the premise that any Cathay Pacific e-business initiative had to prove its value, not only from a soft benefits standpoint but also in terms of satisfying the payback and ROI deliverables presented and endorsed by the Executive Committee in the first place.

---

1. J. Reginald Campbell, "Does Technology Deliver?" *Bankers Monthly*, March 1992.

Cathay Pacific and e-business

Founded in 1946, Cathay Pacific was the flagship airline of the Hong Kong Special Administrative Region (HKSAR). It was voted the world's number two carrier by Best Airline Trans-Pacific and rated the best airline in Asia in a global poll of more than four million travellers conducted by Skytrax in the period August 2001 to March 2002. The airline offered scheduled passenger and cargo services to over 50 destinations in over 30 countries and territories and operated a fleet of more than 70 wide-body aircraft. In 2001, Cathay carried 11.3 million passengers, and turnover for the year was US$3.8 billion. It employed more than 14,000 staff worldwide.

The Company's vision was to make Cathay the most admired airline in the world. Despite the difficult operating environment in 2001, with the economic downturn and the impact of the tragic events of September 11 on the whole airline industry, Cathay remained profitable and committed to providing passengers with superior products and services. Its philosophy was to compete on product and service rather than on price. During tough times when competition was intense, Cathay thought it more important than ever to offer a premium product, to commit to product enhancements rather than cutbacks. During the year, Cathay launched its New Business Class, which featured one of the longest and widest stretch-flat seats in the sky, an exclusive bar and reception area for passengers to meet and mingle inflight, and a private dressing room. It was also the only airline in the world to offer an onboard high-speed data network for in-flight email.

In October 2000, just before the economic downturn, Philip Chen, Cathay's Director and Chief Operating Officer, announced Cathay's intention to invest US$256 million over three years in Internet-related technologies to fulfil the vision to be Asia's leading e-business airline. Over 30 projects were identified, including a new flagship Website, a new cargo Website, an online travel exchange and an investment in an aviation e-marketplace, Aeroxchange, jointly with 12 other international carriers. The projects were grouped into five areas: Passenger, Cargo, Procurement, CX team (helping staff to increase productivity and acquire new skills) and Future Opportunities. A dedicated e-Business Programme Office was established to direct the airline's e-business projects.

Through these projects, Cathay expected to generate a substantial increase in revenue and achieve significant cost savings. e-Business was expected to reduce total expenditure by more than US$30 million a year by 2003.[2] Most of the savings were expected to come from online purchasing, including a substantial reduction in inventory and its carrying costs. The Executive Committee made it clear at the outset that the over-riding goal was to improve efficiency rather than to cut staffing.

Procurement at Cathay prior to adopting CXeBuy

The procurement system and process

Procurement was broadly divided between non-technical and technical goods and services. Technical goods referred to items such as aircraft equipment and spare parts, including powerplants as well as maintenance and engineering services. Non-technical goods included such items as office supplies, in-flight consumables, information technology, fuel and marketing services. Prior to implementing CXeBuy, all paper-based purchase orders were raised by a system called Engineering Maintenance

---

2. M. Rosario, "Cathay Pacific implements e-procurement initiative", *New Straits Times Press (Malaysia) Berhad*, 20 May 2001.

Planning and Control System (EMPACS). EMPACS also acted as the inventory management system. It had originally been conceived 25 years earlier and evolved as an in-house system through the years. It was used primarily for acquisitions of technical goods purchased through purchase orders (POs) sent either by fax, mail or more recently the EDI Spec 2000 format. EDI Spec 2000 was an electronic data interchange (EDI) format approved by the Air Transport Association (ATA) for use by the airline and aerospace industry to satisfy the specific needs of parts tracking and approval within a regulatory framework. The system also started to be used in the mid-1970s for raising purchase orders and managing the inventory of non-technical items.

Prior to the implementation of CXeBuy, there were 750 suppliers of non-technical goods and services worldwide on EMPACS and a wide variety of requisitioning processes and purchase order approval processes in operation. Some categories of spend relied heavily on paper-based processes while others were stand-alone-system based workflows. (See Exhibit 1 for an example of the purchasing process for an Inflight Services stock item using EMPACS.)

An Electronic Inventory Reporting system (EIR) retrieved information from EMPACS for reviewing stock quantities. Requisitioning staff used information contained in EIR to determine which items required replenishment and to calculate the quantities to be ordered.

Unit charges incurred by aircraft, such as fuel, landing and deplaning, were captured in the Flight Operation Data System (FACTS). The Accounts Payable Purchase Order (APPO) system would gather data from FACTS and match the individual charges with the invoice entries. Once verified, FACTS would send an electronic instruction to the Financial Management Information System (FMIS) to trigger

Exhibit 1 Example of purchasing process flow prior to CXeBUY inflight services department

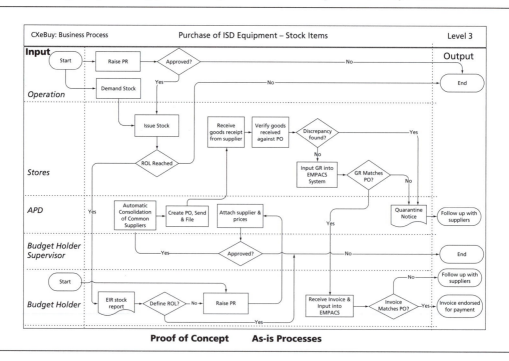

payment to suppliers and various airport and government authorities.

To process payments and general bookkeeping activities, FMIS carried supplier address and billing information. Whenever new suppliers were added or their details changed, this information was manually keyed into both EMPACS and FMIS.

FMIS in turn drew information from the SHARE database, which housed the common exchange rates information that many departments needed to use during the course of their business operations. These included, for example, inter-airline billing rates as agreed with other airlines and exchange rates in settling invoices raised by overseas suppliers. The exchange rate to be used for each business transaction with an overseas supplier or partner was contractually specified. Hence SHARE held many different exchange rate tables for the same period at any one time. Up to five or six years listing of exchange rates were kept in SHARE. The advantages of having access to a common database were: (1) resources were not wasted in building and maintaining such data sources for each department; and (2) there was consistency in the data extracted and used.

The role of the airline purchasing department

The Airline Purchasing Department (APD) came into being in 1996 and consisted of about 50 staff who served the five major user departments and respective spend categories: Marketing, Fuel Services, Information Technology, Ground Services and Inflight Services. They held commercial responsibility for all non-technical purchases including the sourcing of goods, negotiating supply agreements, and, in some cases, even the placing of orders. Prior to CxeBuy, an authorised Inflight Services user would typically requisition items such as napkins or inflight blankets by sending a paper requisition via fax or e-mail to a colleague in

APD who was responsible for handling procurement for the Inflight Services Department. The APD staff would then identify an appropriate supplier, enter the information into EMPACS and generate a purchase order that was printed through the IBM mainframe located at Quarry Bay, 20 km away from Cathay's head office at Cathay City near Hong Kong International Airport. Every few days a batch of purchase orders would be physically transported from Quarry Bay to Cathay City, where they would then be distributed to various department managers for approval to purchase. Bearing in mind that purchases of different values required different levels of authorisation, the approval process in itself could take a few days. There could be as many as seven approval, validation and distribution steps. Once approved, the purchase order would be mailed or faxed to the supplier. The long procurement cycle meant that significant lead times were necessary for making purchases, and inventory had to be maintained at a high level. Within the Inflight Services Department alone, the value of inventory held within the central stores was around US$3 million. The responsibility for managing inventory was left to the user departments, who were also the budget holders.

In the case of generic-type goods such as office supplies, goods were received centrally for checking and distribution to user departments and payment to the supplier was instructed by APD through the FMIS.

CXeBuy

Expected benefits

Central to achieving Cathay's e-business vision was the impetus to apply Internet-based tools to building the most efficient purchasing process and capability in the industry. CXeBuy was the first Oracle Internet Procurement (OIP) solution ever implemented by Oracle for an airline. As such, the project commanded the utmost attention of both Oracle and Cathay staff. OIP was adopted to streamline and enhance the procurement process for the non-technical spend categories, providing better spend and supplier information, and providing access to new suppliers through electronic marketplaces. It was anticipated that CXeBuy would help Cathay to better manage and control its expenditures, and to reduce the cost of purchasing and of goods purchased. In other words, it would strengthen Cathay's position and leverage its purchasing power as a procurer of a variety of supply items across the globe. Predicted savings in operating expenses were estimated at around US$38 million per year, of which inventory reduction would contribute US$10 million.[3] CXeBuy was expected to handle between 35 and 50 per cent of Cathay's non-technical purchases, which accounted for approximately US$385 million in 2000. In effect, this meant taking the non-technical procurement out of EMPACS and

standardising and simplifying the airline's procurement ("req-to-cheque") processes across five spend categories and departments. In this way, Cathay would be able to leverage its corporate buying power and suppliers would benefit from a more efficient and integrated requisition-to-payment process. CXeBuy would also provide improved information on company-wide expenditure and supplier performance for better corporate management decision making. (See Exhibit 2 for a summary of the expected benefits and Exhibit 3 for a summary of the system requirements.)

Interfaces with new and existing systems were planned. CXeBuy, as an e-procurement system, lacked the inventory management function that was previously supported by EMPACS. While EMPACS itself was to be replaced by a new engineering procurement and planning system called Ultramain, it was necessary to identify a suitable inventory management system with which CXeBuy could be integrated to. Using Ultramain was an option but it was

Exhibit 2 Project benefits

The benefits of the project were identified as follows:

For APD
● Improved supplier and spend information
● A more efficient supplier sourcing process that generates added value
● Reduced "Request for Proposals" and "Request for Information" costs
● Increased market visibility.

For user departments
● Easier to use
● More product information in a more accessible format
● Customised product and supplier information to meet individual and departmental requirements
● Faster order fulfilment.

For suppliers
● Easier and direct access to Cathay buyers
● Lower cost of sales
● Access to new markets
● A more efficient order-handling process.

3. "Cathay eyes big saving with Oracle", Joseph Lo, *South China Morning Post*, 3 April 2001.

Exhibit 3 Extracts from the summary of system requirements

Catalogue
- The system needs to be able to display and enable purchase of products from multiple suppliers
- It needs to have a search engine for finding the required catalogues

Requisition
- The system should support the automated requisitioning process for:

  (i) Direct purchase order to supplier
  (ii) Inventory request to Cathay's inventory system
  (iii) Electronic requisition forms for non-catalogue items

- It should allow requisitioning of multiple items from multiple suppliers for multiple delivery addresses with multiple currencies
- It should provide the requisitioner with an update on the status of the requisition
- If the line amount is over the requisitioner's limit, the requisition will be auto-forwarded to approver

Purchasing limits
- It should be able to restrict certain individual employees or groups of employees from buying specified products

Approval and review
- It should allow the approver to justify or reject a requisition
- It should be able to route a requisition to multi-level or different approvers based on the line amount or product
- It should allow the approver to delegate the authority to another person or to re-assign it to another approver for specific tasks/projects or a specific time period
- It should be able to route the requisition to the next-level approver after a pre-defined time period had lapsed

Contract management
- It should automatically notify the budget holder/buyer when a supplier contract expires
- A contract filtering function is necessary to allow Cathay managers to limit the products that a specific department within the Company can see

e-Commerce with suppliers
- The system should be able to automatically trigger and send a "delivery reminder" to suppliers for items that are outstanding (i.e. unfulfilled orders/items)
- It should automatically inform suppliers of any discrepancies on receipt against orders via electronic means

Access control
- The system should be linked to the Cathay corporate network (Novell) to verify a user's password

---

considered too complex an integration to undertake. At the end of 2001, CXeBuy was integrated with EMPACS. CXeBuy was also connected with the existing back-office finance and planning systems (APPO and FMIS) and Cathay's management information systems.

External systems integration with e-marketplaces was also anticipated and this was a significant motivating factor for the whole CXeBuy initiative. The Oracle platform was chosen to a large extent because other immediately identifiable vertical and horizontal e-marketplaces that Cathay wanted to connect with were also using an Oracle platform. Sharing a common technology platform provided the foundation for future connectivity. Cathay's ultimate objective was to get the suppliers who were supporting CXeBuy to eventually move onto the e-marketplaces, thus shifting the burden of maintaining an electronic catalogue from Cathay to the e-marketplaces.

Implementation

CXeBuy was implemented in three phases over 14 months, starting with the pilot rollout in October 2000, to validate the CXeBuy model for adoption by the airline's business units across the board. The scope of the pilot project was defined and the key stakeholders (appropriate APD staff, a selection of suppliers and a selection of users) were identified. The OIP solution needed to be configured to meet Cathay's requirements on the corporate, departmental and outport levels. Ten weeks later, the second phase began with a configured and parameterised solution for access by over 100 Hong Kong-based users and a larger supplier base. March 2001 saw the operation of the system on a production basis. Phase 3 concentrated on ramping up the number of suppliers on CXeBuy and on its full integration with other Cathay systems.

Through the processes of customisation and parameterisation, a number of issues had to be resolved:

1 Streamlining the number of suppliers: The PSC, led by Robert Lamoureux, saw an opportunity to rationalise the number of suppliers to be carried over from EMPACS. Following a time-consuming exercise of identifying all the non-technical goods suppliers and the goods they each supplied, decisions had to be made to forgo supplier relationships with those that were of less value in terms of the range of product offerings and price differentiation. A multi-dimension priority selection framework was used to assess and prioritise those suppliers, products and user departments that were favourable to CXeBuy adoption, and efforts were concentrated on these suppliers in the first two phases. Only 400 suppliers were carried over to CXeBuy, all of which had contractual supply agreements with Cathay.

2 Cataloguing: Once the suppliers were selected, a supplier adoption programme was introduced to prepare them for the move to the electronic platform. Through the three implementation phases, 400 electronic catalogues were created for the system. Over 4000 items were available through the catalogues by the end of 2001. Cataloguing removed the ambiguities over part standards and item definitions, for example. Furthermore, contractual details such as product specifications and, where relevant, even drawings or pictures, were built into the electronic catalogues.

Catalogues could be hosted by CXeBuy, suppliers or e-marketplaces, such as MartPOWER, for generic non-aviation supply items.[4] Terms for maintenance of the catalogues had to be negotiated with suppliers and the e-marketplaces and these included, for example, the frequency of updating catalogues.

3 Incorporating the spend authorisation protocol: Clarification with all the heads of department was necessary to confirm the business requirements for the new system in terms of who would have access to the system, what information and which catalogues they would have access to, spend limits and authorisation structure. Such information had to be programmed into CXeBuy to ensure that the requisition-to-payment process could be electronically executed in an efficient and timely manner. Where the value of a purchase was within the user's expenditure limit, the order was sent directly to the supplier. If the expenditure limit was exceeded, the order was sent to the manager with the appropriate authorisation level via e-mail with a hotlink attachment that would take the recipient into the CXeBuy system to view the order before approving it electronically. In the majority of instances,

---

4. MartPOWER was an online collaborative environment that allowed buyers and suppliers to come together to conduct business over the Internet through spot purchases, forward auctions, reverse auctions, catalogue searches and online inquiries.

the purchase approval and validation steps were reduced from seven to two, leading to significant process efficiencies.

For those spend categories that were procured through CXeBuy, users could buy only from the authorised suppliers, although some degree of flexibility was built into the system to allow for the procurement of non-catalogued items. A request for a non-catalogued item would be sent to APD, which would carry out the appropriate sourcing process, identify the appropriate supplier and order the item through CXeBuy. CXeBuy significantly reduced if not eliminated the level of maverick spend that used to take place when users would directly purchase items such as PC software or mobile phones using their company credit cards.

4 Business Process Reengineering (BPR) of procurement practices: A BPR Team first took on the time-consuming task of collating purchasing intelligence data to assess actual spend by department or user. After validating the spend data, the BPR team mapped out the "As-is Ordering Processes" for all five spend categories. The ordering and re-stocking processes were different not only between categories, but also sometimes between items within the same category. Hence, following an intensive round of meetings with each of the users, the team was able to sketch the various processes and sub-process flows to identify the commonalities and redundancies in the processes as well as the various points of interaction between EMPACS and the other information systems. With this information, the Team set about designing and developing new business processes with the various user groups, identifying the system and process improvement opportunities. These new processes based on CXeBuy were known as the "To-be Ordering Processes". Working closely with the Change Management team, issues such as lack of clarity or

understanding of the project's purpose and objectives were tackled. Questions such as, "What's in it for me?" and "How will it affect my job?" were also addressed by the Change Management team through a series of departmental focus groups to win support from the users. Users were made aware of the changes in the procurement tasks that they were each responsible for, based on a very detailed process flow analysis. Revised business processes had to be agreed with representatives from each user group. A comprehensive step-by-step training programme for users was necessary as the system was rolled out. The Change Management team handled the first series of user training using the Oracle training material. Then, Cathay Pacific Training Department (TDC) supported and funded the design and production of a Computer Based Training (CBT) programme for the long-term training support and deployment of the system. User manuals were also produced to provide clear user guidelines.

5 Systems integration: CXeBuy had to be fully integrated with EMPACS and FMIS such that the purchase requisition process could be linked with the goods-receiving and goods-payment processes (see Exhibit 4). The CXeBuy/EMPACS interface eliminated the need for catalogue searching by transferring the item identity number whose inventory level had fallen below the reorder limit to CXeBuy. Certain CXeBuy users were assigned responsibility for specific goods/items. Requisitions would be automatically created in the "to do" list of the user assigned to those goods/items. The requisition quantity was defaulted to the recommended reorder quantity programmed into the CXeBuy stock table. Stock requisition information was interfaced between CXeBuy and EMPACS daily.

The purpose of the CXeBuy/FMIS supplier interface was to enable supplier information that had already been created

Exhibit 4 Overview of CXeBUY interfaces

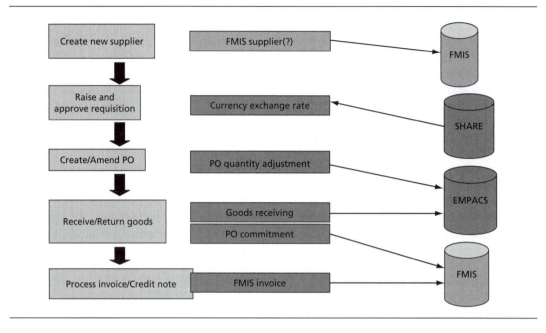

within CXeBuy to be copied automatically to FMIS to facilitate billing and bookkeeping activities. The interface allowed for daily automatic creation, deletion or modification of FMIS supplier records, thus removing a significant administrative burden.

Goods available for purchase on CXeBuy could be sourced from local or overseas suppliers and could be contracted in foreign currencies. All goods in CXeBuy were displayed in the contracted currency. To speed up the requisition approval process, all items in the shopping cart were converted and displayed in Hong Kong dollars. Once the requisition was approved, it was converted to a purchase order and issued to the supplier in the contracted currency. However, the purchase order commitment interface with FMIS took place in Hong Kong dollars. Due to the fluctuations in foreign exchange rates, it was necessary for Cathay to regularly review the rates used in the CXeBuy system conversion table. The purpose of the currency exchange rate

interface, therefore, was to allow relevant exchange rate information to be automatically transferred from SHARE to the CXeBuy exchange rate conversion table whenever these were updated.

Impact on procurement processes

The transmission of orders was electronic and required no printing, signature or manual handling. The purchasing staff in APD no longer needed to be involved in the raising of orders. The user departments could access CXeBuy directly to make their orders, thus decentralising the process and giving users greater control. APD staff time was freed up to engage in strategic sourcing and managing the performance of suppliers. The delivery of goods was made directly to the requesting department, thus removing the need for orders to be separated from distribution. As invoice matching was handled online through CXeBuy, this provided the opportunities to centralise, outsource or even remove altogether the need to process invoices. A common, core procurement process was in place with variations to accommodate the specific categories of goods and services (see Exhibits 5 and 6).

In addition to benefiting from better supplier management, APD was also able to negotiate better contract terms with suppliers for the whole airline. CXeBuy also provided a more systematic use of purchasing intelligence, that is spend and supplier performance data, resulting in more structured supplier management functions and centralisation of the accounts payable function.

In the whole of 2001, 4600 purchase orders were processed through CXeBuy. EMPACS and CXeBuy ran in parallel during that year. At the beginning of 2002, the running of parallel systems was stopped and all non-technical goods, as far as they had been transferred onto CXeBuy, were procured through CXeBuy. For the month of March

2002, 1330 purchase orders were processed through CXeBuy.

Future plans for CXeBuy

We have completed all inventoried goods and services, creating more than 400 e-catalogues. We are now moving to non-inventory contractual spend, i.e. items or services that cannot easily be itemised or catalogued and that are not normally acquired or contracted through a purchase order. We are also planning to deploy the e-procurement solution worldwide to any ports whose level of spend and number of transactions justify the deployment.

– Robert Lamoureux

Towards the end of Phase 3 the total value of procurements through CXeBuy was around US$50 million. The next stage was to identify other e-procurable goods and services, such as catering, marketing and IT goods and

Exhibit 5 Example of purchase order creation process flow using CXeBuy inflight services department

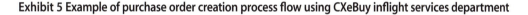

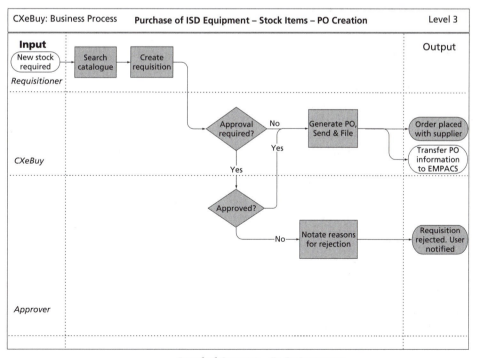

Exhibit 6 Example of goods receipt-to-pay process flow using CXeBuy inflight services department

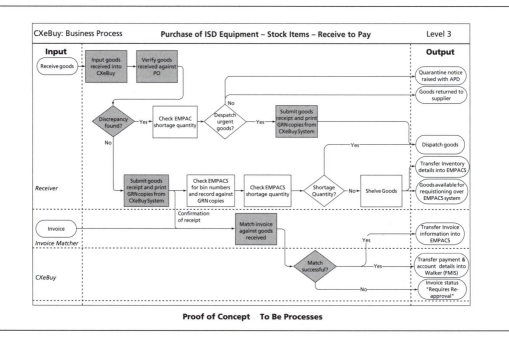

Proof of Concept   To Be Processes

services that could be adopted on the e-procurement platform. However it became clear, as the PSC began to focus on the more complicated and intangible spend items, that CXeBuy would not be an appropriate or cost-effective system for certain items, such as housing spend and government charges, that is those expenditures not contracted via a Purchase Order. Whereas at the start of the project, the PSC identified that potentially 67 per cent of Cathay's spends (after excluding fuel and maintenance & engineering spends) could benefit from CXeBuy, by March 2002 this forecast had to be scaled back considerably. Where there was no or little value to be gained from using CXeBuy, the procurement process for those services would remain unchanged. It became clear that efficiencies brought about by e-procurement had to do with the automation of requisition and the reduction of the order cycle. Significant improvements were realised where there was a high number of transactions of goods that were of relatively small value. It also became clear that the level of spend

going through CXeBuy was not necessarily an accurate measure of the success of the implementation.

The rollout of CXeBuy started in Hong Kong, where the system was deployed across different departments and spend categories. In March 2002, the global rollout commenced, with Australia identified as the first location that could benefit from adopting CXeBuy due to the potential of linking its six ports under a common purchasing process and supply base. The consolidation of its suppliers on a nationwide scale could achieve the same benefits for users, APD and suppliers that were expected from the Hong Kong rollout. With 48 outports around the world, the PSC was in the process of reviewing the cost and benefits of CXeBuy adoption at each location and was looking first at those multi-port countries where process and supply base rationalisation was most needed. Japan, with its five ports, was slated to be the next target for adoption. It also represented an opportunity to activate an OIP functionality that had never been tried before: foreign language cataloguing and ordering. In locations where spend volume was low it made little sense to carry out the deployment.

Cathay planned to further broaden its Internet procurement strategy to include participation in a number of vertical and horizontal e-marketplaces. Oracle had demonstrated marketplace connectivity, and security protocols for affecting this had been validated soon after Phase 1. Cathay decided to adopt a leading role in the definition of airline e-marketplace standards through Aeroxchange, a vertical market exchange established by 13 airlines (see Exhibit 7).[5] However, by March 2002, the exchanges (Aeroxchange and MartPOWER) had not reached the level of maturity that could support services such as the aggregation of orders. They could provide only limited visibility of airline spares and allocation at common ports, which were considered to be functions that would deliver real value to the participants. Therefore, the issue was as much to do with the technology (full airline-exchange system integration) as it was with the business value proposition.

During the implementation of CXeBuy there were intentions to build a data warehouse to bring together spends and supplier information from the three procurement systems used by Cathay (see Exhibit 8). CXeBuy provided purchasing intelligence and visibility that could be made available for analysis in a common, Company-wide database.

---

5. Cathay was a founding member of Aeroxchange, an aviation e-marketplace that could host supplier catalogues, run electronic auctions, engage in e-sourcing, provide repair management services for its 13 airline members and engage in collaborative purchases of goods/items that were specific to the industry, such as seats for airplanes. A number of e-auctions run by Aeroxchange in 2001 showed an average of 21 per cent savings on certain goods/items. Significant benefits were gained by all participating airlines through aggregated orders. 2002 was Cathay's turn to chair the executive committee of the exchange.

A new position – Manager e-Purchasing – was proposed to head up a new section within APD (see Exhibit 9). With CXeBuy up and running and in view of the longer-term strategy of using supplier-hosted and marketplace-hosted catalogues, the PSC saw the need for a Content Administration and Catalogue Aggregation team. Other support functions on the technical and systems side were also required.

Project costs

At its peak there were 27 people working full-time on the CXeBuy implementation project, of whom 19 were external IT (Oracle) specialists and management consultants. The core group consisted of eight Cathay staff, paired with eight staff from PricewaterhouseCoopers, providing the management consulting and process design expertise for the project. Three Oracle staff were stationed at Cathay City for almost nine months for system development and configuration.

e-Procurement valuation

The impetus

The call for a valuation of CXeBuy came from the PSC, which actually had two Cathay Pacific Airways Executive Board members sitting on it, Ian Riddell, Director of IT, and Tony Tyler, Director of Corporate Development. Surrounded by frequent news of Internet-based or dot-com investments and ventures that had gone wrong, there was a genuine concern about whether the CXeBuy project was taking the airline in the right direction and that measurable benefits had been realised to justify its expenditure to date. Like all other capital investment projects at Cathay, ranging from the construction of the Cathay City head office to the implementation of its Intranet, the Expenditure Control Committee (ECC) chaired by Philip Chen would review the achievements of each project to ensure that targets had been met. A similar kind of

Exhibit 7 Proposed common gateway to aeroxchange

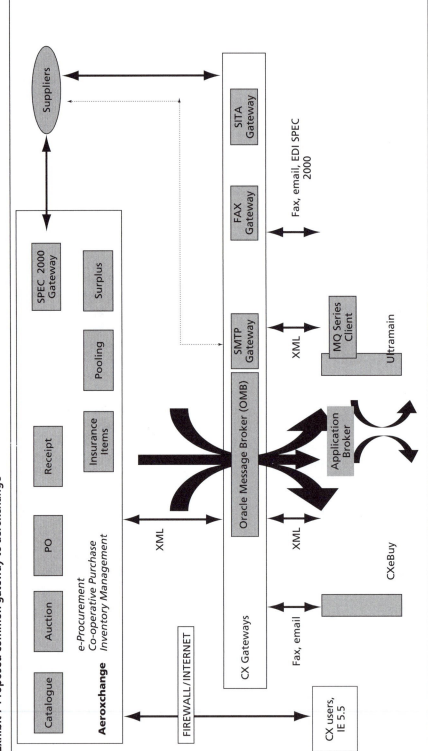

Exhibit 8 Potential for data warehousing

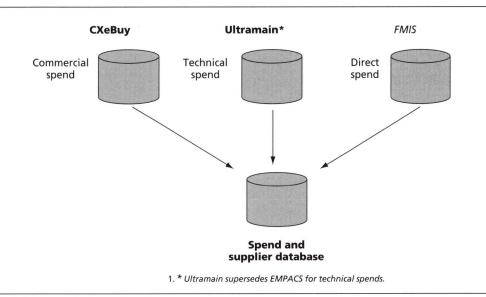

1. * *Ultramain supersedes EMPACS for technical spends.*

assessment was expected of the CXeBuy project as it had been through the rigours of the ECC approval process twice already during the proof-of-concept and rollout phases.

The PSC generally welcomed the idea of a valuation exercise, mainly because it would help the user departments to identify the areas of savings and encourage them to redeploy their resources accordingly to fully benefit from CXeBuy. It was also felt that there was a surplus of low-level, administrative staff in many areas now that the req-to-cheque process was synchronised

onto the Internet platform. However, neither the APD nor the PSC was prepared to take charge of the valuation exercise as the consequences or the need to act on results was clearly the responsibility of the business units. Rumours were already spreading among staff across the departments that, in view of the deepening recession and the tragic events of September 11, this could turn out to be a staff-cutting exercise. Robert felt that it was not the Project Team's mandate to tackle such issues and that it was beyond the scope of the PSC, which was simply to implement an e-procurement system successfully. Other

Exhibit 9 The new e-purchasing team in APD

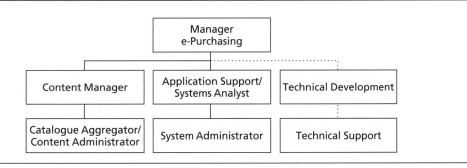

concerns related to the timing of such a valuation, what should be measured and how, and the usefulness of the information collected, were all challenged.

Just a matter of timing?

Some PSC members wanted some hard figures to show the beneficial impact of CXeBuy on Cathay's operations. Others thought that it would be premature to carry out such a valuation. To look at just the immediate benefits (and costs) of CXeBuy would not present a realistic assessment of the longer-term value of Cathay's new e-procurement strategy. While the system was operational, the implementation was by no means complete. The implementation team was still in the process of identifying and transferring onto the system some of the more complex spend items, including other categories that would benefit from being procured electronically. The airline was also in the process of rolling out CXeBuy to its outports worldwide where deployment was warranted.

From a corporate perspective, CXeBuy was one of the first in a number of other e-business initiatives that the airline was pursuing. Within the purchasing function alone, other systems and applications would be brought into play in the near future, notably the new procurement system for technical spends called Ultramain (EMPACS's replacement) and potentially a new electronic sourcing application. The benefits to be gained from all this would include the purchasing intelligence that could be aggregated and analysed into appropriate reporting formats, which would allow for a birds-eye view of spend behaviour, major expense categories, supplier performance and the like. From this perspective, CXeBuy was simply one of the infrastructure systems that would have to be in place to affect Cathay's e-business strategy. Therefore, how could a value be attached to CXeBuy's impact on Cathay's overall corporate strategy to turn the airline into Asia's leading e-business airline?

It was not intended for e-procurement at Cathay to stop with the implementation of CXeBuy. The PSC had clearly stated to the Executive Committee the value of e-marketplaces, such as MartPOWER and Aeroxchange, as well as the potential of adopting an e-sourcing strategy for the airline. CXeBuy had to be viewed as a vehicle automating requisition and ordering as well as meeting the internal systems requirements that would enable integration with external exchanges in the future. By March 2002, integration with external exchanges had been achieved. However, it would take some time before a substantial user and supplier base could be established to reap the full benefits. Aeroxchange had recently achieved a 30 per cent cost saving on a recent aggregation, with four other airlines, of orders for blankets. The potential to realise greater savings was immense.

Measuring what?

The impact of CXeBuy adoption on Cathay's business operation extended beyond the APD to its various business units and other departments. There was a general consensus among APD staff and the PSC that the system had contributed to improved performance, faster response times and additional functionality, as supported by a one-off valuation exercise on one item (napkins) that was regularly purchased by the Inflight Services Department (ISD) (see Exhibit 10). The process, which would normally take 22 steps, took only seven steps using CXeBuy. The step-by-step transaction cost reduction exercise had to take into account the level or grade of the staff performing each task (and their corresponding average pay) and the length of time it took to complete each task (which could also vary depending on the job ranking of the staff performing each task). From this exercise, the total amount of time required to procure napkins using CXeBuy was found to be 44 minutes. However, this

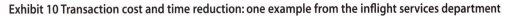

Exhibit 10 Transaction cost and time reduction: one example from the inflight services department

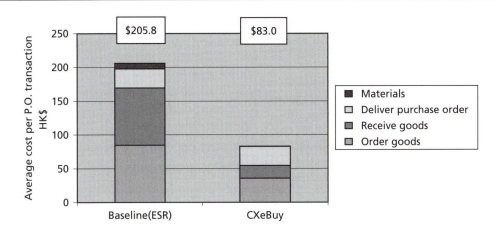

Average Time Per P.O. Transaction

Average activity time is estimated based on the observations conducted by the BPR team under a testing environment.

Transaction steps	Baseline (ESR) Minutes	CXeBuy Minutes	% of PO	Ave minutes
Complete ESR form	15	6	100	6.0
Fill request	15	10	20	5.0
Process purchase order	15	3	100	8.0
Prepare packaging of order	10	10	50	5.0
Deliver order	30	0	100	0.0
Check and sign-off of delivery	5	5	100	5.0
Process invoice/filing	10	5	100	10.0
Process payment	5	5	100	5.0
Totals	105			44.0

could not be translated to 61 minutes of savings in one person's time as a number of staff would have contributed to the procurement process. Neither could this result be applied across the board. Although CXeBuy had streamlined the vast array of procurement processes, the procurement steps were not identical. Some goods, notably computer hardware and software, were more complex due to the technical requirements set by the Information Management Department (IM). Therefore,

the savings in terms of process efficiency in IM were not as high as in ISD, for example. There were many more non-catalogued items to handle for IM. Even with the catalogued items, much more time was required to maintain and manage the catalogue to keep it up-to-date, as systems and software upgrades were frequent.

There were also other benefits that would prove difficult if not impossible to measure in monetary terms. For example, many of the users had commented on its ease of use and the automation of the requisition authorisation process as factors that had contributed to greater job satisfaction. How could these be measured? These were points that had to be made known to the Executive Committee.

Robert knew that the task of measuring and quantifying all the benefits and savings gained through CXeBuy would be a challenge. In focusing on the tangible benefits, Robert came across an article issued by the *AberdeenGroup* in March 2001 entitled "e-Procurement: Finally Ready for Prime Time".[6] The article identified six key business benefits that had been quoted as justification for adopting an e-procurement system. These were:

1 reduced procurement administration costs;

2 improved information intelligence for reporting purposes;

3 improved compliance with corporate spend policies and supplier contracts;

4 shortened req-to-cheque cycles;

5 strengthened negotiating muscle with suppliers; and

6 freeing-up of purchasing staff to engage in strategic tasks.

Robert could identify with all six points as benefits that had been realised through CXeBuy. But how could the full extent of these benefits be measured and quantified without turning the task into a tedious academic exercise?

Methodologies

His suggestion to the PSC was to provide user departments with a methodology that could help them to measure and quantify the benefits and savings as they related to the procurement functions handled by their departments. For starters, he decided on the following approach in designing the methodology:

- identify the relevant benefits measures, according to the six points defined by the *AberdeenGroup*;

- agree on the capture mechanisms and targets with APD managers and CXeBuy user departments;

- carry out data capture; and

- analyse the results.

He thought that this self-measurement proposal would satisfy all PSC members, both those who were for and those who were against benefits measurement at this stage. It would be up to the user departments to adopt the given methodology to evaluate the benefits and savings they had achieved through CXeBuy. They would then be able to use the results to assess the need for redeployment of resources and/or restructuring of their departments for greater efficiency. He felt that this would instil a sense of accountability in the department heads and relieve the implementation team of a task that they were not mandated to perform in the first place.

Some members of the PSC still objected to this approach as it would create an administrative burden on the user departments. The transaction cost reduction exercise using the napkin example had proved this point. To apply metrics for assessing the "before and after" impact of CXeBuy on all the various procurement processes would take a considerable amount of management time and could turn into an academic exercise that no one wanted to take charge of. Staff would view the exercise as a threat to their job security, and seeking their co-operation in collecting data could prove to be difficult or otherwise result in data inaccuracies. Furthermore, the value in carrying out such an exercise was questioned. By allowing departments to

---

6. "e-Procurement: finally ready for prime time", *AberdeenGroup*, vol. 14, no. 2, 21 March 2001.

adopt the methodology voluntarily, the data and results would only be useful for the respective departments to fine-tune their procurement process. There could be no aggregation of cost savings for the whole company, for example.

Robert's suggestion was insufficient for meeting the requirements set by some members of the PSC. They wanted to know how, in the broader scheme of Cathay's e-business strategy, the CXeBuy project fared. More specifically, questions were asked about the return on investment, whether the project served Cathay's strategic mission to be Asia's leading e-business airline, and the aggregated cost savings of all the user departments as a result of CXeBuy. Lee Tak Ming, a member of the PSC, suggested using the Balanced Scorecard technique to look at the performance of CXeBuy against enterprise, project and process level targets. Scorecard objectives and performance measures would have to be designed to assess:

- *Financial gains*: cost reductions (i.e. staffing, inventory, etc.)
- *User satisfaction*: reduced time engaged in routine and often mundane tasks, better time management and greater control over the working environment
- Procurement process alignment with overall business objectives
- Future potential for improvements, value creation and adaptability to change.

Objections were also raised against the Balanced Scorecard approach. Robert viewed CXeBuy as a tool to speed up and, where possible, automate the requisition and ordering process for improving tactical procurement and providing the required spend and supplier management intelligence for strategic procurement. He argued that the level of analysis should be at the process level where the benefits and savings were immediately apparent. Falling short of designing a methodology along the six key business benefits, he began to toy with the idea of drafting a report to the PSC explaining the shortcomings of a valuation exercise. He argued that CXeBuy should not be assessed as a stand-alone system, and that the timing of such an exercise could generate inaccurate results that would not serve any meaningful purpose and could pose a risk to the smooth global deployment of the solution.

Pauline Ng prepared this case under the supervision of Dr Ali Farhoomand for class discussion. This case is not intended to show effective or ineffective handling of decision or business processes.

With Cathay Pacific's consent, pages 1, 2 and 8–11 contain fabricated information to stimulate case discussion only.

e-Business infrastructure development

e-Business infrastructure: the building blocks

Objectives

❑ To establish the importance of e-business infrastructure

❑ To place e-business infrastructure in the context of evolving enterprise technologies

❑ To gain an understanding of the building blocks of e-business infrastructure

❑ To explore how Internet technology is being leveraged by e-business vendors

❑ To establish how emerging technologies can enhance competitive advantage

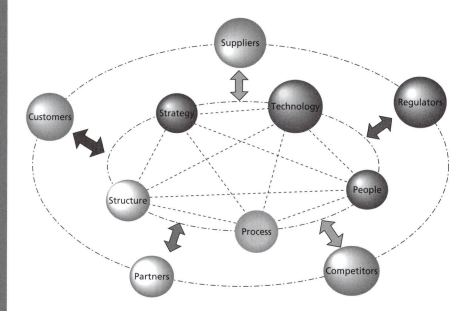

> In the early days, top IT executives were primarily technically oriented, concerned with computer capacity planning, and used such terms as "million instructions per second," and "megabytes of memory." That is what they tracked and focused on, something few executives outside of IT understood or cared about.
>   – Paul Strassmann, President of the Information Economics Press[1]

---

1. Strassmann and Bienkowski (2001).

Following our discussion of *structure* and *strategy* in Part 1, we shift our attention now to the *technology* issues in the DOT framework. The function of this chapter is to establish the need for senior management involvement in strategic decisions relating to development of the organization's e-business infrastructure. We present the material with a view to making it accessible to a non-technical audience. The chapter begins with a historical overview of the major advances in organizational computing – from the mainframe-computing environment of the 1960s to the expansion of the computing function beyond organizational boundaries, made possible with the advent of Internet open protocols.

After placing the development of infrastructure in historical context, we will examine the building blocks of an e-business infrastructure from a participant viewpoint of how they relate to an enterprise's core functions and processes. To better understand the interrelationships between information technology (IT), end users and the larger issue of enterprise management, we undertake an examination of what is meant by infrastructure and more precisely, those aspects of infrastructure foregrounded in the context of e-business transformation.

In this chapter you will learn about the key components of e-business infrastructure: enterprise resource planning (ERP) – the transactional backbone supporting the enterprise – and the applications and technologies which help an enterprise manage its relationships with customers, suppliers and internal employees. These important building blocks are represented within an e-business components pyramid that will offer a conceptual representation of what constitutes an e-business "infrastructure". This chapter establishes the groundwork for the material that follows in the next chapter: integration, standards and security. Throughout the chapter we place emphasis on a managerial perspective through which to view and evaluate options and opportunities.

Innovation and solutions to the problems of e-business crop up at a bewildering pace. Traditionally, faced with a rapid pace of technological change and an overwhelmingly complex vendor landscape the senior management let the burden of infrastructure decisions fall squarely on the shoulders of IT staff. With the transformation of modern enterprises towards e-business models, however, IT has been employed strategically in a firm's dealings with customers, partners, suppliers and regulatory bodies.

As modern enterprises make the transformation into e-businesses, success is largely determined by infrastructure performance. This is the simple reality dawning on managing executives who now find that traditionally "technical matters" have a direct strategic impact on many business issues. No longer can company executives afford to delegate decision-making on crucial infrastructure investments to IT people without thoughtful consideration of measurement and accountability issues. Nor can blind faith be placed in external consultants telling executives in various industries what percentage of revenue should be spent on their firms' computing function in order to remain profitable.

To oversee the successful implementation of an e-business initiative, it is important for the top management to be involved in charting the course of a firm's infrastructure. IT spending is the largest capital expense in many organizations and budgeted funds have been rising, even in industries where IT spending has traditionally not been as substantial. Notwithstanding weak economic conditions, companies still spend on IT initiatives when they can cost justify direct savings related to purchasing, the supply chain or overall growth as a result of customer management applications. The economic downturn of the early 2000s actually led to a spike in the outsourcing segment[2] – particularly with respect to infrastructure services, as companies wary of new spending, nevertheless recognized the long-term importance of infrastructure in realizing their e-business ambitions.

The IDG group's CXO Media reports that IT executives devote an average of nearly one full day each week to brush up on their professional knowledge – relying on industry publications, business journals and communication with their peers in the field.[3] Obviously, it is neither practical nor advisable for executives with responsibility over the functional range of their companies to devote this amount of time to understanding the minutiae of e-business technology.

In the light of the strategic importance of e-business to many firms a firm's senior executives should be versed in the many aspects of infrastructure at three levels. First, they should possess a concrete understanding of how the core technical issues at hand impact enterprise strategy. IT has increasingly become a strategic necessity; a commodity without which a firm's strategy will be affected. As such, top management need to understand the dynamic interplay between strategy and technology. Second, senior management need to have an adequate comprehension of the building blocks of e-business infrastructure to be able to communicate and collaborate effectively with internal technical staff as well as the myriad of external parties including vendors, consultants, and solutions providers in the IT arena. Third and perhaps most importantly, today's decision-makers must hone their facility to recognize and exploit technological opportunities as they arise, and to strategically lay the infrastructural foundation necessary for a business environment characterised by intense competition, unpredictability and swift innovation.

Advances in organizational computing

When seeking an understanding of e-business infrastructure, it is particularly important to have a firm grasp of how the shape and character of organizational computing has evolved over years. In this section we examine the historical role that IT infrastructure has played in creating the conditions for change as well as in providing the tools necessary for change.

Mainframe computing (circa 1960s)

In the 1960s, many corporations embarked on the task of automating a number of information-intensive tasks – particularly those of a clerical nature – with the aid of newly available mainframe computers. The term "mainframe" originally referred to the main central processing unit (CPU) cabinet, but nowadays is by

---

2. Gartner Group (2001), "Downturn fails to stem IT spending", *South China Morning Post*.
3. EIU (2001).

and large used generically in reference to a large computer system. The first main-frame vendors included such companies as IBM, GE, Univac, RCA, NCR and Honeywell (IBM continues to be the market leader to this day, competing against companies such as Hitachi Data Systems, Amdahl/Fujitsu and Unisys). Programmers went about developing applications to automate routine and tedious back-office tasks relating to accounting, basic resource planning and other functions. These relatively rudimentary applications were deployed in the hopes of improving efficiency and mitigating the need for avoidable repetition within functional departments at a particular location, with access to information available only to internal employees of that unit. As the aim was purely to replicate tasks, the level of management involvement in these initiatives was minimal.

Mainframe computing dominated the business mainstream for many years, and its presence can still be felt in enterprises around the world. Mainframe computers continue to play an important role in modern information systems (IS), offering several important advantages.[4] They provide superior computing power, extreme reliability (much of the circuitry in a mainframe is designed to handle errors, which is why the mean-time between errors is often as much as 20 years) and straight-forward scalability (mainframes can be expanded by adding CPUs to a system or by adding clusters of systems). These systems, once considered highly complex, now seem very manageable. Their centralized architecture requires far less programming and maintenance expertise than today's sprawling modern enterprise networks involving diverse platforms. With the value of existing mainframe applications amounting into the trillions, it is likely that these systems will continue to play a major role in enterprise computing for some time.[5]

End-user computing (mid-1970s)

Low-cost hardware became affordable, initially in the form of minicomputers (or "minis"). Minicomputers were smaller than mainframes and available at the then astonishingly low prices, yet at times performed better than their monolithic counterparts. In the early 1980s computer users developed higher levels of computer literacy as computer manufacturers built systems to satisfy demand for greater ease of use and improved functionality. A wide variety of user-friendly software titles began to appear on the market, greatly reducing the need for custom programming.

End user computing led to improved communication between users and IS specialists – the former group became more adepts at using computer technology, while the latter gained a better understanding of business issues. With end users assuming a portion of the overall systems workload, IS specialists were able to concentrate their efforts on the maintenance and development of organizational systems. The minicomputers of this era were so well received that in the late 1970s microcomputers began appearing on the market, advancing towards the modern-day personal computer (PC).[6]

---

4. Computer Desktop Encyclopedia (2000).
5. Ibid.
6. Computers featuring small silicon integrated circuit chips called a "microprocessor".

Client/Server computing (mid-1980s)

In the 1980s, technology had become smaller and less expensive. Computer expertise was fairly widespread, end-users had become highly sophisticated and the corporate world began to experience the growing use of microcomputers to complement mainframe systems. By the mid-1980s a distinct trend had materialised towards client/server architectures. Under such a platform most of the application programs and databases are kept at the server, which acts as the supplying machine, while the PC acts as the client, requesting applications and data from the server. All the clients are connected via a local area network (LAN) or wide area network (WAN) to a server.

An important enabler of client/server computing was the timely commercial production of various Relational Database Management Systems (RDBMS) such as DB/2 from IBM and Oracle from Oracle Corporation. Relational databases eliminated the need, as was the case with the first-generation DBMSs, for complex programs to be developed for answering even simple queries. The outcome of these advances was the physical and conceptual separation of the application from the database, allowing for the decentralization of organizational computing. The essential function of the PC was not to store the needed data, but rather to act as a gateway to those data. No longer was access to information confined to a particular business division or geographical regional unit. Employees throughout an organization, irrespective of location, could now access the same information through the same applications simultaneously. As implementations grew more advanced, the client/server architecture evolved from a simple client and server to multi-tier architectures in networked environments (Figure 4.1).

Figure 4.1 Client/Server architectures

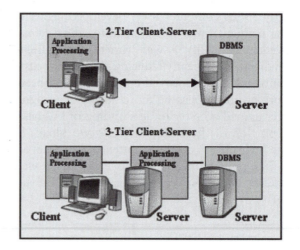

Source: Computer desktop encyclopedia (2000).

With processing divided between clients and servers, individual machines can be assigned the functions they are most suited to. The typical user interacts with the system-at-large through a graphical user interface (GUI) on the client machine. Most commonly, the database is queried by means of specially written programs which allow users to access the data they are after without any direct interaction with the DBMS, as is the case in processing of tickets at airline check-ins. The data can then be analysed as needed, updated or reported, using software packages such as spreadsheets, word processors or graphics applications on the client machine. The server machine might be a mainframe, a supercomputer or simply another desktop computer, which stores and processes shared data and may also perform back-end functions not visible to users, for example managing peripheral devices and controlling access to shared databases.

There are a number of reasons for adopting client/server architecture:

● cutting computing costs

● promoting knowledge workers' productivity

● accessing information faster

● enabling collaborative work across geographical divides

● providing a better match with flattened organizational structure.

In spite of these benefits client/server computing has several disadvantages. For instance, a specific server can get bogged down easily when too many users attempt to access a hosted service at once. Also the complexity of administering numerous PCs with independent processing power increases as the client software must be installed manually on every desktop, something which typically consumes a large portion of the total capacity of the end-user's workstation.

The client/server architecture is based on a set of communications protocols known as the Open System Interconnection (OSI) seven-layer model developed by the International Standards Organization (ISO). This protocol establishes rules governing the requests between clients and servers in the form of instruction sets accompanying all communications over a network. As the name implies the seven layers are designated to define particular aspects of how information is to be handled (Table 4.1).

e-Business (mid-1990s[7])

The Internet opened up new possibilities for transforming activities and relationships along a company's internal processes, as well as supplier, partner and

---

7. The Internet started in 1969 as the US government funded ARPAnet – a network of high-speed links between supercomputers, research and educational sites, primarily in the USA. By the 1990s, so many networks had become assimilated that the Internet gave rise to an increasing number of ventures. In 1995, large commercial Internet service providers (ISPs) assumed responsibility for the backbones, giving rise to the surge in Internet usage and commercial applicability.

Table 4.1 OSI seven-layer model

7	Application layer	Defines the language and syntax used to communicate between programs. Common functions at this layer include opening and closing files, obtaining directory information and email
6	Presentation layer	Negotiates and manages the way data are represented and encoded. Also used for encryption and decryption
5	Session layer	Coordinates communications and manages the dialogue between different parties. Makes sure that a request is satisfied before the next one is sent. It allows for recovery in case of failure
4	Transport layer	Is responsible for ensuring a valid end-to-end transmission. It detects if a data packet is lost somewhere along the network and ensures that files are received in their entirety
3	Network layer	Routes data from one node to another. The functionality of this layer is only required when stations exist on separate segments of the network
2	Data Link layer	Is responsible for the physical passing of data from one node to another by means of transmitted bits, divided into frames
1	Physical layer	Is responsible for managing data on and off the network media. This layer simply deals with the electrical and mechanical characteristics of the signalling methods

Source: International Standards Organization (2001).

customer relationships, towards the ultimate end of creating value for customers. e-Business transformation allowed companies to develop the capabilities needed to improve the flow of information and business intelligence among all their stakeholders. What made this possible is that the Internet is an open, public communications infrastructure. A company can now connect and exchange information with any customer, supplier or partner without the need for establishing and maintaining costly proprietary networks.

The Internet is founded on the de facto Transmission Control Protocol/Internet Protocol (TCP/IP Protocol), which was developed to connect dissimilar systems. Under TCIP/IP, layers 5 through 7 of the OSI model are combined into one application layer (It is also important to realise that the physical and data link layers do not pertain to TCP/IP but serve as a necessary underlying base). TCP provides the transport functions, ensuring valid end-to-end transmission, while the IP part provides the routing capability. With TCP/IP, messages can be sent to multiple parties within an enterprise, or beyond company boundaries anywhere around the world as long as they possess an IP address, which is either permanently assigned or dynamically assigned after a connection has been established. The rapid expansion of the Internet can be largely attributed to this departure from proprietary protocols, which allowed a large variety of service and content providers to share the existing infrastructure: the basic phone network. Open access to the network has led to many innovations on which much of the network economy is based. As an open system, new Internet protocols are added through a process of industry consensus and can be introduced without much cost.

The Internet provides companies with many advantages. Two major ones are:

1 *Easy and customised access*: The browser is a universal access application that provides the user interface for a variety of information sources. Using Hypertext Markup Language (HTML),[8] one page at a time is displayed to the user. Protocols such as Common Gateway Interface (CGI)[9] provide further access to information from back-end databases. Although browsers provide universal access, features can be added to customise it by, for example, limiting the functionality to numerous HTML capabilities and avoiding vendor-specific add-ons.

2 *Unlimited and continuous access*: An open Internet application is accessible to anyone with a browser. This provides companies with an unparalleled degree of scalability, thus allowing them to plan for and manage fluctuating market demand. At the same time the Internet provides continuous access.

The e-business infrastructure

Before progressing to our discussion of the core components of "e-business infrastructure", let us first shed some light on what exactly is meant by the term. Infrastructure, as a term, has been identified with the mainstay hardware, software, data, networks and human resources constituting the underlying foundation of an enterprise computing utility.

e-Business infrastructure encompasses the conventional components of a system infrastructure, but the focus is increasingly on the importance of applications technology to tackle the information management issues and problems that companies have been addressing throughout modern times. e-Business, with the Internet as enabler, can be seen as a culmination of the process, which from the time of early mainframe systems has seen the emphasis shift from technology-versed humans to human-versed technology. The foundation of e-business infrastructure is vast in scope and can be represented by the remarkable amount of innovation that has been driven by the Internet in a quest for the seamless exchange of information, inside and outside the modern organization.

The e-business components pyramid (Figure 4.2) offers a conceptual representation of the components of an e-business infrastructure.

8. HTML is the document-formatting language used to define layout and hypertext links on web pages.
9. CGI scripts are compact programs written in languages such as PERL or Tcl serving as mechanisms for the Web page to interact with databases or server-based applications.

Figure 4.2 e-Business components pyramid

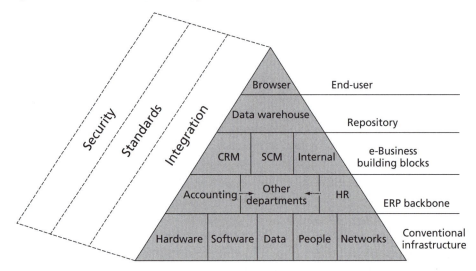

Source: Adapted from Shields (2001).

Conventional infrastructure

The conventional infrastructure, represented by the base layer of the e-business components pyramid, supports all other systems. Its composition determines how the system at large will function and how flexible it is to meet the future requirements of the enterprise. It comprises:

● *Hardware* refers to the devices and equipment that accept, process, display or broadcast data. Hardware is designed to accommodate certain instruction sets (the machine language instructions that tell it what to do). Typical examples of hardware include processors, modems, keyboards, monitors and printers. The hardware can only be as effective as the instructions it receives.

● *Software* refers to instructions for the hardware on how data should be processed. Sets of instructions designed to accomplish certain tasks are referred to as programs. There are two major categories: system software and application software. System software refers to programs that manage processes related to the computer operations. It includes programs such as the Basic Input Output System (BIOS) and the operating system (OS), which serve as an intermediary between hardware and application programs. Application software refers to the programs that process data for the user, within the capabilities of the systems software. Examples include word processors, presentation packages and electronic mail.

● *Data* are the raw facts, figures and descriptions that are processed into information. Data are stored and classified within database systems. A database is a set of logically related files that are created and managed by a Database

Management System (DBMS), which makes the data accessible to various programs. Databases have now grown in sophistication to accommodate virtually any form of digital data, including text, graphics, sound and video.

- *Networks* are the linkages, comprised of software, cables, and related hardware that transmit data among users. The providers of access networks fall under four categories: telecom, cable, wireless and computer-based online information services. The main network classification includes local area networks (LANs) which connect two or more devices within 2000 ft, and wide area networks (WANs) which encompass network connections surpassing that range. Value-added networks are third-party managed WANs, that provide additional services such as error-detection, message storing and protocol conversion. Virtual Private Networks (VPNs) are another form of WAN, taking the shape of a private network configured within a public network. VPNs allow organizations to leverage the shared Internet infrastructure and enjoy economies of scale (discussed further in Chapter 5). Backbone networks encompass the countrywide and trans-national linkages that have been put into place over recent decades by telephone, cable and satellite companies.

- *People* are an often-overlooked component of infrastructure. Any study of infrastructure should include the people who work with the system and who enforce the procedures for working with the system.

ERP backbone

The second tier of the e-business components pyramid is the enterprise resource planning (ERP) backbone that serves departments of the enterprise. ERP systems encompass multiple parts of application software catering to the various business areas of the firm. This will be further discussed in this chapter and covered extensively in Chapter 6.

e-Business building blocks

The next tier of the pyramid contains the core *e-business building blocks*, the applications technology catering to vital participants of the firm's business – customers, suppliers, partners, employees and other parties. These "building blocks" are the primary focus of this chapter. In Chapter 7 we will discuss various aspects of customer relations management, while Chapter 8 is devoted to the issues related to supply chain management.

Repository

The next tier in the pyramid is the *data warehouse* – the central repository integrating massive quantities of enterprise-wide corporate data to support management's analysis and decision-making process. A typical enterprise may possess data in a variety of databases associated with its ERP systems or e-business applications. The range of data can be expansive and is largely intended to support specific transactions. A data warehouse may be used to extract pertinent data from a variety of application-level databases and to structure it in a form that supports management queries, reporting and analysis.[10]

End-user

Finally, the browser, as we have discussed, serves as the universal application by which end-users reap the functionality offered in an e-business environment.

Enabling components

The enabling components of infrastructure (*standards, integration, security*) are represented by the sloping face of the components pyramid. These components, in addition to *payment*, are of crucial importance in realizing a secure, operational and efficient e-business environment. They will be our focus in Chapter 5.

The advent of client/server computing and later ERP platforms lowered barriers between business units within the enterprise. But the options available for achieving this level of integration outside of company boundaries had previously been impractical and limited to all but the largest businesses. In past times, employees were required to devise stopgap measures and procedures to tackle the many disconnects that typically occur in the flow of information, not only within the enterprise but involving customers, partners, suppliers and regulatory organizations. These included resorting to old-fashioned legwork, word of mouth, telephones, fax machines, macros and various tools.

Before the Internet became a factor in the corporate realm, the only possibility for establishing the automated exchange of information with external organizations was through electronic data interchange (EDI), the direct computer-to-computer communication of business transactions such as orders and invoices. The operation of EDI is highly structured, requiring proprietary networks and applications. While the possibilities for lowering costs and accelerating order cycles are significant, the price tag for implementing EDI has been prohibitively high for many organizations, especially small and medium enterprises (SME). The advent of the Internet has allowed information architects to circumvent the need to establish traditional EDI by exploiting the public infrastructure and employing open standards such as XML (see Chapter 5).

Core e-business applications

Our focus in the remainder of this chapter will be on the ERP backbone and e-business building blocks tiers of infrastructure. We will examine key e-business applications and technologies that relate to the essential relationships of the enterprise. Appendix 1 provides an accompanying discussion of the impact

---

10. Shields (2001).

that wireless technologies are having on e-business. We begin here by providing an introduction to some major trends in the applications arena that are having a profound impact on the working relationship between a company and three major stakeholder groups: customers, suppliers and internal employees. With respect to all three, we have witnessed a fundamental shift from applications geared to performing particular functions to more ambitious offerings developed to manage an enterprise's relationships from end-to-end. This is in keeping with the ultimate e-business ideal of establishing a seamless flow of information within and outside the firm towards the goal of creating customer value.

ERP: integrating enterprise resources

The business climate of the 1980s was characterized by ageing legacy systems, rising customer expectations, increasing globalization of operations and mounting administrative complexity. This in turn resulted in immense demand for ERP packages from organizations seeking tighter integration along their internal value chains and managers asking for real-time information and greater control over internal operations. ERP rose to prominence through the offerings of vendors such as SAP, Baan, Oracle, J.D. Edwards and Peoplesoft. Because of the complexities associated with implementing such systems, a bevy of consulting specialists also benefited by providing expertise necessary for the analysis, customization, implementation and maintenance of these systems.

ERP evolved from applications used in the manufacturing industry, typically called Materials Resource Planning (MRP). It was widely seen as a major advance towards the goal of streamlining the flow of reliable information and integrating the internal transactions that take place throughout an organization. ERP systems standardize the data relating to an enterprise's business processes, thereby generating useful information in support of decisions made at all levels of the business. When an action occurs at some point in the internal value chain, information is dispersed throughout the system and the resulting effect on other areas of the business is automatically determined. For example, the sale of a unit will result in the necessary updates to information pertaining to relevant departments and processes such as manufacturing (scheduling), human resources (sales commissions), warehouse (procurement planning), accounting (accounts receivable and general ledger) and so forth.

The decision to implement ERP is not one to be taken lightly, as it can easily require an investment of millions for a central application. More importantly, it usually entails redesign of many business processes, with likely disturbances to established methods and corporate culture and legacy. Indeed, there have been well documented cases of disastrous ERP implementations, such as the one undertaken by FoxMeyer Drugs, which according to company management, led to its filing for bankruptcy protection in 1996 and a much publicized lawsuit against German software company SAP's US subsidiary, and Andersen Consulting (now Accenture).[11] FoxMeyer accused SAP – the world's

---

11. "SAP share price hit by FoxMeyer allegations", *Financial Times*, Friday, 28 August 1998.

second largest business software maker – of misrepresenting the capabilities of its R/3 software and charged Andersen of negligence in its implementation.

In the hope of broadening their position beyond that of pure information-backbone, a number of major ERP vendors have extended the functionality of their current releases to reflect the trend towards e-business. Many of the leading solutions with respect to customer, supplier and internal aspects of business relationships, however, have been developed by fast-rising vendors such as Siebel Systems and Manugistics, which have considerable expertise in these particular areas and whose offerings have special appeal in the age of e-business (see Appendix 2: Major e-business vendors). While large enterprises may have the option of developing ERP systems in-house, the great majority opt for commercial packages to limit the internal resources that must be committed to ongoing maintenance and updating. In addition, commercial ERP packages are commonly designed around industry "best practices" and this is thought to ease the transition en route to new business processes. The importance of ERP for e-business will be explored in greater detail in Chapter 6.

Customer relationship

Customer Relationship Management (CRM) has become a principal IT initiative for many businesses. In the wake of globalization, where customer satisfaction is not merely the key to success but a requirement for continued existence, the need to satisfy customer expectations has risen to the height of managerial consciousness. The global reach of the Internet and an abundance of increasingly affordable technologies have lowered traditional barriers to competition. As such, companies increasingly find it difficult to differentiate themselves solely on the basis of their products and services.

The perception a customer has of a company is largely based on the interactions that take place over the length of the relationship. This encompasses initial inquiry, sales and after-sales service among other steps that today transpire by means of a variety of communications media. It has become widely known that the cost of bringing in new customers is many times that of retaining existing ones.[12] It is then no surprise then that so many companies try to gain an edge by acquiring valuable information about the customer whenever possible in order to leave positive impressions whenever contact is established. CRM allows companies to lay the foundation necessary to meaningfully interpret the information gathered from the customer with a view to identifying and catering to the most profitable ones. Such capability allows firms to customize their offerings, thus increasing their customer retention rate by creating barriers to exit.

This intensified customer-orientation requires dramatic change to the focus of the company, and as a result, changes to the way the entire organization works. It has become all the more crucial to have accurate and timely information at the disposal of the sales team. This is especially important when there is high

---

12. Peppers and Rogers (1997).

turnover among account representatives and it is critical for new representatives to acquire expertise, establish rapport and maintain relationships with minimal inconvenience to the customer. A variety of existing technologies are increasingly converging under the "CRM" umbrella to lay claim to providing seamless, integrated solutions to managing the customer relationship activities of the firm.

Sales force automation

A class of applications, termed *Sales Force Automation* (SFA), began emerging in the late 1980s. This was in response to the need for sophisticated technological support for what has traditionally been a function heavily revolving around personal relationships. SFA software typically includes wide-ranging capabilities that correspond to the requirements and responsibilities of the account executive. Responsibility for customer accounts is generally apportioned across the sales force according to region, industry, account size, volume and various other classifications. Each account executive is typically assigned a notebook computer on which the installed SFA serves as a customer database management system for a particular territory. A regular process of "synching" with a central repository is necessary to ensure that information residing on the client and server are kept current. Through this process, generated leads can filter through to the appropriate executive's SFA. When making a sales call, representatives have at their disposal a wealth of information such as product configuration, pricing, customer sales history, contract details, contact information, maintenance records, competitive intelligence and a range of analytical tools. In addition, the SFA package might include functionality for developing proposals, report generation or for managerial users to monitor the selling cycles of those under their supervision.

The implementation of sales force automation can be highly complex and requires a fair amount of training and commitment on the part of each executive to maintain information pertaining to their customers. Very often, in the absence of necessary incentives much of these functionalities are unused while information grows outdated. Account executives may have neither inclination nor motivation to update data that are housed securely in their minds. Tighter integration of SFA with other features of CRM technology may reduce some of this burden, but the challenge will remain largely one of human dimensions.

The advent of Internet-based computing and mobile productivity technologies (see Appendix 1) stand to elevate the utility of SFA to new heights. Through these devises universal access to real time information is available not just to the account executive, but also to related third-party groups such as retailers and resellers and perhaps directly to the customer.

Data mining: exploring and analyzing customer transactions

The customer relationship does not lie with the sales function alone, but also includes marketing and after-sales service. Accordingly, CRM suites have set their sights beyond sales force automation functionality by bringing automation to activities that span the range of the customer relationship. Data warehousing (see Figure 4.2) techniques have been around since the mid-1980s and are intended to provide a repository for the flow of data from operational systems to decision-support environments. This is done through the process of *data mining*, with the objective of exploring and analyzing business transactions to uncover useful patterns of activity. The practice of data mining aims to address the problems and high costs associated with the delivery of management information that is used to identify patterns from all customer interactions.

A recent study conducted for a multi-billion dollar corporation resulted in some interesting findings:[13]

● Eighty per cent of data used by the various data warehouses across the corporation were derived from the same 20 per cent of sources.

● New processes to extract, clean and integrate data from various sources were devised for each new data warehouse project, even though much of the same data had been "mined" for past projects.

● The data housed in a particular warehouse was generally based on the requirements of a specific group within the corporation, with little or no consideration given to other possible uses.

Many companies are failing to exploit economies of scale when embarking on data mining projects. Available funds would be put to better use if companies focus primarily on the crucial sources from which the bulk of useful data are derived. Similarly, the benefit from these projects should be aimed at audiences wider than just the initiating party.

The ability to address the pitfalls of traditional data mining methods has become an important component of leading CRM systems. The information garnered from data mining may be used for a variety of purposes, ranging from the design of customized services to the profiling and targeting of a specific customer segment. Data mining continues to attract interest, but many projects have fallen short of expectations. They have surpassed their original budgets, becoming more time-consuming and labour-intensive than originally anticipated. This is often a result of too much emphasis being placed on the technological tools rather than the underlying processes necessary to ensure data quality.

Customer interaction management

An area of CRM, the managing of customer service interactions, has seen a boom in technological innovation through the development of applications and associated infrastructure. Today's enterprises are under enormous pressure to provide a variety of means by which the customer can interact with their representatives. Customer interaction management systems bring together all channels

---

13. Manning (2000).

of customer interaction on a unified platform to create a knowledge base for the handling of customer issues. Modern customer service is epitomized by the growing prominence of the call centre, which can be established internally, but is increasingly outsourced to third-party specialists. The key technological enabler of the modern call centre is the automatic call distributor (ACD), a computerised phone system that routes incoming calls to the next available operator or agent based on the requirements as specified by the customer. With the growing sophistication of corporate Web sites, we are now seeing the use of Web-enabled call centres – call centres that are able to receive calls from a link on a Web page. By installing the necessary voice encoding and decoding plug-ins, these Web sites allow visitors to obtain additional information from a human via IP telephony directly at their computers.

The future of CRM

Applications that support different aspects of the customer relationship are increasingly becoming subsumed into all-encompassing CRM or ERP platforms. Notwithstanding the marketing hype of leading proponents, CRM packages still have some way to go to achieve true integration within the e-business architecture.

We will discuss the full CRM mix, including a bevy of lesser-known software specialties such as click stream analysis, Web site personalization, auto response applications and segmentation algorithms in greater detail in Chapter 7.

The supply chain

Supply chain management (SCM) software is designed to enhance interactions between an enterprise and its suppliers. The supply chain is the linkage of all activities and processes to supply a product or service to the end-consumer. The classic supply chain begins with the acquisition of raw materials, progresses through a distribution system involving a number of intermediaries such as wholesalers, warehouses and retailers before concluding with the delivery of finished goods. The critical importance of effectively managing the supply chain is well illustrated in this account by Victor Fung, former Harvard professor and Chairman of Li & Fung, one of the largest international export-trading companies:

> At Li & Fung, we think about supply chain management as "Tackling the soft $3" in the cost structure. What do we mean by that? If a typical consumer product leaves the factory at a price of $1, it will invariably end up on retail shelves at $4. Now you can try to squeeze the cost of production down 10 cents or 20 cents per product, but today you have to be a genius to do that because everybody has been working on that for years and there's not a lot of fat left. It's better to look at the cost that is spread throughout the distribution channels – the soft $3. It offers a bigger target, and if you take 50 cents out, nobody will even know you are doing it. So it's a much easier place to effect savings for our customers.[14]

14. Magretta (1998, p. 108).

There is no one-size-fits-all answer to the problem of optimizing the supply chain, as different strategies are better suited for different products. With so many theories floating about for improving supply chain performance – vendor-managed inventory, quick response, mass customization, postponement, and supplier partnerships among others – it can be an overwhelming prospect determining the right plan of action.

A framework for designing supply chains centres on the distinction between *functional* and *innovative* products.[15] Functional products are staples that tend to experience very stable demand and long product life cycles. These products tend to be under immense profit margin pressures and require highly efficient supply chains, where customer demand is met at the lowest cost. The supply chain environments for functional products are characterized by minimization of inventory throughout the chain, low-cost suppliers and short lead times. By contrast, innovative products are new products that tend to have highly unpredictable demand and require responsive supply chains that are able to adapt to fickle customer requirements. The supply chains for innovative products are characterized by the need for "safety" inventories, short lead times and an adaptive, flexible group of suppliers.

Supply chains can involve any number of supplier–customer relationships (a customer may also serve as a supplier to other customers), with products and services flowing from supplier to customer ("moving downstream") while demand information flows from customer to supplier ("moving upstream").

SCM software functionality is usually comprised of these major components:[16]

- *Demand planning*: The process for forecasting demand for products and services. By accurately forecasting customer demand, customer service can be improved while reducing uncertainty.

- *Manufacturing planning*: The process that optimizes manufacturing order scheduling with the enterprise's production capacity. This process is optimized by combining material requirements planning systems with capacity requirements planning to create the most advantageous production plan.

- *Supply planning*: The process that meets customer demand based on inventory status and transportation resources. This includes distribution requirements planning, which monitors warehouse inventory levels.

- *Transportation planning*: The planning process for optimizing the scheduling and delivery of shipments to customers under stated deadlines, given constraints such as available transportation, carrier preferences and so on.

- *Collaborative capabilities*: SCM packages are fast evolving to incorporate collaborative functionality such as collaborative sourcing, planning (e.g. Web-based exchange of forecasts among partners) and design.

15. Fisher (1997).
16. Clarkston Group (2000).

The difference between SCM software and ERP is often unclear to many observers who see similarities in the functionality of both. Leading SCM products generally offer many more enhancements than comparable ERP packages. Many employ graphical representations of the entire supply chain, showing where problems are. Several overlapping features do exist, however. The fundamental distinction between the two is that ERP software generally strives to encompass all facets of the business – order entry, distribution, procurement, production, logistics, inventory and finance – towards the primary purpose of controlling the flow and execution of transactional information. SCM systems on the other hand focus on providing support for managerial decisions that must be made *prior* to the execution of a transaction.[17]

For these reasons, companies on the cutting edge of SCM tend to implement tightly integrated SCM and ERP systems that are able to adapt to changing company needs. As was the case with CRM, ERP and SCM solutions are increasingly encroaching on each other's territory. Nevertheless, major ERP vendors are gradually providing more application programming interfaces that can be interfaced through the use of middleware. This, however, requires that these vendors change their interface software on a regular basis through a largely trial-and-error process that can lead to frustrating complications. Newer forms of specialized software promise to provide a better solution to this problem by eliminating the chore of developing specific interfaces to every other vendor's offerings. We will explore SCM technologies in greater detail in Chapter 8.

Internal communication and collaboration

The major remaining piece of the e-business solutions puzzle concerns a category of applications designed to facilitate employee interactions within company walls. These applications are intended as a source of competitive advantage that enhances efficiency, supports collaboration and makes highly relevant information readily available.

The popular catchphrase in this arena is "Knowledge Management" (KM) targeted at gathering, analyzing and disseminating the knowledge of groups and individuals across the enterprise. The objective is to enhance organizational performance through shared knowledge. This movement corresponds to a shift in emphasis on the part of many companies from rewarding individuals for amassing knowledge and expertise to encouraging them to share their knowledge with others so that the entire organization will benefit.

The case that follows this chapter takes a detailed look at how PriceWaterhouseCoopers sought to develop its "KnowledgeCurve" intranet and knowledge management platform as a cornerstone of its e-business strategy following the merger of Price Waterhouse and Coopers & Lybrand.

In the past, knowledge workers practised improvizational KM, making use of email and a haphazard arsenal of communications methods to share their problem-solving expertise. As we saw in Chapter 2, the foundation of modern

---

17. Ibid.

business is increasingly shifting from physical resources to knowledge capital. As such companies are exploring how knowledge is being used and shared by and among their workers. Early innovators set about developing systematic approaches to knowledge sharing, based on the dynamics of the networked organization.

Groupware software such as Lotus Notes and Microsoft Exchange constitute a relatively long-established class of applications that fall under this category. The concept of groupware is an evolving one that aims to provide a mechanism for coordinating and tracking ongoing group projects. Groupware is built around a messaging system supported by applications such as document sharing and document management, group scheduling, group contact and task management, threaded discussions, text chat, data conferencing and audio and videoconferencing. Workflow, which allows messages and documents to be routed to the appropriate users, is also often included in groupware systems.

The widespread implementation of enterprise portals (Figure 4.3), accessible through the company intranet, provide proprietary information to company employees and in some instances, selected third parties (e.g. partners, suppliers, prime customers). The essential attraction of the enterprise portal lies in its ability to serve as a common interface and access point to all data inside and outside the organization and to ultimately facilitate the location and retrieval of information. Through enterprise portals users are able to access either structured or unstructured data without having to know its actual location or format.

A complete portal solution should include provisions for security, an intuitive user interface, a search engine, indexing/cataloguing, document management, business intelligence tools, personalization and a host of other functionality.[18]

Figure 4.3 Basic architecture of an enterprise portal

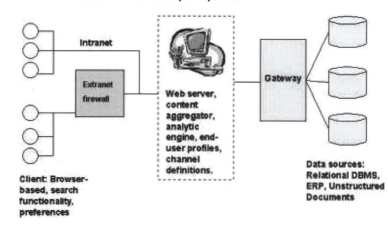

Adapted from Szuprowicz (2000).

---

18. Enterprise portal start-up costs (including the software to develop customized interfaces and aggregate sufficient data) range from US$150,000 to $300,000. The development of a major enterprise portal system over a two-year period could require a budget of approximately $1.5 million (Szuprowicz, 2000).

PriceWaterhouseCoopers' KnowledgeCurve began as a global repository of small databases, but developed into an expansive, feature-rich resource regularly accessed by its vast pool of geographically dispersed consultants.

A number of vendors specialize in highly sophisticated tools for the design and maintenance of portals to assist organizations in realizing their internal collaboration goals. For instance, Semio's flagship product, Taxonomy, automatically builds hierarchical structures of categories out of immense collections of unstructured data. The growing sophistication of enterprise portals promises to offer employees a highly effective, standardized interface to the mass of information that they must deal with.

Collision of ERP and e-business

It is no coincidence that many of the most recognizable names on the e-business landscape hail from the first-tier of established ERP vendors. Growing acceptance of Internet technology in the business world and a decline in the sales of ERP software has forced many of these vendors to extend the orientation of their products to go beyond the back-office functionality they were largely identified with.

In response to changing customer requirements, ERP software providers initially provided some degree of "Web-enabling" by making their products accessible through a browser. While this allowed users to access the ERP system remotely, it was a far cry from fully leveraging Internet technology as the fundamental architecture. To compete with Web-based software, a new generation of ERP suites are becoming increasingly common. Extended ERP refers to the number of extended applications that vendors have developed and are promoting as complementary to the core system for addressing today's e-business requirements (Figure 4.4).

With the merging of ERP and Internet technologies, the role of ERP is increasingly that of an internal hub for the enterprise. The addition of Web-based technology extends the information infrastructure into the marketplace

Figure 4.4 Extended ERP applications

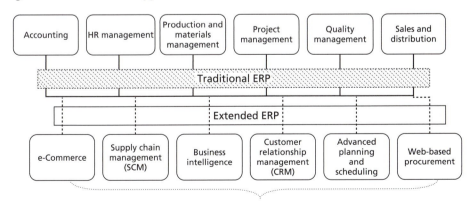

Users access these applications through a portal interface

Adapted from Callaway (2000).

for dealings with a host of external parties. We present detailed discussion of ERP in Chapter 6.

Summary

The form and function of IT infrastructure are now almost indistinguishable from those of the early mainframe period. As IT has increasingly become a strategic necessity it is essential for decision-makers to have a solid grasp of infrastructural issues in their e-business transformation initiative. Technology is advancing at breakneck speeds and myriad vendors are developing and marketing solutions for virtually every aspect of a business. In such fast-moving landscape, senior management must have a high level understanding of technical issues in order to devise e-business solutions that are cost effective, feasible and customer-centric. The strategic implications of e-business infrastructure issues are too important to be left to technical people; management involvement is vital to success of transformational initiatives.

In the next chapter we will turn our attention to the enabling technologies that are crucial to realizing a secure, operational and efficient e-business.

Questions for discussion

1   What are the advantages of mainframe computing?

2   What were the factors behind the proliferation of end-user computing?

3   How did the shift to client/server computing affect information access within the enterprise?

4   What are the advantages and disadvantages of client/server computing?

5   What are the characteristics of the Internet that distinguish it from earlier architectural environments?

6   What are the components of *conventional infrastructure*? What are the *e-business building blocks* from a participant viewpoint? What are the *enabling components*?

7   How are e-business technologies lowering the barriers between units within the enterprise and along the value chain?

8   How did ERP packages rise to prominence? How might an ERP system ease the transition towards new business processes?

9   What issues must a company address when striving to achieve a customer-orientation?

10 What is the function of sales force automation software? What other applications and technologies fall under the CRM umbrella?

11 What is meant by data mining? What are its pitfalls?

12 What are the major functionalities of supply chain management (SCM) software?

13 What is knowledge management?

14 What is groupware?

15 What are the benefits of implementing a corporate portal?

16 How are traditional ERP and specialised e-business software encroaching on each other?

17 What relationships exist between the economic climate and managerial attitudes towards e-business spending and infrastructure projects?

18 To what degree should senior management be involved in infrastructure decision-making?

Appendix 1: Wireless e-business

The promise of a wireless future is one we have been hearing of for quite some time. However, there have so far been some disappointments in this arena. These include widespread consumer indifference to Wireless Applications Protocol (WAP),[19] the dearth of available Bluetooth[20] devices, and of course, the repeated postponement of 3G deployment – the third generation of mobile communications systems designed for high-speed Internet access, rich multimedia and global roaming.

In the media frenzy over consumer aspects of wireless innovation, the immense potential of wireless technology for enterprise productivity is often overlooked. As with Internet-enabled business, which was initially considered almost entirely in terms of consumer e-commerce, we are seeing that the near-term payoff in the wireless arena will be in the enterprise arena.

The rush to invest in consumer-focused wireless initiatives by many companies seeking competitive advantage has largely overshadowed the many possibilities for business-wide wireless initiatives to enhance accuracy, speed, productivity and ultimately customer service. In some circles, the perception of wireless devices and applications has long been associated with trendy and gimmicky novelties. However, wireless innovations are now widely employed in critical business environments – in conveying buy-sell orders on the NYSE trading floor, by field professionals in transportation and logistics, towards materials management on production lines, even by medical professionals who make use of mobile devices for storing patient history details and for making prescription calculations. Today's employees are constantly on-the-go and companies are finding that wherever there are physical disconnects or gaps in the flow of information, the best solution is often to go wireless. Environments where frontline employees need instant access to critical systems lend themselves especially well

---

19. A standard for providing cellular phones and other handheld devices with access to e-mail and text-based Web pages. WAP functions by employing Wireless Markup Language (WML) and WMLScript – a scripting language that requires little memory.

20. A wireless personal technology established in 1998 by Ericsson, IBM, Intel, Nokia and Toshiba ("Bluetooth Special Interest Group"). Bluetooth is an open standard for up to 720 Kbps transmission of digital voice and data between mobile devices (laptops, PDAs, phones) and desktop devices over short ranges.

to wireless solutions, as do situations involving applications based on the location or status of assets and inventory.[21] Areas such as sales force automation, field service, shipping and logistics and operations monitoring are especially likely to benefit from wireless advances.

Unlike other forms of infrastructure investment, wireless solutions are often able to produce near-term value by offering relatively clear evidence of ROI. They significantly enhance business responsiveness, yield high productivity, reduce travel time, lower telecommunication charges and lower demand on call centres.

With so many opportunities to consider, technology managers must take a disciplined approach to how and where to invest and take care to work through the business process implications of their mobile solutions in advance. Wireless devices found in companies today include Web-enabled mobile phones, pagers, barcode scanners, payment consoles, notebooks, and of course PDA (personal digital assistant) products. These devices may run one of several operating systems (e.g. Palm OS, Pocket PC, Epoc) and utilise any number of communications and productivity applications. Universal acceptance of wireless devices and applications as a component of technology infrastructure is far from complete in the corporate IT world. Consequently, PDAs and their associated applications are often chosen and purchased by individual owners rather than the company, resulting in a smorgasbord of platforms and applications in use throughout the business. Decision makers must realise the strategic firm-wide importance of wireless technology so that they can set about devising appropriate policies and planning the IT architecture and support necessary for this new reality. More importantly, sound planning for wireless is of crucial importance for mitigating the hassle of integration when it is time to leverage these innovations to achieve seamless business-wide functionality.

With this in mind, a host of vendors have responded by offering comprehensive end-to-end solutions that include terminals, servers, middleware, applications, encryption and even airtime on commercial wireless networks. The importance of establishing a sound platform and strategy cannot be understated, whether by vendor or proprietary means. Value can be derived from wireless applications only if they are developed with the end user in mind within the context of the device, network and underlying enterprise infrastructure. Many mobile interfaces, which were developed merely as after-the-fact supplements to existing PC-based applications, have subsequently failed to fully leverage the possibilities of wireless. The coming years will bring unforeseeable advances in the wireless field and the difficulty of incorporating new technology will be compounded manifold under haphazard approaches. IT people must bear in mind that deficiencies such as poor application design, awkward interfaces and roaming difficulties will only hamper the adoption of mobile applications at the enterprise level.

In the wireless era, decision-making authority will shift to employees on the frontlines. Wireless solutions must link to a fully integrated e-business infrastructure,

---

21. Deloitte Research (2001).

allowing for device compatibility and a consistent user experience. From the greater business viewpoint, it is important that senior management anticipate the important changes to business processes and corporate culture that can result from wireless implementations. Most significantly, as geography-based reporting relationships will diminish in importance firms will re-evaluate and re-align organizational relationships to reflect this new reality. Restructuring the broader business to streamline processes and enable flatter organizations is a distinct possibility.

Wireless standards

In recent years, we have witnessed the explosive growth of mobile technology which started with the modest prospect of wireless voice communications. Let us take a chronological examination of the extraordinary advancement of wireless network technologies:

- *First Generation (1G)*: The history of popular mobile communications started with analogue-based, voice-only 1G networks; the handsets were bulky and inconvenient, and the fees expensive. 1G services were used in the 1980s and early 1990s before they became obsolete.

- *Second Generation (2G) (Speed: 10 Kbps)*: Second generation was a digital, voice and data communications platform that became popular in late 1990s. Widely used technologies applied towards 2G networks included Personal Digital Cellular (PDC), which was popular in Japan; Code Division Multiple Access (CDMA), which was widely used in South Korea; and Global System for Mobile Communication (GSM), which was widely used in the Asia-Pacific region and Europe. Time Division Multiple Access (TDMA) was heavily adopted in the Americas, as well as CDMA and GSM to a lesser extent. 2G networks allowed a simple non-voice data transmission service called text messaging, also known as Short Message Service (SMS) in many countries. Users of the service could send each other telegram-like messages of up to 160 characters through their mobile phones, usually at a rate cheaper than voice calls.

- *2.5G (Speed: 64–144 Kbps)*: An interim network technology between 2G and 3G, 2.5G was a less-costly upgrade to existing 2G networks than 3G, but still capable of delivering significantly higher data transmission rates. It was also "always-on" and operated as a packet-switched network. There were two types of 2.5G networks, namely General Packet Radio Service (GPRS) and IS-95B.[22]

- *Third Generation (3G) (Speed: 384 Kbps to 2 Mbps)*: Third generation is technologically a quantum leap from 2G. It allows broadband, packet-switched transmissions of voice, data and images at a maximum speed of

---

22. GPRS was evolved from GSM and TDMA; IS-95B was developed from CDMA.

2 Mbps. The voice transmission quality of 3G is equivalent to fixed lines. 3G can easily handle multimedia content, as well as download videos and hold videoconferences, while with the present network services, one can only receive slow, rudimentary graphics. 3G will also bring about benefits such as satellite communications or the use of Global Positioning Systems (GPS) on mobile phones and handheld devices (see Table 4.2).

The international standard for 3G mobile communications, as set out by the International Telecommunications Union (ITU), was called International Mobile Telecommunications-2000 (IMT-2000). Companies and organisations worldwide have formed the consortia 3GPP

Table 4.2 Services that represented the majority of the near-term 3G demand

Service name	Service description
Mobile Internet access	A 3G service that offers mobile access to full-fixed Internet service provider (ISP) services with near-wireline transmission quality and functionality. It includes full Web access to the Internet as well as file transfer, e-mail and streaming video/audio capability
Mobile intranet/extranet access	A business 3G service that provides secure mobile access to corporate Local Area Networks (LANs), Virtual Private Networks (VPNs) and the Internet
Customised infotainment	A consumer 3G service that provides device-independent access to personalised content anywhere, anytime via structured-access mechanisms based on mobile portals
Multimedia messaging service (MMS)	A business and consumer 3G service that offers non-real-time, multimedia messaging with always-on capabilities allowing the provision of instant messaging. Consumer service are targeted at closed user groups that can be services provider- or user-defined; business service are targeted at closed business communities that can be services provider- or customer-defined
Location-based services	A business and consumer 3G service that enables users to find other people, vehicles, resources, services or machines. It also enables others to find users, as well as enabling users to identify their own location via terminal or vehicle identification
Rich voice and simple voice	A 3G service that is real-time and two-way. It provides advanced voice capabilities such as Voice over Internet Protocol (VoIP), voice-activated net access and Web-initiated voice calls, while still offering traditional mobile voice features such as operator services, directory assistance and roaming. As the service matures, it would include mobile videophone and multimedia communications

Source: Report No. 9, "The UMTS Third Generation Market – Structuring the Service Revenue Opportunities", UMTS Forum, September 2000, and Telecompeition Inc., March 2001, as cited in Report No. 13, "The UMTS Third Generation Market – Phase II: Structuring the Service Revenue Opportunities", UMTS Forum, April 2001.

(Third-Generation Partnership Project) and 3GPP2 (Third-Generation Partnership Project 2) respectively to promote two competing IMT-2000-compatible radio interfaces, namely Wideband Code Division Multiple Access (W-CDMA) and cdma2OOO.

A basic wireless Internet process consists of several steps. A browser application on the mobile phone or handheld device first sends a request to a service platform or interface known as a gateway server,[23] which then sends a request to the relevant Web server on the Internet. The Web server sends the requested file to the gateway (the file should be written in a language compatible with the browser) and the gateway then transmits the file to the browser. Communications between the wireless device and the gateway take place over a mobile network such as 2G, 2.5G or 3G. The service platform might be operated by a network operator, an Internet Service Provider (ISP), or, more generally, a Mobile Virtual Network Operator (MVNO). Content providers, advertisers, wireless application service providers and aggregators could work with any of these. The browser and the content language constituted the Internet technology, which commonly includes:

- *Wireless Application Protocol (WAP) and Wireless Markup Language (WML)*: In 2000, WAP was the dominating wireless Internet technology worldwide (much of the US used WAP's precursor, Handheld Device Markup Language (HDML). WAP content was written in WML, which had some significant differences from the widely used Hypertext Markup Language (HTML). WAP/HDML services were operated in Europe, the United States and Asia-Pacific countries including Korea, Japan and Hong Kong. Outside Japan, the wireless Internet was dominated by WAP technology: in early 2001, there were 10,000 WAP sites from 95 countries, some five million WAP-readable pages and 50 million WAP-enabled handsets worldwide.[24] But, despite these figures, many industry observers stated that WAP was not successful. They quoted service weakness as the major problem; glitches were relatively frequent compared with normal voice communications, and the number of useful services and WML pages for the general market were limited. Because WAP services are operated over circuit-switched networks users have to pay time-based connection fees and wait for 15–30 sec of log-in time, reasons that led to lacklustre adoption of this protocol.

- *Compact Hypertext Markup Language (CHTML)*: The content language used by Japan's NTT DoCoMo for its popular i-mode service. Because CHTML is a subset of HTML the fixed-line Internet pages can be easily converted – initially this was an advantage over WML.

---

23. A gateway is a computer that converts protocols, allowing interaction between different types of networks or applications.
24. Quoted by Scott Goldman in "WAP 2001 Update", WAP Forum, presented on 11 January 2001. URL for online version http://www.wapforum-org/new/WAP2001UDdate.vpt.

- *Extensible Hypertext Markup Language (XHTML) Basic*: A higher level wireless Internet language, XHTML Basic was the mobile subset of the XML standard. XHTML Basic is expected to be used widely in the future wireless Internet in conjunction with more advanced cellular networks such as 3G.

Consumer and mass-market wireless initiatives typically involve massive infrastructure investments and gambling on new-fangled standards and applications. Many wireless enterprise projects are based on fairly established technologies that are available at lower cost and often implemented relatively easily. While the arrival of 3G and higher bandwidth ability will almost certainly bring a major boost to wireless implementations, reliable standards and technologies are already available for mobile productivity implementations that can generate value in the near-term. Wireless LANs (local area networks) are suitable for small- to large-scale implementations (Figure 4.5). They are relatively easy to install and work by transmitting data over unlicensed frequencies such as the 2.4 GHz band.[25] They do not require the lining up of devices for line-of-sight transmission, as with infra-red data association (IrDA), but rely on wireless access points that transmit radio frequencies capable of penetrating walls and travelling up to a thousand feet. Users can be transferred from one access point to another whilst roaming, much like what is done with conventional cellular phone systems.

Going beyond the possible boundaries of a local area network, wireless computing may be realised on a wide-area scale by employing the cellular digital

Figure 4.5 Wireless LANs

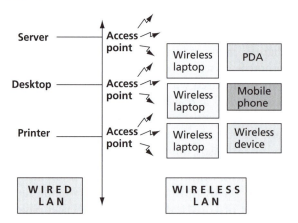

Source: Adapted from Computer Desktop Encyclopedia (2000).

---

25. Wireless LANs rely on the IEEE 802.11 standard that provides for either 1 or 2 Mbps data transmission using either a Frequency Hopping Modulation Technique (FHSS) or Code Division Multiple Access (CDMA). Small wireless LANs are sometimes called "personal area networks" (PANs) and are mainly used to connect a laptop or PDA to a desktop machine.

packet data (CDPD) standard[26] – a digital wireless transmission system that is deployed by enhancing existing analogue cellular networks or by means of WAP.

Wireless security (see Chapter 5)

In the new reality of wireless computing, technology managers must understand and appreciate the difference between wireless security and traditional PC security. Security applications must account for the limited memory of wireless devices and will likely have to support multiple protocols. The Wireless Application Protocol (WAP) is the present de facto wireless standard, but newer protocols promise greater functionality. The majority of wireless transactions will originate from outside corporate firewalls and, by their very nature, will be easier to intercept and have a much higher rate of failure. As such, the wireless security strategy must be developed in conjunction with the overall e-business security strategy. Policies governing passwords, authentication and access profiles should be the same for cell phones and PDAs as for notebook computers and PCs.

Mobile devices are location-independent, personal, portable and widely available. They are well suited to become the dominant enablers for carrying out

Figure 4.6 Mobile Internet development towards 3G

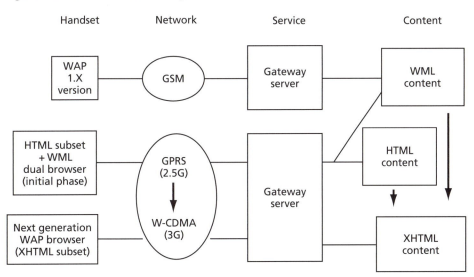

Source: "Global Strategy and Investments in U.S. and Taiwan", NTT DoCoMo, Inc., URL: http://www.nttdocomo.com/corporate/ir/kss/fi00_1201.pdf, 30 November 2000.

---

26. CDPD is based on IBM's CelluPlan II and moves data at 19.2 Kbps over unused intervals in voice channels on the analog cellular phone network. When all channels are in use, the data is stored for future forwarding. CDPD modems are widely available in PC-card form for notebook computers and handheld devices.

financial transactions and other activities relating to e-business and consequently will incorporate applications that also demand security functions. At
present, security levels in wireless environments lag behind fixed-line standards.
Network operators cannot always guarantee that confidential information will
be transmitted in a secure way. With mobile devices now challenging the domi-
nance of PCs, public key infrastructure (PKI) is being extended to the wireless
environment and is poised to become the preferred system for implementing
secure communications and authentication procedures. The same PKI concepts
that have been employed in stationary TCP/IP networks also carry over to the
wireless environment. A PKI is considered wireless when the front-end devices
used to communicate to other parties are wireless. The back-end of these connections can be integrated into fixed networks such as the Internet – in other
words, a "wireless network" need not be entirely wireless by nature.

Appendix 2: Major e-business vendors

e-Business function	Description	Major vendors
Enterprise resource planning (ERP)	Information system to support the business processes of all functional areas of the enterprise	SAP, Baan, Oracle, J.D. Edwards, Peoplesoft
Customer relationship management (CRM)	Information systems that allow companies to manage every aspect of their customer relationships	Siebel, Amdocs, Vantive (Peoplesoft), Pivotal
Data warehousing	Database-driven systems for storing, managing and retrieving large amounts of enterprise data	Hyperion, Brio Software, Cognos, Business Objects
Supply chain management (SCM)	Systems with functionality for planning, scheduling and management of the supply chain	Manugistics, i2, Ariba, J.D. Edwards, MySAP, Aspen Technologies
Groupware and collaboration	Software to support communication and collaboration among different users at separated workstations	IBM/Lotus, GroupWise, Microsoft (Exchange)
Enterprise portals	Software that facilitates the development, maintenance of corporate portals for aggregating information and optimizing efficiency	Semio, Information Advantage (MyEureka), Sybase
Integration	Integration servers and other products that serve as a common connecting point for other applications	Tibco, WebMethods, Vitria, Asera, Portera
Mobile productivity	Solutions that make productivity-enhancing applications available through wireless devices	Avantgo Enterprise, Palm Enterprise, Zimba

References

Callaway, Erin. (2000) *ERP: The Next Generation; ERP is Web enabled for e-Business*, Charleston, SC: Computer Technology Research.

Clarkston Group (2000) *Supply Chain Management Primer*, Durham NC: Clarkston Group.

Computer Desktop Encyclopedia (2000) The Computer Language Co. Inc., Point Pleasant, PA.

Deloitte Research (2001) *Mobilizing the Enterprise: Unlocking the Real Value in Wireless*, New York: Deloitte Consulting.

EIU (2001) "On-the-job learning is crucial to IT execs", *Ebusinessforum.com* [online], 1 August, available from: http://www.ebusinessforum.com/index.asp?layout=rich_story&doc_id=4148&categoryid=&channelid=&search=on+the+job+learning [accessed 1 August 2001].

Fisher, M. (1997) "What is the right supply chain for your product?" *Harvard Business Review*, March–April.

Magretta, J. (1998) "Fast, global, and entrepreneurial: supply chain management, Hong Kong style – an interview with Victor Fung", *Harvard Business Review*, September–October, p. 108.

Manning, I. (2000) "Data warehousing – what exactly is it?" *ittoolbox.com* [online], available from http://www.ittoolbox.com/peer/dwarticle.htm [accessed 22 August 2001].

Peppers, D. and Rogers, M. (1997) *The One to One Future: Building Relationships One Customer at a Time*, New York: Doubleday.

Phan, A. (2001) "Downturn fails to stem IT spending", *South China Morning Post*, 4 December, Business, P. 12.

Shields, M. (2001) *e-Business and ERP*, New York: John Wiley & Sons.

Strassmann, P. and Bienkowski, D. (2001) "IT in the 21st century: speaking the language of business", *ABTCorporation White Paper*, available from http://www.strassmann.com/pubs/abtcorp/ [accessed 24 November 2001].

Szuprowicz, B. (2000) *Implementing Enterprise Portals: Integration Strategies for Intranet, Extranet, and Internet Resources*, Charleston, SC: Computer Technology Research Corp.

Further reading

Amor, D. (2000) *The e-Business (R)evolution: Living and Working in an Interconnected World*, Upper Saddle River, N.J.: Prentice-Hall.

Economist Intelligence Unit (2000) *e-Business Transformation*, New York: Economist Intelligence Unit.

Gloors, P. (2000) *Making the e-Business Transformation*, London: Springer.

Kalakota, R. and Robinson, M. (2001) *e-Business 2.0: Roadmap for Success*, Reading, MA: Addison-Wesley.

Kalakota, R. and Whinston, A.B. (1997) *Electronic Commerce: A Manager's Guide*, Reading, MA: Addison-Wesley.

Keen, P. and Mackintosh, R. (2001) *The Freedom Economy: Gaining the M-Commerce Edge in the Era of the Wireless Internet*, New York: Osborne/McGraw-Hill.

Macsweeney, G. (2001) "Building an e-business infrastructure", *Insurance & Technology*, vol. 26, no. 3 (February), pp. 24–9.

McLeod, R. et al. (2000) *Management Information Systems*, Upper Saddle River, N.J.: Prentice-Hall.

Norris, G. et al. (2000) *e-Business and ERP: Transforming the Enterprise*, New York: John Wiley & Sons.

Porter, M. (2001) "Strategy and the Internet", *HBR OnPoint*, March, pp. 63–79.

Radding, A. (1999) "ERP: more than an application", *Information Week* [online], 5 April, available from: http://www.informationweek.com/728/28iuerp.htm [accessed 5 August 2001].

Ranadive, V. (1999) *The Power of Now: How Winning Companies Sense and Respond to Change Using Real-time Technology*, New York: McGraw-Hill.

Sawhney, M. and Zabin, J. (2001) *The Seven Steps to Nirvana: Strategic Insights into E-business Transformation*, New York: McGraw-Hill.

Strauss, J. and Frost, R. (2000) *e-Marketing*, Upper Saddle River, NJ: Prentice-Hall.

Turban, E. et al. (2001) *Introduction to Information Technology*, New York: John Wiley & Sons.

Weill, P. and Broadbent, M. (1998) *Leveraging the New Infrastructure: How Market Leaders Capitalize on Information Technology*, Boston, MA: Harvard Business School Press.

Weill, P. and Vitale, M. (2001) *Place to Space: Migrating to e-Business Models*, Boston, MA: Harvard Business School Press.

Case study   The PricewaterhouseCoopers KnowledgeCurve and the spinning off of PwC Consulting

We are generally very early adopters of technology, which is great in the beginning, but you pay a price for it because it's very difficult to change technology that's already in place. And in fact Lotus Notes is a classic case of that because we adopted it so early, it's very deeply embedded in our organisation, which also means it's very hard to change.

– Stephen Langley, CIO Asia Pacific, PwC Consulting

By May 2002, over 99 per cent of PricewaterhouseCoopers' 150,000 staff worldwide were actively using the KnowledgeCurve (KC), based on Lotus Notes databases, for their daily business activities. The KC had become the lifeline of the Firm. New knowledge was pumped into it, and shared knowledge and experiences were drawn from it, on a daily basis from and to anywhere across the globe where PwC conducted business. Growing dependence on the KC and the maturing of the Firm's business strategy raised a number of concerns that were to have major implications for the future of the KC. In March 2002, PwC announced that it had begun the process of changing the name of one of its businesses, PwC Consulting, the consulting arm of the Firm, in preparation for an IPO that was expected to take place in August. Stephen Langley – CIO Asia Pacific – and his counterparts in the US and Europe were engaged in pressing issues pertaining to the separation of the fabric of the KC in preparation for the spin-off. The technical infrastructure of the KC had been built upon legacy systems inherited from the two merged companies, Price Waterhouse and Coopers & Lybrand, in 1998. Since then, newer technologies and Internet-based applications had emerged and it seemed illogical to duplicate the legacy infrastructure with the spin-off. Furthermore, users were constantly pushing

for newer functionalities that would, for example, allow them to access and retrieve information not only from PwC's knowledge base, but also from the wealth of external information service providers. The technological infrastructure upon which the KC sat was stretched and tested to its limit. In response to these changes and emerging demands, PwC Consulting started work on building a portal, to be launched in Q4 2002, that would encompass the Intranet as it existed at that time. The migration from the legacy infrastructure to the portal was posing a few technological challenges. Should it adopt a full portal integration approach, buy in middleware to enable the integration of certain applications, or simply link the existing KC to the portal to provide data access?

The PwC Firm and PwC Consulting

PwC was formed in July 1998 following a merger of Price Waterhouse and Coopers & Lybrand, both global companies in their own right, offering professional services well beyond accounting.[1] The merger created the world's largest professional service organisation, surpassing Arthur Andersen which had previously been considered the industry's giant in terms of asset size. Total global revenue for the fiscal year ended 30 June, 2000, was $21.5 billion. On announcing these results, CEO James J Schiro commented: ". . . we laid the groundwork for our impending restructuring . . . Our focus now is to

---

1. Farhoomand, A., McCauley, M., Fukagata, M. and Lovelock, P., "PricewaterhouseCoopers: Building a Global Network", *Centre for Asian Business Cases*, The University of Hong Kong, 2000.

Figure 1 PwC revenue for the year ended 30 June 2000

Revenue by PwC LOS (in millions)	Gross 2000
ABAS	8,737.0
MCS	6,644.2
Tax	3,993.0
FAS	1,519.5
BPO	218.0
GHRS	719.9
Total	21,467.6

Figure 2 PwC Consulting's core solution areas

Development	Deliver	Operate
Strategic change	Customer relationship management Financial management Human capital Supply chain and operations Information technology	Application management and business process outsourcing

further enhance our innovative leadership in the networked economy by building on our traditional skill set."

Immediately following the merger, the Firm was organised into six lines of service (LOS): Audit; Assurance and Business Advisory Services (ABAS); Business Process Outsourcing (BPO); Financial Advisory Services (FAS); Global Human Resources Solutions (GHRS); Management Consulting Services (MCS or "PwC Consulting"); and Global Tax Services. Figure 1 shows the revenue split between the six lines of service.

Two years later the Firm announced its intention to spin off various parts of its organisation. As part of this strategy, the separation of the management consulting business, PwC Consulting, through an IPO was announced at the end of January 2002.

PwC Consulting was one of the world's leading providers of management consulting and technology services to some of the largest and most successful organisations spread over 20 industries. With more than 32,000 employees operating in 52 countries and territories on six continents, PwC Consulting's expertise lay in seven core

solution areas (see Figure 2). This, combined with its extensive industry-specific and solution area expertise, together with knowledge of a region's people, language and culture, helped PwC Consulting achieve annual revenue of $7.5 billion in 2001.

PwC Consulting provided services spanning five industry groups covering 20 industry sectors (see Figure 3). Through alliance relationships with various leading technology providers such as EDS, HP, Oracle, PeopleSoft, SAP, Siebel and Sun, PwC Consulting was rated the number two consultancy in e-business worldwide in 2001.[2]

The Information infrastructure of PwC

You really have to keep in mind that a system like [the KC] is organic. Think of it as an organic system, as a living, breathing thing that needs to be fed and watered. It's like growing a

---

2. Dresdner Kleinwort Wasserstein, March 2001.

Figure 3 Industry groups and sectors served by PwC Consulting

Products	Government and services	Financial services	Information, communication and entertainment	Energy and utilities
Pharmaceuticals Consumer packaged-goods	Government Defence Aviation	Banking Capital Markets Insurance	Communications Entertainment and media	Oil and Gas Utilities
Technology Industrial Products Automotive Retail	Posts and Surface transport	Investment management	Hospitality and leisure	Mining

Source: "PricewaterhouseCoopers Reports Fiscal 2000 Revenues of $21.5 Billion", PwC Press Release, 18 January 2001.

plant; you've got to keep feeding it, talking to it nicely, and keeping an eye on it, otherwise it doesn't work, it dies. We need to ensure that out of date content is removed. You've got to keep things fresh, up to date.

– Stephen Langley

Bringing together technology and competitive strategy

Following the merger, PwC developed the KnowledgeCurve, its award-winning intranet that connected its global organisation of partners and employees. On the understanding that synergies were to be gained through the sharing of knowledge and expertise of the two companies, swift action was taken to integrate the information systems that held the knowledge base in various legacy systems. As the central communications and knowledge-sharing tool for all of PwC, KC became the forum and foundation for its knowledge-management strategies and initiatives. Apart from the KC other applications (in finance and HRM) were also part of the intranet. However, the most significant part of the intranet was the KC.

Implementation of the intranet infrastructure was a key element of the Firm's e-business strategy for the 21st century. The strategic priority of the Firm was to become "the new knowledge enterprise". The KC brought

together the best intellectual capital and the global information, knowledge and skills of more than 150,000 people in the home pages for each line of business. For example, it provided a central source of information for all tax professionals, gave an overview of global tax practices and the latest tax news from around the world, and provided information about PwC policies, recent client engagements, new business opportunities and technology updates. Its multi-dimensional design supported knowledge sharing, communications, continuous learning and virtual office strategies. PwC claimed that the KC helped it to serve its clients better, win new engagements and bring the organisation's professionals together. By taking a "knowledge perspective", PwC perfected the art of integrating processes and learning across the value network and the use of knowledge and experience acquired through interactions with clients.

The KnowledgeCurve framework

The KC started off simply as global repositories of small databases. Over the course of 18 months of development and migration, the KC took shape. It was designed so that each line of service had its own Web page (e.g. www.pwcconsulting.com) and there was also a global homepage (www.pwcglobal.com) that spanned the whole Firm (see Exhibit 1).

Exhibit 1 Accessing the global and local KnowledgeCurve

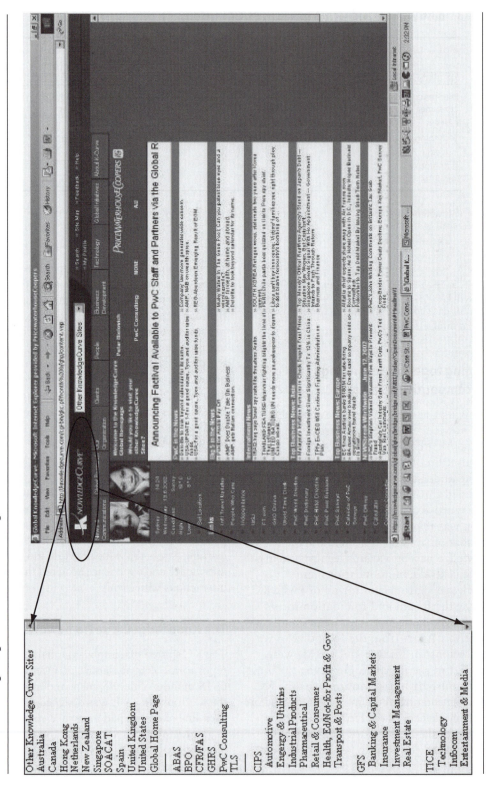

Through the Web pages of each line of service, applications and content specific to each line of service were deployed. For some of the more strategic locations, country-specific sites would provide a knowledge base to communicate, for example, HR-type information that was appropriate only to the local community of PwC staff. Other information that could be accessed through the KC included the industry-specific sites that were often used as a base for collaboration across the six lines of service.

The global homepage provided access to information on global initiatives, Firm-wide projects, know-how and expertise in the areas of, say, technology, business development, staff directories, the PwC dictionary and Firm policies. The Global Research Centre housed in the global homepage was also the gateway to external information providers such as Factiva, Goldman Sachs and S&P.

PW and C & L were both early adopters of Lotus Notes. Hence, about 60 per cent of the content of the KC was stored in Lotus Notes databases. The other primary content holder was the Oracle system (see Figure 4). The KC provided Web-based access to a series of Dominized Notes databases. These databases were organised by community and were equipped with a Content Management Workflow. The three servers (Domino, Oracle and SUN) formed PwC's data centre. The data centre was replicated in three locations or "theatres", namely, Tampa to serve the Americas, London to serve Europe, the Middle East and Africa, and Sydney to serve the Asia Pacific region. Stephen gave two reasons for replicating the data centres: firstly, the cost of ensuring adequate bandwidth globally to access one data centre was prohibitive; and secondly, it reduced the global risk to the Firm in the event that one theatre's system was down, although it did

Figure 4 The framework of the KnowledgeCurve

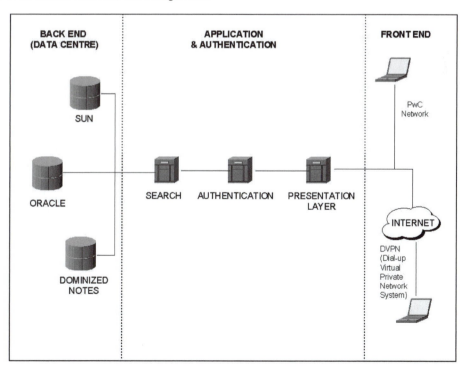

not go as far as to provide cross-theatre backup in the event of systems failure.

About 80 per cent of the time, consultants would access the KC from outside of the office. The system architecture enabled them to access the KC for information while on the road. While PwC offices provided direct access to the KC, remote access was possible through the dial-up virtual private network (DVPN) system. PwC deployed the Verity full-text search engine that allowed users to search across all of HTML and in Dominized Notes. Verity enabled searching across both environments. It maintained an index of the content of documents based on keywords. In order to make searches more productive, a taxonomy structure for storing content was used. So for example, if a consultant was searching for a certain form of proposal document, instead of searching the whole of the KC, he/she could go to the proposal database and search within that limitation. The taxonomy was set up in alignment with the types of knowledge consultants needed to leverage in delivering work, such as best practices, benchmarks, templates and tools, example deliverables, industry points of view and so on.

Over 99 per cent of PwC staff had access to the KC. The remainder were those in remote locations where telecommunications were restricted or too costly.

Management and maintenance

> I think what makes [the KC] work is the knowledge management processes, the quality of content, and I guess the other key factor is the combination of search and navigation.
> – Petar Bielovich, KM Programme Leader for Asia Pacific, PwC Consulting

The KC infrastructure was built inhouse by the Global Technology Systems (GTS) team, the internal IT department of PwC. GTS managed the maintenance of the three data centres. A core team of about five people managed the overall technical architecture, while local IT staff consisting of three to four people were deployed in each of the theatres to look after the groupware-type support of the whole intranet. They were also responsible for the graphics, layout and navigation of the KC as these related to the site for each line of service.

Content management followed a comprehensive content management policy and guidelines known as the Content Management Workflow. The site for each line of service was owned by a particular group of people or content managers at the theatre level who were responsible for organising, maintaining and refreshing content. These owner groups were well briefed on business needs through surveys and discussions with subject matter experts and business leaders on a regular basis in order to identify the type of content that they needed to harvest from projects. The workflow in the databases was such that it allowed them to engage in dialogue with subject matter experts, who in turn would review the content and highlight various points in a best-practice type document. The workflow also incorporated an automatic reminder function that triggered certain key staff to review certain content based on specified dates. The content managers would, on a regular basis, review documents under their ownership based on the current business environment and decide whether to keep or trash documents in the databases. However, even with such a rigid content-management framework, one big challenge was in ensuring that the databases had a critical mass of content on the various subject areas with variety in the content to make it useful to users. They were also responsible for liaising with the global Knowledge Management Team to ensure that deployment of new applications or new HTML content fell in line with the appropriate technical standards of the Firm. Applications would then be deployed via the KC and the local IT staff would address any technical problems.

The databases were updated with new information between one and three times every 24 hours. The technology allowed PwC to publish, form best-practice guidelines or share a thought-leadership piece of information to anybody in the organisation overnight.

Functionalities

Apart from the search capabilities, the KC also provided e-learning and e-training services. Within PwC Consulting's Website, for example, *ecademie* allowed staff to select from over 100 different courses that they could download onto laptops and play when they were on the road or in a plane. The hosting, technology, maintenance of course records and maintenance of access authorisations for *ecademie* were outsourced.

The KC also provided access to the external information service providers such as Goldman Sachs and Dow Jones. It gave PwC greater buying power in bringing all the location-based contracts with these organisations together and having one global contract with each of the service providers. It thus realised a saving of over $7 million.

To the user, the mass of databases were presented as a single unified system, even though the searched result could come from a number of databases. As a B2E solution, all staff had access to all information in the KC. Other applications on the Intranet, such as the Financial Client Portal, had restricted access rights.

Limitations

From the user's standpoint perhaps the biggest limitation is revealed when travelling or at a client's office, which is frequent in consulting. The physical bandwidth of the connection simply makes it slower to use applications, research and find information. Of course we have techniques for working around that; for instance, we can replicate some databases and information onto our machines. Another limitation: despite the good technology for access, it is often best to use knowledge management specialists to make the most use of the assets available to us. A conundrum is the trade-off between people most experienced with finding information and those who engaged in the projects. But what this really highlights is the vast, and growing amount of organizational knowledge we have at our disposal, either singly or as a group. I think we do a very good job of putting information into

[the KC], particularly the major methodologies, new practices and research, and getting it out. Still, our business is knowledge and experience, so it will always be nice to have more.
 – Brian Eccles, Principle Consultant, PwC Consulting

The culture of the organisation was very much ingrained in a code of behaviour set by Lotus Notes. However, as users began to demand greater functionality, the capabilities and limitations of the KC infrastructure were tested to their limit.

People just keep wanting more and more. This is the real problem . . . No matter how much you give them they always want more.
 – Stephen Langley

Another challenge was trying to keep up with the increasing expectations of the users in terms of navigation and functionality. As Stephen put it, "One of the problems is that most of our consultants are IT consultants anyway, so they are always checking out what is the latest thing on the Internet and they want to have it on the system right away . . . The problem is, having sunk a lot of investment into a particular set of technology, you can't always move as quickly as you would like onto new technology." In addition, in order to ensure that all information on the KC got searched the search engine had to be continually improved.

The original intention was for the KC or parts of it to be accessible by PwC clients. However, this did not materialise mainly because the KC was a closed system and the whole issue regarding information security and access authorisation to facilitate client access was not investigated.

Content ownership and information infrastructure issues for PwC Consulting

At the end of the day, we all share the same infrastructure and in some cases we share the same content. So we do have real IP issues to

negotiate and we do have real infrastructure issues to negotiate. I guess that shows the strength of having the infrastructure that we have because it has really tied us together.
                                    – Petar Bielovich

In January 2002, PwC announced the separation of PwC Consulting through an IPO expected in August. This raised a number of immediate issues that had to be resolved, the first with regard to the intellectual property (IP) rights of the knowledge in the shared databases, and the second concerning the technological infrastructure for housing PwC Consulting's knowledge base.

PwC Consulting developed 34 integrated global databases that were used solely by the consulting arm of the business. These databases allowed documents to be viewed by content type and gave communities (these were essentially practice areas of the consulting organisation) the ability to edit only their content. All 34 databases were housed in one KC server in each of the data centres. IP issues arose with the other databases that were shared across the Firm. These included the industry and best-practice

information. With two more months to go before the IPO, a resolution that would satisfy both organisations had to be found quickly.

The infrastructural framework for housing the PwC Consulting knowledge bases also had to be decided upon. Given the limitations of the existing infrastructure based on legacy systems, Stephen and his counterparts in the other two theatres did not see any value in duplicating the existing KC infrastructure for PwC Consulting. Furthermore, a project was in place for the launch of a PwC Consulting portal in Q4 2002.

The portal project

> Moving from the technology we have now to the portal is a very big step because we want to take advantage of all of today's technology, so there are many more things we have to think about.
>   – Stephen Langley

Justification

The value propositions for moving to the Internet platform are summarised in Figure 5. The mission to be achieved by

Figure 5 Value propositions for the portal

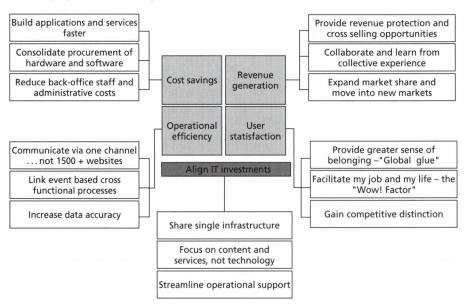

Exhibit 2 Core functionalities of the portal

Core Functionality	
• Authentication	**Authentication:** Verifying users' identities when they come to the portal.
• Authorisation	**Authorisation:** Giving users permission to access applications (or parts of applications) and content.
• Aggregation & Enablement of Applications/Content	**Aggregation and Enablement of Applications/Content:** Single point of access and session management.
• Profiling (firm driven)	**Profiling (firm driven):** Information presented based on role or other information we have about the user.
• Personalisation (user driven)	**Personalisation (user driven):** Individuals structure their views of the site to meet their needs and preferences.
• Search	**Search:** Ability to find relevant material across heterogeneous systems.
• Content Delivery (PwC and third party)	**Content Delivery (PwC and third party):** Easy access to timely relevant information with intuitive navigation.
• Collaboration	**Collaboration:** The ability to question, collaborate, and share information with other users.
• Payment Processing	**Payment Processing:** Applications that allow users to conduct business, e.g., purchase a subscription.
• Metrics/Reporting	**Metrics/Reporting:** Monitoring and measurement of usage and operating performance.

the PwC Consulting portal was to enhance connectivity and build on existing relationships with clients and staff. It was hoped that cost savings would be gained and the user experience would be improved through the shared infrastructure and common policies. As well as providing a single point of access to the business, significant built-in functionality was to be incorporated into the portal design. Exhibit 2 shows some of these core functionalities. The vision was not only to migrate the KC onto the Internet platform but also to design a comprehensive B2E online strategy as well as B2B and B2C initiatives.

Co-ordinating design and development

A Firm-wide portal project had been in progress for two years. In the beginning, it was decided that it would make more sense to have one team of people working on this project for the whole Firm in order to avoid having many unco-ordinated portals. Design, planning and development were organised through eight workstreams that looked into various aspects of the portal, such as content management, security, the enterprise directory and applications integration. Rollout and content

integration were expected in 2003–2006. However, with the impending IPO, the revised plan was to have a separate PwC Consulting portal by Q4 2002 with its own separate identity. The portal architecture adopted by PwC Consulting mirrored the Firm's portal architecture (see Figure 6 and Exhibits 3 and 4). Designing and developing a single portal platform required the implementation of a rigorous control and co-ordination process to guarantee the same user experience ("look and feel") across the business. In a large organisation such as PwC Consulting, where applications development could take place simultaneously in several locations, common technological and security standards had to be communicated to application developers, in order to avoid incompatibility and to ensure a common "worldview" (that is the design, look and feel of the portal).

The portal architecture

To realise the full benefits of the portal, a number of challenges were identified, including the need for a scalable, global, "always-on" infrastructure with 24/7 support. The industry trend was towards open, XML based applications to minimise integration

Figure 6 The portal systems architecture

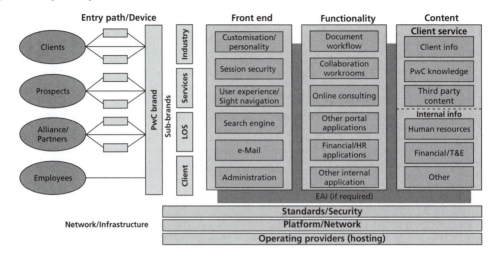

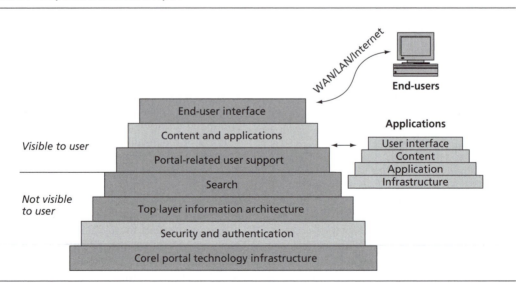

costs. PwC Consulting decided to develop a global, open XML-standard-based architecture. This would enable the core functionalities to be rapidly implemented and leveraged across geographies.

The open architecture would allow not only employees but also clients, prospective clients and business partners to access the portal. This made security and permission management one of the most important issues in the design of the portal.

In a portal, what you want to do is to have a single sign-on; you don't want to have to login 10 separate times for 10 separate applications. So how do you integrate the security for different applications? Those are the types of difficult questions we are having to deal with.
                                                    – Stephen Langley

Exhibit 3 The portal architectural layers

Exhibit 4 The portal framework

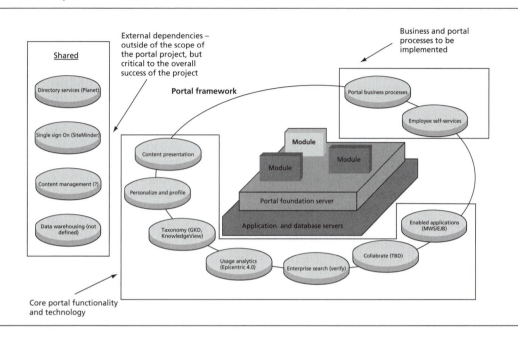

Notes

- *Content presentation* refers to the core portal engine. It is the system that creates the framework of the portal.
- *Personalize and profile* refers to the ability to personalise the portal (a standard portal functionality).
- *Taxonomy (Global Knowledge Objects)* refers to the way in which data is structured.
- *Usage analytics* are statistical tools that keep track of page hits, most frequently searched information, etc. Modifications to the site are often based on such statistical information.
- *Enterprise search* refers to the search engine. Verity is the search engine used for searching the KC. PwC intended to continue using Verity for its portal.
- *Collaborate*: The portal would enable PwC to consider adopting new technologies such as Groove (groove.net) that provided features such as discussion databases, real-time chat, instant messaging and so on for work groups to operate in a peer-to-peer collaborating environment. While Lotus Notes has served PwC well, users are demanding more of the system. Lotus Notes was not developed to be a global real-time, networked database system.
- *Enabled applications* are applications that are fully integrated with the portal such as the online leave-management application.
- *Employee self-services* enable the Firm to more efficiently manage information pertaining to employees and company policies and procedures for HR administration.
- *Portal business processes*: New business processes are created by building new services at both the source and target application side.

Front end

The intention of the portal project was to integrate applications and the knowledge base to make them more useful and personalised to the users. Employees could create their own homepages with different portlets that would push new information of interest to them from a wide range of different sources on a daily basis. Senior staff could be alerted to review and approve leave applications by simply clicking on a link that would take them directly to the page where they would sign an electronic approval. So even without having to search for information of interest, the personal homepage would alert the user to any new piece of information as it arose.

Functionalities

The portal could provide access to a much broader range of applications. Existing HRM and financial applications could be accessed through the portal as well as collaborative applications that would allow work groups to operate in a peer-to-peer collaborating environment. Sixteen PwC Consulting application areas were identified and grouped for deployment through the portal (see Exhibit 5). Other applications could be deployed as demand required them.

Content

The content layer was equally, if not more, important than the front end and functionality/applications layers to PwC Consulting, since content management determined its competitiveness in the industry. Choosing a common content architecture that enabled easy location and use of the organisation's knowledge content was critical. PwC Consulting recognised that the shelf life of knowledge was shortening, and therefore the transfer of knowledge to the content layer had to be embedded into the organisation's standard work processes. To achieve this, it was decided to adopt a metadata architecture based on the open standard, XML GKO version. In line with this, a rigorous management process had to be created to ensure that valuable assets were captured and leveraged. Ultimately, the plan was to do away with the current database content-management

Exhibit 5 Applications and major modules for operational readiness and rapid and responsive deployment in PwC Consulting

- Financials
  - General ledger
  - Accounts receivable
  - Accounts payable
  - Asset register
  - Cash management/Treasury
  - Budgeting
  - Tax management
  - Payroll
  - Financial and regulatory reporting
- Asset management
  - Procurement
  - Asset tracking
  - Software distribution
- Engagement management
  - Project management
  - Engagement financials
  - Engagement billing
  - Time and expense
  - Methodologies/Project tools
  - Document management
- Risk management
- Business intelligence/Decision support
- HR management
  - HR administration
  - Benefits
  - Executive/Partner affairs

- Recruiting
- Resource management
- Learning and professional development
  - Training administration
  - On-line training
  - Career development
- Knowledge management
  - Web Site
  - Search engine
- Marketing management
- New product/Service development
- Client relationship management (CRM)
  - Sales forecasting
  - Contact management
  - Opportunity management
- Enterprise portal
- Collaboration
  - E-mail
  - Calendar
  - Workflow
  - Desktop video conferencing
  - Virtual white board
  - Instant messaging
- Venture capital management
  - Investment modelling
  - Portfolio management

systems and move towards tagging and data structures. The categorisation of content accessed through the portal would take many man-hours. Data tagging had to be standardised to allow for the online searching and drilling of information. Common taxonomies for managing and sharing content had to be agreed upon.

Applications integration

Attention to the functionalities of the portal necessarily raised concerns regarding its ability to integrate with the front end and with other applications. PwC considered three options to tackle the issue of applications integration:

1 A full portal integration approach. The portal would include in its design navigation, security, standards compliance, content hosting, access authorisation, etc. A fully integrated portal would require the applications to be designed and built from scratch to run on the portal architecture. This would take time, resources and considerable expense.

2 Simply link applications to the portal. In this way, existing databases such as Lotus Notes could be accessed through the portal through the dumb-link, but no intelligence would be built into the system to allow for manipulation of the information or data. Under this approach, integration was only minimal. Nevertheless, depending on the requirements of the business and user, such an approach could provide a low-cost yet adequate solution.

3 Integrate content by linking applications to the portal through the use of enterprise application interface (EAI) systems. EAI software was bought-in middleware that would automatically perform certain information retrieval tasks from secondary systems. For example, an EAI system could pull relevant data from a financial management system that operated on a mainframe, and transform the data into a format that could then be pushed out into

the portal. So from the user's point of view, it would not matter that the information was stored in a system that was 15 or 20 years old.

The question for PwC Consulting was whether to simply link the existing applications and systems to the portal, rewrite the systems and applications to customise interfacing with the portal, or buy in an EAI system. PwC had experimented with designing custom interfaces with global service providers such as American Express (AMEX), which issued credit cards to PwC staff to manage their travel expenses. By linking AMEX to the portal, data from the AMEX system could be automatically pushed into PwC's financial systems for easy access by PwC employees. An alternative to customised interfacing was to buy in commercial EAI systems, but PwC considered this to be too complex and expensive to implement. Unlike manufacturing businesses, where real-time information was critical to the performance of the company, consulting businesses had less need for real-time updating of their databases.

[S]o do you invest in an EAI system and just keep your foundation? I guess that the real benefit of an EAI system is that you can leave your back-end systems untouched. Or do you scrap the back-office systems and replace them with systems that integrate with the portal?
– Stephen Langley

Governance and maintenance of the portal

PwC Consulting's strategy was to outsource the management and operation of the infrastructure layer. In this regard, it was looking to partner with a truly global infrastructure provider that could provide network security and reliability. On-going maintenance of the portal (content and applications) required a more formal governance structure that would encompass a steering committee, special interest groups and a programme management office.

Resolutions sought

With the IPO scheduled for early August and the PwC Consulting portal launch in late 2002, time was pressing on Stephen and his team to come up with some immediate solutions. Intellectual property issues in relation to the knowledge base had to be resolved. But more importantly, what was the most timely and cost-effective solution for transferring the relevant databases in the KC to the online medium, given that the portal would not be ready for launch until Q4? It seemed inappropriate to replicate the legacy systems that currently housed the KC.

There were also longer-term issues related to the portal. The challenges with respect to the technology and the applications integration approach had to be resolved before the portal project could go any further. Furthermore, while the KC was replicated in three theatres, managers remained undecided whether the portal should be replicated. Replicating the portal architecture could

determine the performance of the network as well as provide a disaster recovery site in the event of a systems failure. Having said that, Internet bandwidth was forever increasing and the cost of having all the bandwidth necessary was decreasing. The portal promised to be "everything for everyone". It was crucial that it lived up to its promise, particularly in marking a new page in the history of PwC Consulting under a new identity and brand name.

Pauline Ng prepared this case under the supervision of Dr Ali Farhoomand for class discussion. This case is not intended to show effective or ineffective handling of decision or business processes.

e-Business infrastructure: integration, standards and security

To establish the importance of integration as the cornerstone of successful ❑ e-business transformation

To introduce multi-tiered architectures and examine the characteristics of ❑ integration servers

To learn about the XML messaging standard and its key role in facilitating ❑ B2B transactions

To explore how emerging technologies are causing computing to evolve ❑ into a utility

To learn about important issues relating to security, virtual network services ❑ and the payment solutions arena

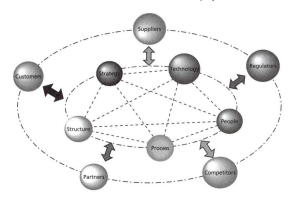

> I know it's hard to imagine what the world was like before the World Wide Web became widely used, but remember there was no common access to content. There were no browsers. There was no HTTP. There was no notion of Web sites, and therefore you couldn't access anything. Then, because of the agreement on standards, all of a sudden the World Wide Web flourished and the rest is history.
>
> – Irving Wladawsky-Berger, Vice President for Server Group Technology and Strategy, IBM[1]

---

1. Wladawsky-Berger in IBM Corp. (2002).

In Chapter 4 we introduced the building blocks of e-business infrastructure. Our focus in this chapter will be on integration, standards and security – the enabling components of e-business infrastructure (as represented by the sloping face of the e-business components pyramid – see Figure 5.1). We will discuss in detail the importance of integration in achieving a successful e-business implementation. With a basic understanding of the building blocks of e-business infrastructure, we are able now to delve into greater technical detail to appreciate how the goal of integration, the application of standards and the issue of security must be grasped by decision makers. These three enabling components are crucial to the success of any e-business initiative.

An organisation's legacy systems are often a significant investment built up over years of operation. As we saw in Chapter 2, a company's efforts to achieve its e-business objectives is usually hampered by inflexibilities ingrained in such systems. Because information is the basic resource of any e-business transformation effort, the underlying infrastructure should therefore be conceived and designed such that it can readily access critical information from legacy systems for sharing with both internal and external e-business applications in a standardised and secure manner.

In response to rapid technological advances, a multitude of vendors and standards bodies keep developing and marketing solutions for seemingly every aspect of business. A sound conceptualisation of the organisation's business processes will assist in achieving the integration of legacy, Web-based and newly developed applications. A secure, operational and efficient e-business should utilise key standards, integration, security and payment solutions to "weave" the latest applications with pre-existing financial, ERP and back-office products.

In this chapter we will discuss a particular open standard called XML because of its importance in the proliferation of e-business, particularly with

Figure 5.1 e-Business components pyramid

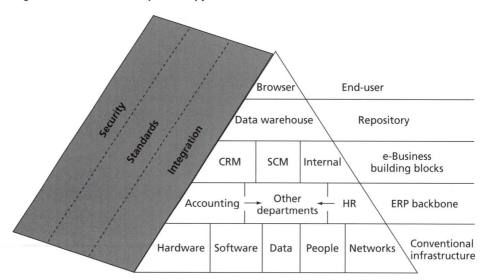

Source: Adapted from Shields (2001).

respect to traditional electronic business-to-business transactions, or electronic data interchange (EDI). Since e-business transformation entails the exchange of sensitive business information, particularly customer records and financial transactions, we will also provide an overview of security considerations and the mainstay solutions (firewalls, virtual private networks, public key infrastructure and digital certificates). Finally because payment issues are integral to most e-business initiatives we will shed some light on this important area.

A successful e-business implementation involves the attentive weaving together of various information technologies to ensure that the solution in place is functional, secure, scalable and founded on the ultimate objective of making the organisation more customer-centric, and thus more competitive.

The overriding theme in achieving an e-business infrastructure is that of integration. An enterprise that successfully integrates existing and new systems throughout its value chain can open up new avenues of business opportunity and experience tremendous cost, resource and time savings. A standardised foundation of open data formats is essential in supporting integration efforts, making e-business accessible to businesses of all sizes and allowing companies to transact with a high degree of confidence. As such, standards have become the most important issue for regulating and governing the e-business landscape. Finally, the data and information concerned must be secured against tampering and unauthorised access.

Integration, standards and security are closely interrelated matters that should be anticipated and planned for at the highest levels of management. Some of the key technologies behind these efforts have existed for some time, but their importance has been greatly elevated in the context of the Internet as a medium for business transaction. Others such as the various XML-based frameworks have emerged as revolutionary means of making electronic business more accessible than ever before.

The importance of integration

By modern standards, applications in the early mainframe period were uncomplicated in design and intended to process simple, repetitive transactions. As such, there was little need to integrate corporate data. With the proliferation of enterprise-wide applications, it became vital for companies to leverage existing data and the diverse array of processes, software, standards and hardware. Integration became even more crucial as e-business applications crossed organisational boundaries, and the confluence of Web, legacy and new applications became necessary for conducting business.

Traditionally, companies achieve integration through tedious programming of custom middleware.[2] This type of software links one application with

---

2. Middleware is software that liaises between applications and enterprise networks, generally with the capability of managing interactions between disparate applications and across divergent computing platforms. In other words, middleware lets developers avoid the issues involved in getting applications to interact with one another across multiple environments.

another on a point-to-point basis within closed proprietary settings. Today's businesses however, face a myriad of challenging issues and imperatives that call for intra- and inter-corporate integration of business processes, data, standards, applications and platforms. As a result, integration is evolving beyond *internally* oriented enterprise application integration (EAI) and a variety of technologies that are being deployed to achieve B2B integration (see Figure 5.2).

The process of integration is usually costly and highly complex and requires consideration of many parties as well as a host of technical and organisational dimensions:[3]

● *Business processes*: The underlying processes for exchanging enterprise information within and across the business must be clearly defined and conceptualised. Organisations must manage business processes with attention to (i) minimising costs (ii) improving responsiveness and

Figure 5.2 Integration shifting from internal to B2B dimensions: (a) enterprise application integration and (b) B2B integration

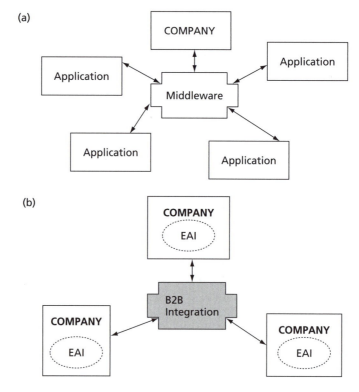

Source: Adapted from Linthicum (2001).

---

3. Gormley (2001).

(iii) streamlining operations. Modelling techniques and workflow integration are some of the practices employed towards these ends.[4]

● *Data*: Before integration at any other level may proceed, enterprise data must be identified and catalogued – this process of "data-mapping" is of vital importance because it reduces the effort necessary for further integration. Metadata models (repositories of data describing other database's structures, attributes or changes) are typically developed so that data can then be shared across disparate systems.

● *Standards*: Standard formats for data and information must be established. The issue of standards is perhaps the most important in the IT field, where the absence of regulation has resulted in a set of innumerable data formats and languages. Some of the emerging and increasingly accepted standards with potential to promote the sharing and distribution of data in e-business are extensible mark-up language (XML) and Common Object Request Broker Architecture (CORBA).[5]

● *Enterprise applications*: Application integration is commonly required for B2B integration, integrating legacy applications with ERP implementations, integrating CRM systems with backend applications and a host of other integration requirements. The objective is to transport data from one application to another, or to extend functionality across applications so that software on multiple machines from multiple vendors can communicate. Custom development is often necessary to supplement a packaged integration solution.

● *Platforms*: Finally, the architecture, hardware and software must be integrated. This level of integration deals with the processes and necessary tools to ensure that diverse systems on a heterogeneous network are able to communicate effectively in a secure manner.

Integration servers

A sound integration solution is increasingly considered a precondition for the development of agile systems, capable of fine-tuning in response to the unpredictable realities of business. A currently favoured approach is to employ *integration servers* (also termed "message brokers") and other specialised integration products that can be established as a common connecting point for the various enterprise applications. Since the advent of the Web, these pre-package solutions have become widely used to leverage existing data and the diverse array of processes, software, standards and hardware that comprise the e-business landscape. There are significant differences in the product architectures of the available

---

4. "Workflow" refers to the automated routing of documents to the appropriate user.
5. CORBA is a middleware platform that allows programs written in different languages and operating on various platforms to work together. It is suited for situations where processing performed by one computer requires processing from another.

solutions. This makes the selection of an integration server an important decision to be based on the enterprise environment and specific application needs.

Integration servers typically include packaged connectors or adapters[6] for the most common enterprise applications (often in a graphical environment with point-and-click functionality), toolkits for performing custom development and integration, and engines[7] for translating data between systems.[8] With integration servers, the integration of highly disparate systems, ranging from databases to e-business applications, is greatly facilitated. Middleware identifies what data are required to perform a transaction and which of the enterprise's applications need the data. It then standardises the format of the data and transmits them through the integration architecture.

Integration servers are typically built around one of two architectural configurations: hub and spoke model or bus architecture (often referred to as a messaging bus or an information bus).[9] In the hub and spoke architecture, all integrated applications are linked to the integration server at a central connecting point (Figure 5.3). Under this configuration, new systems or applications can be automatically integrated by means of a connection to the server at the nucleus. This integration server functions as a broker, performing data conversion and the necessary processes to allow interaction among the connected systems. Hub and spoke integration approaches can be centrally managed and do away with the need for convoluted point-to-point integration. By contrast, in bus architecture, all applications are linked by adapters to the message or information bus which serves as a communication backbone. Messages are channelled through the bus to the integration server, which then translates the data and redirects them to the receiving node. The bus architecture offers greater scalability and the potential of better performance, but its implementation is more complex and increasingly difficult to administer as the environment grows.

The choice of what architecture to implement is a function of the applications involved and available resources. Hub and spoke architectures are thought to be better suited to companies with moderate IT resources, a smaller number of systems to integrate and moderate transaction volumes.[10] Bus architectures are more complicated to manage and usually require larger outlays, but are better suited for larger-magnitude integration efforts involving numerous systems and high transaction volumes.[11] Integration servers can constitute a major portion of the overall IT budget and must sometimes be looked at as a strategic technology investment for facilitating future integration as the enterprise brings more e-business technology into its fold.

---

6. Layers between the integration server and the targeted application that allow one system to interact with another. Adapters may employ "libraries" (collections of data) to map differences between application interfaces.
7. Software that performs a repetitive function, for example a graphics or database engine.
8. "Integration Powered", Informationweek.com, 28 May 2001.
9. Ibid.
10. Ibid.
11. Ibid.

Figure 5.3 Integration servers

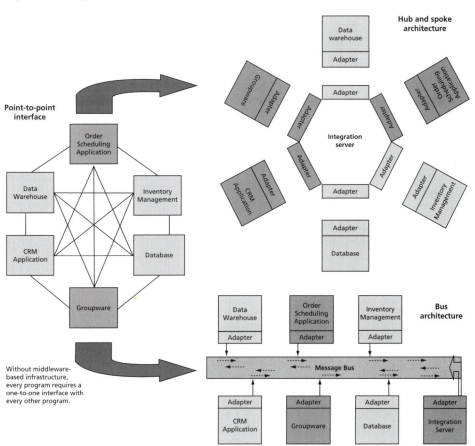

Source: Adapted from Sanchez et al. (2001).

Multi-tiered architectures to ease integration

In the age of extended computing environments, developers are increasingly favouring multi-tiered architectures (also referred to as "N-tiered architectures"), which distribute systems and software across front end, Web-servers, application servers, integration servers and databases (Figure 5.4). Effectively, an additional, independent application layer is added to the traditional 2-tier architecture (see Chapter 4), which has the effect of separating the business logic from front and back ends (presentation and database management functions), both physically and in the software design.[12] When properly implemented, the hardware and software for each layer within the architecture may be modified and upgraded independently – making it much easier to integrate new applications into the environment.

---

12. Intel e-Business Center White Paper (2001).

Figure 5.4 A multi-tiered architecture

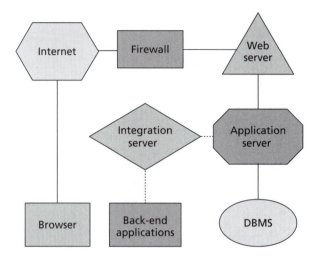

Adapted from Intel e-Business Center (2001).

Through this departure from simple 2-tier client/server configurations, a building block approach to infrastructure design and implementation can then be applied, with e-business applications designed, deployed and integrated with greater agility and cost-effectiveness. By standardising the hardware and software at each layer, the benefits of multi-tier architecture may be extended further to allow for the reuse of core components to facilitate integration and simplify the computing environment.[13] Individual applications can be designated access to only certain levels of data from the ERP system, allowing for better data security when deployed to a variety of external users.

XML: a critical standard for integration

The task of integrating an enterprise's internal applications has always been a difficult one, but one that is often further complicated by the requirement to extend integration efforts beyond the enterprise. With the recent decline of tech companies, it is difficult for businesses to embark on integration projects with confidence that vendors and partners will remain in business long enough to support their proprietary technologies. In the light of these circumstances, the adoption of open standards will be a crucial determining factor of success in integration projects and the seamless operation of e-business in general. Industry bodies have been working to establish standardised functionality for formerly proprietary standards and a number of these emerging standards promise to revolutionise the way data are defined.

---

13. Ibid.

Extensible Markup Language (XML) is a promising messaging standard that was introduced by the World Wide Web consortium (W3C) in 1996 for describing data elements on Web pages and B2B documents. XML provides an open format for information exchange between otherwise incompatible applications. It is expressed in a very similar way to the traditional Hypertext Markup Language (HTML) used for Web-page design, but while HTML is used to convey data together with formatting information, XML contains the data together with its associated descriptive metadata.[14] Although XML employs similar tags to HTML, it does not convey any formatting information to the browser. Rather, XML conveys the essential data and leaves layout and formatting to the developer of whichever application will read the data, allowing Web pages to function much the same as a database record. This fundamental difference facilitates the integration of information and enhances interoperability, thus making XML extremely valuable for information exchange and data warehousing. Table 5.1 provides a side-by-side example of HTML and XML.

In the example above, to display a customer's name and address using HTML, data must be formatted using tags to indicate font size, font family (e.g. Times New Roman, Arial) and so. Thus, the data are merged with its formatting elements. Under XML, the element is defined in the Document Type Definition (e.g. Identity) with its attributes (Name, Date of birth, Town of birth, State of birth). Data in XML are then added according to the schema that has been defined. Any formatting particulars will be dealt with by the developer of the application that will read the data. Hence, data and formatting are separated. For more details on XML terminology consult Appendix 1.

The advantages offered by XML – platform independence and a clearly defined structure – have made it a promising standard for the implementation of B2B integration. Its ability to eliminate variations that occur in dealing with

Table 5.1 HTML and XML comparison

Hypertext Markup Language (HTML)	Extensible Markup Language (XML)
<font size = "4">Barry White</font> <font size = "2">September 12,1944 Galveston, Texas</font>	<Name>Barry White</Name> <Dateofbirth>12-09-1944</Dateofbirth> <Townofbirth> Galveston </Townofbirth> <Stateofbirth> Texas </Stateofbirth>

Document Type Definition (DTD)

<! Element Identity (Name, Dateofbirth?, Townofbirth?, Stateofbirth?)>
<! Element Name (#PCDATA)>

etc…

#PCDATA declaration identifies an unformatted string of text.

Question marks indicate these fields are optional.

---

14. Data that serve to describe other data.

HTML among different browsers led to speculation that it might eventually replace HTML altogether. Rather than replacing HTML, however, XML has become a behind-the-scenes data management system and a general enabler of e-business.[15] By separating the user interface from the content, XML has greatly simplified the task of keeping information current in electronic communications.

XML and EDI

Against the backdrop of increasing industry-wide cooperation, XML-based technologies are well positioned to pick up where EDI left off as an enabler of inter-corporate transactions. The origins of EDI can be traced back to 1960s when the automobile industry started to devise ways to electronically interchange business documents. EDI is based on a set of highly structured transaction sets that govern inter-company transmission of various business documents such as purchase order or bill of lading. It is usually based on direct computer-to-computer communications involving third-party proprietary value-added networks. EDI implementation is, however, complex and its cost relatively high for most organisations, especially for SMEs because of their low transaction volumes.

XML provides an accessible, standardised and inexpensive means for information to be exchanged between companies in environments that do not share common platforms. It promises to improve the speed and flexibility of B2B applications because it is not a proprietary development of any private concern. The development of XML specifications is supervised by the XML Working Group and various special interest groups drawn from different industries. Special purpose XML languages and standards are announced on virtually a daily basis and nearly every vertical industry now has XML efforts underway to establish its own data definitions and schemas for exchanging data.[16]

An XML-based framework for supply chain partners

The growing drive to convert EDI systems to XML-based frameworks is particularly well exemplified by the fast-advancing RosettaNet Internet Standard (www.rosettanet.org) that makes heavy use of XML as the lingua franca for electronic transactions (EIU, 2001). RosettaNet is a consortium of major information technology, electronic components and semiconductor manufacturing companies, including key members such as Intel and Cisco Systems. The consortium works to implement industry-wide, open standards for a wide range of e-business processes.

The fundamental concept behind RosettaNet is the use of XML to standardise highly specialised communications between partners. These inter-partner dialogues are known as Partner Interface Processes, or PIPs, which function as the governing lexicon, defining the properties behind all aspects of a particular

---

15. Abualsamid (2001).
16. Marshall (2001).

business transaction. For example, the PIP relating to "Request Price and Avail-ability" enables a buyer to obtain product price and availability information from a supplier. To facilitate communications between the two parties the request allows the supplier to include both the requested information and addi-tional product information as appropriate, and return the information to the buyer, who in turn analyses this information.

PIPs serve as the interface between partners in a supply chain and specify the activities, decisions and interactions that pertain to a transaction between the parties.PIPs are designed for ease of integration and serve as ready-made solu-tions for more than 100 common business requirements. Companies can use a grouping of PIPs to rapidly and efficiently fulfil a wide range of activities such as pricing, managing inventory and tracking orders, to mention a few. This is a major advance from the EDI alternative that was limited in scope and required costly setting-up for each partner relationship.

There are presently more than 100 PIPs arranged in the following seven pri-mary "clusters":[17]

1   Partner product and service review

2   Product information

3   Order management

4   Inventory management

5   Marketing information management

6   Service and support

7   Manufacturing.

For a more detailed breakdown of PIP clusters, see Appendix 2.

As PIPs specify the processes for particular transactions, they are guided by the RosettaNet Implementation Framework (RNIF) and rely on a body of busi-ness and technical data dictionaries. The RNIF uses XML to provide specifica-tions for the exchange of information between trading parties and regulates the transport, routing and packaging, security, signals, and trading partner agreements (Figure 5.5). A set of business and technical dictionaries, meanwhile, serve to provide common attributes to avoid the disorder that would result from trading partners independently defining their own terminology. The business dictionary designates properties for business transactions, while the technical dictionary designates processes for defining processes and services.

RosettaNet is positioned to become a leading framework for supporting e-business transactional exchanges. In contrast to EDI, which requires all parties to use a shared (generally proprietary) network and application suite, RosettaNet takes advantage of the Internet as a medium for communication. By serving as a

17. RosettaNet.org.

Figure 5.5 RosettaNet structure

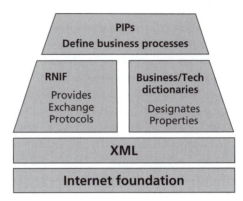

Source: Adapted from RosettaNet Source.

common language, B2B implementations become more manageable with a less unwieldy volume of data and processes. From the perspective of distribution, RosettaNet offers a broad, supply chain-wide standard rather than the knotty interfacing that is required of EDI. Perhaps more significantly, development cycle times can be reduced considerably from what is presently the norm. The essential attractiveness of RosettaNet is its promise of a standardised interface, agreed upon by all parties so that individual companies are no longer burdened with the need to invest in developing unique processes.

RosettaNet receives technological and corporate support from some of the industry's largest players, including leading companies from IT, electronics components and semiconductor sectors. RosettaNet partners make contributions throughout the development process, providing technical input, their expertise in process methodology, and knowledge of best practices. The non-profit consortium structure is intended to encourage the best minds from notable companies to contribute to developing non-proprietary standards to address the needs of the entire industry. While at present RosettaNet is primarily focused on high-tech sectors, indications are that it may expand in due course to encompass other supply chains such as that of the automotive sector.

The ebXML framework

While RosettaNet is an example of an influential XML framework for the supply chains of vertical industries, the horizontal electronic business XML (ebXML) initiative promises to bring the benefits of XML-based transactions to enterprises of all sizes, operating in any industry. We have seen that the closed nature of traditional EDI suffered many inadequacies that made it accessible only to the largest enterprises. ebXML is jointly sponsored by the Organisation for the Advancement of Structured Information Standards (OASIS) and the United Nations Centre for Trade Facilitation and Electronic Business (UN/CEFACT) to promote a vendor-neutral messaging framework for electronic business. Similar to RosettaNet, it is a platform-independent open standard with complete sets of specifications available for programmers to follow. The ebXML infrastructure provides a set of industry-neutral "core components" that contain formatting information for a wide range of business data for companies to employ the framework. For more detailed explanation of terminology related to ebXML consult Appendix 3.

Since ebXML software is less expensive and easier to implement than proprietary EDI, the first and immediate beneficiaries will be SMEs, operating in industries that have long been excluded from the realm of electronic business (Cottrill, 2001). A second virtue of ebXML is that it has intrinsic security features. When compared to other XML standards, the ebXML framework pays significant attention to the issue of security in its specifications. The support of point-to-point communication makes ebXML attractive because responsibilities for message transfer are clearly defined. Before a message is sent to a trading partner, security is the sender's responsibility. Once it arrives at its destination, security becomes the responsibility of the receiving partner. This capability averts the disputes that commonly occur in business transactions.

In order to join the ebXML community, a company needs to publish its profile in the ebXML registry using ebXML specifications. An ebXML registry is similar to a telephone directory that stores all telephone numbers. Suppose that company A and company B have published their profiles to the registry and have installed systems for implementing ebXML. When company A wants to conduct businesses with company B, it must download company B's profile from the registry. Once it has done this, the parties then need to establish a contract defining the business operations and security measures to be employed in the deal. Once the contract has been agreed upon, both companies need to install these new terms in their respective systems for implementation. Company A and company B are now able to conduct businesses with each other. Table 5.2 compares and contrasts traditional and ebXML-based business transactions.

Table 5.2 ebXML vs traditional transactions

Traditional business transaction	ebXML-based transaction
Business partners have registered their phone numbers in a telephone directory	Companies register their company profile in the ebXML registry
Phone, video phone, fax and other kinds of communication devices are installed	Companies install a system to get ebXML running
Parties search the telephone directory for business partner's telephone number	Companies download business partner's company profiles from the ebXML registry
Agreement on the channel of communication, for example, making an international call, using video phone, or using the facsimile	Agreement on the terms of conducting businesses such as business operations included; security measures employed, etc.
Business communication is established	Companies proceed with business transactions

The above scenario illustrates a one-to-one relationship. However, an important feature of ebXML is its capability of supporting collaboration over multiple business transactions. Such collaboration can be constructed by aggregating services over multiple business transactions. For example, unlike the case with EDI, a buyer's request for a product price quotation is not restricted only to those suppliers, which with it has already existing agreements. Instead, as ebXML standardises the transaction specifications, it does not require the trading partners to have one-to-one connection, thus facilitating electronic trading. In the above example, ebXML allows the buyer to use the services of an intermediary, such as a market hub, to post its request on the Internet. The hub broadcasts this information to appropriate registered members, who would in turn respond to the request.

While ebXML may seem a more broadly applicable standard than vertical industry initiatives such as RosettaNet, it is expected that the two will serve complementary rather than competing roles. Vertical standards are driven by participants intimately familiar with the industry and hence able to develop more appropriate message definitions in the context of their unique business needs. ebXML, on the other hand, provides interoperability in message definitions, which enables communication between multiple buyers and sellers. It is expected that the capabilities of ebXML may eventually be incorporated as a messaging layer for vertical standard frameworks. In effect, ebXML will eventually become "...the envelope the message is deposited into, while the verticals provide the content."[18]

Computing as a utility

The adoption of open standards such as XML will be important in enabling integration, but is not in itself enough to tackle the immense complexity inherent in bringing together different software systems. Programs by major vendors such as SAP and Oracle have been popular largely because they are offered as readily integrated packages. A number of innovative start-ups, referred to as Managed Service Providers, are vying to provide solutions based on the assumption that companies will want to outsource this aspect of their infrastructure simply to avoid the bothersome task of integration.

Web services are capable of interacting with other such applications using open messaging protocols such as XML. They are developed with the goal of allowing one application to locate and exchange data with others that supply its needed services. Specialised integrators focus on linking disparate systems within a company. Others have secured solid positions in the B2B integration market but are working towards realising the greater ambition of developing end-to-end platforms for business automation. Recent years have seen the

---

18. Bill Smith, as quoted in Montalbano (2000).

growing realisation that no single vendor can be the leader in all areas of innovation. Consequently, companies are linking these various "best-of-breed" components and offering them under the umbrella of a unified service, in some cases even charging on a rent-like basis for the particular applications used.[19] The pinnacle of integration may well be this Web-driven weaving together of services and the subsequent repositioning of software usage from periodic purchase to ongoing utility.

The future: grid computing

As Web-based methods of delivering application functionality are increasing in popularity, another technology that is gaining recognition for its potential to radically alter the computing landscape has been *grid computing*. Grid computing is essentially a means of harnessing the power of computers located on a network that would otherwise have gone unused. Grid computing can be used to tackle problems that require processing power greater than a single personal computer can provide without having to resort to far more costly alternatives of supercomputing or networked-servers (so-called "server farms"). Rather than using a network merely to transmit data, grid computing uses the network to share processing power.

As with the Internet itself, the concept originated from research communities where grid computing has been employed for collaborative scientific computation and data analysis. The technology behind grid computing is not particularly complex, nor is the concept a new one – in 1965, MIT academic Fernando Corbats envisioned a computing facility akin to a power or water company.[20] It was not until recent advances in bandwidth capability, networking technology and the trend towards mobile devices (with limited processing capability) that the conditions for grid computing ripened such that industry heavyweights like IBM and Sun Microsystems have become key proponents of the technology.

The single most important factor for the success of grid computing will be agreement on standards. Increasingly, industry forces are pushing for the merger of Web-service protocols with corresponding grid computing protocols. As the concept of Web services converges with the power of grid computing, the implications for e-business are tremendous. Companies can drastically reduce technology expenses by harnessing grid computing for power-intensive problems such as economic forecasting or risk analysis. The burden of constant hardware upgrades will be alleviated as applications utilise idle network resources. Perhaps most significantly, end-users will increasingly interact with front-end devices that serve primarily to identify the user, receive and display a stream of content and return simplified responses.[21]

---

19. For example: Asera, Jamcracker, Portera.
20. Foster (2002).
21. Shear (2002).

GRID ARCHITECTURE

Close to a decade of focused R&D and experimentation has produced considerable consensus on the requirements and architecture of Grid technology. Standard protocols, which define the content and sequence of message exchanges used to request remote operations, have emerged as an important and essential means of achieving the interoperability that Grid systems depend on (Figure 5.6). Also essential are standard application programming interfaces (APIs), which define standard interfaces to code libraries and facilitate the construction of Grid components by allowing code components to be reused.

Protocols and APIs can be categorised according to the role they play in a Grid system. At the lowest level, the fabric, we have the physical devices or resources that Grid users want to share and access, including computers, storage systems, catalogues, networks, and various forms of sensors.

Above the fabric are the connectivity and resource layers. Because the protocols in these layers must be implemented everywhere they must be relatively small in number. The connectivity layer contains the core communication and authentication protocols required for Grid-specific network transactions.

Communication protocols enable the exchange of data between resources, whereas authentication protocols build on communication services to provide cryptographically secure mechanisms for verifying the identity of users and resources. The resource layer contains protocols that exploit communication and authentication protocols to enable the secure initiation, monitoring, and control of resource-sharing operations. Running the same program on different computer systems depends on resource-layer protocols.

The collective layer contains protocols, services, and APIs that implement interactions across collections of resources. Because they combine and exploit components from the relatively narrower resource and connectivity layers, the components of the collective layer can implement a wide variety of tasks without requiring new resource-layer components. Examples of collective services include directory and brokering services for resource discovery and allocation; monitoring and diagnostic services; data replication services; and membership and policy services for keeping track of who in a community is allowed to access resources.

Figure 5.6 Grid architecture as a series of layers

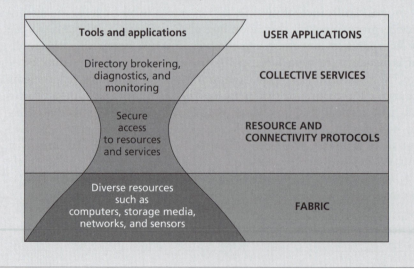

At the top of any Grid system are the user applications, which are constructed in terms of, and call on, the components in any other layer. For example, a high-energy physics analysis application that needs to execute several thousands of independent tasks, each taking as input some set of files containing events, might proceed by:

- **obtaining** necessary authentication credentials (connectivity layer protocols);
- **querying** an information system and replica catalogue to determine availability of computers, storage systems, and networks, and the location of required input files (collective services);
- **submitting** requests to appropriate computers, storage systems, and networks to initiate computations, move data, and so forth (resource protocols); and
- **monitoring** the progress of the various computations and data transfers, notifying the user when all are completed, and detecting and responding to failure conditions (resource protocols).

Many of these functions can be carried out by tools that automate the more complex tasks. The University of Wisconsin's Condor-G system (http://www.cs.wisc.edu/condor) is an example of a powerful, full-featured task broker.

Reprinted with permission from Physics Today Vol. 55 #2, p. 42, 2002. © American Institute of Physics. © 2002, American Institute of Physics.

Security considerations

e-Business makes data security a vital imperative for all parties conducting business, whether via the corporate intranet, over the Internet or by means of a location-independent wireless device. Security refers to the safeguarding of corporate information utility including hardware, software and data. Threats to data security most commonly originate from computer viruses, but also consist of unauthorised access of the corporate network, interception of data transmitted over the Internet or plainly physical damage to hardware components. There is quite simply no "out-of-the-box" security solution that offers protection against every possible scenario. A comprehensive and reliable solution can only be achieved through a mixture of sound technologies and most importantly, education on the part of employees as to the potential dangers.

The major components that comprise the portfolio of computer security can be classified according to five major groups[22] (we will further examine three leading security technologies – firewalls, virtual private networks and public key infrastructure):

- *Physical security*: The most obvious, but often overlooked form of security concerns the physical security of the hardware itself. Special locks and cables can prevent the removal of computer hardware by unauthorised parties. Where necessary, higher end security systems such as surveillance and tracking devices are employed.

---

22. Security Overview, ittoolbox.com.

- *Content filtering*: The most widely known and applied form of content filter is the anti-virus utility (the most popular titles include McAfee VirusScan and Norton AntiVirus) which scans incoming files to identify binary signatures (patterns) of known viruses that may be attached to scripts and executable programs. Whenever new viruses are discovered, a signature database (or virus definitions library) is updated and made available by major vendors who typically offer the latest downloads online. There are two fundamental types of anti-virus scanners[23] – one type simply scans every file on the system at start-up and again before any file is accessed. The other type takes inventory of all executable files residing on the system and scans them only when they have changed. While the first type of scanner offers a higher level of security, the second appreciably reduces the amount of computer processing that needs to be performed. Aside from anti-virus utilities, widely used content filters include URL blockers (used by corporations, schools and parents to restrict access to irrelevant, inappropriate or offensive sites), spam-blockers and email filters.

- *Protocols and encryption*: Various network protocols are in place to ensure that transmitted data will not be intercepted. Secure Socket Layer (SSL) is the most widely used protocol on the Internet. When sessions are initiated, a public key[24] is sent from server to browser. The browser then uses this to randomly generate a secret key that is sent back to the server in exchange for a corresponding key to enable the session. SSL is being combined with other authentication protocols and techniques by the Internet Engineering Task Force[25] (IETF) to form the Transport Security Layer (TSL) – a backwards compatible protocol expected to become a major security standard. In addition to network protocols such as SSL, data encryption is often employed to ensure that messages cannot be read even in the event that they are intercepted. Encryption uses algorithms to encode data so that only the correct key can restore it to its original form.[26]

- *Intrusion prevention and network monitoring*: Firewalls, virtual private networks (VPNs) and intrusion detection systems (IDSs) are frequently used to secure a network. Firewalls are widely used to allow users to access the Internet, while separating the company Web server from the corporate

23. Computer Desktop Encyclopedia (2000)
24. A "key" in cryptographic terms refers to a numerical code, usually ranging from 40 to 128 bits in length (with a higher number of bits in the key, more combinations exist, making it increasingly difficult to break the code). Encryption involves mathematically combining the key with the contents of a file in some manner. Keys are typically published in two parts – a "public key" that is publicly accessible, and a "private key" known only by the owner.
25. The IETF (www.ietf.org) is an international volunteer organisation comprising network designers, operators, vendors, and researchers who propose solutions to common problems and issues relating to the Internet. The work of the IETF is accomplished through working groups that are organised by topic, with much of the collaboration coordinated through mailing lists and tri-annual meetings.
26. A mathematically expressed set of ordered steps for solving a problem.

intranet. A firewall can be a single router[27] that regulates traffic and restricts access to unwanted packets, or may be a more sophisticated combination of routers and servers. An IDS is a software that detects when a computer system has been accessed without authorisation. IDSs typically detect "cracker"[28] attempts and signal an alert or interpret irregularities in the normal routine as indication of a possible attack. VPNs are networks that are configured within a shared wide area infrastructure (discussed further below). They perform like private networks to the user but physically share a common backbone with other parties.

● *Authentication and access control*: This aspect of data security involves establishing policy that specifies which parties are to be granted access to different levels of information. Corporate data can be protected at the most basic level by employing user passwords. However, systems programmers and technical support personnel will ultimately have access to these codes. A further limitation inherent in the use of passwords is that they offer no assurance that the authorised party is in fact using the password. Data access control can be further enhanced through solutions such as smart cards, and increasingly through the use of biometrics[29] to verify identity. Public key infrastructures (discussed in greater detail below) may also be used to confirm the identity of a user, or to ensure that the integrity of a message has not been compromised.

The company firewall

The most widely known mechanism by which intruders are barred from networks is the company firewall, which enforces a security policy by regulating data traffic between networks. Firewalls are commonly used to allow enterprise users to access the Internet securely, or to separate the company's public-accessible servers from the goings-on of its internal network. A company may also implement internal firewalls to add an additional layer of security between internal boundaries – for instance, keeping the human resources network secure from unauthorised access from within the enterprise. While in many enterprises, certain departments (e.g. R&D, Accounting) tend to be privy to more sensitive data, strong authentication and access controls may in many cases provide adequate protection. A firewall can also serve an important central auditing function, providing systems administrators with information about the volume of traffic passing through and any attempts made to break into the network.

Conceptually, a firewall consists of two mechanisms – one to deny traffic and one to permit it. The notion of firewall protection is a metaphorical construct,

---

27. A router is a device that forwards packets of data from one network to another.
28. A cracker is someone who breaks into computer systems and causes damage, typically using fairly basic skills.
29. "Biometric" technology is more fail-safe than other currently available security technologies and involves the biological identification of a person through fingerprint, eyes or other characteristics.

which typically is accomplished through some combination of the following techniques:

- *Packet filters*: Most routers include some form of packet filtering technology as a fairly basic form of firewall protection. Also known as "screening routers," packet filters work by screening out traffic originating from specific IP addresses or blocking a particular type of application (e-mail, ftp, chat, etc.), which is identified by port number.[30] Packet filtering is an aspect of firewall protection that is notoriously difficult for administrators to manage. Traffic is permitted or denied according to established rules. The order in which a set of rules is applied affects how all traffic is dealt with, meaning that the governing rules must be conceptualised and tested very rigorously.[31]

- *Proxy firewalls*: This is generally the most secure form of firewall protection. Proxy firewalls receive every incoming packet from the Internet, submit them to detailed inspection and translate the data before they are relayed to the internal network.

- *Network address translation (NAT)*: This IETF standard (in its most common implementation) works by converting all IP addresses from individual client stations on the internal network into a single IP address visible to external parties. Often used in conjunction with proxy firewalls, NATs perform these translations back and forth, thus concealing all individual IP addresses from the outside world.

- *Inspection*: Through various inspection techniques, transactions are monitored to ensure that the receiving user in fact requested incoming packets of data.

Although firewalls are often upheld as the definitive security solution, they are highly prone to configuration error and only guard against one possible avenue to an organisation's proprietary data. Because there are too many viruses and methods of encoding files, it is not safe to merely rely on firewalls as a panacea to solve all security problems. For example, attacks may take place without passing through the firewall, such is the case when a dialup connection is established by modem from within the network. Neither are firewalls effective in protecting against viruses nor "tunnelling," the practice whereby data structured under one protocol are transmitted within the format of another.[32]

Firewalls have clear limitations and must be configured according to carefully crafted security policies if they are to be an effective component of the company's

---

30. A number assigned to an application running on a server.
31. Dynamic packet filters are a more sophisticated type of packet filter that compare the pattern of transfer against norms and examine the protocols and contents of a packet rather its header alone.
32. The concept of tunneling is important in network design. It involves transmitting data over a public network for an intended internal use within a private network.

overall security solution. Depending on the particular circumstances, enterprises generally adopt either an aggressive or a moderate stance on security:[33]

● *Moderate stance*: "Permit all traffic, unless explicitly denied"

● *Aggressive stance*: "Deny all traffic, unless explicitly permitted"

A company with a moderate stance on security may be content with the most basic firewall set-up. Under this configuration, firewall protection is installed at the "boundary of trust" between the Internet and the company's internal network.

The aggressive stance is clearly the more secure and is suited to a firewall configuration known as the "demilitarised zone" (DMZ). The DMZ (Figure 5.7) is an intermediate network zone with firewall protection on either end to separate the internal network from the Internet. A company's public (non-proprietary) information is housed in servers within this zone so that external parties can obtain it without accessing the internal network. Firewalls under this configuration have three network interfaces corresponding to the three zones. The internal network is thus further secured from breaches of access. Alternative configurations are possible, each with implications for security, speed and administrative complexity.

Traditional firewall protection has its focus on the network level, but the circumstances surrounding the rise of Web-based applications requires a new

Figure 5.7 A DMZ network

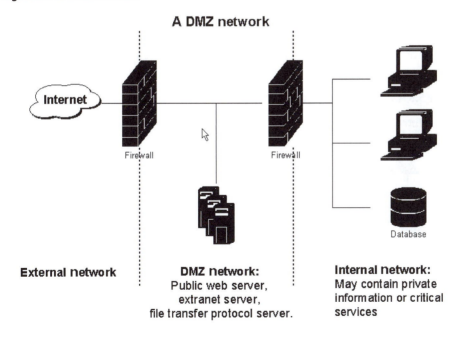

---

33. CTR Corp., "Global Network Security".

generation of firewalls that focus on the application level. Integration server and a host of Web services vendors have long been frustrated by the lack of support for their protocols and the impediment posed by traditional firewalls. As a result, many have devised means of tunnelling in order to transmit data over the HTTP protocol, thereby circumventing enterprise security policy. To address this, firewalls are evolving to include capabilities for examining the contents of transmissions to implement application-specific security capabilities.

Virtual private networks: outsourcing network security

Organisational computing has traditionally been supported by in-house IT departments, with application functionality made possible by an underpinning of fixed network connections between the central enterprise and its branch offices. Companies today are grappling with an explosion of process integration and redesign that affects not only the internal audience, but increasingly the external suppliers, customers and partners. The distributed nature of e-business applications necessitates an underpinning of internal and external network infrastructure. Faced with the complex nature of networked e-business applications and the rise of new, external requirements, enterprise IT has struggled to develop and support traditional physical networks to meet increasing requirements, while ensuring high levels of security. As an appealing alternative, businesses are increasingly opting to take their architectures "virtual" by partnering with network service providers who typically offer a range of professionally managed communications and network services on IP backbones capable of handling major traffic (Figure 5.8).

A virtual private network (VPN) is a private network that has been configured within a shared public network infrastructure and acts as its transportation

Figure 5.8 A virtual private network (VPN)

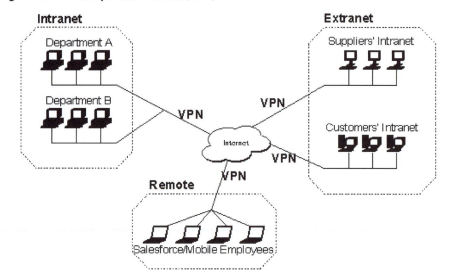

backbone, connecting branch offices, partners and mobile users. A VPN appears as a private network to its users, but may physically share the same backbone with other customers and unrelated parties. VPN architectures employ authentication and firewall mechanisms; connections are commonly established by means of encrypted software tunnelling of dialup access lines to secure data traffic between external users and the receiving party. VPN connections can also be "switched" – a process by which a temporary connection is established for a fixed duration or for the transmission of a certain quantity of data packets. The architectural nature of VPNs makes them applicable to network configurations of virtually any scale, thus making secure business communications affordable for small enterprises. Enterprises may opt to manage their own VPNs, but a considerable level of in-house expertise is required under this option. Most companies opt either to fully outsource VPN services or to arrive at some form of shared management.[34] With VPNs, companies of all sizes can enforce high standards of security and employ access controls and encryption, while exploiting the economies of scale and management capabilities offered.

The key advantages of virtual private networks may be summarised in terms of the following major areas of benefit:[35]

● *Cost*: The cost of building a VPN can be substantially lower than that of building a proprietary network in-house. The traditional mode of enterprise networking is achieved through leased lines installed between all points of access. This quickly leads to large numbers of dedicated lines traversing any necessary distance to interconnect the enterprise and a geometrical growth in leased line expenses. The need for this tangle of leased lines (and associated services) is eliminated in the VPN scenario, resulting in large savings in networking expenses. The company may also realise cost savings by implementing centralised applications, rather than installing applications at each location. With the engagement of an outsourcing partner, the enterprise itself is spared the need for large capital investments, ongoing network maintenance and monitoring, and the need for upgrades. Many companies are eager to shield themselves from the cost and complexity of building a traditional private network. By leaving the question of development and maintenance to a service provider's expertise, the enterprise can dedicate its resources and manpower to the support of its essential business activities.

● *Flexibility and simplification*: In the VPN scenario, network configuration and reconfiguration are straightforward. VPN implementations usually incorporate traffic control mechanisms that allow the enterprise to control network access and manage traffic flow. The prospect of extending

---

34. Under certain shared management arrangements, in-house IT personnel may adjust configuration and security policies through a Web-based interface while the outsourcing partner maintains the underlying infrastructure.
35. Based on "Ultimate enterprise architectures: the worldcom guide to e-infrastructure integration", http://content.techweb.com/custom/ultimate/70/document_741.html.

networks by means of point-to-point leased lines to every intranet and extranet site can be overwhelming in complexity. The result is often a convoluted architecture that is difficult to modify and manage. In a VPN scenario, each enterprise site requires only a high-speed link connected to the provider's point-of-presence. This greatly simplifies the process from the enterprise perspective and otherwise complex architectural configuration issues can be quickly resolved using software tools.

- *Performance*: With leased line networks, the potentials for performance are largely fixed once installation is complete. Should more bandwidth be required, a higher speed line must be ordered and installed. In a VPN scenario, the service provider's backbone links are typically many times faster than those of a typical corporate backbone and designed to surpass peak traffic loads. Service agreements guarantee that latency (the temporary delays when data packets are stored, analysed and eventually forwarded) is kept below stipulated levels.

- *Reliability*: With demands on corporate networks escalating over the course of an e-business transformation, enterprise IT faces an immense challenge in maintaining secure and reliable private networks. Consequently businesses are increasingly disposed towards the option of outsourcing much of their networking infrastructure. A first-rate VPN provider typically has a very large team of highly specialised network engineers and technical specialists who ensure that users have excellent reliability.

- *Scalability*: Only the largest corporations can undertake the task of building international private networks that extend to all branches, mobile users, customers, partners and other parties along the global value chain. In a VPN scenario, this magnitude of international reach is made available to companies of all sizes. One of the best arguments in favour of VPNs is the ability to scale from a handful of sites to thousands of sites without major changes to the system. In traditional networking, every major connecting point in the corporate backbone must be manually reconfigured when a site is added. This could affect network performance and require a significant amount of downtime. By contrast, adding a site to a VPN requires merely a software operation.

The case of VPN implementation highlights the rise to prominence of outsourcing partners and a desire on the part of many companies to relieve themselves, whenever strategically possible, of the hardware, software and support burdens that detract from core business activities. Network architectures are gradually becoming rid of capacity, flexibility and geographic limitations. In the new reality of extended enterprises, technology managers are increasingly finding they can best realise their goals by partnering with service providers who theoretically assume the burden of network maintenance and security, freeing them to focus exclusively on supporting essential business activities and on custom application development. It is likely in future that enterprise/provider-blended architectures will become widespread, with the two co-existing in close integration.

Public key infrastructures and digital certificates

The idea behind most conventional security systems is to restrict access by parties outside the enterprise and to place restrictions on access to the organisations' proprietary information and computing resources. However, this frame of mind is not especially conducive to the requirements of e-business, namely that organisations are seeking tighter integration with the (external) customers, suppliers and partners along their value chains. As a result, security solutions based on authentication techniques are becoming especially important in light of this need for "openness".

In a public key infrastructure (PKI) system, each user is issued a public key and a private key, which are mathematically related.[36] Messages intended for particular recipients are encrypted with their public keys. The message recipient is then able to decrypt the message using his private key (this process is called authentication). Similarly, messages sent by one party are signed by a private key and may be decrypted by any party with access to the corresponding public key (this process is called non-repudiation). A growing number of companies are deploying PKI so that they can use digital certificates to authenticate their dispersed users. A digital certificate may be considered a form of digital identification used in conjunction with a PKI system. PKI and digital certificate systems function according to the following procedure (Figure 5.9):

Figure 5.9 Digital certification process

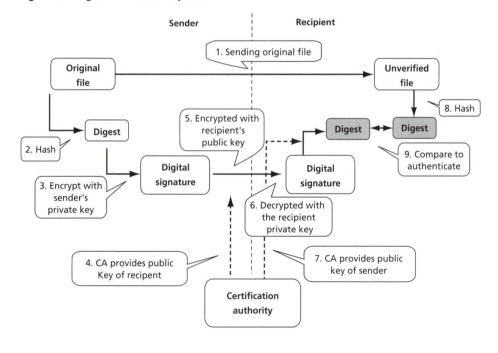

---

36. Public and private keys are numerical codes for encrypting data.

1   The sender transmits an unprotected version of the original file to the recipient.

2   Through a process known as **hashing,** an algorithm is used to transform the string of characters in the original file into a shorter fixed-length value. The result of the hashing process is known as a **digest,** which is a unique code generated based on the content of the original content of the message. If anything is added or subtracted from the original message, intentionally or unintentionally, the resulting digest would be different.

3   The resulting digest is then encrypted with the private key of the sender. The result is known as a **digital signature,** an electronics means of authentication.

4   The sender makes a request for the public key of the recipient. The **certification authority** (CA) – a highly trusted third party (such as Verisign) issues public and private key pairs and serves as a repository for public key information. It sends out a **digital certificate** containing this information to the sender. The public key provided is encrypted with the private key of the certification authority for authentication purposes.

5   The sender decrypts the digital certificate with the widely known public key of the CA. The digital signature is further encrypted with the public key of the recipient before it is transmitted.

6   Upon receiving the message, the recipient decrypts the file with its own private key.

7   A digital certificate containing the sender's public key information is sent to the recipient by the CA. The recipient uses this to decrypt the file received from the sender and to generate a digest.

8   The recipient hashes the original unverified file received in Step 1.

9   The two digests are compared to authenticate. Upon authentication, the recipient is assured of the sender's identity.

Under such a model, both the sender and the recipient can be assured of each other's identity and that a third party has not altered or tampered with the file. While this process may seem complex, in reality the recipient's client performs the process of verifying digital certificates automatically. Through the process of encryption and the safekeeping of private keys, digital certification systems can be highly effective at ensuring confidentiality and detecting if data has been tampered with. Businesses that want to issue digital certificates to their partners, suppliers and customers must either purchase software (thereby assuming the role of a certification authority) from vendors or subscribe to the services of a CA.

As digital certification has become an increasingly important component of overall security strategy, many companies are hurrying to implement PKI infrastructure. A PKI however, can be highly difficult to implement and does not come without risk. Companies must strive for overall security by building a portfolio of solutions that will not be compromised by one weak link. While on a theoretical level, PKI technology may appear sound, it is important to realise that other factors are at play. Can the certification authority itself be trusted and what is its liability (these issues are also examined from a legal perspective in Chapter 10)? How secure is the computer system on which the private key is stored? Should longer keys be employed for greater security, or shorter keys for higher speed? These and other questions must be considered when considering PKI implementations and potential certification partners. Nevertheless, the use of PKI and digital certificates is likely to grow. The Windows 2000 operating system incorporated PKI, indicating that a preponderance of enterprise desktops will be fitted to use digital certificates in coming years.

The issue of payment

Although consumer and business purchasers have been making larger and larger volumes of purchases online, the great majority of these transactions are still being paid for by traditional methods. B2C transactions over the Web are largely settled on credit and debit cards, while B2B sales are often settled through electronic funds transfer, automated clearinghouses or EDI.[37] Credit cards, a popular means of payment, have been especially problematic for companies selling online. Attempted fraud is widespread and merchants must often incur losses in the event of disputed transactions. Moreover transaction costs associated with credit cards are steep for merchants, especially with regard to low value transactions (so-called "micropayments") with slim profit margins. While many companies are compelled to accept these forms of payment, in the long run, they are inadequate for e-business as they carry security risks, higher costs and often impede the completion of transactions.

In recent years, a host of organisations have been promoting various solutions as an alternative to credit card payment schemes. Many have been centred on the concept of digital money in an effort to address the issue of micropayments. Digital money can be downloaded from participating banks into a digital wallet on the user's PC or the servers of a Web payment service. A digital wallet, as suggested by the name, is the digital equivalent of a wallet for storing money.[38] The wallet will in most cases employ a digital certification process to validate the identity of the user. The account is debited during a transaction and the required funds are transmitted to the merchant – under encryption for security. To further enhance security, password protected smart cards are available as another means of user authentication, but the costs are often prohibitively high as consumers and companies would need to purchase and install the appropriate card-readers to make online purchases.

---

37. Rosen (2001).
38. Yahoo! Wallet and Microsoft Passport are popular examples of digital wallets.

An alternative payment solution could come in the form of a server-based authentication system, such as the "three domain secure electronic transaction" (3D SET) effort headed by Visa and Mastercard, which transfers the workings of a digital wallet to a server at the card-issuing institution and authenticates a purchaser to the merchant and vice versa. In Germany, Deutsche Telekom has launched a prepaid online payment card called "MicroMoney". The card can be purchased in various denominations from 80,000 retail outlets across Germany (including places like gas-stations), and users scratch off the covering of a code number. The code can then be used to pay for online purchases with participating merchants.[39] Other alternative payment solutions include systems by which micropayments are linked to a purchaser's telephone bill or pre-purchased single-use authorisation codes.

In the context of B2B e-business, all payment transactions must be tightly integrated with the internal billing and settlement processes that take place in enterprise back office systems. For this reason, it is likely that the systems most likely to gain favour will be those offered by ventures involving established financial institutions and their technology partners. A venture that has garnered much attention for its potential to establish a widespread payment standard has been the tentatively named Project Eleanor, launched by Identrus – a third party trust system backed by leading global financial institutions including Bank of America, ABN Amro, Chase and Citibank. Identrus aims to address the lack of feasible payment solutions aside from credit cards for small transaction amounts, and full-fledged financial EDI (an option only available to large companies with abundant resources). Project Eleanor promises a complete e-payment solution for banks and their customers that will offer:[40]

- open specifications that allow multiple, interoperable solutions (including functional specifications in addition to XML-based technical specifications);

- flexibility to encompass conditional payments and other payment processing options; and

- globally viable operating rules that transcend geography.

Through payment systems such as Project Eleanor, trading partners may initiate payment requests, establish credit, specify the terms and conditions for the transaction, and ultimately direct their respective banks to transmit the necessary electronic payments. Since it functions through open XML-based specifications, any vendor can develop a system with complying standards to operate with the Identrus network. As it is browser-based, the implementation hurdle should be considerably lower than that for conventional EDI;

---

39. http://www.micromoney.de.
40. Identrus Project Eleanor Overview.

users will be able to access the system using browser plug-ins in conjunction with smart cards and smart card-readers to authenticate personnel and establish credit limits.[41]

Identrus is not the only behemoth in the online settlement arena. The case study following this chapter details the efforts of TradeCard, a venture launched by the non-profit World Trade Centers Association to build a viable international electronic payment system addressing credit, connectivity and compliance. Tradecard was conceived as a mechanism for facilitating international trade through open Internet standards that would allow users to continue using their existing systems and hardware platforms. To date, company managers have indicated a disapproval of "niche solutions", meaning that electronic payment will only truly take off when widely accepted standards emerge. Until then, businesses and consumers will continue to draw from the existing payments infrastructure to facilitate online payment.

Summary

To brace themselves for e-business transformation, companies must take a highly proactive approach in deploying the right technologies and forging the vendor and service relationships that will position them for success. As the technology portfolio necessary for e-business grows all the more complex, issues relating to integration, standards and security – particularly in the light of the arrival of exciting new technologies (wireless, payment, Web services) – become increasingly crucial. In a few years, the enterprise technology portfolios will be virtually unrecognisable from those of a mere decade ago.

To conclude our infrastructure part, we provide a brief descriptive case study to illustrate how the Hong Kong Exchange transformed from a closed, proprietary system to an open architecture.

Building an open system architecture: Hong Kong Exchanges and Clearing Ltd[42]

Hong Kong Exchanges and Clearing Ltd (HKEx) is the second largest stock market in Asia and ninth largest in the world. Faced with constant pressure to upgrade systems with new technologies that provide more features and capabilities to brokers and investors, and recent attention in the industry to the formation of global alliances, HKEx addressed these challenges by adopting a new open architecture. Automated Matching System/3 (AMS/3) enables HKEx to compete more effectively on the global stage, allowing interconnectivity with existing and future business partners and scalability for growth.

---

41. Rosen (2001).
42. Adapted from Farhoomand, A. and Ng, P. (2003).

In adapting the traditional trading processes to an open environment, HKEx had to comply with the stringent confines of resilience and performance requirements of the new US$38 million project. Among daunting challenges facing HKEx were:

- coordinating systems development, testing and rollout through concerted harmonisation and mobilisation of resources among HKEx, hardware and software systems vendors, and various market participants, including brokers;

- preparing all market participants for the introduction and adoption of the new application;

- testing and seamless integration of end-to-end trading processes; and

- Formulating and executing a well-planned migration strategy.

Planning, development and rollout necessitated over 2000 man-months and involved more than 140 external consultants at its peak. More than 500 critical project activities with complex intra- and inter-dependency across project segments required detailed planning. With over 500 brokerage firms, as well as a large number of information providers and software vendors, a tightly managed timetable with clearly defined checkpoints was necessary.

Planning for AMS/3 began in January 1997, just 10 months after the launch of AMS/2, its predecessor, which was a closed system with no connection to external networks or to the 500 plus members' computer systems. HKEx saw the need for continuous improvements and innovations in trading mechanisms and efficiency, such that all market participants could be fully equipped to capitalise on greater trading turnover. There were two main objectives driving the adoption of AMS/3: (i) to open up the trading system to brokers and to individual investors and (ii) to provide new functions and features that would improve the efficiency of the market. AMS/3 was to establish a securities trading architecture that would provide expanded business accessibility and technological capabilities for HKEx to achieve success in the global financial markets. AMS/3 was also to be a trading platform that would pave the way for straight-through processing by automating the complete trading process, from the point of entering investors' instructions to buy or sell, through to the point of entering the details of the transaction with the Registrar (Figure 5.10). In this regard, AMS/3 would seamlessly integrate end-to-end trading processes from investors to brokers to markets.

Figure 5.10 Steps in processing a trading transaction

AMS/3 is a complete overhaul of AMS/2. It encompasses a new host system, a new network and new technical platforms. AMS/3 offers two approaches for brokers to trade through, namely the terminal approach and the gateway approach (Figure 5.11).

The terminal approach is similar to the on-floor and off-floor terminals of AMS/2 in terms of operation and functionality. The gateway approach, however, is more complex. An open gateway device enables the interchange of electronic data between the host system and the brokers' systems. Brokers can use the electronic data to support their back office operations, market analysis or to perform other trading operations.

Should brokers choose to connect to the host using the open gateway, they have a choice of two trading facilities: the Multi-Workstation Systems developed and provided by HKEx, or Broker Supplied Systems (in-house systems developed by the brokers themselves). One Multi-Workstation System is able to carry a maximum of eight workstations. However, there is no limit to the number of workstations that can be connected to Broker Supplied Systems. The Multi-Workstation System is a broker front-end system that supports multiple users and remote access to the host trading system, and concurrent execution of trading functions. It provides risk management functionality to support multi-level, investor, trader risk measurement, and limit setting. It also enables the import and export of data to support the back office systems of brokers. The Broker Supplied Systems, on the other hand, gives brokers the

Figure 5.11 AMS/3 trading system

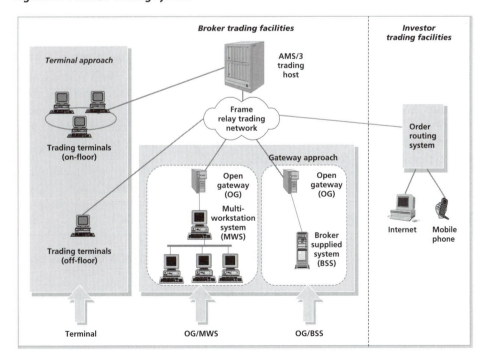

flexibility to create their own system that could include those trading functions found on trading terminals and the Multi-Workstation Systems, plus other customisation and integration with backend systems to support their own operational needs. For the larger brokers, Broker Supplied Systems presented enormous opportunities for business growth and greater operations efficiency.

The open gateway gives investors more choice and convenient channels for accessing the market. Individual investors can purchase a mobile phone that facilitates online trading. The SIM card installed in the mobile phone contains PKI access codes. Once the investor purchases the phone, he/she opens an account with a broker of his/her choice. Order and inquiry transactions through the Internet, mobile phones and proprietary network systems can go through an order routing system, which was developed by HKEx, to the Multi-Workstation System or Broker Supplied System adopted by the investor's designated broker. An authentication service would be performed before the broker sends the order or inquiry to the host system via the Multi-Workstation System or Broker Supplied System.

AMS/3 was designed to support platform-independent interfacing among various components and external systems. The AMS/3 host uses a multi-node architecture that ensures optimal performance and resilience in handling high volume, real-time processing and throughput. The open gateway, Multi-Workstation Systems and trading terminals run on the Windows NT platform. The order routing system developed on a separate Sun Solaris platform supports connectivity to different order routing channels, such as the Internet and mobile phones.

Unlike AMS/2, which only supported single-market trading, AMS/3 was built around a multiple-market trading model. This means that it can support concurrent and continuous trading in multiple markets, with each market having its own products, trading hours, trading methods and trading rules. AMS/3 is capable of running more than 20 hours per day for each market. With AMS/3, it is possible for brokers to conduct trading activities in different stock markets. Also built into AMS/3 is the capability to handle new order types such as enhanced limit orders, special limit orders, average value orders, at auction orders and auction limit orders. HKEx can now introduce new trading methods and new order types according to market needs.

Questions for discussion

1   Why is integration an overriding issue of e-business infrastructure? What aspects must be considered?

2   What are the two common integration server architectures? What are their advantages?

3   How does XML differ from HTML? Why is it a valuable standard?

4   What is RossettaNet and what does it aim to achieve?

5   What is ebXML and how does it differ from the RosettaNet framework?

6   What implications will Web services and grid computing have on business computing?

7   Which are the major components of computer security?

8   What functions does a firewall serve? Can it be considered a complete security solution?

9   How does a PKI system function?

10   What is the role of the Certification Authority in a digital certification system?

11   What factors affect the security of the PKI system?

12   What is a digital wallet? How does it function?

13   What is a VPN? What are its key advantages?

Appendix 1: Assorted XML technologies

XML may be regarded as an assortment of technologies centred on **XML 1.0** – the specification that defined its essential tags and attributes. In addition, there are a growing number of optional parts[43] that supplement XML 1.0 with specifications for further tags, and attributes specific to certain tasks.[44]

Examples include XML Linking Language (**XLink**), which provides rules for adding hyperlinks to XML documents and XML Pointing Language (**XPointer**), which enables a specific part of an XML document to be referenced rather than the entire page.

● The standard language used to describe the contents of an XML document is known as a document type definition (**DTD**[45]), which helps to establish an understanding of metadata between parties exchanging XML.

● Extensible Stylesheet Language (**XSL**) is used to generate Web pages based on XML data, with each XSL page containing a set of template rules, each rule corresponding to one or more XML tag.[46]

● A Document Object Model (**DOM**) is an application-programming interface (API) that allows other programs to access XML files to update content, structure or style as necessary.

● **XML Schemas** are representations for assisting developers to form their own XML-based definitions; as opposed to DTDs, XML schemas are written in XML's own syntax.

---

43. A "part" here refers to a self-contained software component programmed to handle a specific task. Parts facilitate the development of large-scale projects.

44. www.w3.org.

45. DTDs are eventually expected to be replaced by an XML schema by the W3C, which will contain a wealth of database-oriented relational information.

46. XSL may be thought of as the XML equivalent of Cascading Style Sheets (CSS) used for HTML.

Appendix 2: RosettaNet partner interface processes

Clusters	Segments
1. Partner, Product and Service Review	**1A**. Partner Review **1B**. Product and Service Review
2. Product Information	**2A**. Preparation for Distribution **2B**. Product Change Notification **2C**. Product Design Information
3. Order Management	**3A**. Quote and Order Entry **3B**. Transportation and Distribution **3C**. Returns and Finance **3D**. Product Configuration
4. Inventory Management	**4A**. Collaborative Forecasting **4B**. Inventory Allocation **4C**. Inventory Reporting **4D**. Inventory Replenishment **4E**. Sales Reporting **4F**. Price Protection
5. Marketing Information Management	**5A**. Lead Opportunity Management **5B**. Marketing Campaign Management **5C**. Design Win Management **5D**. Ship from Stock and Debit
6. Service and Support	**6A**. Provide and Administer Warranties, Service Packages and Contract Services **6B**. Provide and Administer Asset Management **6C**. Technical Support and Service Management
7. Manufacturing	**7A**. Design Transfer **7B**. Manage Manufacturing WO and WIP **7C**. Distribute Manufacturing Information

Note
1. Cluster 0 is RosettaNet Support, which is concerned mainly with administrative duties.

Source: RosettaNet.org.

Appendix 3: ebXML terminology

Registry: A central server that stores a variety of data necessary to make ebXML work. Amongst the information a Registry makes available in XML form are: Business Process and Information Meta Models, Core Library, Collaboration Protocol Profiles, and Business Library. Basically, when a business wants to start an ebXML relationship with another business, it queries a Registry in order to locate a suitable partner and to find information about requirements for dealing with that partner.

Business Processes: Activities that a business can engage in (and for which it would generally want one or more partners). A Business Process is formally described by the Business Process Specification Schema (a W3C XML Schema and also a DTD), but may also be modelled in UML.

Collaboration Protocol Profile (CPP): A profile filed with a Registry by a business wishing to engage in ebXML transactions. The CPP will specify some Business Processes of the business, as well as some Business Service Interfaces it supports.

Business Service Interface: The ways that a business is able to carry out the transactions necessary in its Business Processes. The Business Service Interface also includes the kinds of Business Messages the business supports and the protocols over which these messages might travel.

Business Messages: The actual information communicated as part of a business transaction. A message will contain multiple layers. At the outside layer, an actual communication protocol must be used (such as HTTP or SMTP). SOAP is an ebXML recommendation as an envelope for a message "payload." Other layers may deal with encryption or authentication.

Core Library: A set of standard "parts" that may be used in larger ebXML elements. For example, Core Processes may be referenced by Business Processes. The Core Library is contributed by the ebXML initiative itself, while larger elements may be contributed by specific industries or businesses.

Collaboration Protocol Agreement (CPA): In essence, a contract between two or more businesses that can be derived automatically from the CPPs of the respective companies. If a CPP says "I *can* do X," a CPA says "We *will* do X together."

Simple Object Access Protocol (SOAP): A W3C protocol for exchange of information in a distributed environment endorsed by the ebXML initiative. Of interest for ebXML is SOAP's function as an envelope that defines a framework for describing what is in a message and how to process it.

Source: ebXML.org and adapted from Mertz (2001).

References

Abualsamid, A. (2001) "XML: the big picture", *Network Computing*, 16 April, available from http://www.networkcomputing.com/1208/1208f3.html [accessed 11 November 2002].

Computer Desktop Encyclopedia (2000) The Computer Language Co. Inc., Point Pleasant: PA.

Cottrill, K. (2001) "Global: EbXML; creating a global language for electronic trade", *Ebusinessforum.com*, 16 January, available from http://www.ebusinessforum.com/index.asp?layout=rich_story&doc_id=1986&categoryid=&channelid=&search=ebxml [accessed 24 April 2002].

EIU (2001) "*All about XML*", *Ebusinessforum.com*, 12 April, available from http://www.ebusinessforum.com/index.asp?layout=rich_story&doc_id=3068&categoryid=&channelid=&search=ebxml [accessed 20 April 2002].

Farhoomand, A. and Ng, P. (2003) "Creating sustainable competitive advantage through Internet-worked communities", *Communications of the ACM*, vol. 46, no. 9 (September), pp. 83–8.

Foster, I. (2002) "Grid computing: a new infrastructure for 21st century science", *Physics Today*, vol. 55, no. 2, p. 42, the American Institute of Physics.

Gormley, L. (2001) "EAI overview" *ittoolbox.com* [online], available from http://eai.ittoolbox.com/browse.asp?c=EAIPeerPublishing&r=%2Fpub%2Feai%5Foverview%2Ehtm [accessed 24 August 2001].

IBM Corp. (2002) "Interview: IBM's Wladawsky-Berger explains grid computing", IBM.com, March 2002, available from http://www-1.ibm.com/linux/news/grid.shtml [access 20 May 2002].

Intel e-Business Center (2001) "N-tier architecture improves scalability, availability and ease of integration", Santa Clara, CA.

Linthicum, D.S. (2001) B2B Application Integration, Boston, MA: Addison-Wesley.

Marshall, M. (2001) XML: "Like the air that we breathe", Informationweek.com, 5 March 2001, Available from: http://www.informationweek.com/827/xml.htm [accessed 27 April 2002].

Mertz, D. (2001) "Understanding ebXML: untangling the business Web of the future", IBM developerWorks, June.

Montalbano, E. (2000) "ebXML: a room for two", CRN, 18 October, available from http://www.crn.com/Components/printArticle.asp?ArticleID=20753 [accessed 10 May 2002].

Rosen, C. (2001) "Seamless b-to-b online payment systems readied", Informationweek.com, 10 September, available from http://www.informationweek.com/story/IWK20010907S0040 [accessed 9 May 2002].

Sanchez, E. et al. (2001) "Integration powered", Informationweek.com Tech Analyzer, 28 May, available from http://www.informationweek.com/839/integration.htm [accessed 26 April 2002].

Shear, P. (2002) "Grid computing the next 'killer app,' Delphi Says", Gridcomputingplanet.com, available from http://www.gridcomputingplanet.com/news/article/0,,3281_1025741,00.html [accessed 18 May 2002].

Shields, M. (2001) *e-Business and ERP*, New York: John Wiley & Sons.

Worldcom (2001) *Ultimate Enterprise Architectures: The Worldcom guide to e-Infrastructure Integration*, Clinton, MS: The Worldcom Group, available from: http://content.techweb.com/custom/ultimate/70/document_741.html [accessed 24 October 2000].

Further reading

Amor, D. (2000) *The e-Business (R)evolution: Living and Working in an Interconnected World*, Upper Saddle River, N.J.: Prentice-Hall.

Cameron, D. (2000) *Global Network Security: Threats and Countermeasures*, Charleston, S.C.: Computer Technology Research Corp.

Economist Intelligence Unit (2000) *e-Business Transformation*, New York: Economist Intelligence Unit.

Gloors, P. (2000) *Making the e-Business Transformation*, London: Springer.

Grant, N. et al. (2000) *e-Business and ERP: Transforming the Enterprise*, New York: John Wiley & Sons.

Kalakota, R. and Robinson, M. (2001) *e-Business 2.0: Roadmap for Success*, Reading, MA: Addison-Wesley.

Kalakota, R. and Whinston, A.B. (1997) *Electronic Commerce: A Manager's Guide*, Reading, MA: Addison-Wesley.

McLeod, R. et al. (2000) *Management Information Systems*, Upper Saddle River, N.J.: Prentice-Hall.

Porter, M. (2001) "Strategy and the Internet", *HBR OnPoint*, March, pp. 63–79.

Sawhney, M. and Zabin, J. (2001) *The Seven Steps to Nirvana: Strategic Insights into e-Business Transformation*, New York: McGraw-Hill.

Szuprowicz, B. (2000) *Implementing Enterprise Portals: Integration Strategies for Intranet, Extranet, and Internet Resources*, Charleston, SC: Computer Technology Research Corp.

Turban, E. et al. (2001) *Introduction to Information Technology*, New York: John Wiley & Sons.

Case study   TradeCard: building a global trading electronic payment system

While the Internet is enabling millions of businesses worldwide to buy and sell in ways never before imagined, the tools and methods used to conduct trade have gone unchanged for several hundred years and do not fit into the world of electronic commerce (e-commerce). TradeCard represents a new payment alternative for international trade.

– Kurt Cavano, TradeCard Inc.,
Chairman and CEO[1]

TradeCard (www.tradecard.com) was a business-to-business e-commerce transaction enabler focused specifically on cross-border trade. It was conceived as a new payment alternative for international trade that provided a solution that was easier to use than a letter of credit, more secure than open accounts, and available for one flat fee per settled transaction. TradeCard was designed to provide an on-line payment mechanism for large-dollar cross-border transactions. TradeCard's aim was to increase the volume of cross-border trade and lower the cost of transactions.

To successfully implement TradeCard, however, required that the technical infrastructure be able to provide a seamless on-line settlement transaction and a secure electronic solution involving a network of global players. Could the TradeCard platform be able to synchronise all the databases involved in international transactions on an open Internet standard that allowed all parties to use their own tools, operating systems and hardware platforms? TradeCard's aim was to become an alternative on-line payment mechanism for most b-to-b hubs as well as an alternative payment mechanism for existing traditional international trade tools. How could TradeCard integrate an on-line

payment mechanism to these b-to-b hubs and be an accepted trade settlement tool amongst buyers and sellers? Likewise, TradeCard, Inc., the company, required the building of a network of players in international trade and aggregating the disparate services necessary for international trade onto the TradeCard system. Without the participation of the traditional trade services providers, TradeCard would not be able to gather information that would facilitate future transactions, and TradeCard members could not deal with traders who were non-TradeCard members. What was the best means of getting traders and trade services providers to sign on and become TradeCard members? How could TradeCard change the mindset of global traders who conduct large-dollar transactions to use TradeCard rather than the traditional off-line settlement methods such as through banks?

The International Trade Payment Environment

The methods used to conduct trade had remained unchanged for several hundred years as international trade was still a complex, paper-based and labour-intensive business. The greatest obstacle to trade was the high cost of financing for small and medium-sized traders. The fees associated with doing business with letters of credit were prohibitively high for some smaller transactions. The three payment methods for international trade had various risks and costs associated with them. (Please refer to Appendix 1 for the trading terminology and Exhibit 1 for the average costs of the financial settlement process.)

---

1. URL: http://www.tradecard.com, 18 January 2000.

Appendix 1: Trading terminology

The following is a glossary of some of the major types of transactions and documents used in trade finance.

Advance payment	An agreement that payment be sent before goods are sent to the buyer (such an arrangement is typically made informally).
Bill of lading	A transport document that details the contents of shipment, often in great detail. It functions as a receipt of goods, evidence of transport and a document of ownership.
Documentary collections	A formal contract where the ownership of goods is not transferred to the buyer until the seller receives certain documentation and payment. Documentary collections are often used when the two parties to the trade do not yet have a long-standing business relationship.

Two types of documentary collection:

Documents against payment, the bank releases the documents to the buyer/importer only against a cash payment in prescribed currency. In many cases, however, the title document has already been transferred, through supply chain mechanisms, making this protection meaningless.

Documents against acceptance, the bank releases the documents to the buyer/importer against acceptance of a bill of exchange by the buyer guaranteeing payment at a later date by the buyer. Again, the title document is transferred prior to payment.

Document of title	A document that gives the holder the right to possess certain assets.
Letter of credit (LC)	A formal contract where the bank guarantees that the buyer of goods will pay the seller. Letters of credit are used when trading partners might not have established trust yet. LCs are more formally called documentary letters of credit because the banks handling the transaction deal in documents as opposed to goods. The terms and conditions listed in the credit all involve presentation of specific documents within a stated period of time, hence the formal name documentary credits. The documents the buyer requires in the credit may vary, but at a minimum include an invoice, packing list and a bill of lading. Other documents that the buyer may specify are certificate of origin, consular invoice, insurance certificate, inspection certificate and others.

| Open account (payment) | An agreement that the buyer of goods will pay for them after they are received. |
| Waybill | A transport document that functions as a receipt for goods and evidence of transport, but not as a document of title. |

Source: Faulkner & Gray Inc., Bank Technology News International (August 1998) and TradeCard, Inc.

Traditional trade settlement methods[2]

- *Letters of Credit*: the most common method of making international payments as they reduced the risks in the transaction. According to the Boston Consulting Group, businesses spent about US$420 billion[3] each year on administrative costs, mainly on document handling and transmissions related to trade transportation.

- *Documentary Collection*: with banks acting in a fiduciary capacity and ensuring that payment was received, but were liable only for the correct execution of the collection instructions, and were not committed to paying the seller/exporter themselves should the buyer/importer default on its financial obligation.

- *Open Account/Cash-in-Advance*: credit extended that was not supported by a note, mortgage, or other formal written evidence of indebtedness. This method posed a risk to the supplier as the buyer's integrity was essential.

Other secondary methods that were available included:

- *Credit Insurance*: offered to exporters who were seeking protection against commercial and political risks, often layered on top of an open account transaction.

- *Credit Cards*: created for businesses in the form of purchasing cards, but were still limited by their ability to purchase large-dollar items.

- *Escrow*: a method used as an intermediary device during the transfer of and payment for goods.

- *Cheques*: similar to open accounts without the immediate availability of funds provided by electronic funds transfer.

TradeCard's competitors

There was no other company offering the same kind of services as TradeCard. However, TradeCard was often compared with Bolero Ltd., a joint development of the Through Transport Club and the Society for Worldwide Interbank Financial Telecommunication, or SWIFT, which tested an electronic registry for global trade. The Bolero system was like a repository for LCs and the system was used mainly for bulk shipments of commodities, such as crude oil, whereby market participants could trade their positions in a cargo several times during a voyage.[4] With the TradeCard system, a trade would be made and paid for at the same time, and a transaction would be completed. Moreover, TradeCard targeted importers and exporters that deal in finished goods, such as toys, electronics and clothing.

TradeCard, Inc.: the company

The World Trade Centres Association (WTCA) in New York office, headed by its president, Guy Tozzoli, formulated the TradeCard concept in 1994 to help international traders, particularly small and

---

2. TradeCard, Inc., "A Revolution in Payment Settlement for an On-line Global Trading Community", March 2000.
3. US$1 = HK$8.

4. Platt, G., "Global Trade 'Credit Card' Planned: Transactions Can Be Done Without Letters of Credit", *Journal of Commerce*, 2 July 1997.

Exhibit 1 Average costs of financial settlement process (as of August 2000)

	Letters of credit	Documentary collection	Open account with credit insurance	Open account without credit insurance
Per cent of International Trade	20–25	10–20	35	35
Characteristics	• Paper-based transaction • Compliance based on stringent documentation requirements • Credit risk is assumed by a bank	• Paper-based transaction • Compliance based on buyer's acceptance of goods, bank facilities transfer of documents only • High amount of risk is assumed by the seller	• Paper-based transaction based on trust • Compliance based on buyer's acceptance of goods • Insurance mitigates risk but limitations on coverage may exist	• Paper-based transactions based on trust • Compliance based on buyer's acceptance of goods • Unsecured extension of credit
Average Fees Paid by Buyer & Seller*	$1,000–$1,500	$250–$500	$50–$200 plus variable cost of premium	$50–$200
Payment Guarantee	Full, if documents are in compliance	None	Full, but may have coverage limitations	None
Compliance Check	• Time-consuming • Done by bank	• Time-consuming • Done by buyer	• Simple procedures • Done by buyer	• Simple procedures • Done by buyer

Note

1. * Based on an average international trade transaction for manufactured goods of US$50,000.

Source: TradeCard, Inc.

medium-sized companies, automate their transactions. Tozzoli established the Full Service Trade System (FSTS), the company that completely developed and operated the TradeCard product, in 1994. General Electric Information Services, American Management Systems and General Electric Capital were among the 80 shareholders in the firm.

Dubbed as the first "credit card" for international trade, the TradeCard system empowered the small and medium-sized companies to compete with the bigger companies. It was the world's first and only e-commerce service that contained all the three "C's" of an international trade transaction: credit, connectivity and compliance.[5]

TradeCard started with a series of private tests with interested companies in the United States between 1996 to 1998, with the first actual pilot carried out in 1998 with a US importer. TradeCard's strategy then was "to start small, but start successful".[6]

Warburg Pincus takeover of FSTS

TradeCard did not get off the ground until February 1999, when the private equity investment firm of E. M. Warburg Pincus & Co., LLC, the biggest private fund management company in the US East Coast, saw the potential in the TradeCard system and committed up to US$53 million capital in TradeCard. TradeCard, Inc. became an independent company with Warburg Pincus as the major shareholder. The new management team, composed of aggressive and experienced banking, international trade and technology professionals from different backgrounds, immediately introduced changes in TradeCard. In that same year, *Future Banker* magazine named TradeCard as one of the "Top 25 Technology Deals of the Year". Cary Davis, Warburg Pincus Managing Director, said:

We seek opportunities to invest in companies that have unique products or services, technological superiority, unusually talented management and the potential for significant growth. We certainly see those factors in TradeCard.[7]

TradeCard's organisational structure

By March 2000, TradeCard had increased its total workforce from 20 staff to 80 in their New York office. One of its management challenges was the continued weekly growth of its workforce. TradeCard however maintained a flat organisational structure that involved the following departments:

- *Marketing*: management of advertising, public relations and direct marketing of the TradeCard service
- *Technology*: implementation of business specifications into the technology system
- *Alliance Management*: management of customers and network alliances
- *Business Development*: supervision of sales and servicing to the right customers
- *Operations*: management of Member and Application Services, Client Managements, Training and Product Quality Assurance
- *Product Management*: development and direction of TradeCard's Compliance and Financial Settlement application.

(Please refer to Exhibit 2 for TradeCard's organisational structure.)

TradeCard: the system

TradeCard leveraged the benefits of Internet applications, building the TradeCard technology that would enable full transaction capability, featuring:

---

5. URL: http://www.iserve.wtca.org/infosvcs/Tcorland.html, 18 January 2000.
6. URL: http://www.webcom.com/pjones/wtcglo.html, 18 January 2000.

7. URL: http://www.wtcsd.org/newsletter.html, 19 January 2000.

Exhibit 2 TradeCard organisational structure

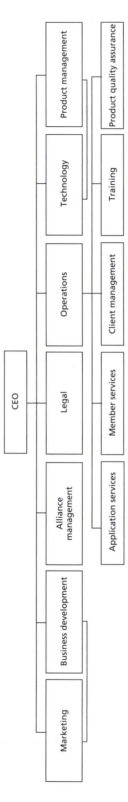

- integration of multiple data formats within a single transaction;
- digital signatures on all documents, which would enable trust between global parties;
- managed global transactions between multiple parties with automatic workflow and alerts;
- single-point tracking and reporting on all transactions;
- 24 × 7 global real-time data access; and
- Open Internet standards that would allow all parties to use their own tools, operating systems and hardware platforms.

TradeCard technical architecture[8]

TradeCard was built on an Enterprise Java Beans-based architecture and all application code was Java.

- *Application Server*: The BEA WebLogic Enterprise Application Server managed the Java-based components. This sessionless architecture enabled each incoming request to be serviced as an independent event, which allowed for automated failover and linear scalability. The Presentation Server, a client of the application server, accepted and created the HTML pages delivered to the user's browser. All the HTML pages were generated using Java Server Pages (JSP) technology.[9]
- *Message Queuing*: An IBM MQSeries (an application often known as *business integration software* or middleware, whose components tie together other software applications) based eventing service provided asynchronous processing, which

ensured that long running background tasks did not interfere with peak in-line usage patterns. MQSeries also managed the message queuing requirements of the Message Broker.

- *Rule Engine*: This custom software was at the heart of TradeCard's patented compliance engine. The TradeCard Rule Engine encapsulated all business rules, which allowed the addition of custom products or business services without affecting the basic architecture of the system, and determined the workflow requirements of all transactions in the system.
- *Message Broker*: TradeCard's Messaging Infrastructure enabled the web browser and non-browser access to TradeCard, such that messages received from non-browser access were converted to TradeCard XML formats. Non-browser access could be achieved by messaging delivered in a variety of mediums, including SMTP, FTP, EDI and custom formats.

TradeCard systems security

The authentication and validation with Coface and Thomas Cook, two alliance partners in the TradeCard network, during registration were designed to minimise transaction risks for all parties and provided a secure and responsible environment so members would have the proper assurances to conduct their affairs. There was also the assurance that data provided to TradeCard by the buyer and seller should remain private and secure. (Refer to Appendix 2 for TradeCard Privacy and Confidentiality Policies.) TradeCard was aware that in conducting global transactions, security was a critical issue. Thus, aside from the stringent application procedure and registration done through Coface and Thomas Cook, TradeCard built three security levels into the architecture of the system: server authentication, 2-factor user authentication and digital signatures (refer to Figure 1).

---

8. See "The TradeCard Solution: On-line International Trade Transactions—Technical Overview", TradeCard, Inc., 1999. See also http://www.tradecard.com/privacy/data.html.

9. JSP is a technology for controlling the content or appearance of web pages through the use of servlets, small programmes that are specified in the Web page and run on the web server to modify the web page before it is sent to the user who requested it. See URL: wysiwyg://def.557/http://www.whatiscom./jsp.html.

Figure 1 TradeCard systems' three levels of security

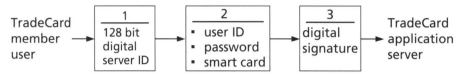

Appendix 2: TradeCard privacy and confidentiality policies

Visitors to our website

When you visit our web site, www.tradecard.com, TradeCard does not collect personally identifiable information about you except when you specifically and knowingly provide it. For instance if you request information from TradeCard, you will be asked to provide basic contact information, including your name, company, title, country, and e-mail address. Any additional information, such as industry and average transaction size, is provided on a purely voluntary basis.

TradeCard will never sell, trade, or rent to any third party any personally identifiable information. We will use the information you provide to respond to your requests for additional information and for inclusion in future mailing initiatives. If you would like to opt-out of receiving future mailings, send us an e-mail with your name referencing "no updates" in the subject line to: unsubscribe@TradeCard.com.

TradeCard's corporate web site does not use "cookies," small text files placed on your browser. Our system does, however, log some basic and generic information about your computer, including its:

● IP address (your computer's unique signature)
● Operating system (i.e. Windows NT)
● Browser software (i.e. Netscape Navigator).

TradeCard uses this information about your computer to perform routine web site maintenance and to generate aggregate web site traffic reports so we can develop and enhance our web site.

TradeCard is committed to providing reasonable and practical access to you to identify and to correct any inaccuracies in the information you may provide. Visitors who have provided information on our web site can contact TradeCard Member Services to correct any inaccuracies.

TradeCard members

If you choose to apply for membership in the TradeCard global e-commerce network, you will be asked to provide detailed personal and business information. This information will be shared with our credit risk provider and payment agent to enable your company to qualify for credit risk and payment services. During this registration process, TradeCard will allow you to choose whether or not you would like us to contact your trading partners for membership and other services related to transactions.

Once you become a member of the TradeCard global e-commerce network your personally identifiable information, confidential business data, and transaction details will be shared with other members *participating in your transaction* as well as TradeCard's alliance partners. TradeCard will not disclose your personally identifiable information, confidential business data, or transaction details to parties outside of the TradeCard network without your consent.

When you log onto our transaction site TradeCard uses "session cookies", small text files placed temporarily on your browser, to maintain user session records. These cookies are destroyed as soon as you log out and close your browser and cannot be used to track other information about you or your computer. They are required; you cannot use TradeCard unless you accept these session cookies.

TradeCard will use the information you provide to contact you, if necessary, to service your account or for other administrative purposes. We may also access your information to resolve disputes, to troubleshoot problems, to enforce our Member Agreement, or for marketing purposes. In addition, the TradeCard system uses your transaction details to automate and to streamline your international trade transaction by checking for electronic data compliance, providing reporting features, and transferring data from previous forms to those of the current transaction.

As a TradeCard member you have the right to opt-out of being listed in the TradeCard Membership Directory, which only members and alliance partners will be able to access. This means that TradeCard allows you to determine how "visible" your organisation will be to other organisations within the TradeCard network. These visibility options become available when other organisations are creating communities and when other organisations are searching for trading partners during new document creation.

If your organisation is listed as Public, any TradeCard member will be able to add your organisation to its private community. Your organisation will also be available when a party search is performed during document creation.

If your organisation is listed as Protected (sellers only), any TradeCard member will be able to see that your organisation is a TradeCard member; however, your organisation must accept an invitation to join another organisation's community before your organisation can be added.

If your organisation is listed as Private, no organisation will be able to add you to its private community unless your organisation's administrator accepts an invitation to join that community. Your organisation will also not be visible in a party search during the creation of a new document.

TradeCard is committed to providing reasonable and practical access to you to identify and to correct any inaccuracies in the information you may provide. TradeCard members can use the system's administrative function on the transaction web site or contact TradeCard Member Services to maintain up to date account information.

Privacy and confidentiality FAQs

1. What information does TradeCard collect about my business or me?

When you visit TradeCard's web site, TradeCard will collect only the personally identifiable information or confidential business data that you specifically and knowingly provide. TradeCard's system will also log some basic and generic information about your computer, including its IP address, operating system, and browser software.

If you choose to apply for membership in the TradeCard global e-commerce network, you will be required to provide detailed personal and business information. Please review the section titled *Required Application Information* for more details on the application requirements as well as how your application data is used to qualify your company for TradeCard membership and for credit risk and payment services.

2. How does TradeCard use the information that I provide?

Data collection	How data is used
Request for Information Form Join the TradeCard Network Form	● Respond to requests ● Inclusion in future mailings (if you do not opt out)
IP Address Operating System Browser Software	● Conduct routine web site maintenance ● Develop and enhance our web site

➤

(cont'd)

Data collection	How data is used
TradeCard Membership Application Form	● Qualify your company for TradeCard membership ● Qualify your company for credit risk and payment services ● Marketing and sales purposes (if you do not opt out) ● Contact your trading partners (if you do not opt out) ● Provide member support ● Administrative purposes, i.e. service your account, troubleshoot, resolve disputes
Transaction Details	● Automate and streamline your international trade transaction by checking for electronic data compliance, providing reporting features, and transferring data from previous forms to those of the current transaction ● Provide member support

3. Does TradeCard sell or share the information that I provide?

TradeCard will never sell, trade, or rent to any third party any personally identifiable information, confidential business data, and/or transaction details. Once you become a member of the TradeCard global e-commerce network your personally identifiable information, confidential business data, and transaction details will be shared with other members *participating in your transaction* as well as TradeCard's alliance partners. TradeCard's alliance partners include, but are not limited to, payment agents, credit risk providers, cargo insurance providers, country managers, freight forwarders, inspection agents, logistics providers, pre-and post-financing providers, and sales, support, and marketing agents. TradeCard will not disclose your personally identifiable information, confidential business data, or transaction details to parties outside of the TradeCard network without your consent.

4. Can I update the information that TradeCard has about my business or me?

TradeCard is committed to providing reasonable and practical access to you to identify and to correct any inaccuracies in the information you may provide. Visitors who have provided information on our web site can contact TradeCard Member Services to correct any inaccuracies. TradeCard members can use the system's administrative function on the transaction web site or contact TradeCard

Member Services to maintain up to date account information.

5. What choices are available to me regarding the collection and use of the information that I provide?

Visitors to TradeCard's web site who request additional information, will be included in future mailing initiatives. If you would like to opt out of receiving these mailings, send us an e-mail with your name referencing "no updates" in the subject line to: unsubscribe@TradeCard.com.

During the registration process, TradeCard will allow you to choose whether or not you would like us to contact your trading partners for membership and other services related to transactions.

As a TradeCard member you have the right to opt-out of being listed in the TradeCard Membership Directory, which only members and alliance partners will be able to access. This means that TradeCard allows you to determine how "visible" your organisation will be to other organisations within the TradeCard network.

6. How do I know TradeCard is adhering to its Privacy and Confidentiality Policy?

The TradeCard proprietary system is protected by a VeriSign Global Secure Site Certificate. TradeCard is also a member of the International Chamber of Commerce (ICC) and plans to abide by the ICC rules and guidelines for electronic contracting when they are finalised. Further, TradeCard is committed to having our privacy and confidentiality policies and procedures audited by an independent third party.

7. What about children's online privacy protection?

TradeCard understands the importance of protecting children's privacy. The TradeCard web sites are not intentionally designed for or directed at children 13 years of age or younger. It is TradeCard's policy never to knowingly collect or to maintain information about anyone under the age of 13.

8. Whom may I contact at TradeCard to find out more about your privacy practices?

Please contact our Privacy Office by e-mail at *privacy@TradeCard.com*. You may also call TradeCard and ask to speak to the Director of e-Compliance. We welcome your comments and suggestions about how we can improve our privacy and security procedures. You may also contact us if you believe we have not complied with our Privacy and Confidentiality Policy with respect to your personal or confidential business data.

Although TradeCard adheres to industry standard practices to protect your personal information and your company's confidential data, we cannot ensure that this information will never be disclosed in ways not otherwise described in this Privacy and Confidentiality Policy.

Source: URL: http://www.tradecard.com/privacy/policy.html, 18 August 2000.

Server authentication: 128 bit digital server ID

A Verisign Global Secure Site Certificate protected the TradeCard system wherein the Global Secure Site ID provided the client browser with the communications encryption of 128 bit (using a US domestic web browser) and 40 bit data encryption (using an exportable web browser). Both Microsoft Internet Explorer 4.0 or later and Netscape Navigator 4.0 or later support this function.

All TradeCard servers were located in key-locked racks, in a code-locked room that was only accessible by employees responsible for maintenance and operation of the equipment. Each server was protected by a user ID password to gain access to the machine, two layers of firewall configured to only allow network transactions over set protocols/machines. Any irregular activity was logged. There was no direct access to the database as this was prohibited. All data access would have to be directed through the Application Servers, which add another level of security for accessing data from the system.

2-Factor user authentication: physical challenge/response token

Two-factor user authentication comprising a valid user name or ID and password and an authentication code by using a smart card technology with a wireless handheld reader to match up a challenge code prior to gaining access into the system. The 128-bit encryption provided by the Secure Socket Layer (SSL) session between the browser and server protected the user ID and password. The encryption, however, was not a guarantee for protection of the user ID and password as these could be easily obtained, e.g. by looking over someone's shoulder. Thus, TradeCard provided additional protection to all approved members through the smart card and reader, known as the TradeCard e-identity security system, which generated a one-time access code.

The password would be known only by the user; only hash values would be stored in TradeCard's database and this information was not accessible to TradeCard employees. The user would also be protected as at login time a token would be generated for the login session and stored in the user's web browser as a session cookie for that session only (persistent web browser cookies were not utilised). Login session also required an inactivity time-out such that the user would need to re-enter the user ID and password to re-authenticate the user's identity.

Digital signatures

Digital signatures were required at initial login time in the TradeCard system as these authenticated electronic data and verified that a specific user created an electronic document. An invalid digital signature prevented a transaction from being processed and any attempt to conduct a transaction using an invalid digital signature would be logged.

TradeCard issued a unique digital key pair – a password encrypted private key and public key – to the approved users of the system the first time they accessed the TradeCard system. The private key was required every time a user signed a document in the system during a transaction. The public key validated the authenticity and integrity of an electronic document when the document was received and as a means of verifying a document at any time in the future.

Creating a digital signature involved user browser passing the user's encrypted private key, password and document data into a digital signature creation algorithm. The algorithm result would be the document signature. The document data and document signature would then be forwarded onto the TradeCard application server for processing. Validation of the electronic document was through the TradeCard application server passing a user's public key, electronic document and digital signature into a digital signature verification algorithm. This would confirm that the digital signature on the document was valid and that the document was not altered after it was created.

How TradeCard worked

TradeCard's global e-commerce trade settlement network was described as:

> When a buyer and seller agree to transact, the TradeCard system allows them to negotiate contract terms and conditions on-line. Once a transaction is established in electronic form with both parties in agreement, the seller will formally approve the terms of the purchasing contract. Each purchase order is then attached with an assurance of payment through Coface and their @rating service ensuring that the seller will receive payment upon receipt of goods. When the goods are shipped, TradeCard's patented compliance engine compares the shipping information with the purchase order. If the terms are met, the payment is made automatically. The buyer gets its goods and the seller gets its money.[10]

Based on the process flow of transaction, TradeCard acquired a patent for the TradeCard solution. Filed on 13 October 1994, a U.S. patent was issued on 10 February 1998. A Taiwanese patent was just granted in June 2000 with pending acceptance in seven foreign countries as of June 2000. The patent described TradeCard as a system that stores criteria specified by a funder relating to trade transactions for buyers and sellers. The system compared the criteria with a proposed purchase order (PO) to determine whether the system could generate a payment guarantee on behalf of the funder for the buyer to the seller. The system also compared subsequent PO documentation with the original PO to ensure that the terms of the PO were properly fulfilled. (Please refer to Exhibit 3 for the TradeCard process.)

TradeCard Internet document workflow

TradeCard controlled all the business transactions created by the TradeCard system through the TradeCard Workflow Processor. The TradeCard workflow processor managed all business documents that were organised into sets of folders and contracts. When an action was required against a document, all the parties involved were automatically alerted. Also, when a document or folder went through a business level change, the workflow processor would initiate an internal event (an example of an event would be the application of a digital signature to a document).

---

10. URL: http://www.tradecard.com, 24 March 2000.

Exhibit 3 The TradeCard process

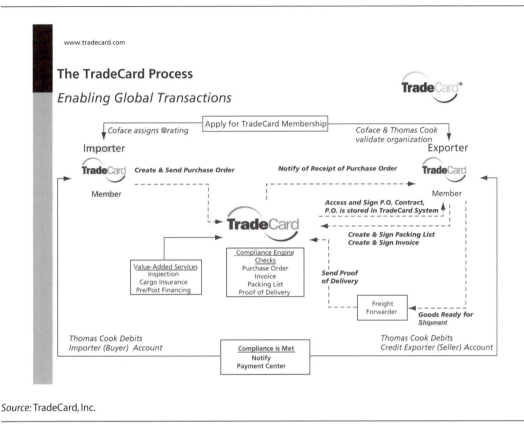

The TradeCard Process

Enabling Global Transactions

Source: TradeCard, Inc.

The TradeCard Rule Engine that determined the workflow requirements of all transactions would be informed of every event in the system. There was a set of business rules that examined the event and processed or assigned the next work item required for the transaction.

All transactions in the TradeCard system contained a list of required work items against the documents within that transaction. This list was made available through a reporting engine that allowed users to request and receive transaction reports via a web browser. Users could track the entire trade transaction workflow and view the individual steps in real-time. The user could download these reports to a local system in a variety of formats including HTML, Adobe PDF and Microsoft Excel.

TradeCard had a rule-based architecture – Dynamic Business Logic – that allowed the standards of a particular buyer/seller community to be defined once. All subsequent transactions within the community would then follow the predefined rules or standards. The rules managed the workflow of the transaction by determining the required documents, their routing, and compliance characteristics. Dynamic business rules could be created for specific individual parties, communities and regions.

TradeCard's e-value chain

The two major parties involved in any transaction were the buyer and the seller.

The traditional model of the trading process involved the following steps:

- *Discovery*: seller displays goods and buyer selects the goods to purchase
- *Negotiation*: buyer and seller negotiate a price and buyer formally confirms the order
- *Ordering*: buyer and seller agree to transact
- *Fulfillment*: movement of goods from buyer to seller
- *Compliance*: documents are checked against one another
- *Settlement*: buyer pays and seller receives the payment.

Predominantly, b-to-b trading sites, or online marketplaces, offered Discovery, Negotiation and Ordering; the last three processes required dropping off-line. TradeCard provided the financial link that completed the value chain on-line. (Please refer to Exhibit 4 for the TradeCard E-Value Chain.) Like Amazon.com, where users were guided through the buying process from source (Amazon.com) to settlement (credit card) to shipment (DHL) all in one seamless transaction, TradeCard created a platform for all the data and information involved to be displayed in one window in the electronic compliance process that could be viewed by all parties involved. The system was designed to let the buyer and seller control the transactions without having to rely on banks to approve the deal. When all the appropriate conditions for payment were met, TradeCard would initiate an automatic settlement.

TradeCard had the International Chamber of Commerce (ICC) rule as its standard in the documentation process, similar to a LC with an ICC stamp, but was not replicating everything. For example, TradeCard was not creating the bill of lading or all other cargo documents; only the freight forwarder would notify TradeCard that they had prepared the documents. In such cases, TradeCard like LC would facilitate trade by guaranteeing payment for sellers, but only when the documents were in order. It would also protect the buyers by ensuring that sellers complied with terms and conditions of a transaction before releasing payments.

Becoming a TradeCard member

All the network users and partners in the trading process had to be part of the TradeCard network to enable transactions to be conducted on-line. To become an approved member of the TradeCard network, users had to complete an on-line application that would be evaluated by TradeCard and its two core partners:

1 *Thomas Cook*: performed OFAC and anti-money laundering checks, collected bank/account information from buyers and sellers that would guarantee that they were authorised to approve and transfer funds.
2 *Coface*: provided a credit rating to the buyer and assurance of payment to the seller.

Since TradeCard provided payment assurance and movement of funds, the registration procedure had to look for credit ratings and the financial background of the company or user lodging the application. The process was similar to applying for a credit card in which applicants had to provide detailed information for TradeCard to verify the company credentials and the user involved, a process that would normally take about two weeks.

Costs of using TradeCard

Fees involved in the TradeCard system included an annual membership fee of US$250 per company, and a flat fee of US$150 per settled transaction for transactions between US$10 000 and US$100 000, applicable to either trade import or export party. With the TradeCard system, the seller normally had to pay for the transaction fee, but TradeCard was designing this liability such that it could be negotiated

Exhibit 4 TradeCard e-value chain

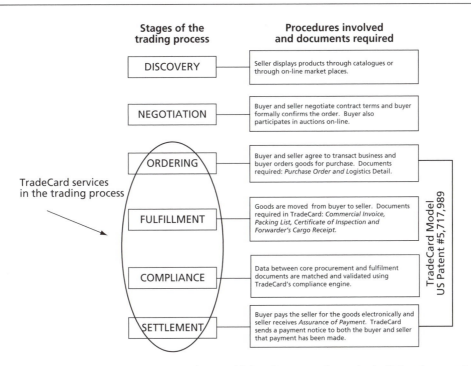

- *Purchase Order (P.O.)*: a required document that establishes the terms of an order by listing the quantity, type, and price of goods to be purchased.
- *Logistics Detail*: a required document that defines the shipping terms and conditions for a Purchase Order.
- *Commercial Invoice*: a bill for the goods from the seller to the buyer.
- *Packing list*: lists the number of items shipped, describes the items shipped and provides shipping information.
- *Certificate of Inspection*: a certificate attesting to the specifications of goods shipped, required by some purchasers and countries; may also be referred to as an Inspection Certificate.
- *Forwarder's Cargo Receipt*: proof of delivery document.
- *Assurance of Payment*: provided to the seller by the Coface Group for the amount of the invoice up to the buyer's @rating limit in case the buyer defaults on payment. This assurance of payment applies only to TradeCard transactions that are fully compliant to the terms and conditions of the purchase order between a specified buyer and seller within a given time frame.

Source: TradeCard, Inc.

and apportioned between the buyer and seller. With the US$150 fee TradeCard members would get value-added services including:

- access to third-party services;
- transaction security for all parties;
- assurance of payment to the seller;
- electronic movement of funds; and

- 24 × 7 real-time access to accurate transactions.

The US$150 fee was about one tenth of the cost of a LC per transaction. According to Klausner, the average shipment of finished goods such as toys, electronics, etc. based on the US government statistics was about US$43 000 per transaction and the fee to use a LC on a US$43 000 transaction was from US$1000 to US$1500, usually paid by the seller.[11]

Implementation issues

The new management team that came along in 1999 identified three major issues that hampered the full implementation of the TradeCard system from 1994 to 1998: the system, specifically data synchronisation; marketing strategy; and business model.

Implementation problems from 1994 to 1998

Data synchronisation

FSTS developed TradeCard on a Windows-based software application that was a distributed data system that had to be installed in every single PC at all locations and had to be synchronised to enable traders transact on-line incorporating electronic compliance.[12] A single transaction between a buyer and a seller using the system was a massive effort as it involved linking up all trading parties involved and synchronising the database. Data were often difficult to access and out-of-date. Logistically it was impractical to use the system when the users involved were in countries where TradeCard was not available, because the software had to be physically installed in the PC.

Marketing strategy

As TradeCard's strategy was "to start small, but start successful", the companies involved in the first transactions were small and medium-sized companies. The first transactions were carried out on 30 April 1998, involving a US-based importer, Avalon Products, importing US$21 600 worth of baby strollers from a Taipei-based manufacturer, Most-Brite. The transactions also involved the participation of the following:

- the NationsBank's Atlanta office granted credit for the transactions, and Most-Brite's account at Standard Chartered Bank in Taipei received payment;
- the Best Freight International of Hong Kong provided Freight Forwarding services; and
- the GE Information Services' global network assisted with installation and technical support.[13]

Since TradeCard was targeting companies in the global trade industry, focusing on small and medium-sized companies did not help build trust and credibility for TradeCard in the marketplace.

Business model

"TradeCard unsuccessfully tried to set up a business model that included banks," according to Avivah Litan of the Gartner Group.[14] Although owned and developed by private companies, TradeCard was marketed by banks and they were allowed to focus on the provision of financing services and access to a payment network. According to the Boston Consulting Group, the trade finance business was dominated largely by a relatively small number of banks that were reluctant to share their scale. In the US alone, the 10 largest trade finance banks account for 75 per cent of LC.[15] TradeCard could be a contender for the banking business, which makes it crucial for banks to actually market the TradeCard service.

---

11. Interview with Michael Klausner, TradeCard Vice President for Marketing, 13 March 2000.
12. URL: http://www.dbassoc.hu/WTC/11–96NWS.HTM, 19 January 2000.
13. URL: http://www.webcom.com/pjones/wtc$$$.html, 18 January 2000.
14. Marjanovic, S., "Two Web Trade Systems Ready for Launching", *American Banker*, 24 September 1999.
15. Platt, G., "Automated Payments Will Cut Costs, Report Says", *Journal of Commerce*, 17 September 1999.

Solutions implemented by TradeCard, Inc. in 1999 and 2000

Realising the three key issues in the implementation from 1994 to 1998, the management team started working to address the three key issues in February 1999.

A new system built on the Internet

The new management changed the whole medium of providing electronic settlement services by abandoning the client server system in preference for developing an entirely new system on the Internet. TradeCard, Inc. built the new TradeCard system around the old client service system model on an Internet-based system that allowed the buyers, sellers and the network partners to access one application through a web browser based on the HTTP and HTML protocols.

The TradeCard system was built on a HTML platform with HTML incorporating Java programming. TradeCard's formulas and electronic documents were based on XML (Extensible Markup Language) Schema Document Type Definitions, which provided a mechanism for translating and integrating business data from disparate systems.

All types of business documents were stored internally in the TradeCard system as XML; although TradeCard customers were not required to have XML-compliant interfaces on their systems. For example, a seller could upload an invoice from an automated supply chain system directly into the TradeCard system, the buyer could view the invoice in HTML via a web browser, and a freight forwarder could send the advance shipping notice in EDI format.

TradeCard was developing a standard XML-based schema that would be published for every service provider to utilise. In special circumstances, TradeCard would provide translation services for standard industry accepted formats into its own schema. In countries where paper documents were still required, these documents could be faxed to the TradeCard system. The documents would then be stored as images that would be accessible via a web browser. This allowed businesses with paper-based requirements to participate in TradeCard transactions.

Marketing strategy: build alliances with best-of-breed international trade service providers

TradeCard's aim was to change traditional trading practices globally. TradeCard faced the challenge by building its brand and establishing trust, and implemented the concept of trust by association. TradeCard was building trust and credibility in the marketplace through developing alliances with best-of-breed companies instead of small and medium-sized companies. With the support of WTCA, GEIS, and Marsh & McLennan Cos. (an insurance brokerage and consultant), TradeCard also built alliances with companies such as:

- Coface Group – world's leading source of credit information and the manager of the French Government's export guarantee
- Thomas Cook Group Ltd., London – London-based payments and foreign exchange specialists and the world's leading international travel and financial service provider
- Tradelink Electronic Commerce Ltd. – the "electronic gateway" for Hong Kong traders
- Information Technology Pioneer International Inc. – a financial information integration service leader in Taiwan
- SGS International Certification Services, Inc. – the world's largest inspection, certification and verification organisation
- Bureau Veritas/ACTS Testing – a leading inspection, certification and verification organisation
- Inspectorate – a global inspection, certification and verification organisation

- Intertek Testing Services (ITS) – an international inspection, certification and verification organisation
- Comerica – 24th largest bank holding company in the United States
- Bank SinoPac – Taiwan-based international bank
- Dah Sing Bank – Hong Kong-based multi-service bank.

TradeCard's New York office dealt primarily with the North American companies that were buyers and whose trade counterparts were predominantly located in Asia. Therefore, TradeCard's plan for expansion was to start in the Asia-Pacific region with a business coverage of the initial rollout looking at four countries concurrently: Hong Kong, Taiwan, Singapore and South Korea. Hong Kong was the first physical office established, and it served as the regional headquarters that would look after the TradeCard offices in the other Asian countries. TradeCard's target was to secure 100 exporters and sign up with TradeCard within the first quarter of 2000. Overall, TradeCard aimed to have 2000 users conducting at least one transaction in the system. In the years 2000–2001, TradeCard's plan was to roll out its services in Europe and South America.

The business approach was the same in all countries: to forge alliances with established local trading companies or institutions that had developed strong links with the local community. These alliances would serve as TradeCard's main sales force on the ground. Marketing of the TradeCard service would be through:

- Referrals from the core group of invited customers or early adopters who had used TradeCard. If they were buyers, TradeCard would request a listing of their major sellers and consequently TradeCard would conduct a direct marketing approach to their referrals.

- Companies and institutions such as Tradelink in Hong Kong which understood trading practices and had an established database of traders. TradeCard would work with Tradelink and come up with a direct marketing programme to promote TradeCard as a new international trade settlement tool to the Hong Kong trading community.

A public relations and direct marketing firm, Ogilvy, worked with TradeCard to create the TradeCard brand image and disseminate the service to each region or country where TradeCard would be commercially launched. Ogilvy prepared all the marketing promotion material and documentation necessary to launch the service in the region.

In March 2000, TradeCard Inc. in co-operation with Tradelink introduced the TradeCard system to members of the Tradelink trading community. On 28 March 2000, TradeCard announced its worldwide service launch in Hong Kong.

Thomas Cook as "money mover"

Thomas Cook served as the "money mover" for TradeCard, whereby the agreement between the two companies allowed buyers and sellers who would transact with TradeCard to maintain their individual bank relationships. Thomas Cook provided global payment and foreign exchange functions to buyers and sellers using the TradeCard network, and conveyed funds between the banks of the parties to a trade.

Issues and challenges

Network of international players

TradeCard's need was to gather information from the traditional trade providers to facilitate future transactions. TradeCard had to decide on how to build up the network of players in the international trade to

TRADECARD'S ALLIANCE WITH TRADELINK IN HONG KONG

In June 1999, TradeCard decided to expand into Asia, targeting first the Hong Kong market as it was the most active international trading hub in Asia. (Refer to Exhibit 5 for Hong Kong's total export in 1996 to September 1999) TradeCard announced its alliance with Tradelink Electronic Commerce Limited in November 1999. Tradelink was a joint venture between the Hong Kong Government and 11 private sector shareholders that served as the local "electronic gateway" for the Hong Kong trading community and had 43 000 customers. Tradelink, an established institution had the market penetration for international trade, which mirrored the TradeCard model. Tradelink offered their customers EDI-based trade declaration services, whereas the TradeCard system focused more on an on-line financial settlement network with a value-added service to current Tradelink customers.

The agreement required Tradelink to provide TradeCard with its primary sales and marketing resource and customer service support for TradeCard customers in Hong Kong. This would entail Tradelink setting up the TradeCard call centres to support TradeCard customers and provide services under the TradeCard name. As Tradelink had already built the infrastructure, TradeCard only had to train the workforce from a TradeCard perspective.

Exhibit 5 Hong Kong export trade statistics

Year	Total exports*	Total trade*
1996	1,397,917	2,933,499
1997	1,455,949	3,071,040
1998	1,347,649	2,776,741
1999**	976,731	1,985,082

Notes
1. ** In Hong Kong dollars.
2. * January to September only.

Source: Hong Kong Monthly Digest of Statistics (November 1999).

incorporate TradeCard members. This entailed approaching traditional providers of trade such as:

- logistics providers
- credit and financial providers
- inspection providers
- other trade service providers.

Building the network of players in the TradeCard system was crucial as this would provide solutions to the issue regarding geographical limitations in using TradeCard. As of March 2000, use of the TradeCard system was only possible in countries such as the US, Hong Kong, Taiwan, Korea and Singapore. For example, if traders in Hong Kong wanted to do business with mainland China, TradeCard was not yet in a position to do so, as they had not established the appropriate facilities, due to capacity issues and some regulatory issues that were out of their control.

Negative perception associated with electronic transactions

TradeCard's aim was to change traders' approach to trade. In doing so, TradeCard had to tackle issues relative to the needs and expectations of international traders. Traders were accepting the concept and the idea of b-to-b e-commerce, but were unsure what the next step was with regard to payments and making sure that payments were secure. Banks had traditionally provided a secure method of facilitating large transactions across international borders. When TradeCard approached the banks, the banking community initially was apprehensive because they perceived the TradeCard system as a threat to their LC business. Moreover, buyers and sellers had accounts in various different banks and they were concerned that they would have to change their account relationships. The three levels of security built in the TradeCard system were considered secure. TradeCard's main concern was how to change the negative perception associated with conducting secure on-line transactions. Michael Klausner, TradeCard Vice President for Marketing, expressed their challenge as:

> It's a marketing play to reach people and get them to sign up. We need buyers and sellers who are both members of the TradeCard network. This is quite similar to the credit card model where you need members who are cardholders and merchants who accept the card. But how do you get both sides of a transaction on the first day? Who will sign up first? We are in a similar situation right now to what the credit card companies must have faced when they first launched.[16]

Technical Infrastructure

TradeCard completed building its technological infrastructure, an "open box" of how everything worked, that would seamlessly aggregate all the necessary disparate services in international trade. TradeCard had also completed its Customer Service Management System.[17] Its data centre was co-located at PSINet and a separate disaster recovery facility became operational. Klausner said that speed and capacity were big issues for TradeCard. There were other intrinsic issues in global e-commerce that TradeCard had to consider, including, among others, the telecommunications infrastructure that would be able to accommodate all users and all types of data, updated standards to keep up with the changing laws associated with the Internet, and other technical and electronic transmissions standards.

Marissa McCauley prepared this case under the supervision of Dr. Ali Farhoomand for class discussion. This case is not intended to show effective handling of decision or business processes.

This case is part of a project funded by a teaching development grant from the University Grants Committee (UGC) of Hong Kong.

---

16. Interview with Michael Klausner in Hong Kong, 13 March 2000.

17. The Customer Relationship Management System was a web-based system designed by TradeCard that would follow the cycle of the transaction process. There would be one database into which all the departments in TradeCard could feed information. The departments would in turn have access to that data. For instance in the acquisition of the customer, the Marketing department would have to input information to the system. When a marketing prospect become a customer, it would be passed on to Customer Service department so they too could monitor the transactions, and so on.

e-Business process management

Enterprise resource planning systems

Guy Gable

Objectives

❏ To establish the importance of ERP in an e-business context

❏ To examine ERP's role as the backbone of a firm's e-business capability

❏ To understand how integrating ERP with the Web can create opportunities for enhancing the firm's operational efficiency.

❏ To consider alternative e-business strategies for the ERP-enabled firm

❏ To explore the future of ERP and how this future might impact e-business models

❏ To consider the potential costs and benefits of maintaining and evolving ERP and e-business applications

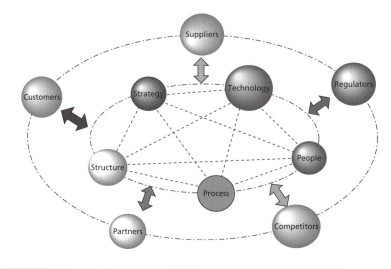

ERP has for some time been the primary enterprise application and the architectural framework into which most other applications plug. This role is being challenged. Some argue that in their rush to become an (e)Business many companies, because of the compatibility issues involved in making 3rd party (e)Business applications work fluidly with ERP, will decide against implementing an ERP system, stop a current ERP development in its tracks, or even backtrack away from ERP as the technology of transaction processing.

– Norris et al. (2000)

Having covered some key technology issues and gained an understanding of the infrastructure decisions underpinning modern e-business, we now move on to our coverage of **e-Business Process Management** which entails the *process* dimension of the DOT framework. We will concentrate on illustrating the interdependence of internal and external processes and the challenge of integrating highly technical systems with the diverse processes that exist across an organisation's value chain. Within this part, we devote this chapter to examining ERP – the corporate-wide backbone that caters to the transactional needs of various business areas. Chapter 7 will explore the theme of customer relationship marketing in the e-business context, while Chapter 8 examines the business concepts behind supply chain management and the challenges companies face in adopting new technologies to enable their traditional supply chains for e-business.

As we discussed within our building blocks framework in Part 2, the function of ERP systems has traditionally been to organise and standardise the data relating to an enterprise's core processes. The standing of ERP systems as the necessary starting point for organisations with e-business ambitions has been cast into doubt by third-party e-business applications that increasingly supplant the functionality of ERP systems. Yet ERP continues to be the most fitting solution in scenarios where organisational processes are heavily tied with physical production needs and under circumstances where vast amounts of financial and human resources information must be processed. In such situations ERP continues to provide the context and the platform for enterprise-wide consistency in data, processes and integration efforts.

In a competitive environment where the strategic value of information is vital, enterprises are transforming themselves from vertically integrated organisations into agile outward-looking entities positioned strategically in the business web comprising customers, suppliers and many partners. The demand on ERP solutions to address this shift has resulted in its evolution to encompass these outward-facing elements. ERP systems are increasingly wed to e-business applications in order to extend their core functionality to external nodes in a business web.

Because implementation of a full-fledged ERP system constitutes a major investment, senior management need to be attentive to industry developments, the relation between ERP and key e-business functionality and, perhaps most importantly, the challenges related to the integration of e-business initiatives and ERP.

In this chapter we explore the present and future relationship of Enterprise Resource Planning (ERP) systems with e-business. Many organisations seeking to develop e-business capabilities, build on an existing base ERP investment. Others who do not, possibly should. This chapter thus takes an ERP-centric perspective, extending from key concepts introduced in Chapter 4 on infrastructure to explore several pragmatic issues faced by organisations considering "where to from here".

Background

What is ERP?

In Chapter 4 we described ERP as software that evolved from early Materials Resource Planning (MRP) applications used in the manufacturing industry. A main driver behind this evolution was the aim of integrating internal transactions and streamlining related information flows. We should note at the outset that there is no consensus with regard to the role that ERP should, or can, play in e-business transformation.

Predecessors of ERP include MRP (1950s), MRP II (1970s), and CIM (Computer Integrated Manufacturing; 1980s). MRP II extended the functionality of MRP to let manufacturers to optimise materials, procurement, accounting, distribution and manufacturing processes. In essence it made possible the integration of MRP with other manufacturing and business functions.[1] CIM expanded this role by integrating management of information for all business and technical functions of a manufacturer.[2] ERP strived for more integration by integrating logistics, manufacturing, financial and human resource management functions within a company. The ultimate goal is to enable enterprise-wide management of resources.[3] Although this historical sequence implies a continuous and temporal evolution of process modelling in different industries, a quick review of similarities and differences across these predecessors is revealing.[4]

MRP II software solutions, in the form of Production Planning and Control systems, can be regarded as predecessors of ERP software. Like MRP II systems, ERP support a range of typical business functions. Subsequent CIM models provided the conceptual basis for the development of integrated software application packages and simpler techniques for data and process modelling. The concept of one (logically) integrated database with a common user interface led to the emergence of ERP.

Despite these similarities, several key differences separate ERP from MRP II and CIM. While MRP, MRP II and CIM are based on widely researched and debated models developed independent of any specific vendor solution, such a common reference model for ERP does not exist. This is a major reason for the lack of academic and practitioner consensus on ERP-related concepts and terminologies to date.

Also, while MRP, MRP II and CIM reflected the continuous extension of production functionality, ERP can be implemented without any production-related functionality. Today ERP are widely installed in non-manufacturing sectors, including services, finance and government. We should note that while CIM included many technical functions like CAD/CAM (computer aided design/manufacturing), ERP solutions typically do not have embedded parts for these functions.

---

1. Howe (1993).
2. Scheer (1994, p. 2).
3. META Group (1998).
4. Klaus et al. (2000).

In fact, difficulties in integrating an ERP solution with other highly technical systems are a major challenge for many companies.

Finally, MRP, MRP II and CIM concentrated exclusively on processing functions internal to the firm. They were not designed to enable integration of business partners' processes through the entire value chain. In contrast, ERP have capacity to underpin Supply Chain Management (SCM) and Customer Relationship Management (CRM). MRP covered all functions related to material management, and MRP II and CIM indeed concentrated on manufacturing issues, but they did not provide integrated solutions for inter-corporate processes.

Set in this background let us understand what ERP is, and what it is not. First, ERP are concerned with both resources and processes in the organisation. Second, planning functionality is neither a primary nor a universal strength of current ERP packages, which emphasise the execution of operational transactions like sales order processing, rather than sophisticated planning capabilities in the areas of procurement, production, sales or finance.[5] Third, as discussed earlier, the term "enterprise" in ERP is now too narrowly focused to take account of process integration across multiple business partners in the value chain. Thus it is incorrect to assume that ERP literally means enterprise-wide planning of resources.

Further, new innovations have given rise to what might be called eXtended, cross organisational (X-organisational), or "neXt generation ERP" (perhaps "X-ERP" is an appropriate term), and supplier-and-customer integration functionality (these extended ERP were initially referred to as "ERP II" by Gartner). ERP vendors eager to unbundle and market new functionality on offer (e.g. CRM and SCM) have themselves moved away from exclusive use of the term "ERP". Thus, the term "ERP" is not ideal.

Regardless, practitioners have adopted ERP as a ubiquitous "island of technology" term. "ERP" and "Enterprise Resource Planning" are terms now commonly used to signify integrated business application packages and these terms are pervasive in the commercial press as well as in academic literature.[6]

How big is an ERP?

Transformational initiatives fall into three categories: projects, programs and endeavours. Because each type of initiative requires a quite different management approach, vision and philosophy, and measures of success, confusing the scope of an initiative, such as ERP, can place the organisation at great risk (Figure 6.1).

A project has an identifiable scope and owner, a definable goal, and a start and finish. Programs tend to involve multiple objectives, changes in business processes,

---

5. Having said this we note that ERP are evolving rapidly, and support for planning constantly increasing.
6. We recognise that alternative terms are being used in some quarters. For example, the term "Enterprise Systems", in most usages, is synonymous with ERP as defined herein.

Figure 6.1 How big is an ERP?

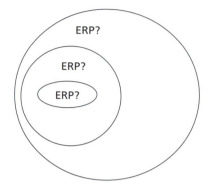

a multi-layered business case, evolving scope, and cross-organisational boundaries. They are not just larger and longer projects. Examples include sales force automation, total quality management, or creating a Web presence. Endeavours are "strategic initiatives concerned with major and fundamental changes to business models and industry structures, how customers interact with enterprises . . ."[7] Examples include e-business, supply chain management, customer relationship management and globalisation.

Both programs and endeavours involve multiple projects. A given project may be deemed a success, but the program or endeavour a failure. Conversely, an endeavour may be deemed a success, though one or more of its component projects or programs have failed.

A key distinguishing feature of programs and endeavours from projects is that their scope evolves in the face of changing organisational culture, structures and competitive environment. Consequently, when a firm faces a challenging program or endeavour, even the most disciplined project management approaches may not deliver the required business benefits.

ERP implementation is often an example of a program. Others refer to ERP as "grand designs" – perhaps more akin to an endeavour – suggesting that:

> [Such] approaches to solving organisational challenges are based on long-term, fundamental assumptions about the organisational environment and a planned, systematic effort to solve a number of related problems over a long period of time. Here some powerful assumptions about the environment are needed; as one grand design is chosen, experimentation with other designs will be limited, and a significant resource commitment will have to be made over a long period of time.[8]

Endeavours require the organisational will and commitment to manage ambiguity over an extended period. A retailer's decision to move to an e-business

---

7. Broadbent and Ragow (2000, p. C02).
8. Laudon, K.C. and Laudon, J.P. (2000, p. 570).

model may of necessity be a life-or-death endeavour. The possibly simpler (though not simple) decision to deploy ERP usually should not be.

While many now consider ERP a competitive necessity – perhaps foundational to an endeavour – it is important to recognise that it may be only one component of a much larger initiative. Part of the confusion stems from ERP often being necessary, but not sufficient for success with an endeavour such as e-business. It is thus important to recognise that the ERP is often a mechanism of broader change, rather than the target of change.

ERP vs e-business

In Chapter 1 we saw that the propagation of business process reengineering efforts in the mid-1990s shifted firms' attention from isolated business activities to entire value chains. Nevertheless, the scope of these efforts were in most cases limited to departmental or corporate boundaries – obstacles within these areas were often overwhelming by themselves.[9] As we discussed in Chapter 4, the functionality of ERP systems is extending beyond the boundaries of the enterprise. Parties along value chains are taking an increasingly integrated view of their internal processes and trying to understand how their systems relate to those of their customers, suppliers, partners and competitors.[10]

e-Business is causing ERP applications to evolve

Until the late 1990s ERP was the primary enterprise application and the architectural framework into which most other applications plug. This role was recently challenged by some advocates of e-business. It is believed that Web-based technology can effectively supplant internal information systems, and that transaction processing inside the enterprise can be carried out via the software of these front-end communication systems and passed from one to the next. In their rush to become e-businesses many companies will struggle to resolve the compatibility issues involved in making third-party e-business applications work fluidly with ERP. The proponents of this view think that some companies will decide against implementing an ERP system, stop a current ERP development in its tracks, or even backtrack away from ERP as the technology of transaction processing.

However, the issue is in fact far more complex than some e-business evangelists suggest. Some companies currently building e-business applications are largely ignoring ERP development, hoping that someone someday will integrate the back-end. As a result, companies whose e-business applications have no order-fulfilment and order-status capabilities may either lack this data or need to recreate it. Any company requires an internal transaction engine, independent

---

9. Scheer and Habermann (2000, p. 60).
10. Laudon, K.C. and Laudon, J.P. (2000, p. 555).

of the supplier- and customer-facing front-ends, and to date the best of these are driven by ERP software.

This brief discussion already suggests several possible future scenarios:

- a successful front-end e-business software vendor builds a viable transaction engine component;

- a customised in-house transaction engine to link and integrate e-business front-ends;

- ERP products evolve to increase their compatibility with third-party front-ends;

- more flexible, more easily implemented ERP with e-business functionality will emerge; and

- application service providers enable the firm to undertake collaborative commerce via a "metaprise" capability.

e-Business is undoubtedly causing ERP applications to evolve. Given the continued expansion of ERP systems beyond the firm's traditional boundaries to enable e-business partner interactions, the boundaries between first-generation ERP (or "back office") and new extended-function (or "front-office") solutions and e-business applications have become blurred.

While traditional ERP systems catered to various business areas of the firm (refer Figure 6.2), next generation ERP systems must extend functionality beyond enterprise boundaries (refer Figure 6.3). ERP vendors are consequently repositioning themselves to provide e-business software solutions.

Market and technological uncertainty has led some in the "solutions industry" to predict that e-business applications will supplant ERPs. There are two major problems with this forecast:[11]

1 The [firm] . . . with internal processes that have to do with physical production needs an ERP or comparable enterprise-wide transaction processor to keep track of money, people, raw material, work-in-progress, and finished goods inventory.

2 Once any organisation grows to a certain size . . . it must consolidate financial and human resources information in such a way that ERP becomes appropriate.

As we saw in Chapter 4 ERP is now considered the "transactional backbone" that supports advanced applications such as CRM, SCM and e-procurement. ERP continues to be centrally important and has become a basic assumption in doing business of substantial scale. For a truly e-enabled enterprise, quality information must be available in real-time anywhere it is needed. Scattered

---

11. Norris et al. (2000, p. 28).

Figure 6.2 Traditional ERP

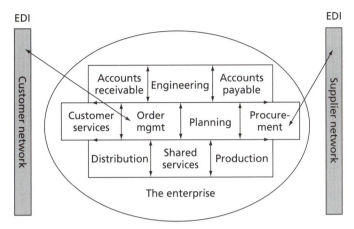

Figure 6.3 Next generation ERP: extending beyond enterprise boundaries

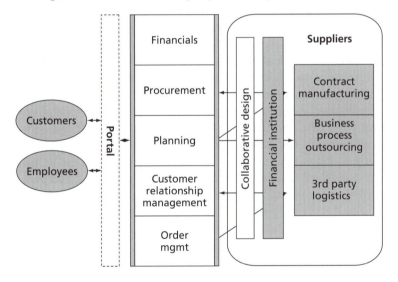

islands of information hinder the development of e-business – increasing costs and coordination difficulties, decreasing accuracy and reducing flexibility, and increasing processing and development time.

Nonetheless, while every manufacturing company needs some level of ERP capability to keep the wheels of business turning, few ERP systems actively help the business grow or stave off competitive pressures. Since most ERP systems do not provide end-to-end solutions for business needs, manufacturers need to foster multiple vendor relationships and integrate business growth applications with the core transactional ERP system.[12] The complete solution must enable

12. Ford (2000, p. 213).

enterprise-wide access to current, and particularly Web-based, information and allow portability between ERP systems.

Lack of integration between ERP and e-business systems

To achieve maximum benefits, ERP and e-business technologies must be fully integrated across the enterprise. e-Commerce software and back-end systems, including ERP software, must be integrated in order to manage the fulfilment process seamlessly. Very few organisations have implemented a fully integrated ERP suite across the enterprise.[13] A recent survey of UK manufacturers found that the main problems encountered when selling online are:[14]

● lack of integration between ERP and e-business systems (52 per cent);

● the resulting need to re-key orders into the ERP system (47 per cent); and

● non-automated order processing (44 per cent) (resulting in the need to re-confirm order details by fax).

It seems that a lack of integration with ERP systems could be a major setback for e-business implementations. Manufacturers will face pressure to upgrade their ERP systems for Web compatibility or find alternative solutions.[15]

Both current and prospective ERP-enabled organisations need to be aware that ERP extensions sometimes sit outside the core ERP software and database. In other words, these extensions can be quite different from, and almost physically separate from, the original, core functionality of the software. This may be by design, as part of a vendor's strategy for unbundling new functionality from the original, holistic model, or it can be due to acquisition of the extension from a third-party software provider. Depending on how well the ERP provider has managed integration of the parts, this implicit segregation can impact system performance and its robustness during system changes.

Caution when evaluating vendors' integration claims can pay off later in implementation. Vendors often extend their core ERP software by retrofitting new extensions obtained through acquiring or partnering with third parties. Organisations evaluating the capabilities of prospective products must therefore determine exactly how, and how tightly, any e-business extensions are integrated with the core ERP system.

Integration of applications can be achieved in several technically different ways:[16]

1 *The ERP has open APIs.* Applications in the ERP are able to communicate with other software via layers of code called *application programming*

---

13. Norris et al. (2000).
14. Callaway (2000).
15. Tinham (2000, p. 39).
16. Callaway (2000).

interfaces (APIs). However this does not mean that the applications can be simply "plugged together". A programmer must write code that facilitates communication between the systems. The existence of APIs can simplify this task considerably.

2 *The ERP system and its e-business extensions are connected at the database level.* When the same database structure is shared by two systems the same database fields (e.g. general ledger account codes) can be used by each, leading to data management efficiencies. However simply linking the systems at the database level does not mean that the applications can communicate in real-time or that they necessarily share a common graphical user interface. If data in one application changes, the systems must be reintegrated.

3 *The applications share data via data extraction.* Data is extracted from one application, placed in a file to be translated into a format that the other application can understand, and delivered periodically to that application. Batches of data can be sent as often as every few minutes or as infrequently as once per day.

4 *The applications share a common user interface.* The applications *appear* so similar that the user is unaware that s/he has stopped using one and started using another. However "integrated" applications often do not have a common user interface: one application merely allows the user to launch or access the other application.

5 *The applications share data in real-time.* Also known as "event-level integration", connections are developed to allow one application to instantly update the information in the other application.

So the degree of integration between a core ERP and its e-business extensions can vary. At one extreme, integration could be considered "loose" when the ERP has the necessary APIs but does not share a common user interface or database structure, and can exchange data only in batches. At the other extreme, integration would be considered "tight" where the ERP core and the e-business extension are delivered integrated at the database level, sharing a common user interface and exchanging data seamlessly and in real-time.

Web-enabled ERP

The Internet has rapidly become the applications platform of choice. Its ubiquity makes it readily accessible to distributed customers, suppliers and employees alike. As a result, ERP vendors have moved quickly to extend the functionality of their systems to reflect the trend towards e-business.

As most traditional ERP are client/server applications (see Chapter 4), a significant amount of code and logic run on both the workstation (client) and the server. This "fat client" architecture is not well suited to deploy over the Internet as large amounts of data and information need to be shared between the client and the server at run-time. Importantly, instead of being accessible through simple browser software, specialised client software must be installed on all workstations that access the server.

Web-enabling a software product so that it can be accessed via a browser is now reasonably easy. The basic software can remain much the same, however it may not perform well over the Internet's architecture. For this reason, ERP vendors have been careful to Web-enable only those parts of their systems that do perform well in a "thin client" arrangement. Unfortunately, simple retro-Web-enabling of client/server software is a far cry from software specifically developed for the Internet.[17]

Earlier in this chapter we noted that companies looking to manage the fulfilment process seamlessly must ensure that e-business software and back-end systems, including ERP, are tightly integrated. Back-end integration helps companies to closely manage and track their Internet-based transactions. Companies can then coordinate the data they collect from online transactions with information they gather from other channels, such as the telephone, traditional retail stores and in-person transactions. We have already seen how integrating front-office and back-office systems to achieve dynamically coupled internal and external processes can be a strategically important capability. Tight integration enables a company to better identify, manage and transact with online customers, with data gathered from all channels residing centrally in the ERP, and allows them to present an organised and professional image to their trading partners and customers. To achieve such tight integration, however, companies must overcome the following legacy issues inherent in the original design of ERP systems:

● ERP designs were initially based on an enterprise-centric paradigm;

● ERP are fundamentally internal transaction oriented systems;

● ERP designs were conceived in the client/server era, while e-business is, by definition, Internet based;

● ERP e-business functionality is often behind that available from next-generation competitors; and

● ERP systems are notoriously rigid and difficult to change once implemented, while e-business systems must be flexible, responsive and dynamic.

ERP as a platform for e-business

In this section we discuss the potential of using ERP as a platform for pursuing new sources of e-business value.[18]

Contemporary applications of ERP are still undertaken with the intent to integrate a firm's internal systems in order to present an enterprise-wide view of

---

17. Callaway (2000).
18. Much of this section is based in Davenport (2000).

business processes. However, there is now a clear trend towards firms leveraging their ERP capabilities to enable process integration beyond the enterprise boundaries and into customers' and suppliers' realms.

ERP can serve as a platform from which the organisation may pursue these new sources of e-business value. However to be a central component of the firm's strategic response, ERP will need to acquire new functionality, or integrate cleanly with other applications. Shortfalls in current ERP functionality represent opportunities for ERP vendors to evolve their software to add value associated with these trends, either through enhancing existing products or through facilitating ease of integration with third-party e-business technology solutions. ERP are likely to evolve to reflect the changing concerns of corporate management, potentially addressing:

- globalisation
- rapid-sense-and-respond business models
- corporate realignment
- virtual organisations.

Globalisation

ERP systems already support relatively straightforward capabilities such as multiple-currency handling and reporting by country. However, major requirements that ERP may potentially satisfy include:

- adaptability to local regulatory structures (current ERP integrated database and complex structures can present difficulties for companies looking to adapt their processes to local conditions);
- adaptability to local cultural expectations (standardising processes can generate economies of scale, but the trade-off may be a poor fit to local requirements and low customisation of products and services); and
- global production management (integration of globally sourced data on site capacity, production and transportation costs, tariffs, and demand, supporting production scheduling across multiple sites in order to optimise overall operational efficiency).

As consolidation may be an inevitable consequence of globalisation, Davenport (2000) suggests that ERP must evolve its capacity to combine multiple ERP instances through:

- ease of merging data definitions;
- ease of merging processes; and
- adaptability to local regulatory and cultural differences.

Rapid-sense-and-respond

Rapid-sense-and-respond capability provides value by learning what an individual customer wants at a particular time and responding by quickly providing a tailored product or service. To achieve this, an information system must maintain a tight real-time link between customer contact and production or service processes. Also known as "lean production", "mass customisation", or "customer-centric" production, this requires:

- process integration throughout the supply chain;
- production management;
- product configuration;
- the integrated applications and database of ERP *within* the firm; and
- SCM *across* firms.

Some ERP vendors now offer functionality or utilities supporting integrated applications, integrated database, production management and product configuration.

In recent years major ERP vendors have begun introducing SCM applications. ERP and SCM functionality will continue to evolve to support the trend towards rapid-sense-and-respond business models.

Corporate realignment

Firms' motivations for realigning horizontally (splitting off non-core or incompatible functions) may arise from the complexity of managing very large structures and the need to decrease costs. In the logistics sector, for example, businesses such as Federal Express supply inventory management to specialist retailers. Similarly, some professional employment organisations provide HRM services to SMEs.

Firms seeking to combine a renewed focus on their core competencies with expansion into global markets must not only divest certain functions, but may also need to organise these in new ways to survive. While ERP can in some ways facilitate merging of data and processes, there are no clear models of how to disaggregate data and processes when organisations restructure.

To remain relevant and continue to create value ERP will need to accommodate structural change throughout the organisational lifecycles. In essence, while we have a good understanding of cross-firm integration of supply chains, we are still faced with challenges relating to cross-firm integration.

Virtual organisations

A virtual organisation is based on a network of companies, which unite quickly (configuration and alternation of it) in order to exploit an apparent chance to compete. In a virtual organisation partners share costs, risks and knowledge. They act together in national and global markets whereby each "player" contributes its "comparative advantages". A critical success factor is a sophisticated information infrastructure that connects the dispersed member companies over large distances. If a market task is accomplished, whether it be after a year or a century, the organisational structure disbands respectively to make space for new alliances.[19]

Virtual organisations require an integration/disaggregation capability that is vastly superior to that needed by traditional organisations undertaking occasional realignments.

A large portfolio of relationships between past, present and potential business partners handling parts of processes gives rise to a near continual state of flux characterised by high transition costs.

For these organisations, building and sustaining competitive advantage depends on the strategic use of difficult-to-imitate core capabilities based on dynamically coupled internal and external processes. The uniqueness and complexity of these capability tends to result from effective combinations of other capabilities, competencies and resources. Strategic advantage may depend not only on strong collaborative relationships between diverse business partners and on value-added products and services, but also on integrated enterprise views of knowledge about internal and external entities and processes. As represented in Figure 6.4, core capabilities based at least in part on superior knowledge management are increasingly becoming strategic differentiators in industries and markets where changing business conditions have levelled the playing field.

ERP capabilities can offer strategic potential when leveraged to complement the firm's business context and other capabilities. As a central component of this approach, ERP must:

● facilitate ease and speed of bundling and unbundling; and

● support differing levels of integration of data and processes (appropriate to those firms that comprise the virtual organisation).

Current ERP systems do not support rapid, flexible and secure integration and disaggregation of data and processes to the degree required by emerging virtual organisations, nor the kinds of analyses necessary to evaluate value chain member benefits.

Figure 6.4 Knowledge management as source of strategic differentiation

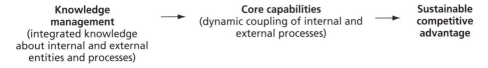

---

19. Published in Mertens, P. and Faisst, W. (1996).

Future systems will need to support vastly extended value chains. Firms must be able to use their ERP to support strategic evaluation of the relative value offered by membership in alternative value chains. Existing members of a given value chain must be able to evaluate the potential benefits offered by allowing new members. Evaluating entire value chains and membership potential suggests deep sharing of data amongst allied firms, requiring consolidation of data across multiple data systems.

Investing in ERP vs e-business

In this section we explore the issue of when to invest resources into ERP or e-business capabilities in order to maximise the effectiveness of both over the long term. To inform such decisions we will look at a framework for understanding e-business opportunities that arise from the context of a traditional enterprise and its ERP infrastructure. This discussion is based on several key assumptions:[20]

- e-Business will only work with clean internal processes and data;

- Web-based technology extends traditional core ERP technology, which tends to be large, technologically unwieldy, and often of dubious value; and

- ERP will integrate and evolve with several other technologies, in ways that cumulatively support the e-business model.

The existing internal infrastructures of today's global enterprises represent a huge sunk investment in technology. The most successful companies will be those that leverage this investment by implementing e-business solutions supported by sound, existing infrastructures based on well-functioning ERP systems. Rather than discarding past gains, today's executives should be asking themselves: How do we get the most out of our current investment in infrastructure? How do we penetrate the Internet marketplace with current assets? How do we compete against pure dot-com companies?

The ERP/e-business matrix

In order to make rational decisions about allocating resources to e-business, ERP, or both, an organisation must be able to identify alternative ways of moving from where it is now, to where it wants to be. Obviously, not all parts of the organisation, especially a conglomerate, will necessarily be at the same starting point. The ERP/e-B matrix depicted in Figure 6.5 is a decision-making tool advanced by PriceWaterhouseCoopers.

---

20. Norris et al. (2000).

Figure 6.5 The ERP/e-B matrix

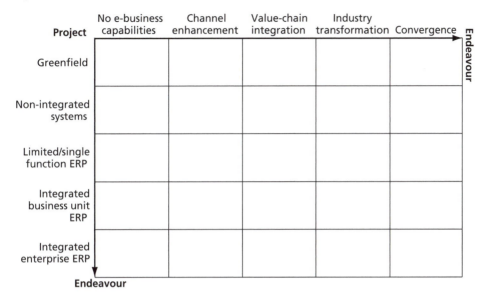

Source: Adapted from Norris et al. (2000). © 2000 PriceWaterhouseCoopers LLP. This material is used by permission of John Wiley & Sons, Inc.

The horizontal axis in Figure 6.5 depicts five positions along an e-business continuum, while the vertical axis shows an organisation's ERP status. In reality they are not as discrete as depicted here. Although it is possible that an enterprise may not map neatly to one of these positions, the framework provides a useful basis for discussion.

The horizontal axis shows how as an organisation moves from left to the right along the continuum, its business model is increasingly determined by its e-business strategy:

1   Most firms start with *no e-business capability*.

2   Using Web technology as an enabler, companies make inroads into an e-business through *channel enhancement*. They modify existing business processes aimed at improving business performance. e-Commerce – the marketing and selling/buying of products or services over the Internet – is an example.

3   Often the next step is to seek improved integration of business processes with customer and supplier operations, or *value-chain integration*. CRM and SCM are examples discussed earlier in this chapter, and more extensively in previous chapters.

4   *Industry transformation* may be sought by industry leaders looking to create a competitive advantage. Some realign their business strategies according to core competencies and use the Internet to offload non-core processes or to

take on the management of their customers' and suppliers' non-core processes where this fits their competence.

5 *Convergence* refers to the coming together of companies from different industries. In addition to the Internet's influence, it can be a function of deregulation, globalisation, and simply new strategic ideas. The Internet has made convergence easier and cheaper by enabling companies to more readily partner, providing customers with a "one-stop shop" experience.

The vertical axis in Figure 6.5 depicts the position of an organisation with regard to ERP implementation:

● In building its e-business capability, a *greenfield* organisation has no legacy of information systems to consider.

● *Non-integrated systems* typically entail high maintenance costs, rigidity and myopic or fragmented views of organisational performance.

● *Limited/single function ERP* refers to implementation of a few ERP parts across all business units, often suggesting a cost-cutting IT strategy and a lack of process orientation.

● *Integrated business unit ERP* implies wall-to-wall ERP in at least one of several business units in the overall organisation. This situation assumes distinct business units, with little value from cross-unit integration of processes.

● Finally, *integrated enterprise ERP* assumes the ERP has been fully implemented across the enterprise, enabling holistic and integrated views of enterprise-wide processes.

Taking these concepts a step further, Figure 6.6 divides the 25 cells of the ERP/e-B Matrix into six regions to consider the question, "Where might an organisation go and why?"

● *Region 1* is the default for a new dot-com entering the business world. As this company grows it must very quickly decide whether it will focus resources on moving along either the e-business or ERP continuums. This decision will be based on the firm's unique competitive and business circumstances.

● Moving into *Region 2* is an option, with the firm focusing on best-of-breed Web-based technology. Yet, lack of a supporting technological infrastructure limits internal organisational complexity and scale, possibly limiting growth. Although e-business front-ends might be sophisticated, internal processes might be manual or desktop-oriented. With little or no integration, partnering is difficult.[21]

---

21. Norris et al. (2000).

Figure 6.6 The ERP/e-B matrix: where might an organisation go and why?

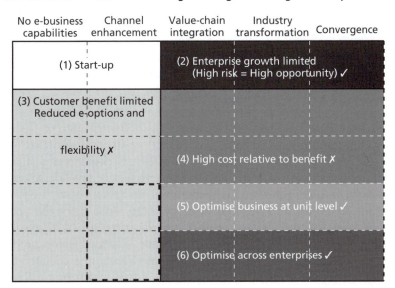

Source: Adapted from Norris et al. (2000). © 2000 Price WaterhouseCoopers LLP. This material is used by permission of John Wiley & Sons, Inc.

- *Region 3* is bounded by the other regions and has few positive attributes. Simply opening an e-business channel (channel enhancement) is not enough. These firms will soon find they cannot satisfy customer and supplier needs and expectations. While it is conceivable that a start-up would be initially positioned in the first two columns of the matrix, it should soon be seeking to shift its position (to the right). Unfortunately, moving to the right from Region 3 can be problematic, except from the sub-region bounded by the dark-dashed line.

- In *Region 4*, much effort is required to gather data, to process transactions and to maintain technology. If e-business efforts are successful, human-capacity and the infrastructure are overwhelmed by orders coming through the e-business front-end.

- *Regions 5 and 6* are the ideal positions that all firms should aspire to achieve as quickly as possible. To integrate with value-chain business partners and create an extended enterprise that changes the basis of competition in an industry, the firm must have a transaction and information-processing engine powerful enough to manage internal information flows.

Maintaining ERP and e-business systems

Virtually all ERP today are packages, though there are several notable exceptions. The standardisation of business applications has changed the patterns of development and use of software, as well as many aspects of their maintenance.

In this section we briefly consider the future maintenance implications of ERP. Though widely perceived as the more mundane side of these systems, maintenance has now become *the* major IT operating expense of many ERP-using organisations. It can be expected that maintaining e-business extensions to these systems will be no less taxing on the firm's resources.

Figure 6.7 presents a framework for understanding the key dynamics of maintaining large application software packages. It begins with the simple observation that maintenance generates benefits as well as costs. Maintenance strategy is influenced by a range of factors, including (a) software-source; (b) support-source; (c) organisational context; and (d) environmental context. Within a "distributed" maintenance arrangement, four key stakeholders are affected: the user-organisation, the software vendor, third-party service providers, and society (through participating in the broader economy).

Important economic and business strategy issues arise from the probability that various software and related support-sourcing alternatives have substantial maintenance implications in terms of the incidence of costs, benefits, and responsibilities. The complexity of standard business software and associated commercial arrangements calls for organisations to adopt appropriate knowledge strategies. Decisions on sourcing maintenance knowledge are made in anticipation of maintenance knowledge requirements across the software lifecycle. Optimising maintenance thus requires all stakeholders to have a lifecycle-wide view

Figure 6.7 Key dynamics of maintaining ERP

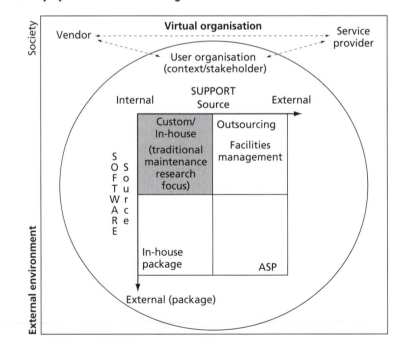

Source: Adapted from Gable et al. (2001).

of maintenance costs and benefits, considering the four key factors listed above, and taking into account the differing perspectives of the stakeholders.

ERP-to-ERP vs e-hub

[M]ost of the Net markets operating today are modelled on price competition – pitting buyers against sellers to get the best price for indirect materials or excess inventories. These exchanges aggregate catalogues, facilitate auctions and bring large numbers of buyers and sellers together via the Internet, thus creating a degree of price transparency not available offline.

The price competition model of the net markets is coming under pressure to change because such models discourage buyer/supplier relationships built on added value. Competition on price is making way for an emerging e-business model that is collaboration-based and takes advantage of price transparency for sourcing. New terminology such as "collaborative commerce" has emerged to describe software- and Internet-enabled collaboration among employees, business partners and customers through a trading community or market. As such, some industry experts recommend that companies should plan to extend, open and secure their application architectures for access to a much wider universe of potential business partners.[22]

As we saw in Chapter 5 ERP-to-ERP direct connection using XML over the Internet has supplanted EDI as the preferred approach for electronically transacting between two large companies. Though these direct connections offer substantial efficiencies, because information can be moved across enterprises directly into key systems, substantial complexities of inter-organisational communication and collaboration remain. Collaborating firms must yet address how to integrate their respective business processes and related information. Even where two companies have the same ERP, they may have configured these quite differently.

Typically ERP-to-ERP connections entail employing integration tools to translate one party's information into the format needed by the other. The advent of XML and Web services and evolving ERP capabilities are making this easier. Key advantages of this approach include the level of control the small number of participants have over the systems and their data. The key disadvantage is cost per connection, which limits the extensibility of the approach to large, high-volume partners.

Not everyone is keen on ERP-to-ERP connectivity. The concern is that smaller suppliers cannot afford ERP and do not have sophisticated production planning systems. The case study accompanying this chapter, *Return of the JEBI* gives an account of the Queensland State Government's consideration of an ERP-to-ERP procurement strategy amid concerns that the Australian state's SMEs might be placed at a disadvantage.

---

22. Gartner Group (2000).

An alternative to ERP-to-ERP approach is the concept of private eHubs (also called extranets or metaprises). This approach focuses on coordinating cross-enterprise processes, where the metaprise is the coordinating layer that ties together all of the individual companies in a business web.

The eHub software is not owned by any one firm, but is used by all members of a shared environment at the same time. While this approach largely supplants ERP-to-ERP arrangements, member ERPs can link directly with the eHub systems. Smaller members without ERP may be able to use functionality available from the eHub in their purchasing, invoicing, inventory, forecasting and planning systems.

Firms can reap potentially enormous benefit – such as reduction in costs and product lead times – from the implementation of eHubs. By making a single connection the users can access all the members of the consortium. Potential disadvantages include failure of the consortium and shallow integration.

Grander, longer-term potential from this direction includes "industry transformation" and "convergence" as described in the preceding section. Metaprise-like software and consortia, though not sufficient, are necessary for transition to these e-business states.

Key advantages and disadvantages of ERP-to-ERP and group integration through joining a consortium are listed in Table 6.1.

Table 6.1 ERP-to-ERP vs e-hub

ERP-to-ERP	Consortia
Advantages	**Disadvantages**
● Can establish a small number of key relationships more quickly	● Must have critical mass of relationships
● More likely to succeed	● More complex, more stakeholders and little guarantee of success
● Can be readily made very secure and private	● Security and privacy tend to be more of a concern, as members do not control the system
● Easier to achieve deep integration with one or a small number of partners	● Likely to yield shallow integration with all partners/members
Disadvantages	**Advantages**
● More expensive per relationship	● Less expensive for large number of relationships
● Can establish a limited number of relationships	● Can establish a large number of relationships more rapidly
● Very expensive to extend to another industry	● Easier to extend to further industries
	● Potential for early/instant visibility of transactions across the inter-organisational value-web

Source: Adapted from Davenport (2002).

Firms should adopt a portfolio of approaches to maximise the likelihood of success in e-business. ERP-to-ERP connections should be one "bet" within the portfolio. If a company already participates in an industry group that has made progress on process and information standards, it should encourage the consortium to develop ERP–hub interconnection capabilities. If there is no such association, a better strategy will be to pursue ERP-to-ERP interconnection with the firm's largest partners.

Summary

In this chapter we have sought to make the case for strong back-office systems as a launching pad for e-business. We have also suggested that ERP and e-business applications are morphing to facilitate increased access to integrated business information that spans the entire business web. We suggested a natural progression from channel enhancement to value-chain integration to industry transformation to convergence.

The distinctions that can be made between CRM, SCM and ERP are useful but ultimately, as with the historical classification of applications by internal organisational function (the "Finance system", the "HR system", etc.), these terms also become constraining. In practice, customers, partners, suppliers, employees and other stakeholders are all interconnected and may even hold multiple roles. Strategies towards industry transformation and convergence demand a much wider and more complete view of the business web than has been available to date. In the new world, the analogy of a "chain" becomes enchaining. As enterprises have inexorably moved to synchronised intra-enterprise processes, so too is the movement to synchronised inter-enterprise processes inevitable.

In practice, most business processes are inter-enterprise, so the ideal towards which we should aspire is synchronisation of information across the entire business web. The more and the earlier each stakeholder knows about what is coming, and what is happening in the business web, the better able they are to prepare, plan and execute. Logistically, the more accurate their understanding is of what they should be doing, and what is expected or required of them, the better able they are to deliver when the time comes. The need to maintain contingency stocks of inputs to, or outputs from, their physical processes in order to address "projected" requirements is virtually eliminated.

ERP systems were a boon to the integration of systems within organisations yielding a synchronised view of internal information. They are now morphing to play a larger role in inter-enterprise systems. In the next e-business wave, "metaprises" will be a boon to inter-organisational visibility and synchronisation of information across the business web.

We started the chapter reviewing the origins of ERP systems, the assumption being that solid, integrated back-office transaction processing is a necessary but not sufficient requirement for e-business. We then considered the importance of close integration between the back-office and all e-business applications and cautioned against naïve acceptance of claims made in this regard by vendors. We highlighted difficulties faced by entrenched competitors in the enterprise software marketplace and suggested various short-term and long-term strategies some of these vendors are pursuing. Insight into these directions, motivations and limitations are clearly of value to executive managers.

We next looked at several broad trends in business that are pushing ERP and e-business vendors to evolve their software offerings to meet the new demands of globalisation, rapid-sense-and-respond, horizontal corporate alignment, and virtual organisations.

Next, we looked at alternative ways forward from an ERP-base, and introduced the ERP/e-business matrix which cross-references five alternative states or destinations of ERP, with five states or destinations of e-business. Having considered the practical value of knowing where a firm is starting from, we explored the future of metaprises.

Questions for discussion

1   What capabilities must ERP and e-business software have in the face of continuing trends towards globalisation, rapid-sense-and-respond (mass customisation, customer centric), over-capacity and corporate realignment (horisontal corporate realignment), and virtual organisations?

2   Can Web-based technology effectively supplant internal information systems? Will it develop the transaction processing power necessary? Will organisations continue to require an ERP-type transaction-engine?

3   Should organisations shelve their ERP efforts and shift resources to e-business? Will Web software make ERP, as we now know it, redundant? How safe are current ERP investments and for how long?

4   How can organisations build on what they have?

5   To what extent should a business be integrated itself (e.g. with ERP) before it can open its e-business shop-front?

6   What key technological developments are impacting the future of ERP?

7   What impact will the advent of Application Service Provision (ASPs) have on the fortunes of client organisations, ERP vendors, e-business software vendors and consultants?

8   Which future scenario is more likely and why? (a) successful front-end e-business software vendor builds a viable transaction engine component; (b) custom, in-house transaction engine that processes transactions between e-business front-ends; (d) increased ERP product compatibility with third-party front-ends; (e) more flexible, more easily implemented ERP with e-business functionality; or (f) application service provision.

9   What are the advantages and disadvantages of ERP-to-ERP connection vs an eHub? Is one or the other of these more likely to be appropriate for small vs large enterprises?

References

Broadbent, M. and Ragow, S. (2000) *Australian*, 9 May, p. C02.

Callaway, E. (2000) *ERP – The Next Generation: ERP is Web Enabled for e-Business*, Charleston: Computer Technology Research.

Davenport, T.H. (2000) "The future of enterprise system-enabled organisations", *Information Systems Frontiers*, vol. 2, no. 2, pp. 163–80.

Davenport, T.H. (2002) "Connecting enterprise solutions across organisations", *Next Generation Enterprise Solutions*, no. 7 (26 April), pp. 1–3, Accenture Institute for Strategic Change, www.accenture.com/isc.

Ford, D. (2000) "Beyond ERP", *Manufacturing Engineer*, October, pp. 210–13.

Gable, G.G., Chan, T. and Tan, W.G. (2001) "Large packaged application software maintenance: a research framework", *Journal of Software Maintenance and Evolution: Research and Practice*, vol. 13, pp. 351–71.

Gartner Group (2000) Gartner Insight vol. 2, no. 3, May.

Howe, D. (1993) *Free On-Line Dictionary of Computing*, Imperial College Department of Computing, available from http://wombat.doc.ic.ac.uk/foldoc/[accessed 13 November 2003].

Klaus, H., Rosemann, M. and Gable, G.G. (2000) "What is ERP?" *Information Systems Frontiers*, vol. 2, no. 2, pp. 155–76.

Laudon, K.C. and Laudon, J.P. (2000) *Management Information Systems: Organisation and Technology in the Networked Enterprise*, Upper Saddle River, NJ: Prentice-Hall.

Mertens, P. and Faisst, W. (1996) "Virtuelle Unternchmen: Eine Organisations form für die zukunft?" in *Das Wirtschaftsstudium* (translated from German by Ulrich Franke), vol. 6, pp. 280–50.

META Group (1998).

Norris, G., Hurley, J., Hartley, K., Dunleavy, J. and Balls, J. (2000) *e-Business and ERP: Transforming the Enterprise*, New York: John Wiley.

Scheer, A.W. (1994) *CIM: Towards the factory of the Future* (3rd edn), Berlin: Springer.

Scheer, A.W. and Habermann, F. (2000) "Making ERP a success", *Communications of the ACM*, vol. 43, no. 4, pp. 57–61.

Tinham, B. (2000) "e-Business in manufacturing new understanding dawns", *Manufacturing Computer Solutions*, vol. 6, no. 11, pp. 36–9.

Further reading

Carvalho, M. (2002) "What everyone needs to know about private eHubs", available from http://logistics.about.com/library/weekly/uc010101b.htm [accessed 9 July 2002].

Deise, M.V., Nowikow, C., King, P. and Wright, A. (2000) *Executive's Guide to e-Business: From Tactics to Strategy*, New York: John Wiley & Sons.

Gartner Group (1999) The ERP Vendors Market. Symposium/ITexpo. Brisbane, 19–22 October.

Case study   Return of the JEBI

The Joint Electronic Business Initiative (JEBI) was a central e-procurement service envisaged by a State Government. On a sunny winter's day in mid-2002 George, the manager responsible for JEBI, received the go-ahead to revive the project. Eighteen months earlier, following a formal public Expression of Interest for this service, the government had postponed the JEBI project due to uncertainty and fallout among "e-marketplace" providers. Some companies that had built or provided e-marketplaces were going out of business and the government could not determine whether the companies that had expressed interest in providing JEBI would survive this fallout.

The e-business landscape had changed since August 2000, when George, who built government technology infrastructure, formulated a plan to construct an electronic (e-) procurement marketplace hub. Rather than construct this hub in-house, it was envisaged that a third-party provider would build and operate the hub service, initially for government suppliers, and eventually for all e-enabled state businesses.

Since the initial shelving of JEBI, Mary, Head of Procurement in the State Health Department, the biggest-spending department, had been building advanced materials management systems based on the Enterprise Resource Planning (ERP) system, SAP R/3. The department's approach had been to establish technological materials management superiority and so better position itself to pursue an ERP-to-ERP e-procurement strategy, initially with its major suppliers and then extending to all suppliers.

In addition, Taizan from State Purchasing, a division responsible for government purchasing policy and practice, had further developed the State Government Buyers' Catalogue to allow government purchasing officers not only to locate goods on pre-arranged government contracts but also to automatically generate SAP purchase orders for these items.

George was confident that the surviving e-marketplace providers were viable and could supply the envisioned hub service. George and the JEBI team's preference was for all departments, including State Health, to process transactions via the JEBI e-marketplace hub and so improve the viability of the third-party hub service. Further, he wanted to realise the government's broader agenda of creating an e-procurement hub that could be extended to transactions between small and medium businesses across the State, empowering them in the global information-trading community.

As the sun streamed into George's office he wondered how he could convince the other departments of the merits of the JEBI approach.

"This Government is Committed!"

e-Procurement policy solidified in the State government when in January 2001, the Minister for Information and Communication, in his foreword to the report "Strategy for Promoting State-wide E-Commerce", stated:

> The strategy identifies electronic procurement as a strategic priority for the Government in promoting e-commerce.
>
> – Hon. John Doe

Envisaging the prospect of cost reductions to both business and government, and access to wider supply markets, policy-makers saw e-procurement also as a way to promote the uptake of e-commerce in the business community. Regardless, the government insisted that any strategy must not disadvantage small or regional businesses. The State was geographically large (~2.0 million sq. km.), its relatively small population of 4.0 million being concentrated in the southwest corner and along the coast. A section of the government's e-procurement policy platform had been to e-enable small and medium-sized enterprises (SMEs) in the wider electronic marketplace. The strategy paper further stated, ". . . any government not engaged in e-procurement is not showing leadership in e-commerce."

The State government had demonstrated e-procurement leadership in several ways. State Health, from a position of strength based on its sound ERP materials management systems and its strong buying power (approximately $6 billion per year), had been negotiating business-to-business (B2B) transactions standards with its major suppliers.

Diagram 1 shows State Health's e-procurement strategy: direct ERP-to-ERP transactions with its major suppliers and the use of a fax gateway to transact with its minor suppliers.

George and his colleagues in the Department of Information and

Communication had developed plans for an e-procurement hub, taking the first steps to e-procurement-enable SMEs in the State. Diagram 2 shows the two stages envisaged for JEBI. Stage I shows the central hub system that translates both ERP and non-ERP e-procurement transactions into formats suitable for the target suppliers. Suppliers can load and manage their product catalogues directly into JEBI. Diagram 2(b) shows JEBI Stage II, where e-procurement transactions can take place not only between the government and its suppliers but also amongst the JEBI supply community. Taizan and his colleagues in the State Purchasing Department provided sound procurement policy and advice and a business perspective to these initiatives, ensuring that e-procurement outcomes did not, inter alia, unwittingly take business away from SMEs that supplied government agencies in their locale. They had also been extending the State Government Buyers' Catalogue to provide some of the functionality envisioned within the JEBI project. Diagram 3 shows the State Government Buyers' Catalogue system where government purchasers could browse the

Diagram 1 State Health's approach to e-procurement

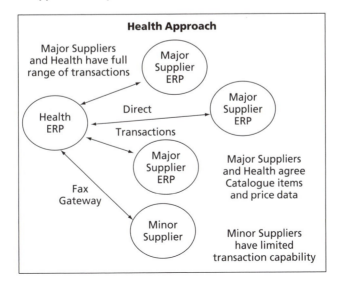

Diagram 2 JEBI e-procurement strategy: (a) stage I and (b) stage II

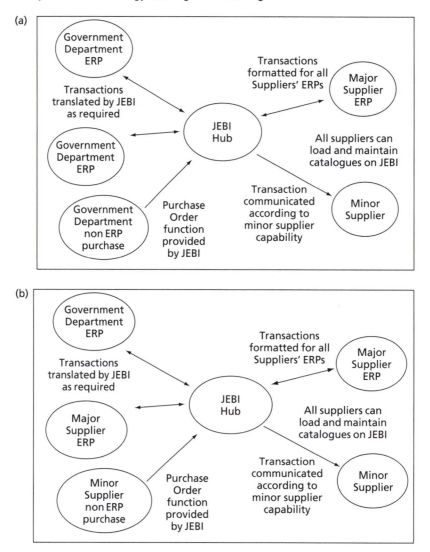

catalogue (outside of their ERP system) and select a product. The information would then be passed back to their ERP system to help produce the purchase order detail. Catalogue item details were managed by government personnel.

The importance and application of the ERP systems varied in the strategic approaches taken and promoted by State Health, State Purchasing and the JEBI team. For State Health, with a large-scale materials management need and large numbers of transactions, direct interorganisational ERP integration with suppliers was a rational way to gain e-procurement efficiencies. State Purchasing's "Buyers' Catalogue" built on its management of pre-contracted arrangements for common products and services across government and so was designed to service and interface with multiple departmental ERP systems. The JEBI team saw ERP as just another technical interface.

Diagram 3 The government buyers' catalogue

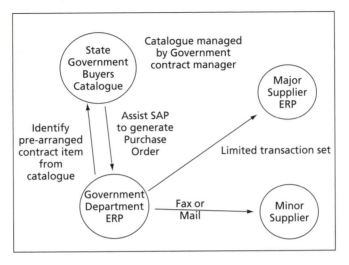

In an uncertain world of failing electronic marketplace vendors, expensive ERP support, continually changing competing solutions, possible competition (or co-opetition) from other more e-enabled communities, and an increasingly stretched government dollar, the question remained: how to integrate these e-procurement strategies in a balanced way for the benefit of all State citizens.[1]

State Government purchasing policy

The State PurchasingPolicy contained the government's procurement policy agenda.[2] This document stated:

> The objectives of this policy are to advance the Government priorities, achieve value for money, and ensure probity and accountability for outcomes . . .

> In doing so, each agency should use its best endeavours to ensure that competitive local firms that comply with relevant legislation are given a full, fair, and reasonable opportunity to supply the State Government.

Table 1 lists three of five overarching Government priorities. Cross-referenced with these are a few points directly or indirectly related to e-procurement.

---

1. "In most of the modern theories of business, competition is seen as one of the key forces that keep firms lean and drive innovation. That emphasis has been challenged by Adam Brandenburger of the Harvard Business School and Barry Nalebuff of the Yale School of Management. In part using some of the ideas of game theory, they suggest that businesses can gain advantage by means of a judicious mixture of competition and cooperation. Cooperation with suppliers, customers and firms producing complementary or related products can lead to expansion of the market and the formation of new business relationships, perhaps even the creation of new forms of enterprise. They chose coopetition for this concept (a blend of cooperation and competition), which they used as the title of their 1996 book explaining their theories, a book which has become a best-seller and which has since come out in paperback. However, it seems that they didn't coin the word: it was Ray Noorda, the founder of Novell, who did that. The concept, and the word, seem to have been taken up most enthusiastically in the computer industry, where strategic alliances are common in order to develop new products and markets, particularly between software and hardware firm." http://www.quinion.com/words/turnsofphrase/tp-coo2.html.

2. According to the Oxford English Dictionary on-line, the terms "procurement" and "purchasing" are virtually synonymous. However in practice procurement usually means the acquisition by any means, including by purchase, rental, lease or conditional sale, of goods, services or construction. So purchasing is seen as direct payment for goods and services and is therefore a subset of procurement.

Table 1 State Government priorities and their relation to e-procurement

Priority	Some points relating to e-procurement
More jobs for the State – Skills Innovation – The intelligent State	• Promoting innovation and entrepreneurial culture across all sectors of the State community, the state's industry and Government (such as enabling e-business capability) • Improving workforce skills for current and future needs (such as e-business skills)
Community Engagement and a Better Quality of Life	• Improved and integrated Government service delivery including e-business delivery of services
Building State Regions	• Increasing state-wide development by enabling businesses for global trading • Building and encouraging infrastructure to support State-wide development such as JEBI • Expanding export markets by encouraging e-enabled businesses

Using purchasing to achieve these priorities

State Purchasing estimated that the State government issued around three million purchase orders per year, of which around 1.2 million purchase orders were for items that could be recorded in a catalogue. Example of items not amenable to cataloguing included consultancy services or made-to-order goods. These 1.2 million purchase orders were worth around $1.2 billion, with an average of $1000 per purchase order. Total government purchases approximated to $4.9 billion for non-capital and core department services.

The average cost per transaction (e.g. purchase order) was $78 when it was not supported by a computerised financial management system such as SAP R/3, which was the standard ERP system implemented in State government departments. This cost per transaction dropped significantly when it was supported by a financial management system, to $24–28 per transaction for a non-catalogued item and $12–14 for a catalogued item. These costs, however, did not include the sunk cost in the SAP R/3 systems or any activity in identifying the product or supplier (i.e. sourcing).

Government agencies were required to analyse their purchasing patterns, suppliers and supply markets, in order to identify opportunities for advancing government priorities. As depicted in the Figure 1, two major factors influenced the nature of government purchasing:

(a) the "difficulty of securing supply" of goods and services, which meant the degree to whichthe goods or services presented risks or were critical to the agency, as well as the extent to which a competitive supply market for the goods or services existed; and

(b) the relative expenditure for the goods and services, which meant their cost relative to the total purchasing expenditure of an agency.

Having geographically devolved control over purchasing of quadrant three goods, the government tried to spread expenditure equally across the State, thereby supporting the priority listed above, "Building State regions", or supporting regional businesses.

The government's procurement policy targeted goods and services in quadrant four as those where it could secure value for money by minimising process-related costs

Figure 1 Types of goods and services

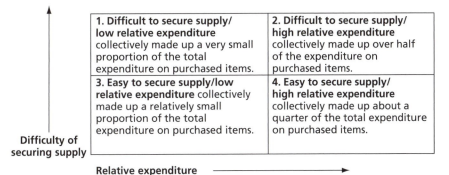

1. Difficult to secure supply/ low relative expenditure collectively made up a very small proportion of the total expenditure on purchased items.	**2. Difficult to secure supply/ high relative expenditure** collectively made up over half of the expenditure on purchased items.
3. Easy to secure supply/low relative expenditure collectively made up a relatively small proportion of the total expenditure on purchased items.	**4. Easy to secure supply/ high relative expenditure** collectively made up about a quarter of the total expenditure on purchased items.

Difficulty of securing supply

Relative expenditure ⟶

through effective electronic interfaces with suppliers and by negotiating price reductions based on volume sales.

When determining value for money, the government advised its agencies to consider the full transaction costs, including:

- establishing the need for the purchase;
- planning for the purchase;
- identifying sources of supply;
- approaching the market to seek supply;
- selecting suppliers;
- ordering and processing payments; and
- managing relationships with suppliers, including supplier performance monitoring and management.

As the largest purchasing agency in terms of both expenditure and the number of transactions, State Health was often a leader in the implementation of purchasing policy and practices. In the absence of a suitable government-wide mechanism, the department developed an ERP-to-ERP e-procurement strategy.

Purchasing in State Health

State Health employed over 50,000 people, and ran hospitals and other health services throughout the State. Annual procurement

expenditure on goods in State Health exceeded $430 million. State Health had 60,000 corporate catalogue items. Forty-seven separate purchasing groups issued 330,000 individual purchase orders annually. Fifty-one per cent of these purchase orders originated outside of the State capital city and major population centre. State Health placed approximately 205,000 of all purchase orders (62 per cent) with only 3.3 per cent of its vendors, representing expenditures of around $345 million.

State Health faxed 15,000 (out of 27,000) orders automatically through a gateway facility (12 lines). The gateway also automatically faxed 12,000 remittance advices every month. In October 1999 only 31 per cent of the value of payments was made electronically to suppliers. Following promotion of the benefits of direct payments to suppliers' bank accounts (as an alternative to cheques), the value of payments made electronically rose to 90 per cent of total expenditure by the end of 2001.

Supporting procurement processes had been the Materials Management & Finance Information System, or MEMFIS. This fully integrated supply, finance and asset management system had 4000 internal users. MEMFIS began operation in June 1999 and had been operating in all of State Health's 38 districts. It was a single instance of SAP

R/3 version 4.6B.[3,4] This system had been supporting all districts, corporate business units (e.g. Pathology) and Corporate Head Office. Since introducing the materials management module, MEMFIS had been e-procurement-ready.

The goal of the department's purchasing and supply management was "to provide the right product in the right place at the right time in the most cost-effective manner, to efficiently serve health care consumer needs."

The Health department's expectation was that e-procurement would provide improved efficiency of requisition to supply process, easier request processes and reduced time to supply, and would be workflow-driven. Further, they were expecting a reduction in the cost of supplies through increased use of pre-negotiated contracts arrangements, and reduced pricing.

The e-procurement pilot in State Health

State Health had established extensive efficient and effective internal materials-management processes. Staff in hospital wards had the ability to reserve and order goods electronically from central stores and warehouses. Inventory levels were automatically updated (real-time) with every internal requisition, external purchase order, withdrawals from stores and warehouses, returns and delivery. The department paid suppliers by electronic funds transfer.

To extend automated materials management into its supply chain, State Health had implemented a pilot project or "proof of concept" of e-procurement in a controlled and limited way. The pilot built on the SAP R/3 platform by implementing SAP's

Enterprise Buyer Professional (EBP) module, part of the Supplier Relationship Management (SRM) set of products. This module was SAP's standard software offering to manage large-scale e-procurement functions and integrate them with other materials-management and accounting processes.

The pilot project started in the West Complex in The State capital in early 2002. The West complex comprised three of the largest hospitals under State Health's management: State Hospital, State Women's Hospital and State Children's Hospital. All were co-located at the edge of the Central Business District, close to State Health's head office and across the road from the MEMFIS support team. The Supply Services Unit in the nearby suburb of South-end (about two kilometres away) was also included in the pilot project. The West complex location was chosen for its sound purchasing practices and related skills, and for its potential role as a future purchasing hub/distribution centre.

Management stressed the importance of process measurement and the identification of key performance measures before and after the pilot project. These performance measures included system-based processing efficiency and price reductions from supplier efficiency. Both pre-negotiated contract purchases and non-contract purchases were included in the project's scope.

The scope of the pilot project initially involved an existing purchasing hub/skill centre with six to eight purchasers and 10 to 15 requisitioners. Functionally it included on-line ordering, order acknowledgement and invoicing.

Three of the top 20 (largest) suppliers were chosen to participate. Within this group of 20, the choice of pilot suppliers was based on how e-procurement-ready each supplier was. Discussions with the Health department's largest suppliers over the previous 12 months had indicated that they were generally not e-procurement ready.

---

3. Meaning that all business entities within State Health are considered part of a single, over-arching organisation in the structure implemented within R/3 (rather than separate instances with ERP-to-ERP interfaces).
4. SAP, the world's fourth-largest software provider and by far the largest ERP vendor, introduced version 4.6B in 2000.

Having been made aware of this lack of supplier readiness, State Health employed a strategy whereby it would invest several million dollars in its ERP systems to implement a strong internal materials management and logistics environment. It was reasoned that the department would thus be ahead of industry in terms of e-procurement readiness, and would therefore be in a position to play a lead role. As things transpired, the department's leading-edge materials management systems and supporting technology served to cushion pressure from its main suppliers, who had been pressing for a supplier-driven and dominated e-procurement model. State Health's materials management systems and e-procurement-readiness enabled it to "take a seat at the table" to discuss and negotiate such issues as transaction standards, document definitions and contractual terms suitable for electronic trading.

The advanced ERP functionality in State Health allowed requisitioning staff in hospital wards (e.g. nurses) or in other functions (e.g. clerical staff) to order goods by swiping bar codes in corporate catalogues. This requisition flowed through the SAP ERP systems, initially to reserve those items in a State Health warehouse or hospital store. Depending on stock levels in the store, transactions also triggered the re-ordering process.

The process in its barest form, assuming no complications, looked like this:

State Health's intention had been to extend the electronic reach of the transaction to enquire about stock in its suppliers' warehouses, reserve this stock and automatically purchase pre-identified and pre-negotiated goods from suppliers' stores (triggering delivery, invoicing, payment). The department pre-identified and pre negotiated contracts for many goods purchased in a traditional fashion. It needed to extend contract terms and conditions to cover electronic transactions.

The difference between the internal interaction with local stores and warehouses, and supplier stores and warehouses, arose mainly because of the different management information systems in each organisation. If both State Health and the supplier had ERP systems capable of the range of functions required (e.g. real-time inventory, stock reservation) and these ERP systems were integrated and fully implemented, then the challenge would be in designing the inter-organisational transactions between the two ERP systems. If, however, the ERP in the supplier organisation was only partially implemented, then a given functionality might not always be available to QH (e.g. querying the stock holdings). This reduced the effectiveness of the e procurement processes between the two organisations and increased the complexity of inter-organisational transactions, particularly when State Health's e procurement strategy extended to many suppliers running different ERPs.

Process	ERP functions
Stock enquiry Reservation of goods in store	Inventory Warehousing
Requisition Ordering	Purchasing
Delivery trigger	Logistics
Usage	Inventory Finance (expenditure)

The State Government buyers catalogue

State Purchasing, the government body responsible for the State Purchasing Policy, purchasing training, monitoring and advising on purchasing practices, also co-ordinated Government-wide contract arrangements such as travel, fuel, stationery, office products and supplies, some information technology and telecommunications products and services and office furniture.

These government-wide contracts and some contracts put in place by other departments had been made available to the government purchasing community. This community was made up of an estimated maximum of 14,000 potential purchasers, but these were mostly casual and very intermittent purchasers. There were 200 purchasing officers who bought large quantities of products and services, and around 750 regular purchasers, registered on the State Government Buyers' Catalogue (SGBC) system.

There were approximately 40,000 line items on the State Government Buyers' Catalogue. These line items all belonged to pre-arranged contracts put in place by departments. The departments created contracts for open use by all departments or restricted their use to a few departments or just themselves. Government contract managers, not the suppliers, maintained the data in the catalogues.

The system was a SQL Server database and employed a SAP R/3-compliant interface. This allowed departmental purchasing officers to enter the system through SAP, transfer to the SGBC interface, search for and select the line items in the SGBC, and place the selected items in a shopping cart. On returning to the SAP system, an SAP-based purchase order was composed.

Initially, State Purchasing charged departments for their use of the SGBC, but stopped doing so because the cost of measuring and charging usage was very high; so high that it was approaching the cost of providing the base system and discouraging use by purchasing officers. Charges were subsequently dropped and absorbed into State Purchasing's funding allocation on the basis that the system was generally improving government purchasing practice.

The Joint Electronic Business Initiative (JEBI)

Two blocks across town, a new JEBI team was geared up again to execute their strategy. The project manager was drawn from within the Department of Public Works. Project management and sole sponsorship rested with George in the Department of Information and Communication, which was responsible for government technology infrastructure.

A central messaging/database hub or marketplace was the core idea in the JEBI concept. Suppliers to government would post and maintain their catalogues on the marketplace and government buyers would choose catalogue items and order them. StateNet, the whole-of-government Intranet, was to serve as a secure messaging backbone for all e-procurement transactions, providing access to government buyers and routing transactions through the central marketplace hub.

It was anticipated that orders would be placed either directly into the marketplace, or initiated from departmental SAP R/3 systems. The marketplace system would forward that order to the supplier in an appropriate format: electronic transaction, fax stream, email, etc. It would then be up to the supplier to fulfil this order and communicate, according to their technological capability, with the purchaser. Suppliers did not need to have catalogues or even an ERP to participate in this system. The government would provide them with a catalogue facility in the marketplace, opening up new markets for them not only in government but also in the wider business community as this marketplace concept developed. They also planned to develop, perhaps in concert with a major software supplier, some sort of ERP "lite", a cut-down version of a full ERP system that could manage a range of standard e-procurement functions. The vision was that once this marketplace was established for transactions between government and suppliers (and especially SMEs and regional suppliers) then part of it could be isolated for use amongst those businesses already participating. In other words, the government would provide businesses with an opportunity to apply the same technology to conduct e-procurement amongst themselves and eventually to the wider national and the global business community.

The source of revenue to cover the costs of the marketplace was never fully decided. A number of models were considered and each had its advantages and disadvantages. These models included a cost-per-transaction borne by the purchaser, a cost-per-transaction borne by the supplier, a budget allocation from a central agency to cover all costs; a flat fee for participation, a percentage of the transaction total, and finally some combination of the above.

Uncertainty: the force that shelved the JEBI

The original JEBI team had released an expression of interest to potential suppliers of e-marketplaces in late 2000. While several responses were received at the time, it was an uneasy period for e-marketplace initiatives. The dotcom crash had already happened but e-marketplaces survived for a while longer. Ariba and other e-marketplace companies were suffering major losses and a drop in investor confidence. In considering a long-term arrangement, the government was unable to assess the future of those companies offering this type of business model and function. Furthermore, the potential for enticing State Health to participate in this e-marketplace was weakening as the department pursued its independent e-procurement strategy.

In 2001, State Purchasing examined the JEBI model, conducting a detailed study of which departments were likely to buy using this marketplace. They concluded that JEBI needed State Health's participation because that was the only department with the scale of transactions that would justify the initial investment in the then-proposed JEBI infrastructure.

Facing these and other uncertainties in the cadre of suppliers and builders of e-marketplaces, the State government shelved the JEBI project until the e-marketplace commercial alternatives became clearer (and the survivors were identified) and there was more certainty about the potential service providers (and their offerings) to any tender for an e-marketplace solution.

But now JEBI has returned!

In mid-2002, George again geared up a team to lead the rejuvenated JEBI project. It was anticipated that the JEBI strategy would remain relatively unchanged from that described above.

> During the time that JEBI was shelved, alternatives to its central e-marketplace strategy had arisen in State Health with its ERP-to-ERP approach, and in State Purchasing with its central catalogue system. George and his team faced a difficult task: to combine the strengths of e-procurement systems developing in State Health and State Purchasing to build a JEBI system that could support e-procurement activities not only in government but also among the State's small and medium businesses.

Greg Timbrell prepared this case under the supervision of Guy Gable and Ali Farhoomand for class discussion. This case is not intended to show effective or ineffective handling of decision or business processes. The names of organisation and people have been disguised throughout the case.

e-CRM: evolution from traditional relationships

Shamza Khan

Objectives

❑ To identify CRM as a *process*

❑ To learn how businesses can benefit from CRM processes

❑ To demonstrate how CRM can change competitive positioning

❑ To recognise CRM's strategic and economic value

❑ To identify the critical value of brand equity in an online environment

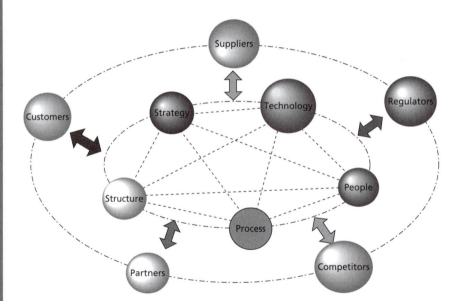

Continuing our focus on the process dimension of the DOT framework, this chapter examines the fundamentally vital concept of customer relationship management. We touched on CRM as a core e-business application in Chapter 4 and presented an overview of various existing technologies that are converging under the "CRM" umbrella. In this chapter, we take a less technical view and aim to identify CRM as a process, explain how businesses can benefit from CRM-related processes and explore how these can affect a company's competitive position.

The CRM function caters to one of the most important external forces of the DOT framework: the organisation's customers. Our discussion will focus on building a conceptual understanding of CRM strategy. Specifically, we present a framework for understanding how existing customer relationships can be leveraged to bring about a meaningful transformation from traditional relationship management to CRM within an e-business environment. We will also discuss how a hybrid between digital and embedded business environments can exist, and how "e-CRM" can enhance a company's ability to employ knowledge management processes and create business intelligence within the structure of a customer-centric organisation. The modern practice of CRM is a holistic approach towards attracting and retaining customers. Broken down into its most basic steps, CRM entails identifying current and prospective customers, discerning the highest-value segments according to established criteria and implementing customised marketing to meet needs and exceed expectations in a highly competitive landscape.

The "e-CRM" incarnation of this age-old concept has been subjected to much hype and CRM has quickly become as hot a buzzword as ERP before it. Yet underlying this exuberance, the promise of a technology-enabled foundation for interpreting and harnessing customer information bears tremendous appeal for companies looking to gain a source of competitive advantage. Potentially, e-CRM offers businesses a powerful range of tools for managing and making the most of the myriad interactions that occur between diverse customer groups.

The topic of customer relationship management (CRM) has garnered widespread attention in recent years as businesses aim to create deeper and longer-term relationships with new and existing customers. The art of managing relationships is an age-old managerial imperative. Companies have always tried to leverage customer relationships to achieve their business objectives; however, in the contemporary business environment, the focus on customer interactions has intensified. Firms are beginning to appreciate the underlying financial and strategic value in building customer-centric businesses.

Recent customer relationship trends involve adopting cost-effective and dynamic methods of customer acquisition and retention. A major business emphasis continues to be building customer relationships by interaction through the online medium; the Internet constitutes a powerful platform to acquire detailed customer information. This information can then be organised, profiled and disseminated throughout an organisation with the purpose of advancing personal relationships with customers – thereby building loyalty. This view redefines the traditional role of marketing, and marketers – who are now able to meet the challenge of forging deeper customer relationships with the assistance of e-business architecture and Internet technologies.

Historically businesses have focused on single market transactions, or a series of transactions. By contrast, the concept of CRM challenges this view by emphasising long-term customer relationships and advocating the lifetime loyalty of customer business within a particular space. In a nutshell, CRM is an organisational, strategic and technical process of change through which a company can re-orient its entire business towards the customer by basing enterprise management on customer interactions.

CRM: a cornerstone of lifetime value management

A traditional relationship marketing perspective serves as a strong foundation for CRM, because both concepts reflect the process nature of marketing:

> Marketing is to establish, maintain, and enhance relationships with customers and other partners, at a profit, so that the objectives of the parties involved are met. This is achieved by a mutual exchange and fulfilment of promises. Such relationships are usually but not necessarily long term. Establishing a relationship, for example with a customer, can be divided into two parts: to attract the customer and to build the relationship with that customer so that the economic goals of that relationship are achieved.[1]

The emergence of relationship marketing occurred to replace marketing's four principles (the so-called 4P's of marketing – product, price, promotion and place) as a resource allocation framework for planning and managing customer relation activities. The literature and research contributing to Relationship Marketing (RM) theory can be traced to services marketing theories, the network approach to business marketing, and quality management.

A customer relationship orientation also connotes the possibility of a strategic shift in managerial thinking from emphasising the *value of transactions* to developing the *value in relationships*. Until recently, relationship-oriented concepts had not exerted significant influence on mainstream marketing practices, which emphasised product-related issues over issues relating to service. Famous marketing strategist, Philip Kotler, characterises the importance of a strong service orientation as such:

> Companies must move from a short-term *transaction-oriented* goal to a long-term *relationship-building* goal; a movement away from focus on exchange – in the narrow sense of transaction – and toward a focus on building value-laden relationships

---

1. Grönroos, as cited in "Measuring and Valuing Customer Relationships", *Business Intelligence* (1999).

and marketing networks. Businesses think about how to hold on to existing customers . . . The thinking therefore is moving from a marketing mix focus to a relationship focus.[2]

Mutually satisfactory relationships and customer retention make it possible for customers to avoid significant transaction costs involved in switching supplier or service providers.

If CRM is viewed across all marketing, sales and customer service functions, there are three main areas where firms can realise efficiency:

1 *Marketing efficiency*: Customer segmentation based on knowledge from interactions with the firm allows firms to respond to valuable customers with targeted marketing programs. This leads to lower expense-to-revenue ratios.

2 *Back-end efficiency*: Automating customer management processes allows greater business volume. For example, building an e-commerce corporate website increases a firm's distribution channel and also allows it to manage customer orders and manage inventory; this creates efficiency, for example, by realising a shorter sales-cycle time (which in turn affects the bottom line).

3 *Service-centre efficiency*: Call centres empowered with comprehensive customer information can lower transaction durations and reduce customer management costs, while improving customer service.

Unlike traditional CRM, which often captures disparate information, electronic customer relationship management (e-CRM) focuses on transforming a firm's information into competitive intelligence. The use of technology in building and managing long-term and sustainable relationships forms a mechanism for achieving customer *intelligence*. Technology enables a company to integrate all the information collected from its customer-base, and the transactions and interactions that occur throughout the demand and supply chains, and to use analytical tools to understand the effectiveness and value of these transactions. As we showed in Chapter 2, such integration offers total visibility throughout a firm's demand and supply chain. This allows companies to improve the efficiency and effectiveness of their marketing, sales and customer service resources, with the final aim to increasing profits.[3]

To understand how traditional business assets like customer information and portfolios can be better leveraged, in the next section we provide a useful comparison between traditional relationship building, CRM and e-CRM (Table 7.1).

---

2. In an interview in the *Marketing Science Institute Review* in 1991.
3. Eklektik Consulting (2001).

Table 7.1 Comparison of RM, CRM and e-CRM

Variables	Relationship marketing	CRM	e-CRM
Definition	Marketing seen as relationships, networks and interactions	The business strategy, process, culture and technology to enable organisation to optimise revenue and increase shareholder value through better understanding of customer needs	e-CRM involves optimising the customer experience and implementing web-based CRM strategies to provide integrated e-services
Characteristics	• an exchange process • interaction between suppliers, customers, competitors and others • suppliers and customers are often co-producers, they create value for each other in a joint effort • all parties carry collective and active responsibility in the relationships	• CRM process is driven from the outside in • understand customer interaction history at any touch point • interaction takes place with the customer to identify what their needs are (as part of the learning relationship) • it is built on a customer-driven strategy geared towards customer information management and leveraging long-term relationships.	• relationship management strategy is integrated with Internet technologies • customer data, information and knowledge are used to build customer loyalty • leading-edge customer service technologies are implemented • the Internet is used to deliver scaleable, process-oriented and cost-effective customer service • a complete, single and accurate view of the customer service business environment is developed • companies open internal operations to customers; customers share information; high information exchange and analysis between the company and customers
Channel	• intermediaries • wholesalers	• direct-to-customer • mass-market	• web (B2B, B2C, intermediary, full-service provider, virtual market)
Theoretical and practical base	Built on the basis of the 4 P's v traditional marketing management, services marketing, the network approach to marketing, quality management and organisation theory	Built on the principles of relationship marketing and organisational strategy integration. Product information and services delivery systems are critical to CRM success	Integrated principles of business process, Internet technology, organisational management and marketing strategy with customer relationship management theories

Links to management	It is more than marketing management; it focuses on marketing-oriented management. For example, a marketing plan becomes part of the business plan	It focuses on having strategy and management commitment to a customer-service environment. It originated from call centres where customer-service agents served the customers. Putting a CRM package in place involves putting together sets of skills in different areas including marketing, customer service, e-business, call centres and technology and project management	It is an "across the board" implementation of CRM that brings all marketing, sales, service and other back office systems into one customer-centric management environment
Advantages to a firm	• increases customer retention and duration • increases marketing productivity • increases profitability and security	• matches workflow and processes with a core company strategy • enables employees to implement strategy • improves bottom line.	• preserves revenues • manages a scaleable customer base • increases customer loyalty • lowers costs and improves revenues • taps cross-selling opportunities • reduces business volatility • improves employee productivity
Advantages to customers	• creates competition • customisation • seller has personal knowledge of customer	• reduces response time • results in better value for money • facilitates one-to-one marketing.	• provides targeted information and services • provides multiple sales and customer service channels • allows personalisation of customer service • allows customisation of products

How CRM fits into e-business

The main impetus for CRM growth during the 1990s was the growing complexity of the marketing, sales and customer service environment. New channels such as the Web and wireless communications increased the complexity of managing customer relationships. In addition, pressure of a competitive business environment has forced companies to work "smarter" in order to win customers and retain them. This intelligent marketing strategy involves understanding the customer and offering customised services with convenient means of access. Firms have become committed to building customer loyalty because although it requires more strategic planning and organisational commitment, in the long run, it is financially rewarding. Also, it is much more costly to focus solely on winning new customers rather than keeping them.

Table 7.2 highlights some facts on how expensive it is to mismanage customers. There are three primary reasons why focusing on CRM makes good business sense:[4]

1 Managing customer relationships represents a "cheap growth" option by using appropriate technology to tap into their customers' interaction and purchase behaviour.

2 Investments in CRM can be made incrementally, with the possibility of generating immediate cash flow benefit. CRM frameworks can be built so that technology can be adopted according to a firm's individual requirements.

3 The ability to manage valuable customers is a strategic capability that will increasingly influence the competitive performance of a company. CRM allows the marketer to stay close to its customers and to respond quickly to their changing needs and behaviour. The better the marketer knows the customer, the more efficiently and effectively it can customise

Table 7.2 Customer maintenance facts and figures

● It costs six times more to sell to a new customer than to sell to an existing one.

● A company can boost its profits 85 per cent by increasing its annual customer retention by only 5 per cent.

● The odds of selling a product to a new customer are 15 per cent, whereas the odds of selling a product to an existing customer are 50 per cent.

● Seventy per cent of complaining customers will do business with the company again if it quickly takes care of a service snag.

Source: Kalakota, R. and Robinson, M. (2001) *e-Business 2.0: Roadmap for Success.*

4. Nucifora (2001).

its relationship. At a tactical level, this means more cross-selling, up-selling and customer service and, in many instances, seeking out more opportunities to collaborate with the customer via a customised, individual approach.

Company experiences to date suggest that opportunities to gain from CRM exist in all industries, particularly in those with high fixed-cost structures, multiple product/service offerings to clusters of customers, high volumes of customer interaction and relatively low dollar values per transaction. Firms can leverage existing customer bases by gathering and analysing knowledge about customer needs, attitudes and behaviours. As a result, firms can optimise their resource allocation to CRM strategies towards specific segments.

In recent years, the Internet has changed basic customer behaviour in three major ways:[5]

1 The Internet provides an environment which allows a diffusion of text, media and audio tools; it has the capability of bringing together technologies, products, services and information from widely disparate sources.

2 The Internet gives consumers greater control over their search for and acquisition of decision-making information relevant for consumer buying decision-making.

3 Consumers can interact with the medium by becoming active participants in the marketing process. No longer do they need to be passive receivers of marketing communications since they can view focused information on the Internet.

Intense competition and new methods of leveraging the Internet as a business platform are forcing companies to focus their operations and processes even more towards customers. In the customer-centric enterprise, customers are key assets and customer interactions are a critical element of a firm's business. As a result, CRM impacts bottom-line performance, as well as employee and customer satisfaction. CRM allows firms to minimise costs by targeting the right customers, expand revenues through better customer attraction and retention and maximise profits through better cross-selling and up-selling.

Lifetime customer relationship management framework

Businesses are learning to harness the Internet to create new sales channels and acquire new customers. Companies are increasingly finding that the only way to sustain growth is to shift the focus from customer acquisition to customer retention. The overall strategic business objective of CRM is to build loyal

---

5. Farhoomand and Lovelock (2001).

profitable customer relationships. Companies can anticipate their customers' needs and use information to personalise their relationships with their customers.

In order to achieve integrated customer service, companies have to grapple with the challenge of synchronising online operations with existing business processes. e-CRM, then, becomes part of the overall e-business strategy, through which companies try to use shared infrastructure and Internet-based solutions to deliver superior customer service and manage lifetime customer relationships.

Table 7.3 shows a framework that identifies the building blocks of lifetime CRM from traditional relationships. This framework can be used in developing the vision and necessary strategies in developing successful CRM. It can also be the basis for assessing the enterprise's existing and required CRM capabilities, understanding its current position and charting its future strategy.

This framework emphasises balance between enterprise and customer requirements. Many CRM initiatives suffer from an inward focus on the enterprise. However, to build and maintain mutually beneficial relationships, a CRM should achieve a balance between value to shareholders on the one hand, and value to customers, on the other hand.

The four building blocks of CRM illustrate how traditional companies must adopt a holistic approach to customer satisfaction and make technology investments to support specific business and financial objectives. Many enterprises have launched broad efforts to build better customer relationships in order to get ahead of competition. However, many appear to lack a strategic approach to customer satisfaction which could in turn drive shareholder value.

To increase customer satisfaction and be profitable, companies must build a customer-centric organisation that can offer a strong client value proposition. This can be achieved by defining a clear strategy that generates higher sales from their most valuable customers. In the process, firms should use technology investments to become more effective in identifying high-value customers and satisfaction drivers, create tailored solutions to improve satisfaction and continuously measure results to ensure they capture value.

In the next section, we look at each of the four relationship building blocks stage more closely with a view to analysing what it takes to deploy CRM to build and maintain customer-sustainable customer relationships.

Table 7.3 Four building blocks of lifetime CRM

1. Strategy	Customer value proposition, customer segments, customer-oriented business models
2. Processes	Trust-Building processes, customer–firm relationship cycle, lifetime-value management
3. Technology	Applications, IT Architecture, CRM technologies
4. Measurement	Value, retention, satisfaction, loyalty, cost to serve

Building block 1: CRM strategy

In formulating a CRM strategy, it is critical to put together various components of the customer relationship into a coherent system. The key difference between a traditional company and a customer-centric company is that the business model in the latter is based on customer needs. Therefore, the firm must articulate its value proposition to the customer. As we discussed in Chapter 2, firms must begin by answering three key questions regarding customers:

1 Which customers are key to our business and what are their needs?

2 Why are the existing alternatives inadequate in satisfying these needs?

3 What distinctive value can an e-CRM initiative create for customers?

By answering these questions, the value proposition becomes driven by customers' needs, not company processes. In essence, the value proposition should be designed to allow customers to conduct business their way, not the company's way.[6] By coupling its value chain dynamically to those of individual customers, a firm can attract customers from rivals and also increase its customer retention rate. Attracting new customers and retaining existing customers can both be sources of sustainable advantage.

Once the value proposition is established, a firm needs to understand what factors build a relationship between the customer and itself, however, any organisation's fundamental CRM strategy should be creation and maintenance of trust-based relationships. Therefore, as in traditional business interactions, building *trusting* relationships is key to understanding the real business transformation being ushered in by the Internet.

In CRM strategy process, customers may go through four transition stages in their relationship with a firm:[7]

1 At the **bonding** stage in the customer–firm relationship, companies pursue longer-term relationships based on customer information and delivering products and services which exceed customer expectations.

2 In the **personalisation** stage, companies move away from transaction-based exchanges to relationship-based exchanges. Customer information is of key importance here. Firms take extra steps to intimately know and understand customers and demonstrate that knowledge proactively. This is also the acquisition stage during which a business designates strategies to secure the customer through a unique value proposition, with the purpose of establishing a customer's trust through knowledge of the customer.

---

6. Tapscott et al. (2000).
7. PriceWaterhouseCoopers (2001).

3 During the **empowerment** stage, firms empower customers because they are more interested in capturing a share of client's total wallet. By establishing mutual trust, the firm will seek to convert buyers into loyal customers.

4 In the final stage, **customer loyalty** is established and customers become fully "vested" in the company. Firms employ a long-term strategy to maintain customer value through established mutual trust and aim to build a lifetime relationship with the client through dialogue management. Trust and customer loyalty is sequential, building up from one stage to another. Because consistent delivery of these trust-building dimensions is important, firms need to develop a coherent customer relationship strategy to fulfil customer expectations and build relationships.

Traditional customer-focused companies must determine whether enabling technologies will allow them to move from the first stage – where customer interactions are transactions oriented, into the relationship-oriented stage. Firms need to ensure that the foundations are in place to customise products and services, and ultimately, to deliver increased value by building an understanding of who their customers are.

Building block 2: CRM processes

Many firms have traditionally made the mistake of reacting to customers based on inflexible internal organisational structures. A customer-centric enterprise, however, adopts business processes based on its competencies and by using enabling technologies to ultimately segment and satisfy needs of their profitable customers.

During the late 1980s, businesses focused attention towards reducing costs and increasing efficiency through internal workflow processes. However, throughout the 1990s, firms have begun focusing on providing a holistic customer view, integrating customer management processes and building and managing trust with customers. The *processes* of customer relationship building are key in understanding how business value can be created through CRM. We identify four distinct processes in a lifetime relationship management framework:

1 customer acquisition

2 customer retention

3 customer loyalty

4 lifetime value management.

Customer acquisition

During the customer acquisition process, brand management plays a critical role in affecting customer perception and behaviour. At this stage, CRM can help companies to use enabling technologies to:

- Gain a deeper understanding of customers' needs (with the aim to maximising marketing ROI).

- Identify customers who exhibit similar behaviours and cluster them in terms of purchase behaviours (market segmentation).

- Cluster customers in terms of lifetime value and profitability to the organisation.

- Model churn behaviours by profiling customers who stop using a firm's products/services.[8]

In an increasingly complex economy, customers demand the ability to interact through multiple communication channels, and to move seamlessly from one medium to another. A customer may wish to initiate a transaction online, receive instructions from an agent, click on a button to have a telephone conversation with that agent to answer one question and then return to the Web to complete the transaction. Businesses must provide their customers, partners and suppliers with the flexibility of integrated Internet, telephone, e-mail and fax interactions. This will enable companies to appeal to a wider customer base and execute customer acquisition strategies more effectively.

Customer retention

Customer retention is a critical aspect of an online firm's overall marketing strategy. The focus during customer retention shifts to "locking in" customers with strong customer information and a strong brand, or differentiated service. However, customers are not "acquired" – they are merely "rented".[9]

The Internet's ability to integrate value from different businesses becomes apparent when competitors create strategic alliances for mutually beneficial business strategies. For online firms to calculate expected customer value, they can predict the cash flow a new customer will generate over time and discount it to determine the customer's net present value. An economically rational

---

8. Churn rate refers to the number of participants who discontinue their use of a service divided by the average number of total participants. It provides insight into the growth or decline of the subscriber base as well as the average length of participation in the service. See http://www.investorwords.com/cgi-bin/getword.cgi?857 for more details.
9. Swigor (1999).

merchant should be willing to pay less than the expected value to acquire customers. However, in real life it is difficult to measure such values as average customer expenditure and customer turnover. For example, Marriott Hotels measures its success by hotel occupancy rates, revenue per available room and revenue per available customer. A CRM application consolidates customer data and offers customers a highly personalised experience based on a rich profile of information. The CRM application enables Marriott to manage its marketing activities based on accounts information, thus extracting higher revenue per customer.

Customer loyalty

Loyalty is traditionally defined in terms of its consequences: repurchase intent, referral intent, share of purchase and actual repurchase. In the new business environment, firms committed to gaining loyalty can use the Internet platform as a means for managing all the stages of customer relationship building. For example, American Airlines launched an online application to manage customers. The goal was to increase customer interaction, enhance customer feedback to improve operations and develop a strategy to maintain loyal customers. The specific CRM solution was creating a database for its most loyal customers and developing an online site as a vehicle for customer feedback and airline bookings.

Lifetime value management

Aligning CRM strategy with a business process means all initiatives and infrastructure development should be linked to a core cycle of interdependent and continuous customer-related activities. Integration arises from the interdependence of processes as some activities cannot be implemented without others. Gradual change is required for a business to manage information exchange and data analysis, and to employ integrated technologies to capture and consolidate information. Another key element is implementing a cost-effective, direct linkage from front-end marketing, sales and service to the supply chain and ERP backbone.

Not only does e-CRM focus on providing optimal value to the customer – through the way businesses communicate with them, market to them and service them – it also helps companies through the traditional means of product, price, promotion and place of distribution. In other words, customers make buying decisions based on their experiences, which take into account product and price, but also include the nature of their overall interactions with the business.

While companies traditionally have been very good at sourcing, processing and distributing their products, to compete in an information economy, companies must become adept at using CRM architecture to manage customer knowledge and develop business intelligence.

Building block 3: integrated CRM architecture

Traditional businesses can transform into customer-centric firms with the aid of an e-CRM architecture. The initial focus of firms on providing transaction-oriented customer services needs to evolve towards the long-term analysis of customer revenue generation. Relationship-oriented stages and dialogue management approaches, for example, are more focused on customer retention and customer relationship management; they are a function of the same underlying rationale behind relationship marketing. However, an e-business infrastructure enables firms to become more customer-centric. If firms can consistently deliver on marketing, sales, service and support interactions, lifetime value can be built and companies can leverage customer loyalty to enhance economic returns and gain competitive advantage.[10]

Relationship marketing is an old business concept because creating value and loyalty in business dealings is as old as the merchant trade itself. What is new in e-CRM is a re-examination of how this can be achieved. This involves an organisational and process shift and a transformation of the company's CRM architecture which involves learning new customer management, new business processes and new systems and technologies to collect, process and manage customer data.

As the customer focus increases, organisations begin placing more importance in streamlining information and pursuing integration to enhance the customer experience. This is tied to the importance of providing an effective knowledge management system, where customer data is transformed into valuable information and is accessible to the employees interfacing with customers.

Figure 7.1 illustrates how a firm can become customer focused by making essential internal process changes using various technologies and external interfaces. A firm's customer interaction management tools, also referred to as operational CRM tools, facilitate more effective interaction with the customer. The three main stages of business transition to leverage data from a database include:

1 gathering data from various customer interaction points

2 implementing analytical CRM technology

3 selecting operational CRM technologies and customer interaction channels.

As shown in Figure 7.1, companies have to tightly integrate their back-end and customer-interfacing processes in order to be able to provide personalised marketing and targeting of the profitable customer.

---

10. White (2000).

Figure 7.1 An integrated e-CRM architecture

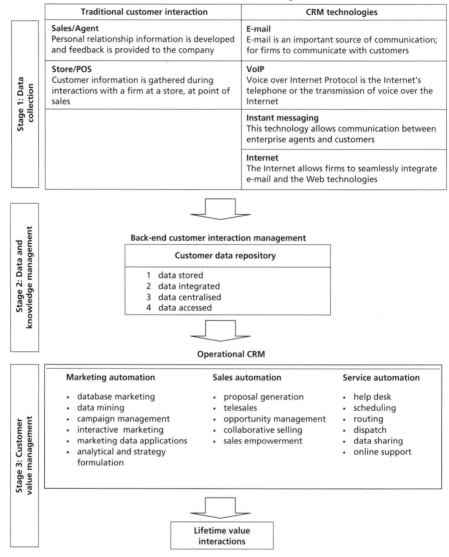

Front-end customer interface management

Traditional customer interaction	CRM technologies
Sales/Agent Personal relationship information is developed and feedback is provided to the company	**E-mail** E-mail is an important source of communication; for firms to communicate with customers
Store/POS Customer information is gathered during interactions with a firm at a store, at point of sales	**VoIP** Voice over Internet Protocol is the Internet's telephone or the transmission of voice over the Internet
	Instant messaging This technology allows communication between enterprise agents and customers
	Internet The Internet allows firms to seamlessly integrate e-mail and the Web technologies

Stage 1: Data collection

Back-end customer interaction management

Customer data repository

1 data stored
2 data integrated
3 data centralised
4 data accessed

Stage 2: Data and knowledge management

Operational CRM

Marketing automation	Sales automation	Service automation
• database marketing • data mining • campaign management • interactive marketing • marketing data applications • analytical and strategy formulation	• proposal generation • telesales • opportunity management • collaborative selling • sales empowerment	• help desk • scheduling • routing • dispatch • data sharing • online support

Stage 3: Customer value management

Lifetime value interactions

Stage 1: data collection

At the first stage, firms begin gathering data about customers. CRM technologies are changing the way firms can interact with customers and manage data received. Traditional relationship management is being overshadowed by a new Web-centric model that opens the front office for collaborative e-business, for example, by permitting customers greater access to the enterprise's internal processes.

As shown in Figure 7.1, CRM provides a variety of channels for firms to gather customer information. Regardless of what channel a company uses, the Internet specifically has revolutionised business by allowing 24-hour services, which in turn has led to the transformation of the call centre into the contact centre. In addition, traditional customer interaction methodologies, such as voice-only call centres and Internet-only electronic services and sales channels, can be replaced by multi-channel customer interaction systems that combine telephone, the Internet, e-mail, fax and chat services. Customer-facing technologies, such as e-mail response systems, self-service portals, Web collaboration and chat services, are being integrated with traditional call-centre technologies to provide more seamless and efficient customer interaction. A flexible, integrated Internet architecture allows integration of different touch points of customer communications, thus enhancing visibility throughout the selling chain.

E-mail, for example, is increasingly being used by firms to communicate with customers. Customers use e-mail as a channel to contact firms for inquiries or information; however, this also puts pressure on firms to provide prompt, accurate responses. Also, the Voice over Internet Protocol (VoIP), the transmission of voice over the Internet, can be combined with e-mail to interact with customers. Similarly, instant messaging technology allows communication between enterprise agents and customers. Two Web technologies in particular are increasingly used to boost efficiency in customer problem-solving:[11]

1 *Web chat problem-solving* enables online, text-based communications between customer and service representative. When used with forms, it can facilitate routing to service representatives with particular skills. In addition it provides both customers and service representative with a record of the dialogue.

2 *Web collaboration problem-solving* can be used in conjunction with other technologies, such as Web chat or VoIP, to enable service representatives to direct the customer's browser to a particular Web page. It also provides customers with rapid access to specific information without the need to go through the entire website to find the information.

Companies that successfully integrate these technologies into their CRM systems will deliver higher levels of customer satisfaction. These customer interaction management tools not only facilitate more effective interaction with the customer, they also allow firms to change process flows as they become necessary or redesign CRM solutions as needed.

Stage 2: data and knowledge management

The key challenge at this stage is to identify and unlock general data characteristics necessary to recognise and analyse profitable customers. CRM databases can aggregate data from various sources (during Stage 1) and synthesise it into

---

11. CommerceNet (2001).

useful information. The trick is to integrate data from websites, call centres, ERP systems, cross-functional operations databases, third-party data, sales force reports and so forth.

There are three content management tools, which are critical to building CRM databases:

1 *Information mining*: A text-crawling "spider" program that gathers topic-specific documents.

2 *Information extraction*: A software program that pulls information from text and generates personalised summaries.

3 *Information classification*: An automatic classification software program that funnels these summaries into a customised directory.

Knowledge management becomes critical in developing CRM initiatives and building customer strategies. Customer profiles and customer information are then integrated and provided to all customer touch points. In addition, customer analysis tools such as data mining allow an enterprise's marketing function to segment customers, analyse their propensity to buy, churn, cross-sell and up-sell.

Firms can enhance value to customers simply by providing access to real-time data. The value of real-time data to customers is most visible in the mobile and wireless technology areas. Since firms are focusing on improving efficiencies and enhancing customer relationships, they realise that access to real-time data can provide a competitive advantage. Companies such as DHL and FedEx provide their workforces with wireless devices including personal digital assistants to improve customer service. Financial services companies, for example, are making the wireless play as a smart way to improve customer satisfaction by extending the channels through which real-time data and services can be delivered. In addition, telecom and transportation companies are embracing customer-centric technology to provide 24-hour customer services and field operations.

Consider how adding information to generic products (i.e. commodities) enhances their overall economic value. For example, Amazon.com personalises book recommendations based on customer feedback, customer interactions and purchases from its website. By using these data to analyse customer tastes, Amazon builds personal information about a customer's choices. In the next section we show how by creating knowledge about their customers, companies such as Amazon can personalise their offerings, ultimately increasing lifetime value of their customers. This strategy also directs the purchase decision away from price allowing Amazon to focus on service and product differentiation as a means of increasing the company's value proposition.

By adding intelligence to CRM initiatives, abstract intellectual assets can be linked with practical business solutions. Databases are a key enabling technology for changing business processes and organisational structures. CRM databases and attendant applications create a business culture of customer intimacy. Customer decision support and customer information management facilitate and improve customer interaction through the integration of information about customer contact points, the channel they employ and the marketing content they use.

Stage 3: customer value management

This stage of the CRM framework focuses on the ability to leverage CRM technology to deliver personalised customer services. e-CRM technologies have been very effective at managing information at specific customer touch points and distributing information during customer interactions with a firm. Each system is built with a technology layer that utilises databases, rules engines and data capture mechanisms and is designed to manage interactions within their specific environment, or context. For example:

● Call centres leverage new-data retrieval and call-scripting technologies.

● E-mail blasters use the latest in personalisation and HTML to produce personalised e-mails.

● Sales force automation tools can now connect disparate sales forces together via wireless and mobile client/server systems.

The integrated touch points indicated in Figure 7.1 highlight how companies can automate their relationship management through:

1   marketing automation

2   sales force automation

3   customer service automation.

Companies can integrate these touch points with front- and back-end functions in order to enhance customer lifetime value. Consider the case of Grey Worldwide, a communications enterprise, presented in the case study following this chapter. As CRM is a broad concept that involves both hardware and software, Grey wanted an infrastructure that focused on communications, which included understanding CRM, tailor-making marketing campaigns and programs leading towards providing a full CRM strategy, and online and offline strategic consulting. The existing customer data and customer knowledge residing in Grey's specialised companies provided tremendous opportunities for knowledge integration, creating not only a single customer database (that was easy to catalogue and retrieve using the modern systems), but also a system that collected hidden knowledge in existing data.

Grey's model allows us to see how CRM tools and customer data management strategies enable companies to discover which customers are profitable. This impact on real business value has very significant implications. Companies discover who their core customers really are and find ways to cater to their needs. For example, wine.com, a leading online purveyor of wine and gourmet products, originally believed its core customers were wine connoisseurs. A careful assessment of data, however, showed that its best customers were wine novices. With this knowledge, wine.com significantly modified its website to deliver the kinds of features these less experienced customers wanted, particularly recommendations and educational content.

As is the case in Grey Worldwide, each touch point uniquely manages customer interactions and requires highly specialised tools to facilitate customer dialogues. Each touch-point-specific tool leverages an application-specific database. Businesses that centralise their e-CRM, provide each touch point with real-time accessibility (vs physically storing them at each touch point). This way, every touch point has access to the same set of rules, providing a consistent and continuous customer experience from one touch point to the next. As a result, meaningful customer information is built within the organisation, allowing specific strategies to be developed.

Building block 4: CRM measurement

The final building block of our CRM framework is CRM measurement. It addresses the issues of "value" and how to value customers, information and online businesses. Return on Relationship (ROR) captures a new group of business behaviours. It requires companies to look beyond customer satisfaction to strive for customer loyalty by focusing on the relationship, not just the sale, and by staying one step ahead of their customers' needs and desires. In customer-driven firms, ROR drives return on investments and financial value is created by fostering customer loyalty.

Consumer relationship management financials are no longer limited to increased revenues and cost savings measurements. While the financial impacts of CRM systems are enormous, the cause-and-effect connections are still not clear. Senior executives are not entirely sure which tools are useful for measuring benefits of returns to CRM projects. A harsher financial environment is forcing companies to ask the question: "How do we justify this investment?" The broader or more comprehensive those CRM solutions are, the more difficult it is to pinpoint specific causes for business improvement. Correlating CRM's impact on values like customer satisfaction is even more challenging.

Two broad CRM measures are derivatives of traditional business practices: increased revenue and reduced cost. However, intangible efficiency is particularly relevant to CRM and these are difficult to quantify. Benefits of CRM on the sales side are relatively easy to quantify like increased revenue, for example; shortened sales cycles, faster product-to-market, customer acquisition costs, and so on can also be measured. Likewise, there are quantifiable benefits from enabling new sales channels. If a website, for example, is enabled to deal with product complexity that formerly required the attention and expense of a direct sales force, then the cost of sales drops and the operating margin rises.

There is a strong correlation between building customer loyalty and ROI, a dynamic which forces companies to shift from transaction-based customer interactions to relationship-based customer interactions. For example, to protect what has been invested in customers, companies concentrate on the time value of their customers. They focus on the potential dollar value of repeat and referral business both over time (through the customers shifts in age, spending patterns and other demographic changes) and over a broad range of products and services.

In general as customer relationships with a firm matures, its return on investment increases. The value-added stages of customer relationship are rewarding both to the customers, since they are privy to receive personalised service, and for firms, which gain the opportunity to increase revenues through cross-selling and up-selling opportunities.

LIFETIME VALUE METRICS

A "hurdle rate" is another simple tool which uses customer activity levels to assess customer significance under a "recency, frequency, and monetary value" (RFM) model. It gives the percentage of customers who have engaged in a behaviour since a certain date (recency), engaged in that behaviour a certain number of times (frequency) or have purchased a certain amount (monetary value). Because of the link between RFM and lifetime value, it can be concluded that:

- If the percentage of customers over each hurdle (recency, frequency, monetary value) is growing, the business is healthy and thriving. Customers are responding positively to their experiences, and as a group are more likely to engage in profit-generating behaviour in the future.

- If the opposite is true, and the percentage of customers over each hurdle is falling over

time, high-value customers are defecting and the future value of the business is declining. Customers as a group are responding negatively to the overall service they are receiving.

- If a business has an understanding of the customer life cycle, the logical hurdle rates to set for recency, frequency and monetary value would equate to customer behaviour at primary changes in the customer life cycle. If the business is very new or has never studied its customer life cycles, then a good default position to use is based on the 20/80 rule (20 per cent of customers generally generate 80 per cent of the behaviour – sales, visits, etc.) The analysis would default to a starting hurdle rate of 20 per cent for each behaviour (purchases, visits), and examine the customer base to determine RFM values corresponding to the 20 per cent hurdle.

OVERALL CUSTOMER RETENTION

A simplified application of RFM is called "hurdle rate analysis", where hurdles are selected for recency, frequency and monetary value, and the entire customer base is evaluated against these hurdles as a group.

Under this example, the business should look at the top 20 per cent of their customers for each of the recency, frequency and

monetary value parameters, and examine the "tail end" customers – the bottom customers of the top 20 per cent. These values would constitute the hurdle that the customer base is judged against. Customers would have to exceed the activity levels of these tail-end customers to be considered "over the hurdle".

For example, to determine the recency hurdle using the 20/80 rule (assuming a database of 10,000 customers):

1 Select the behaviour to be profiled – purchases, visits and so on.

2 Sort customers by most recent date of the behaviour.

3 Starting at the most recent customer, count down to customer number 2000 (20 per cent of 10,000) in this sorted database. Examine the group of customers near this target level (perhaps from customer 1950 to customer 2050).

4 Determine how long ago (recency) these customers, on average, engaged in the behaviour you are profiling.

5 Should you find that these customers last purchased an average of 60 days ago, the recency hurdle becomes 60 days for the "today" or starting hurdle rate of 20 per cent. Regardless of whether the hurdle rate is set using the customer lifecycle or the 20/80 rule, the operational implementation is the same. Each week or month, sweep the database and determine the percentage of customers who have engaged in the behaviour within the hurdle definition. For a 60-day hurdle, it would be the percentage of customers engaging in the behaviour in the past 60 days.

If the percentage of customers "over the hurdle" (engaging in the behaviour less than 60 days ago) grows over time, the future lifetime value of the customer base is rising. If the percentage of customers "over the hurdle" is falling, the future value of the customer base is falling as well.

For example, if you started with 20 per cent of customers having 60-day recency for purchases, you would like to continue seeing 20 per cent of your customer base purchase within the past 60 days. Ideally, you would see 21 per cent, then 22 per cent, then 23 per cent, and so on, purchasing in the past 60 days. If this percentage is rising, this means the future value of the customer base is growing, the high-value customers are being retained and promotions will have increasing response rates.

Reprinted by permission of Etailers Digest, from "Measuring Customer Retention and Value in Online Retailing," by Jim Novo, 18 October 2000. Available from: http://www.etailersdigest.com/resources/Specials/CustomerRetention.htm [Accessed 14 July 2002]

Summary

The desire to be customer-centric is a significant strategic business shift. Accordingly, business processes are moving ownership of customers away from sales and marketing towards embedding customers into the enterprise as a whole. New technologies can be a source of risk as well as opportunities for firms. Success rates differ widely, since the transition from traditional customer management to an e-CRM environment is a fundamental change in the way an entire business operates. The change affects aspects of strategy, organisation design, business processes and performance measurement. However, rewards are realised as firms begin to retain business by developing customer loyalty and better transforming data into knowledge.

The intelligent e-CRM enterprise is engaged in sharing, collecting, understanding and proactively using customer information. For a successful firm, information exchange and knowledge management become a focus of the entire CRM-oriented firm. Firms can extract competitive advantage by delivering real-time service combined with core knowledge capabilities and embedded in a multi-channel communications infrastructure. In effect, e-business enables enterprises to build lifetime value relationships through engagement and knowledge of customers. Such capability provides transparency both to the firm about its performance and to customers about the firm. The chain of engagements between customers can be more accurately measured as more readily available customer information greatly enhances the analysis of transactional and behavioural data.

Questions for discussion

1   Discuss some of the business theories that can be applied to understand CRM.

2   What are the key differences and similarities between traditional marketing and e-CRM?

3   Describe the role of information in building a customer-centric business strategy.

4   How can e-business be used as a platform to create customer loyalty?

5   What are the benefits to a firm, of developing lifetime customer value?

6   How does the Internet impact traditional marketing practices?

7   How can firms use CRM technology and applications to achieve lifetime value with customers?

8   What are some of the difficulties in measuring CRM?

9   What is the relationship between ROI and customer building?

References

Business Intelligence (1999) "Measuring and valuing customer relationships", *Business Intelligence* [online], available from http://www.eccs.uk.com/resources/CRMChapters/mvchapter1.pdf [accessed 6 December 2001].

CommerceNet (2001) "Using Internet-based technologies to enhance customer support" [online], available from http://www.commerce.net/projects/ongoing/pdf/SSAPilot.pdf [accessed 10 July 2002].

Eklektik Consulting (2001) *Putting Customer Relationship Management into Context: 2001 Summary Research Report*, commissioned by New Zealand Direct Marketing Association [online], available from http://www.dma.co.nz/pdfs/crm_summary_results.pdf [accessed 10 July 2003].

Farhoomand, F. and Lovelock, P. (2001) *Global e-Commerce: Text and Cases*, Singapore: Prentice-Hall (Asia).

Kalakota, R. and Robinson, M. (2001) *e-Business 2.0: Roadmap for Success*, Reading, Mass.: Addison-Wesley.

Novo, J. (2000) "Measuring customer retention and value in online retailing", *Etailers Digest*, 18 October, available from http://www.etailersdigest.com/resources/Specials/Customer Retention.html [accessed 14 July 2002].

Nucifora, A. (2001) *CRM is Best Marketing Defense in a Down Economy* [online], available from http://www.robersondesign.com/alfarticles/article1.html [accessed 4 March 2002].

PriceWaterhouseCoopers (2001) "e-CRM live: making your customers love you best", PriceWaterhouseCoopers [online], available from http://e-business.pwcglobal.com/pdf/pwc_ecrm_whitepaper.pdf [accessed 6 December 2001].

Swigor, T. (1999) "Retention strategies smart catalogers and retailers know: you must have a customer's attention if you're to have a shot at retention", *Epsilon* [online], available from http://www.epsilon.com/home.nsf/EpsiArticles/001297F8D4630AA4852568A800774427? OpenDocument [accessed 6 December 2001].

Tapscott, D. Ticoll, D. and Lowy, A. (2000) Digital *Capital: Harnessing the Power of Business Webs*, Boston, Mass.: Harvard Business School Press.

White, R. (2000) "Integrating e-CRM, struggling to unify your CRM applications? a new type of application provider promises relief", *ebizQ* [online], available from http://eai.ebizq.net/crm/white_1.html [accessed 6 December 2001].

Further reading

Grönroos, C. (2000a) *From Marketing Mix to Relationship Marketing: Towards a Paradigm Shift in Marketing*, Key Note Paper [online], available from http://www.mcb.co.uk/services/conferen/feb96/relation.mar/new_phil/backgrnd.htm [accessed 6 December 2001].

Grönroos, C. (2000b) *Service Management and Marketing: A Customer Relationship Management Approach*, New York: John Wiley & Sons.

Heskett, J. (1976) *Marketing*, New York: Macmillan.

O' Loughlin, D. (1997) *Towards a new Perspective of Service Brand Equity*, University of Limmerick.

Nykamp, M. (2001) CRM: what it's really all about, New York: AMACOM Book.

Reichheld, F. (2001) *Loyalty Rules! How Today's Leaders Build Lasting Relationships*, Boston: Harvard Business School Press.

Sheth, J.N. and Parvatiyar, A. (2001) *Handbook of Relationship Marketing*, Thousand Oaks: Sage Publications.

Stewart, E. and Mason, D. (2000) "CRM strategy development", *Datawarehouse* [online], available from http://www.datawarehouse.com/iknowledge/whitepapers/Base_759.pdf [accessed 6 December 2001].

Storbacka, K. (1994) *The Nature of Customer Relationship Profitability: Analysis of Relationships and Customer Bases in Retail Banking*, Doctoral dissertation, Helsinki: Swedish School of Economics and Business Administration.

Swift, Ronald S. (1998) "CRM for high productivity in telecommunications", in Proceedings of Conference on Effective DataBase and Management Information Systems Uses, Beijing, China, August.

Swift, Ronald S. (2001) *Accelerating Customer Relationships: Using CRM and Relationship Technologies*, Upper Saddle River, N.J.: Prentice-Hall PTR.

Wanninger, L.A., Anderson, C. and Hansen, R. (2001) "Designing servicescapes for electronic commerce: an evolutionary approach", Working Paper [online], available from http://misrc.umn.edu/wpaper/WorkingPapers/9701.pdf [accessed 6 December 2001].

Wittreich, W. J. (1969) "Selling A Prerequisite to Success as a Professional", paper presented in Detroit, Michigan, 8 January.

Case study   Grey Worldwide: strategic repositioning through CRM

Chaotic media and communications market conditions and downward industry pressure on commission margins forced Grey Worldwide Hong Kong and China (Grey WW-HK/China) to conceive a CRM philosophy called Grey Relationship Management (GRM) in 2001, to reposition itself through defined e-marketing and CRM strategies for the Asian market, particularly China.[1] Facing threats from a changing and fiercely competitive communications industry, Grey WW-HK/China did not want to compete on cost. Instead, it needed a differentiation strategy to leverage the growing Asian CRM market and compete with other players such as management consultants, traditional agencies and pure online players who were also building a CRM business focus.

Although communications agency Grey Worldwide had very strong umbrella brand equity, the brand capital needed to be invigorated through a renewed e-marketing focus. In particular, Grey WW-HK/China needed to re-evaluate its market environment and redefine its value proposition to its clients.

Viveca Chan, CEO of Grey Hong Kong and China, was questioning to what extent the GRM concept should merge technology with traditional marketing philosophy to develop a CRM proposition for its local clients. She asked her core strategy team to deliver a proposal outlining which CRM tools Grey WW-HK/China should engage in to reposition the Company's brand and build customer loyalty. She wanted to know how the Company could build an Asia-specific CRM process blueprint for their internal customer management process and transfer that knowledge to its clients. The strategy team had a four-week deadline to present its solutions.

Background

Grey Global Group was a full communications enterprise with 16 global partner companies focused on distinct communications disciplines and engaged in a wide range of marketing and communications activities (refer to Exhibit 1 for details of each partner company).

Grey Worldwide Hong Kong and China

Grey Worldwide Hong Kong and China was established in 1978 as part of the Grey Global network, focusing on "communications" as its core business and following eight principles to provide client services (refer to Exhibit 2). Grey Worldwide's (or Grey) Asia strategy focused on building partnerships with local agencies and developing local management talent to allow quick recognition of indigenous opportunities. This communications strategy proved successful for Grey WW-HK/China; its billings have grown steadily since 1986 (refer to Exhibit 3).

Grey Hong Kong started as a small agency, and delivering integrated marketing expertise was its core strategy. Integrated marketing was its strategy cornerstone because agencies in Asia, as compared to the US, were generally required and expected to do everything – customer interaction, advertising, design and public relations – without relying on specialised departments for individual expertise. In addition, due to the importance of one-to-one customer relationships in Asian business, companies delivered "integrated" marketing because it was the most cost-effective client service approach. "The one-to-one customer relationship strategy originated from the

---

1. CRM can be defined as a comprehensive set of processes and technologies for managing the relationships with potential and current customers and business partners across marketing, sales and service, regardless of the communications channel.

Exhibit 1 Global partner companies

1. *Alliance*: Alliance has developed a strong network within a vast array of industries that has allowed it to create strategic partnerships that provide solutions and create opportunity. It specialises in creating global alliances between brand companies, entertainment properties and new media.

2. *APCO Worldwide*: APCO specialises in public affairs and major corporate issues including issues management, litigation support, communications regarding mergers and acquisitions, government relations, corporate positioning, strategic philanthropy, community relations and general issue communications.

3. *Beyond Interactive (BI)*: BI is a full-service interactive marketing agency specialising in customer acquisition and customer retention. It focuses on increasing clients' exposure and maximising customers' lifetime value through interactive marketing. BI develops marketing strategies to promote existing sites and traditional brands; the objective is to improve clients' return on investment from interactive marketing efforts.

4. *Elemental Interactive*: An award-winning global interactive communications firm that specialises in helping companies communicate effectively with their critical stakeholders by leveraging the power of the Internet and other interactive technologies. Its work focuses on investor, corporate and employee communications including annual reports, investor relations Websites, fact books, leadership profiles and other interactive resources.

5. *G2*: G2 specialises in brand communications; it has a team of strategic consultants and multimedia designers who have experience across virtually every communications discipline and product category. With its BRAND EXTENSION(tm), G2 is involved from strategic consultancy to communications design and implementation.

6. *GCI*: GCI is one of the world's largest global public relations agencies, recently named Agency of the Year by a leading industry journal. It has expanded traditional services into an ever-widening group of practices, including brand marketing, corporate affairs, healthcare, technology, change management and financial relations.

7. *Grey Direct*: Grey Direct is a leading global marketing services company targeted towards business marketing to individuals and other businesses. Grey Direct services include: direct marketing solutions (for the analogue world); electronic direct marketing support (for the digital world); database optimisation and implementation; and aggressive sourcing and print production management.

8. *Grey Directory Marketing, Inc. (GDMI)*: GDMI specialises in yellow pages and other specialised directory media. One of the top ten companies in its industry, known for its disciplined marketing approach and media innovations, GDMI pioneered the use of metered testing and other tools to measure its clients' return on investment from the medium.

9. *Grey Healthcare Group*: Grey Healthcare Group established itself as one of the world's largest healthcare marketing agencies. It provides education, consulting, advertising, public relations and online patient relationship and loyalty programmes for pharmaceutical and healthcare companies.

10. *Grey Interactive (GI)*: Grey Interactive offers full interactive marketing services in support of business and brand building through the use of e-commerce, Internet advertising, research, consulting and relationship marketing tools.

11. *Grey Worldwide*: Grey Worldwide develops highly creative solutions to marketing problems including brand positioning, brand planning, creative development and production.

12. *G WHIZ*: G WHIZ is an integrated, multi-disciplined marketing company created in 2000 by the merger of G WHIZ Youth Marketing and Grey Entertainment. It specialises in understanding the youthful mindset of today's consumer. G WHIZ offers advertising and media services, Internet and interactive content, promotional marketing, and proprietary research, consulting and brand planning for entertainment-related products and services.

13. *J. Brown/LMC Group*: J. Brown/LMC Group, the leading co-marketing agency in the US, helps companies leveragemarketing budgets through retail partnerships, which result in stronger merchandising, consumer impact and brand equity communications. It also offers product and technology demonstration and sampling programmes, and through LMC, adds value to local radio programming.

Exhibit 1 (cont'd)

14. *Mediacom*: Mediacom creates media solutions that build business for a wide range of local, regional and worldwide clients.

15. *Visual Communications Group (VCG)*: VCG specialises in investor and marketing communications: the investor communications group develops strategies and designs creative media for IPO roadshows, investor conferences, annual reports and investor relations websites; the marketing communications group provides an integrated approach to brand-building and corporate identity by developing innovative print collateral and websites.

16. *Wing Latino Group*: Wing Latino Group, a merger of Grey Global Group's US Hispanic marketing agency (FOVA) and its Puerto Rico-based agency (West Indies & Grey), provides full-service capabilities in advertising, media, research, merchandising, promotions, direct marketing, interactive and public relations for major corporations.

Source: Adapted from Grey Global Group (2001), "A full spectrum of marketing communications," at http://www.greyglobalgroup.com?frameset.asp, 16 July.

Exhibit 2 Grey global's eight principles (promises)

Promise 1: We provide clients with an experienced and consistent team.
Promise 2: We promise true partnership attitude.
Promise 3: We apply strategic knowledge and disciplines to add value.
Promise 4: We consistently deliver high quality services.
Promise 5: We leverage global "best practice."
Promise 6: We fight for the best prices for our clients.
Promise 7: We create ideas that sell.
Promise 8: We turn your brand into a showcase of success.

Exhibit 3 Grey WW-HK/China's billings growth

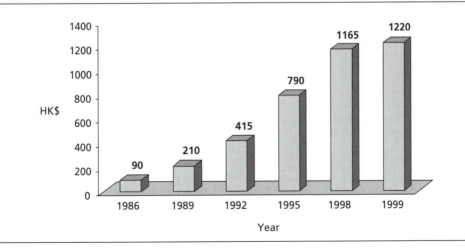

East and this age-old concept is actually nothing new to the Eastern culture," said Peter Boulter of the Peppers and Rogers Consulting Group.[2]

The integrated marketing communications (IMC) concept referred to the "integration" of specialised communications functions that had previously operated with various degrees of autonomy. It was only in the early 1990s that US agencies merged various marketing communications functions. The market factors included:[3]

- communications agencies' mergers and acquisitions
- higher level of client and retailer sophistication
- the increased cost of traditional advertising media
- the rise of global competition
- pressure on organisations' bottom lines
- the decreased effectiveness of traditional media and the loss of message credibility.

The American Association of Advertising Agencies defined IMC as "a concept of marketing communications planning that recognises the added value of a comprehensive plan that evaluates the strategic roles of a variety of communications disciplines, for example general advertising, direct response, sales promotion and public relations – and combines these disciplines to provide clarity, consistency and maximum communications impact."[4]

2. Loh Chyi, J. (2000) "Using CRM tools to attract customers," *New Straits Times*, Kuala Lumpur, 6 September, p. 10.
3. Dilenschneider, R.L. (1991) in Duncan, T. R. and Everett, S. E. (1993), "Client perceptions of integrated marketing communications," *Journal of Advertising Research*, 33(3), May/June, p. 30.
4. Duncan, T.R. and Everett, S.E. (1993), "Client perceptions of integrated marketing communications," *Journal of Advertising Research*, 33(3), May/June, p. 30.

A changing media industry

In the early 1990s, while US agencies began moving towards an "integrated marketing" approach, Asian agencies began moving away from "generalisation" towards the "specialisation" model. The late 1990s in Asia also saw market competition change dramatically, and various departments began specialising in different areas (i.e. advertising and PR). This culture change led to the creation of a CRM philosophy called Grey Relationship Management (GRM), an initiative designed to give the agency a more holistic approach to advertising in the new world order. It was a move considered ahead of the expected convergence of new and traditional media.

Traditionally, advertising agencies concentrated their skills in building brand equity, direct marketing companies in direct communications/database and interactive agencies in one-to-one marketing. To position Grey WW-HK/China in the 21st century, Viveca Chan felt strongly the need to combine these skill sets to develop a bigger picture in order to leverage all touch points to build both brand and the customer base. "My challenge is how to expand the vision of our people, how to manage the different company roles and how to create process that cross all these disciplines," Viveca said.

Viveca Chan elaborated on GRM's business role:

> GRM has emerged because, in Asia, we are moving towards specialisation. In fact, Grey WW-HK/China is moving towards "integrated specialisation" because now creativity is converging with knowledge.

In the 1980s, Grey WW-HK/China concentrated on brand-building and management; by 2001 the focus was not simply brand management, but now involved customer management as well. Therefore, Grey WW-HK/China needed to manage brand equity as well as customer equity. Grey had already developed a strong brand in the marketplace; however, it had to build a customer knowledge base to enable customer relationship management.

The existing customer data and customer knowledge residing in Grey's specialised companies provided tremendous opportunities for knowledge integration, creating not only a single customer database (that was easy to catalogue and retrieve using the modern systems), but also a system that collected hidden knowledge in existing data. This "database" or knowledge base captured Grey WW-HK/China's biggest asset and helped in segmenting customers, predicting loyalty and analysing market needs. The main goal of the GRM philosophy was an integrated approach to create, identify, evaluate, capture, enhance, share and apply Grey's intellectual capital (refer to Figure 1).

As CRM was a broad concept that involved both hardware and software, GRM would focus on communications, which included understanding CRM, tailor-making campaigns and programmes leading towards a full CRM strategy, and online and offline strategic consulting. This whole package was called GRM, and a specialised team was needed to develop and build a CRM strategy in Asia. To implement GRM, Grey WW-HK/China utilised the resources of Grey Worldwide partners such as Grey Direct, Grey Interactive and Beyond Interactive (an Internet advertising agency). In particular, Beyond Interactive's competence – educating consumers and unique understanding of gathering data, and optimisation, among others in the front-end as well as the back-end of using the Internet – was fundamental to Grey WW-HK/China's new CRM focus. Beyond Interactive was considered an expert in using DoubleClick's DART systems and had global contracts with DART (refer to "Competition" section below for additional discussion on DoubleClick's DART system).

The media market in 2001

By the late 1990s, competition in the communications industry was not only limited to advertising agencies; management consultants, marketing businesses and consultants also began competing in the same space by developing a CRM focus. By 2001, the media market was in chaos, as technology and the market were driving companies across several industries (consulting, branding, media, etc.) to redefine their roles in terms of media,

Figure 1 The GRM framework

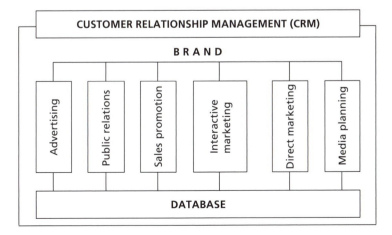

marketing and content. Specifically, three overarching trends were pushing communications companies to focus on improving their client attraction and retention processes:

1 increased competition

2 new technology

3 rising customer expectations.

Competition

With the advent of heightened global competition in nearly every industry, clear demarcations between core communications agencies such as Grey Worldwide, traditional consulting firms (McKenzie, Arthur Andersen), pure online media firms (DoubleClick, Yahoo) and online design outfits (Razorfish) were becoming blurred. The main change-driver was technology.

Internet technologies provided companies with tools to adapt to changing customer needs, and could be used for economic, strategic and competitive advantages. For example, after media company DoubleClick was launched, it started licensing its proprietary ad-placement technology, even though DoubleClick's advertising sales force was competing with some of the websites that used the technology. "It was one of the toughest but smartest decisions we made," said Barry Salzman, President of global media at DoubleClick.[5] The system known as DART (Dynamic Advertising Reporting Targeting) was used to manage marketing e-mails as well, and had become the bulk of DoubleClick's business.

In addition, pure online firms had a low cost base and began producing competitive high-quality products. This general industry trend created tremendous cost pressures on traditional businesses. Marketing and advertising industry players were faced with

constant margin squeezes; between 1988 and 2001, commissions had fallen from a standard of 15 per cent to as low as 2 per cent of sales.

Media and Internet CRM technologies

The Internet's growth and new media technologies (refer to Exhibit 4) provided innovative communications solutions such as:

● Internet-centric technologies that integrated with existing business infrastructures (e.g. telecommunications, data communications and other connectivity could provide cross-media business solutions and enhance customer value).

● Enhanced Internet telephony and e-marketing communications that leveraged new media technologies, including IP telephony, visual communications, Internet kiosks, interactive responses and messaging portals.

Rising customer expectations

A concurrent trend driving industry change was rising customer expectations; this meant that agencies had to refine their ability to identify and serve their "best" customers – and create loyal customers. As a result, previously ad hoc and fragmented techniques for dealing effectively with customers were giving way to a more methodical CRM approach: identifying, attracting and retaining the most valuable customers in order to sustain profitable growth.

Renewed customer focus, driven by technology, market and media infrastructure changes, was a new industry trend. Historically, regulation and minimal competition encouraged communications companies to look inward in search of process efficiencies to fuel margins, rather

5. Angwin, J. (2001) "DoubleClick keeps two steps ahead of rivals," *Wall Street Journal*, New York, 26 April, p. B.6.

Exhibit 4 Selected e-marketing customisation tools

	Level	
	Small segment/group	Individual
Company-side tools (push)	Collaborative filtering Data mining and profiling Outgoing e-mail	Cookies Web log analysis Real-time profiling Outgoing e-mail
Client-side tools (pull)	Agents Experiential marketing	Individualised Web portals Wireless data services Web page formats Fax-on-demand Incoming e-mail

Company-side tools

- *Collaborative filtering* software automatically gathers the opinions of like-minded users and returns those opinions to the individual real-time.
- *Data mining and profiling*: Data mining software is used to find patterns of interest, such that predictive information is extracted in large databases through statistical analyses.
- *Outgoing e-mail*: The use of e-mail to provide useful, appropriate, valuable, timely and unobtrusive information to its clients.
- *Cookies* are small files written to the user's hard drive after visiting a website, which is used to personalise a website for a user returning to the site.
- *Website log* records every visit of a user in the Web server's log file, including pages visited, duration of visit and whether there was a purchase or action. Web log analysis allows a company to customise Web pages based on visitor behaviour, something that makes users feel that the firm knows them and is trying to provide better service.
- *Real-time profiling*, also known as tracking user clickstream in real time, allows the analysis of consumer online behaviour and makes instantaneous adjustments to site promotional offers and Web pages.

Client-side tools

- *Agents* are programmes that perform functions on behalf of the user; for example, shopping agents and search engines are software agents that match user input to databases and return customised information.
- *Experiential marketing* is often used in bricks-and-mortar; it gets the consumer involved in the product to create a memorable experience.
- *Individualised Web portals and wireless data services*: Clients can create personalised Web pages so users can get a standard Web page with a company's or client's name on it. Each client can edit and select things they want to see, thus providing a completely client-specific information source. Customised information can also be offered to clients with cell phones, pagers, PDAs, or tools that can receive wireless Internet transmission.
- *Web page format* (or HTML format) is the technical term for a Web page format that has designated places for the user to type information. This can be used for purposes such as site registration and survey research.
- *Fax-on-demand*: customers phone a firm, listen to an automated voice menu, and through selection options request that a fax be sent on a topic of interest.
- *Incoming e-mail* is initiated by clients or prospects. E-mail queries, complaints or compliments can be used as an opportunity to cross-sell, up-sell or ask for more information to build the customer's profile.

Source: Adapted from Strauss, J. and Frost, R. (2001) E-Marketing, 2nd edition, New Jersey: Prentice Hall, 290–292.

than outward for market share. During the 1990s, even though the business landscape was undergoing tremendous transformation, an inward-looking mindset still prevailed in many communications companies' service organisations. The net result was a customer service environment struggling to meet the needs of an increasingly complex marketplace and at the same time retain and grow its embedded customer base.[6]

Focused customer relationship management provided some business solutions. As Mary Wardley, director of IDC's CRM applications research, said: "In an era in which the competition is one mouse click away, the need to solidify and deepen relationships with valuable customers has never been more important."[7]

The customer service area presented the communications industry with tremendous opportunities for achieving breakthrough differentiation and competitive advantage. Although most senior communications executives knew intuitively that managing customer relationships was critical, the fundamental dilemma was determining which customer relationship management capabilities had the greatest financial impact. If a company was unable to quantify a capability's financial impact, the wrong investment decisions were often made, resulting in high opportunity costs.

A huge issue with CRM was its lack of accountability. Measurement of effectiveness was difficult, and while some return-on-investment methods were tested, they lacked the necessary tools to determine specific costs or to assess the behavioural changes resulting from CRM, and whether the behaviour changed once or 50 times, for

example. Sources from Charles Schwab reported some customer service and maintenance costs in the US across four different categories:[8]

1 face-to-face (F2F) communication – US$10 per contact

2 call-centre agents – US$7.50

3 voice response unit (VRU) – US$2.48

4 Internet – US$0.18.

In addition, a study by Arthur Andersen in 2000 was the first to quantify the value of specific CRM capabilities; the research found that CRM performance accounted for 50 per cent of the variance in communications companies' return on sales.[9] Therefore, 50 per cent of return on sales could be directly attributed to CRM activities (sales, service and marketing), while the other 50 per cent was not related to CRM (refer to Exhibit 5).

The CRM industry in Asia

Between 1995 and 2001, CRM technology and practice exploded to create a whole new market, one that AMR Research claimed would be worth US$16.8 billion by 2003. However, the Asian CRM pie was relatively smaller, but higher growth rates were expected than in North America (refer to Exhibit 6 for CRM industry growth figures).

> The market size for Asia-Pacific isn't yet close to growth in the US. We can say the market size for Asia-Pacific is less than eight per cent of the US; although its growth rate is almost

6. Raaen, D. and Wolfe, M. (1999) "CRM takes the driving seat for shareholder value," *Telecommunications*, 33(8), Dedham, August, pp. S60–S65.

7. Perez, B. (2001) "IT companies lie in wait for opportunities in CRM business," *South China Morning Post*, Hong Kong, 15 May, p. 8.

8. Loh Chyi, J. (2000) "Using CRM tools to attract customers," *New Straits Times*, Kuala Lumpur, 6 September, p. 10.

9. It was found that just three out of 19 key customer service capabilities – an effective billing system, attracting the best talent and measuring customer service effectiveness – accounted for 43 per cent of the available ROS impact of moving from average to top-tier performance in customer service.

Exhibit 5 The contribution of CRM to return on sales (ROS)

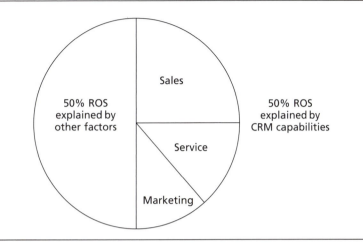

Exhibit 6 CRM industry growth in Asia

Year	Asia-Pacific* CRM Market Growth (in millions US$)
2000	206
2001	351
2002	501
2003	716

Note
* Excluding China, Japan, India and South Korea.

Source: Anonymous (2000) "Asian e-commerce market booming, customer service takes front seat," *Electronic Commerce News*, 5(26), Potomac, 26 June, p. 1.

200 per cent – even faster than the growth lines we saw in the US two years ago.[10]
– James Vogtle, CRM Industry Expert

However, Asian markets began to understand the importance of CRM. Primarily, the interest was led by traditional customer management economics. It cost the industry five times as much to acquire a new customer than to retain an existing one (refer to Exhibit 7); therefore, building long-term and sustainable customer relationships was a good strategy, from the point of view of both building life-time value relationships and the business cost savings involved. Consequently, customer management benefits became more apparent. Successful customer relationships cost less because promotional costs were reduced, higher response rates to promotional efforts yielded more profits, sales teams could be more effective when they got to know individual customers well and loyal customers cost less to service.

Meanwhile, Europe and North America specialised and focused on sophisticated and high-end CRM solutions because market needs

---

10. Anonymous (2000) "Asian e-commerce market booming, customer service takes front seat," *Electronic Commerce News*, 5(26), Potomac, 26 June, p. 1.

Exhibit 7 Maximising the number of customers

Acquisition emphasis		Retention emphasis	
Gain 6 new customers ($500 each)	$3000	Gain 3 new customers ($500 each)	$1500
Retain 5 current customers ($100 each)	$500	Retain 20 current customers ($100 each)	$2000
Total cost	$3500	Total cost	$3500
Total number of customers	11	Total number of customers	23

Source: Peppers and Rogers (1996) in Strauss, J. and Frost, R. (2001) *e-Marketing*, Second edition, New Jersey: Prentice-Hall, p. 293.

were sophisticated. Therefore, a lot of customer management technology available in the US was not available in Asia, such as radical mail or rich e-mail. Nevertheless, the Asian market, particularly China, had no legacy systems that required conversion, which provided Grey WW-HK/China the opportunity to introduce state-of-the-art CRM tools. Hong Kong was a technology centre in Asia, but the market was small; hence China was more interesting because of the huge market size, and it had the potential to leapfrog. In order to develop CRM initiatives for Asia, Viveca Chan felt that certain Asian specificities needed to be recognised:

- Asian consumers needed to be educated in e-business and enabling technologies;
- the Asian market was more fragmented in its CRM needs; and
- the strategy, execution and knowledge mix in Asia would differ.

Asia-Pacific's technology adoption rate was slower, as compared to Europe and the US. For example, in the US, easy access to customer information was available through various channels.[11] Also, a large portion of capital investment in Asia was in information technology, but relatively little investment was channeled to supporting technologies and enabling functions (such as CRM).

Another issue was the size of Asian markets; they were smaller, and CRM needs were fragmented. For example, industry-specific stages of development in finance, insurance or health were also important considerations in understanding how to implement CRM in Asia.

Software firm Interact Commerce's Asia sales director, Devin Nair, said Asian organisations were becoming more focused on retaining existing customers. He confirmed CRM's particular importance in critical industries such as telecommunications, banks and financial institutions, where customer service was a key focal area. Devin said the global economic slowdown forced companies to cut down on information technology spending, but at the same time, the market needed a quicker return on investment:

> The solution lies in CRM, which can help companies manage customers better, and subsequently secure more new clients. Asia-Pacific is the largest growing market for CRM.[12]

The main attractive Asian market was China; size and strategy were major reasons why China was critical for Grey WW-HK/China's growth in Asia. For example, industry experts believed that building a CRM product for 600 million people was no more difficult than

---

11. Early CRM adopters in Asia included the financial and telecommunications sectors, while insurance and pharmaceutical companies were trying to catch up.

12. Pardas, A. (2001), "Growing market for CRM adoption," *Computimes Malaysia*, New York, 16 April, p. 1.

building a product for 60 million; however, in China the product would have scale opportunities due to a large user base.

> China leapfrogs the rest of the world. It's a virgin technology and methodology base. Asian brand owners in China are finding new ways to compete and align their business technology and practices to global standards. Whereas players in other countries are constrained by legacy systems, local players are free to develop their own methodologies to meet local demand in a more effective way.
>
> – Theresa Franklin, Grey Wordlwide Hong Kong and China CRM Director

Grey Worldwide Hong Kong and China: e-marketing strategy

By July 2001, Viveca Chan was pushing her Company to identify where its strengths lay, what traditional business resources it could leverage and what new media tools it could use to redefine customer value in the face of dramatically changing market conditions. She advised her team to consider several issues when developing strategy ideas:

- how to tackle a dramatically changing industry cost structure where there was downward pressure on profit margins;
- to understand the specific market forces that were driving media and communications changes, and to identify how Grey WW-HK/China could manage its business model in the light of these changes; and
- how to attract and retain high-calibre talent, since agencies were pressured to cut costs.

Service industries in Asia were becoming increasingly aware of the importance of customer relationship services as the market was becoming more competitive; CRM was also a method to avoid destructive price wars as products became less and less differentiated in an open market. However, it was less clear how CRM could be implemented, as the region had idiosyncratic economic maturity and fragmented CRM needs.

China was a huge potential market for CRM opportunities. Companies were investing significant resources there; for example, Avaya's main focus was Hong Kong and China, based on its growing relationships with major service providers and the fact that enterprises were increasing the use of Internet-based communications to run their businesses.[13] During 2001, Avaya planned to invest between US$80 million and US$100 million into the Asia-Pacific region to expand its operations in the key markets of China, Hong Kong, Taiwan, Singapore, South Korea and Australia.[14]

It planned to focus its CRM products on enterprises and build market share through a combination of direct presence, distributor partners and alliance partners to create solutions that it would offer in the marketplace. Avaya believed there was tremendous opportunity in China for data networking and an even bigger opportunity in the telephony area. Avaya's main differentiating factor was its CRM technology focus and implementation experience.

However, successful CRM implementation, according to Viveca Chan, hinged on a company's ability to execute a strategy with the right market knowledge; she felt no such player existed in the market yet (refer to Figure 2). Despite cost pressures, though, Grey WW-HK/China decided not to compete on price; instead, it would differentiate itself through a CRM proposition – the GRM concept. To become that player, Grey WW-HK/China viewed its Asian challenges in two specific ways: by managing knowledge and by executing strategy through managing technology.

---

13. Avaya – the former business-communications systems unit of Lucent – offered voice, converged voice and data, customer relationship management (CRM), messaging, multi-service networking and structured-cabling products and services.
14. Chua, J. (2000) "HK stands to benefit from Avaya Asia-Pacific key to plan of Lucent spin-off," *South China Morning Post*, Hong Kong, 3 October, p. 1.

Figure 2 Grey Worldwide Hong Kong and China's CRM implementation

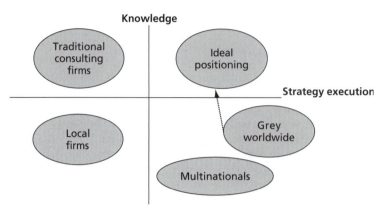

Managing knowledge

Viveca Chan commented that "knowledge management is critical to capture best practices and detailed information about customer usage behaviour, contact history, product enquiries and corporate data that marketing people can use to their advantage." A US cable company executive supported this notion: the company had remarkable information about its customers that the customer service department was uninformed about; this meant they continued to struggle with how best to extract actionable insights about customers from the data.

Communications companies faced the daunting challenge of integrating multiple customer databases to create a single customer profile. In particular, creating a holistic view of a large business customer with complex organisational hierarchies, geographic locations and custom-designed products required an enormous amount of knowledge integration. Theresa Franklin said:

> Knowledge is information gathered on customers through various events and media. Sharing customer knowledge is our biggest future asset. Our main challenge is how to develop a system to build "customer equity". In addition to "brand equity"; customer management has become key in this business. This means managing the multiple customer contact points, managing CRM.

Managing technology

In pursuing the Asian CRM market, Grey WW-HK/China was taking the view that it would extract relevant CRM components and "add on" technology as client needs developed. It still emphasised its strength in marketing strategy; Grey WW-HK/China felt technology was an enabler, a part of its strategy sum, not the sum of its CRM strategy. Viveca Chan elaborated:

> We want to enhance our "total customer experience". Our definition of CRM is focusing on what we do best: enhancing brand equity and enhancing customer loyalty and retention. We want to manage multiple consumer touch points such as the Internet, multimedia, TV and other customer information channels to achieve customer information integration knowledge. Beyond Interactive is expert on educating consumers, but now we are focusing on managing customer feedback and moving prospective customers into loyal prospects.[15]

Grey WW-HK/China was convinced that customer "strategy" would remain its leading edge, while technology would be incorporated as part of its strategy

---

15. Beyond Interactive is Grey Worldwide's full-service marketing agency, specialising in customer acquisition and customer retention.

implementation tactic. Technology would help make the implementation of its customer relationship philosophy both faster and cheaper. In addition, Grey WW-HK/China was planning to use technology to enhance value, for example, by offering clients "database management" including data mining and customer profiling tools.

Grey WW-HK/China's management considered that applying technology at a brand level was a successful strategy because Grey's core strength was brand; however, integrating technology with brand by incorporating database management into its value proposition meant it could offer a knowledge edge.

> Technology is part of our total communications process, but not necessarily part of our strategic processes. It is part of sharing information about our clients, enhancing our business efficiency and as an alternative for traditional media in building media presence on-line. Our focus is still our brains.
>
> – Candy Wan, Director of Grey Direct

Grey relationship management

The GRM concept was a four-principle philosophy developed with a specific customer management focus:

1 build brands

2 develop and manage customers

3 create a positive brand experience for clients

4 build brand through knowledge about the customer through constant dialogue.

The GRM concept referred to the philosophy Grey WW-HK/China was trying to blueprint, with an emphasis on strategy but allowing technology to help build a better, efficient and cost-effective CRM strategy. Data mining and customer profiling, for example, were key areas in Grey WW-HK/China's CRM strategy.

Grey WW-HK/China's tools for implementing the GRM concept were two proprietary products – "Brand Futures+" and "GRM Charter" (refer to Figure 3). Brand Futures+ was designed to help assess clients' competitive environments and help

Figure 3 Grey Worldwide Hong Kong and China tools for GRM

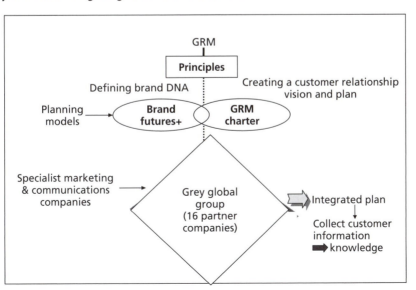

them build brands. GRM Charter was a customer management model for more sophisticated clients who understood their competitive positioning and had scanned their environment to determine the focus of their CRM strategy.

Brand Futures+ targeted companies that had traditional marketing needs: defining and building brands. Brand Futures+ tapped a partner or a group of Grey's partners, such as specialist marketing and communications companies, to create personalised strategies to meet clients' needs. For example, Brand Futures+ could be used to assess Company A's marketing and branding needs. Depending on the assessment outcome, Grey WW-HK/China would tap its pool of specialist marketing and communications companies and select the most appropriate company to map out a plan for defining and building the brand for Company A. Brand Futures+ allowed Grey to leverage its strength in turning brands into "a showcase of success" (refer to Figure 4).

GRM Charter catered to the needs of companies that had strong marketing and brand strategies in place and wanted to develop a customer relationship vision and plan. GRM Charter could build an integrated plan that involved the participation of all of Grey's global talent. For example, if Company B already had an established brand but wanted to build lifetime customer loyalty,

GRM Charter could be used to collect customer information that could be translated into practical knowledge. Technological advances and Web-based tracking capabilities were some of the new tools that GRM Charter could leverage to profile customers, thus allowing Grey WW-HK/China to build a CRM strategy. The GRM Charter would help Company B to turn customer raw data from bricks-and-mortar stores, catalogues, websites and other sources into practical knowledge, so that the company could make better-informed business and marketing decisions (refer to Figure 5).

The complexity involved in building relationships with customers meant that Grey WW-HK/China had to capitalise on the strengths of each of its diversified communications partner companies in order to create the best solution. One of the changes introduced at Grey Worldwide was the elevation of a new generation of management; some of Grey's most senior executives had moved up to the parent company, where all of Grey's companies benefited from their wisdom and experience. This new management structure, combined with the use of innovative CRM technology, was used by GRM Charter to serve its targeted clients with CRM needs.

Theresa Franklin conceded that selling GRM's philosophy was not difficult because it

Figure 4 Brand Futures+ process

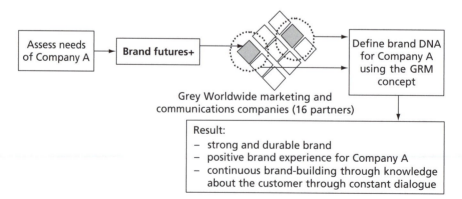

Assess needs of Company A → Brand futures+ → Grey Worldwide marketing and communications companies (16 partners) → Define brand DNA for Company A using the GRM concept

Result:
- strong and durable brand
- positive brand experience for Company A
- continuous brand-building through knowledge about the customer through constant dialogue

Figure 5 The GRM charter process

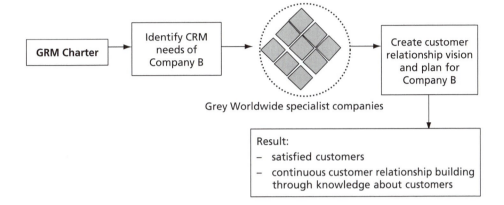

Grey Worldwide specialist companies

catered to market needs. The Brand Futures+ and GRM Charter tools were a strategic fit with consumer needs, so the Company was not pushing an unnecessary product onto the market. The core task was still how to provide brand value to clients, but the components of brand value were changing. Theresa Franklin elaborated on Grey WW-HK/China's plan to capitalise on changing values:

> Database management is the backbone of CRM. We plan to build our credibility in database management through understanding how to use and apply technology.

In building a customer-focused process blueprint, Grey WW-HK/China needed to keep in mind its back-end ability and front-end processes. On the front-end, its employees were key; they were required to think strategically in the context of clients' needs. Grey WW-HK/China typically put together key stakeholders to brainstorm ideas, and an outside consultant was hired to help institutionalise key processes and strategies being developed through client interaction; Grey WW-HK/China was still trying to create a blueprint for the CRM process for Asia.

From an internal perspective, Grey WW-HK/China's challenge was for employees to adapt to a new way of thinking, incorporating a GRM focus at every level.

It was easier for employees to shift their thinking and adapt to this new GRM philosophy as they became a part of building it; however, Grey WW-HK/China was also planning to train employees through client CRM case studies.

Viveca Chan's final thought on Grey WW-HK/China's e-marketing strategy was:

> Strategy is strategy. "e" is part of it now, but there is no change in fundamentals! "e" is just a tool for us to change brand experience.

Challenges

Grey WW-HK/China had not yet devised its CRM processes and applications internally, but was testing various processes to build a CRM blueprint; these processes would represent Grey's CRM perspective and reflect its spin and value in terms of strategy and technology to its clients. Gartner's eight CRM blocks provided a simple framework for Grey WW-HK/China to understand what its strengths and weaknesses were and how it would position itself in the complex communications marketing space. However, the key challenges Viveca was facing kept resurfacing in her mind:

● Grey WW-HK/China would need to operationalise adopted CRM processes for all employees at all levels of the organisation

Table 1 The eight building blocks of CRM[16]

1.	CRM Vision	Leadership, Market Position, Value Proposition	
2.	CRM Strategies	Objectives, Segments, Effective Interaction	
3.	Valued-Customer Experience	• Understand Requirements • Monitor Expectations • Satisfaction vs Competition	• Act on Feedback • Customer Communications
4.	Organisational Collaboration	• Culture and Structure • Customer Understanding • People: Skills/Competencies	• Incentives/Compensation • Partners and Suppliers
5.	CRM Processes	Customer Life Cycle, Knowledge Management	
6.	CRM Information	Data, Analysis, Market Research	
7.	CRM Technology	Applications, IT Architecture	
8.	CRM Metrics	Value, Retention, Satisfaction, Loyalty, Cost to Serve	

- management knew Grey had strong brand equity, but it needed a renewed marketing focus to sustain competitive advantage

- brand equity alone was losing its magic as a value to customers; Grey WW-HK/China needed to reinforce customer value through GRM

- Grey WW-HK/China faced price pressures and was losing high-calibre people to clients.

While it was generally understood that a properly deployed CRM could boost Grey WW-HK/China's bottom line in Asia, Viveca realised the monumental task at hand. She would need to make company-wide transformations in order to implement the GRM philosophy and culture. Grey WW-HK/China would have to embrace a willingness to implement CRM platforms across the organisation and develop skills for setting realistic, measurable ROI goals.

Gartner Research Company's eight key characteristics of a successful CRM strategy could be used to identify the critical success factors important to GRM (refer Table 1).

Gartner's research showed that the companies selected in the study had achieved a level of CRM success and that each had exhibited one or more of the eight characteristics. According to Gartner, companies needed to exhibit one or more of the eight key characteristics in order to be profitable and a key winner in CRM.

Shamza Khan and Marissa McCauley prepared this case under the supervision of Prof. Julie H. Yu and Dr. Ali Farhoomand for class discussion. This case is not intended to show effective or ineffective handling of decision or business processes.

This case is part of a project funded by a teaching development grant from the University Grants Committee (UGC) of Hong Kong.

16. Close, W., Ferrara, C., Galvin, J., Hagemeyer, D., Eisenfeld, B., and Maoz, M. (2001), "CRM at work: Eight characteristics of CRM winners," 19 June, http://web.bentley.edu/empl/c/lchin/mk/crm.htm, 1 August.

Supply chain management

Shamza Khan

To understand the business concepts behind SCM ❑

To review traditional supply chain mechanisms ❑

To discuss the challenges of SCM integration ❑

To develop an understanding of the key differences between traditional, ❑
integrated and collaborative supply chains

To highlight collaborative SCM's importance and why we view it as a future ❑
SCM trend

To learn about SCM metrics ❑

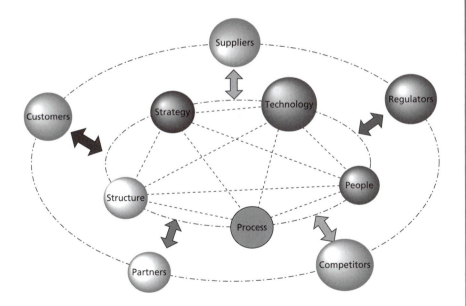

In the first two chapters of this *e-Business Process Management* part, we discussed the role of enterprise-level processes and customer management processes. In this chapter, we examine the last major set of processes that a firm must deal with: supplier-related processes. The term "supply chain management" encompasses the end-to-end process of manufacturing and distributing goods from the supplier of raw materials to the final customer. A major focus of our discussion will be on two key challenges facing companies today: how to integrate and synchronise the business processes associated with a supply chain's upstream and downstream. This integration challenge also involves a discussion of the emerging collaborative SCM model.

Supply chain management (SCM) is the practice of manufacturing and distributing physical goods as efficiently as possible. In Chapter 4, we looked at the role of SCM technologies in enhancing the interactions between an enterprise and its suppliers. Here, we take a more conceptual view of the evolution of SCM. As was noted in our discussion of CRM, the emergence of the Internet has empowered customers to seek out products they want at the prices they are willing to pay. From the supplier's perspective, the "one size fits all" view is no longer valid in today's marketplace. Suppliers must adopt methods that will allow them to respond rapidly to changes in demand.

Modern SCM practices enable companies to optimise their processes and collaborate beyond enterprise boundaries to deliver products to customers in an efficient and timely manner. Inefficient supply chains are a liability in the e-business era with customers unwilling to absorb costs associated with long lead times while being able to migrate to competitors with merely a mouse click. SCM practices, supported by leading technology, offer companies a cost-effective means of aligning internal processes with the realities of the marketplace. SCM is thus one of the most powerful enablers of e-business transformation and in many cases a competitive necessity.

We will proceed by examining some theoretical underpinnings and important concepts relating to SCM. We explore how *downstream* and *upstream* SCM have changed over the years, and emphasise the importance of integrating the two streams. Next we discuss the evolution of SCM, considering the idea of a supply web instead of supply chain. We then present an integrated SCM framework before discussing the collaborative model. Finally the integration challenges are discussed before we explore some of the major issues surrounding SCM performance and metrics.

In the present global environment, many organisations are adopting business models that place greater focus on customer needs. This trend in turn is leading to both an intensified focus on supply chain integration within organisations and greater collaboration between supply chain partners. Companies are increasingly leveraging the Internet's potential for organising information, facilitating demand management, and managing procurement. The Internet is widely viewed as a platform to optimise logistical processes.

The Internet technologies have allowed firms to manage inventory and supply chains in new ways, support changing business models such as direct selling online (Amazon), and develop new ways to improve performance efficiency and resource utilisation.[1] The Web represents an opportunity for supply chain optimisation across geographies, plants, shipping costs, labour, tariffs, processes and customers. By automating supply chains, traditional businesses can evolve into integrated networks of business-to-business (B2B) collaboration. Some corporations have even developed their own marketplaces to serve partners or clients in their supply chains. For example, vendors such as Global Exchange (GE), also provide marketplace development technology enabling businesses to develop their own marketplaces.

The surge in interest in SCM can be attributed to the ever-increasing role that the Internet plays in integrating different processes across and within organisations. The Web provides a low-cost medium for all parties in the business web to communicate. It enables effective and complete information flow at low costs, thus lowering the need for physical ownership of assets. It provides cost-effective connectivity, and increasingly secure transactions built on standards that make communicating simple and straightforward. The Web also works as a universal networking standard, creating seamless interactions amongst business partners and within the organisation. More significantly, the Web has caused a major shift from proprietary business processes towards a more collaborative model. As the competitive global business environment requires businesses to forge tighter relationships with their supply chain partners, the need to extend internal information systems to include partners has become critical. The Web provides such platforms; it leverages legacy resources while at the same time allowing companies to streamline both their internal processes and inter-corporate relations in an integrated manner.

The Web has emerged as the main platform to build an integrated enterprise. It facilitates transformation of supply chains, enhances business visibility through access to real-time information, allows faster time-to-market through process synchronisation, and above all enhances customer centricity through enhanced service. The true power of the Web, however, is unleashed only if companies can approach and manage inter- and intra-corporate processes in an integrated manner. An integrated company can streamline the buying and selling processes, improve interactions with customers and suppliers, and develop outsourcing alliances with partners. Such integration involves not only integrating and managing the supply chain but also the selling chain. This means, managing end-to-end business processes from the time a customer orders a product/service, to the time a customer receives the product/service. Real-time information to deal with suppliers, customers and partners, and extended advantages of integrated information, affect a company's bottom line.

Supply chain and selling-chain process integration changes the way businesses operate. For example, companies engaged in B2B are moving routine aspects of sales processes to the Internet by selling commodity and repeat-purchase products via their e-commerce programs, putting catalogues and product information online, tracking orders and even negotiating prices for some deals. Such front-end

---

1. Hurwitz Group (2001).

integration allows clients themselves to engage in many tasks, such as taking orders or reorders. Integrated supply chain systems result in many benefits, including:

- faster order processing
- better tracking of inventories
- more accurate order fulfilment
- better customer service.

It is now widely believed that since customers are at the centre stage of today's businesses, we should study business process flows in reverse, beginning from customer demand and ending with the sourcing of that product.

In spite of the apparent advantages of integrated SCM, the plight to convince business partners to support interconnectivity and participation in an integrated supply chain is often fraught with obstacles. The case study following this chapter, for instance, gives an account of Eastman Chemical's efforts to elicit support for its integrated electronic supply chain effort by easing the adoption process through the application of XML standards.

Stages in supply chain

Figure 8.1 exhibits the five stages in traditional SCM. Stages 1 and 2 relate to the buying side, or upstream side of the supply chain; they refer to material procurement and material management. Stage 3 relates to manufacturing and production. Stages 4 and 5 refer to the selling, or downstream, side of the supply chain; they include fulfilment and post-sales maintenance with the customer.

Upstream transformation

The Internet allows firms to automate many of their purchasing tasks. These include:[2]

Figure 8.1 Stages in traditional SCM

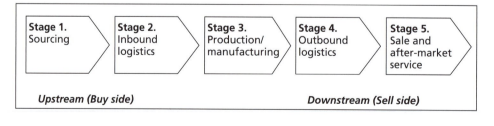

---

2. Chanaron (2001).

- auction/bidding;

- online price quoting;

- order management and follow-up;

- inventory management;

- real-time purchase accounting;

- online quality and logistics problem management;

- budgeting, planning and scheduling;

- marketing and business intelligence;

- data interchange.

The current environment is marked by international competition pressures and rapidly changing technologies driving the business change. As such the trend is to leverage product information throughout the supply chain to shorten product life cycles, and to enhance product customisation. These pressures have forced firms operating in the upstream SCM area to reassess their sourcing strategies and to make procurement processes more efficient.

The Internet's open standards and its global reach make it an ideal platform to achieve these objectives. Firms using the Internet can connect with each other's business processes, flexibly and cheaply. The Web has become an invaluable sourcing tool that saves time and redirects human resources to focus on more strategic management issues. In fact, firms have begun to use the Internet for a wide variety of sourcing-related tasks:

- seeking out sales contacts;

- looking for product information, including prices;

- finding new sources of supply;

- finding delivery information and tracking orders;

- negotiating terms and conditions; and

- receiving technical advice.

The Internet platform allows firms to streamline sourcing processes, reduce market discovery costs and improve overall material procurement. Such cost savings are relatively easy to achieve through consolidated and improved purchase processes. For example, not only does electronic purchasing reduce costs but it also produces more complete data for both buyers and sellers, saves time and enhances security. Traditional firms complain of spending a bulk of their time on operational support activities, such as requisition and purchase order processing, supplier selection and material receipts processing. Technology allows automation of these lower-value processes and relocation of valuable human resources to higher value-added decision support. The Internet allows new business models to emerge in sourcing and aggregation. For example, large buyers are exercising their buying power on the Internet by using reverse auctions sponsored by market makers on an Internet trading platform. In a reverse auction:[3]

- a buyer places a request for quotation (RFQ);

- the market maker qualifies potential bidders; and

- the market maker arranges for bidders to participate in a time-definite reverse auction.

Reverse auctions eliminate information asymmetries and drastically reduce search costs since buyers and sellers seem to operate in a perfectly competitive environment. Procurement aggregation is based on developing volume discounts by consolidating many small buyers together into conglomerates to order goods. By using an Internet aggregator, smaller companies can better manage inventory levels and reduce inventory holding costs. Since a community of buyers consolidate orders, overall costs are reduced through better price negotiation and improved inventory management. Such reduction in coordination costs creates overall efficiency.

SCM integration can only happen when information, material and products flow smoothly and freely, in synchronisation with demand. For example, by extending organisational boundaries to integrate processes between two agents (business and suppliers), suppliers can access information on inventory and replenish it, thus reducing costs associated with carrying high inventory.

Even prior to automating processes, customers and businesses were moving towards integration and interfacing to respond to customers' demand for quicker on-time delivery and better pricing. Today, enabling technologies have dramatically changed the nature of supply chains. Internet technologies, concepts of collaborative demand and supply planning, better forecasts of customer needs and importance of information exchange between suppliers, partners and customers have been radically enhanced through the introduction of technology.

Downstream transformation

Increasing pressure by customers for information transparency and order processing efficiency is pushing firms to provide customers with real-time visibility on product inventory, processing time required and delivery schedules. However, this is contingent on an organisation's ability to translate information into accurate order status and delivery information for customers. As the Internet

---

3. In reverse auctions, a buyer receives bids from multiple sellers and the price decreases as these bidders compete for the buyer's business.

has forced a fundamental shift in consumer buying behaviour and customer service expectations, order fulfilment and customer relationship management have taken centre stage. Effective use of technology has allowed firms to streamline the sell-side of the SCM process, allowing efficient and effective transfers of information to and from customers.

Technology's impact on downstream supply chains is mainly visible through firms' greater ability to configure products to customer orders, confirm availability and track orders and delivery schedules in real time. Improved technology and enhanced process management systems have also dramatically reduced costs of creating and processing purchase orders and keeping inventory. In addition to contracting process chains and improving customer relationship management, technology and process improvements have also created a new dynamic marketplace for conducting B2B e-commerce. These benefits result from implementation of a solid infrastructure capable of delivering the right product/service, at the right time, to the right place, while keeping customers informed along the way.

Information visibility, specifically, as a marketing advantage has helped firms win and retain customers. As companies shorten their supply chain and rely upon more frequent shipments from their trading partners, information on the components' whereabouts becomes even more crucial. As inventory management becomes more of a joint venture, both partners need updated information on goods in production or in transit. Visibility of information translates into logistics value, such as the ability to promise delivery dates or track the delivery process.

Traditional fulfilment and distribution models are based on the push concept: the distributor holds forward inventory to be picked and delivered to an end customer's demand. Now, suppliers can also act as shipment consolidators; distributors receive inbound shipments that are cross-docked to outbound staging lanes for store-level shipment. In order to integrate downstream processes firms must be able to effectively manage customer information from all contact points, including the toll-free call service centre, the voice response system and all sales channels. In the case of an e-commerce firm, firms have to accurately capture orders, move goods from warehouses to customers, track changing inventory levels, capture payment information, and make sure that customer inquiries are handled appropriately and timely.[4]

Evolution of supply chain management

Information technology plays the key role in linking all components of an efficient supply chain, points of production to the points of delivery or purchase. The information which is generated at each stage of product movement allows planning, tracking and estimating lead times to be developed. It is available

---

4. In addition to these demands, companies also have to be concerned about customers in other countries.

internally, or it can be made available to customers. On-time information allows the workings of a seamless supply chain. It gives companies the ability to move swiftly and decisively, and eliminate mundane and repetitive processes in order to manage business with more effectiveness.

Since the 1970s, automobile manufacturers have been trying to improve supply chain workflows and information amongst suppliers through ownership. During the 1980s, forward or backward integration was thought critical to improving supply chain management. SCM tools of the 1980s and 1990s, including material resource planning, just-in-time production, kanban, continuous improvement, time-to-market, and total quality management focused on traditional issues of cost control and improving operating performance. Today, power has shifted to buyers where delivering superior customer service through long-term customer relationship management has become the ultimate priority for many firms. In such environment, enterprising organisations have moved to a collaborative model of supply chain management, where geographically dispersed business partners use shared infrastructures to manage their end-to-end selling and buying chains.

Supply chain management refers to the complex network of relationships that organisations maintain with trading partners to source, manufacture and deliver products. It is the coordination of material, information and financial flows between and among the participating enterprises. The supply chain can then be described as ". . . the network of facilities and activities that perform the functions of product development, procurement of material from vendors, the movement of materials between facilities, the manufacturing of products, the distribution of finished goods to customers, and after-market support for sustainment."[5] In this context, as we show in the next section, it is perhaps more appropriate to regard the supply chain as a web or network of organisations that are involved in different upstream and downstream processes and activities, with the objective of producing value in the form of products and services in the hands of the ultimate customer.[6]

Supply chain or supply web?

As shown in Figure 8.2, in a traditional supply "chain" material and information flow from the suppliers to the manufacturer to distributors to retailers, before reaching the customer. In traditional supply chains, the internal functions are less integrated and interaction between business units is low. In addition, the flow of information is relatively slow and decision-making is based on past information. Logistics management is more labour intensive and supply chain business models lack information or product flow transparency.

As discussed before, the traditional linear supply chain model is by its nature sequential in both physical and information flows. From a physical flow

5. Mabert and Venkataramanan (1998).
6. Lysons and Gillingham (2003).

Figure 8.2 Traditional supply chain

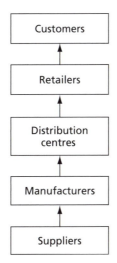

perspective, raw materials and components are purchased before products are produced and marketed. When enough finished products are manufactured, they are moved to warehouses and distribution centres. Ultimately these products are delivered to points of sale or end-users/consumers. From an information-flow perspective, most of the business processes in a linear supply chain (e.g. forecasting, warehousing, procurement, etc.) are typically fully connected only to immediate upstream and downstream activities. A lack of interaction within the organisation creates a culture of independent decision-making between different business units such as supply planning and inventory management. The treatment of supply-related processes as sequential activities, however, has rendered the traditional view of supply chain problematic. Like a waterfall, sequential processes flow from one upstream to the next downstream level. Such sequential flow of information usually leads to one of the most significant problems encountered in supply chain management, that is *bullwhip effect*.

The bullwhip effect occurs when information about the demand for a product gets distorted as it passes from one node in the supply chain to the next. Inaccurate forecasting is at the heart of many of these problems. Observers have noted increases in variance further up the supply chain due to responses made to small changes in consumer demand. For instance, when a retailer notices a drop in inventory levels, it may respond to the short-term spike in demand for a particular product by increasing the size of its next order in hopes of creating a buffer. This action in turn works like a snapping bullwhip, amplifying in effect as distributors, manufacturers and raw-material suppliers upstream adjust their forecasts and production levels in response. Later, the same retailer may find it is carrying too much stock and responds by reducing or postponing a subsequent order, thus creating an inaccurate picture of demand. Poor communication and coordination means that entire supply chains can gradually become prone to large swings as each member seeks to respond to new information from its own perspective. The bullwhip effect has been observed across many industries, and is commonly cited as a precursor to increased costs and poorer service.

As a countermeasure to the bullwhip effect and other supply chain-related problems, leading organisations are pursuing integration and seeking to enhance coordination along their supply chains. Figure 8.3 shows a network representation of today's supply chain.[7] The new era in SCM requires companies to fully understand their roles in the business web in which they operate, synchronise the processes in the supply chain and find new ways to serve their customers better. Traditional companies are coming under pressure to unleash underutilised strategic value within the supply chains.

The glue that puts together such a network – or web – is information. But for such information to be useful it needs to be up-to-date, on-time and accessible to all concerned parties. Integration of supply chain is necessary to ensure that events triggered by any of the participants are synchronised throughout the whole network.

In sum, the traditional supply chain was asset-based, relatively customer-insensitive and slow to acclimate to new business conditions. The objective was to connect individual processes between trading partners, for example EDI transaction sets for purchasing or shipment status. In contrast, the Web-based supply chain is designed to manage one collaborative process rather than multiple processes in an enterprise. This holistic view of supply chain entails collaborative execution between supply chain partners, streamlines the workflow processes, and provides visibility to inventories, purchase order status and transportation status.

Figure 8.3 Supply web

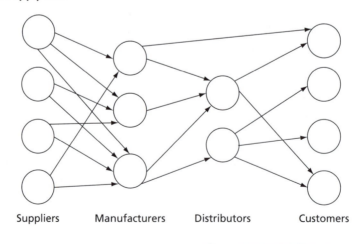

Suppliers   Manufacturers   Distributors   Customers

---

7. In order to prevent confusion we use the term *supply chain* throughout the book.

Integrated supply chain management

Figure 8.4 illustrates the processes involved in developing a tightly integrated supply- and selling-chain framework; it covers the major process areas on the demand side and supply side. The framework can help us assess where supplier and customer values are emerging and how we can use e-business to manage these processes more efficiently. It is based on the premise that since companies cannot internally achieve excellence in all areas of business they increasingly focus on pulling together requisite skills and expertise through partnerships and alliances to achieve quality across a full spectrum of business processes.

We can use this framework of business processes to see how to add value through e-business transformation. As we discussed, by using the Internet as a universal networking standard, business partners can create seamless, automated supply chain systems. Technology allows connectivity within a supply chain and enables the development of an extended enterprise. This enterprise differs from the traditional one because of its ability to link its logistics and manufacturing processes with customers, suppliers and other business partners. Network application

Figure 8.4 An integrated SCM framework

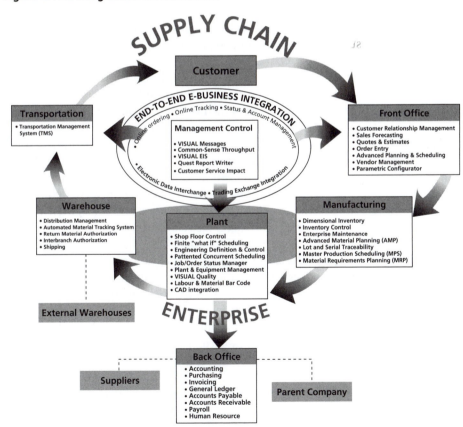

Source: Figure courtesy of Lilly Software Associates, Inc.

technologies can be used to extend processes from within the supply chain enterprise and make them visible to business partners externally. The key principle is to provide a holistic business model that involves the customer throughout.

The integrated SCM enterprise in Figure 8.4 also indicates that to link all the selling- and supply chain nodes, firms must rely heavily on shared global networks, shared information and mutual collaboration among all parties along the chain. Each node is a strategic key and every link adds value to the chain. For example, inventory management point should be able to access any data in the system from a single point of contact and any component should be able to analyse relevant business decisions based on the information from the entire supply chain. The integrated SCM approach unites all steps in the business cycle: from initial product design and the procurement of raw materials, through production, shipping, distribution and warehousing until a finished product is delivered to a customer. Because any network is as good as its weakest node, every node in the supply chain is of strategic significance.

Collaborative supply chain management

Today customers and suppliers have become mutually dependent in businesses. They need to collaborate through the sharing of relevant information and focus on managing both the demand and supply process. In such environment, businesses and their suppliers are moving away from conflicting goals towards building an integrated supply chain.

New business dynamics, driven by technology, integration, customer focus and tighter business partnerships, are creating the need for new, nonlinear SCM business models. The collaboration management philosophy emerging for SCM is a long-term, strategic management perspective of how to view supply chains. Continuous business pressure emanating from a need for real-time information, faster-to-market product delivery and high visibility with partners will further expedite the development and proliferation of tighter collaborative supply chains. We should anticipate continuing evolution of SCM towards collaborative models where value is added through on-time information, tighter integration with supply partners, or deeper customer relationship.

We are already witnessing changes to traditional SCM as companies are increasingly focusing on building investment visibility and clearer strategic and financial objectives. Achieving objectives such as lowering costs, shortening lead times and facilitating updated information flow require supply chains to evolve towards a collaborative business model. Because of increased visibility throughout the collaborative supply network, all participants gain more control of what is happening at each step in this complex process. In essence, moving SCM away from handling of discrete events allows improvements in costs, quality, time to market, and sales.

Table 8.1 highlights the fact that by taking a holistic management view, SCM emerges as a comprehensive methodology for handling logistics activities when integrated with production and marketing aspects. The pressure to build an integrated collaborative supply and selling chain is a result of the growing focus on customers and their rising power. Customers demand shorter order

Table 8.1 Evolution of supply chain management

	Traditional supply chains	Integrated supply chain management	Collaboration supply chain management
Procurement	● Leverage purchasing knowledge to procure at the lowest price ● Low interaction with other organisational units	● Integrated decision making amongst other organisational units ● Cost minimisation major business objective ● Long-range planning developed to reduce costs	● Strategic sourcing ● Supplier segmentation – differentiation between key suppliers ● Access to exchanges and auctions as a means to secure supply of raw materials, etc.
Planning	● Supply planning based on historical production records	● Integrated demand forecasting, planning and scheduling ● Execute sales and operations planning	● Collaborative planning, forecasting and replenishment (CPFR) ● Higher frequency of sales and operations planning
Scheduling	● Minimise manufacturing costs ● Low interaction with supply planning unit	● Higher interaction with customer service units ● Stronger interaction with supply chain planning	● Collaborative scheduling, involving interaction with the front-end (customers) and back-end (internal)
Inventory Management	● Inventory treated as independent business variable ● Slow information gathering and dissemination	● Align inventory policies with customer service levels ● Low inventory key to maintaining low costs	● Network optimisation ● Collaborative replenishment and vendor managed inventory
Logistics and Warehouse Management	● Labour intensive ● Low transparency	● Automation of logistic functions such as packing and shipping ● Value added to customer through more customer information	● Real-time information provided to other organisational units on tracking, tracing and shipment status ● Value added to customers through information visibility
Sales/Customer Service	● Reactive customer service ● Minimal interaction with manufacturing unit ● Low customer history information	● Align customer service levels according to customer segmentations	● Integrated customer relationship management ● Higher collaboration around all business process extending beyond the enterprise to key customers and suppliers

Source: Muzumdar and Balachandran (2001). Reproduced with Permission by Aspen Technology Inc.

processes, effective systems to manage feedback to their inquiries and sales order, and efficient delivery infrastructures. In essence, customers are demanding more value. In return companies are reacting by investing in a wide range of capabilities to integrate, automate and manage sales interactions throughout an enterprise by catering to individual customers.

In the past, each enterprise treated SCM processes as an internal matter. Such inter-organisational incompatibility however made streamlining and automating inter-corporate processes difficult. This problem was ameliorated to a certain degree through the use of standardised EDI transaction sets in the 1980s and 1990s. But the widespread adoption of EDI was retarded, among other things, by high cost and the proprietary nature of most value-added networks. The Internet, intranets and extranets largely changed that by allowing companies to design common interfaces embedded in an open e-business architecture. By building their e-business on such open architectures, companies have been able to closely integrate their business processes with those of their trading partners, thus extending their market reach, increasing sales and improving customer service.

For example, several research studies reveal that the use of Point of Sales (POS) information can significantly improve demand management, including transferring information from one part of the supply chain to the other. But this was not possible before the dawn of the Internet because single EDI transaction sets were not integrated with POS and demand forecast information. The Internet allows integration of POS data and forecast data to be provided simultaneously to all collaborators participating in a supply chain. The availability of up-to-date and cost-effective information enables quick adjustments, unified planning and improved communication within the supply web.

In the past approach of application integration, firms built point-to-point integration, one application at a time; but that is changing. In recent years the Internet has allowed firms to use open standards such as XML to connect various components of the supply chain, including interface devices, communications, databases and open architectures. Such business shift has resulted in improved market efficiencies, increasing rates of change, and a far greater number of customer choices.

Integration challenge

Supply chain management integration remains challenging and management has to ensure that it continues to identify, minimise and solve problems. Even well-tuned supply chains can become inefficient over time, for several reasons:

- changing demand creates expensive, unplanned changes and setup charges;
- incorrect forecasts lead to inventory problems;
- ad hoc changes in processes create high labour costs; and
- last-minute orders mean high freight and express charges.

Inter-organisational technologies allow a firm to be flexible, support core company processes and extend a firm's reach beyond the firm. Not only has e-business allowed firms to cut costs by automating their transactional processes, it has also lead to improved customer services through rapid response times. But companies can reap the benefits of e-business only if they can successfully reengineer their internal processes so that these processes are in synch with those involved in the selling and supply chains of their trading partners. Such integration is perhaps one of the most difficult and challenging jobs facing businesses today.

Through appropriate deployment of technology, companies could accomplish operational excellence by streamlining and integrating their supply and selling chains. The upshot of such process integration is that all business units can work in tandem with one another in terms of goals, processes and customer relations. The critical factor is maintaining a tightly integrated supply and selling chain within which each process is designed to add value to customers. Because interweaving the selling and supply chains requires management of many complex and interrelated links, interactions and partnerships, it is a very difficult part of formulating and implementing an e-business strategy.

Firms are realising that to tie sales processes to back-end logistics requires applying enabling technologies to traditional processes. However, while technology implementations and collaboration with supply partners have allowed firms to create broad efficiencies cost-effectively across a firm, they have also created many risks, including increased investment costs and possible loss of relationships with existing suppliers. Table 8.2 summarises several risks and benefits of transforming traditional SCM to an integrated SCM model.

Table 8.2 Summary of risks and benefits

Risks	Benefits
Downward pressure on prices	Savings in procurement costs such as transaction and operation administration
Increasing IT costs	Direct revenues from the exchange system through commissions, transaction fees and service fees
Standardisation as opposed to customisation and variety	Design cost savings through standardisation
Supply base expansion	Savings due to a more efficient supply chain, i.e. less components in the supply chain process
Losing a world-class supplier	Promoting and leveraging supplier efficiency
Increased risk of lost corporate data	Optimising purchasing processes
	Transparency across the supplier base
	Satisfying OEM requests

Source: Chanaron (2001).

Cost-savings through integration of the supply chain reduces costs and time necessary to exchange transactional information between the supply chain partners. Consider, for example, the savings in procurement costs. As suppliers are able to access inventory and procurement information automatically, they can shift attention from low value transaction activities towards more strategic activities such as vendor sourcing and supplier relationship management, or savings in inventory cost made possible through better channel visibility. But as more competitors adopt these cost-saving technologies, the savings are passed to customers, putting pressure on prices. Another risk is exposing internal processes to partner suppliers and other relationships within the integrated supply chain.

Many existing SCM businesses have found it difficult to develop tightly integrated systems or to reinvent their traditional processes. For most firms the most difficult barrier is perhaps to overcome the traditional view that various functions involved in the business cycle are separate entities. Adopting an integrated organisational method, as we discussed, represents a holistic perspective from which a business is seen as part of an ecosystem – a network of firms. By seeing each firm within the supply chain as an interdependent partner, and by regarding logistics as an integrated part of the entire business system, a company can move closer to its ultimate purpose: enhancing customer service through flawless delivery of customised service.

Another problem is management focus on cost-minimisation: it is a timid objective and short sighted for strategic planning and long-term sustainability. Instead, supply chain network optimisation models should seek to maximise net revenues by incorporating demand management decision options. Related objectives, such as maximising return on assets also need to be incorporated in senior management decisions.

In spite of these difficulties, and given the competitive nature of today's business environment, firms must build trusting relationships with suppliers and customers. The risks and costs of losing business partners are too high. It is near impossible to function effectively without collaboration with business partners. For example, through its integrative supply chain, the "Dell Model" has reduced complexity, increased personalisation and reduced costs. Interestingly these benefits have been achieved by outsourcing all aspects of the product to many different partners.

Supply chain metrics

The existence of overlapping supply chains – so common in today's business environment – makes the development of supply chain metrics difficult. Nevertheless, managers are keen to increase their visibility over both the areas they do control and those which indirectly impact their company's performance. To gain this type of insight, businesses need to build metrics to track and measure their success in implementing SCM solutions and to devise outward-looking performance assessments of their business partners. Comparing existing performance to benchmarked performance metrics can be useful in helping companies determine whether they can benefit from becoming more integrated and externally focused. The performance measurement framework we presented in Chapter 3 may be applied when measuring the success of SCM solutions: managers must go about charting a linkage of needs and responses (for internal stakeholders and external business partners) to identify the most essential goals relating to SCM practices and subsequently, to determine the most appropriate measures for evaluating performance.

There are a variety of supply chain performance indicators that can be used; determining a set of metrics and then collecting the associated measurement data is a simple yet effective way to analyse program performance. However, managers should pay careful consideration to ensure that the chosen measures are relevant to the work of purchasing staff and affected departments, and that all stakeholder groups understand what is being measured and in principle view the measurement effort as being credible and flexible enough to adapt to changing circumstances.

Some possible SCM metrics include:[8]

- *Delivery performance*: requested versus actual dates at the line-item level.
- *Percentage of on-time deliveries.*
- *Percentage of incoming defects requiring refurbishment or return to suppliers.*
- *Total cycle time*: from requisition to production.
- *Cash-to-cash cycle time*: measuring the time it takes to close the loop between funds utilisation (material acquisition) and collection (invoice payment).
- *Pay on receipt*: measure the time required to match and reconcile invoices.
- *Material availability*: the number of days required to achieve a sustainable increase in production.
- *Total supply chain costs*: the total cost, as a percent of sales, to manage order processing, acquire materials, manage inventory and manage supply chain finance, planning and MIS costs.
- *Order accuracy*: products delivered versus what was ordered.
- *Replenishment*: the time it takes to replenish inventory and the accuracy of the replenishments.
- *Customer service level/fill rate*: items available in stock for delivery per purchase order.

In the domain of SCM, the balanced scorecard technique (see Table 8.3), which we covered in Chapter 3, is especially popular with managers. While it was not

8. Rabin (2002).

Table 8.3 Sample balanced scorecard metrics for measuring supply chain performance

Scorecard area	Sample metrics
Financial	Estimated operating expenses, Cost of warehousing, Transfer cost of supplies, Return on assets controlled by supplies, sales dollars per purchasing employee
Customer perspective	Order fill rate, On-time deliveries, Quality assurance measures (e.g. shipments without damage)
Internal business processes	Forecasting accuracy, Manufacturing cycle time
Ongoing learning and innovation	Professionalism of purchasing staff, internal stakeholder satisfaction

specifically designed for SCM measurement, it offers an effective means for tracking several key measures under the four scorecard areas. By gauging performance through a balanced scorecard approach, managers can make sure that they focus on several core measures which reflect the context of their business and which are aligned with enterprise objectives.

Some businesses however, are becoming weary of implementing complex performance targets which are difficult to review or understand. Some firms may want to concentrate on a fundamental financial analysis before implementing an SCM project and traditional financial metrics can be simple, yet effective tools to review SCM performance (perhaps more applicable for firms with disparate SCM functions). A fundamental financial analysis approach is one which may be considered in the case study *Shun Sang (H.K.) Co. Ltd: Streamlining Logistical Flow*, which gives an account of a small business that invested heavily in experimental IT solutions to streamline operations.

A "back to basics" focus would necessarily include using free cash flow (FCF) as a tool to evaluate investments; in traditional accounting, a FCF stream is indicative of a business' general health. FCF analysis can provide a financial overview. It can also highlight the status of various SCM-related efficiencies, such as inventory churn, or if appropriate trade credit is being used to finance growth, and even help firms to balance transaction costs appropriately with the asset cost itself. Another basic method to understand SCM performance under the FCF mechanism is to understand if customers, suppliers, products, and services contribute or consume free cash flow. This analysis has become especially critical in tough economic conditions, as investors are willing to pay premiums for companies generating strong and quality cash flows. In addition, measuring the percentage of FCF to sales (a term referred to as the *cash velocity*) for each customer, for example, enhances a firm's ability to understand the true value of each customer. Given that a likely scenario for many companies is that approximately 20 per cent of the customers or product lines create 80 per cent of the FCF within the company, and 20 per cent of the customers consume 80 per cent of the cash that is consumed below the line.

By developing simple metric and performance criteria, firms can arrive at sound conclusions on an SCM project's viability and better determine asset allocation within the SCM value chain and how to use resources efficiently. Developing a strong SCM metric framework also helps companies execute focused SCM strategies; performance criteria can guide firms on using SCM implementations to focus on containment of operating costs, effective capital deployment, effective risk management and using the SCM as an integral business model through which to generate revenue and create customer value.

Summary

Supply chain management has been deemed a useful tool for businesses to enhance their competitiveness, and to build up their trust relationship with upstream and downstream businesses. Transaction cost economics and core competency theories are some major reasons why firms may want to effectuate a shift, however, management must understand the fundamental shift in upstream and downstream SCM transformation to make the transition effectively.

The Internet is a compelling platform to conduct many back-end and front-end functions; new technologies such as HTML and XML are creating new methods for companies to integrate processes, transform data into information and manage business relationships with internal and external clients to create value. Eastman Chemical, for example, developed XML infrastructure to initiate purchase orders with companies that did not have the means to fully adjust their business processes for integration with Eastman's electronic supply chain initiative. In order to link the whole value chain, information technology (IT) application has been essential for enterprises. In conclusion, enterprises must converge ERP, by combining electronic SCM and CRM with competitive advantage.

However, SCM integration challenges remain. While collaborative SCM is a strategic and comprehensive model to manage a firm's business, there are several risks in facilitating a shift from traditional supply chain processes. Businesses need to understand how their supply chains can evolve from traditional models to collaborative models, how customer value will be impacted and whether the changes in procurement, inventory management and customer service can benefit a firm's bottom line, add strategic value or provide firms with a competitive advantage.

The financial and strategic visibility of technology investment issues has gained tremendous importance; as a result, metrics are becoming critical in evaluating whether new technologies provide adequate returns on investment. Firms need to focus on building appropriate performance benchmarks to evaluate their supply chain efficiency. Finally, value can be discovered from SCM processes or SCM strategy – collaborative SCM however has emerged as a strategic business model through which firms can cut costs, build a competitive edge, create loyalty with business partners and build long-term *sustainable* firm value. Firms can also capitalise on new technologies to manage inventory and supply chains in new ways or to customise existing and new technologies to support changing business models.

Questions for discussion

1 Discuss three business theories managers can think about when planning to improve existing supply chains?

2 Discuss the Internet's impact on upstream SCM?

3 What are some of the risks and benefits with transforming traditional supply chain processes?

4 Highlight the key differences between integrated SCM and collaborative SCM?

5 How does information visibility impact downstream SCM?

6 Develop four key strategies on how traditional firms may leverage the integrated SCM model to improve their process management?

7 Outline problems of traditional firms in effectively integrating their SCM processes?

8 What are the key benefits of adopting a collaborative SCM approach vs an integrated SCM approach?

9 Discuss how incorporating metrics can impact a firms SCM outlook?

References

Chanaron, J. (2001) "Rationale and future of digital procurement: the case of the automotive industry", paper from the CoCKEAS-Meeting, 4–5 October, available from http://www.e.u-tokyo.ac.jp/itme/grnbl/papers/JJC-FJWorkshop-10-2001.pdf [accessed 20 July 2001].

Hurwitz Group (2001) *e-Business Infrastructure Management: The Key to Business Success*, Framingham, MA: Hurwitz Group.

Lysons, K. and Gillingham, M. (2003) *Purchasing and Supply Chain Management*, Prentice-Hall.

Mabert, V.A. and Venkataramanan, M.A. (1998) "Special research focus on supply chain linkages: challenges for design and management in the 21st century", *Decision Sciences*, vol. 29, no. 3, pp. 537–52.

Muzumdar, M. and Balachandran, N. (2001) "The supply chain evolution: roles, responsibilities and implications for management", *AspenTech* [online], 1 October, available from http://www.aspentech.com/publication_files/APICS10-01.pdf [accessed 18 June 2002].

Rabin, S. (2002) "Measuring collaborative performance: metrics for inter-enterprise e-business", *line56.com* [online], 7 January, available from http://www.line56.com/articles/default.asp?articleid=3273 [accessed 5 February 2003].

Further reading

Bruce, H. (2000) "Five steps to successful eFulfillment", paper from the DCI's eB2BWorld Conference and Exposition, 7 December.

Clark, T.H. and Lee, H.B. (1999) "Performance, interdependence and coordination in business-to-business electronic commerce and supply chain management", *Information Technology & Management*, vol. 01, no. 1–2, pp. 85–105.

Davenport, T.H. and Short, J.E. (1990) "The new industrial engineering: information technology and business process redesign", *Sloan Management Review*, vol. 31, no. 4, pp. 11–21.

Davenport, T.H. (1993) *Process Innovation*, Boston, MA: Harvard Business School Press.

Gossain, S. and Kenworthy, R. (2000) "Winning in the third wave of e-business: beyond net markets", *NerveWire* [online], December, available from http://www.nervewire.com/pdf/winning.pdf [accessed 23 August 2001].

Greenbaum, J. (2001) "Evaluating the supply chain: the case for business analytics and peoplesoft's supply chain insight", *PeopleSoft* [online], September, available from http://www.peoplesoft.com/media/en/pdf/209.pdf [accessed 2 August 2002].

Kalakota, R., Robinson, M. and Tapscott, D. (1999) *e-Business: Roadmap for Success*, Reading, Mass.: Addison-Wesley.

Kulkami, S. (2001) "Beyond the bricks: organisations look to create extended supply chains over the Internet", *Wipro Technologies* [online], 1 January, available from www.wipro.com/pdf_files/beyond_the_bricks.pdf [accessed 3 October 2002].

Malhotra, Y. (1998) "Business process redesign: an overview", *IEEE Engineering Management Review*, vol. 26, no. 3, Fall, available from http://www.brint.com/papers/bpr.htm [accessed 12 December 2001].

McKendrick, J. (1999) "Procurement: the next frontier in e-business", *Midrange Systems*, Spring House, vol. 12, no. 11, p. 27.

Michael, T. and Fath, M. (2001) "Streamlining supply chain management through e-procurement", presentation at 2001 OFDA Dealer Strategies Technology Summit, March, available from http://www.ofdanet.org/Content/2002TechSummit/Presentations/KPMG.pdf [accessed 25 October 2002].

NxTrend Technology (2001) "Optimising the supply chain from back office to e-business", NxTrend Technology, Inc., June, available from http://www.idii.com/wp/nxtrend_optimize_SC.pdf [accessed 17 April 2002].

O'Brien, K.P. (2000) "Value-chain report: the supply chain of the future looks more like a web", *Industryweek.com* [online], 3 April, available from http://www.iwvaluechain.com/Columns/columns.asp?ColumnId=598 [accessed 10 December 2001].

Porter, M.E. (1985) *Competitive Advantage*, Free Press: New York.

Reddy, R. (2002) "The evolution of supply chain technologies", *Intelligent Enterprise* [online], 14 January, available from http://www.intelligententerprise.com/020114/502infosc1_1.shtml?/supply_chain|supply [accessed 20 August 2002].

Srinivasan, M., Reeve, J. and Singh, M. (2000) "e-Business in the supply chain", paper from SSGRR Conference 2000, 2 August, available from http://www.ssgrr.it/en/ssgrr2000/papers/217.pdf [accessed 13 February 2003].

Schmidt, G. (1998) "Supply chain management", *The McDonough School of Business*, December, available from http://www.msb.edu/faculty/bios/schmidt/SupplyChain.PDF [accessed 19 June 2000].

Case study 1   Constructing an e-supply chain at Eastman Chemical Company

Considering how many companies we deal with around the world, we only have 22 companies connected at this stage. We still have a long way to go. We have an infrastructure that would allow us to connect with hundreds of strategic partners, but it is slow for partners to take it on board . . . One of the hurdles now is with companies having sufficiently integrated systems internally to actually get the value from connecting with us . . . In pushing others to adopt the technology, we are trying to get the industry to adopt the e-business approach.
– Craig Knight, Digital Business & Customer Services Manager – Asia Pacific

It was a sultry day in the middle of June 2002. Craig Knight, Asia Pacific Digital Business and Customer Services Manager of Eastman Chemical Company, was heading out of his Singapore regional head office on another two-week trip to Tokyo, Shanghai and Kuantan in Malaysia. The mandate he had been given was to sell Eastman's philosophy for an integrated electronic supply chain, otherwise known as the Integrated System Solution (ISS), to its business partners in the region, and to encourage adoption. Having invested in a state-of-the-art technical architecture that would support interconnectivity with all parties along the supply chain, Eastman was keen to realise the full benefits to be gained from an integrated e-supply chain on a global scale. Following numerous rounds of discussion with key business partners in the Asia Pacific region, some progress had been made. Nagase & Co., Ltd. of Japan had agreed to adopt ISS connections with Eastman, but had some reservations regarding the extent of integration. Although the benefits of integration were proven, suppliers, customers, distributors and other interested parties were faced with numerous limitations and considerations that would have significant implications on their established business processes and even the shaping of their corporate strategy. Adoption was not a simple choice. Craig understood

these shortcomings and was making every effort to ease the adoption process by identifying the longer-term benefits to Nagase and other business partners of applying XML technology to their businesses.

The chemical industry

The chemical industry consisted of manufacturers of basic and immediate chemicals, specialty chemicals, agricultural chemicals, petrochemicals, plastics and fibres, and paints and coatings. It provided intermediate and raw materials for industry and a variety of synthetic and formulated products for industry, agriculture, business and individual consumers.[1] At the same time, it was dependent on many of these same industries for raw materials, including, for example, agriculture and petroleum. The relationship between the industries is illustrated in Exhibit 1.

The industry was unique in many ways. Unlike, say, the steel industry, which made a group of products from only a few key raw materials, the chemical industry took low-cost basic chemicals and converted them into a series of intermediaries that would, in turn, be reacted or formulated into a wide variety of end products, usually of high unit value and for a diverse range of industries. In this way, many chemicals were actually the raw materials for making usable end products.

Synthesis and formulation were the two basic technologies used in the industry. Formulation involved mixing the chemicals by blending, emulsification, solution or other physical manipulation. Synthesis was a newer processing technique used to create new

---

1. "Economics of the Industry: US Specialty Chemicals, 1999, GAPS Sheet", Kline & Company, http://www. klinegroup.com/Practices/chemicals/industry_business.htm, accessed 4 June 2002.

Exhibit 1 The chemical industry: materials and product flow

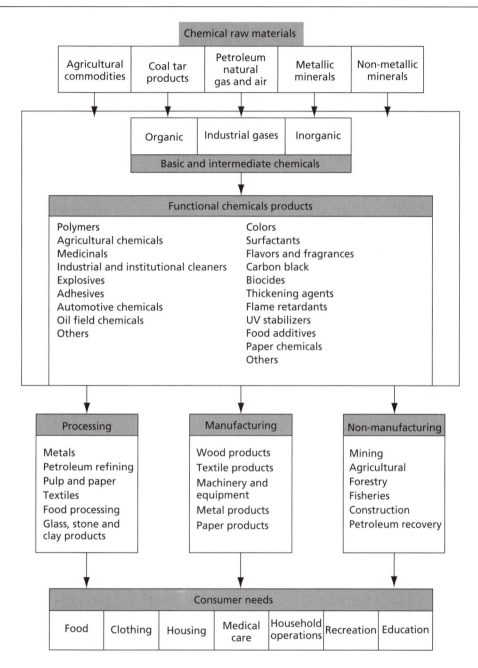

Source: "Economics of the Industry: US Specialty Chemicals, 1999, GAPS Sheet", Kline & Company, http://www.klinegroup.com/Practices/chemicals/industry_business.htm, accessed 4 June 2002.

synthetic products. Through these technologies the industry grew by 2.9 per cent annually in terms of physical output between 1985 and 1998.[2] Formulated products could achieve proprietary positions as they were continually modified to meet customers' changing needs.

The chemical industry was also unique in terms of capital investment, ranking second in the world when measured by annual expenditure. The cost of building a new facility would often be hundreds of millions of dollars. Large plants were needed to incorporate efficiencies and economies of scale.

The demand for chemicals was directly correlated to the demand for consumer products. The industry was highly dependent on the automobile, manufacturing and housing business sectors, which were very cyclical. Supply and demand imbalances resulting from economic cycles were a major concern for chemical companies. The imbalance was also partly due to the limited flexibility of the continuous and semi-continuous manufacturing processes requisite for producing chemicals. Such processes complicated overall supply chain planning.

Most continuous, semi-continuous and batch processes operated 24/7. The processing of materials was transferred automatically from one stage to the next, with monitoring and self-adjusting flow and quality forming part of the automated process. The only human intervention involved checking the system. The enormous capital investment meant that maximising operating time was a major concern for manufacturers. Furthermore, the nature of the processes was complex and procedures for shutdowns and start-ups were costly. Hence, the manufacturing cycles were more or less fixed and measured in weeks or months. Unexpected fluctuations in demand or unexpected problems with equipment created

major problems for inventory management and customer service performance. Another factor affecting inventory management was the practice of "optimal transition wheels", where multiple products shared one reactor and production was restricted by a time sequence. For example, a paint manufacturer might make green paint only once every 45 days due to product sequence restrictions.

In 1999, the chemical industry reported a very difficult year, impacted by weakened international economies, slackening demand, over-capacity and a squeeze on prices and margins.[3] These factors made for some of the poorest results in many years. Players in the industry resolved to find new and innovative ways to improve profitability while delivering superior customer service, reducing operating costs, improving plant efficiencies and lowering inventory costs.

The traditional strategies were to extract additional value from existing assets: improving sales and operations functions, reaping economies of scale and capturing synergies. However, the most forward-thinking companies were beginning to see the need to improve supply chain planning processes as the key to future success. The characteristics of the chemical business (notably its finite capacity and cyclical-based manufacturing processes) required a three-way balance of agile demand planning, agile production scheduling and efficient distribution of inventories.[4]

Eastman Chemical and its e-business strategy

Eastman Chemical Company, headquartered in Kingsport, Tennessee, manufactured over 1,200 chemicals, fibres and plastics. It was

2. "Economics of the Industry: US Specialty Chemicals, 1999, GAPS Sheet", Kline & Company, http://www.klinegroup.com/Practices/chemicals/industry_business.htm, accessed 4 June 2002.

3. "2001 Chemical Industry Review", *Chemical and Engineering News*, http://pubs.acs.org/cen/topstory/7952/7952bus1.html, accessed on 4 June 2002.
4. "Chemical Companies Discover Supply Chain Planning is Key to Increasing Revenues", http://wamsystems.com, accessed on 3 June, 2002.

the world's largest supplier of polyester plastics for packaging; a leading supplier of coatings raw materials, specialty chemicals and plastics, and a major supplier of cellulose acetate fibres and basic chemicals. In addition, Eastman was one of the top 10 global suppliers of custom-manufactured fine chemicals for pharmaceuticals, agricultural chemicals and other markets. Its chemicals and polymers kept paints and coatings from cracking and extended the shelf life of foods; were used in the manufacture of safer medical equipment, film for smaller electronic devices and more efficient circuit boards for computers; retarded mould in animal feed; enabled garden hoses to bend; contributed to the manufacturing of packaging for beverages, foods, electronics, cosmetics, pharmaceuticals and household products; were raw materials for producing credit and debit cards, electrical connectors, medical devices, vending machines, signs, display cases, carpet fibre, binding fibre for car interiors and upholstery, heavy-duty shipping sacks and pond liners, toothbrushes and tool handles, sports equipment and movie and X-ray film; and were used as ingredients for artificial sweeteners, pain medication, bleach activators in laundry detergent, safety glass, vinyl flooring, disposable gloves, toys and countless other consumer products. As the needs of its customers evolved, so did its product offerings.

Eastman employed 15 800 people in more than 30 countries, with manufacturing sites strategically located in 17 countries. Sales in 2001 amounted to US$5.4 billion, of which the Asia Pacific Region accounted for US$547 million. In the 5 December 2001, issue of *Chemical Week*, Eastman was ranked 43rd by sales, 59th by profitability and 29th by innovation in the US$1.7 trillion global industry.

Our primary rationale for making digital business investments has been to enable Eastman to help transform the way the chemical industry does business and to help create industry standards.

– Roger Mowen, CIO and VP – Global Customer Solutions[5]

Eastman was a recognised industry and world leader in e-business transformation. It was the first chemical company to offer customers an easier way to do business with the Company through a portfolio of Web-enabled options. Its e-business strategy included an online store-front and transactional Customer Centre; Web-enabled auctions; alliances and investments in digital business ventures, and system-to-system (S2S) ERP connections. The foundational principles for its e-business strategy were:

- to focus on creating customer-centric solutions;
- to hold a portfolio of options, choices and solutions for customers via electronic channels;
- to invest in technologies/capabilities that bring real value to customers;
- to be externally focused;
- to form partnerships ("We cannot do it alone");
- to build an "e-brand" to attract customers, suppliers and technology partners; and
- to leverage its intellectual capital, industry knowledge, network of contacts, credibility, brand and customer base.

The Customer Centre (at www.eastman.com), launched in July 1999, enabled registered users to access Eastman's product information (including technical specifications); check the status of orders; access certificates of analysis, material safety data sheets and other compliance-related documents; track railcar shipments and access the Technical Help service desk. Other e-business related initiatives and capabilities that were introduced are listed in Exhibit 2.

---

5. "Eastman Announces e-Business results for 2000 Establishes e-Business Goals for 2001", News Archive, http://www.eastman.com, 26 February, 2001, accessed on 28 May, 2002.

Exhibit 2 Eastman's e-business initiatives and capabilities

July 1999	Launched Customer Centre on its Website in North America. This enabled registered users to access Eastman's product information (data sheets, etc.), check the status of orders, access certificates of analysis, material safety data sheets and other compliance-type documents, track railcar shipments and access the Technical Help service desk. This made Eastman the first chemical company to do business online. ($300 million + online revenue reported in 2000.)
September 1999	Announced Eastman's equity investment in ChemConnect, the largest global Internet exchange, making it the first charter Member. The horizontal marketplace provided an open neutral environment where buyers and sellers from around the world met, in real time, to negotiate transactions for all types of chemicals. ChemConnect's World Chemical Exchange was the world's largest Internet chemical exchange, with over 2000 members.
October 1999	Established relationships with Dell Computer Corporation and UUNET to create a Customer Enabling Program that would make it easier for Eastman customers in the US to engage in e-commerce via eastman.com. The program aimed to help customers who did not have computer hardware or Internet access to obtain these capabilities through Dell and UUNET, thus removing barriers to e-commerce.
November 1999	Launched EastmanMarketPlace.com, an online solution to quickly liquidate certain materials on an as-needed basis. Auctions are private – by invitation only – in order to ensure that the audience contains valid and qualified participants.
December 1999	Launched Customer Centre globally.
February 2000	Announced its first B2B pilot programme to provide a direct link via the Internet from Eastman's backend systems to the IT infrastructures of its customer, Albemarle Corporation, and its supplier, Rayonier. The link was enabled by webMethodsB2B. This demonstrated the ability to link separate systems not originally designed to communicate with one another using a Web-enabled platform. Also affirmed the value of supplier-customer partnerships. Eastman pioneered B2B e-commerce in the chemical industry.
February 2000	Announced a strategic alliance with SESAMI.com to pioneer e-commerce for the chemical industry in Asia. Eastman became the first tenant on SESAMI.com's chemical portal and implemented SESAMI.com's Web-based eMRO (materials, repairs and operations materials) solution at its plants across Asia. The portal provided a comprehensive online catalogue, auction services, information and e-procurement for direct and indirect goods and services. For Eastman, the vertical portal reduced search and information transfer costs and enhanced matching for buyers and sellers.
February 2000	Nagase & Co., Ltd.(Headquarters: Tokyo), Eastman's largest distributor in Asia Pacific, began placing orders online through eastman.com.
August 2000	Completed migration from IBM DB2 to the Oracle®Database for its SAP R/3 environment in August 2000. The migration was to ensure scalability and the high availability of its databases and performance features, thus promoting Eastman's e-business infrastructure to become faster, more reliable and cheaper.
January 2001	Completion of Chem eStandards initiative with Chemical Industry Data eXchange (CIDX). CIDX was a global trade association and standards body whose mission was to improve the ease, speed and cost of conducting business electronically between chemical companies and their trading partners. Eastman was one of 60 companies that actively participated in the development, use and promotion of XML-based Chem eStandards. They were designed to facilitate the electronic buying, selling and delivery of products across the industry. CIDX also offered a neutral foundation to explore collaborative solutions.
April 1997	Implemented Logility Voyager Solutions to enable collaborative forecasting based on the latest sales data rather than historical trends. Logility's top customer award ("*John Hewson* Sailing to New Heights with Logility" award for supply chain excellence) was named in honour of an Eastman employee who contributed significantly to Logility's product development, and who sadly passed away in 2000.
April 2002	Partnered with Yantra to streamline direct procurement with its small and medium-sized suppliers (those companies that did not plan to build a direct connection to Eastman's SAP ERP system). These suppliers represented up to 30% of direct and 70% of indirect procurement spend.

Other significant achievements:
- The first chemical company to go global on one instance of SAP
- Dell's first customer to have a global desktop standard
- CommerceOne's second customer
- webMethods flagship customer and partner in chemicals supply chain
- The first chemical company to adopt Saqqara, Yantra, ePrise, Idiom, Moai and others.

Eastman announced significant achievements towards its e-business goals in 2001. Electronic sales were approaching 30 per cent of total annual sales through all electronic channels such as eastman.com, eastmanmarketplace.com, online marketplaces, EDI and ISS. Over 30 per cent of total procurement for direct and indirect materials was procured electronically. It managed to establish over 20 system-to-system connections with key trading partners. Three digital business ventures were launched in 2000: PaintandCoatings.com, a provider of marketing and commerce solutions for the paint and coatings industry; Cendian Corporation, a virtual logistics provider for in-transit freight and services; and Asia BizNet, an organisation that aimed to facilitate chemical industry e-business solution investments in China and Asia. These ventures were aimed at creating new solutions and reducing inefficiencies in the chemical industry.

Eastman's mission was to make it easier for business partners to do business with Eastman and to invest in technologies that would bring value to customers. The goals were to change the way the Company interacted with customers and other business partners, and to transform its internal business processes.

Linking the front end and the backend

In 1992, Eastman adopted the SAP enterprise resource planning (ERP) system, making it probably one of SAP's largest customers at the time. The system managed information throughout the Company across the supply chain, including bringing raw materials into the plants, operating the manufacturing processes within the plants and fulfilling customer orders. At the production level, production planning tools for continuous manufacturing were deployed to enable manufacturing line changes between product runs, variable supply sourcing, managing maintenance schedules and so on. Eastman later deployed SAP's Advanced Planner and Optimizer (APO) for these functions (see Figure 1 for the standard APO architecture). The APO provided functions that enabled intra- and inter-company planning of the supply chain and for scheduling and monitoring various processes. For Eastman's business, acquiring rapid, accurate external data for planning purposes was critical, and for this same reason, the XML integration across its supply chain was strategic. Early versions of SAP were designed for batch and repetitive manufacturing. Eastman worked with SAP in an attempt to apply "discrete" logic to a continuous manufacturing environment. In R/3, additional functionalities such as continuous display of inventory consumption and output were incorporated, but the continuous Available-to-Promise function was not yet available.[6] The Production Planning and Detailed Scheduling (PP/DS) functions would select best manufacturing sequences to minimise

6. Available-to-Promise (ATP) was a multi-level, rule-based availability-checking function with due consideration for inventories, allocations, production and transportation capabilities, and costs.

Figure 1 SAP's standard architecture of the APO

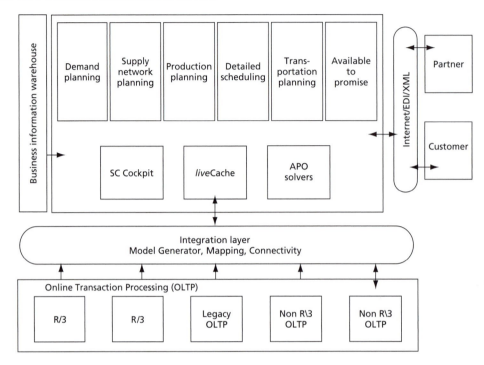

Source: Adapted from Knolmayer, G., Mertens, P. and Zeier, A. (2002) *Supply Chain Management Based on SAP Systems,* Springer-Verglag Berlin Heidelberg, p. 117, Figure 3.1. Original source: SAP AG.

costs and/or time and/or other "penalty factors". Variable supply sourcing could be handled by having multiple R/3 production versions (otherwise known as Production Process Models in SAP lingo) for manufactured items, or if necessary, multi-vendors could be set up with associated transportation lanes to offer selection options for sourcing raw materials. Maintenance Schedules for plant maintenance work were incorporated manually by adding downtime for any equipment resource in APO; production scheduled for these periods would then be "blocked".

With Demand Planning, Supply Network Planning, Production Planning and Detailed Scheduling integrated in APO, the planner could display and make decisions regarding demand, supply and inventory data at one plant or many plants. Demand Planning and

Supply Network Planning handled aggregation when desired, while Production Planning and Detailed Scheduling aggregated at the plant level.

Forecasting was performed by another system – the Logility Voyager Solution – that helped Eastman create a single forecasting process based on real-time sales data collected from its worldwide sales force via the Company's Intranet, not historical trends and guesswork. Eastman manufactured a diverse product line. Furthermore, chemical manufacturing was very different to electronics components manufacturing for instance, in that it was a lot more difficult to anticipate market requirements. For example, some products were fourth step or fifth step derivatives of a raw material, e.g., propylene. The continuous manufacturing processes branched off into other processes. Depending on which branches of products were in most demand, production would need to be adjusted to place emphasis on certain branches at any given time. In the past, forecasting was performed by "departmental islands". Logility Voyager enabled Eastman to dynamically combine all those individual forecasts. Aggregating market demand and funnelling this information down to the "individual product" assessment of which products were going to sell in the next 3–12 months therefore demanded accurate forecasting. The supply chain started off with demand planning and ended with fulfilment (transportation planning).

Eastman also engaged in Vendor Managed Inventory (VMI) scenarios with key customers and used data communication technologies (provided by Integrated Support Systems, Inc.) to acquire timely inventory and forecast data, and to respond to order commitments. Furthermore, Eastman engaged in projects to acquire tank telemetry signals via XML directly into its ERP systems for automatic replenishment requests. Re-order points were agreed for each tank so the tank, in effect, would request Eastman's ERP to schedule a shipment to keep the inventory at specific levels.

The ability to link supply chain computing systems together afforded all the trading partners the opportunity to re-engineer their business processes. It was possible for Eastman to remove work and unnecessary tasks from its internal processes and to re-think the inter-company processes, thus removing work in the extended relationships also. For example, sales and delivery systems were linked such that the systems audited each other as the orders progressed in real time. This eliminated the need for staff to identify discrepancies at the end of each month.

SAP was Eastman's core technical infrastructure. Data and information about nearly every aspect of its business was contained in SAP. This kind of infrastructure provided connectivity to multi-parties beyond simply point-to-point interactions. Based on

this infrastructure, the value of ISS was in its ability to make available to all connected parties the information necessary to manage their businesses. As Craig put it, "You have to really leverage the network effect you get out of visibility to data from this kind of infrastructure."

The integrated systems solution

Integrating supply chain activities with key customers and suppliers represents a tremendous opportunity to provide more value at reduced cost.

   – Mary Kay Devillier, Director – e-Business & Information Resources, Arbemarle Corporation, an Eastman customer[7]

our vision is to link our production directly to our customers' manufacturing need. This is more than e-commerce. It is industry-to-industry e-business.

   – Lynne Taylor, Manager – Market Development, Rayonier, an Eastman supplier[8]

There were four elements to Eastman's e-business strategy (see Figure 2), and one of Craig's areas of responsibility fell within the system-to-system integration (Integrated Systems Solution or ISS) element. ISS was a means by which Eastman could leverage Internet and XML technologies to enable it to connect its core computing platform or ERP system with the core computing platforms of other companies. This would allow direct data transfer between core systems.

Since 1999, Eastman had invested heavily in a technological infrastructure that would enable it to deploy collaborative supply chain solutions and services based on XML technology (see Figure 3). Upon this

7. "Eastman Pilot Links IT Infrastructure with Supplier and Customer; Based on webMethods B2B", News Archive, http://www.eastman.com, 23 February 2000, accessed on 28 May 2002.
8. "Eastman Pilot Links IT Infrastructure with Supplier and Customer; Based on webMethods B2B", News Archive, http://www.eastman.com, 23 February 2000, accessed on 28 May 2002.

Figure 2 Four elements of Eastman's e-business strategy

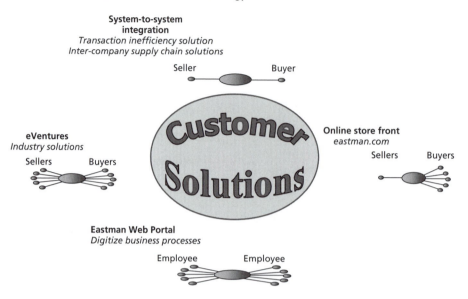

Figure 3 The integrated system solution architecture

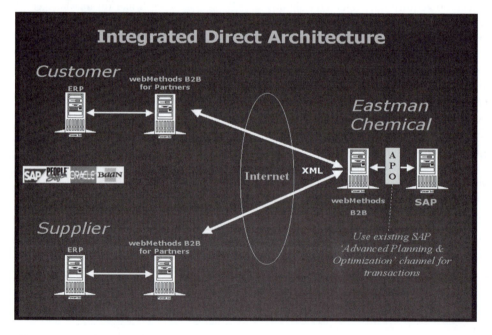

infrastructure, Eastman was able to build e-business solutions that would facilitate direct or exchange/marketplace connections with its sales channels, fulfilment channels, financial services providers and logistics services providers (see Exhibit 3). By giving trading partners the option of deploying a webMethods server to process XML messages between Eastman's SAP system and the Internet, and using webMethods

Exhibit 3 Connecting the various business partners

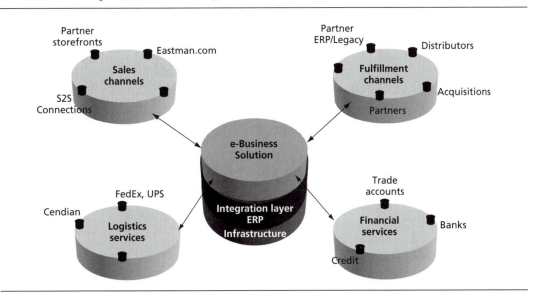

Trading Networks and a CIDX[9] Adaptor to mediate communication between trading partners' and Eastman's systems, the Company intended to build in collaborative supply chain management capabilities that would deliver value to Eastman and its business partners (see Figure 4). Fundamental to its strategy was the anticipated ability of ISS and collaborative supply chain management to optimise working capital and increase the Company's flexibility to market changes. Reducing working capital through integrated production planning systems across the supply chain was a priority at Eastman. However, the reduction of working capital was possible only via the deployment of integrated collaborative planning processes in which customers sent electronic demand data, goods receipts and inventory

positions, and Eastman automatically replenished the customer's stock and sent electronic replenishment notifications. Almost all of Eastman's trading partners wanted to start with the integration of the basic order-to-cash transaction cycle to prove the viability of the technological concept and realise modest savings in data entry relief.[10]

The webMethods partner server software, Trading Networks and CIDX Adapter licence, were offered to business partners free-of-charge to encourage adoption, although they could select any other XML software provider that used a standard protocol for transporting data through the Internet to connect with Eastman. In this way, regardless

---

9. Chemical Industry Data eXchange (CIDX) was a global trade association and standards body that built the XML-based Chem eStandards to define business messages required by chemical companies to carry out highly secure transactions with business partners over the Internet.

10. The order-to-cash cycle refers to the following sequence of information flow: a customer submits an order to Eastman; Eastman acknowledges the order; the customer requests changes to the order; Eastman acknowledges these changes; Eastman advises the customer of the shipment details; Eastman invoices the customer; the customer pays Eastman; the customer advises Eastman of the payment.

Figure 4 Applying the webMethods B2B solutions

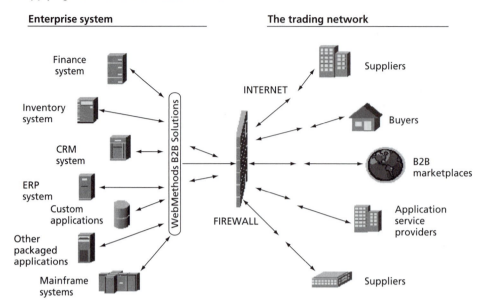

of whether the partner's system was an ERP, a legacy system or an EAI engine, systems-to-systems communication could be established. The webMethods Integration Modules could deliver simple files into a legacy system and facilitate XML-to-EDI operations without a VAN. The layout costs for partners included the hardware and network services for installation of the webMethods technology and user training provided by webMethods. Connections typically took 8–12 weeks. Once connected, partners had to ensure sufficient support for the technology at their end. It was also up to the partners to explore and develop the options for multiple tiers of integration with their business partners.

When ISS was launched on a trial basis in 1999, Eastman invited a few of its large customers and suppliers in the US to experiment with the technology in a production environment. Albemarle Corporation and Rayonier were two of the early adopters. At the time, CIDX had not arrived at the Chem eStandards that were subsequently introduced in 2001. Eastman therefore had to work initially with its own

agreed definitions and terminologies for, say, export shipment and hazardous warnings, etc. The results were encouraging, with basic purchase orders, sales orders and acknowledgements exchanged electronically after negotiating the business process and data formats with the pilot trading partners. For example, a strategic customer would key in a purchase order to Eastman. Once the order was confirmed, the customer's system would be programmed to recognise that it was an Eastman order and would automatically generate an XML transmission to Eastman's receiving system via standard HTTPS Internet protocol. By the end of 2001, Eastman reported monthly transaction volumes in excess of 30,000 XML documents. Eastman saw a lot of potential in the ability to operate a system that could capitalise on other people's systems and information.

By June 2002, Eastman's ISS allowed for the issuing of certificates of analysis, the placing of orders, order changes, order cancellations, the issuing of order acknowledgments, ship notices, invoicing and payment notices. Other mainstream transactions including production planning and logistics transactions, and vendor-managed inventory enablement were under development.

Other connections established included service providers such as Cendian. Cendian was an independent chemical logistics service provider that had been spun off from Eastman. The industry benchmark was that a global supplier of chemicals would typically spend 8–10 per cent of revenue on logistics and trade compliance (e.g. regulations for shipping certain products into certain countries, safety warnings, etc.). Many business processes were unique to shipping chemicals. In the formative period, Eastman invested significant amounts in Cendian's technological infrastructure to build a business that would become one of the first specialists in chemical logistics. Cendian used software from Global Logistics Technologies (GLT) to manage and optimise freight movements so as to balance different shipments coming from different countries across the same routing. As a specialist in handling chemical products and with established XML connections with Eastman, Cendian handled all of Eastman's logistics requirements. Eastman's relationship with Cendian was vital, as every order that needed to be fulfilled, except airfreight shipments, which were handled by FedEx and UPS, was handled by Cendian. Only on rare occasions were goods transported by air. Many thousands of documents were exchanged between the two companies every month, by far the most heavily trafficked connection. The benefits to Eastman were improved customer service, reduced transportation costs, timely deliveries and reliability, significantly reduced logistics planning time (as the logistics function was now outsourced to Cendian), high visibility and improved control over the tracking of shipments, and optimisation of transactions and processes. Having the technical infrastructure in place enabled Cendian to benefit from connecting

not only with Eastman but also with freight forwarders and other Cendian business partners.

> we expect these system-to-system links with major trading partners to account for at least half of our online revenues (by 2005).
> – Fred Buehler, VP – e-Business[11]

Linking the Chain

> In Asia, Eastman will step up efforts to establish several integrated direct system-to-system digitised connections with its leading trading partners and increase the adoption rate of XML technology and the associated chemical industry standards.[12]

In the Asia Pacific region (AP), online sales accounted for approximately 25 per cent of Eastman's revenue – the highest out of all the regions – at the end of June 2002. The target was to see sales from all electronic channels (refer to Figure 2) increase to around 40 per cent in 12–18 months' time worldwide. Eastman operated six manufacturing plants in the region that manufactured different products from different raw materials, with each serving different markets. The location of a plant was therefore dependent on access to raw materials, customers and markets. The ISS concept took off much faster in the US, where the majority of the earlier connections were based. The AP region presented some new challenges.

One of the major hurdles companies faced was that they did not have a sufficiently integrated systems infrastructure to fully benefit from connecting with Eastman. Some of the companies that Craig had approached were keen to make the connection with Eastman but wanted to undertake the project

---

11. "Eastman announces 15 system-to-system connections; Computer-to-computer links may account for half of the company's online revenues", News Archive, http://www.eastman.com, 23 January 2001.
12. "Eastman Commences Online Trading in Japan", News Archive, http://www.eastman.com, accessed 28 May 2002.

as part of their broader business strategy rather than on a piecemeal basis. Many were in the process of planning for or implementing an ERP layer before considering making the Eastman connection.

Eastman ranked its trading partners by volume of exchanged purchase orders and sales orders to identify the largest opportunities for integration. A modest percentage of its trading partners comprised 50 per cent of the total order transaction volume (not revenue or spend), providing a focused opportunity set. When engaging these key trading partners, business experts from both sides examined processes that required significant labour to manage, and considered these pain points for re-engineering projects. For example, processes for monthly invoice reconciliation, pricing change management and pricing support all required significant human attention by both parties, sometimes resulting in mutual write-offs to clear the books. Part of the ISS value proposition was to analyse and discover new process-integration solutions that could extend the value of interconnectivity beyond order-to-cash data-entry labour savings. Integrated collaborative planning, evaluated receipt settlements and so on were part of a growing portfolio of solutions that leveraged the efficiencies of system-to-system e-commerce.

Nagase & Co., Ltd

In May 2002, Nagase and Eastman celebrated their 50th year of doing business together. Nagase was a major distributor, headquartered in Tokyo. It comprised 102 member companies worldwide and provided trading, marketing, R & D, manufacturing and processing functions to its customers in the chemicals, plastics, electronics and healthcare industries. Japan was Eastman's single largest market in the AP region. Nagase represented Eastman in the Japan market in almost all business segments. Annual purchases from Eastman totalled

around JPY3 billion.[13] The two companies transacted a huge number and a broad cross-section of business interactions. Hence, Craig anticipated that the integration with Nagase would truly be a test case for the technology in a complex business environment.

In spring 2002, Nagase agreed to go ahead with the XML connection with Eastman. As an international trading company, Nagase had thousands of customers and suppliers worldwide. XML technology was considered to be the key to engaging in e-business with these business partners. In preparation for connecting with Nagase, Eastman sent two technical staff from Singapore over to the US for training in implementation, which was planned for Q3. Eastman had provided Nagase with information about what they needed to do to prepare to run the connection. Discussions took place concerning the processes and systems involved, and the mapping of data. Nagase did not have an ERP system. Even before it could embark on connectivity with Eastman, Nagase had to engage in the painstaking task of customising its systems and work processes. The very complex business interactions between the two companies (including understanding the CIDX standards application and agreeing on business process event flows for order-to-cash transactions) and the language difficulties presented challenges for both parties.

Nagase's information systems consisted of two separate components that handled import/export orders and domestic orders respectively (see Figure 5). PRONETS was the import/export system used to manage foreign order fulfilment, including logistics and customs clearance. APORO was the domestic order management system that was also used to manage the whole company's inventory. Typically, purchase order requests would be keyed into either system by staff in the Sales Department. Orders were then passed to the

---

13. JPY3 billion = US$25 million.

Figure 5 Nagase's import workflow (simplified)

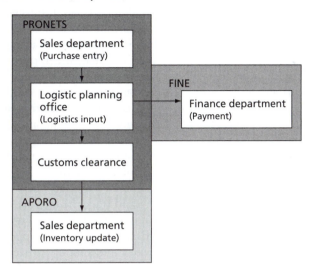

Logistics Planning Office, which instructed shippers and administered shippers' and goods invoices through an accounting system (FINE) that was linked to the Finance Department. From there, the Finance Department would handle payments and a Nagase Logistics Subsidiary would handle customs clearance. When goods reached Nagase's warehouse, the inventory database in APORO would be updated. A stand-alone system was used by Nagase for order forecasting.

Connecting the two companies required integration not only of technical systems but also of business processes. The trading partners had to assess their business needs and technical proficiency before deciding on the extent to which the business processes could be transferred onto the electronic medium. While the CIDX standard did define processes to handle a multitude of situations, variances in these standard processes were foreseen. These included:

- agreeing on transaction response timeframes;
- handling of unmatched order quantities (i.e. when Eastman could not satisfy the order in full); and
- changes in shipment dates.

Electronic solutions to some of these variances were dependent on the technical capabilities of both companies and their willingness to tackle some of the more complicated issues.

Of the order-to-cash cycle, the initial phase of development concentrated on the order and acknowledgment processes. Processes for future consideration included invoicing and shipment notification.

Only as Strong as the Weakest Link

> The true value is really being able to connect across the whole value chain from raw materials through to our customers.
> – Craig Knight

Before the management of Nagase could decide on the degree of investment they wanted to make in the interconnection with Eastman's information systems, both sides were to meet to discuss the business needs of each company; the systems and business processes that would require integration, including data mapping, and the likely value added of each integrated process to both companies. Craig focused his thoughts on these issues as he was leaving his office.

Labour savings from electronically exchanging purchase-order-related documents for any two companies were typically not significant enough to justify any one connection. Each company had to have strategic plans for multiple connections with high-volume trading partners to begin to realise cumulative savings. How could Craig convince Nagase of the strategic benefits of its investment?

Without doubt, Eastman wanted not only to ride the wave of the transformation that was taking place in the industry but also to lead it. To do so, it had packaged a technological solution that would facilitate interconnectivity in different ways with its business partners. For example, besides the ISS solution, Eastman benefited from the use of its XML infrastructure to initiate purchase orders with companies that did not have the true ISS connection with it. Eastman was confident that the full backend XML integration would deliver productivity gains of seven per cent in the procurement of direct materials through its supplier portal. All that was required of the suppliers was an interface with a browser-based system. This solution worked well with the non-strategic trading partners or those companies that were not pursuing a comprehensive IT strategy.

On the grander scale of things and beyond the simple order-loop connections, Eastman was also leading a CIDX CPFR Business Process Guidelines Committee to define the initial steps in a standard collaborative planning, forecasting and replenishment (CPFR) process in the chemical industry. Adoption of initial CPFR guidelines would allow more process automation in supply chain management, opening the door to more opportunities to leverage Eastman's B2B expertise. Along the way, the re-engineering of traditionally linear business processes was giving way to dynamic and simultaneous business processes that would capture value for all parties concerned. This was enabled through "day-in-the-life" interviews with strategic partners whereby Eastman staff would trace the interactions that the various staff in the partner company had with Eastman to identify opportunities to capture value and simplify processes or shorten cycle times.

With all these options presented to Nagase, it had to decide which option would be most beneficial to its business.

Pauline Ng prepared this case under the supervision of Dr Benjamin Yen and Dr Ali Farhoomand for class discussion. This case is not intended to show effective or ineffective handling of decision or business processes.

Ref. 02/148C 25 September, 2002

Case study 2   Shun Sang (H.K.) Co. Ltd.: streamlining logistical flow: Background and issues

Introduction

In November 2002, Mr. Tsui Kwok-choy, Managing Director of Shun Sang (H.K.) Co. Ltd., reflected upon the IT-enabled measures that his company had been putting into place since 1998 to improve its logistical and operational efficiency. The results were obvious. Not only had there been significant improvements in operational parameters such as order-to-delivery time and average inventory turnover, with near-real-time information and tracking capability at their fingertips, the staff had more time to do their job better, resulting in higher customer satisfaction and better profitability. But Tsui was not content with the status quo. As he looked back at how the company had transformed and what it had achieved, he wondered what other measures the company should embark upon to further improve its competitiveness.

Company background

When it was founded by Mr. and Mrs. Tsui in 1986, Shun Sang (H.K.) Co. Ltd. (hereinafter referred to as Shun Sang) had only three employees in a 1800-square-foot office in Sheung Wan[1] and did not have its own warehouse. It started as a wholesaler of pharmaceuticals and fast-moving consumer goods serving drug stores and retail outlets in Hong Kong. By 1994, Shun Sang had grown into a company of 18 people, serving some 700 accounts. The year also marked a watershed in Shun Sang's development as it was appointed by Proctor and Gamble (P&G) as one of its two distributors in Hong Kong.

In December 1997, Shun Sang started to set up its own warehouse and became a fully fledged distributor supporting P&G with sales, merchandising, warehousing and goods-delivery services. The same year, a subsidiary, Shun Sang (Technology) Ltd., was established to provide IT-related solutions to both Shun Sang and third-party companies. In 1998, Shun Sang reached another milestone as it achieved over HK$200 million (US$25.64 million) in sales.[2] In 2000, the two Shun Sang companies were regrouped. Shun Sang Holdings Limited was formed, with Shun Sang (H.K.) Co. Ltd. and Shun Sang (Technology) Ltd. (hereinafter referred to as Shun Sang Technology) as its subsidiaries.

Tsui was always keen to bring in new ideas or management concepts to improve Shun Sang's competitiveness. He was on the board of the Hong Kong Article Numbering Association (HKANA, an organisation that promoted the use and standardisation of bar codes and preached the concepts of supply chain management in Hong Kong) and actively participated in field trips organised by the HKANA in order to keep abreast of the latest developments and best practices around the world. He also put emphasis on developing and rewarding his employees. On average, Shun Sang's training budget was about 10 per cent of its total salary expenses. In addition, Shun Sang was one of the few unlisted companies in Hong Kong to offer stock options to its employees. Shun Sang's achievements were publicly recognised in 1998 when it won the Best Managed SME Silver Award of the first Hong Kong Small and Medium Enterprise (SME) Awards in 1998 (a campaign co-organised by the Hong Kong General

---

1. Sheung Wan is located west of Central or the central business district of Hong Kong.

2. The Hong Kong dollar is pegged to the US dollar at US$1 = HK$7.8.

Chamber of Commerce and the Hong Kong Productivity Council[3]). In 2001, Shun Sang won the Good People Management Award organised by the Labour Department.

In December 2001, Shun Sang moved to a 2700-square-foot office in San Po Kong, with its own 16,000-square-foot warehouse just across the street.[4] By 2002, Shun Sang had grown to a company of 36 people (see Exhibit 1). Its clientele consisted mainly of some 400 drug stores, and, to a lesser extent, chain stores, department store, supermarkets, cosmetics shops, hotels and movie theatres, with a total of about 1900 orders and 50,000 cartons of goods sold each month.

Sales and order fulfilment: the early years

Shun Sang's customers were mainly small to medium-sized drug stores and retail outlets scattered around the territory. To serve them, Shun Sang's salespersons needed to meet them in person and take orders directly. Order forms were then filled out by hand and faxed back to the company at night. The following morning, staff from the invoice-processing department would first verify the orders and then prepare the invoices and packing lists. Packing lists were passed to the warehouse (which was outsourced until December 1997), where the ordered items were issued, packed and cross-checked manually. The delivery service was outsourced to a transportation service provider, which only allocated trucks when it saw the packing lists on the spot.

Tsui reasoned that they faced four major problems with this process. First, the order

forms might not be filled out correctly or clearly, and the faxing of the forms could further diminish their readability. Second, sending orders by fax could in itself be problematic – for instance, the line could be busy or the fax machine at the receiving end could be out of paper. Third, staff from invoice-processing were required to spend time verifying each order and the order quantity, and there was still no guarantee that a verified order was error-free. Fourth, as there was little information about the demand for various goods, it was very difficult to control inventory levels.

Since errors could be introduced at various steps of the entire process, when a customer complained that an order was not correctly fulfilled it was nearly impossible to pinpoint what went wrong and when. As Tsui put it, "The customer is always right." The only thing that Shun Sang could do was to apologise to the customer and put things right. Even when everything went smoothly, the best time that Shun Sang could manage from order placement to goods delivery was 48 hours.

Sales and Order Fulfilment in 1998

Small and medium enterprises (SMEs) must apply information technology appropriately in order to avoid laying people off.
– Mr Tsui Kwok-choy, Managing Director of Shun Sang (H.K.) Limited

Tsui attended a number of supply chain management seminars organised by the HKANA in early 1997. He was convinced that supply chain management and IT would be the future direction for Shun Sang. To get his middle management's buy-in, Tsui encouraged them to take courses in supply chain management. After the Asian economic crisis of late-1997, the economy of Hong Kong started its downward spiral. Businesses were hit hard. To survive, some resorted to layoffs to cut costs and improve efficiency. As a small/medium enterprise, Shun Sang was

---

3. A quasi-governmental body in Hong Kong whose mission is to promote productivity excellence through the provision of integrated support across the value chain of Hong Kong firms, in order to achieve a more effective utilisation of resources, to enhance the value added content of products and services, and to increase international competitiveness.
4. San Po Kong is a light industrial district in Hong Kong.

Exhibit 1 Organisational chart of Shun Sang (H.K.) Co. ltd. as of late 2002

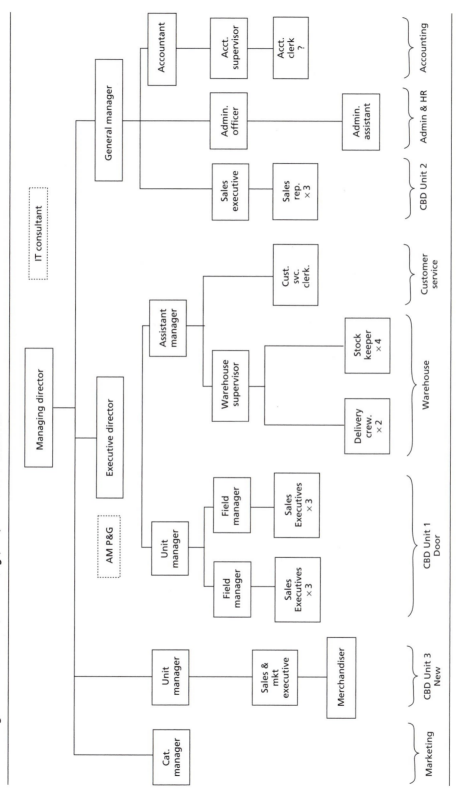

already very lean on its manpower structure. To weather this difficult period, Tsui was more convinced than ever that supply chain management concepts and IT would be the answer to streamlining Shun Sang's operations.

After studying the feasibility, a team from Shun Sang Technology started the development work. The team spent six months developing an Intranet ordering system and a Web-based trading system to improving the ordering and invoice processing, and two months on the inventory control system to streamline the inventory operations. In addition, Shun Sang invested over HK$350,000 (US$44,870) on hardware and software for the various systems. Meanwhile, time and resources were also invested to educate and retrain its employees. As Tsui put it, "Most importantly, we have to educate our staff to be open-minded to accept new things and new challenges." Thus, outside consultants were hired to evaluate, advise and provide training to Shun Sang's employees.

In October 1998, the Intranet ordering system and the trading system were introduced. Under the new working mode, all salespersons were equipped with a notebook computer. They could download customer information from the Company's server any time they wanted. While they still needed to meet their customers and take orders in person, they only needed to log on to the Company Intranet at night through dial-up access to fill out the online order form. Stock availability was checked instantly and out-of-stock items would be flagged and no order could be placed for such items. Tsui recalled, "We did consider desktop computers, which were obviously cheaper than notebooks. But it would be difficult to bring them back to the office for service. It was timely that the price of notebooks came down to an affordable level. So, we decided to use notebooks."

In November 1998, an inventory control system was also implemented using barcode technology to monitor inventory status. Over 95 per cent of Shun Sang's stock-keeping units[5] (SKUs) were barcode-enabled using the same standard (mainly due to the fact that the majority of Shun Sang's SKUs were P&G products and they were all bar-coded when they were delivered to Shun Sang). Through the use of scanners, the in-and-out movements of SKUs were recorded and the inventory records were updated real-time.

All orders uploaded the night before were processed at 8 am the following morning by the trading system. Packing lists and invoices were generated automatically at the warehouse. Equipped with barcode readers, staff at the warehouse scanned and confirmed the issuance of goods. All goods were then packed in accordance with orders, which, along with the packed goods, were verified by another staff member before being picked up by the transportation service provider for delivery.

The results

These new systems delivered a number of obvious benefits. The automated Intranet ordering system eliminated many of the error-prone steps in the old system. Although dial-up access could be very slow, and even got cut off totally at times, the system greatly improved order accuracy, and hence customer satisfaction. Similarly, the inventory system enhanced inventory record accuracy and made the warehouse operations more efficient. With accurate and real-time inventory data, Shun Sang was able to better plan its inventory and, as a result, to decrease the average turnover period of fast-moving consumer goods from 12 to 13 days to seven to eight days and the average inventory value, saving 10 per cent in inventory interest costs and effectively increasing the warehouse space by 15 per cent. Savings were also achieved in the following areas.[6]

---

5. Stock Keeping Units or SKUs are the items for which inventory records are kept.
6. Internal documents of Shun Sang.

	Savings/ Improvements (in %)
Invoice processing time	40
Human resources	50
Report processing time	75
Goods return rate	70
Paper consumption	80

With these systems in place, Shun Sang successfully launched a 24-hour delivery service, thus reducing its customers' stock replenishment time by 50 per cent and increasing the reliability of product supply.

A failed attempt

While notebooks were portable by nature, they were still too heavy to be carried around all the time. Thus, in 1999 Shun Sang seriously considered hand-held devices or Personal Data Assistants (PDAs) as an alternative to notebook. As an authorised distributor of P&G, Shun Sang learned about what P&G did with PDAs in Mainland China. Encouraged by P&G, Shun Sang went ahead and bought a supply of PDAs, and Shun Sang Technology started developing applications for Shun Sang's own use. However, only later did they realise that the PDA technology at the time was not suitable for Shun Sang's unique requirements, so eventually they had to pull the plug.

Sales and order fulfilment in 2002

Although the first attempt to implement a PDA-based system was unsuccessful, Shun Sang was not discouraged. In 2001, when the right PDA technology was available in the market at the right price, the project was promptly revived and development work went full-steam ahead. Once again, system development was led by Shun Sang Technology. After five months of development and trial and an investment of over HK$600,000 (US$76,920) in hardware and software, a new PDA-based ordering system with links to the Web-based trading system was launched in February 2002.

Equipped with a PDA, Shun Sang's salespersons would synchronise the database on their PDAs with the Company database at home via their notebooks with broadband Internet access so that their PDA had the most updated customer information and details of product availability (see Exhibit 2). Orders could be entered right in front of their customers on the PDA, and any requested items that were out-of-stock would be indicated. Once an order was filled out, it could be transmitted wirelessly via a CDMA phone card back to the Company Intranet. Alternatively, the salesperson could also upload all the orders all in one go via broadband Internet access at the end of the day.

Back in the office, a new Web-based trading system was implemented to integrate sales, administration, warehouse management and reporting functions. All orders were uploaded to the Web-based trading system, where they would be processed. The transportation service provider that was responsible for picking up the ordered goods and delivering them to Shun Sang's customers could log on to Shun Sang's Intranet to preview the preliminary delivery order summary for the following day after 11 pm, so that it could effectively plan the vehicle deployment well in advance. Because of this promise to provide advance information to the transportation company, salespersons were required to alert their co-workers in invoice-processing if for whatever reason they could not upload the orders in time.

As before, packing lists and invoices were generated automatically at 8 am the following morning in the warehouse, where goods were issued by the warehouse staff with the aid of a barcode scanner. As soon as the scanner was placed back in the cradle, the mapping process would be initiated to check whether the goods issued matched

Exhibit 2 Workflows: from sales to order fulfilment

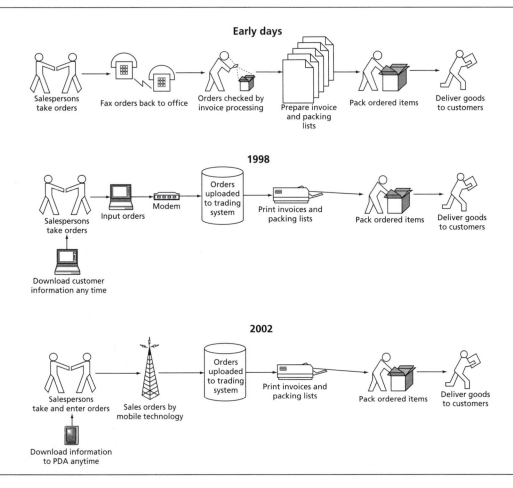

with the goods listed in the packing list. If there were any mismatches, an error report would be generated instantly and the error would be corrected before the goods were shipped.

In April 2002, an invoice-tracking system was also put in place after two months of development work and investment of HK$18,000 (US$2300) in hardware and software. Under this system, the barcodes of the invoice number and the ordered goods were printed on the invoice. The processing times of each invoice for each step in the process (e.g. invoice creation, delivery, delivery confirmation and completion) were recorded in the system. If the customer also employed the barcode technology, they could also use the barcodes on the invoice for goods inspection and for data capturing purposes.

The results

While PDAs could still not totally replace notebook computers, this new ordering system further simplified the workflow and reduced errors. And on average, each salesperson now spent one less hour per night to complete each day's work. This not only reduced stress but also allowed more time for the salespersons to do their job properly. The integrated Web-based trading system helped by reducing duplicate work and saving about two man-hours per day, and by reducing human errors. The full-blown barcode system in the warehouse delivered many benefits as well. Not only were inventory records updated real time, since the system was a closed loop, the accuracy of the inventory records was also improved. The use of scanner in the cross-checking procedure helped reduce the probability of shipping the wrong goods. The system also made inventory tracking and monitoring, and movement control, possible. Data were available to evaluate the performance of the inventory operations. According to Tsui, the fact that they were confident about their accuracy level made the transportation service provider more cautious, as it knew that if an error occurred, Shun Sang could pinpoint the exact step that caused it. Also, with the invoice-tracking system in place, queries from customers could be answered promptly and accurately, thus increasing customer satisfaction. For the management, the system provided them with online and up-to-date reports. For instance, the sales manager could pull out a salesperson's record and review his/her performance versus targets. When Tsui looked at the quantitative measures, he was very pleased and proud of the achievements of his team.

Goods acceptance and issuance processes	Saved 50% manpower
Logbook updates	Saved 99% manpower
Inventory record accuracy	Approaching 99%
Accuracy of goods movements	Approaching 100%
Follow-up on errors	Saved 99% of time

What next?

> Looking back, we made quite a few things happen in the past few years. And I've been thinking, "What next?"
>
> – Tsui Kwok-choy, Managing Director of Shun Sang (H.K.) Co., Limited

Tsui admitted that not too much thought had been put into considering the potential return when Shun Sang first invested money and resources to streamline its operation. This was not to say that the decisions were made without weighing the cost and benefit. In fact, Tsui and his team were very conscious and cautious about the cost. They also knew that they were addressing the right areas to improve the Company's competitiveness. But it was not until recently, when he looked back at the financial results, that he realised that the return had been very encouraging (see Exhibit 3). But Shun Sang also learned its lesson.

Exhibit 3 Selected company statistics

Year	No. of staff	Annual turnover (million HKD)	Profit margin growth rate (97 base)
1986	3	5	–
1989	40	20	–
1993	30	88	–
1994	20	141	–
1997	30	170	–
1998	30	214	−2.9%
1999	32	202	138.4%
2000	33	211	146.2%
2001	34	202	124.4%

Tsui recalled the first and unsuccessful attempt to adopt PDA technology saying, "We jumped in too quickly." "If we could do it all over again, we would do a small scale trial first," said Tsui. Looking ahead, he wondered about the next big stride his Company should take in order to stay competitive.

Andrew Lee prepared this case under the supervision of Dr. Benjamin Yen (1) as a source of reference for Hong Kong's SMEs, and (2) for class discussion. This case is not intended to show effective or ineffective handling of decision or business processes.

This case is part of the **Trade & Industry Department SME Case Series** funded by the Hong Kong Special Administrative Region Trade and Industry Department SME Development Fund. Any opinions, conclusions or recommendations expressed in this material/event (by members of the project team) do not reflect the views of the Government of the Hong Kong Special Administrative Region, Trade and Industry Department or the vetting committee for the SME Development Fund.

Part IV

e-Business implementation and globalisation

e-Business change management: effective implementation of e-business strategies

Lynne Markus

Objectives

- ❏ To establish the importance of e-business change management
- ❏ To conceptualise e-business change management in terms of the DOT model
- ❏ To provide familiarity with common e-business change management situations
- ❏ To explore why people sometimes resist e-business initiatives
- ❏ To illustrate the tradeoffs between the design and implementation of e-business initiatives

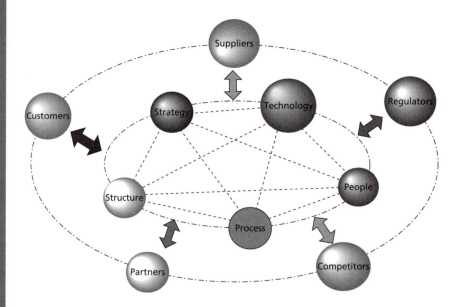

We arrive now at the last part where we focus first on the *people* dimension of the Dynamic Organisational Tension (DOT) framework before proceeding to examine some of the legal and regulatory issues associated with e-business transformation in Chapter 10. In this final part we aim to put the pieces together. We began this book by discussing some of the reasons that transformation initiatives do not succeed: "people problems" such as top management's failure to change, rigid organisational cultures, and fear or distrust by people affected by the change. This chapter is about ways to ensure that e-business initiatives succeed through effective management of the human aspects of change. In particular, we aim to show how the DOT framework can be used to diagnose change management situations and develop effective responses to them.

No matter how promising a new e-business model or business practice appears on paper, if no one adopts it and uses it well, all strategising, planning and development efforts will go to waste. This means that the success of e-business strategies depends on *other people's behaviour*. And unfortunately, the e-business strategist has no direct control over other people's behaviour. However, e-business strategists can significantly improve their chances of success by understanding why people sometimes resist e-business innovations and by knowing about the tradeoffs between the design and implementation of e-business innovations.

A major reason why e-business transformation initiatives often meet resistance is that any major organisational change involves some form of sacrifice by those affected. The adoption of information technology and e-business practices is very likely to have a fundamental effect on organisational structures. Astute managers appreciate that managing a transformation effort involves anticipating and managing the reactions and behaviours of those affected. Affected stakeholders are more likely to commit to the necessary change when a clearly understood imperative has been established. Enterprises that successfully make the case for this imperative, convey it effectively, and reinforce it throughout the transformation effort will experience less resistance. A failed transformation effort bears tremendous costs for the organisation. It can lead to low employee morale, customer dissatisfaction, diminished senior management credibility and resistance to further change. This chapter offers guidelines on how managers can navigate this terrain and shows that effective change management is the key to the success of e-business strategies.

Change management is the process of designing and introducing e-business initiatives in a way that takes into account people's likely reactions to these initiatives. Change management covers a range of implementation strategies from communicating well with the people affected by the change and involving them in the design process to designing (or redesigning) the change initiative in a way that minimises negative impacts on people affected by the change.

The need for change management arises every time the e-business strategist has a great idea and someone (colleague, employee, customer, business partner) raises serious objections to the idea or fails to play along. If people appear to resist your plans, or if "you build it, but they don't come," you have a situation that can profitably be examined as a change management problem. (Of course, you should also try to manage change proactively – anticipating where resistance or non-adoption of your plans might occur and taking steps to avoid it before it happens.)

Put this way, managing change is a bit like feasibility-testing an e-business strategy for its success potential. Naturally, many things other than people's reactions to an idea can affect the success of strategy. Other important factors in e-business success include the technical quality of an e-business product or service, responses by competitors and the impact of relevant government policies. However, since negative reactions by people affected by the change can derail the best-laid e-business plans, the effective management of change is a necessary ingredient in e-business success. The more radical an e-business innovation, the more important change management is to its success.

Sometimes people object that change management "waters down" e-business initiatives, making them less effective. It is true that attending to people issues sometimes slows the pace of change. But the tradeoff for a faster pace or a more radical innovation can be failure of the change effort. Conversely, attending to the human aspects can result not only in a higher probability of success but also in better innovations, that is, ones with more positive business outcomes.

Effective e-business change management means making good tradeoffs and appropriate adjustments among the major elements of the DOT framework: strategy, structure, process, technology and people. As we have previously noted, equilibrium of these elements is neither possible nor desirable. However, problems arise when one element of the model is seriously out of alignment with the others. Attempting to make major change in only one element of a situation is unlikely to succeed unless the other elements can be made to harmonise with it.

Unfortunately, many e-business strategists neglect this fundamental principle. A persistent challenge in IT work is the pervasive belief that problems are best solved by technology (alone). (This is sometimes called the "magic bullet" theory of IT-enabled change.) Unfortunately, new technologies often run afoul of business processes and management systems, such as incentives, that can lead to resistance to the new technology. Nor is it a good approach to assume that top management is responsible for making people use the new system or technology. Similarly, human resource specialists often focus solely on the people aspects of change, neglecting processes, technologies and structures. And strategists sometimes neglect implementation issues: people, processes and technology. Each of these views is a dangerous oversimplification; all aspects of the DOT framework must be considered together.

Most e-business opportunities and many of the problems arising when e-business strategies are implemented can be addressed in a variety of ways. For example, they might be tackled with technical improvements, with procedural changes, or with efforts directed at people, such as training or persuasion. The secret of effective e-business change management is to find *the best* approach or the best *combination* of approaches for *each* particular situation. "Best" here is defined as accomplishing the business goal with fewest negative side effects (e.g. people's resistance).

Consider the implementation of the Electronic Tendering System (ETS) for online procurement by departments of the Hong Kong government[1] – the subject of the

---

1. Markus et al. (2002).

case study accompanying this chapter. The system involved a Web-based front-end to the government purchasing department's legacy purchasing systems. Technically, it was possible and elegant to make a direct link between the front-end and back-end systems. But people in the purchasing department were concerned about the security risks of a direct link. If these concerns were not effectively addressed, purchasing department employees might not have used ETS, leading to its failure.

How could these concerns be effectively addressed? One response would have been to add technical features to ensure security – an expensive solution. Another response would have been to educate people about Internet security and to try to convince them their fears were groundless. The solution finally chosen was sensitive both to people's fears and to their pocketbooks – an inexpensive "sneaker net" with low security risk. Tender documents submitted to the Web-based front-end were burned onto CDs and manually uploaded to the back-end system. (This solution could work, in part, because the volume of tender documents was quite low.)

In the ETS example, the solution involved changes in business processes that complemented change in the technical system. In other cases, the best solution will involve more than two elements of the DOT framework. The example shows that effective e-business change management is often not particularly difficult or esoteric. And it may be difficult to distinguish clearly between effective e-business change management and good strategy formulation or technology development. What characterises good change management is *simultaneous and holistic attention to all five elements of the Dynamic Organisational Tension framework: strategy, structure, process, technology and people.*

Two types of knowledge are central to the effective management of e-business change:

1 understanding why people sometimes fail to adopt e-business innovations; and

2 knowing the tradeoffs between the design and implementation of e-business innovations.

In this chapter, we consider each topic in some depth. First, however, let us examine some examples that show the usefulness of change management knowledge in typical e-business initiatives.

e-Business change management scenarios

In this section we consider three common e-business change management situations:

1 an innovative e-business product or service offered to *individual members of the public at large*;

2 an e-business initiative requiring cooperation of other *companies* (e.g. customers or suppliers); and

3 an e-business initiative affecting people from several *countries or national cultures*.

Naturally, these scenarios may overlap, as when an e-business design team with people from several countries works on an e-business initiative for use by the general public in several countries. For each scenario, common change management issues are presented, along with examples of effective and ineffective change management tactics.

Building a better mousetrap

A common e-business scenario involves an entrepreneur offering a radically new e-commerce service to the public. Radical innovations always face an uphill battle to gain acceptance. First, people need to learn that an innovation exists, and they need to understand what the innovation will do for them. They need to believe that the innovation will provide them with benefits that outweigh the costs of adopting the innovation.

The costs of adopting an innovation are not all financial. It takes time and effort to unlearn old practices and to learn new ones. In addition, some innovations require people to change the way they work *with other people*. Changing the way one works with others, in turn, can change *interpersonal relationships*. People tend to value their relationships with other people above and beyond what these relationships mean to them in instrumental terms. In other words, there is an emotional element to every relationship. People often strongly resist changes in their emotional relationships with others. Therefore, radical innovations are often resisted, even if they offer great benefits, because people perceive the emotional costs of the change to be too high.

Another problem with radically new e-commerce services is that people may not perceive them to be as beneficial as e-commerce entrepreneurs do. Entrepreneurs, like system developers, are often guilty of unrealistic thinking about the benefits of their efforts. When system developers think, wrongly, that technology will solve all the world's problems, we call it "magic bullet" thinking. When entrepreneurs think, wrongly, that their new product is a sure thing, we call it "building a better mousetrap" (because the obvious reaction is: "Does the world *really need* a better mousetrap?")

Consider the true story[2] of a system developer hired by a software company to create an electronic marketplace for "talent" in the Hollywood entertainment industry. The developer (we will call him Dave) built a prototype system with a catalogue of the various creative inputs to a film or TV show. "Suppliers" (independent producers, actors, post production services companies, and so forth) were supposed to enter into the catalogue their capabilities and their availability to work on new projects. "Buyers" (people in the studios and film production companies) were supposed to use the catalogue to find and hire talent.

Let us examine this e-commerce service from a change management point of view. First, where do talent agents fit in? In Hollywood, many actors and other "suppliers" use agents to help them find employment. The system as designed

---

2. David Petrie learned about this example while doing his doctoral dissertation research.

cuts the agents out of the hiring process. How would you expect the agents to react to this system? Would all actors welcome this "disintermediation"? Second, suppose people in the industry actually decided to use this electronic marketplace. How do you think the relationships between "buyers" and "suppliers" might change? Would people welcome the shift from direct personal interactions (the famous Hollywood lunch) to impersonal transactions mediated by the computer? Third, would the electronic marketplace really be able to handle the nuances of the needs of "buyers" and the "capabilities" and "availabilities" of "suppliers"?

Here is what people in "The Industry" told Dave when he held a series of focus groups to get their reactions to his prototype system:

- "How can you represent my creative capabilities accurately in the system? Directors provide a very general statement of what they want; they leave it up to talent like me to work out the details of the solution. I can create solutions to many more situations than I can easily describe for your system. I don't want to miss opportunities because someone thinks I can't do the job."

- "What do you mean by 'available'? I'm *always* available for work, no matter how busy I am! If Steven Speilberg calls, believe me, I'm *available*! If I tell your system I'm not available, I might miss the deal of a lifetime!"

- "Why would I pay money to list myself in this service when I already have a network of relationships with directors and producers who know what I can do?"

- (From a potential "buyer" in a movie studio) "I don't need your system. We've outsourced production to independent producers. They find the talent, not me."

There are two ways to look at these comments. One is to view the situation as *a problem requiring change management*. If you view the situation this way, you will have to develop a strategy for changing people's attitudes and behaviour. What would your strategy be?

The second way to look at these comments is to decide that the electronic marketplace for Hollywood talent is *not a good idea*, because it is unlikely to succeed without a vast amount of additional resources in system redevelopment and change management activities.[3] What would you decide? Why?

Resistance to change can be a signal that you need to take steps to communicate with and educate people about the change – or it can be a signal that the change is a bad idea and needs to be redesigned. It is usually a good idea to evaluate the second possibility before spending time and money to implement the first solution.

---

3. This is what Dave's employer decided: Dave left the company when his project was cancelled.

Part of the job of effectively managing IT-based strategic change is to try to anticipate (*before* spending lots of money on development and promotion) whether an entrepreneurial idea is good enough to outweigh the human costs of change.

Falling through the cracks

Many situations of IT-based change occur entirely within a single organisation. An example is the implementation of the Web-based version of an ERP system. Managing change that affects people in a single organisation can be relatively straightforward, because all affected people report to the same executive. If worse comes to worst, the executive might be willing and able to use managerial power to handle any problems that arise. (But coercion can backfire and is rarely the most effective change management tactic. Effective change managers do not rely on it.)

Increasingly, electronic business is creating change situations that involve people *from several organisations*. These situations can be very challenging, because there is no common authority, the parties' goals and objectives are different, and no common organisational culture exists to promote cooperation across organisational lines. This does not mean that change will not occur, only that managing inter-organisational change is quite difficult, and it requires different strategies and tactics than managing intra-organisational change.

An example of inter-organisational change is the partnerships that industrial buyers and suppliers attempt to forge in order to reap supply chain efficiencies. Sometimes, buyers initiate these partnerships; sometimes, suppliers do. Many companies that try to create supply chain partnerships often run into difficulties because of a long history of antagonistic relationships between buyers and suppliers. In the American automotive industry, for instance, relationships between suppliers and the big-three automakers have been notoriously troubled. The large automakers historically exercised their considerable buying power over suppliers in ways that led to much resentment. Consequently, the automakers' more recent attempts to cooperate with suppliers are sometimes hindered by lack of trust. Inter-organisational change is difficult enough when the parties trust each other; lack of trust *adds* considerably to the challenges of an already difficult situation.

Let us consider an example of inter-organisational e-business change and the problems that arise in attempting to implement it. Although IT plays only a supporting role in this story, the lessons are applicable to situations where, for example, supply chain management software is the driver of the change or the vehicle by which it is supposed to occur. The example concerns Pellton International,[4] a multi-national chemical company that wanted more efficient supply relationships with its customers. Pellton supplies a generic chemical product to automotive industry suppliers. Although the product is generic, it can be

---

4. Corbett et al. (1999).

formulated in different ways and supplied in many sizes. Having to supply many different formulae and sizes of the same product adds to Pellton's production costs, and having to store many product combinations adds to customers' inventory carrying costs. Therefore, it can benefit both parties to streamline the number of product combinations ordered, manufactured and stored, and to have the vendor (in this case Pellton) responsible for managing inventory on a consignment basis.[5]

Basco is Pellton's largest customer, and Pellton's products are a key component of the products Basco makes and supplies to the major automobile assemblers. Basco faces heavy cost pressure from automakers, so saving money on Pellton's products would benefit Basco a lot. However, relations between Basco and Pellton had long been adversarial, and, although *executives* at the two companies recognised the value of cooperation, there was considerable mistrust between the two companies, especially at lower management levels.

A key change management challenge is different reactions to the same initiative by people with different jobs or different levels in the management hierarchy.

Pellton set up a workshop with Basco's corporate purchasing department to discuss ways to reduce the cost of supplying Pellton's products. Pellton's commercial director told workshop attendees that a single Basco plant stocked more than sixty different combinations of Pellton's products. A Basco manager claimed that was not true. It turned out the Basco manager was wrong – the plant *did* stock that many product combinations – and the Basco manager later became convinced that cooperating with Pellton to reduce costs was a good idea. But at the workshop the Basco manager was surprised by Pellton's data, and probably embarrassed as well – embarrassed for not knowing the data, and embarrassed because the data might imply that he was not doing his job well. Many change efforts fail owing to resistance by people who are embarrassed or threatened by a proposed change.

Proposing a "new improved" business activity implies that the old one was bad and that the people responsible for the old one were not doing a good job. The resulting embarrassment can generate great resistance to change – even when the new idea really is better.

In subsequent workshops, Pellton and Basco participants agreed on a series of pilot projects that would illustrate the savings potential of extending the change to all of Basco's plants. Setting up pilot projects can be a good change management tactic, because pilot project results can convince skeptical people that the benefits of change outweigh the costs. However, although both Pellton and Basco expected to benefit from reducing the number of Pellton products that Basco stocked, project participants did not clarify how the benefits would be shared between the companies. Later, that lack of clarity proved to be a mistake, since without a benefit-sharing arrangement, Basco managers had no incentive to supply Pellton with the information Pellton needed to manage inventory for Basco.

---

5. In a consignment situation, the buyer does not pay for the product until it is used. Vendor-managed inventory shifts inventory carrying costs from the buyer to the supplier.

A common change management challenge is lack of alignment between people's incentives and the required new behaviours.

As the project continued, a major barrier to project success surfaced. Basco was highly decentralised. This meant that purchasing managers at individual plants made their own purchasing decisions. Basco's corporate purchasing organisation (which was working with Pellton on the supply chain improvement project) did not have authority over plant purchasing managers and their purchasing decisions. There was no guarantee that the people in the plants would agree with Basco's corporate purchasing department about the benefits of cooperating with Pellton. And there were several reasons that plant purchasing managers might resist the changes that Pellton and Basco's corporate purchasing department were trying to implement. (What do you think they are, and how would you try to deal with them?)

The tactics available to change managers depend on who the change managers are (e.g. in terms of organisational position, hierarchical status, etc.).

In fact, Basco's Antwerp plant manager voiced major opposition to the Pellton cost reduction project. It is possible that the plant manager was concerned about a reduction in his decision-making autonomy. Autonomy is a key resource that managers try to preserve, because it is related to their ability to get things done. In other words, autonomy is related to managers' success as managers. It is also possible that the plant manager was rewarded according to the size of his budget. His budget might have been significantly reduced if he no longer controlled the purchasing of Pellton's products. Finally, it is possible that he resisted the project simply because it was started without his knowledge, approval and involvement. (This is an embarrassing and potentially threatening situation.)

New e-business initiatives may threaten to reduce people's autonomy. Threats to autonomy often generate resistance.

It would have been much easier to achieve the changes Pellton sought if Basco had a centralised purchasing policy. But change project participants (Pellton and Basco's corporate purchasing department) did not have the authority or resources to change Basco's purchasing policies. Making *that* change could only be done by Basco's chief executives. Basco's corporate purchasing department could have tried to convince Basco's chief executives to centralise purchasing in order to reduce costs. But we do not know how successful this tactic would have been. The change would surely have been resisted by the plants, and Basco's chief executives have many important considerations in addition to cost reduction. One of them is to keep plant managers happy.

Lower-level change managers often bemoan the failure of senior executives to "support" the change effort. But supporting the change effort may not be the senior executives' top priority. It is sometimes a better strategy to design the change initiative and/or the implementation strategy such that the support of senior executives is less needed.

Once the Antwerp plant manager calmed down, a pilot project was started in Antwerp. But after three months, inventory levels of Pellton products had not decreased. Lower inventory levels required accurate forecasts, and Basco employees had little incentive to improve forecast accuracy – incentive that a benefit-sharing arrangement might have been provided. Pellton refused to expand the pilot project to other Basco plants until inventory levels at Antwerp decreased. When the Antwerp plant manager learned about the high inventory levels, he was shocked and took steps to reduce them. Together Pellton and the Antwerp plant mapped the flows of forecast information and designed a better communication process involving electronic data exchange. By this time, Basco was cooperating freely with Pellton, and inventory levels decreased to the target level. Owing to strong advocacy by the Antwerp plant manager, senior managers at Basco approved an extension of the project throughout the company. Relationships between the companies improved, and Pellton solidified its position as Basco's preferred supplier.

This case illustrates many important lessons about the barriers facing IT-based changes that cross organisational lines and about effective and ineffective change tactics. Two lessons in particular stand out:

1   IT-based inter-organisational changes can affect people in various jobs and at various levels in two or more organisations. *All* affected people can influence, for better or worse, the success of the outcome.

2   An important consideration in devising effective change management strategies is the level and types of resources (including authority) available to the *change managers*. In the Pellton case, Basco's Antwerp plant manager could employ change tactics that Basco's corporate purchasing department could not use. Thus, it is important to decide *who* should be part of a change project. And it is important to select change tactics appropriate for the change manager's role.

Making the world go away

Many e-business initiatives involve people from two or more different countries. Cross-national e-business projects add complications to the already difficult process of managing IT-based change. Four different scenarios of cross-national IT-based change frequently arise.

In the first scenario, a global company tries to implement an e-business initiative in organisational units located in several countries. Because many global companies are highly decentralised, implementing an e-business initiative in different companies is a lot like implementing that initiative in several companies. Country managers often have considerable autonomy, and they tend to conduct business in locally appropriate ways. Corporate decision-making in Denmark and Israel, for example, is highly democratic, whereas it is much more authoritarian in China and Germany. This means that it is common for country managers to try to go their own ways where e-business projects are concerned.

---

6. Galliers and Newell (2001).

For example, a major international bank[6] decided to create a corporate network after losing a major account through failure to act like "one company" in locations around the globe. Fact-finding revealed that various bank departments in several different countries had set up over 150 separate intranets. When a two-day workshop was held to resolve the problem, business managers attended on the first day, but left their technical colleagues to sort out the details on the second day. Not surprisingly, the IT representatives decided that the solution was a corporate portal that would tie all the intranets together. When they went back to their business homes, several attendees began working – independently – on *the* corporate portal: within 10 days at least 6 or 7 "corporate" portals could be found at the bank.

Intra-organisational change in global companies can involve challenges similar to inter-company change.

Even when a standard solution has been agreed upon, the different circumstances found in different countries can make it quite challenging to achieve a uniform result. For example, when Allied Signal Inc.[7] tried to implement an ERP package in 18 sites in 11 countries, in which 9 different languages were spoken, implementers encountered a number of problems in addition to language differences. One problem was the different levels of IT and business skills in different plants. French workers did not understand modern production planning methods, and a special training program had to be developed just for them. There were also differences in local business practices. French managers created very narrow jobs for workers and demanded extensive documentation; Irish managers created broader jobs that required cross-functional training.

The implementation strategy for a global e-business initiative must often be tailored to differing local conditions.

Allied Signal attributed the success of its ERP implementation in part to an implementation project team whose 15 members included people from all 11 countries. "It never would have worked if they were all Americans." But managing teams of people from different national cultures involves its own special challenges. For example, Philippine team members would not be comfortable in feedback sessions where names are mentioned, and US team members would not be comfortable with the family-like relationships common in Philippine teams.[8] Teams tend to work better when team management styles fit local practices – something difficult to achieve in an international team. The problem becomes ever more complex when the international team is "virtual", that is, distributed in time and space, because people of different cultures have varying levels of comfort with impersonal means of communication. For example, the international members of Air Products Company's global virtual teams strongly felt the need for "face-mail", that is, travel between sites for face-to-face meetings, to deal with

7. Schneider (1999).
8. Kirkman et al. (2001).
9. Massey et al. (2001).
10. Ngwenyama (1998).

challenging problems.[9] But in another company, the Japanese members of a global software development team preferred email to telephone conference calls, because they had an easier time communicating in written, than in spoken, English.[10]

The cultural challenges of change often start with the change management team. But successful change management does not end there.

Another common scenario involving cross-cultural complications in e-business initiatives arises around B2C e-commerce websites. It is well known that people of different national cultures have different values: some value individuality, others value membership in a collective; some are comfortable with high "power distance" (deference to authority), whereas others adopt a more democratic orientation. These cultural values influence the kinds of information people seek from websites. And websites designed by people in different cultures exhibit systematic cultural differences.

For example, comparisons of similar transportation company websites in Malaysia and the US show differences that can be explained by differences in national cultural values.[11] The Malaysian site prominently featured a graphic of an imposing building, detailed information about the company mission, and profiles of senior managers and the members of the board of directors. High quality information about transportation, travel and tourism also had a place on the site, but this information was subordinated to corporate information. By contrast, the American site was oriented around helping passengers to purchase tickets. Information about the company and its board of directors was "buried" under "News and Views". What do these differences have to do with national culture? Malaysia is a country with much higher power distance than the US. "Malaysians want to know who is in charge of an organisation and how it is staffed." Americans, on the other hand, are very task-focused.

Successful global e-business initiatives must address differences in cultural values.

Because of these and many other national culture differences, e-commerce developers are often advised to customise websites to national preferences. However, there are other important considerations in successful global e-business initiatives. One study found that young Internet users in Turkey were much less likely than those in Britain and Denmark to accept Web-based marketing. But the differences were not well explained by differences in cultural values: the lower level of acceptance in Turkey had more to do with problems with Turkey's IT infrastructure than with cultural values.[12]

Problems with IT infrastructure are one example of what might be called "structural factors" that influence, along with cultural preferences, consumer adoption of e-commerce.[13] Consider another example. Consumers in Hong Kong are very Internet savvy and they frequently use the Web, but they generally do not purchase online. The reason is that Hong Kong is a dense urban area with

---

11. Gould et al. (2000).
12. Kucuk and Arslan (2000).
13. Markus and Soh (2002).

great public transportation and a wealth of shopping options convenient to most people's homes and workplaces. According to one Hong Kong shopper: "I once bought a book online from an online store. I bought it online because I couldn't find the book anywhere else. But I never bought online again. It took two months for me to get the book, and usually I want books *now*. So I go shopping in the bookstore. Online shopping is a last resort for me."

Other examples of structural factors that can influence e-commerce adoption in other countries include: language, credit card usage and consumer protection policies. The e-business change manager must take structural as well as cultural issues into account when devising a strategy to capture global consumer business. (Structural factors are an issue in the success of single country, as well as multi-country, e-business initiatives. For example, some consumers may be unable to access websites requiring a particular browser or an up-to-date browser version.)

Successful global e-business initiatives must also address differences in structural conditions around the globe. Structural conditions include income, access to technology, costs of telecommunications services, language issues and so forth.

The fourth common multi-country change management scenario concerns business-to-business initiatives. Again, cultural values may influence the outcomes. And, again, structural factors may underlie or reinforce cultural differences.

Consider B2B e-marketplaces. Successful Asian e-marketplaces exhibit many differences from successful North American e-marketplaces. Asian e-marketplaces are more likely to deal in direct goods (i.e. primary raw materials), whereas many US e-marketplaces deal in indirect goods (such as office supplies, lubricants and travel services). Direct goods often pose greater challenges for e-marketplace operators, because the products and services are less standardised and hence more difficult to describe online. But the benefits of e-marketplaces for direct goods are greater in Asia, where there are many intermediaries and inefficiencies. Finally, the lack of supporting infrastructure in much of Asia means that e-marketplaces have to provide numerous complementary services in the areas of logistics, payments, assurance and credit checks for a successful launch.

These differences are well illustrated by i-Metal.com, an Asian B2B e-marketplace in the nonferrous metals industry (e.g. aluminum and copper).[14] B2B marketplaces are believed more likely to flourish in fragmented industries, and the nonferrous metals industry in China is much more fragmented (many small companies) than in the West. In addition, B2B marketplaces are more likely to be successful in China, because spot buying (which is facilitated by marketplaces) is more common in China that in the West.

On the other hand, the quality of the e-commerce infrastructure in China is still quite poor in ways that might contribute to e-marketplace failure. For example, China lacks a well-functioning electronic payment system. Most business funds transfers involve currency: business checks are uncommon, and use of credit cards is considered an unsound practice. Business interruption insurance is unknown; banks do not provide escrow services to facilitate large transactions; and inventory

---

14. Hempel and Kwong (2001).

financing is unavailable (i.e. banks do not accept warehouse receipts as collateral for business loans). Chinese businesses have been quite loath to adopt ERP systems and other technologies that formalise and routinise business practices. And Chinese managers are relatively unversed in some modern business practices, such as the use of hedging in the metals industry.

These structural factors suggest that an electronic marketplace would not flourish in the Chinese nonferrous metals industry – unless something could be done to change them. Tackling these structural conditions was an important part of the change management strategy, and indeed the e-business strategy, of i-Metal.com. i-Metal.com is a successful B2B marketplace with services that include industry news and market information, online futures trading via the Shanghai futures exchange, online spot trading of primary and scrap metal, catalogue and quotation model purchasing and ancillary services such as transportation and payment. To attract members and induce them to use its services, i-Metal.com had to overcome the structural barriers to e-commerce in Chinese financial services industry. To do so, i-Metal partnered with three leading Chinese financial institutions:

1   i-Metal.com partnered with a leading bank to develop a Web-based payment system and to implement procedures for freezing funds (to emulate escrow arrangements – a service not offered by Chinese banks). The company is also working with banks to introduce more flexible inventory financing.

2   i-Metal.com worked with a leading futures brokerage to enable electronic funds transfers to brokerage accounts for online futures trading.

3   i-Metal.com worked with the Shanghai futures exchange to develop new business practices that would ensure that buyers and sellers would honour their online transactions despite the high price volatility that gives them an incentive to renege.

i-Metal.com also worked with warehousing and transportation companies to provide critical logistics services. In addition, the e-marketplace started a partnership with China Telecom to introduce the use of digital certificates.

The point of this example is that successful business-to-business initiatives may require careful attention to cross-national change management issues. As in business-to-consumer initiatives, cultural values may be important, but structural conditions should also not be neglected. The case of i-Metal.com shows that the most effective change management strategy may be to build change management solutions into the product or service offering rather than relying on implementation tactics like education and training to overcome difficulties when the product or service is introduced. Good change management is integral to successful e-business strategising.

Successful e-business strategists try to build change management solutions into their products and services. Good solutions must often address cross-national differences in cultural values and structural conditions.

Change management knowledge

The examples above illustrate a number of change management situations, challenges, and effective and ineffective responses. This section formalises the lessons of those examples as two categories of change management knowledge:

1   why people sometimes fail to adopt e-business innovations; and

2   tradeoffs between the design and implementation of e-business innovations.

Why people sometimes do not adopt e-business innovations

When change is viewed as problematic, it is natural to start thinking about the obstacles or barriers standing in the way of change. This can be a useful line of thinking because it is often easier *to remove obstacles* than to enable people to overcome them. However, the very term "resistance to change" implies that the problem of change is people. The implication is that if something can be done to fix (or remove) problematic people, the problem of change is solved. This idea is very seductive and there is *some* truth in it. Therefore, many change management strategies focus on changing the people who are *affected by* change.

However, the idea that people are the problem is incomplete at best, and often suggests very ineffective change tactics. The idea can blind us to problems arising from *other* elements of the DOT framework – these additional obstacles to change that may also need to be addressed before the desired change can happen. In e-business initiatives, one common source of change obstacles is the behaviour and attitudes of the *people who are trying to promote change*. Much research suggests that the roles and tactics of change *managers* can be as much a problem as the attitudes and behaviours of change *targets*.

A second set of obstacles concern the *nature of the change* itself. Some changes have very undesirable properties from the perspective of people affected by the change: a new technology may be very hard to use, a new system may do away with some people's jobs, a new way of working may erode valued social relationships and disrupt "organisational politics". Change managers tend to see the positive sides of change, but it is essential to know that others may be more aware of the negatives. If change managers fail to see the potential negatives of change, they are more likely to design changes that fail, and they may fail to see opportunities to design better changes. (Better changes are changes that are adopted and that have the desired positive outcomes with minimal negative outcomes.)

In other words, there are different ways to think about resistance to change. Each view of resistance suggests different courses of action for change managers. If a theory of resistance fits a situation well, the actions based on the theory are more likely to be effective than if the theory does not fit. Therefore, effective change managers are skilled at diagnosing resistance and formulating change tactics appropriate to their diagnosis. The discussion below makes explicit several alternative theories of resistance (theories that focus on the change target, theories that focus on the change manager, and theories that focus on the change itself) and the change tactics each theory implies.

Psychological issues

Since the most common theory of change challenges is that "people resist change", it is useful to review the psychology of change and resistance. At least three psychological dynamics can manifest themselves as resistance to change.[15]

Psychological loss: People can view the introduction of something new as the death or loss of a valued something old. Mourning is a normal response to the passing of something we held dear. And when the loss is felt intensely as "loss of control" – the inability to cope with the changes in organisational life – people can respond to loss by failing to "let go" of the old. Symptoms include people stubbornly digging in their heels, exerting whatever forms of control they retain and attempting to keep things as they are. *When people stubbornly insist that things must remain just as they are, they are often in denial or mourning – a symptom of psychological loss.*

Psychological "limits to growth": There is an old saying: "nothing fails like success." It means that when something has worked for us in the past, we naturally expect it will continue to work in the future. We keep doing the same things over and over, even when they no longer work. We become trapped in our outdated "mental models".[16] Further, if we let ourselves see that the old ways are not working, we may start to believe that the problem is *us*: we are *not good enough to* succeed. Then our confidence goes, and we think that nothing we can do will ever make a difference. This makes us *unable* to change, even when we are willing. *When people become apathetic and lack the energy or enthusiasm to try new things, psychological limits to growth may be operating.*

Psychological defensiveness: Psychological defensiveness often kicks in when other people tell us that we need to change. This message can trigger a chain of negative psychological reactions: "If we were good enough to begin with, we wouldn't have to change, would we? So the very fact that we are being asked to change means that we're somehow deficient or bad. This is insulting! And it's embarrassing! How can we retain our dignity and self-respect? We must fight back (or retreat) in face of this challenge." *When people respond to change with rage, aggression or extreme withdrawal, it is a sign that psychological defensiveness has been aroused.*

Unfortunately, as natural as these human responses to change are, they are often misinterpreted by the people who are trying to bring change about. "Negative" reactions to change are often taken as evidence that the change targets

---

15. DeLuca (1993).
16. Senge (1990).

are the problem: "If people resist change, they must lack *the motivation* to change." Change managers who have these beliefs may try to motivate the change targets by instilling a sense of urgency or crisis. "This company will be out of business in six months if we don't do something now." "Your job is on the line." This tactic is sometimes called creating a "burning platform" mentality. (The thinking goes that if your oil platform is burning, you will not think twice about jumping into the ice-cold sea.)

While the crisis strategy sometimes succeeds, it can arouse even more anxiety and defensiveness in the change targets, making it a self-defeating approach. Generally, motivational experts believe that people respond more positively to *moderate* amounts of challenge, to situations in which they believe they can succeed, and to activities that are engaging and fun. This view of human motivation is not consistent with the strategy of trying to fire people up by manufacturing a sense of crisis.

Similarly, change managers who believe that change targets do not have *the ability* to change may spend great effort on educational programmes. The expectation is that people need training to "think out of the box" (i.e. think creatively) in a reengineering project. Or, the assumption may be that, if people only knew more about modern inventory management principles (or supply chain management), then they would not be so opposed to an ERP (or SCM) system. It *is* true that the failure to educate and train people properly has been identified as a major failure factor in IT-enabled change. However, there are dangers in relying too heavily on training and education as ways to "overcome resistance to change". There may be many other major barriers to change that training cannot address (e.g. inappropriate leadership by senior executives, incentive systems that reward behaviour inconsistent with the change, technology that is hard to learn and use and so on).

The most important conclusions one can draw about "psychological" theories of resistance to change are:

- Change targets' negative responses to change are normal and natural and they need to be "worked through". Change managers can often help best by patiently and skillfully working with change targets' emotions.

- Change targets' negative responses to change may have causes other than the targets' personal deficiencies. For one thing, negative responses to change may be provoked by the ill-advised behaviours of *change managers* (e.g. manufacturing a crisis). For another, they may be provoked by ill-conceived *changes*.

- Relying too heavily on psychological theories of resistance is not a good idea, because it can lead change managers to pursue solutions (e.g. creating a crisis mentality, or educational programs) that do not fully address the obstacles to change.

The next two sections examine alternative causes of resistance to change: inappropriate change manager behaviour and "bad" changes.

Change managers and the process of change

It is sometimes said, "people don't resist change, they resist *being changed*". This saying implies that the behaviour of those who are trying to introduce change may somehow contribute to the failure of change efforts.

As early as 1954, a now famous, much-reprinted, article on dealing with resistance to change pointed out that people do not resist change, they resist changes in their social relationships with staff specialists.[17] Writing about relationships between factory operators and staff industrial engineers, the author of the article showed that

> by his brusque manner and by his lack of explanation, [the industrial engineer] led the operator to fear that her usual work relationships [where she was viewed as someone with valuable skills and knowledge and some sense of responsibility about her work] were being changed. And she just did not like the new way she was being treated.

This quote rings equally true today when "the staff specialists" are IT specialists or members of reengineering or ERP system implementation teams and when "the factory operators" are accountants, sales representatives, inventory control people and their managers. Today, as 50 years ago, how change managers behave can be a major factor in the success of the change effort.

It is useful to know that there are many different ways to define the change manager's role, whether the change manager is an information systems (IS) professional, a manager, a third-party consultant, or – increasingly common in the case of e-business initiatives – a change *team*, composed of all of the above and *representatives* of the areas affected by the change. (No matter how many representatives there are on a change team, it is impossible to include everyone. Therefore, there is always the chance of "us–them" dynamics between the change team and everyone else.) In e-business initiatives, there are three broad ways of conceptualising the role of the change manager:[18] technocrat, facilitator or advocate.

The technocrat – "If we build it they will come". In the technocratic model of change management, *technology* causes change. The role of the human change manager(s) is to build the technology. Technocrats are technical experts. They do not pursue their own objectives. Rather, they design technology that serves the objectives of the organisation's executives. The technocrat's responsibilities end with designing the change – it is up to the executives and others to see that the technology is used and that the desired objectives are achieved.

The facilitator – "We can work it out". In the facilitator model, change is caused by *the people affected by the change*. The facilitator promotes change by helping people increase their ability to change – by educating and training them, or

---

17. Lawrence (1969).
18. Markus and Benjamin (1996).

by providing conditions in which people can participate in designing the change themselves. The facilitator serves the interests of many stakeholders: the organisation's executives, the people affected by the change, and others, such as customers and stockholders. The facilitator's responsibilities end with creating the conditions in which others can do the right things. The facilitator is not personally responsible for achieving the objectives set for the change effort.

The advocate – "Whatever it takes". In the advocate model, change is caused by *change managers* – the advocate and those with whom the advocate works to bring about change (including those affected by the change). Advocates see themselves as responsible for making change happen. They advocate change by increasing change targets' awareness of the need for change, their motivation and their ability to carry out change. The tactics used by change advocates include communication, persuasion, shock, manipulation, and the direct exercise of personal power and organisational authority.

These differences in change manager roles help explain why successful change management requires as much attention to the attitudes and behaviours of the *change managers* as to the change targets. Choice of change manager role and approach is a key factor for the success of change efforts.

It is important to note that *none* of these roles is always better than the others. Each has strengths and weaknesses.

1 The technocrat role reflects the reality that staff specialists (including change teams) do not have the authority to *make* changes; they can only *recommend* changes to executives. On the negative side, by focusing mainly on technical and economic issues and by disclaiming responsibility for outcomes, technocrats may design failure-prone change efforts. (One result is low credibility of the technocrats.)

2 Advocates are most likely to achieve their objectives. On the downside, staff specialists and lower-level organisational members can rarely play the advocate role successfully. In addition, the advocate role can generate negative fallout: people may feel manipulated; the burning platform mentality may burn *people* out, and so forth.

3 The facilitator role builds the capabilities of the people affected by change. And many facilitated changes are well accepted by change targets. However, by assuming that participation will automatically produce good change designs, facilitators often contribute to the design of changes that do not meet objectives.

Ultimately, change managers' roles and tactics must fit their structural positions relative to the change targets. For instance, in the Pellton case considered earlier in the chapter, Basco's Antwerp plant manager could be an effective advocate whereas Basco's central purchasing department members were limited to the technocrat and facilitator roles.

Bad ideas

A another view of resistance to change is that "people don't resist change, they resist *bad changes*". Here the focus is on the solution that is implemented, not on who is leading the change or how it is implemented. According to this view, to avoid (or overcome) resistance, the change manager should change the e-business initiatives so that it is no longer bad.

There are a number of ways in which e-business initiatives can be bad. They may have obvious technical flaws or fail to fit the nature of the work people do. They may require people to work in new ways that conflict with organisational (or national) culture. Or they may disrupt organisational political systems. Let us consider each possibility in more detail.

Technology and technology-task misfits: As mentioned earlier, change managers who adopt the technocrat role tend to have high opinions of technology and tend to minimise technology's problems. For them, debugging technology glitches can be fun. But for ordinary mortals, misfits between technology and one's work can be frustrating at best and disastrous at worse. The package delivery company FedEx used to evoke smiles with its commercials depicting hapless businesspeople telling another delivery company: "if it's not there tomorrow, I'm out of business". (The next scene showed the business shuttered with an "out of business" sign on the door.) For many people, "I'm out of business" is the reality of unreliable technologies. It is sad but true that technology often lets people down.

One small company president interviewed for a research project explained that his successful business had nearly failed owing to a botched ERP-system installation. There were many factors in the disaster – it was not just the software that was at fault, the company also received bad advice from a variety of technical and management consultants. Whatever the cause, the bottom line was awful. For six weeks, the company was unable to issue an invoice or pay a supplier. And that was only part of the disruption. As a result, the company lost some customers – permanently.

Technology does not have to be so glaringly bad to engender "resistance". It can merely be difficult to learn and to use. In another company, customers tended to return products for repair in batches of 10 or more at a time. The company's old systems allowed customer service personnel to open a single repair ticket for all the equipment returned in the batch. The company's new system required them to create a new repair ticket for *each item* in the batch and to reenter all customer information from scratch each time. As a result, customer service personnel could not finish in twelve hours what they had formerly done in eight. Fortunately, the company's managers viewed the problem as an unavoidable negative side effect of a system that would provide great benefits for the company as a whole. To avoid rebellion or even sabotage by the customer service department, they supplied the resources to hire new staff.

Cultural misfits: Sometimes, changes and systems are "bad" because they do not fit the organisational or national culture. For example, when Lotus Notes was introduced to consultants in one professional services firm, the technology was not initially used, because people in the company thought they got ahead by hording, not sharing, their expertise. They failed to submit their work papers and lessons learned to the Lotus Notes database for fear that others in the organisation would use their work to earn a promotion at their expense in the company's "up or out" career structure.[19]

Ultimately, this company succeeded with its knowledge management programme by changing *the change*: *in addition to* providing Lotus Notes, change managers convinced senior managers to model effective information-sharing behaviour, and they changed the reward scheme for junior consultants – people were told that they would not be promoted if they did not make valuable contributions to the organisation's knowledge base.

Changes and systems can also conflict with *national culture*. For instance, a geographic information system in India did not have the hoped-for results, in part because India is not "a map culture".[20] (That is, people there tend not to draw or consult maps, and they often have trouble reading maps.) In Singapore, admissions personnel in hospitals had trouble using SAP, because that package required users to enter names in Western format (first, middle, last), and the operators had to parse the names of Chinese, Malay, Indian and Western patients, whose name formats differ.[21]

Change managers often become very impatient with cultural misfits. Reengineering advocates like Michael Hammer have been known to advise "nuking the culture" if culture stands in the way of radical improvement in business processes and organisational performance. But it is worth bearing in mind that one definition of culture is "that which was successful in the past".[22] This means that attempts to forcibly change culture are likely to generate extreme psychological defensiveness. A far better approach is to try to work *with* the culture – changing only those aspects of culture that really block the change, modifying the system or change when possible, introducing supportive interventions, and showing how the change is consistent with certain valued traditions.

Political misfits: For many people "politics" is a dirty word. The word conveys illicit deals, paybacks and other forms of corruption. But politics can be more positively viewed as "the way things get done in organisations". If you want something to happen – particularly if that something is not likely to happen on its own, surely the case for major strategic change! – you need to find the people who can make it happen and make it worth their while to help you. Conversely, failure to play politics can spell the failure of your project.

The political perspective on resistance reminds us to look at power. Who in the organisation has it; who does not? Who could support the change; who could oppose it? Furthermore, who might *want to* oppose the change, because

19. Orlikowski (1993).
20. Walsham and Sahay (1999).
21. Soh et al. (2000).
22. Schein (1992).

the change threatens their autonomy or power? In one company,[23] each of the major divisions was managed as a fiefdom. The corporate offices did not have enough information to manage the divisions, and the divisions did not want to give it to them. By introducing a new financial system that gave access to detailed divisional financial data, corporate financial specialists hoped to gain power over the divisions. Naturally, divisional accountants resisted. (In this case, there were many other reasons for their resistance, including the non-involvement of divisional accountants in system implementation, technical problems and technology-task misfits in the divisions.)

Another useful way to think about politics is in terms of incentives. As complex social systems, organisations allocate rewards and punishments to motivate certain behaviours and discourage other ones. In many cases, resistance to a new system or innovation can be attributed to conflicting incentive systems. And changing the incentive systems can reduce or eliminate resistance to change. For example, in the Lotus Notes case mentioned earlier, the promotion system for consultants acted as an incentive system for competitive information-hording behaviour.

Political misfits often go hand-in-hand with technology problems, technology-task misfits and cultural misfits. This means that, even if you find and fix one type of problem, but you neglect the others, your initiative may fail. Successful e-business initiatives require a good understanding of *all* major potential sources of "resistance to change". And to identify these sources, two useful guides are the DOT framework and the various theories of resistance discussed in this chapter.

Tradeoffs between the design and implementation of e-business innovations

It should be clear by now that successful e-business change management is not just about overcoming resistance to an innovation that has already been designed and introduced, it is also about designing innovations so that, in addition to accomplishing their intended goals, they are not resisted in the first place. It is particularly important to build change management into the design of e-business initiatives because, with e-business initiatives it is often not possible to employ "after the fact" change tactics such as persuasion and training. This is particularly the case in e-business services targeting the general public: because an extensive education campaign is prohibitively expensive, successful e-business initiatives must almost be *self-implementing*.

Even for e-business initiatives inside companies, it is useful to assume that you will not have the luxury of protracted communication and training or of senior managers willing to mandate use of a particular technology or process. This suggests that extraordinary attention should be paid to human issues and usability

---

23. Markus (1983).

testing *during* the innovation design process. It also suggests that e-business change managers should be willing to go "back to the drawing board" when their plans encounter resistance.

Consider the story of Roger,[24] a chief information officer who wanted to introduce an e-procurement system in his company. Working with the Chairman and CEO of his company, Roger identified a pressing competitive need to reduce costs and increase profitability. One of the most promising opportunities involved the purchasing of indirect goods and services (e.g. office supplies, travel services). Through careful analysis, Roger identified six categories of spending that accounted for 40 per cent of total indirect purchases; he calculated that savings of 10–25 per cent were possible if the company aggregated purchases to obtain volume discounts from key suppliers.

Key to obtaining these savings was people's compliance with the company's new purchasing agreements. Savings would be greatest if 100 per cent of purchasing was done against the volume contracts, but if purchasers ignored the volume contracts and purchased from other suppliers, no savings would result. Roger computed that every 3 per cent increase in compliance would drive $1.2 million to the company's bottom line – a very significant improvement.

Unfortunately, the company was highly decentralised in both structure and culture. Changing these elements of the organisation just to achieve purchasing efficiencies was not a sound option, so Roger conceived the idea of installing an e-procurement package. Roger knew that installing an e-purchasing package was not the only technical option: many suppliers have procurement portals from which the people in Roger's company could make their purchases. But Roger wanted the e-procurement system, because it would be integrated with his company's general ledger: this integration would allow him to easily track, without a lot of manual number crunching, the level of compliance with corporate purchasing agreements.

Here is how Roger described people's reactions to his proposed e-procurement system:

> Well, the human side [of the situation was] they didn't want [compliance] measured. We ran into a tremendous amount of passive/aggressive resistance . . . Plus I made just a huge mistake in trying to go from a very decentralised purchasing approach to one that completely centralised the purchasing overnight [in order to cost justify a major expenditure for the e-procurement system].

> The CEO and I had a conversation [and decided to take] a huge step back and said, how do you redesign our approach that will enable us to get most of the benefits without anywhere near the investment [in IT, so that we would see a financial return in] about one quarter.

> And we came up with the approach [of breaking up the six categories of spending] into functional discipline ownership. Because one of the fundamental rules that I probably should have mentioned is that [with centralised purchasing] you are taking away

---

24. David Petrie learned about this example while doing his doctoral dissertation research.

something that was really enjoyed by the groups. In other words they got all kinds of perks, and now this central procurement organisation has all that access to what [the groups] used to very much enjoy. [Now] we still have the responsibility for negotiating the national contracts, but we did not take away the local groups' access to the vendors.

Roger learned the hard way that some types of innovations generate major resistance. But he also learned that, by changing the innovation, it was possible to get even better results than he initially anticipated. How was the outcome better? First, the new solution did not require a very expensive investment in information technology – Roger and the CEO "mothballed" (shelved) the proposed e-procurement system. Second, the new solution achieved the desired result without external compliance monitoring: "[The groups] now feel part of the process and as a result they're voluntarily holding themselves accountable for compliance." Trying to get people to do what you want with external monitoring and rewards is far more costly than gaining their voluntary compliance.

Roger summed up his learning as follows:

We were trying to meet organisational change with technology. All that does is increase . . . risk, because if you do not deal with the people issues up front . . . all you're doing is postponing [the need to deal with people issues]. And they will find a way to sabotage the tremendous advancement in IT. I'd rather lose a few battles [with IT] and win the war [of getting business results].

Roger resolved his change management situation without technology, but in other cases, technology is a key lever of change. All elements of the DOT framework are potential levers in the design of effective changes.

Another way to design better changes is by improvising a sequence of smaller change efforts. e-business strategists occasionally succumb to the temptations of "big bang" organisational change. They set up large change teams with big budgets to acquire expensive software and introduce it everywhere at once. While this approach sometimes yields great results, it is risky and visible – if you fail, you do so in public, damaging your credibility and the chances that your future change efforts will be successful.

The big bang is not the only or best approach to achieve radical business improvements. It is often possible to gain impressive results quickly using a more incremental approach that involves:

- identifying and implementing the "minimum critical" kernel of change;

- assessing results and identifying unintended consequences; and

- making "fast cycle" extensions and improvisations that progressively urge results in the desired direction.

In the case of Roger's e-procurement project, the minimum critical ingredient was *information* about the need for procurement savings and how to obtain them. Once the most important categories of indirect spending had been identified and volume discounts negotiated, people in his organisation were voluntarily motivated to comply and business results were achieved in a single step. In other organisations, however, the budgets and reward processes might not initially provide enough incentives for voluntary compliance. In that case, a second change management step might be to create a public scorecard of purchasing results. Without an e-procurement system tied into the general ledger, a public scorecard could require a burdensome manual data-gathering process. However, on a one-time (or infrequent) basis, the effort could pay off by encouraging executives to modify their management control processes. Through a rapid series of such "plan, do, check, correct" cycles, e-business change managers can often get better results at much less expense and risk than through a big-bang project.

Summary

Change management involves synchronising the human aspects of e-business initiatives with the other elements of the DOT framework. An ineffective approach is to think about change management for the first time after an initiative has been designed and introduced and has provoked resistance. A more effective strategy is to try to anticipate people's reactions in advance and to build a response to them into the design and implementation of the e-business initiative. Then, through an iterative process, the effective change manager monitors results and makes modifications to keep the direction, level and pace of change on the desired track.

Questions for discussion

1   What is change management? What factors affect the success of a change management strategy?

2   On the basis of the Hollywood talent system example, what questions should you ask about a proposed innovation to anticipate people's likely reactions? (Hint: how can the DOT framework help?)

3   What problems might arise when implementing inter-organisational change?

4   What further complications arise in cross-national e-business projects? How do Asian e-marketplaces differ from North American e-marketplaces?

5   What psychological factors make people resist change and how can managers address these issues?

6   What are the roles that a manager can assume during change management?

7   What are some ways in which e-business initiatives can be bad?

8   How might an innovation be changed to get better results?

References

Corbett, C.J., Blackburn, J.D. and Van Wassenhove, L.N. (1999) "Case study partnerships to improve supply chains", *Sloan Management Review*, Summer, pp. 71–82.

DeLuca, J.R. (1993) *Overcoming Resistance to Change*, New York: Evergreen Business Group.

Galliers, R.D. and Newell, S. (2001) "Electronic commerce and strategic change within organisations: lessons from two cases", *Journal of Global Information Management*, July–September, pp. 15–22.

Gould, E.W., Zakaria, N. and Yusof, S.A.M. (2000) "Applying culture to Website design: a comparison of Malaysian and US Websites", *IEEE Technology & Teamwork*, pp. 161–71.

Hempel, P.S. and Kwong, Y.K. (2001) "B2B e-commerce in emerging economies: i-Metal.com's nonferrous metals exchange in China", *Journal of Strategic Information Systems*, vol. 10, no. 4, pp. 335–55.

Kirkman, B.L., Gibson, C.B. and Shapiro, D.L. (2001) " 'Exporting' teams: enhancing the implementation and effectiveness of work teams in global affiliates", *Organisational Dynamics*, vol. 30, no. 1, pp. 12–29.

Kucuk, S.U. and Arslan, M. (2000) "A cross cultural comparison of consumer's acceptance of Web marketing facilities", *Journal of Euro-Marketing*, vol. 9, no. 3, pp. 27–43.

Lawrence, P.R. (1969) "How to deal with resistance to change", *Harvard Business Review*, vol. 4, no. 12 (January–February), p. 176.

Markus, M.L. and Soh, C. (2002) "Structural influences on global e-commerce activity", *Journal of Global Information Management*, vol. 10, no. 1 (January–March), pp. 5–12.

Markus, M.L., Farhoomand, A.F. and Ho, P. (2002) "Government e-procurement: electronic tendering system in the Hong Kong SAR", *The Centre for Asian Business Cases*, The University of Hong Kong, June.

Markus, M.L. and Benjamin, R.I (1996) "Change agentry: the next IS frontier", *MISQ*, vol. 20, no. 4 (December), pp. 385–407.

Markus, M.L. (1983) "Power, politics, and MIS implementation", *Communications of the ACM*, vol. 26, no. 6 (June), pp. 430–44.

Massey, A.P., Hung, Y.T.C., Montoya-Weiss, M. and Ramesh, V. (2001) "When culture and style aren't about clothes: perceptions of task-technology 'Fit' in global virtual teams", *Proceedings of GROUP '01*, Boulder, CO, pp. 207–13.

Ngwenyama, O. (1998) "Groupware, social action and emergent organisations: on the process dynamics of computer mediated Distributed Work", *Accounting, Management and Information Technology*, vol. 8, no. 4 (September), pp. 127–46.

Orlikowski, W.J. (1993) "Learning from notes: organisational issues in groupware development", *Information Society*, vol. 9, no. 3 (July–September), pp. 237–50.

Schein, E.H. (1992) *Organisational Culture and Leadership*, 2nd Edn, San Francisco, CA: Jossey-Bass.

Schneider, P. (1999) "Wanted ERPeople skills", *CIO Magazine* [online], available from http://www.cio.com/archive/030199/erp.html [accessed 1 March 1999].

Senge, P. (1990) *The Fifth Discipline: The Art and Practice of the Learning Organisation*, New York, NY: Doubleday Currency.

Soh, C., Sia, S.K. and Tay-Yap, J. (2000) "Enterprise resource planning: cultural fits and misfits, is ERP a universal solution?" *Communications of the ACM*, vol. 43, no. 4 (April), pp. 47–51.

Walsham, G. and Sahay, S. (1999) "GIS for district-level administration in India: problems and opportunities", *MIS Quarterly*, vol. 23, no. 1 (March), pp. 39–65.

Case study   Government e-procurement: electronic tendering system in the Hong Kong SAR

The Electronic Tendering System (ETS) was the first Government to Business (G2B) initiative to operate under a legal framework to promote electronic commerce in Hong Kong. Launched in April 2000, ETS was an online tender box that directly linked suppliers with the Government Supplies Department of the Hong Kong Special Administrative Region (HKSAR), enabling tender issue, submission and notification of award over the Internet. ETS was part of the Hong Kong Government's strategy to develop Hong Kong into an "Information Hub". It was also one of the world's first web-based electronic tendering systems for e-government applications.

By 2002, ETS had gained significant recognition in the e-business arena, including a number of industry awards.[1] After two years of implementation, subscription rate exceeded 30 per cent with a total of 1800 online subscribers out of the existing 5000 registered suppliers. With this initial success, the HKSAR Government planned to extend the electronic system to all other Government procurements (except Works tenders), with a goal of issuing 80 per cent of all procurement tenders online by the end of 2003. The Government also planned an Electronic Marketplace System (EMS) for the small value purchases, eventually expected to link the two systems in a "Total Procurement Solution". This would be a formidable task given the diversity of the existing processes across the procuring departments. How should a common infrastructure be built for these procurements across the Government organisations? How should the implementation be sequenced among the procuring departments? How should organisational change management issues be dealt with?

In light of the current economic downturn and fiscal constraints, how should the Government position itself in further IT investments?

Digital 21 and e-procurement strategies

In his 1997 Policy Address, HKSAR Chief Executive Tung Chee Wah announced his vision for Hong Kong to be *a leader and not a follower in the information world of tomorrow*, to use Information Technology (IT) to retain Hong Kong's competitive edge, and to drive overall economic expansion. To this end, the Digital 21 Strategy was formulated under the auspices of the Information Technology and Broadcasting Bureau (ITBB) in 1998. The primary focus of the Digital 21 Strategy was to build capabilities and infrastructure to support a thriving information economy, and to create a strong foundation for growth in the use of IT in the HKSAR. The objective was to develop Hong Kong into a leading digital city in the globally connected world.

In 2001, a comprehensive E-Government Strategy was promulgated including set targets for the provision of public services online. Flagship projects fell under the following four categories:

● *Government-to-Business (G2B)*: government departments would transact with suppliers online to improve efficiency and reduce compliance costs of the business sector, thus enhancing competitiveness.

● *Government-to-Citizen (G2C)*: government departments would provide online public services to individual citizens to improve service level, and to enhance public confidence in conducting electronic transactions, thus promoting a wider adoption of IT in the community.

1. The project won the Hong Kong e-Award for Design and Innovation in the category of E-Public Services in 2000, and the UUNET/Economic Times Business Web Site of the Year Awards 2000 for the Best Public Sector Site.

- *Government-to-Employee (G2E)*: government departments would use electronic means in communication and transactions with employees to enhance internal management efficiency and reduce administrative costs, thus fostering an E-Government culture within the civil service.

- *Government-to-Government (G2G)*: government departments would adopt electronic transactions to communicate internally and with other departments, thereby promoting the use of IT in the Government.

The e-Procurement strategy was the key initiative under the G2B scheme. Its goal was to provide an electronic medium for the entire procurement process, from integrated supplier database, invitation to tender, receipt and negotiation of tenders, to contract signing and payment. The Electronic Tendering System (ETS) was the first implementation under the e-Procurement Strategy to enhance and transform the existing Government procurement process.

The government procurement process

The procurement policy of the Government of the HKSAR was to obtain goods and services at the best value for money in support of the Government's programmes and activities. Procurement policy mandated providing equal opportunities to domestic and foreign suppliers and service providers through open, fair, competitive and transparent procedures. The process was governed by the Stores and Procurement Regulations (SPR) issued by the Financial Secretary and the regulations were supplemented by Financial Circulars issued by the Secretary for the Treasury. The procedures laid down in these regulations and circulars are consistent with the provisions in the World Trade Organisation Agreement on Government Procurement (WTO GPA).

In general, the Government procurement services were classified and administered as follows (see Exhibit 1 for the detailed procurement practices of the HKSAR):

Exhibit 1 Existing procurement practices of the HKSAR

(i) Minor Purchases
Bureaux/Departments are delegated with the authority to make direct purchases of stores of a value not exceeding $0.5M. This financial limit is raised to $0.75M for departments with Supplies Officers, $1M for departments with Senior Supplies Officers, and $1.3M for departments with Chief Supplies Officers or above.

(ii) Purchases of Stores and Related Services Exceeding the Departmental Direct Purchases Limit
Purchases of stores and related services exceeding the departmental direct purchases limit are processed by GSD.

(iii) Procurement of Goods by Other Departments
A few departments also conduct their own procurement of goods. These include the purchase of vehicles by the Government Land Transport Agency, boats by the Marine Department and printing machines and paper by the Government Printer.

(iv) Construction Services
Construction services are procured by the individual works departments concerned, under the general supervision of the Works Bureaux.

(v) Tender Boards
The Financial Secretary has appointed 5 tender boards for consideration of the acceptance of offer for procurement of stores and services under various financial limits.

Source: Guide to Procurement by the Government of the HKSAR, http://www.info.gov.hk/fb/tender.

1 *small purchases under HK$1.3 million* were handled by individual Government departments with their own processes (Request For Proposals, Request For Quotations, formal tender, etc.);

2 *procurements between HK$1.3 and 10 million* were co-ordinated by the Government Supplies Department (GSD), the central purchasing, storage and supply organization for the HR SAR Government (described below);

3 *procurements over HK$10 million* were governed by the Central Tender Board (CTB), an oversight body reporting to the Secretary of the Treasury; and

4 *works or construction-related procurements* were administered by the Works Bureau.

Government supplies department

GSD was the central purchasing, storage and supplies organization for the HKSAR Government, serving over 80 Government departments, subvented organizations and a number of non-Government organisations. The objective of GSD's procurement service was to obtain, at best value for money and in a timely manner, the goods and services required by the procuring departments. This was achieved through open competitive tendering procedures following the SPR guidelines. The Department was currently responsible for procuring around HK$5000 million worth of goods and services each year.

GSD was responsible for the provisioning, storage and distribution of a wide range of common user items, such as stationery, pharmaceutical products, hospital sundries, furniture and household goods, that were used across the service by Government departments and other public bodies. In addition, GSD acted as the purchasing agent for stores and equipment required by specific procuring departments. These departments relied on GSD for expertise in sourcing,

tendering, negotiations and contract administration. The goods purchased by GSD on behalf of these departments were diverse, including aircraft for the Government Flying Service, electronic parking devices for the Transport Department, arms and ammunition for the Police, chlorine for water treatment plants, gases for medical and industrial purposes, and food and beverage for public hospitals.

Electronic tendering system

Under the Government's e-Procurement Strategy, the objectives of the ETS project were:

- improved Customer Services;
- less paper-work and re-keying for GSD and suppliers;
- increased visibility of the tender process;
- foundation for full electronic commerce;
- testing ground for other e-Government applications;
- more competitive trade environment; and
- improve value for money in purchases.

(See Exhibit 2 for fuller descriptions of these objectives.)

In April 1999, after a competitive bidding process, the ETS contract was awarded to Computer and Technologies Ltd. (C&T), a rapidly expanding IT services provider in Hong Kong. C&T had subsequently spun off its application services unit to its subsidiary, GO-Business, which then took over the operations of the ETS project (see Exhibits 3A and 3B). The HK$3.8 million contract involved the building of the online tender system, operating and maintaining the system for two years at a annual service fee of HK$600,000, and an option for the Government to extend the contract for another three years.

The project was implemented in three phases. Phase 1 was launched in April 2000 and involved the building of an online

Exhibit 2 Objectives of electronic tendering system

Improved Customer Service
- Shorter times for receiving invitations and submitting bids
- Less paperwork for suppliers
- Round-the-clock downloading of invitations and submission of bids
- Reduced postage and packaging costs
- More convenient customers access through the Internet
- Electronic access to tenders by procuring departments.

Less paperwork for GSD
- More time available for value-added procurement activities instead of routine tasks.

Less rekeying
- More accurate transcriptions
- Less time needed for corrections.

Increased visibility
- Increased visibility of GSD's procurement processes by suppliers and the public
- Improved perceptions of fairness in procurement.

Foundation for full electronic commerce
- Significant benefits from utilizing the Internet in future for full electronic commerce
- Stepping stone towards the paperless office within GSD
- Expandability for contract monitoring and issuing payment functions.

Testing ground
- Pilot project for other Internet applications in Government
- Increased technology usage in Hong Kong.

More competitive trade environment
- More efficient and competitive trade environment in Hong Kong
- Hong Kong companies in a better position to trade effectively abroad.

Improve value for money in purchases
- Larger supplier base for Government purchases, increasing price and quality competition
- Lower prices through lower transaction costs
- Better bids through increases time for suppliers to produce their bids (especially foreign suppliers).

Source: Computer & Technologies, *Application Scoping Document, Electronic Tendering System,* March 2000.

Exhibit 3A GO-business

Global e-Business Services Limited (GO-Business) is a wholly-owned subsidiary of the rapidly expanding Computer And Technologies Holdings Ltd (C&T). Formed as one of four business units after C&T's listing in the Hong Kong Stock Exchange in 1998, GO-Business provides application services for the e-business. Building on the strengths and networks of its parent company, GO-Business focuses on application services for Operations Resource Management Systems (ORMS), including back-office enterprise applications, Human Resources solutions, tendering solutions, workflow and document solutions. Its recent acquisition of IPL, an established local Human Resources management systems provider, reinforces its strategic focus in this area.

Exhibit 3B Four business units at C&T

Integration Services (C&T Integration Ltd)	Solution Services (C&T Solutions Ltd)	Application Services (GO-Business)	Distribution Business (Maxfair Technologies Ltd)
Provision of systems and network integration service and industry-specific IT application solutions, with a focus in China	Provision of IT services, solutions and custom-developed systems for large enterprises in public and private sectors	Provision of B2B and enterprise e-business application services	Distribution of multi-media digital processing products and networking products

Source: C&T Business Review for the 6 Months Ended June 2000, p. 1.

platform for the existing tender process for GSD procurements between HK$1.3 and 10 million. Phase 2 was launched in December 2001 and extended the online capabilities to GSD-originated tenders over HK$10 million, currently administered through the Central Tender Board (CTB). Phase 3 was planned to be launched by the end of 2003 to deliver an end-to-end online tendering system, providing connectivity between the ETS platform and the individual purchasing departments, and enabling the staff of the departments to be more involved in the operations of their own tendering processes. Concurrently, GSD was pursuing an Electronic Marketplace System (EMS) for the small tenders under HK$1.3 million, currently procured internally by the procuring departments.

Phase 1: pilot implementation

For the initial project implementation, procurements between HK$1.3 million and 10 million were selected for electronic tendering. This class of procurements was chosen because it was a stand-alone process centrally co-ordinated by GSD. It also represented the majority of all Government procurements, making it the most cost-effective category of procurements to automate in an electronic platform.

Phase 1 involved building an Internet platform to enhance the existing paper-based tender process for GSD procurements. The existing tender issuing process was labour-intensive and time-consuming, involving the physical transfer of documents between GSD and the suppliers. The process also had numerous variations depending on the type of procurement (Purchase of Products, Purchase of Services, Sales of Products, etc), the dollar value of the procurement, and the policies of procuring departments (See Exhibits 4 and 5 for details of the tendering process.)

ETS made significant improvements in various aspects of the tendering process, including:

● tender document storage and transmission;

● supplier notification of tender opportunities;

● supplier access to, and submission of, tender documents;

● receiving and responding to suppliers' enquiries; and

● contract award notices.

Systems architecture

The ETS consisted of three sub-systems:

1 *ETS Front-End*: web-based application enabling general public viewing, supplier registration, document downloads and uploads.

2 *ETS Data Centre*: electronic tender box for storing the submitted tender offers in encrypted format, until they are decrypted and opened in the ETS back-end system.

Exhibit 4 The government tendering process

[Excerpt from document available at www.info.gov.hk]

Tender Documents and Specifications
Procuring departments are required to provide in the tender documents all the necessary information to assist the bidders to prepare their tenders. In drawing up tender specifications for goods or services to be procured, departments are required to ensure that the characteristics laid down for the products or services are based on functional and performance requirements. Where standards are referred to, these should, where practicable, be international standards. Tender specifications should not be drawn up to suit a particular brand or country of origin.

Tender documents normally include standard contract forms covering the general aspects of tender and contract requirements, special conditions of contract, detailed price schedules, additional information and instructions applicable to a particular contract. Tender documents are generally issued free of charge but procuring departments may levy a non-refundable sum from tenderers to cover the cost of the tender documents.

Tender Notice
Invitations to tender include:

- a broad description of the requirement;
- estimated quantities and timing;
- the closing date and time for tenders;
- the place for lodging tenders;
- whether the procurement is covered by the WTO GPA;
- where to obtain tender documents; and
- name of the office or officer and a telephone contact for enquiries.

Normally, at least three weeks are allowed for tenderers to submit their bids. Where the procurement is covered by the WTO GPA, the time allowed for submission of tenders is 40 days except in the case of extreme urgency.

Submission and Opening of Tenders
Tenderers must submit their tenders before the tender closing date and time stipulated in the tender notice. We will not open any tenders received after the tender closing time. Tenderers must also ensure that their tenders are deposited correctly in the tender box specified in the tender notice.

At the closing time of tenders, the designated tender opening team, comprising members who are not involved in the procurement process, will open the respective tender box. Only tenders which are due are opened and authenticated by the tender opening team. The tender opening team will make appropriate records on file of the tenders received and then send the originals of the authenticated tenders to the procuring department for evaluation.

Evaluation of Tenders
The procuring department is responsible for evaluating the tenders to determine whether they meet the conditions and specifications laid down in the tender document. To ensure the best value for money, these conditions and specifications may include the time of delivery/completion, quality of goods offered, designs proposed, maintenance and spare parts provision, warranty and guarantees as appropriate. Usually, the department will recommend acceptance of a tender which fully complies with the tender conditions and specifications and is the lowest in tender sum. Where pre-determined factors other than price are included in the tender assessment, the recommended tender is the one which attains the highest combined technical and price score. The procuring departments will then submit their recommendations in the form of a tender report to the relevant tender boards for approval.

Tender Boards
The Financial Secretary has appointed the following tender boards, each consisting of not less than three persons, to consider and decide on the acceptance of tenders

- **Central Tender Board** chaired by the Secretary for the Treasury to deal with high value tenders which exceed those values specified for the subsidiary tender boards. Currently tenders for supplies and general services exceeding $10 million and tenders for construction services exceeding $30 million are considered by the Central Tender Board.

Exhibit 4 (cont'd)

- **Government Supplies Department Tender Board** chaired by the Director of Government Supplies to deal with tenders, except works contracts, of a value not exceeding $10 million.
- **Public Works Tender Board** chaired by the Deputy Director of Architectural Services to deal with tenders for works and related contracts of a value not exceeding $30 million.
- **Marine Department Tender Board** chaired by the Deputy Director of Marine to consider marine tenders of a value not exceeding $5 million.
- **Printing Department Tender Board** chaired by the Government Printer to consider Printing Department tenders of a value not exceeding $5 million. (*The above financial limits of the tender boards reflect the position as at 3 May 1999. They are subject to regular review.*)

On considering a department's tender report, the tender board takes into account the department's recommendation and justifications. The board may seek clarification from the department before accepting the department's recommendation. The decision not to accept any tender in a tender exercise must be made by the relevant tender board.

Award of Tenders
Upon notification of the tender board's approval, the Government Supplies Department or other procuring department will inform the successful tenderer in writing of the acceptance of his tender and invite the supplier/contractor to execute a contract with the department. The procuring department will also inform unsuccessful tenderers of the outcome of their bids and generally the reasons why their tenders are unsuccessful. Given our commitment to respect commercial confidence, we ensure that the details given will not disclose tender information provided by another tenderer in confidence.

The name of the tenderer awarded the contract is published, along with the contract sum of all contracts awarded in the preceding month in the Government of the Hong Kong Special Administrative Region Gazette and on the Internet in the following month.

Delivery Requirement
Delivery of goods is usually made on a consignment or on an as and when required basis. Tenderers are required to quote their prices at **FOB** (Free on Board), **CIF** (Cost, Insurance and Freight), or **DDP** (Delivered Duty Paid) or **FIS** (Free into Storehouse including stacking) terms as stipulated in the Tender Schedule.

Payment Terms
Detailed payment terms and methods are stated in the tender documents. Local suppliers are mostly paid by cheques and overseas suppliers by telegraphic transfer, bank draft or letter of credit. In supplies contracts, payment is normally made upon acceptance of goods though milestone payments related to performance targets may apply for contracts of high value and complexity. In service contracts, milestone payments related to performance targets or service provided is the norm.

---

3 *ETS Back-End*: platform for monitoring and interfacing with GSD's legacy system, the Procurement Management System Upgrade (PMSU).

The PMSU ran on Hewlett-Packard servers with Microsoft's Windows NT 4.0. The system handled the entire procurement process, maintained the master copy of the tender information, and the temporary/registered/nominated suppliers information. While the ETS platform provided a means for the transportation of information between GSD and its suppliers, the PMSU acted as the single source of the most up-to-date tender and supplier information. The principle of maintaining one master copy of tender information was to prevent inconsistency in the information used by both PMSU and ETS, and to guarantee the data ownership in one single source within the Government organization (See Exhibit 6 for the ETS process flow, and Exhibits 7A and 7B for the physical and logical components of the system).

Legal and regulatory concerns

During project implementation, a number of concerns were raised by the various legal and regulatory agencies, posting unique challenges to the project. Since this was the first Government project involving the electronic submission of documents in a legal process, the *Department of Justice* was concerned about the enforceability of the online submission. This led to such questions as whether the process was secure enough to prevent information leak to competing suppliers, and how to ensure that tender offers submitted online were the actual offers for consideration. The *Independent Commission Against Corruption* (ICAC) was concerned about the integrity of the entire online process and the potential for abuse by Government staff.

The Information Technology Services Department (ITSD) was responsible for providing technical advice and quality assurance services to GSD and other key stakeholders. Since the ETS was among the first Government projects to use a service outsourcing approach in its delivery, ITSD's role was to ensure the appropriate execution of this delivery from a technical implementation perspective. Both GSD and ITSD were tasked with ensuring the efficiency and effectiveness of the project and that it would deliver its benefits in a quantifiable fashion. This was particularly challenging due to the lack of precedence in such service delivery, even on a worldwide basis.

To address these concerns, GO-Business, the ETS service provider, worked with GSD to implement changes in perspectives, the legal framework governing procurement, procurement policy and procedures, and technology. The Electronic Transactions Ordinance (ETO) was established to give

Exhibit 5 Life-cycle of a tender

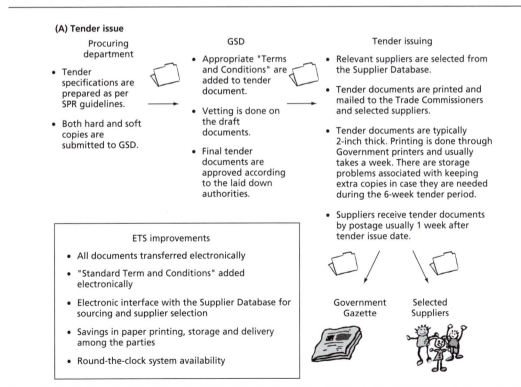

(A) Tender issue

Procuring department
- Tender specifications are prepared as per SPR guidelines.
- Both hard and soft copies are submitted to GSD.

GSD
- Appropriate "Terms and Conditions" are added to tender document.
- Vetting is done on the draft documents.
- Final tender documents are approved according to the laid down authorities.

Tender issuing
- Relevant suppliers are selected from the Supplier Database.
- Tender documents are printed and mailed to the Trade Commissioners and selected suppliers.
- Tender documents are typically 2-inch thick. Printing is done through Government printers and usually takes a week. There are storage problems associated with keeping extra copies in case they are needed during the 6-week tender period.
- Suppliers receive tender documents by postage usually 1 week after tender issue date.

Government Gazette   Selected Suppliers

ETS improvements
- All documents transferred electronically
- "Standard Term and Conditions" added electronically
- Electronic interface with the Supplier Database for sourcing and supplier selection
- Savings in paper printing, storage and delivery among the parties
- Round-the-clock system availability

Exhibit 5 (cont'd)

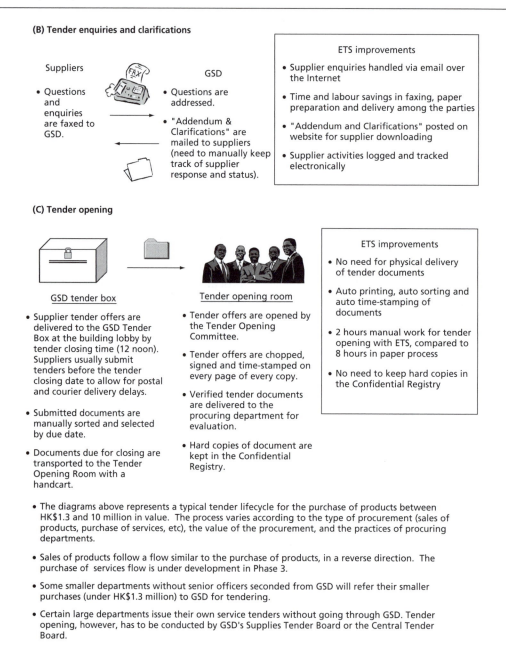

(B) Tender enquiries and clarifications

Suppliers

GSD

- Questions and enquiries are faxed to GSD.

- Questions are addressed.

- "Addendum & Clarifications" are mailed to suppliers (need to manually keep track of supplier response and status).

ETS improvements

- Supplier enquiries handled via email over the Internet

- Time and labour savings in faxing, paper preparation and delivery among the parties

- "Addendum and Clarifications" posted on website for supplier downloading

- Supplier activities logged and tracked electronically

(C) Tender opening

GSD tender box

Tender opening room

- Supplier tender offers are delivered to the GSD Tender Box at the building lobby by tender closing time (12 noon). Suppliers usually submit tenders before the tender closing date to allow for postal and courier delivery delays.

- Submitted documents are manually sorted and selected by due date.

- Documents due for closing are transported to the Tender Opening Room with a handcart.

- Tender offers are opened by the Tender Opening Committee.

- Tender offers are chopped, signed and time-stamped on every page of every copy.

- Verified tender documents are delivered to the procuring department for evaluation.

- Hard copies of document are kept in the Confidential Registry.

ETS improvements

- No need for physical delivery of tender documents

- Auto printing, auto sorting and auto time-stamping of documents

- 2 hours manual work for tender opening with ETS, compared to 8 hours in paper process

- No need to keep hard copies in the Confidential Registry

- The diagrams above represents a typical tender lifecycle for the purchase of products between HK$1.3 and 10 million in value. The process varies according to the type of procurement (sales of products, purchase of services, etc), the value of the procurement, and the practices of procuring departments.

- Sales of products follow a flow similar to the purchase of products, in a reverse direction. The purchase of services flow is under development in Phase 3.

- Some smaller departments without senior officers seconded from GSD will refer their smaller purchases (under HK$1.3 million) to GSD for tendering.

- Certain large departments issue their own service tenders without going through GSD. Tender opening, however, has to be conducted by GSD's Supplies Tender Board or the Central Tender Board.

Source: Interview with Mr. Allen Lee, Chief Technical Officer, GO-Business, 1 March 2002.

electronic records and digital signatures used in electronic transactions the same legal status as that of their paper-based counterparts. To instil public confidence in electronic transactions, the Government set up a local Public Key Infrastructure (PKI) through the Hongkong Post Certification Authority. The objective was to ensure the security and

Exhibit 6 The electronic tendering process

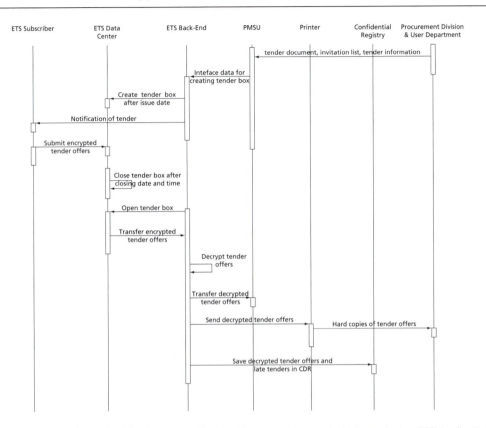

Source: Computer & Technologies, "The Government Supplies Department Electronic Tendering System (ETS) Application Scoping Document, March 2000.

integrity of transactions conducted over the Internet through the use of digital certificates. A stringent audit process for the ETS project was also conducted by the Hong Kong Productivity Council to address concerns of accountability and best practices. Lastly, the project was justified on the basis of the Government's vision of promoting an information-based economy in Hong Kong, rather than on projected project revenue and cost savings.

Security concerns

Because tender documents were considered highly confidential, it became apparent at an early stage that the security of ETS was a major concern. With documents available online, they became vulnerable to unauthorized access. To counter these concerns, the network configuration included two levels of firewalls and intrusion detection software at each operating site and at GSD. For document transfers between the ETS platform and outside suppliers, the system utilized the Public Key Infrastructure (PKI) to enable authentication, non-repudiation, integrity and confidentiality of the tender documents.

Interfacing between the ETS Back-End and GSD's PMSU system required more elaborate considerations. A direct electronic transfer between the two systems might be subject to potential hacking on either end. After a detailed review among all parties, a simple

Exhibit 7A Physical components of the electronic tendering system

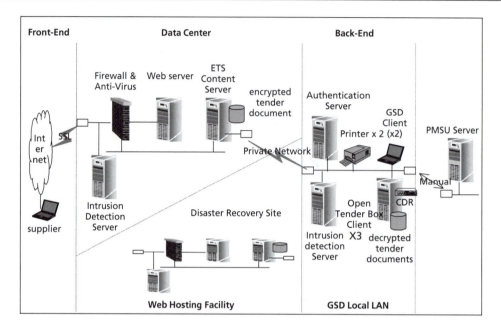

Source: Computer & Technologies, "The Government Supplies Department Electronic Tendering System (ETS) Application Scoping Document, March 2000.

Exhibit 7B Physical components of the electronic tendering system

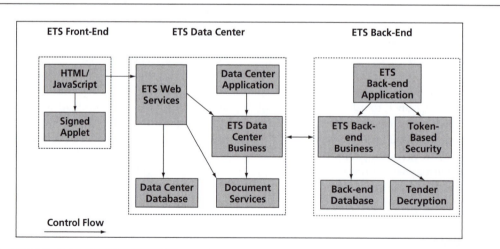

Source: Computer & Technologies, "The Government Supplies Department Electronic Tendering System (ETS) Application Scoping Document", March 2000.

and secure approach was selected in which a CDROM would be generated from the PMSU, which would then be input into the ETS Back-End nightly. The interface process thus involved NO direct physical network connection between the two systems. This method could guarantee PMSU to have a foolproof protection from Internet hacker through ETS. As PMSU rode on GSD's backbone network, which in turn connected to the whole Government backbone network, this prevention of backdoor attack was of vital importance.

As stated by Mr. Peter Yan, Chief Executive Officer, GO-Business,

> The reason for this rather low-tech approach is not that technology is not advanced enough, but the human factor that people are more comfortable using this approach to manage the security concern. This is also the most cost-effective solution that people can understand the best.

User acceptance

During initial project launch, resistance was encountered both internally within GSD and externally from suppliers. Both user groups had well-established procedures for the paper-based procurement process and did not welcome the change. They had to be educated about the purpose and benefits of the new system, before they could be trained in the new way of conducting business.

> This is typical of any large-scale project roll-outs when project benefits were not apparent in the beginning. There would even be the impression of duplicate efforts to run the two systems side by side . . . Externally, we did not anticipate we needed to do so much to increase the supplier take-up rate. Internally, we had anticipated the resistance from our staff, but did not expect that it would last for so long.
>
> – Mr C.T. Chan,
> Principal Supplies Officer, GSD

To overcome this inertia to change, a partnership approach was adopted between GO-Business and GSD for promoting the new

system to both internal Government staff and external suppliers. Working groups and training sessions were held for Government staff members. A "Train the Trainer" approach was used to provide staff with hands-on experience using the new system. Externally, a series of workshops and seminars were organized to introduce the new system to the suppliers. Invitation letters were sent to the most active 3,000 suppliers and a total of 22 briefing sessions were held, with 40–50 suppliers per session. A Help Desk was established to answer questions from the front line and to assist smaller suppliers with limited experience in Internet technology.

Despite the initial resistance, user subscription reached 18 per cent after the first year of implementation (higher than the projected 14 per cent from the project feasibility study). Subscription increased to over 30 per cent in the second year, with a total 1800 online subscribers out of the 5000 registered suppliers. In April 2001, GSD extended the contract with GO-Business for another three years to continue the ETS development.

Phase 2: service extension to CTB

Phase 2 was launched in December 2001 and extended the online capabilities developed in Phase 1 to GSD-originated tenders over HK$10 million, administered through the Central Tender Board (CTB). This service extension called for changes in organisation structures, policy and procedures, human resources, and technical enhancements to the ETS system.

Organization and process changes

To facilitate online tender submissions, a major challenge lay in the timing and physical location of tender opening. CTB tenders were traditionally opened at 12 noon in the CTB building in the Central District, while GSD tenders were opened at 9 am in GSD's North Point office. With online submission enabled for both tender types, the timing and locations of tender openings had to be synchronized. The resulting procedure was a 12 noon tender opening at the GSD location. To accommodate this change, substantial amendments had to be made in the operating procedures of the two departments. Examples included:

- changes in staff roster to ensure that the Tender Opening Room in GSD building was staffed with a senior officers (required for CTB tenders) during the tender opening schedules;
- changes in GSD's Tender Opening Procedures to enable the opening of the CTB tenders;
- changes in security procedures in the Tender Opening Room for the extended usage for CTB tenders; and
- an 8-week transition period to alert suppliers of the change in tender opening time and location.

Technical enhancements

A number of technical enhancements[2] were made in the system to support the Phase 2 service extensions.

Digital certificate verification

In Phase 1, suppliers using the ETS must obtain digital certificates, called i-Certs, issued over the web by Computer & Technologies, under the Public Key Infrastructure (PKI). i-Certs were, however, not recognized digital certificates under the ETO. An enhancement was therefore made in Phase 2 to support the use of e-Certs, the ETO-recognized digital certificates issued by the Hongkong Post, the first Government-designated Certification Authority in Hong Kong. e-Certs carried a HK$500 000 liability insurance for any

damages to the users as a result of the electronic transaction. Hongkong Post required a face-to-face authentication for issuance of the e-Certs to Hong Kong residents holding valid identity cards and companies with business registration certificates. To avoid trade barriers to overseas suppliers, ETS was enhanced to accept both digital certificates: i-Certs for suppliers outside Hong Kong and e-Certs for suppliers in Hong Kong.

Two-envelope proposals

For procuring high dollar value products and services, the HKSAR Government usually employed the two-envelope proposal approach. In two-envelope tendering, suppliers submitted two separate proposals: a technical proposal and a cost proposal. The cost proposals were only opened after the technical proposals were deemed to respond adequately to the Government requirements. To accommodate this procedure, enhancements were made in the online system for a sequenced opening of the tender documents.

Document transfers

High value procurements tended to involve much larger documents (both requests for tenders and tender submissions). The system was enhanced to allow document downloads and uploads by "sessions", where the system automatically broke documents into smaller chunks for transmission. This would prevent system failures associated with high Internet traffic and lengthy document transfers. In the case of transfer interruptions, the system was configured to allow the document transfer to resume at the last failed point. Maximum document size was also increased from 4 to 12 MB to accommodate the larger size of the CTB tenders.

Account management

With the enhanced supplier database and online document delivery, GSD was able to maintain contacts directly with the individual

---

2. *Source:* Computer & Technologies, *The Government Supplies Department Electronic Tendering System (ETS) Application Scoping Document for ETS Enhancement Phase II,* June 2001.

departments of the supplier organisations. This was particularly useful for large corporations with multiple supplier departments and separate tender personnel and procedures in each department.

Supplier file management

The user interface of the system was enhanced to allow suppliers to save their electronic forms on their local workstation for submission at a later time. This allowed the suppliers more convenience in preparing tender documents. It was also an incentive to secure supplier participation in the online system.

Phase 3: integration with operating departments

While Phases 1 and 2 had targeted GSD and GSD-originated CTB tenders, Phase 3 aimed to extend the ETS to include non-GSD-originated tenders such as cleansing service tenders and security service tenders, currently procured by other departments/bureaux. The objective was to issue 80 per cent of all Government tenders (except Works tenders) electronically by 2003. The second objective of this phase was to build a consolidated supplier database for centralized supplier information. The project proposal was endorsed by CTB in August 2001. Initial consultation with individual departments/bureaux was completed in October 2001, and the project implementation proposal was scheduled for completion in mid-2002.

User consultation

A major challenge of Phase 3 was the diversity of tendering processes and procedures across the procuring departments. Service tenders had always been the responsibility of the procuring departments, and while each department conformed to Government SPR, each had its own internal systems, including manual and electronic processes. Exceptions and special procedures

were the norm. Based on the size of establishment and the size of tenders, the departments could be classified into four categories (see Exhibit 8):

1 *small departments with small tenders* had no capability to handle tenders on their own, and online tendering was not a critical function;

2 *small departments with large tenders* would benefit the most from a common procurement infrastructure to standardize current processes;

3 *large departments with small tenders* recognized the importance of a common procurement infrastructure and online tendering platform; and

4 *large departments with large tenders* were most supportive of online tendering for efficiency gains and other value-added services.

The change management challenges are different for each type of department. Overall, system implementors must address the following questions in Phase 3:

● How much did the automated system have to mirror existing procedures? What approach would best address the needs of most departments?

● To what extent should a policy-driven (top-down) approach be used? To what extent should the approach be user-driven (bottom-up)? What would happen when noncompliance with Government policies became much easier to monitor?

● How should organisational change management issues be dealt with? Which operating departments were likely to be most supportive/resistant? How should these departments be sequenced for implementation? How could consensus be built? How should the concern of unenthusiastic departments be addressed?

● Should the departments get rid of their own legacy systems and outsource to

Exhibit 8 Classification of procuring departments for Phase 3

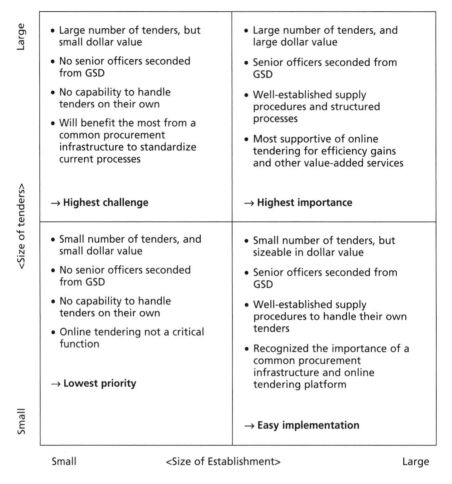

Source: Interview with Mr Allen Lee, Chief Technical Officer, GO-Business, 1 March 2002.

GSD? (From a policy perspective, GSD was mandated to provide value-added services for the departments. It was not staffed to take over the supply logistics of the procuring departments.)

It will not be practical, or economically viable, to assume all 90 Government departments can be integrated. There are the top departments who have the most needs for systems integration. This is not a technical issue, as technologies such as XML can bridge the gap between the different systems. The most difficult part is the process re-engineering, as it will interrupt the status-quo of the departments. In light of the current economic environment, this is particularly challenging . . . From past experience, IT is an expenditure, rather than a cost saving vehicle. The challenge ahead is to change the mentality, and to increase the IT acceptance in the Government departments. A Joined-up Government approach will improve all department's individual operations in the long run.

– Mr Alan Wong, Director,
Information Technology Services Department

Technical challenges

From a technical perspective, this phase would deliver an end-to-end online tendering system, providing direct connectivity between the ETS platform and the individual procuring departments, and enabling the staff of the departments to be more involved in the operations of their own tendering processes. The current ETS system supported a single interface with the GSD PMSU legacy system. To connect to the procuring departments, multiple interfaces would be constructed to the legacy systems of the procuring departments.

Two connectivity options had been identified:

● Option 1: Internet
● Option 2: Government Network (GNET).

The proposed configuration was to use the existing Government Network (GNET) connection. The procuring departments would follow the hyperlinks from the Central Cyber Government Office (CCGO) Website to the system and the data traffic would go through the GNET to the GSD departmental network. This would ensure a secure, reliable and expandable system, while making use of existing resources and integrating with existing systems. Other considerations included the use of shared or stand-alone databases, time and data synchronization between the servers and databases, and resource utilization across the servers and databases.

Future extension: the electronic marketplace system

The planned extension of the project involved building an Electronic Marketplace System (EMS) that would provide a trading exchange for minor purchases, each not exceeding HK$1.3 million (currently handled by procuring departments). With the electronic platform, buyers and sellers would be brought together without the need for quotations and tenders. Additional value-added services such as e-sourcing, relationship management, and reverse auctions would also be considered. The ultimate vision for the Government was to bring ETS and EMS together in a "Total Procurement Solution". The project was currently under scope definition for potential implementation in 2003.

While the EMS concept was sound from a strategic viewpoint, the implementation and maintenance of the system would be costly, involving the provision of graphics-rich supplier catalogues online. A bigger concern was whether the Hong Kong business community (comprised mainly of small to medium sized enterprises) was technologically savvy enough to accept this radical procurement approach.

> We have done a trial with our departments in online procurements of these small purchases. In general, 42% of the purchases are cheaper and can be procured faster, but the commodities that are available online are more limited in variety, and are usually smaller items . . . for low value purchases where profit margins are small, it is questionable if the investment will be worthwhile.
> – Mr C.T. Chan,
> Principal Supplies Officer, GSD

Major issues in the development of EMS included:

● What were the key business drivers? What would the best business model be?
● What was the current state of development and the competitive landscape among e-marketplaces?
● What were the development options (in-house development, outsourcing, partnerships, acquisitions, etc.)?
● What additional value-added features should be provided on EMS, and what were their benefits (e.g. e-sourcing, online supplier catalogues, order placement, relationship management, reverse auctions, etc.)?

● How should supplier participation be secured?

Technical issues

In addition to the business and change management issues, EMS 4 raised a number of technical issues:

● What were the technical options for implementation?

● What were the major systems integration challenges within the Government (back-end integration)?

● How should the challenges of integrating with supplier networks be addressed?

Phoebe Ho prepared this case under the supervision of Lynne Markus and Ali Farhoomand for class discussion. This case is not intended to show effective or ineffective handling of decision or business processes.

Legal considerations of global e-business

To understand the major issues surrounding the development of a legal ❑
framework for e-business

To learn about the concept of jurisdiction ❑

To examine threats to intellectual property rights and ways in which businesses ❑
can protect their IPR

To review recently enacted Digital Certificate Laws pertaining to electronic ❑
transactions

To address privacy issues posed by the e-business environment ❑

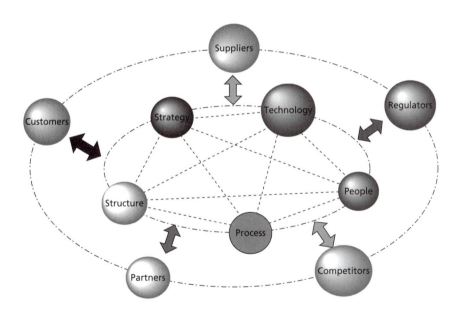

Like an exuberant, self-confident kid, Web business has discovered that
it needs to learn some lessons about how the world really works.
– Bill Zoellick, Author of *CyberRegs*

We conclude our discussion of e-business transformation by devoting this final chapter to examining some of the legal considerations of global e-business. The experienced manager has almost certainly dealt with a range of regulatory issues covering conventional business practices and in the process, acquired some level of awareness of the laws affecting traditional business. Since the late 1990s, the Internet has raised a host of issues that have altered the legal landscape and raised unanticipated concerns.

In a recent survey of 300 decision-makers at UK Businesses,[1] nearly 20 per cent did not view the legal status of online transactions as important, and almost 40 per cent were uncertain if current online transactions held any legal status. Since an online presence has become a mandatory enabler for e-business, senior managers, technologists and content developers will find themselves under growing pressure to demonstrate an understanding of the emerging regulatory framework for the various aspects of conducting electronic business.

As the full range of e-business-related legal topics go far beyond the scope of one chapter, we will focus our discussion on four key areas of particular importance to e-business professionals in an effort to depict the contemporary legal environment and provide a foundation for deeper exploration. The first part of this chapter explores the concept of jurisdiction in a borderless marketplace. The next section outlines issues that have emerged regarding intellectual property rights in an age where information is routinely reduced to digital form. We then turn to an examination of the role of digital certificates for enabling and enforcing e-business transactions. Finally we will explore the question of privacy where individual data is collected and processed in online business. In each of these areas we must consider the appropriate legal frameworks, the relevance to e-business and how business leaders can align their interests with emerging frameworks.

In the early days of the Internet, there was a prevailing sense that the rise of the medium heralded an era where content would move freely, that anything on the Internet was in the public domain and with the example set by companies such as Amazon, conventional distribution chains would soon become a thing of the past. Now these expectations have moderated considerably; the dot-com crash exposed many startup companies as being built on unworkable business models that did not account for the complex interplay between an evolving framework of laws and existing power structures. Those that have survived are tackling the issues that have emerged and are defining how business is conducted in an electronically driven environment.

Napster, the company that infuriated the recording industry with its music file sharing service and epitomized the obstinate challenger to established modes of business, was forced to shut down its service in July 2001 and has now re-emerged as a division of Roxio Inc. – a major digital media software company with partners including Samsung and Microsoft. The law has also clashed with the Internet medium over issues including the use of trademarks in registered

---

1. Commissioned by digital certification authority De La Rue InterClear in 2000.

domain names, online privacy, resolving disputes in transnational dealings, and the enforceability of electronic transactions among many other matters. Before the commercialization of the Internet, the volume of transnational transactions was significantly lower and was commonly initiated by individual consumers or businesses. Since commercial websites are now accessible in all countries, electronic transactions abound between parties who may have had no cause to establish dealings in the past. This foregrounds the issue of jurisdiction and governing law in transactions between businesses and consumers based in different countries. Some governments have advocated an alternative dispute resolution (ADR) system to serve as an avenue for resolving disputes as opposed to costly international litigation. Meanwhile the European Union recently adopted the so-called "Brussels I Regulation" in an effort to harmonize member states' laws to achieve legal uniformity in the light of e-commerce developments.

We are undergoing a period of transition where governments and stakeholder groups are assuming a more prominent role in fostering acceptable levels of legal certainty and uniformity. Businesses around the world with vested interests in the evolving legal landscape are exerting their influence on policy makers and governing bodies. Against this backdrop, a sound grasp of the regulatory climate is essential in the management of modern enterprises.

e-Business jurisdiction

Jurisdiction is the authority to interpret and apply laws within a territorial range. Web sites are commonly available to a global audience, so the issue of jurisdiction is important for anyone planning to do business on the Internet. In the past it was plainly clear where a transaction took place, but online transactions have muddied the picture, causing governments around the world to update their laws to catch up with technology. If a British retailer orders goods online from the US that are found to be defective, in which country can it sue? Questions like this concerning how laws are applied across borders must be thought-out by businesses operating online so that they may protect themselves in the event of a dispute. Moreover, some measure of clarity is necessary to reassure clients and partners that there is a reliable avenue for obtaining relief if something should go wrong with the transaction.

The concept of personal jurisdiction

Under legal doctrine, courts cannot act unless they have *personal jurisdiction* – "the ability to exercise dominion over the parties . . . so that it can compel their obedience to its judgment in the case."[2] If a court were to issue a judgment in a case where it does not have personal jurisdiction, the judgment may not be recognized by courts elsewhere. In many countries, the question of whether a court

---

2. David G. Post (1998).

has personal jurisdiction depends on (i) whether there are statutes granting it authority to exercise jurisdiction over the defendant and (ii) whether *due process* (the idea that laws and legal proceedings have been fair) has been satisfied.

Statutory authority

Statutory authority refers to a court's authority to exercise personal jurisdiction over residents. The particulars of statutory authority vary significantly across geographies. In the US for instance, there are so-called "long-arm statutes" which empower courts to assert personal jurisdiction over non-residents of a state when certain criteria are met. For example, New York's long-arm statute allows its courts personal jurisdiction over any defendant who "in person or through his agent":

1 transacts any business within the state or contracts anywhere to supply goods or services in the state; or

2 commits a tortious[3] act within the state, except as to a cause of action for defamation of character arising from the act; or

3 commits a tortious act without the state causing injury to person or property within the state, except as to a cause of action for defamation of character arising from the act, if he

   (i) regularly does or solicits business, or engages in any other persistent course of conduct, or derives substantial revenue from goods used or consumed or services rendered, in the state, or
   (ii) expects or should reasonably expect the act to have consequences in the state and derives substantial revenue from interstate or international commerce; or

4 Owns, uses or possesses any real property situated within the state.

Source: New York Long-Arm Statute, Section 302: Personal jurisdiction by acts of non-domiciliaries

In spite of the complicated language, it is plainly clear that long-arm statutes can be far-reaching and may be applicable to a wide range of business scenarios.

Due process

The concept of due process in law requires that certain "minimum contacts" exist for a finding of personal jurisdiction against a defendant who is not physically present in territory. This requirement concerns the quality and nature of the activity that is being disputed. If the quality and nature of the activity is

---

3. Tort is defined as "a wrongful act other than a breach of contract for which relief may be obtained in the form of damages or an injunction." *Merriam-Webster's Dictionary*.

deemed continuous and systematic, courts may be allowed to decide any claim against a defendant, even if it transpired in other territories. If the activity was isolated in nature, the court may only decide any action that arose from the defendant's activities within its jurisdiction.

In addition to the minimum contacts standard, courts often consider the following:[4]

- *Reasonable anticipation*: whether the defendant purposefully took advantage of the privilege of conducting business within the territory.

- *Purposefully directed activities*: Some courts have found that mere awareness that a product will find its way to a certain territorial jurisdiction is not sufficient to satisfy the minimum contacts standard. There must be an action "purposefully directed toward the forum" such as advertising or regularly providing product information to customers.

- *Effects cases*: When defendants know their actions will be damaging to a claimant, they can reasonably anticipate being taken to court where the injury took place. This principle has been applied in claims of libel against print publications that are distributed to geographically dispersed markets, and is particularly relevant to e-business because online practices may have effects in numerous jurisdictions.

Personal jurisdiction and the Internet

The question of whether online activities meet the standards we have discussed is problematic due to innate characteristics of the Internet. When a merchant creates a Web site for his/her business, does this in itself satisfy the reasonable anticipation requirement, since it can be expected that customers anywhere in the world may access the site? It can be perceived that anyone who establishes an online presence has effectively entered into every jurisdiction in existence, since it is beyond the means of most site operators to prohibit groups of users based on geography. Clearly assertions that all Web site operators are subject to personal jurisdiction under every court seem highly impractical. Yet there have been cases where foreign courts have reached far to assume jurisdiction over e-business. The case study accompanying this chapter, *Multi-jurisdictional Compliance: Yahoo! Inc.*, gives the account of how several non-profit organizations sought to prevent the sale of Nazi memorabilia by taking action against Yahoo! in French courts.

As the courts attempt to elucidate more concrete guidelines for the personal jurisdiction of Internet transactions, a number of recent court decisions have shed some light on how disputes will likely be handled. An early precedent in international law involved Eileen Weber, an American who attempted to sue an Italian hotel in American Courts. Weber – who had been injured while staying at

---

4. Kesan (1999).

the defendant's hotel, took the matter up in a New Jersey court since the hotel had been advertised on the Internet. The judge presiding over the case refused to find personal jurisdiction, citing three categories of cases dealing with online jurisdictional issues – those where the defendant is actively soliciting business online, those where a user can exchange information with the host site, and those concerning only passive sites that exist to provide information. The judge found Weber's case to fall under the third category, thereby not constituting "continuous and substantial" contacts necessary for a finding of personal jurisdiction. This case constituted an early precedent, giving rise to the notion that mere presence on the Web is not sufficient grounds for personal jurisdiction over a foreign defendant. Assessments based on the distinction between *interactive use* and *passive uses* have also become increasingly important in determining whether a court can assert personal jurisdiction over Web site operators (Blaustein, 1998).

1   *Interactive use* refers to two-way online communications aimed at establishing or maintaining a business relationship. A Web site is considered interactive when online transactions can be conducted or information is exchanged with potential customers for the purpose of soliciting business.[5]

2   *Passive use* refers to situations where information is merely available to viewers.

The greater the commercial nature and level of interactivity of a Web site, the more likely that it may be considered to be "purposefully availing itself" to claims of personal jurisdiction. By contrast, courts have generally been less willing to determine personal jurisdiction in cases of passive Internet use.[6] Companies merely engaging in simple advertising and making information available online will not likely be under the personal jurisdiction of foreign jurisdictions where they have not engaged in commercial dealings.

Interactive use and passive use may be considered two ends of a spectrum, but many cases fall somewhere in between. Many sites, for example, are of a mostly informational nature but also feature some level of interactivity by providing an email address, contact details or perhaps a messaging system for user interaction.

In cases such as these, courts have looked to other factors in determining the level of interactivity of the site. This is not to say that the resulting decisions provide clear guidance. In one instance, the fact that a Web site offered interactive features was deemed insufficient by an American court for a finding of personal jurisdiction, as there was no evidence that business activities were specifically directed at outside jurisdictions question beyond mere placement of the site on the Internet.[7] In another case, an operator merely featured a toll-free number on

5. Christopher Wolf (1999).
6. Ibid.
7. Rannoch, Inc. vs Rannoch Corporation, 52f. Supp. 2d 681 (E.D. Va. 1999).

a Web site, but a court perceived this as an attempt to solicit business in its jurisdiction and extended personal jurisdiction over the defendant through a long-arm statute.[8] In a third case, personal jurisdiction was not extended over a Web site operator, even though the site featured a printable mail-in order form, a toll-free number and an e-mail address.[9] The key factor in these cases seems to have been whether the respective courts viewed the existence of elements such as e-mail addresses and toll-free telephone numbers as active attempts to engage users in transactions.[10]

Other factors in jurisdiction

In addition to the concept of personal jurisdiction, the following factors are also often considered by courts in questions of jurisdiction:[11]

- *Subject matter jurisdiction*: a court may have restrictions on the types of disputes it may deliver judgment on. A court is required to dismiss any claims that fall outside its subject matter jurisdiction.

- *Venue*: regardless of whether a court holds personal jurisdiction or subject matter jurisdiction over a dispute, it may not be able to hear the dispute due to certain *venue rules* that are intended to protect defendants from being taken to court in inconvenient places. For example, a venue rule may require that a claim may only be heard in the place where the events leading to the dispute took place.

- *Choice of law*: once a court establishes personal jurisdiction, subject matter jurisdiction and the appropriate venue for a claim, it is then faced with the question of which laws to apply to the dispute – the law where the claimant is based, the law where the defendant is located, the law where the court is situated or perhaps the law where the transaction came about.

Contractual clauses for managing jurisdiction uncertainty

Companies engaged in e-business may potentially find themselves involved in legal proceedings in any country where they engage in transactions. Aside from the extreme measure of transacting only with local parties, a reasonable way to reduce uncertainty is by ensuring that jurisdiction-related clauses are used as a first step towards limiting litigation avenues. A *jurisdiction clause* specifies that only certain courts will have the authority to handle any potential disputes resulting from the contract (see Figure 10.1). More specifically, the following

---

8. Inset Systems, Inc. vs Instructions Set, Inc., 937f. Supp. 161 (D. Conn. 1996).
9. Mink vs AAAA Development.
10. Wolf (1999).
11. David G. Post (1998).

Figure 10.1 Example of a jurisdiction clause

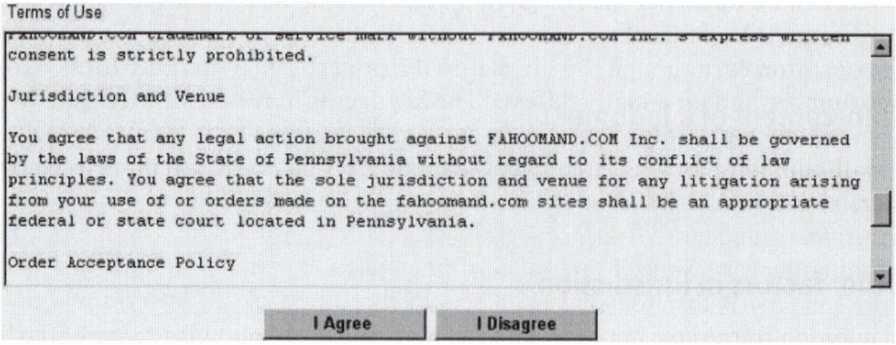

```
Terms of Use

FAHOOMAND.COM trademark or service mark without FAHOOMAND.COM Inc.'s express written
consent is strictly prohibited.

Jurisdiction and Venue

You agree that any legal action brought against FAHOOMAND.COM Inc. shall be governed
by the laws of the State of Pennsylvania without regard to its conflict of law
principles. You agree that the sole jurisdiction and venue for any litigation arising
from your use of or orders made on the fahoomand.com sites shall be an appropriate
federal or state court located in Pennsylvania.

Order Acceptance Policy
```

| I Agree | I Disagree |

clauses may be used to provide some assurance that disputes will be addressed in an acknowledged manner:

- Through a **venue** *or* **forum selection clause,** the parties agree to pursue any legal proceedings arising from the contract in a specified venue.

- A **choice of law clause** states which state/country's laws will be applied in the event of a dispute.

- An **arbitration clause** dictates that the parties must attempt to resolve their dispute through arbitration before pursuing further legal proceedings.

Forming effective contracts

As legislation concerning online transactions continues to evolve, companies should aim to establish contracts in line with traditional principles concerning written agreements. In addition to the contractual clauses mentioned above, online business should pay attention to other aspects of contracts they establish:

- *Conspicuousness*: it should be clear to users that they are agreeing to contractual clauses. The following measures will go some way towards meeting this necessity:[12]

  - display the *User Agreement* or *Terms and Conditions* on the first page, or possibly on each page of a site;
  - require that users scroll down a Web page in order to read the terms;
  - require users to click on an agreement before entering the site; and
  - make the contract highly visible.

- *Unconscionable nature*: Courts are generally reluctant to enforce contracts that are plainly unfair (e.g. contracts that came about as the result of the overwhelming bargaining power of one party).[13]

---

12. Christopher M. Kindel and Deidra Grant (2001).
13. Ibid.

● *Exclusivity*: A jurisdiction clause should be exclusive, that is, it should clearly indicate that the designated venue is the exclusive place where the dispute is to be resolved.

Enforcement of a judgment

Our discussion has thus far focused on how jurisdiction is determined in commercial contracts. An equally important consideration concerns the issue of enforcing judgments. If a losing party does not comply with a judgment, the winning party may need to turn to more drastic measures such as seizing the loser's assets. If the loser has no assets in that jurisdiction, the winning party may have no recourse but to attempt to have the judgment enforced in the country where the loser does have assets. For example, a plaintiff may win a suit against a Dutch company in a British court. However, if the Dutch company has no assets in Britain, the plaintiff must then attempt to have the judgment enforced abroad by Dutch courts. Whether they will be willing to enforce the judgment will depend largely on whether the two countries have signed an international convention. It is therefore important to consider issues of enforcement before deciding whether a claim is worth proceeding in the first place.

The international arena

Without valid clauses or regional laws, the question of which courts have jurisdiction is determined by national laws and international conventions. In many cases, more than one court may apply and a claimant can choose where to pursue the claim. In the international arena, a slight gulf has emerged between EU countries and the US on issues of cross-border regulation of e-commerce.

Member states of the European Union (with the exception of Denmark) have signed on to the jurisdictional rules presented by the Brussels I Regulation that was enacted in March 2002. The Brussels I Regulation maintains that a defendant who is legally resident in a country can be sued in the courts of that country, regardless of nationality. Each member country applies its own law to determine whether a defendant meets the criteria of legal residency in its country.[14] In the United Kingdom for instance, a company is generally considered domiciled if it has incorporated and/or has a registered office or some other official address.[15]

In business-to-consumer contracts, the Brussels I Regulation gives special consideration to consumer interests.[16] As long as a consumer has his or her permanent domicile within a member state, he or she may conclude e-commerce contracts under the same jurisdictional rules even while on a business trip. The protections offered by these rules apply to physical goods, services and electronic materials.[17] The adoption of the Brussels I Regulation has generated

---

14. This is known as the "domicile rule".
15. Simmons & Simmons (2001).
16. Norel Rosner (2002).
17. Ibid.

considerable criticism from European industry, as business interests now face relatively lower levels of protection (Hong, 2000).

The Hague convention

The Hague Convention on Jurisdiction was an effort to negotiate and determine guidelines for international e-commerce disputes. When participating countries, including EU states and the US met in 1999, business and consumer groups offered differing views on how business–consumer disputes should be settled. Work on the convention began in 1996, but the rapid growth of e-commerce introduced new complications and brought the talks to a halt. Negotiations resumed in 1999 and again in 2001, but continually failed to result in agreement.

The main point of contention was a clause that would enable consumers to sue businesses from their home jurisdiction. Consumer advocates maintained that this would bring fairness to customers who lack the necessary resources to file suits in other countries.[18] Some e-commerce groups on the other hand, felt the clause would be an enormous burden on companies hoping to do business online with the monumental burden of considering the laws of many countries. To compound this disparity, US representatives favoured the right of sellers to determine their jurisdiction on business-to-consumer contracts (and the right of intellectual property holders to settle disputes exclusively in the country where the complaining party has registered its trademarks),[19] pitting themselves against the European position (Standeford, 2002).

Alternative dispute resolution

e-Business transactions present a variety of unique characteristics. When purely electronic material is being purchased, the downloading of software or content may last only a few seconds. Furthermore, because of the Internet's wide reach, companies offering goods, services or electronic materials online may expand their reach to serve worldwide markets. The main concern from a regulatory viewpoint is that a company known by its Internet presence may be hard to trace according to traditional criteria.[20]

Given these characteristics, court proceedings often pose challenges for parties with limited resources; it is widely known that legal disputes often last for a very long time and carry significant legal expenses. Companies involved in online commerce are eager to minimize the costs that any court dispute (especially one in a foreign jurisdiction) would require.

Increasingly, out-of-court dispute settlement possibilities are being considered as an alternative to traditional legal avenues. As we have mentioned above, contractual clauses can compel the parties to attempt to resolve their dispute

18. Jean Ann Fox of the Consumer Federation of America, as quoted in Sullivan (2001).
19. Paul A. Greenberg (2001).
20. Norel Rosner (2002).

through arbitration before taking an action to court. Specialized ADR bodies could play an important role in settling online transaction disputes, thus negating the need for overly complicated, costly and time consuming court procedures. A further advantage is that online dispute resolution bodies would likely develop a level of expertise above and beyond traditional legal system's ability to decide issues involving online transactions.

Intellectual property rights

Intellectual property is a concept referring to intangible assets derived from the mental efforts and labour of a person or organization.[21] Any company planning to do business online should take measures to protect its intellectual property rights (IPR), while anticipating and preventing the possibility of infringing on someone else's IPR. The issue of IPR is an inescapable reality of e-business, and is one in which the legal issues are still evolving.

There are five main classes of IPR: trademarks, copyrights, patents, trade secrets and trade dress.

1   A **trademark** can be a name, symbol, device, or combination thereof that distinguishes one's goods and services from those of others. Technically, a trademark (such as Renault or Volkswagen) is used to identify a good or product, whereas a service mark (such as Citibank or Greyhound) is used to identify services. In practice, however, people often use the term trademark in reference to both goods and services.

2   A **copyright** is a form of protection available to a wide variety of works, including literary, musical, graphic, and architectural works, motion pictures and audio recordings. The majority of copyrighted works are literary works – meaning works that can be expressed in words or numbers.

3   A **patent** is an official document granted by the government. Patent holders may exclude other parties from making, using or selling their inventions.

4   **Trade secrets** consist of any information that gives its owner a competitive advantage. Nearly any kind of information can be protected, including customer lists, recipes, formulas, marketing plans, employee rosters, financial information and methods of conducting business. Trade secret protection arises as soon as the information comes into being and lasts as long as the owner makes reasonable efforts to keep the information secret. No registration with any government authority is required. If properly safeguarded, trade secrets can last forever.

---

21. International Accounting Standards (IAS) define *intangible assets* as "identifiable non-monetary assets without physical substance held for use in the production and supply of goods and services, for rental to others, or for administrative purposes."

5 Trade dress refers to the look of a product or its presentation. In e-business, the product may be considered the Web site itself and its design may be considered its trade dress.

The international protection of IPR

In modern economies, technological progress has driven down transaction and production costs; many businesses are fundamentally service-oriented and rely on more intangible assets to generate earnings.[22] As a result, intangible assets have gained great value over the last 20 years and the protection of IPR is becoming increasingly vital to business. A few key points must be understood about the protection of IPR:

● *Intellectual property rights are national*: IPR are primarily the result of national laws. This means that prescriptions for what, when, how and for how long a right may exist varies in different markets. On the other hand, while international law does not dictate the creation of IPR, it does set certain guidelines for IPR harmonization and protection.

● *International protection involves two components*: From the perspective of the party seeking IPR protection (as opposed to the defendant of an infringement claim), the two major components of protection are:

   1 completing any IPR formalities in markets where the rights are to be protected; and
   2 enforcing rights in cases of infringement.

Most existing international accords cover the first of these components. As detailed in Table 10.1 below, the TRIPS Agreement, together with the Paris, Berne and Rome Conventions, and the IPIC Treaty, describe the kinds of IPR protected by national and international law. The two WIPO treaties make it clear that IPR protected by the other treaties are also protected in cyberspace.[23]

IPR and the Internet

In e-business, a Web site is composed of different parts – visible components such as text, graphics and page layout exist on the front-end; code, software and databases work on the back-end to enable transactions. When a designer creates the site, text and art may be incorporated that were originally licensed for different kinds of use. The developer responsible for the site's backend might employ code or tools that are owned by his company or a third party; the resulting system might consist of multiple components belonging to different entities and

---

22. Tapscott et al. (2000).
23. The *WIPO Copyright Treaty* (*Article 8*) states that "authors of literary and artistic works shall enjoy the exclusive right of authorizing and communicating to the public of their works by wire or wireless means."

Table 10.1 International IPR accords

Name of the accord	Purpose

TRIPS agreement
(Agreement on Trade-Related Aspect of Intellectual Property Rights)
	● Offers minimum IPR protection across WTO member countries, e.g. compliance with the Paris Convention, the Berne Convention, the Rome Convention, the IPIC Treaty:
	  – Trademarks: 7 years protection
	  – Copyrights: 50 years protection
	  – Patents: 20 years protection

Year of the accord:
▶ Effective 1/1/2000 (For developed countries)
▶ Effective 1/1/2006 (For developing countries)
 	
Member countries:
All WTO members
	● Extends WTO principles to international IPR, including:
	  – The national treatment principle
	  – The transparency principle
	  – The most-favoured-nation treatment principle
	
	● Member countries are bound by the WTO's dispute mechanism for any IPR disputes

Paris convention (International Convention for the Protection of Industrial Property)	● Establishes a "union" of countries responsible for protecting industrial property rights – rights such as patents, trademarks and industrial designs ● Member countries must follow these principles:

Year of the accord:
▶ Effective on the same dates that apply to the TRIPS Agreement
	– The national treatment principle
	  – The priority principle
	  – The common rules of industrial IPR

Berne convention for the Protection of Literary and Artistic Works	● Establishes a "union" of countries responsible for protecting literary and artistic rights (i.e. copyrights). ● Member countries must follow these principles:

Year of the accord:
▶ Effective on the same dates that apply to the TRIPS Agreement
	– The national treatment principle
	  – The non-conditional protection principle
	  – The protection independent of the country of origin principle
	  – The common rules of copyrights
	
	● Most copyright suits heard today by local courts are based on domestic laws adopted in compliance with the Berne Convention.

World intellectual property organization (WIPO) copyright treaty *Year of the accord*: ▶ Effective in WIPO member states on ratification	● A supplement to the Berne Convention, expanding copyright protection to computer software and data-bases.
Rome Convention (International Convention for the Protection of Performers, Producers of Phonograms) *Year of the accord*: ▶ Effective on same dates as TRIPS Agreements	● Establishes protection for performing artists, recording companies and broadcasters. Protection includes protection against unauthorized recordings, rebroadcasts and other unauthorized use of broadcasts

Table 10.1 (cont'd)

Name of the accord	Purpose
WIPO performances and phonograms treaty *Year of the accord*: ▶ Effective in WIPO member states on ratification	● A supplement to the Rome Convention, expanding the rights of performers, recording companies and broadcasters granted under the Rome Convention. Notably prohibits the circumvention of technological measures, such as encryption, which protect copyrights
IPIC Treaty Treaty on Intellectual Property in Respect of Integrated Circuits *Year of the accord*: ▶ Effective on same dates as TRIPS Agreements	● Member countries must protect the designs used in integrated circuits (such as the design of computer chips) and follow these principles: – The national treatment principle – The common rules of copyrights

may be licensed to a certain company for only limited uses.[24] It is therefore crucial for an e-business operator to understand which parties own the content, the back-end systems and the look and feel of a Web site.[25]

Trademarks and domain name infringement

The characteristics of the Internet have presented a variety of unique problems to business interests, particularly over the issue of domain names. Domain names are the unique identifications of entities registered on the Internet. Domain names are *not* the equivalent of trademarks, and do not offer the same protection as trademark registration. When a domain name is registered, its corresponding trademark is not secured. Similarly, the possession of an existing trademark does not automatically mean that the holder is entitled to the corresponding domain name.

Domain names, such as "IBM.com" or "Amazon.com", are familiar to most of us as the addresses that we type or that are returned by search engines. They may contain trademarks, such as "IBM", but domain names are not trademarks in themselves, unless they have been additionally registered as trademarks (e.g. unless IBM has registered "IBM.com" as a trademark). The problem stems from the fact that domain names may be registered with domain name registrars without any prior check of the relevant trademark registries. Domain name registration entails some rights, but *does not guarantee* that the name being registered is not infringing on another party's rights.

There are four common forms of domain name and trademark infringement:

1 *Cybersquatting* or domain name squatting involves the registration of famous brands or trademarks by speculators, who aim to sell the names to the companies and individuals concerned for large sums of money.

---

24. Brenda Kienan (2001).
25. That is, the "trade dress" of the site.

2 *Deeplinking* refers to the practice of linking a Web page with an external page, bypassing one or more introductory pages on the target site. The problem with deeplinking is that when a link is followed, the user fast-forwards to the linked page and the external site is deprived of potential advertising revenue from the "skipped" pages. Furthermore, the practice of deeplinking may associate the content, product or service described with the originating site. Courts have been divided on the issue of whether deeplinking is illegal.

3 *Meta-tagging* is the practice of inserting invisible words, names or other popular identifiers into a document's hypertext language (i.e. HTML). For instance, a designer may meta-tag the word "Harry Ramsdens" into an unrelated restaurant's Web site, in the hopes that a person searching for restaurant terms might be directed to the site. Metatagging is generally viewed as illegal – constituting a form of trademark infringement.

4 *Framing* is the practice of featuring the content of another site within a frame in your own site. Framing is often combined with deeplinking and therefore the arguments raised against deeplinking can also apply here.

EXAMPLES OF DOMAIN NAME INFRINGEMENT

- *Cybersquatting*: In the UK case of *Marks & Spencer PLC et al.* vs *One in a Million*,[26] the defendant (the company, "One in a Million") registered a large number of domain names representing the names or trademarks of famous companies. It did so with the intention to resell those registered domain names to companies in question. In finding against the defendant, the court held that the practice of premeditated cybersquatting was an infringement of the UK trademark legislation.

  In contrast, a Canadian graphic artist, Anand Ramnath Mani, from Vancouver, British Columbia, who had been doing business under the name A.R. Mani since 1981, won the right to continue using his Internet address, armani.com, despite strenuous efforts by G.A. Modefine SA, the Lausanne, Switzerland-based owner of the Armani trademark. An arbitration panel of the World Intellectual Property Office (WIPO) ruled in favour of Mr Mani, despite G A Modefine's arguments that the former's Web address was "confusingly similar" to the designer's name and that "every day, all over the world, people who are looking for the site of the famous stylist, find, with surprise, the site of Mr. Anand Mani in Vancouver." The panel decided that the company had not proved that such confusion existed, and it held that Mr. Mani had not registered the name in bad faith.[27]

- *Deeplinking*: In the US case of *Ticketmaster Corp.* v *Microsoft Corp.*,[28] Microsoft was sued by Ticketmaster for creating deeplinks connecting a Microsoft Website directly to Ticketmaster's sales pages, bypassing Ticketmaster's home page and advertisements. Microsoft claimed that it had the right to control the manner in which its site was displayed on another Web page. Ticketmaster sued and won against Microsoft for trademark dilution and unfair trade under the Lanham Act and California state law.

- *Meta-tagging*: In the US case of *Brookfield Communication, Inc.* v *West Coast Entertainment Corporation*, the court viewed meta-tagging as a form of infringement. It concluded that using another's trademark in one's meta-tags was much like posting a sign with another's trademark in front of one's store.

---

27. "Canada: a graphic artist may continue using his net address", Montreal Gazette, 3 August 2001.

28. C.D. Cal. 1997, High Court, 28 November 1997.

---

26. High Court, 28 November 1997.

Copyright issues

Copyright laws often require that the original work be fixed in a "tangible form of expression". For instance, to be protected by copyright, any work must be fixed in a book, recording, video, diskette and so on. For this reason, live events, such as corporate speeches and presentations are not protected unless the material is written down in some form or the event is simultaneously recorded.

The extent to which computer software is copied calls for special attention from e-business managers. When copying or modifying a computer program, a programmer should generally be able to do so without infringing on copyright if the new adaptation is created as an essential step in the utilization of the computer program or if the new copy or adaptation is only for archival purposes. Subject to stricter local rules, the buyer of a computer program can (in the course of personal use) tinker with it, for instance to enhance its speed or add features that facilitate its use. It should be noted that such personal use exceptions might not protect business uses. Similarly, modified versions cannot be transferred or sold to other parties – to do so would be an infringement of the author's right to create derivative works.

Vendors of commercial software typically do not sell their programs. Rather, it is licensed to users, with all rights retained. Instead of agreeing by signing a document, a common method of acceptance of the terms of the license is the use of a *shrink-wrap*, or plastic wrap containing the terms of the license (those terms would typically include anti-infringement of copyright clauses). Under this method of acceptance, any unauthorized copy of a program may be traceable and actionable against the buyer of the license. When the license is offered on-line (e.g. by an application services provider), the shink-wrap method is replaced by an acceptance button known as a *click-wrap*. The validity of click-wrap acceptance is being debated by courts in many jurisdictions.

Copyright infringement

Infringement occurs when the exclusive rights granted to copyright owners (that is any reproduction, adaptation, distribution, performance or display right) have been violated. The question often arises as to how much of a work must be taken before infringement exists. Generally speaking, each jurisdiction has its own laws and legal interpretations of how much is enough, yet even within the same jurisdiction, there is often no clear answer.

In the US, copyright protection was updated in 1998 to reflect changes brought about by new technology with the passage of the *Digital Millennium Copyright Act* (DMCA). The DMCA made it illegal for hackers to invade copyrighted material that is encrypted. The legislation was also significant in that it shielded telephone companies and online service providers from infringement liability when pirated works are transmitted through their networks. The act holds service providers liable for infringement if they have actual knowledge of the infringement, profit from it and fail to stop it. The bill brought the United States into line with countries that have signed the WIPO treaties.

Patents

Unlike trademarks and copyrights, which carry the rights to use or exploit them, a patent is a right to exclude others from using or exploiting a patented invention. To be eligible for patent protection, an invention must be new (i.e. never previously disclosed to the public), it must be capable of industrial application (i.e. it must be capable of being made or used in some kind of industry)[29] and not obvious to a person familiar with the technology.

It may be possible to make a single international patent application in one language through a system administered by the WIPO. This method can substantially reduce costs and requires the applicant to specify the countries in which patent protection is desired and make subsequent filings in each of the desired countries.[30] In European Patent Offices, patents are not granted for a variety of inventions, most notably for computer programs (though as we have noted, software is entitled to copyright protection) and for methods of doing business. By contrast, in the United States, it is possible to obtain patents for "business methods" – patent protection for novel methods of conducting business.

AMAZON.COM'S ONE-CLICK PATENT: VALID "BUSINESS METHOD?"

When many people think of e-business and online commerce, they think of a series of open, non-proprietary standards that enable computers to engage each other in a variety of transactions. Some companies have tried to acquire patents on pioneering technologies in an attempt to gain an upper hand in the market.

One of the most controversial examples of this concerned Amazon.com's attainment of a patent for its one-click ordering process. The process is a method for placing an order on a displayed item with only a single click by the buyer. Under this process, identifying information is sent to the server and the customer's previously stored information is used to generate a purchase order. Many critics cried foul, alleging that Amazon's process constituted a fairly routine use of cookies with the sole novelty of skipping further confirmation pages from basic customer orders. As granted, the one-click patent precluded any online business from enabling single-click purchases unless it had licensed the technology from Amazon.com. The question of whether the so-called "one-click patent" is valid is a controversial one.

---

29. This means that the invention must take the form of a device, a product, a substance, or an industrial process or method of operation. The term "industry" is meant in the broadest sense and can include the Internet.
30. Simmons and Simmons (2001).

Electronic signatures

The use of traditional hard-copy agreements poses a challenge to electronic business, prolonging the time needed to finalize transactions, and resulting unnecessarily high costs. In traditional commerce, paper-based signatures serve the fundamental purpose of demonstrating that a party has made a certain promise. In e-business however, electronic signatures may often serve additional functions such as identifying the person making the promise, or ensuring a document's integrity.[31] Online transactions usually take place in real time with the establishment of contracts and agreements commonly done through click-wrap agreements or more simply, by email. We have seen in our discussion of public key infrastructures and digital certification (see Chapter 5) that the central issue behind online transactions is the question of authenticity. The important attributes of signatures have been described by the American Bar Association signatures as such:

- *Signer authentication*: A signature should indicate who signed a document, message or record and should be difficult for another person to produce without authorization.

- *Document authentication*: A signature should identify what is signed, making it impracticable to falsify or alter either the signed matter or the signature without detection.

- *Affirmative act*: The affixing of the signature should be an act that serves the ceremonial functions of a signature and establishes the sense of having legally consummated a transaction.

- *Efficiency*: Optimally, a signature conveys that a transaction has been legally consummated; its creation and verification process should provide the greatest possible assurances of both signer authenticity and document authenticity, with the least possible expenditure of resources.

Source: American Bar Association – Digital Signatures Guidelines, August 1996.

Our use of the phrase "electronic signature" in this context is a generic one and may encompass a variety of acts that serve a similar function to manual signatures, including:

- typing one's name at the end of an email message;

- attaching a scanned graphic of one's manual signature;

- acceptance of a click-wrap agreement;

- digital signatures created by use of a hash function, along with the sender's private key;

---

31. "Creating Enforceable Electronic Transactions," Baker and McKenzie (2002).

● provision of a secret code, password or PIN number; and

● biometric signatures.

We have seen previously that click-wrap agreements have been found to be legally binding by some courts (Watson and Choksy, 2000). In the US, further clarity has been brought to the issue of electronic signatures with the signing of the Electronic Signatures in Global and National Commerce Act (the "e-Sign" Act) by President Clinton in 2000. The e-Sign act serves to harmonize differing regulations by setting the parameters for interstate transactions, largely pre-empting the preceding Uniform Electronic Transactions Act (UETA) that had been adopted by a number of states. Under e-Sign, a signature may not be deemed invalid solely because it has been made in electronic form; electronic signatures are thereby placed on equal footing with manual signatures and subject to the same questions of authenticity that apply to paper-based transactions.[32]

It is important to note that that just because electronic signatures may carry legal weight, governments and organizations may lack the technical means to prevent the fraudulent use of signatures (see Chapter 5). The European Union has undertaken an initiative (known as the European Electronic Signature Standardization Initiative [EESSI]) to develop common standards that encompass two levels of security: a basic level that can be used simply to verify the identity of the party at the other end, and a qualified certificate level in which the electronic signature is but one component of authentication information stored in a certificate.

Government-led initiatives such as e-Sign aim to legitimize electronic signatures, yet do not strictly define how to implement them. A standards-based initiative such as EESSI adds technical depth in determining the legal validity of electronic signatures. The question of whether an electronic signature will be enforceable requires a consideration of the following factors:[33]

● *Authorization*: The electronic signature should be clear in applying to transactions governed by certain laws, for example: laws governing the creation and execution of wills, laws governing family law matters such as adoption or divorce, notices of cancellation or termination of services.

● *Consent*: The law may grant all parties the right to refuse to enter into any transaction conducted in electronic form. On the other hand, it may allow business the right to charge additional fees for paper-based transactions as well as the right to terminate a relationship with parties who do not consent to electronic transactions.

● *Signature*: The law may not specifically define what constitutes an electronic signature or deal with the infrastructure necessary to authenticate signatures.

32. Zoellick (2002).
33. Baker and McKenzie (2002).

- *Record accessibility*: In some jurisdictions, the enforceability of an electronic agreement "may be denied if such electronic record is not in a form that is capable of being retained and accurately reproduced for later reference by all parties or persons who are entitled to retain the contract or other record."[34] Provisions such as this are intended to ensure that parties to an electronic transaction are entitled to download, store or print a record of the agreement.

- *Record-keeping*: Records must accurately reflect the information set forth in the contract and must remain accessible to all people who are entitled under the law.

Since the law may not always offer strict definitions of what expressions qualify as electronic signatures, it is up to the marketplace to determine what forms of signatures should prevail and to develop the necessary infrastructure. Aside from being legally enforceable, the use of electronic agreements must win the trust of consumers and businesses. Consumers are generally concerned with issues of security and liability, while businesses must have confidence that a signature actually belongs to the person believed to be making the transaction and that the signature may not later be repudiated. One of the case studies at the end of chapter, *Digital Certificates and Signatures: Microsoft Corporation* examines an instance of digital certificate fraud, the role of certification authorities and the need to ensure trust in online transactions.

Privacy and data protection

e-Business technology provides companies with advanced tools for collecting data about their customers, partners and employees. Customers must provide information to finalize transactions, but data may also be collected through cookies and other software systems that analyze purchasing behaviour. Information may also be acquired from third parties. Concern over the information gathering ability of technology has increased with the rise of the Internet. Reported examples where customer information has been mishandled include scenarios such as the following:

- the purpose for collecting information has been misrepresented, or the security of collected information has been inadequate;

- customers' personal information has been disclosed or sold to third parties without consent; and

- companies have failed to disclose the use of cookies, or failed to disclose information gathering through "spyware" – software often bundled with downloaded programs that transmit information in the background.

---

34. e-Sign Section 101(e).

The US Federal Trade Commission has identified five key principles of privacy that are generally accepted in Europe and North America:

1 consumers should be made aware of a business' information practices before any personal information is gathered;

2 consumers should have the choice to consent or decline the use of information, whether for the purpose of processing the transaction, or for any secondary uses;

3 consumers should be granted access to their personal data in order to review it and correct any inaccuracies;

4 the data collected should be kept accurate over the course of processing and must be kept confidential; and

5 consumers are entitled to recourse when their information privacy has been violated.

In the United States, laws governing the use of personal data are still evolving. The Children's Online Privacy Protection Act (COPPA) that went into effect in April 2000 was an early instance of legislation designed to compel operators of commercial Web sites to obtain parental consent when collecting personal information (e.g. postal addresses, birth date, gender, social security numbers) from children under 13. Lawmakers there are considering a wide range of legislation at the state and federal levels in an effort to establish clearer standards for online transactions. The possible abundance of varying state laws is alarming industry groups concerned that an unpredictable business environment could result. Meanwhile, e-commerce groups are closely monitoring these developments. Of particular concern is the massive overhaul of infrastructure necessary to provide consumers with the ability to modify personal information without jeopardizing systems security.[35] Opponents of these measures warn that the regulatory burdens may be insurmountable for smaller businesses. Some parties maintain that privacy legislation should focus instead on sensible ways to encourage businesses to regulate themselves.

In the European Union, a privacy directive that has been in effect since 1998 regulates the collection of personal data. Under the EU directive, personal data may only be processed with individual consent, and with stringent adherence to requirements relating to notice about the purposes for which data is collected, the security and integrity of data, and to a consumer's access to collected data and choice to opt out of having information transferred to third parties.[36] In addition organizations are obliged to establish affordable mechanisms for individuals to seek recourse when disputes arise over the handling of personal data.

---

35. Sharon Gaudin, 26 April 2002.
36. Greenstein and Vasarhelyi (2002).

This relatively strict framework places the EU at some level of disharmony with the United States – where until now, the principle of self-regulation has been predominant.

Summary

The rise of the Internet as a medium for commercial transactions introduced new challenges to existing regulatory frameworks. The Web has become an increasingly important facet of business and has raised unanticipated concerns about the authority to apply and enforce laws across jurisdictions. The issue of intellectual property rights is of particular concern to e-business operators; organizations must take measures to protect their intellectual property, while preventing the possibility of infringing on someone else's IPR. Concern over the validity of electronic agreements has been addressed to some extent by legislation, but businesses are largely on their own in developing implementations that meet legislative requirements. Finally, the issue of privacy is of ever-increasing importance as the mishandling of customer information may have negative repercussions for the businesses concerned and adversely affect the general confidence in e-business transactions.

Questions for discussion

1 Explain the concept of personal jurisdiction.

2 What factors do courts consider in determining personal jurisdiction against a defendant?

3 How is the interactive/passive use test being used in determining whether courts can assert personal jurisdiction over Web site operators?

4 What contractual clauses can be used to manage uncertainty in the event of a dispute?

5 What are the five main classes of IPR?

6 What are some common forms of domain name and trademark infringement?

7 What international accords address the protection of IPR?

8 What is a "business methods" patent?

9 What is the purpose of the "e-Sign" Act?

10 Why are some businesses concerned about proposed privacy protection legislation?

Appendix: Duration of copyright

Under the TRIPS Agreement applicable to WTO member countries (see Road-tip #1), copyrights are supposed to be protected for a minimum of 50 years. Member countries are allowed to have protection period exceeding these 50 years. For instance, in October 1998, the US Congress enacted the Sonny

Bono Copyright Term Extension Act (CETA). It extends the term of copyrights created after 1 January 1978:

Works created	Duration of copyright
● prior to 1 January 1978	● 28 years (with option to renew for another 67 years)
● on or after 1 January 1978	● the life of the author +70 years after the author's death

References

American Bar Association (1996) *Digital Signatures Guidelines*, August, available from http://www.abanet.org/scitech/ec/isc/digital_signature.html [accessed 22 June 2002].

Blaustein, R. (1998) "Legal considerations for doing business on the Internet", *Franklin Pierce Law Centre Intellectual Property Mall*, available from http://www.ipmall.fplc.edu/hosted_resources/blaustein.htm [accessed 22 July 2002].

Gaudin, S. (2002) "Privacy bill raises 'grave' e-commerce concerns", *CIO Information Network* [online], 16 April, available from http://cin.earthweb.com/private/special_reports/article/0,,10399_1022951,00.html [accessed 19 June 2002].

Greenberg, P. A. (2001) "It's not a small e-commerce world, after all", *e-Commerce Times* [online], available from http://www.ecommercetimes.com/perl/story/7700.html [accessed 18 June 2002].

Greenstein, M. and Vasarhelyi, M. (2002) *Electronic Commerce: Security, Risk Management, and Control*, Boston, MA: McGraw-Hill/Irwin.

Hong, V. (2000) " 'Brussels 1' Angers EC Businesses", *The Industry Standard* [online], 1 December, available from http://www.thestandard.com/article/display/0,1151,20531,00.html [accessed 8 June 2002].

Kesan, J. (1999) "Personal jurisdiction in cyberspace: brief summary of personal jurisdiction law", *Learning Cyberlaw in Cyberspace* [online], available from http://www.cyberspacelaw.org/kesan/kesan1.html [accessed 18 July 2002].

Kienan, B. (2001) *Managing your e-Commerce Business*, Redmond, WA: Microsoft Press.

Kindel, C.M. and Grant, D. (2001) *Personal Jurisdiction in Cyberspace* [online], available from http://www.unc.edu/courses/law357c/cyberprojects/spring01/Jurisdiction/pj/HomePage.html [accessed 4 June 2002].

Post, D.G. (1998) "Personal jurisdiction on the Internet: an outline for the perplexed", *Cyberspace Law Institute* [online], June, available from http://www.cli.org/jurisdictionoutline.htm [accessed 13 July 2002].

Rosner, N. (2002) "International jurisdiction in European Union e-commerce contracts", *Law Library Resource Xchange* [online], 1 May, available from http://www.llrx.com/features/eu_ecom.htm#Solution [accessed 16 July 2002].

Simmons & Simmons (2001) *e-Commerce Law: Doing Business Online*, Bembridge, Isle of Wight: Palladian Law Publishing Ltd.

Smedinghoff, T.J. (2002) *Creating Enforceable Electronic Transactions*, e-Commerce Practice Group: Baker & McKenzie, available from http://www.bakerinfo.com/BakerNet/Resources/Publications/Recent+Publications/Creating+Enforceable+Electronic+Transactions+-+Chapter+1.htm [accessed 29 June 2002].

Standeford, D. (2002) "U.S. industry, consumers seek input on new Hague convention", *Washington Internet Daily*, vol. 3, no. 84, 1 May.

Sullivan, A. (2001) "Online sales rules still not settled", *The Toronto Star*, Monday, 26 February.

Tapscott, D., Ticoll, D. and Lowy, A. (2000) *Digital Capital: Harnessing the Power of Business Webs*, Boston, Mass.: Harvard Business School Press.

Watson, J.K. and Choksy, C. (2000) "Digital signatures seal Web deals", Informationweek.com [online], 18 September, available from http://www.informationweek.com/804/prrbdigital.htm [accessed 29 May 2002].

Wolf, C. (1999) "The evolving test for jurisdiction", *FindLaw for Legal Professionals* [online], available from http://profs.lp.findlaw.com/netjuris/netjuris_1.html.

Zoellick, B. (2002) *CyberRegs: A Business Guide to Web Property, Privacy, and Patents*, Boston, MA: Addison-Wesley.

Further reading

Amor, D. (2000) *The e-Business (R)evolution: Living and Working in an Interconnected World*, Upper Saddle River, NJ: Prentice-Hall.

Australian Financial Review (2001) "Policing e-commerce", 5 July, p. 53.

Brinson, J.D. et al. (2001) *Analyzing e-Commerce and Internet Law*, Upper Saddle River, NJ: Prentice-Hall.

Computer Desktop Encyclopedia (2000) The Computer Language Co. Inc., Point Pleasant: PA.

Farhoomand, A.F. and Lovelock, P. (2001) *Global e-Commerce: Text and Cases*, Singapore: Pearson Education Asia.

Mellier, P. (2000) "Europe passes stiff e-commerce law", *The Industry Standard* [online], 1 December, available from http://www.thestandard.com/article/display/0,1151,20526,00.html [accessed 8 June 2002].

Parker, C. (2000) "Intangible assets: are they really different?" www.eaccountancy.com [online], 4 August.

Singleton, S. (2001) *e-Commerce: A Practical Guide to the Law*, Aldershot, Hampshire, England; Burlington, VT: Gower Publishing Limited.

Sparrow, A.P. (2000) *e-Commerce and the Law: The Legal Implications of doing Business Online*, London Hong Kong: Financial Times/Prentice-Hall.

Case study 1   Multi-jurisdictional compliance: Yahoo! Inc.

Yahoo! Inc. (Yahoo) operated a number of Websites, including an auction site, a search engine directory at Yahoo.com (written in English) and a regional site at Yahoo.fr (written in French). On Yahoo's auction site, various third parties posted for sale Nazi-related propaganda and Third Reich-related memorabilia, including Adolf Hitler's *Mein Kampf* and "The Protocol of the Elders of Zion" (an infamous anti-Semitic report). In April 2000, the French-based International League Against Racism and Anti-Semitism (also known as LICRA), a non-profit organisation dedicated to eliminating anti-Semitism, sent a "cease and desist" letter to Yahoo. LICRA warned Yahoo that the advertising and/or the sale of Nazi memorabilia and racist literature or objects on its auction site were prohibited in France. Another non-profit organisation dedicated to eliminating anti-Semitism, L'Union des Etudiants Juifs de France, joined LICRA thereafter and took Yahoo to court.[1]

Yahoo said in a statement about the lawsuit: "Yahoo supports the mission of LICRA. Yahoo does not endorse anti-Semitism or racism of any sort."[2] After it received the complaints from LICRA, Yahoo claimed it had removed such postings. However, a few days after Yahoo made that statement, a search of its auction site using the word "Nazi" found 1,173 items.

Mr. Marc Levy, the lawyer who represented LICRA in the lawsuit against Yahoo, said: "The freedom of expression is not unlimited. The law does not permit racism in writing, on television or on the radio, and I see no reason to have an exception for the Internet."[3] Mr. Levy further argued that an ISP could tell where a viewer came from and that blocking French access to particular pages was easy.

French citizens could access Yahoo's auction sites via links on Yahoo.fr. Because of this, the French court concluded that Yahoo's auction sites violated section R645-1 of the French Criminal Code, which prohibited the exhibition of Nazi propaganda and artefacts for sale. On 22 May 2000, the French court ordered Yahoo to block French residents' access to sales of Nazi memorabilia that appeared on one of the Websites it hosted.[4] The court gave Yahoo France two months to come up with a plan for such selective blocking and ordered Yahoo to pay more than US$2000 in fines to the two advocacy groups.

Yahoo agreed to comply with the laws of France, but warned that it was technically impossible to reliably screen out French users from all Internet content hosted in the US. "No technical solution is 100% reliable," said Mr. Philippe Guillanton, Director-General of Yahoo France. Mr. Levy argued that an ISP could tell where a viewer came from and that blocking French access to particular pages was easy. However, Mr. Joe McNamee, spokesman for the European Internet Service Providers Association in Brussels, said it would be difficult for an on-line company to prevent people from one country from viewing a Website. In addition, a determined viewer could easily get around a blocking device by going to a Website that could hide a browser's origin.

Even if this were feasible, the case created a debate over the consequences of such an

---

1. Yahoo! Inc. v. LICRA [The United States Case No. C-00-21275JF (N.D. Ca., 24 September, 2001].
2. USA Today (2000), "Net sleuths track art stolen by Nazis," *USA Today*, USA Today, Arlington, Va., 13 April, p. 03D.
3. Dembart, L. (2000), "Boundaries on Nazi sites remain unsettled in Internet's global village," *International Herald Tribune*, Paris, 29 May, p. 7.
4. USA Today (2000), "French judge orders block on Yahoo's Nazi auctions," *USA Today*, Arlington, Va., 23 May, p. 17A.

action. Yahoo officials had argued that such a filtering would open the way for broader censorship of the Web and further limitations of individuals' rights on-line.

Despite Yahoo's contentions that compliance with the French order was technologically impossible, the French court reaffirmed the order on November 20, 2000, and directed Yahoo to comply with its order within three months or face a penalty of 100,000 francs (approximately US$13,300) per day.[5] Yahoo then posted warnings on its Yahoo.fr's site, prohibiting postings that were in violation of Section R645-1 of the French Criminal Code. It also amended its auction policy to prohibit auctions of items that were directly associated with Nazis.

By late 2000, Yahoo started an action in the US District Court for the Northern District of California and sought a declaratory judgement that the French ruling could not be enforced in the US under the laws of the US. In November 2001, the US District court held that a French court's decision to restrict access to Yahoo auction sites hosted in the US was unenforceable in the US courts. The court determined that it was not obliged, under the principles of comity, to enforce the French Order.

In January 2002, the French court brought criminal charges against Yahoo and Timothy Koogle, its former Chief Executive, for allegedly condoning war crimes by hosting sales of Nazi memorabilia. A trial date was set for January 2003.[6]

The question for most on-line businesses was: if France could prevent Yahoo from hosting these auctions, could one country hold companies from other countries with on-line businesses liable for providing information about issues that were sensitive to that country? What would be the implications of the French court's decision on countries enforcing their laws on a foreign Internet company whose Website content might be objectionable in some countries; for example, could a conservative Persian Gulf country prohibit access to a Website that provides information about birth control? Should France's example be held out as a model? What could be learned from the Yahoo case?

Marissa McCauley and Mary Ho prepared this case under the supervision of Dr. Ali Farhoomand for class discussion. This case is not intended to show effective or ineffective handling of decision or business processes.

This case is part of a project funded by a teaching development grant from the University Grants Committee (UGC) of Hong Kong.

---

5. The French order required Yahoo to (1) eliminate French citizens' access to any material on the Yahoo.com auction site that offered for sale any Nazi objects, relics insignia, emblems, and flags; (2) eliminate French citizens' access to Web pages on Yahoo.com displaying text, extracts or quotations from *Mein Kampf* and "The Protocol of the Elders of Zion"; (3) post a warning to French citizens on Yahoo.fr that any search through Yahoo.com might lead to sites containing material prohibited Section R645-1 of the French Criminal Code, and that such viewing of the prohibited material might result in legal action against the Internet user; (4) remove from all browser directories accessible in the French Republic index headings entitled "negationists" and from all hypertext links the equation of "negationists" under the heading "Holocaust". The order would subject Yahoo to a penalty of 100,000 Euros for each day it failed to comply with the order.

6. Reuters (2002), "Lawyer says Internet outside US law," URL: http://news.com.com/2100-1001-851418.html, 18 March, 2002.

Case study 2   Digital certificates and signatures: Microsoft Corporation

On 22 March, 2001, the Microsoft Corporation warned computer users that an individual posing electronically as a company representative had fooled VeriSign Inc., the leading digital certificate authority, into issuing two fraudulent electronic certificates in Microsoft's name. The certificates were issued on 29 January and 30 January, 2001. Despite the discovery of the fraud and the follow-up investigation by the FBI, the identity of the person who had registered the certificates remained unknown. The flawed certificates in the Microsoft case were used to prove the origin and authenticity of software programmes and data on the Internet, a key requirement for users who downloaded patches or software updates. Similar certificates issued by companies such as VeriSign were also used in creating secure Internet transactions with commercial Websites, sending secure and authentic e-mail, and in related applications.

The accident posed a great risk to computer users and could have affected all users of Microsoft's operating systems, ranging from Windows 95 to Windows 2000. An attacker armed with such certificates could produce digitally signed code and appear to be an official representative of Microsoft Corporation. In this scenario, the party could potentially host a malicious programme on a Website and then try to deceive users into installing and running the software. This meant that unsuspecting users who thought they were downloading an update of Internet Explorer or some other Microsoft software – from a site not affiliated with Microsoft – could end up with a destructive programme that could trash their hard drive or give hackers access to their entire network. The attacker could also choose to package the malicious code as an ActiveX control (an Office document with macros or other executable content) and send it to users by e-mail.

The Microsoft case was the world's first reported case of digital certificate fraud.[1] It raised serious questions about CA's practices in issuing digital certificates. Class 3 certificates, the kind that were given out to software publishers and developers, were supposed to be issued only after the most stringent measures had been applied to ensure that the identity of the applicant was valid.[2] Obviously, something had broken down in VeriSign's technical control and screening procedures.

Officials of VeriSign took responsibility for issuing the certificates via an automatic Internet-based system. Mahi deSilva, Vice President and General Manager of the company, blamed the accident on human error and claimed the company's automated and manual process for examining certificate applications and identifying individuals who submitted them had held up. VeriSign cancelled the certificates on 9 March and 12 March, 2002, but could not be certain as to whether the false certificates had been used. Whilst details of the revoked certificates were included in VeriSign's Certification Revocation List, the list could not be downloaded automatically by Web browsers. This forced Microsoft to develop an operating system update with information about revoked certificates.

The incident highlighted the tricky nature of ensuring trust on the Internet and the sophistication of digital certificates. Consumers did not know, when they were trusting Microsoft, that they were in fact

---

1. Palfreyman, J., "How to ensure e-security for e-biz", *The Business Times Singapore*, 6 August 2001.
2. Certificate Authorities usually offer a range of digital certificates, graded according to the level of inquiry used to confirm the identity of the subject of the certificate.

EXAMPLE 1

Company A entered into an on-line business arrangement whereby it performed a service for a company that held a digital certificate of Company B. The digital certificate that Company A relied on was an erroneous certificate but the certificate authority failed to detect it. When Company A later attempted to enforce its electronic contract and collect from the real Company B, it found that it had become a victim of fraud. Should the certificate authority be liable in contract for its acts and omissions? Given that the certificate authority did not have a contract with Company A, what remedies were available to Company A?

EXAMPLE 2

LCA, a licensed certification authority, duly issued a certificate to Kenny. LCA published the certificate in a recognised repository. Kenny's private key, which corresponded to the public key in the certificate, was kept on his computer's hard disk. Bob, a computer hacker, released a computer virus on the Internet that allowed Bob to gain access into Kenny's computer. Subsequently, when Kenny used his private key, the virus programme sent a copy of Kenny's private key to Bob. Bob immediately used the private key to cash an electronic check drawn upon Kenny's account payable to an anonymous account in a state having rigorous bank secrecy laws. Bob disappeared and could not be found. As soon as Kenny discovered the fraud, he revoked his certificate.

Under the Utah Digital Signature Act, Kenny would be liable for the loss caused by the forgery if he failed to exercise reasonable care in protecting his private key. Thus Kenny would have to obtain the services of an attorney and go to court. He would have to overcome the presumption that the electronic check signed with his digital signature was valid and binding upon him, and he would have to prove that in fact he did not affix the digital signature in question. Furthermore, he would have to show that he did not breach his duty of care in allowing Bob, the criminal, to obtain his private key. Under this Act, a digital certificate subscriber might have to bear an immense amount of risk.

relying on VeriSign's certification policies and procedures. Yet digital certificates issued by VeriSign could not provide absolute proof of identity. This means that similar e business transactions that are conducted and secured by electronic certificates are also vulnerable to such a security flaw (see Example 1).

The situation could be further complicated if the participants lived in different jurisdictions, as it would often be unclear which jurisdiction's laws would apply. Under the Utah Act, a digital certificate subscriber defrauded by a criminal could be liable for the loss caused by a forgery [see Example 2].[3]

How could Microsoft and general subscribers protect themselves against the potential threat posed by these fraudulently acquired certificates or signatures? What possible remedies were available to those

---

3. Biddle, C.B., Misplaced Priorities: The Utah Digital Signature Act and Liability Allocation in a Public Key Infrastructure, 18 October 1996.

who relied on them in electronic transactions? What action could CAs take and how could legislators regulate the conduct of CAs, subscribers and relying parties?

Mary Ho prepared this case under the supervision of Dr. Ali Farhoomand for class discussion. This case is not intended to show effective or ineffective handling of decision or business processes.

This case is part of a project funded by a teaching development grant from the University Grants Committee (UGC) of Hong Kong.

Name Index

Company Index

World Trade Centres Association (WTCA), 229, 239, 253

X

Xerox, 19, 67
XML Working Group, 210
XSAG.com, 39

Y

Yahoo! Inc., 320, 423, 443–4
Yellow Corporation, 113–14

Z

Zimba, 184

Subject Index

DATE DUE

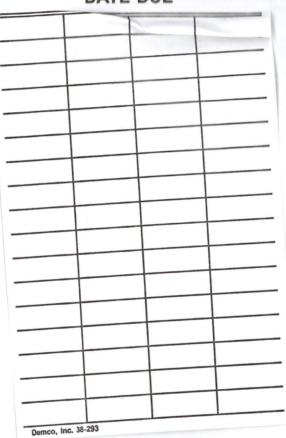

Demco, Inc. 38-293